A Handbook of International Trade in Services

A Handbook of International Trade in Services

Edited by
Aaditya Mattoo,
Robert M. Stern,
and Gianni Zanini

OXFORD
UNIVERSITY PRESS

OXFORD
UNIVERSITY PRESS

Great Clarendon Street, Oxford OX2 6DP

Oxford University Press is a department of the University of Oxford.
It furthers the University's objective of excellence in research, scholarship,
and education by publishing worldwide in

Oxford New York

Auckland Cape Town Dar es Salaam Hong Kong Karachi
Kuala Lumpur Madrid Melbourne Mexico City Nairobi
New Delhi Shanghai Taipei Toronto

With offices in

Argentina Austria Brazil Chile Czech Republic France Greece
Guatemala Hungary Italy Japan Poland Portugal Singapore
South Korea Switzerland Thailand Turkey Ukraine Vietnam

Oxford is a registered trade mark of Oxford University Press
in the UK and in certain other countries

Published in the United States
by Oxford University Press Inc., New York

British Library Cataloguing in Publication Data

Data available

Library of Congress Cataloging in Publication Data

Data available

Typeset by SPI Publisher Services Ltd, Pondicherry, India
Printed in Great Britain
on acid-free paper by
Biddles Ltd., King's Lynn, Norfolk

ISBN 978–0–19–923521–6 (Hbk.)
978–0–19–923522–3 (Pbk.)

3 5 7 9 10 8 6 4 2

FOREWORD

The performance of the services sector is vital for growth and poverty reduction in developing countries. Directly because services are already a large if not the largest part of their economy. Indirectly because services like finance, communication, and transport, as well as education and health, affect other sectors of the economy and the productive potential of the people. Today, in many countries around the world, inadequate access to services hurts people, not just in their role as consumers, it also perpetuates poverty by undermining the productivity of firms and farms as well as their ability to engage in trade.

When we talk about "trade" in services, it is not just trade in the conventional sense—where a product is produced in one country and sold to consumers in another country—but we mean the whole range of international transactions, including foreign investment and international movement of people, as consumers or providers of services. Thus, services "trade" encompasses: cross border trade in road and air transport; consumption by foreigners of tourism services; foreign direct investment in banking, communication, and distribution; and the temporary migration of doctors, teachers, and construction workers. Put this way, it is obvious that trade in services matters, not just for the state of the services sector but for overall economic performance.

The World Bank and others have done considerable work on trade in goods. We have also been engaged in services sector reform in telecommunications, finance, transport, tourism, health, and education. What has received comparatively less attention is trade in services. Many countries have, of course, implemented significant reforms in services sectors, often with World Bank support, and liberalization has been a part of these reforms. But the outcomes have not always been satisfactory, especially in terms of improved access to services. It is essential to understand why. What could we have done better? What can we do better?

This *Handbook* shows that while openness and competition are necessary parts of a reform program, they are not sufficient. There is a need to strengthen the regulatory framework and institute complementary policies that widen access to services. Small countries in particular need also to pursue deeper regional integration to benefit from the economies of scale that are important in services from telecom to transport.

I am glad to see that this *Handbook* builds on previous services sector work and is the result of collaboration between sector experts and trade experts. It builds on course materials that World Bank staff and many outside services trade experts prepared and presented at various learning and knowledge exchange events around the world. It aims at providing an overview of the findings of theoretical and empirical research at the Bank and other international organizations and in academia, as well as the experiences of policy makers and negotiators in shaping the services trade reform agenda. It aspires at being both a useful reference for services trade practitioners in governments and international and national advisory bodies and an indispensable learning tool for students and professionals approaching services trade for the first time. Learning activities by the World Bank Institute (WBI) and research, operational, and advisory activities by the Bank related to services trade will continue to offer the opportunity to expand and update the content of this volume. This will allow future editions of this *Handbook* to reflect progress in knowledge and changes in the international policy regime and negotiating environment with respect to services trade. Hence, I see this *Handbook* not so much as a collection of established facts but as a contribution to a dynamic process of learning and discovering.

François J. Bourguignon

Senior Vice President and Chief Economist
The World Bank
April 2007

CONTENTS

LIST OF FIGURES   ix

LIST OF TABLES   xi

LIST OF BOXES   xv

NOTES ON CONTRIBUTORS   xvii

ACKNOWLEDGEMENTS   xix

LIST OF ABBREVIATIONS   xxi

PART I. THE FRAMEWORK OF TRADE IN SERVICES

1. Overview   3
Aaditya Mattoo and Robert M. Stern

2. The GATS   48
Rudolf Adlung and Aaditya Mattoo

3. The Basic Economics of Services Trade   84
Brian Copeland and Aaditya Mattoo

PART II. ANALYZING TRADE IN SERVICES

4. Measuring Trade in Services   133
Andreas Maurer, Yann Marcus, Joscelyn Magdeleine, and Barbara d'Andrea

**5. Empirical Analysis of Barriers to International Services Transactions
and the Consequences of Liberalization**   169
Alan V. Deardorff and Robert M. Stern

6. Regionalism in Services Trade   221
Aaditya Mattoo and Pierre Sauvé

PART III. SECTORAL AND MODAL ANALYSIS

**7. Financial Services and International Trade Agreements:
The Development Dimension**   289
Wendy Dobson

8. Trade in Infrastructure Services: A Conceptual Framework   338
Philippa Dee and Christopher Findlay

9. Transport Services   356
Christopher Findlay

10. **Trade in Services Telecommunications**   389
   Peter F. Cowhey and Jonathan D. Aronson

11. **Trade in Health Services and the GATS**   437
   Richard Smith, Chantal Blouin, Nick Drager, and David P. Fidler

12. **E-Commerce Regulation: New Game, New Rules?**   459
   Carlos A. Primo Braga

13. **The Temporary Movement of Workers to Provide Services (GATS Mode 4)** 480
   L. Alan Winters

Appendix. A Guide to Services Negotiations   542
   Geza Feketekuty

INDEX   593

LIST OF FIGURES

1.1. Trade in goods and services, 1985–2002   7

1.2. Developing countries' share in world exports of goods and services, 1986–2002   8

1.3. Regional distribution of business services exports   8

1.4. Average growth rate of exports of business services, 1965–2000   9

1.5. Welfare gains from a 3% increase in developed countries' temporary labor quota   11

1.6. Effects of telecommunications costs on trade in goods   12

1.7. Services liberalization indices: telecoms and financial services   13

1.8. Effects of services liberalization on economic growth   14

1.9. Effects of sequencing on mainlines   19

1.10. WTO Members have been reluctant to make market access commitments
      on the movement of natural persons (Mode 4)   25

1.11. Sector focus of current commitments (developed/developing country
      members, August 2003)   27

1.12. Sector focus of current commitments (acceding/non-acceding members)   27

2.1. Sector focus of current schedules, November 2005   55

2.2. Sector policy profile of MFN exemptions, September 2004   65

2.3. The impact of offers on the share of sectors subject to commitments
      under the GATS, November 2005   74

3.1. Welfare effects of service trade   90

3.2. Welfare effects of trade taxes   106

3.3. Effects of an import quota   108

3.4. Foreign direct investment: competitive market   110

3.5. Impact of restrictions on market structure   113

3.6. FDI with average cost pricing   115

3.7. FDI with markup pricing   115

3.8. Trade in professional services with imperfect screening   118

3.9. Trade in professional services with reform of screening   119

3.10. National treatment vs. recognition   121

3.11. External benefit from local production   122

3.12. Local product squeezed out by trade   123

3.13.	Substitution between modes of supply	125
4.1.	World trade in commercial services, total exports, 1980–2004	134
5.1.	Perfect competition and perfect substitution between domestic and foreign services firms	174
5.2.	Imperfect competition and substitution between domestic and foreign services firms	175
5.3.	Domestic services firm with monopoly power and restrictions on foreign firms	175
5.4.	Restrictiveness indexes for banking services for selected Asia–Pacific economies, South Africa, and Turkey	190
5.5.	Restrictiveness indexes for banking services for selected Western Hemisphere economies	191
6.B.6.1.	Regionalism and trade in services in the Americas	280
7.1.	Liberalization indices based on GATS commitments—core banking services	308
7.2.	Liberalization indices based on GATS commitments—direct insurance services	309
8.1.	Separating the natural monopoly and competitive elements of infrastructure industries	347
9.1.	Number of WTO members scheduling transport services	365
13.1.	Remittances from overseas workers as percent of GDP and exports (1990–2000)	487
13.2.	The costs of labor misallocation	494
13.3.	The benefits of a small relaxation of mobility restrictions	495

▌LIST OF TABLES

1.1.	Inadequacies of Statistical Domains with Regard to Modes of Supply	7
1.2.	Developing Country Priorities in Alternative Negotiating Fora	23
1.3.	Commitments for Telecommunications Reform	29
2.1.	Measures that May Affect Services Trade under the Four Modes of Supply	51
2.2.	Structure of a Schedule of Commitments	54
2.3.	Commitments by Country Group, November 2005	56
2.4.	Examples of Pre-commitments to Liberalization in Basic Telecommunications (Mode 3)	62
2.5.	Rationale for Regulation in Services and Potentially Relevant GATS Rules	68
2.6.	Overview of Mode-specific Objectives as Contained in the Hong Kong Ministerial Declaration	76
3.1.A.	Welfare Economics A: Lawyers that Move Counted in GDP of Abroad	91
3.1.B.	Welfare Economics B: Lawyers that Move Counted in GDP of Home	91
4.1.	Correspondence Between Modes of Supply and Statistical Domains	140
4.2.	Countries Reporting Exports of Selected BPM5 Services Components	158
4.3.	Summary of BOP Trade in Services Data Dissemination by International Organizations	159
4.4.	Availability of Inward and Outward FATS Statistics in OECD Countries	160
5.1.	International Services Transactions by Modes of Supply, 1997	170
5.2.	Restriction Categories for Banking Services	180
5.3.	Barriers to FDI	182
5.4.	Components of an Index of FDI Restrictions	188
5.5.	FDI Restrictiveness Indexes for Selected APEC Economies and Selected Sectors, 1996–98	188
5.6.	Constructed Ad Valorem Tariff Equivalent "Guesstimates" by 1-Digit ISIC Services Sectors for Selected Countries	193
5.7.	International Air Passenger Transport: Bilateral Restriction Indexes and Price Impacts	194
5.8.	Tariff Equivalents of Barriers to Telecommunication Services in Major Nations	196

5.9.	Estimated Tariff Equivalents in Traded Services: Gravity-model Based Regression Method	198
5.10.	Average Gross Operating Margins of Firms Listed on National Stock Exchanges, 1994–96 by Country/Region	199
5.11.	Average Gross Operating Margins of Services Firms Listed on National Stock Exchanges, 1994–96, by Country/Region and by Sector	199
5.A.1.	Price Impact of Regulation on Telecommunications Prices, 1997 (Percent of Notional Price Existing under Benchmark Regulatory Regime)	207
5.A.2.	Price Impacts of Regulation on Industrial Electricity Prices, 1996	209
5.A.3.	Estimated Cost Impacts of Foreign and Domestic Barriers to Establishment in Wholesale and Retail Food Distributors	210
5.A.4.	Estimated Price Impacts of Foreign and Domestic Trade Restrictiveness Indexes (TRI) on Net Interest Margins of Banks	211
5.A.5.	Estimated Price and Cost Impacts of Restrictions on Engineering Services	212
5.A.6.	Coefficient Estimates of Technical Efficiency in Telecommunications Services	213
5.A.7.	Welfare Effects of Elimination of Services	216
6.1.	Key Disciplines in RTAs Covering Services	240
6.2.	Key Features of RTAs Covering Services	248
6.3.	Key Provisions of GATS Article V (and V bis)	250
7.1.	An Index of Openness in Financial Services, 1997	305
7.B.1.1.	Main Provisions on Financial Services—Regional and Extra-Regional Agreements of the Western Hemisphere	318
7.B.1.2.	Main GATS plus Component in Financial Services Commitments of Selected Western Hemisphere Countries	320
7.B.2.1.	Foreign Ownership in China's Local Banks	328
7.B.2.2.	Non-performing Loans and Capital Adequacy of Banks	329
7.B.2.3.	Important Events Related to the Qualified Foreign Institutional Investors (QFII)	331
7.B.2.4.	Comparison of Some Indicators between China's Banks and Top Banks in the World	332
7.B.2.5.	China: A Summary of Implementing GATS Commitments in the Financial Sector	333
8.1.	Access Charges with Structural Separation	349
8.2.	Access Charges with Vertical Integration	350
9.1.	Trade in Transport Services: Some Examples	363
9.2.	Example of GATS Commitments	364
10.1.	Wireless Technology Systems	399
10.2.	Participant Commitments	401

11.1.	Articles of GATS of Greatest Relevance to Health Policy	440
12.1.	The Layers of Communication Systems	460
12.2.	Regulatory Environments and Networks: Areas of Relevance for E-Commerce	461
12.3.	Deeper Integration Issues Related to E-Commerce	471
13.1.	The Temporary Movement of Unskilled and Skilled Workers: Estimated Stocks in 1997	484
13.2.	Geographic Origin of Non-immigrants to the United States: Selected Visa Categories of Most Relevance for Mode 4, 2001	485
13.3.	Profile of H1B Beneficiaries by Top Ten Industries, United States, Fiscal 2001	486
13.4.	Overseas Service Workers from the Philippines, by Occupation and Country (1995–2000)	488
13.5.	Commitments on Mode 4 by Type of Person (Horizontal Commitments), April 2002	489
13.6.	Economic Welfare by Region and Class of Worker	501
13.7.	Percentage Changes in the Real Wages of Skilled and Unskilled Workers	501
13.8.	Welfare Decomposed According to Effects of Increasing Skilled and Unskilled Quotas	503
13.9.	Welfare Results for Sensitivity Analysis	504
13.A.1.	Accounting Concepts for the Temporary Flow of Labor from Country A to Country B	539

LIST OF BOXES

1.1.	Why do Services Matter for Development?	10
1.2.	Services Reform and Impact on Comparative Advantage	12
1.3.	The Sequence of Reform Matters	18
1.4.	The Main GATS Rules	25
1.5.	Ensuring Barrier-Free Trade in Electronically Delivered Products	28
2.1.	Classification of Services Proposed by the then GATT Secretariat	49
3.1.	Some Stylized Facts about Services	86
3.2.	Dynamic Benefits of Services Trade Liberalization	98
3.3.	Impact of Restrictions and Substitutability between Modes	102
3.4.	Fiscal Instruments: Is the Difficulty of Substitution Between Policy Instruments Overstated?	109
3.5.	Are There Good Reasons to Limit Entry?	116
4.1.	Measuring Services Production	133
4.2.	Different Types of Movement of Persons, Viewpoint of the Recipient Country	134
4.3.	Patterns of Trade in Services Expansion	135
4.4.	Measuring Trade in Services: The U.S. Statistical Practices—Obie G. Whichard	150
5.1.	Russia's WTO Accession: What Are the Macro-economic, Sector, Labor Market, and Household Effects?—Thomas F. Rutherford and David Tarr	171
6.1.	The Standard Economics of Preferences	225
6.2.	Harmonization and Mutual Recognition in Services: Promise and Pitfalls	243
6.3.	Liberal Rules of Origin Can Minimize Investment Diversion	251
6.4.	Demonstration Effect Regionalism: The Digital Trade Agenda and RTAs	260
6.5.	Liberalizing Services Trade in the ASEAN Region—Carsten Fink	274
6.6.	Regionalism and Trade in Services in the Americas—Sherry Stephenson	278
7.1.	Liberalization of Trade in Financial Services: New Trends in the Western Hemisphere—Patricio Contreras	316
7.2.	China's Financial Sector: Pre- and Post-WTO Reforms—Yan Wang	326
9.1.	Inefficient Internal Transport System Contributes to the Concentration of China's Export Industries in Coastal Regions	357
9.2.	Transport Services Categories in the GATS	361

9.3.	Argentina's Experience in Port Reform	368
9.4.	Derailed British Railway Reforms	373
9.5.	NAFTA and Mexico–U.S. Liberalization of Cross-border Road Transport	381
9.6.	Trade in Transport Services: Competition and Reliability: Issues and Trade-Offs—Marc H. Juhel	384
10.1.	Economic Principles of Telecommunications	392
10.2.	Basic and Value-Added Telecommunications	403
10.3.	Korea's Final Schedule of Commitments on Telecom at the WTO	405
10.4.	The WTO Reference Paper	407
Annex	Commitments of Costa Rica on Telecommunication Services in the Context of the U.S.–Central America–Dominican Republic Free Trade Agreement (DR-CAFTA)—Roberto Echandi	428
11.1.	Health Policy Principles to Guide Liberalization of Health-Related Services	438
11.2.	Points for Policy Makers	439
11.3.	Modes of Service Supply under GATS and Health Opportunities and Risks	441
11.4.	Key Questions for Monitoring the Impact of GATS 2000 on Health Policy	443
11.5.	Checklist for Policy Makers on Trade in Health-Related Services	445
11.6.	Elements of a General Framework for Country Analysis of GATS	445
11.7.	The GATS and the Health of Poor People—Shantayanan Devarajan	457
13.1.	The Indian Proposal on Mode 4	517
13.2.	The United Kingdom's GATS Visa Scheme	518
13.3.	The Recruitment of Nurses in the U.S.	523
13.4.	The European Communities' Offer on Mode 4, 2003	526
13.5.	The Temporary Movement of Service Providers: The U.S. Experience—Demetrios G. Papademetriou	533
13.6.	Mobility of Service Providers in the Caribbean Region—Sherry Stephenson	535
A.1.	The Experience of Brazil in Trade in Services Negotiations—Flávio Marega	590

NOTES ON CONTRIBUTORS

Rudolf Adlung, Senior Economist in the Trade in Services Division of the WTO Secretariat, World Trade Organization

Jonathan D. Aronson, Executive Director, Annenberg Center for Communication, and Professor of Communication and International Relations, University of Southern California

Chantal Blouin, Senior Researcher, Trade and Development, Chercheure Principale, Commerce et Développement, Ottawa, Canada

Patricio Contreras, at the time of writing, Chief Competitiveness Section, Department of Trade, Tourism and Competitiveness, Organization of American States; currently, Office of the Comptroller of the Currency, Washington, DC

Brian Copeland, Professor, Department of Economics, University of British Columbia

Peter F. Cowhey, Dean and Qualcomm Professor, Graduate School of International Relations and Pacific Studies University of California, San Diego

Barbara d'Andrea, Statistician, Economic Research and Statistics Division, International Trade Statistics Section, WTO

Alan V. Deardorff, John W. Sweetland Professor of International Economics and Professor of Economics and Public Policy, Department of Economics and Gerald R. Ford School of Public Policy, University of Michigan

Philippa Dee, Visiting Fellow, Asia-Pacific School of Economics and Government, Australian National University

Shantayanan Devarajan, Chief Economist, South Asia Region, World Bank

Wendy Dobson, Professor and Director, Institute for International Business, Rotman School of Management, University of Toronto

Nick Drager, Senior Advisor, Department of Ethics, Trade, Human Rights and Law, World Health Organization

Roberto Echandi, Director, Small Economy Trade & Investment Center (SETIC), Professor of International Trade and Investment Law, Diplomatic Institute, Ministry of Foreign Affairs of Costa Rica

Geza Feketekuty, Consultant and President of the Institute for Trade and Commercial Diplomacy

David P. Fidler, Professor, Indiana University School of Law

Christopher Findlay, Head of School, School of Economics, University of Adelaide

Carsten Fink, Senior Economist, International Trade Team, World Bank Institute, World Bank Geneva Office

Marc H. Juhel, Transport and Logistics Adviser, World Bank

Joscelyn Magdeleine, Statistician, Economic Research and Statistics Division, International Trade Statistics Section, WTO

Flávio Marega, Counselor, Embassy of Brazil, Washington, DC

Aaditya Mattoo, Lead Economist, International Trade Group, Development Research Group, World Bank

Yann Marcus, Statistician, Economic Research and Statistics Division, International Trade Statistics Section, WTO

Andreas Maurer, Chief of Section, Economic Research and Statistics Division, International Trade Statistics Section, WTO

Demetrios G. Papademetriou, President, Migration Policy Institute

Carlos A. Primo Braga, Senior Adviser, International Trade Department, World Bank Geneva Office

Thomas F. Rutherford, Ann Arbor, Michigan

Pierre Sauvé, Visiting Fellow, International Trade Policy Unit, London School of Economics and Political Science

Richard Smith, Professor of Health System Economics, Department of Public Health and Policy, London School of Hygiene and Tropical Medicine

Sherry Stephenson, Director, Department of Trade, Tourism and Competitiveness, Executive Secretariat for Integral Development (SEDI), Organization of American States (OAS)

Robert M. Stern, Professor of Economics and Public Policy (Emeritus), Department of Economics and Gerald R. Ford School of Public Policy, University of Michigan

David Tarr, Consultant, Development Research Group, World Bank

Yan Wang, Senior Economist, Trade Team, World Bank Institute, World Bank

Obie G. Whichard, Chief, International Investment Division, Bureau of Economic Analysis, U.S. Department of Commerce

L. Alan Winters, Director, Development Research Group, World Bank

Gianni Zanini, Lead Economist, World Bank Institute, World Bank

ACKNOWLEDGEMENTS

In addition to the editors and the authors of the various chapters, boxes, and annexes, many other people contributed to this volume. Bernard Hoekman, manager of the Bank's research complex, and Roumeen Islam, manager of the World Bank Institute or WBI, helped mobilize the funding for this knowledge project and review its outputs. Philip English, now working in the Bank's Africa Region, was instrumental in the original commissioning of the various chapters and in reviewing early drafts. Judith L. Jackson, an assistant to Professor Robert Stern, and Gustavo Garcia-Benavides, a consultant in the WBI, assisted in assembling and editing the contributions of the various authors. Maria Lourdes Penaflor Gosiengfiao and Diane Leslie Billups (staff assistants in the WBI) took care of administrative matters related to the commissioning of the contributions and WBI learning events. Finally, this project would not have been feasible without the financial contribution of the U.K. government through its Department for International Development (DFID) to the Bank's trade research program and to the WBI's capacity building program.

LIST OF ABBREVIATIONS

1993 SNA	System of National Accounts, 1993
ABSs	asset-backed securitizations
ADB	Asian Development Bank
ADSLs	Asymmetric Digital Subscriber Line systems
AITIC	AITIC is an independent organization, based in Geneva, whose goal is to help less-advantaged countries (LACs)
AMCs	Asset Management Companies
ASEAN	Association of Southeast Asian Nations
BATNA	Best Alternative to an Agreement
BOC	Bank of China
BD3	3rd edition of the OECD Benchmark Definition of Foreign Direct Investment
BOP	Balance of Payments
BPM5	5th edition of the Balance of Payments Manual (IMF)
BTA	Basic Telecommunications Agreement
CARICOM	Caribbean Community and Common Market
CBRC	China Bank Regulation Commission
CCB	China Construction Bank
CEPA	Closer Economic Partnership Arrangement
CIRC	China Insurance Regulatory Commission
COMESA	Common Market for Eastern and Southern Africa
CPC Ver. 1.0	Central Product Classification, Version 1.0
CSME	Single Market and Economy
CSRC	China Securities Regulatory Commission
DR-CAFTA	U.S.–Central America–Dominican Republic Free Trade Agreement
EBOPS	Extended Balance of Payments Services Classification
ENTs	economic needs tests
EPA	Economic Partnership Agreement
EU	European Union
Eurostat	Statistical Office of the European Communities

FATS   Foreign Affiliates Trade in Services

FCC   Federal Communications Commission

FDI   Foreign Direct Investment

FSA   Financial Services Agreement

FTA   free trade area

GATS   General Agreement on Trade in Services

GATT   General Agreement on Tariffs and Trade

GDDS   General Data Dissemination System (IMF)

GDP   Gross Domestic Product

GNS/W/120   services sectoral classification list

ICAIS   International Charges for Access to Internet Services

ICANN   Internet Corporation for Assigned Names and Numbers

ICBC   Industrial and Commercial Bank of China

ICE   Costa Rican Institute of Electricity—"ICE"

ICFA   ISIC Categories for Foreign Affiliates

ICSE-93   International Classification of Status in Employment

ICT   information and computer technology

ILO   International Labour Organization

IMF   International Monetary Fund

IPO   Initial Public Offering

IPRs   intellectual property rights

ISCO-88   International Standard Classification of Occupations

ISIC   International Standard Industrial Classification

ISP   Internet service provider

IT   information technology

ITE   Internet traffic exchange

ITRS   international transactions reporting system

ITU   International Telecommunications Union

KT   Korea Telecom

KTF   a subsidiary of KT

LACs   less-advantaged countries

LDCs   least developed countries

LLDCs   landlocked developing countries

M&A   mergers and acquisitions

MBS   mortgage-backed securitization

MERCOSUR	South American Common Market
MFN	Most-Favored Nation
MIC	Ministry of Information and Communication
MSITS	Manual on Statistics of International Trade in Services
MVNOs	mobile virtual network operators
NAFTA	North American Free Trade Agreement
n.a.	not available
NCA	National Communications Authority (Ghana)
n.i.e.	not included elsewhere
NGO	non-governmental organization
NPL	Non-performing Loan
NTB	Non-Tariff Barrier
OECD	Organisation for Economic Co-operation and Development
QFII	Qualified Foreign Institutional Investor
PCS	digital cell phone network
PTO	public telecommunications operator
PTT	Post-Telephone-Telegraph
RIS	Research and Information System (for the Non-Aligned and Other Developing Countries)
RTA	Regional Trade Agreement
SDDS	Special Data Dissemination Standards (IMF)
SET	Secured Electronic Transactions
SMEs	small and medium enterprises
SNA	System of National Accounts
TM	temporary movement of natural persons; temporary labor mobility or migration
TRAINS	TRade Analysis and INformation System
TRIPS	Agreement on Trade-Related Aspects of Intellectual Property Rights
UBO	ultimate beneficial owner
UN	United Nations
UNCTAD	United Nations Conference on Trade and Development
UN-ESCAP	United Nations—Economic and Social Commission for Asia and Pacific
UN ECLAC	UN Economic Commission for Latin America and the Caribbean
UN ESCWA	UN Economic and Social Commission for Western Asia
UNSD	United Nations Statistics Division
UNU	United Nations University (UNU)

USA	United States of America
USAID	U.S. Agency for International Development
USD	United States dollar
USTR	U.S. Office of the Trade Representative
VAT	value-added-tax
VoIP	voice over the Internet
WIPO	World Intellectual Property Organization
WTO	World Trade Organization

Part I

The Framework of Trade in Services

1 Overview

Aaditya Mattoo and Robert M. Stern

Introduction[1]

International trade and investment in services are an increasingly important part of global commerce. Advances in information and telecommunication technologies have expanded the scope of services that can be traded cross-border. Many countries now allow foreign investment in newly privatized and competitive markets for key infrastructure services, such as energy, telecommunications, and transport. More and more people are traveling abroad to consume tourism, education, and medical services, and to supply services ranging from construction to software development. In fact, services are the fastest growing components of the global economy, and trade and foreign direct investment (FDI) in services have grown faster than in goods over the past decade and a half.

International transactions, however, continue to be impeded by policy barriers, especially to foreign investment and the movement of service-providing individuals. Developing countries in particular are likely to benefit significantly from further domestic liberalization and the elimination of barriers to their exports. Indeed, income gains from a reduction in protection to services may be multiples of those from trade liberalization in goods. The increased dynamism of open services sectors can make the difference between rapid and sluggish growth.

But the benefits from services liberalization are by no means automatic. Significant challenges exist in introducing genuine competition, building the regulatory institutions that are needed to remedy market failures, appropriately sequencing service-sector reforms, and establishing mechanisms that promote the availability of essential services especially among the poor.

Even though governments can initiate reforms of services unilaterally, international engagement can play an important catalytic role. In recognition of their rising role in international trade and the need for further liberalization, services were included in the multilateral trade architecture of the World Trade Organization (WTO) in the form of the General Agreement on Trade in Services (GATS). Services have featured prominently as well in the process of WTO accession. And services are increasingly important in the large and growing network of regional, and especially, of North–South trade agreements concluded of late or still under negotiation.

---

[1] Much of what follows in this Overview has been adapted from Mattoo (2005a). See also Mattoo (2001, 2005b, and 2006), Hoekman and Mattoo (2006), and Hoekman (2006).

In the negotiations under the Doha Development Agenda, however, services have received surprisingly little attention. Much of the public discourse has focused on protectionist policies in agriculture. The neglect can be costly. The potential gains from reciprocal liberalization of trade in services are likely to be substantial, and progress in services may be necessary for a positive outcome in other areas. However, for these and future negotiations to be fruitful, countries must recognize mutual interests in reciprocal liberalization, supported by broader international cooperation.

First of all, developing countries must see the advantages of international agreement to increase competition in services, enhance credibility of potential domestic reform, and strengthen domestic regulation. But global cooperation is needed to provide support for developing countries at four levels: in devising sound policy, strengthening the regulatory institutions, enhancing participation in the development of international standards, and in ensuring access to essential services in the poorest areas.

Second, industrial and developing countries must see advantages to allowing the temporary movement of individual service providers. Facilitating such movement will require greater cooperation between source and host countries than has been provided for in the framework of GATS and other regional trade agreements and may be more feasible in a bilateral context. For example, source countries could undertake to screen services providers and to accept and facilitate their return, and host countries would undertake to ensure that skilled migration stays temporary.

Third, all countries must lock in the current openness of cross-border trade in a range of services. Such trade is probably the most dynamic dimension of international trade, in which both industrial and developing countries have a growing stake, but over which looms the specter of protectionism provoked by the potential costs of adjustment.

Finally, there is a strong case for regional cooperation in services. Most regional agreements in services have followed mechanically the precedent of regional agreements in goods, and the framework of the GATS or NAFTA, and focused on the elimination of explicit barriers to the entry of service providers. Preferential liberalization in services is difficult because the required legislative changes are usually easier to accomplish on a non-preferential basis, and services markets are ideally opened on an MFN or non-preferential basis. But perhaps the greatest cost of the existing approach is that it may have diverted attention and negotiating resources away from an area of much greater benefit in the regional context: cooperation on infrastructure services and regulation. Such cooperation we show is both more feasible and desirable in the regional context with proximate countries at a similar level of development than in the multilateral or EPA context.

In view of the increasing importance of international trade in services, ongoing domestic reforms, and the inclusion of services issues on the agendas of the multilateral, regional, and bilateral trade negotiations, there is an obvious need on the part of trade officials, advisors, analysts, representatives of business and consumer associations, and students to enhance their understanding of the economic implications of services trade and liberalization. *A Handbook of International Trade in Services* has been produced with the objective of contributing to this improved understanding.

Before turning to the individual chapters, some additional background information that places the services issues in context may be helpful for *Handbook* users. In what follows, we first discuss the four modes of supply of services that are covered by the GATS, the sources of services data, and the services growth experiences of selected countries and regions. We then discuss how services reform can promote efficiency and growth at the sectoral level and economy-wide, pointing out that the benefits of services liberalization may be diminished by flaws in reform programs, the failure to provide for greater services access for the poor, and the need to take adjustment costs into account.

We argue that domestic policy reforms should recognize the importance of increasing competition among service providers, the need for appropriate sequencing of reforms, and reduction of the importance of national monopolies. Further, we stress that international engagement is crucial to buttress domestic reform in order to achieve reciprocal liberalization, greater credibility of reform, provision of external assistance to facilitate domestic adjustment, reinforcement of the reform process, and promotion of greater harmonization and integration of policies. The ongoing GATS negotiations are an important and essential framework to support the international liberalization of services and should include the design of arrangements for aid to developing countries to help promote services trade and promote greater cooperation on temporary migration. There may also be greater scope for achieving deeper integration of particular services sectors by means of regional services agreements.

Pattern of Trade in Services

Services include activities as disparate as transport of goods and people, financial intermediation, communications, distribution, hotels and restaurants, education, health care, construction, and accounting. In contrast to merchandise trade, services are often intangible, invisible and perishable, and usually require simultaneous production and consumption. The need in many cases for proximity between the consumer and the producer implies that one of them must move to make an international transaction possible. Since the conventional definition of trade—where a product crosses the frontier—would miss out on a whole range of international transactions, the GATS took an unusually wide view of trade, which is defined (in Article I) to include four modes of supply:

- *Cross-border (mode 1):* services supplied from the territory of one Member into the territory of another. An example is software services provided by a supplier in one country through mail or electronic means to consumers in another country.

- *Consumption abroad (mode 2):* services supplied in the territory of one Member to the consumers of another. Examples are where the consumer moves, e.g. to consume tourism or education services in another country. Also covered are activities such as ship-repair abroad, where only the property of the consumer moves.

- *Commercial presence (mode 3):* services supplied through any type of business or professional establishment of one Member in the territory of another. An example is an insurance company owned by citizens of one country establishing a branch by means of foreign direct investment (FDI) in another country.

- *Presence of natural persons (mode 4):* services supplied by nationals of one Member in the territory of another. This mode includes both independent service suppliers and employees of the services supplier of another Member. Examples are a doctor of one country supplying through his physical presence services in another country, or the foreign employees of a foreign bank providing services on a temporary basis.

It would be useful if trade statistics for each service sector were available according to each of the modes of supply. This would enable an assessment both of the relative importance of different modes of supply in a particular sector and of the impact of measures affecting each mode of supply. However, the only services trade statistics available on a global basis are the IMF Balance of Payments (BOP) Statistics, which register transactions between residents and non-residents. According to BOP conventions, if factors of production move to another country for a period longer than one year (sometimes flexibly interpreted), a change in residency is deemed to have occurred. The output generated by such factors that is sold in the host market is not recorded as trade in the BOP. Therefore, transactions involving commercial presence and stay of natural persons for durations of more than one year are not covered by the BOP statistics. The limitations of the existing statistical domains in providing information on trade by different modes of supply are listed in Table 1.1.

Nevertheless, the BOP statistics are revealing. They show that services are the fastest growing sector of the global economy, and, as noted in Figure 1.1, trade in services has grown faster than in goods over the past decade. Developing countries in particular have witnessed even faster growth rates, and, as noted in Figure 1.2, their share in world services exports increased from 14 per cent in 1985–89 to nearly 20 per cent in 1998–2002.

While some developing countries are increasingly investing abroad to provide services—e.g. Malaysia in environmental services, and South Africa in telecommunications—most countries supply services via cross-border sales (e.g. data processing), tourism services for visiting foreign consumers, and the movement abroad of individual services providers (e.g. professional services or construction workers). Developments in information and communication technology have dramatically increased the scope for cross-border exports of services, ranging from software development in the Philippines to data processing in Barbados. The IMF Balance of Payments category *business services* covers trade in all services other than *transport* and *travel* services. As Figure 1.3 shows,

Table 1.1. Inadequacies of Statistical Domains with Regard to Modes of Supply

Mode of Supply	Relevant Data Source	Inadequacies
Cross-border supply (mode 1)	BOP service statistics (categories other than travel)	- BOP does not distinguish among cross-border supply, commercial presence (firms) and presence of natural persons (individuals) for less than one year
Consumption abroad (mode 2)	BOP Statistics (mainly the travel category)	- Travel also contains goods, and is not subdivided into the different categories of services consumed by travelers - Some transactions related to this mode of supply are also in other BOP categories
Commercial presence (mode 3)	FDI and foreign affiliates trade (FAT) statistics	- FDI statistics do not provide data on output (or sales); FDI definition does not match the definition of commercial presence - Until recently, FAT statistics only existed for the United States. Now other Organization for Economic Co-operation and Development—(OECD) countries have also started collecting such statistics using basic concepts and definitions contained in the Manual of Statistics on International Trade in Services (http://www.oecd.org/dataoecd/32/45/2404428.pdf).
Presence of natural persons (independent) (Mode 4)	BOP Statistics (mostly categories other than transport and travel)	- BOP do not distinguish between cross-border supply, presence of natural persons (individuals) and commercial presence for less than one year - natural persons who are residents are not covered
Presence of natural persons (employees) (mode 4)	Employment data from FAT statistics	- not yet available

(compound growth, 1985=1)

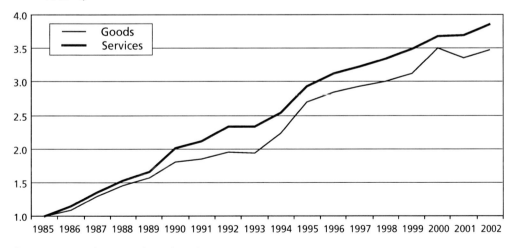

Figure 1.1. Trade in goods and services, 1985–2002

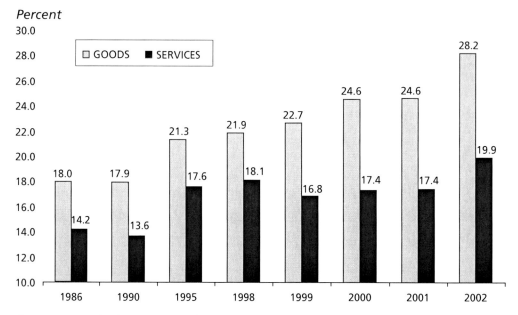

Figure 1.2. Developing countries' share in world exports of goods and services, 1986–2002

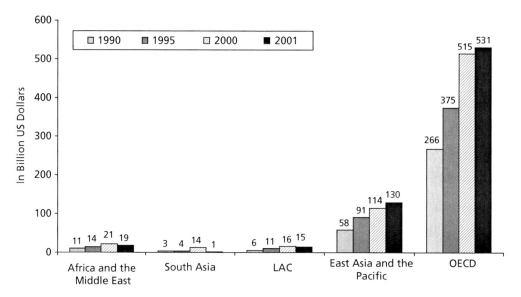

Figure 1.3. Regional distribution of business services exports

Note: The "Business Services" category includes Total Services minus Transportation, Travel and Government Services. Alternatively, Business Services consist of: Communication, Construction, Insurance, Financial, Computer & info, Other business, Personal, cultural and recreational services, as well as Royalties and license fees.

Source: Adapted from IMF Balance of Payments Statistics.

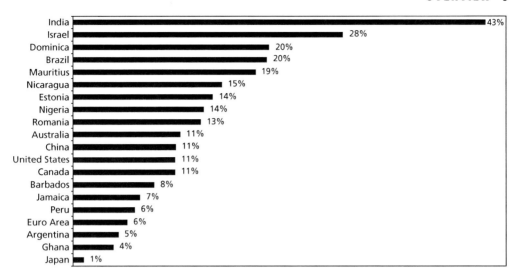

Figure 1.4. Average growth rate of exports of business services, 1965–2000
Source: Adapted from IMF Balance of Payments Statistics.

most exports of business services still originate in OECD countries. But Figure 1.4 reveals that while the exports of the European Union and the United States have grown at respectively 6 and 11 per cent per annum in the second half of the 1990s, the exports of countries like India, Israel, Dominica and Brazil have grown at rates above 20 per cent per annum. Moreover, many other developing countries—including Mauritius, Nicaragua, Barbados, and China—have witnessed high rates of growth.

Service Reforms Can Promote Efficiency and Growth

Liberalization of trade in services, accompanied by the reform of complementary policies, can lead both to sectoral and economy-wide improvements in performance.

SECTORAL EFFECTS

Removing barriers to trade in services in a particular sector is likely to lead to lower prices, improved quality, and greater variety. As in the case of trade in goods, restrictions on trade in services reduce welfare because they create a wedge between domestic and foreign prices, leading to a loss to consumers that is greater than the increase in producer surplus and government revenue. Several empirical sectoral studies support this contention. Since many services are inputs into production, the inefficient supply of such services acts as a tax on

---

Box 1.1. Why do Services Matter for Development?

In developing countries, the average share of services in GDP increased from around 40 per cent in 1965 to around 50 per cent in 1999, while in the OECD countries, the average share increased over the same period from 54 per cent to over 60 per cent. Among the fastest growing sectors in many countries are services like telecommunications, software, and finance. Efficient services not only provide a direct benefit to consumers, but also help shape overall economic performance. An efficient and well-regulated financial sector leads to the efficient transformation of savings to investment, ensuring that resources are deployed wherever they have the highest returns; and facilitates better risk-sharing in the economy. Improved efficiency in telecommunications generates economy-wide benefits as this service is a vital intermediate input and also crucial to the dissemination and diffusion of knowledge—the spread of the Internet and the dynamism provided to economies around the world is telling testimony to the importance of telecommunications services. Similarly, transport services contribute to the efficient distribution of goods within a country, and are particularly important in influencing a country's ability to participate in global trade. Although these are the more prominent services, others are also crucial. Business services such as accounting and legal services are important in reducing transaction costs—the high level of which is considered one of the most significant impediments to economic growth in Africa. Education and health services are necessary in building up the stock of human capital. Retail and wholesale services are a vital link between producers and consumers, and influence the efficiency with which resources are allocated to meet consumer needs. Software development is the foundation of the modern knowledge-based economy. Environmental services contribute to sustainable development by helping to alleviate the negative impact of economic activity on the environment.

---

production and prevents the realization of significant gains in productivity. As countries reduce tariffs and other barriers to trade in goods, effective rates of protection for manufacturing industries may become negative if they continue to be confronted with input prices that are higher than they would be if services markets were competitive.

A major benefit of liberalization is likely to be access to a wider variety of services whose production is subject to economies of scale. Consumers derive not only a direct benefit from diversity in services such as restaurants and entertainment, but also an indirect benefit because a wider variety of more specialized producer services, such as telecommunications and finance, can lower the costs of both goods and services production (Ethier, 1982; Copeland, 2001). In such circumstances, smaller markets can be shown to have a strong interest in liberalizing trade in producer services, since this can offset some of the incentives that firms have to locate in larger markets (Markusen, 1989). (See Box 1.1)

ECONOMY-WIDE EFFECTS

Estimates of benefits vary for individual countries - from under 1 per cent to over 50 per cent of GDP—depending on the initial levels of protection and the assumed reduction in barriers. In simulations of global service-trade liberalization, developed countries gain more in absolute terms—which is not surprising given the relative size of their economies—but developing countries also see significant increases in their GDP. One model predicts gains of between 1.6 per cent of GDP (for India) to 4.2 per cent of GDP (for Thailand) if tariff-equivalents of protection were cut by one-third in all countries (Chadha et al., 2003). The gains from liberalizing services may be substantially greater than those from liberalizing trade in goods, because current levels of protection are higher and because liberalization would also create spillover benefits from the required movement of capital and labor. For instance, one model finds that the welfare gains from a 50 per cent cut in services-sector protection would be five times larger than the gains from non-services sector trade liberalization (Robinson et al., 1999). These results are particularly striking because they are derived from models that do not fully allow for the temporary movement of individual service suppliers—potentially a major source of gain.

Temporary movement of workers offers arguably the neatest solution to the dilemma of how international migration is best managed, enabling the realization of gains from trade while averting social and political costs in host countries and brain drain from poor countries. Recent research finds that if OECD countries were to allow temporary access to foreign service providers equal to just 3 per cent of their labor force, the global gains would be over $150 billion—more than the gains from the complete liberalization of all trade in goods (Walmsley and Winters, 2005). Both developed and developing countries would share in these gains, and they would be largest if both high-skilled mobility and low-skilled mobility were permitted. (See Figure 1.5.)

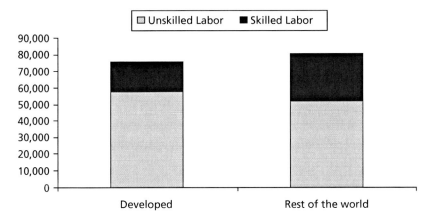

Figure 1.5. Welfare gains from a 3% increase in developed countries' temporary labor quota

Note: Data in million US$.

Source: Adapted from Walmsley and Watson (2005).

Box 1.2. Services Reform and Impact on Comparative Advantage

Reform of services policy has an impact not only on overall economic activity but also on its composition. The profound effect that transport costs have on trade and the distribution of economic activity across regions is increasingly well documented. The impact of communication costs on trade costs has received less attention. Fink et al. (2002) tested this relationship by incorporating alternative measures of communication costs in a model of bilateral trade. They find that international variations in communication costs indeed have a significant influence on trade patterns. More interestingly, estimates using disaggregated data reveal that the impact of communication costs on trade in differentiated products is larger than on trade in homogenous products—by as much as one-third (Figure 1.6). The implication is that lower communication costs can shift a country's comparative advantage towards more sophisticated communication-intensive differentiated goods and away from more standardized primary goods.

Source: Fink et al. (2002).

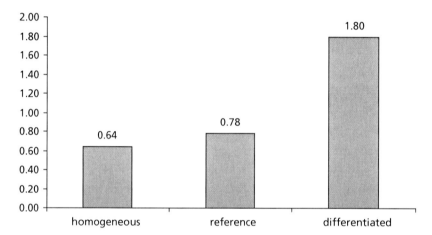

Figure 1.6. Effects of telecommunications costs on trade in goods

Note: The chart is based on 1999 data and uses the Rauch classification of goods.
Source: Adapted from Fink et al. (2002).

ACCELERATOR EFFECTS ON GROWTH

Certain services industries clearly possess growth-generating characteristics. Furthermore, barriers to entry in a number of services sectors, ranging from telecommunications to professional services, are maintained not only against foreign suppliers but also against new domestic suppliers. Full liberalization can, therefore, lead to enhanced competition from both domestic and foreign suppliers. Greater foreign factor participation and increased competition together imply a larger scale of activity, and hence greater scope for generating the special growth-enhancing effects. Even without scale effects, the import of foreign factors that characterizes services-sector liberalization

Figure 1.7. Services liberalization indices: telecoms and financial services

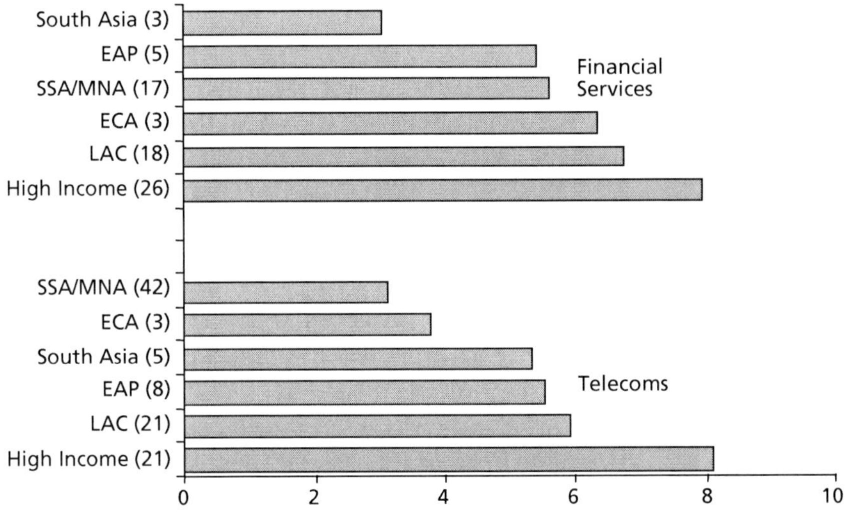

Source: Adapted from Mattoo, Rathindran, and Subramanian (2006).

could still have positive effects because the foreign factors are likely to bring technology with them. If greater technology transfer accompanies services liberalization—either embodied in FDI or disembodied—the growth effect will be stronger.

There is econometric evidence—relatively strong for the financial sector and less strong but nevertheless statistically significant for the telecommunications sector—that openness in services influences long-run growth performance (See Figure 1.7). After controlling for other determinants of growth, countries that fully liberalized the financial services sector (in terms of the three dimensions noted above) grew, on average, about 1.0 percentage point faster than other countries. An even greater impetus on growth was found to come from fully liberalizing both the telecommunications and the financial services sectors. Estimates suggest that countries that fully liberalized both sectors grew, on average, about 1.5 percentage points faster than other countries (See Figure 1.8). While these estimates indicate that there are substantial gains from liberalizing key services sectors, it would be wrong to infer that these gains can be realized by a mechanical opening up of services markets. A flawed reform program can undermine the benefits of liberalization.

EFFECTS OF FLAWS IN REFORM PROGRAMS IN SERVICES

For example, if privatization of state monopolies is conducted without concern to creating conditions of competition, the result may be merely transfers of monopoly rents to private owners (possibly foreigners). Similarly, if increased entry into financial

Figure 1.8. Effects of services liberalization on economic growth

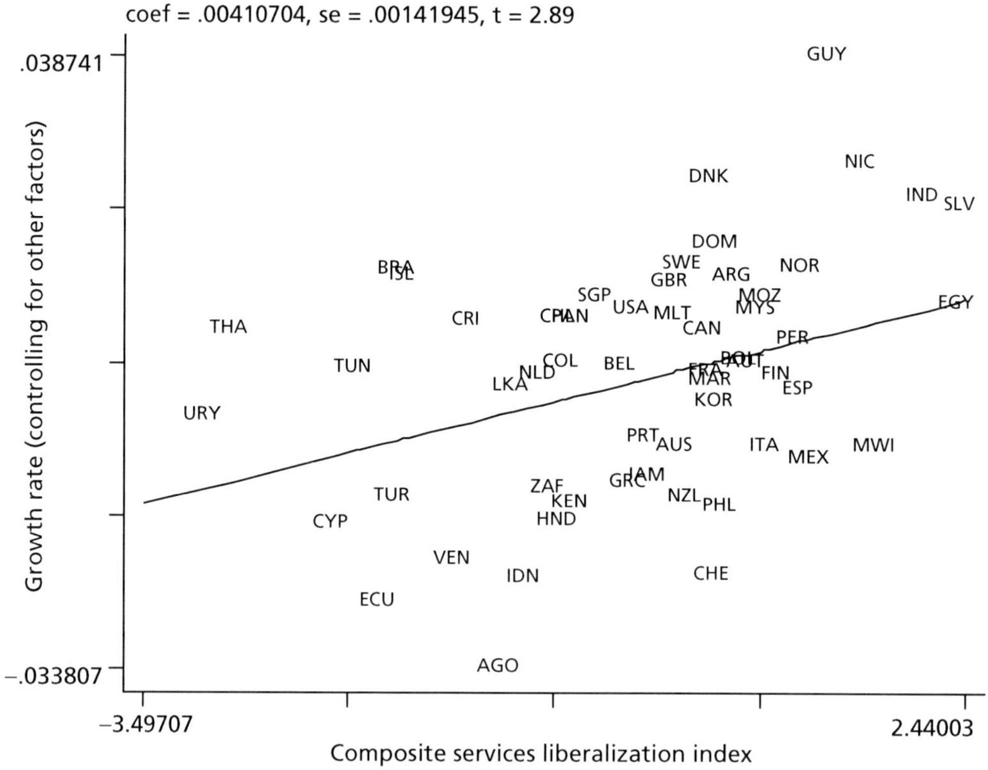

Source: Adapted from Mattoo, Rathindran, and Subramanian (2006).

sectors is not accompanied by adequate prudential supervision and full competition, the result may be insider lending and poor investment decisions. Also, if policies to ensure universal service are not put in place, liberalization need not improve access to essential services for the poor. Managing reforms of services markets therefore requires integrating trade opening with a careful combination of competition and regulation.

South Africa's experience with liberalizing telecommunications services is instructive. The Government recognized the need for a more efficient supply of services. It decided to sell a 30 percent equity stake of the public incumbent, Telkom, to a strategic investor and to grant the newly privatized entity a five-year monopoly period for fixed-line telephone services. It was hoped that market exclusivity would facilitate rapid infrastructure rollout to previously under-serviced areas. But the program has had mixed results. Even though network growth picked up, Telkom did not meet its rollout obligations and sought to renegotiate the targets specified in its monopoly license. The cost of the fixed-line monopoly was also reflected in Telkom's rising price–cost margin, with gains in productivity leading to higher margins rather than lower prices (Hodge, 1999). Finally, despite some improvement, labor productivity was only a quarter that of leading international operators, with the lack of competition in the domestic market identified as a major contributing factor. Continued restrictions on domestic and foreign entry appear to have prevented the realization of the full benefits of competitive markets.

In addition to competition, the institutional and regulatory framework plays a critical role. For example, in the 1990s, financial reforms were introduced in many African countries but have been less successful than expected (World Bank, 2001). Some of the reasons for the disappointing results are directly related to the financial system, while others pertain to the more general economic environment. The restructuring of state-owned banks was not sufficient to change the behavior of the financial institutions. Public authorities still pressured these institutions to lend money to loss-making public enterprises. Liberalization failed to trigger competition in the banking sector, and governments were mostly reluctant to close down distressed state banks. Furthermore, liberalization of interest rates in a setting characterized by uncontrolled fiscal deficits had a pernicious effect on domestic public debt, which in turn led to larger deficits. Finally, and crucially, there was a lack of adequate regulation and supervision mechanisms to monitor the functioning of the financial system.

The collapse of the Korean economy in 1997 also reveals the precariousness of financial liberalization in an imperfect policy environment. Korea did liberalize its financial markets substantially, but it encouraged the development of a highly fragile financial structure. By liberalizing short-term (but not long-term) foreign borrowing, the Korean authorities made it possible for the larger and better-known banks and chaebols to assume heavy indebtedness in short-term foreign currency debt. Meanwhile, the second tier of large chaebols greatly increased their short-term indebtedness in the domestic financial markets (funded indirectly through foreign borrowing of the banks). The funds borrowed were being invested in over-expansion of productive capacity. At the same time, financial regulation and supervision were fragmented with responsibilities spread unclearly between the Bank of Korea and several parts of the Ministry of Finance. In addition, Korea had a restrictive regime in terms of foreign bank entry. Until the 1997 financial crisis, the Korean banking system was virtually closed to foreign banks, in contrast to some other East Asian countries, such as Hong Kong, which was almost completely open for all financial services. This restrictive regime impeded the development of the local institutions and may have contributed to the large capital outflows as foreign creditors refused to rollover their loans.

EFFECTS ON PRICES OF SERVICES FOR THE POOR

Opening up essential services to foreign or domestic competition could have an adverse effect on the poor—which is often cited as a reason for the persistence of public monopolies. However, a more efficient solution is to have regulations with a social purpose.

If a country is a relatively inefficient producer of a service, liberalization and the resultant foreign competition are likely to lead to a decline in domestic prices and improvement in quality. But there is a twist. Frequently, the prices pre-liberalization are not determined by the market but are set administratively and kept artificially low for certain categories of end-users and/or types of services products. Thus, rural borrowers may pay lower interest rates than urban borrowers, and prices of local telephone calls and public transport may be kept lower than cost of provision. This structure of prices is often sustained through cross-subsidization within public monopolies or through government financial support.

Liberalization threatens these arrangements. Elimination of restrictions on entry implies an end to cross-subsidization because it is no longer possible for firms to make extra-normal profits in certain market segments. New entrants may focus on the most profitable market segments ("cream-skimming"), such as urban areas, where network costs are lower and incomes higher. And privatization could mean the end of government support. The result is that even though the sector becomes more efficient and average prices decline, the prices for certain end-users may actually increase and/or availability decline.

The evidence on the relationship between competitive market structures and wider access to services is mixed. In some cases, a positive relationship has been observed in services like basic telecommunications, especially in countries where initial conditions are feeble, as exemplified by a low teledensity or service rationing (long waiting lists for obtaining connections). However, there is also evidence that financial services liberalization in some countries has had an adverse effect on access to credit for rural areas and the poor. There is a need accordingly to create mechanisms to ensure that the poor have adequate access to services in liberalized markets.

EFFECTS ON ADJUSTMENT COSTS

Different modes of supply have different effects on factor markets. Cross-border trade and consumption abroad resemble goods trade in their implications. The impact of the movement of factors depends critically on whether they are substitutes or complements for domestic factor services. Given the structure of factor prices in poor countries, we would typically expect liberalization to lead to an inflow of capital and skilled workers. Such inflows would tend to be to the advantage of the unskilled poor—increasing employment opportunities and wages. Interestingly, it has been shown that even when foreigners compete with local skilled workers in a services sector, the productivity boost to the sector from allowing foreigners access could lead to an increase in the demand for domestic skilled workers—the scale effect could outweigh the substitution effect (Markusen et al., 2000). Given these predictions, why are workers in developing countries sometimes skeptical about the benefits of liberalization? One concern is the possible reduction in employment in formerly public monopolies that have frequently employed surplus labor. For example, Alexander and Estache (1999) find that the privatization of electricity distribution in Argentina led to a 40 per cent reduction in the workforce after privatization.

But there is also evidence that pessimism may not always be justified. For example, a number of developing countries have managed to maintain or even increase employment in their liberalized telecommunications sectors. Since many developing countries have low teledensities (in the vicinity of 5 lines per 100 people), roughly 70 per cent of telecom investment in developing countries is directed towards building wire line and mobile networks that are labor intensive and hence help to maintain or raise employment levels. Petrazzini and Lovelock (1996) find in a study of 26 Latin American and Asian economies that telecom markets with competition were the only ones that consistently increased employment levels, while two-thirds of the countries with monopolies saw considerable declines in their telecom work force.

Domestic Policy: Emphasizing Competition and Regulation

IMPORTANCE OF INCREASING COMPETITION

Many developing countries have moved away from public monopolies in sectors such as communications, financial, and transport services, but are still reluctant to allow unrestricted new entry. Privatization does not axiomatically mean greater competition. Restrictions on foreign presence assume particular significance in the case of services where cross-border delivery is not possible, because consumer prices then depend completely on the domestic market structure. Several studies have concluded that larger welfare gains arise from an increase in competition than from simply a change in ownership from public to private hands (Armstrong, 1997). Foreign investment clearly brings benefits even in situations where it does not lead to enhanced competition. Foreign equity may relax a capital constraint, help ensure that weak domestic firms are bolstered (e.g. via re-capitalizing financial institutions), and serve as a vehicle for transferring technology and know-how, including improved management. However, if restrictions on competition artificially inflate the returns on investment, the net returns to the host country may be negative.

Are there good reasons to limit entry? In some cases, technical limitations may prevent competition, such as those imposed by the scarcity of radio spectrum needed for the provision of mobile telecommunications services, and scarcity of space for department stores or airports in a city. More generally, entry restrictions might be justified by the existence of significant economies of scale, e.g. if there are substantial fixed costs of networks, competitive entry could lead to inefficient network duplication. However, entry restrictions are increasingly difficult to defend in principle, in the face of technological change and the mounting evidence that competition works.

First of all, entry restrictions change the nature of interaction between incumbents and may well make collusion more likely. Second, such restrictions dampen the impact of competition on productive efficiency. Third, the regulator is usually not better placed than the competitive process to determine the optimal number of firms in the market, especially given the difficulty of obtaining information about the cost structure of firms and other sources of regulatory failure. Furthermore, technological advances have significantly lowered network costs in a sector like telecommunications, and vertical separation (e.g. through network unbundling) has widened the scope for competitive entry (Smith and Wellenius, 1999). Therefore, inefficiencies introduced by duplication of networks may be small compared to operational inefficiencies that can result from a lack of competitive pressure. For example, even in telecommunications, a sector where fixed costs are significant, countries in Latin America that granted monopoly privileges to telecom operators of six to ten years in the privatized state enterprises saw connections grow at 1.5 times the rate achieved under state monopolies but only half the rate in Chile, where the government retained the right to issue competing licenses at any time (Wellenius, 2000).

Finally, sequences matter because of the implied changes in the regulatory environment (See Box 1.3): in one case, the incumbent is a relatively inefficient public operator

---

Box 1.3. The Sequence of Reform Matters

Fink et al. (2003) analyzed the impact of policy reform in basic telecommunications on sectoral performance, using a new panel-data set for 86 developing countries across Africa, Asia, the Middle East, Latin America, and the Caribbean in the period, 1985 to 1999. It was found that both privatization and competition can independently lead to significant improvements in performance. But a comprehensive reform program, involving both policies and the support of an independent regulator, produced the largest gains: an 8 per cent higher level of mainlines and a 21 percent higher level of labor productivity compared to years of partial and no reform (See Figure 1.9.).

Interestingly, the sequence of reform matters: mainline penetration is lower if competition is introduced after privatization, rather than at the same time. This result suggests that delays in the introduction of competition—for example due to market exclusivity guarantees granted to newly privatized entities—may adversely affect performance even after competition is eventually introduced. This could happen for three reasons. First, the importance of location-specific sunk costs in basic telecommunications suggests that allowing one provider privileged access may have durable consequences because sunk costs have commitment value and can be used strategically (Bös and Nett, 1990). Second, allowing privileged access creates vested interests that may then resist further reform or seek to dilute its impact. For example, in South Africa, private shareholders (national and foreign) in the incumbent successfully lobbied to reduce the number of entrants that the government was planning to allow from two to one (Lamont, 2001).

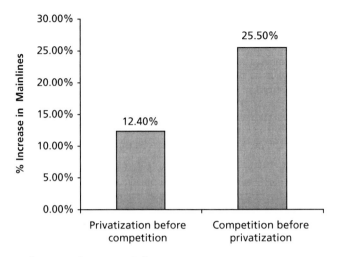

Figure 1.9. Effects of sequencing on mainlines

Source: Adapted from the World Bank/ITU Telecommunications Policy Database and Fink et al. (2003).

and the regulator is well informed about the cost structure; in the other case, the incumbent is a relatively efficient private operator and the regulator is less well informed. It could be argued that new entry is easier to accomplish in the former situation.

We may note that regulation in services, as in goods, arises essentially from market failure attributable to three kinds of problems: natural monopoly; inadequate consumer information; and considerations of equity and protecting the poor.

EFFICIENT REGULATION: MAKING COMPETITION WORK

Existence of Natural Monopoly

The existence of natural monopoly or oligopoly is a feature of the "locational services." Such services require specialized distribution networks: roads and rails for land transport, cables, and satellites for communications, and pipes for sewage and energy distribution (UNCTAD and World Bank, 1994).

Many countries have instituted independent regulators for basic telecommunications services to ensure that monopolistic suppliers do not undermine market access by charging prohibitive rates for interconnection to their established networks. A similar approach is being taken in a variety of other network services, including transport (terminals and infrastructure), and energy services (distribution networks).

Regulation of the interconnection price may not, however, be sufficient. Small markets may not be able to create conditions for effective competition in the supplies of certain telecommunications, transport and financial services, even if they eliminate all barriers to entry. This is the case for two related reasons. First, unlike in the case of goods, national markets are often segmented from the international market due to the infeasibility of cross-border delivery. Second, changing technologies may have reduced the optimal scale of operation as well as sunk costs in these sectors, but not enough for small markets to sustain competitive market structures. Some form of final price regulation may, therefore, be unavoidable. In some cases, such regulation can, at least in principle, be implemented at the national level although, in practice, many developing countries today lack the means to do so. In other cases, the limited enforcement capacity of small states strengthens the case for multilateral initiatives.

Regulation to Remedy Inadequate Consumer Information

In many intermediation and knowledge-based services, consumers have difficulty securing full information about the quality of service they are buying (UNCTAD and World Bank, 1994). Consumers cannot easily assess the competence of professionals such as doctors and lawyers, the safety of transport services, or the soundness of banks and insurance companies. When such information is costly to obtain and disseminate and consumers have similar preferences about the relevant attributes of the service supplier, the regulation of entry and operations in a sector could increase social welfare. However, the establishment of institutions competent to regulate well is a serious challenge, as is revealed by the difficulties in the financial sector—not only in a number of developing countries but also in the U.S., Sweden, and Finland in the 1980s and 1990s. The fact that regulatory inadequacies cannot be quickly remedied raises the issue of how different elements of reform—particularly prudential strengthening and trade and investment liberalization—are best sequenced.

A separate problem is that domestic regulations to deal with the market failure may themselves become impediments to competition and trade, as a result of differences across jurisdictions in technical standards, prudential regulations, and qualification requirements in professional, financial, and numerous other services. In many cases, the impact on trade is an incidental consequence of the pursuit of a legitimate objective, but in some cases regulation can be a particularly attractive means of protecting domestic suppliers from foreign competition. The issue of how multilateral trade rules might shift the legitimate from the protectionist is an issue to which we return in the final section below.

Regulation to Widen Access to Services

Reform programs can accommodate universal-service obligations by imposing this requirement on new entrants in a non-discriminatory way. Thus, such obligations were part of the license conditions for new entrants into fixed network telephony and transport in several countries. However, subsidies have often proved more successful than direct regulation in ensuring universal access (Estache et al., 2001). In 1999, Peru adopted a universal-service levy of one percent to finance a fund dedicated to providing universal access in remote areas. Funds were allocated through a competitive bidding process that encouraged operators to adopt the best technology and other cost-savings practices at minimum subsidy. The Chilean government adopted a similar scheme that permitted it to leverage over $2 million in public funds into $40 million in private investment; this resulted in installation of telephones in 1,000 localities at about ten percent of the costs of direct public provision. Household ownership of a telephone in Chile increased from 16 per cent to 74 per cent in 1988–2000, and all but 1 per cent of the remaining households were provided with public access to telephone.

Public subsidies also are directed to the consumer rather than the provider (Cowhey and Klimenko, 1999). Governments have experimented with various forms of vouchers from education to energy services. This last instrument has at least three advantages. First, it can be targeted more directly at those who need the service and cannot afford it; second, it avoids the distortions that arise from artificially low pricing of services to ensure access; and finally, it is an instrument that does not discriminate in any way between providers.

International Engagement: Buttressing Domestic Reforms

Most developing countries are today engaged in services trade negotiations in one or more fora: in the WTO under the General Agreement on Trade in Services (GATS); bilaterally with a large trading partner like the United States or the European Union, e.g. in the context of the Economic Partnership Agreements (EPAs); and regionally, e.g. in the context of MERCOSUR, ASEAN, and COMESA. The question policy makers and negotiators must address is: what is feasible and desirable in the different negotiating contexts?

In general, international services trade negotiations have not so far been powerful instruments of reform (with the exception of some deeper integration agreements such as the EU, the Australia-New Zealand Agreement and to a more limited extent, NAFTA). Looking ahead, however, it would be wrong to rule out the possibility of beneficial engagement in bilateral, regional, and multilateral fora. In principle, international negotiations can deliver four things:

- *Reciprocal liberalization, i.e., improved access to foreign markets and liberalization at home through a process of mutual market opening.* International trade negotiations offer an opportunity to pit opposition to reform at home and barriers to access abroad against each other constructively through the process of mercantilist negotiations. In principle, improved access to markets abroad provides ammunition in the battle against protectionist vested interests at home, and the existence of such interests at home makes a country a credible negotiator for improved access abroad.

In any case, if a country were to liberalize or bind its liberalization, its own interests are served best by doing so on an MFN or non-preferential basis. By doing so it would give its consumers access to the best service providers in the world. It may improve on the status quo in the short run even from liberalizing on a preferential basis, but granting a first-mover advantage to a second-best provider can have durable adverse consequences in services markets.[2] Therefore, a country should depart from non-preferential market opening only if its trading partners in a regional or bilateral context provide substantial incentives to do so.

- *Credibility of existing and future reform through legally binding international commitments that are costly to revoke.* Where a services market is already open, promising to keep it open creates greater policy certainty that could make the market more contestable and attract new firms. The key issue is whether the gain in credibility outweighs any loss in flexibility. Where there is reason to defer market opening, for example, to give the regulator time to prepare for competition, there is also reason to make reform credible through binding commitments to future liberalization. Such commitments avoid the danger of perpetual infancy and hence perpetual protection by confronting incumbents and regulators with a credible deadline by when they must be equipped to deal with openness.

- *External assistance from more affluent trading partners to facilitate adjustment, improve regulation and institute effective policies for universal access.* The poorer developing countries are currently well placed to mobilize international assistance. The consensus-based approach to international negotiations confers on small countries an important say on the advancement of liberalization, in particular because the interests of these countries are only imperfectly aligned with the broader liberalization agenda. Since they already have preferential access to the markets of the industrial countries, further multilateral liberalization would in certain areas erode rather than enhance their access to these markets. Accommodating the interests of the small and poor countries through providing them with "aid for trade" is desirable in itself, but is also necessary to ensure smooth and expeditious progress in the Doha Round or the EPA negotiations, especially in an intellectual and political climate that is so geared to ensuring a fair outcome for these countries.[3]

- *Deeper integration that creates a single market in one or more sectors through regulatory harmonization and infrastructural coordination.* In order to create stronger incentives for investment, and to reap the benefits of scale without sacrificing competition, small countries need to be part of a more integrated market. Integration often requires a

---

[2] This is because services are often provided through establishment and involve significant sunk costs that give an incumbent a strategic advantage. Once the second-best provider has been established, it may be difficult for the best provider to enter even if the country subsequently liberalizes on an MFN basis.

[3] Conceptually, the world trading system faces a classic conflict between efficiency and distribution. Further MFN liberalization would lead to a more efficient allocation of global resources, but have an adverse distributional effect on those who have preferential access to markets today. The additional twist is that those who would lose (the small and poor countries) have a say in the creation of more efficient arrangements.

certain degree of regulatory harmonization, which has benefits but also costs. The former will dominate where national regulation can be improved, as is often the case in areas like transport and telecommunications. But where national regulations are optimal, the benefits of international harmonization in terms of greater competition in integrated markets must be weighed against the costs of departing from nationally appropriate regulations. For example, harmonizing accounting standards with the European Union (EU) may give a developing country's accountants access to the larger EU market, but it leads to a high degree of local inappropriateness than if standards were harmonized with neighboring countries. The choices are simpler where it is possible to have separate standards, e.g. one for exporters and one for those who serve the domestic market, as may be feasible in accountancy.

Table 1.2 below summarizes how developing countries may decide on priorities in the different negotiating contexts.

Table 1.2. Developing Country Priorities in Alternative Negotiating Fora[a]

	WTO	Bilateral with the U.S. and/or E.U. (e.g., EPA)	Regional (e.g., ASEAN, COMESA, MERCOSUR)
Reciprocal market opening	Abroad: Locking in openness of cross-border trade, seeking greater scope for temporary migration and transport liberalization desirable but all except the first probably infeasible in the short run. Home: Desirable and feasible to open telecom, banking, etc. on an MFN basis	Abroad: Locking in openness of cross border trade, cooperation on temporary migration and transport liberalization desirable and may be feasible. Home: Preferential opening not necessarily desirable	Home and abroad: Reciprocally liberalizing access is desirable and may be feasible, but opening is ideally on an MFN basis.
Credibility of own reforms	Binding existing openness and pre-committing to future opening is feasible and desirable	May be feasible	May be feasible
External assistance	"Aid for trade" is desirable and may be feasible	Desirable and most likely to be feasible	Limited feasibility
Deeper integration	Infeasible in the foreseeable future	Relatively feasible but not always desirable	Regulatory cooperation in professional, financial, telecom and transport sectors, is desirable and feasible.

Note: [a] The assessment of desirability is based on economic considerations; the assessment of feasibility, by our view of the broad political environment.

Four bundles therefore naturally emerge:

- Reciprocal liberalization and enhanced credibility in the WTO context, especially for the large developing and industrial countries.
- Aid for services trade and commitment to reform in the WTO and bilateral (with E.U. or U.S.) contexts.
- Cooperation on migration in the bilateral context (with E.U. or U.S.).
- Deeper integration in the regional (ASEAN, COMESA, MERCOSUR, etc.) context.

USING GATS NEGOTIATIONS TO DELIVER OPENNESS AND CREDIBILITY

Developing countries like Brazil, China, India, and South Africa have significant nego-tiating leverage because of their large services markets, parts of which are still protected. But developing countries, like Haiti, Nepal, and Zambia, have such small markets that they have only limited bargaining power, individually and collectively. Furthermore, the former countries have a growing stake in services exports that face actual or potential protection, but the smaller countries have an interest mostly in areas like tourism where trading partners impose few restrictions (we deal with the issue of labor mobility separately). It follows that the larger developing countries are in a position to play the mercantilist game in a way that the small countries are not.

The GATS was constructed with a deliberately symmetric structure, encompassing the movement of both capital and labor for services provision. In theory, developed and developing countries could indeed bargain to exploit their modal comparative advantage: improved access for capital from developed countries being exchanged for improved tem-porary access for individual service providers from developing countries. But in practice, all countries have been unwilling to grant greater access for foreign individuals (except for the limited class of skilled intra-corporate transferees), and a trade-off between modes of delivery simply has not occurred (Figure 1.10). Moreover, even the negotiating links across services sectors and between services and goods sectors do not seem to have been particularly fruitful. And so, since governments could not demonstrate improved access to foreign markets as a payoff for domestic reform, GATS commitments reflect for the most part the existing levels of unilaterally determined policy—rather than liberalization achieved through a reciprocal exchange of "concessions". The only exceptions are the WTO newly acceding countries, which were induced to make far-reaching commitments to current and future liberalization as part of their accession negotiations—on both a sectoral basis and a modal basis. But even for these countries, commitments on the movement of individuals remain thin.

The overall negotiating context may change with time. First, there is a growing shared interest in cross-border trade where industrial countries dominate but developing countries are experiencing some of the fastest growth. The GATS could help ensure

Figure 1.10. WTO Members have been reluctant to make market access commitments on the movement of natural persons (Mode 4)

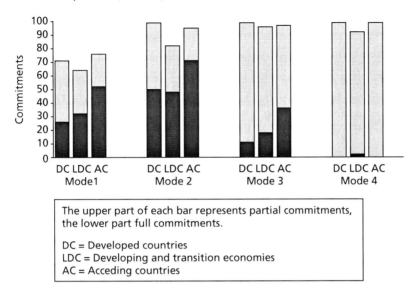

The upper part of each bar represents partial commitments, the lower part full commitments.

DC = Developed countries
LDC = Developing and transition economies
AC = Acceding countries

Note: Calculated on the basis of a sample of 37 sectors deemed representative for various services.

Source: WTO Document S/C/W, 2, March 1999.

Box 1.4. The Main GATS Rules

The GATS rules operate at two levels. First, there is a set of general rules that apply across the board to measures affecting trade in services, and then there is a set of sector-specific commitments that determine the extent of liberalization undertaken by individual countries. The most important of the general rules are *transparency* and the *most-favored-nation* (MFN) principle. The former requires that all measures of general application affecting trade in services be published by a Member, and that other Members be informed of significant changes in trade policy. The latter prevents Members from discriminating between their trading partners.

The specific commitments on market access and national treatment are the core of the GATS, and the impact of the Agreement depends to a large extent on the commitments made by Members.[1] Both types of commitments are made for each of the four modes of delivery of service transactions.

(i) *Market access.* Article XVI stipulates that measures restrictive of *market access* which a WTO Member cannot maintain or adopt, unless specified in its schedule, include limitations on:
  (a) the number of service suppliers;
  (b) the total value of services transactions or assets;
  (c) the total number of services operations or the total quantity of service output;
  (d) the total number of natural persons that may be employed in a particular sector;
  (e) specific types of legal entity through which a service can be supplied; and
  (f) foreign equity participation (e.g. maximum equity participation).

With the exception of (e), the measures covered by Article XVI all take the form of quantitative restrictions.

Three aspects of Article XVI are important. First, the Article XVI list does not include all measures which could restrict market access. Perhaps most significantly, fiscal measures are not covered. Thus, a Member could maintain, without being obliged to schedule, a high non-discriminatory tax on a particular service that severely limits market access.

Second, Article XVI has been interpreted to cover both discriminatory and non-discriminatory measures, i.e., measures of the type "only five new *foreign* banks will be granted licenses" and also measures such as "only ten new [*foreign and domestic*] banks will be granted licenses." Finally, the limitations must be read as "minimum guarantees" rather than "maximum quotas," i.e. a country that has promised to allow five foreign banks entry is free to grant entry to more than five.

(ii) *National treatment.* Article XVII.1 states the basic *national treatment* obligation:

In the sectors inscribed in its Schedule, and subject to any conditions and qualifications set out therein, each Member shall accord to services and service suppliers of any other Member, in respect of all measures affecting the supply of services, treatment no less favorable than that it accords to its own like services and service suppliers.

Unlike Article XVI, Article XVII provides no exhaustive list of measures inconsistent with national treatment. Nevertheless, Article XVII:2 makes it clear that limitations on national treatment cover cases of both *de jure* and *de facto* discrimination.

Consider two examples of limitations on national treatment. If domestic suppliers of audiovisual services are given preference in the allocation of frequencies for transmission within the national territory, such a measure discriminates explicitly on the basis of origin of the service supplier and thus constitutes formal or *de jure* denial of national treatment. Alternatively, consider a measure stipulating that prior residency is required for the issuing of a license to supply a service. Although the measure does not formally distinguish service suppliers on the basis of national origin, it *de facto* offers less favorable treatment for foreign suppliers because they are less likely to be able to meet a prior residency requirement than like national service suppliers.

A Member's specific commitments can be seen as the outcome of a two-step decision. Each Member first decides which service sectors will be subject to the GATS market-access and national-treatment disciplines. It then decides which measures violating market access and/or national treatment, respectively, will be kept in place for each mode in that sector. Granting unrestricted market access with full national treatment would be equivalent to establishing free trade, and the flexible structure of rules reflects the desire of most governments to adopt a gradual and conditioned approach to opening up their markets.

Virtually all existing GATS commitments—with the exception of those for acceding countries—reflect a binding of the status quo rather than liberalization. There are twenty acceding members, including: Albania, Armenia, Bulgaria, Cambodia, China, Chinese Taipei, Croatia, Ecuador, Estonia, Georgia, Jordan, Kyrgyz Republic, Latvia, Lithuania, Macedonia, Moldova, Mongolia, Nepal, Oman, and Panama. In Figure 1.11, the sectoral focus of current commitments by developing and developed countries is presented. Figure 1.12 provides a sectoral focus of current commitments by acceding and non-acceding countries.

Note: [1] The GATS does not apply either to measures affecting natural persons seeking access to the employment market of a member, or to measures regarding citizenship, residence or employment on a permanent basis.

that trade in electronically delivered products will remain free of explicit barriers—should this ever become feasible (see Box 1.5 and Chapter 12).

Second, with severe shortages of skilled labor in the United States and Europe and the powerful constituency of high-technology companies lobbying for relaxation of visa limits, the prospects for serious inter-modal tradeoffs—such as obtaining temporary labor movement in return for allowing greater commercial presence for foreign services providers—are now greater. The challenge is to devise mechanisms that provide credible assurance that

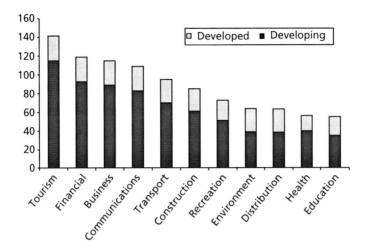

Figure 1.11. Sector focus of current commitments (developed/developing country members, August 2003)

Source: Adapted from WTO.

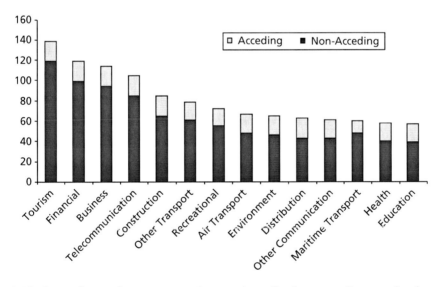

Figure 1.12. Sector focus of current commitments (acceding/non-acceding members)

Note: Acceding Members (20): Albania, Armenia, Bulgaria, Cambodia, China, Chinese Taipei, Croatia, Ecuador, Estonia, Georgia, Jordan, Kyrgyz Republic, Latvia, Lithuania, Macedonia, Moldova, Mongolia, Nepal, Oman, Panama.

Source: Adapted from WTO.

Box 1.5. Ensuring Barrier-Free Trade in Electronically Delivered Products

Trade in electronically delivered products, in which more and more developing countries are beginning to participate and which offers an increasingly viable alternative to the movement of individuals, is today largely free of explicit barriers. The main concern should be preventing the introduction of new barriers, which the dramatic expansion of exports is showing signs of provoking. What then is the best route to preventing the imposition of explicit restrictions?

WTO Members have so far focused on prohibiting the imposition of customs duties on electronically delivered products. It is ironic that considerable negotiation energy has been invested in prohibiting the economically superior (and infeasible) instrument of protection whereas little attention has been devoted to inferior (and possibly more feasible) instruments such as quotas and discriminatory internal taxation. In any case, since the bulk of such commerce concerns services, open trading conditions are more effectively secured through deeper and wider commitments under the GATS on cross-border trade regarding market access (which would preclude quantitative restrictions) and national treatment (which would preclude all forms of discriminatory taxation).

There is considerable scope for an improvement in such commitments. For instance, in data processing, of the total WTO Membership, only 66 Members have made commitments; and only around two-thirds of these commitments guarantee unrestricted market access. Many developing countries have not made sectoral commitments, but the commitments of those who have are frequently superior to those of developed countries. It is particularly striking that in some of the core financial services, about a third of the developing countries that have made commitments guarantee unrestricted cross-border supply whereas none of the 26 developed countries does so. Developing countries have also been more forthcoming than developed countries in audiovisual and entertainment services. One possible approach to improving commitments would be for all Members to agree that no restrictions would be imposed on cross-border delivery, either of all services or of a bundle of whose composition could be negotiated.

movement is temporary, rather than a stepping stone to migration. It may help if host countries make commitments in this area transparently and predictably conditional on, say, their unemployment rate and on source countries assuming obligations regarding certification, accepting and facilitating repatriation, and countering illegal immigration (see below).

Finally, the negotiating currency need not be restricted to the more difficult immediate liberalization but could also include promises of future liberalization. Such precommitment has additional domestic value because policies that are believed are most likely to succeed. Developing countries could thus take greater advantage of the opportunity offered by the GATS to lend credibility to reform by committing to maintain current levels of openness or to achieve greater levels of future openness. In basic telecommunications, the one sector where countries have been willing to make such commitments, there is evidence that the commitments have facilitated reform (Table 1.3).

AID FOR SERVICES TRADE: A PRIORITY IN THE DOHA AGENDA AND BILATERAL (WITH EU OR US) CONTEXTS

The critical elements of the "aid-for-trade" agenda relate to services. The aim for developing country governments should be to present large trading partners or donors with a package in which the country: (a) commits to a program of reform over a certain

Table 1.3. Commitments for Telecommunications Reform

Country	Precommitment to liberalization
	LATIN AMERICA
Argentina	No restrictions as of November 8, 2000
Grenada	Reserved for exclusive supply until 2006. No restrictions thereafter.
Venezuela	No restrictions as of November 27, 2000.
	AFRICA
Cote d'Ivoire	Monopoly until 2005, no restrictions thereafter,
Mauritius	Monopoly until 2004, no restrictions thereafter.
South Africa	Monopoly until 31 December 2003: thereafter duopoly and authorities will consider the feasibility of more licenses
	ASIA
India	Review the subject of opening up of national long-distance service in 1999, and international services in 2004.
Korea	Will raise foreign equity participation in facilities based suppliers.
Pakistan	Proposes to divest 26% to a strategic investor who will have an exclusive license for the operation of basic telephonic services for seven years.
Thailand	Will introduce revised commitments in 2006, conditional upon the passage and coming into force of new communication acts.

time period, and (b) donors would commit to provide the requisite technical assistance. The elements (a) and (b) will be mutually reinforcing both substantively because the ability to use aid fruitfully depends on domestic reforms, strategically because the promise of reform makes the demands for assistance less resistible, and the promise of assistance could make the demands for reform less resistible. Any assistance should be consistent with country's broader development priorities, be additional to and build on existing projects and commitments, and be informed by international principles of aid-effectiveness.

Beyond international negotiations, multilateral support is needed at four levels: in devising sound policy, strengthening the regulatory environment, enhancing developing country participation in promoting international standards, and ensuring access to essential services in the poorest areas.

While there is growing consensus on the benefits of liberalization, there is less agreement on the precise route to liberalization. Certain issues have prompted differing strategies. Should all barriers to entry be eliminated in sectors with significant economies of scale? How far should trade and investment liberalization be conditioned on strengthened prudential regulation? Developing countries in particular could benefit from the experience of other countries on these issues—but the experiences with electricity in California and rail transport in Britain suggest that there is scope for learning in all countries. More work is needed at the national and international levels to take stock of individual and cross-country experience to identify the areas in which there are clear prescriptions for policy and those in which there is need for further research, and therefore, for humility in policy advice and formulation.

Sound domestic regulation—ranging from prudential regulation in financial and professional services to pro-competitive regulation in a variety of network-based services—is critical to realizing the benefits of services liberalization. We have also seen that devising and implementing such regulation is not easy, and there are acute regulatory problems in many developing countries. Regulatory institutions can be costly and may require sophisticated skills. To some extent, such costs can be recovered through fees or regional cooperation—but external assistance could help ensure that adequate regulation is in place. Some technical assistance is already being provided, but often on an ad hoc basis either bilaterally or through international organizations. More systematic efforts—along the lines of the Integrated Framework for least developed countries—are required to assess the needs of individual developing countries and to ensure that the most appropriate assistance is provided in key sectors.

Improvements in domestic standards and qualifications are also needed in order to be able to export services. For example, in the case of professional services, low standards and disparities in domestic training and examinations can become major impediments to obtaining foreign recognition. Thus, inadequacies in domestic regulation can legitimize external barriers to trade. At the same time, developing countries need to participate more actively in the development of international regulations and standards, especially in new areas like electronic commerce. Otherwise, standards could evolve to reflect the concerns only of developed countries and impede the participation of developing countries in services trade.

There will remain certain poor countries, or certain regions within poor countries, where improvements in services policy and regulation will not be sufficient to ensure access to essential services. The criterion for determining whether assistance is needed could be the absence of private-sector provision despite comprehensive policy reform. The effectiveness of international assistance could be maximized by allocating it in a manner similar to that used domestically by countries like Chile and Peru to achieve universal service. For instance, once a country (or a region within a country) has been selected for assistance, funds—such as those provided by certain countries to bridge the digital divide—could be pooled and allocated through international competitive tenders to the firm that offers to provide the necessary infrastructure at least cost. Providing international assistance in meeting the costs of the required subsidy programs could increase the benefits of, and facilitate, liberalization by ensuring that the needs of the poor would be met.

COOPERATION ON TEMPORARY MIGRATION: A PRIORITY IN THE BILATERAL (WITH EU AND US) CONTEXT

Even though international migration offers potentially large benefits to sending and receiving countries, industrial receiving countries have shown little interest in liberalizing the inward flow of the unskilled while being relatively open to the entry of the skilled. A development-friendly migration policy would strive to ensure temporariness. On the one hand, industrial countries may be willing to accept a higher level of unskilled immigration if they could be certain that it was temporary. On the other hand, concerns about brain drain in developing countries would be greatly alleviated if emigration was temporary. The problem is that host countries cannot unilaterally ensure temporariness of unskilled migration because repatriation cannot be accomplished without the cooperation of the source. And source countries cannot unilaterally ensure temporariness of the skilled because repatriation cannot be accomplished without the cooperation of the host—today most temporary migration schemes in the OECD countries are in fact stepping stones to permanent migration.

Hence, there is a strong case for cooperation between source and destination countries in the design and implementation of migration policy so that unskilled migration becomes feasible and skilled migration more desirable. The source would agree to help with the selection and screening of migrants, provide necessary pre-departure training and cooperate to ensure timely return. And the host would agree to repatriate (especially the skilled) by issuing visas that are not renewable except after a certain period in the home country. Bilateral agreements on these lines have been successfully implemented between the Caribbean and Canada, Ecuador and Spain and Poland and Germany.

As noted above, negotiations on the "temporary presence of natural persons" (mode 4) under the GATS have not been particularly successful in the past and prospects in the current Doha round are not bright. We believe that the negotiations under GATS have failed to do better because only host countries are induced to make commitments to allow entry. Such an approach is currently ill-suited to unskilled migration because there is no provision for source countries undertaking binding commitments on screening, selection and facilitating repatriation. The approach is also ill-suited for skilled migrations because it does not enable host countries to undertake binding commitments to ensure temporariness of skilled personnel from developing countries. In the absence of a dramatic change in the multilateral framework, a development-friendly approach to manage migration is more easily developed in a bilateral context.

DEEPER INTEGRATION: A PRIORITY IN THE REGIONAL CONTEXTS

Regional agreements in services have followed mechanically the precedent of regional agreements in goods and the framework of the GATS or NAFTA, and focused on the elimination of explicit barriers to the entry of service providers. Preferential liberalization in services is difficult because the required legislative changes are usually easier to accomplish on a non-preferential basis. Furthermore, as noted above, services markets are ideally opened on an MFN or non-preferential basis. But perhaps the greatest cost of the existing approach is that it may have diverted attention and negotiating resources away from an area of much greater benefit in the regional context: cooperation on infrastructure services and regulation. Such cooperation is both more feasible and desirable in the regional context with proximate countries at a similar level of development than in the multilateral or EPA context. Some of the more obvious priorities are cooperation on telecom and transport infrastructure, air and road transport liberalization, and the development of regionally appropriate professional standards in areas like accountancy, as well as the enforcement of competition policy. At the next stage, countries may consider exploiting economies of scale in regulation by creating common regulators and pursuing deeper integration in other ways. The issues of what to cooperate on, with which partners, and how deeply, need much more analysis.

Handbook Chapters

To complement the foregoing background information and discussion, we now present brief summaries of the chapters that comprise the *Handbook*. Given the length and complexities of the chapters, these summaries should be helpful in guiding the users of the *Handbook* in focusing their attention on the services issues that are of greatest interest and concern to them.

CHAPTER 2—THE GATS BY RUDOLF ADLUNG AND AADITYA MATTOO

This chapter seeks to explain the basic structure of the General Agreement on Trade in Services (GATS), and how it applies to measures that affect trade in services. Although a number of terms and concepts in the GATS have been borrowed from the General Agreement on Tariffs and Trade (GATT), the older agreement covering merchandise trade, there are important differences. For example, the GATS is more comprehensive in coverage. Its definition of trade in services extends beyond the traditional notion of cross-border exchange to cover consumer movements and factor flows (investment and labor) as well; and the reach of relevant disciplines is not confined to the treatment of products, i.e. services, but extends to measures affecting service suppliers (producers, traders, and distributors).

The breadth in scope and coverage of the GATS contrasts with the flexibility of its rules. For example, unlike under the GATT, the use of quantitative restrictions is legitimate under the GATS, unless explicitly foregone by the Member concerned, and national treatment is not a general obligation, but a negotiable commitment. Country-specific schedules of commitments define the extent to which these rules apply to individual service sectors. There are no common templates.

The explanation of the structure of the GATS focuses on accommodating the diversity of the WTO membership and differences in sector-related objectives and concerns. While it is reassuring for governments that there are virtually no policy interests that cannot be accommodated under the GATS, the Agreement's flexibility also implies a formidable challenge: the need to define these interests and translate them, within the existing framework, into a coherent and effective negotiating strategy. Finally, discussion is provided of the achievements to date (or lack thereof) in the current Doha Round of services negotiations, with a focus on the issues especially from a developing-country perspective.

CHAPTER 3—THE BASIC ECONOMICS OF SERVICE TRADE BY BRIAN COPELAND AND AADITYA MATTOO

The authors note that services trade differs from goods trade in two major ways. First, while most goods trade involves shipping goods from one country to another, such cross-border trade is much less important for trade in services. Because many services require personal contact between customers and clients, such trade is possible only via sales through foreign direct investment (FDI) in a foreign affiliate or if either the customer or producer travels across borders. While FDI and labor mobility are also issues affecting goods trade, they are fundamental aspects of trade for some services. A second difference is that services tend to be highly regulated and are publicly provided or produced by regulated monopolies. In contrast to goods, relatively few services are subject to simple discriminatory taxes on trade. Instead barriers to trade in services arise from domestic regulations that often serve the dual purpose of responding to market failures (such as ensuring quality standards for medical practitioners) and protecting local suppliers from foreign competition. This means that identifying and measuring trade barriers in the service sector is very complex. It also means that simple rules for trade liberalization that have worked for goods trade (such as reducing all tariffs by 30 per cent) are not available as an option for service trade liberalization. Instead service trade liberalization is organized around the notion of non-discrimination and is often linked with domestic regulatory reform.

A brief overview is provided on how services are traded and the different modes of service supply that include: cross-border trade, consumption abroad, FDI, and labor movement. The chapter then reviews the reasons for trade in services and discusses the sources of potential welfare as well as the effects of services liberalization on income distribution. It is noted that these issues are very similar to the standard analysis of trade in goods and factors. Next discussed are interactions among the different modes of supply. These interactions are important because restrictions on some modes (such as labor mobility) may either render some services non-tradable, or may force service providers to use another (possibly less efficient) mode. An analysis is then provided of the effects of some of the most common barriers to trade in services, noting in particular how the effects of trade liberalization cannot be analyzed independently of the domestic regulatory system. There follows a discussion of the relative merits of trade agreements versus unilateral liberalization of service trade.

CHAPTER 4—MEASURING TRADE IN SERVICES BY ANDREAS MAURER, YANN MARCUS, JOSCELYN MAGDELEINE, AND BARBARA D'ANDREA

Statisticians often use complex concepts, methodologies and systems to produce reliable numbers. Translating them into simple and readily understandable information for non-specialists can be quite a challenge. The communication gap between producers and users of statistics is particularly wide in the area of trade in services. The recent entry into force of the WTO General Agreement on Trade in Services (GATS) has not only inflated demand for enhanced statistics, it has also highlighted that the scope of international trade in services is far wider than what statistics conventionally measure.

Statistics are best interpreted with a sound understanding of the methodologies underpinning their production. This chapter provides an accurate while simple overview of the newly defined statistical framework for measuring trade in services. It will be beneficial for government officials and trade negotiators as well as business analysts, students, etc. Statisticians new to the domain may also find it useful to understand the more complex and accurate reference documents on the methodology for measuring trade in services.

The chapter begins with a general overview that sets out the economic importance of services and the concept of trade in services as illustrated in the GATS four modes of supply. The relevant statistical framework recently developed on the basis of two major statistical domains is then set out, with a focus on key concepts related to trade between residents and non-residents as defined in international guidelines and with statistics on operations of services foreign affiliates. Subsequent sections deal with the current state of play with regard to statistics on the presence of natural persons, the different methods that statisticians use to collect statistics on trade in services, indications of the statistics that are currently available, and recent developments in the domain of statistics on trade in services.

In an addendum to the chapter, Obie Whichard reviews U.S. statistical practices for measuring trade in services

CHAPTER 5—EMPIRICAL ANALYSIS OF BARRIERS TO INTERNATIONAL SERVICES TRANSACTIONS AND THE CONSEQUENCES OF LIBERALIZATION BY ALAN V. DEARDORFF AND ROBERT M. STERN

This chapter provides an overview of the methods that can be used to identify and quantify barriers to international trade in services. Trade in services is customarily classified into four "modes of supply". Barriers to any of these forms of trade typically take the form of regulations that either restrict supply or make it more costly. In either case, the economic impact of such a barrier can in principle be quantified as a "tariff equivalent," defined as the percentage tax on foreign suppliers that would have the same effect on the domestic market for the service as is caused by the barrier.

Barriers to trade in services are extremely diverse, making it difficult to classify them in any simple yet detailed way. Broadly, they may be separated on the one hand into those that restrict entry of firms versus those that affect firms' operations, and on the other hand into those that discriminate against foreign-service providers versus those that do not. Within these broad categories, barriers have been classified much more finely in terms of characteristics that are appropriate to particular service industries.

Measurement of service barriers can be either direct or indirect. Direct measurement involves documenting barriers that are known to exist, either by extracting information about them from government documents or by questioning those market participants who confront them. Ideally, both of these methods should be based on detailed knowledge of the industries involved, since services differ greatly among themselves in the kinds of regulations that apply to them and in the rationales and effects of these regulations.

Indirect measurement attempts to infer the presence of barriers from their market effects, much as non-tariff barriers on trade in goods are often inferred from price differences across borders. Unfortunately, most services do not cross a border in this way, and even those that do are often differentiated sufficiently that comparable prices do not exist inside and outside of countries. Thus indirect measurement has to be even more indirect, drawing heavily on theoretical models of activity in the absence of barriers.

The chapter illustrates these various approaches by citing in some detail a number of studies that have been carried out, some for broad categories of service trade and others for particular sectors. The chapter concludes with a presentation of guideline principles and recommended procedures for measuring services barriers and assessing the consequences of their liberalization. An annex is included that contains discussion of selected technical issues and summaries of literature pertinent to methods of measurement of services barriers.

The addendum to this chapter includes a presentation by Thomas Rutherford and David Tarr of the macro-economic, sectoral, labor-market, and household effects of Russia's prospective WTO Accession

CHAPTER 6—REGIONALISM IN SERVICES TRADE BY AADITYA MATTOO AND PIERRE SAUVÉ

This chapter aims to take stock of the recent wave of regional trade agreements (RTAs) with a view to informing some of the policy choices that developing countries will typically confront in negotiating regional regimes for services trade and investment. While a country's choice of integration strategy will in most instances be dictated by political considerations, there remains a need for a careful assessment of the economic benefits and costs of alternative approaches to services liberalization.

The chapter focuses on three core issues. The first issue involves the economics of regional integration in services, asking whether services trade differs sufficiently from trade in goods as to require different policy instruments and approaches in the context of preferential liberalization. Also discussed is whether and how RTAs may allow deeper forms of regulatory cooperation to occur. It further highlights the importance for third countries of multilateral disciplines on regional agreements, and the criteria for regional agreements not to be detrimental to non-members.

The second issue relates to the political economy of regionalism in services trade, highlighting a number of lessons arising from the practice of preferential liberalization in services. Based on a comparison of the GATS and a sample of 25 RTAs featuring services provisions, it is asked whether and how regional approaches to services trade and investment liberalization differ from the GATS, both in terms of market access (liberalization) and rule-design. It is also asked whether such differences matter in policy terms.

The third issue addresses the legal dimension of this policy interface, focusing on a number of aspects of rule-design, including the strengths and weaknesses of existing multilateral disciplines on regional approaches to services trade and investment liberalization. There is a summary of the major provisions of Article V (Economic Integration) of the GATS, which governs the relationship between RTAs and the WTO system, and a discussion of the extent to which its disciplines are likely to allow third countries to object to provisions in proposed agreements that are detrimental to their interests. Where relevant, GATS provisions are contrasted with those of Article 24 of GATT and the experience to date of Working Parties that have investigated the compatibility of customs unions and free trade areas with GATT rules.

The chapter concludes with a brief discussion of issue areas that parties to prospective RTAs in services will likely need to confront and seek novel solutions to in advancing the process of services liberalization and rule-making at the regional level.

In the first addendum to this chapter, Carsten Fink discusses liberalizing trade in the ASEAN region, and Sherry Stephenson discusses liberalization in the Latin American region.

CHAPTER 7—FINANCIAL SERVICES AND INTERNATIONAL TRADE AGREEMENTS: THE DEVELOPMENT DIMENSION BY WENDY DOBSON

This chapter begins with an introduction to financial services and their special role in an economy, and distinguishes trade policy reform in financial services, domestic deregulation, and capital account liberalization. The chapter then examines the impact of trade-policy reform and the benefits and risks for broader financial sector development, growth, income distribution, and poverty. The impacts of reform include: increased domestic competition; providing catalysts for further reform and greater regulatory transparency; increased resiliency of the domestic financial system to shocks; encouragement of the diffusion of new skills, products and technologies; and facilitation of access to international capital.

The elements of successful trade-policy reform are noted, based on the experiences of China, Thailand, and Latin America. Issues in need of additional research include the impact on domestic financial performance of foreign equity participation, improvement of available data on and transparency of barriers to cross-border transactions and foreign entry, measures used to moderate unanticipated impacts of liberalization, and further elucidation of the rationales for the WTO Financial Services Agreement (FSA) commitments. One reason for the willingness of governments to make liberalization commitments may be the realization that liberalization is a good idea, and that the WTO offers a useful instrument for consolidating and promoting liberalization, as well as defining and formalizing future liberalization plans. Yet the use of the GATS as a mechanism for lending credibility to liberalization programs has been somewhat disappointing. However, some governments have undertaken unilateral liberalization of financial services regimes to signal their interest in attracting foreign investors and strategic partners in the cross-border supply of services.

The role of international negotiations is addressed in terms of how they can be helpful to individual countries, what can be learned from how international rules have been designed and commitments undertaken, whether there is scope for improvement, whether existing commitments promote desirable policies, possible reasons for refraining from commitments, and issues in need of further research.

In an addendum to this chapter, Patricio Contreras reviews "Liberalization of Trade in Financial Services: New Trends in the Western Hemisphere," and in a second addendum, Yan Wang discusses "China's Financial Sector: Pre- and Post-WTO Reforms."

CHAPTER 8—TRADE IN INFRASTRUCTURE SERVICES: A CONCEPTUAL FRAMEWORK BY PHILIPPA DEE AND CHRISTOPHER FINDLAY

A well-functioning and open infrastructure sector is an important determinant of economic growth and improving living standards. Infrastructure is a significant and qualitatively important determinant of transport costs and bilateral trade flows. Openness in such key infrastructure services as telecommunications and finance influences long-run growth performance. Infrastructure can play an important role in improving health outcomes. The purpose of this chapter is to focus on one key attribute that many infrastructure industries have in common—economies of scale or scope—and to show how this poses some significant policy challenges for successful trade-policy reform. These conditions can lead to natural monopoly in which costs of provision are minimized with only one supplier in the market, but the problem is that the single producer may abuse its monopoly power by restricting the quantity or quality of output and pricing above costs. Opening this market to trade creates opportunity for introducing alternative suppliers but also creates challenges of arranging the transition to a new provider and regulating them appropriately. The chapter then discusses in general terms how international trade negotiations can contribute to ensuring successful outcomes.

Key messages in the chapter are that, while natural monopoly is a common feature of the infrastructure sector, care should be taken not to exaggerate its importance. There are circumstances in which no policy problem arises. Further, even if there is an apparent natural monopoly, it is important to separate that part of the chain of supply from other elements in which competition can develop. However, even so, natural monopoly elements remain. The GATS is relevant to natural monopoly markets and contains some disciplines on policy in those markets. Trade-policy reform can contribute to performance in markets in which natural monopolies have some influence, both in markets for services of the natural monopoly component of a longer chain of supply or in competitive markets for related services. However, market opening has to be complemented by the appropriate regulatory structures to capture these benefits, for example, related to the terms on which competitive firms have access to bottleneck facilities. Commitments made through international trade negotiations can facilitate the necessary regulatory reform.

CHAPTER 9—TRANSPORT SERVICES BY CHRISTOPHER FINDLAY

Lower transport costs are associated with integration of markets within an economy and with the integration of those domestic markets with the rest of the world. These linkages support economic development and contribute to the growth of income. Important determinants of transport costs include policy choices by government.

A wide set of policies affects the performance of the transport sector, but the focus in this chapter is the contribution of trade policy and its reform. The key points emphasized are that the GATS provides a structure in which policy makers can commit to sets of policy changes in the transport sector, including policy with respect to entry by domestic as well as foreign participants. A significant number of WTO Members have already made commitments to policy applied to transport services. However, there are some important exemptions that remain to be negotiated or reviewed, including those in maritime transport and air transport. Foreign participation in the transportation sector offers gains from specialization and trade, from competition and from making available a wider variety of services. Reform in the transport services sector can lead foreign suppliers to establish local operations, which adds to the options available to suppliers of labor in this sector.

There are some special features of the transport sector that complicate the application of trade-policy reform. These are the tendency to natural monopoly, at least in some parts of the sector. Another set of policy issues relates to the sector's contribution to congestion and to environmental problems. The trade-policy interest in the former problem is to ensure that there is sufficient domestic regulation in place to avoid these natural monopoly elements becoming a barrier to entry of new suppliers in other parts of the sector, and to avoid them being captured and exploited by new entrants into the sector. The trade-policy interest in the latter problems of congestion and pollution are to avoid the policy responses being more restrictive of trade than necessary to solve the problems. These complications indicate that successful trade-policy reform in this sector will demand a high level of capacity in government to design a trade-policy reform strategy, and to construct the necessary regulatory institutions. Support in the development of this capacity is an item for economic cooperation between developed and developing countries with interests in these fields. A further concern linked to policy reform in the transport sector will be its impact on poor areas. Research has highlighted the elements of efficient solutions for meeting this concern, including the design of subsidy policies.

The contribution of international negotiations and the related commitments made through the GATS is to add credibility to domestic policy, which is important because of the nature of the investment necessary in the transport sector, to suggest direction of changes in regulatory reform, and perhaps to offer additional market-access opportunities that ease the adjustment costs in domestic markets that are becoming more open. At the same time, the GATS offers sufficient flexibility to policy makers who want to fix a timetable for their reform programs and pursue social objectives while seeking the gains from foreign participation.

In the addendum to the chapter, Marc Juhel discusses issues and trade-offs for competition and reliability in trade in transport services.

CHAPTER 10—TRADE IN TELECOMMUNICATIONS SERVICES BY PETER F. COWHEY AND JONATHAN D. ARONSON

This chapter focuses on issues of negotiations on trade arrangements for international telecommunications and information services. After a brief preview of the key messages, the first part of the chapter provides background on the major changes that have transformed and globalized communications and information technology during the past two decades. The second part of the chapter reviews the agreements that came out of the Uruguay Round (1994), including the Basic Telecommunications Agreement (1997) and other international agreements. It also examines the regulatory choices tied to competition and trade in telecommunications services. The third part of the chapter briefly considers the experiences of Ghana and South Korea as they adapted their national systems to the post-1997 telecommunications reality. The final part of the chapter provides an overview of the international telecommunications/IT issues that are under consideration in the Doha Round negotiations. It seeks to explain what the industrial countries are seeking, why they argue that these additional reforms are desirable, and whether and under what circumstances these arguments might make sense to developing countries and their negotiators.

In Annex 3 to the chapter, Roberto Echandi discusses the specific commitments of Costa Rica with regard to telecommunication services in the context of the North American Free Trade Agreement (NAFTA) with the United States.

CHAPTER 11—TRADE IN HEALTH SERVICES BY RICHARD SMITH, CHANTAL BLOUIN, NICK DRAGER, AND DAVID P. FIDLER

Services of many kinds play important roles in the protection of public health (e.g. sanitation services) and the delivery of health care to individuals (e.g. hospital services).

The GATS affects health-related services in many ways that are essential for health policymakers to comprehend. In addition, the GATS establishes a process designed to progressively liberalize trade in services, and health policymakers must be prepared to participate in this process to ensure that such liberalization unfolds in a way sensitive to the needs of national governments in ensuring the provision and regulation of health-related services.

Any liberalization under the GATS should aim to produce better quality, affordable, and effective health-related services, leading to greater equity in health outcomes. Liberalization should also ensure the necessary policy and regulatory space that governments require to promote and protect the health of their populations, particularly those in greatest need. The GATS creates health opportunities and challenges, especially for developing countries. The GATS accords countries considerable choice, discretion, and flexibility so that proper management of the process of liberalization of trade in health-related services can adequately protect health. Countries are encouraged to embed the following health-policy principles to protect health adequately in the process of managing the GATS:

- Liberalized trade in health-related services should lead to an optimal balance between preventive and curative services.
- Involvement of both private industry and civil society is important to ensure that liberalization of health-related services promotes participatory health policy towards achieving national goals.
- Improving access and affordability of health-related services should be a goal of liberalization of trade in health-related services.
- Developing countries, and least-developed countries, in particular, deserve special consideration in the process of liberalizing trade in health-related services.
- The status of health as a human right should inform and guide proposals to liberalize trade in health-related services.

In an addendum to this chapter, Shantayanan Devarajan notes that the GATS is unlikely to have a direct effect on the health of poor people because the health services they receive are not the ones being liberalized. But the GATS could have an indirect, beneficial effect if it helps countries break out of the trap of capture of the health budget by the rich and the health-service providers, releasing resources for improving the health of the poor.

CHAPTER 12—E-COMMERCE REGULATION: NEW GAME, NEW RULES? BY CARLOS S. PRIMO BRAGA

The rapid expansion of electronic commerce (e-commerce) is impacting economic activities both at the national and international levels. E-commerce is still in its infancy, but it is often identified as one of the main drivers of the economic and social changes associated with the "networking revolution".

There is broad consensus that the establishment of the regulatory environment under which economic agents practice e-commerce plays an important role in shaping the impact and depth of these transformations. Most countries have by now introduced domestic legislation devoted to foster an adequate "digital" environment with special emphasis on the rules and regulations relevant for e-commerce. At the international level, debate is also ongoing not only under the auspices of the World Trade Organization (WTO), but also in many other forums (e.g. OECD, WIPO, ICANN, ITU). This chapter reviews the case for multilateral rules and the challenges faced by regulators around the world to cope with the extra-territorial implications of e-commerce.

The chapter first discusses the economic dimensions of e-commerce and the most relevant regulatory issues for its expansion, and thereafter analyzes the case for multilateral rules concerning e-commerce, focusing on ongoing discussions on trade-related issues in the WTO.

CHAPTER 13—THE TEMPORARY MOVEMENT OF WORKERS TO PROVIDE SERVICES (GATS MODE 4) BY L. ALAN WINTERS

This chapter considers the case and the means for liberalizing the temporary flow of labor between countries for the purpose of providing services: mode 4 of the GATS. Despite being until now a mere bit-player in the GATS, mode 4 is at last starting to command some attention from negotiators and policy makers. The attention is long overdue, especially since serious efforts to liberalize the temporary movement of natural persons (TM) from developing to developed member countries could generate very large mutual benefits.

The very heart of international trade, be it in goods or in factors, lies in exploiting differences. The larger the differences, the larger the potential gains from opening up international trade. In the case of TM, potentially large returns would be feasible if medium and less skilled workers, who are relatively abundant in developing countries, were allowed to move and provide their services in developed countries. The review of existing empirical studies of factor mobility and new estimates agree that there are huge returns to even relatively small movements of labor.

The mass permanent migration of less skilled workers raises fears in developed countries over the erosion of their cultural identity, problems of assimilation and the drain on the public purse. These need be much less pressing with TM, providing that governments correctly inform their citizens and take steps to make "temporary" credible. Objectively speaking, the biggest concern about TM is its competitive challenge to local less skilled workers. This is neither more nor less than the challenge posed to such workers by imports of labor-intensive goods from developing countries, which has been overcome by the economic gain that trade could deliver and by policies to ease adjustment among local less skilled workers in developed countries. Applied with the same sensitivity and the same sorts of policies as trade-policy reform in goods has received in the past, the TM of less skilled workers between countries would offer the chance to reap some very large gains from trade.

For the sake of concreteness, the chapter focuses on the multilateral liberalization of TM via the GATS. Many of the arguments, however, generalize to unilateral, bilateral or regional liberalizations and some of the lessons are drawn from such arrangements. Similarly, the chapter focuses on developing to developed country flows although nearly all of the analysis would equally apply to developing-developing country TM.

The chapter comprises seven parts. First discussed is the extent and nature of TM and the barriers to it. Then there is a discussion of ways in which we might think of and model the liberalization of mode 4. This is based on two polar alternatives—treating it as perfectly akin to goods trade and treating it as perfectly akin to labor migration. The second section summarizes an estimate of the benefits of mode 4 liberalization treating it as akin to migration. This is argued to be a reasonable assumption in the context of the sort of models that economists use for this exercise, and it suggests the very large economic benefits already alluded to. The third section examines the simple gains from TM of persons as part of mode 4 liberalization. To examine these gains, this section presents the logic of computable models to understand the gains of TM of persons as well as its effects on different economic sectors. The fourth section discusses ways in which the polar forms of thinking about TM may be relaxed in future empirical exercises to try to refine the estimates of the effects of liberalization. The fifth section discusses practical issues that may be negotiated in the GATS to make TM a reality. It cautions not to stake everything on achieving a clean, elegant and comprehensive agreement on mode 4. Many issues are still very complex and sensitive and the over-riding requirement is an increase in actual mobility rather than an elegant solution. The sixth section asks what benefits GATS mode 4 may bring to countries wanting to liberalize TM. The final section considers briefly the arguments for and technicalities of compensating domestic workers who are disadvantaged by inflows of workers from abroad.

In the first addendum to the chapter, Demetrios G. Papademetriou discusses the U.S. experience with the temporary movement of service providers. He notes that U.S. policies reveal a strong, continuing, but also schizophrenic interest in the use of TM to enhance U.S. international competitiveness. The challenge remains for the international community to be mindful of the overall tendency toward openness, yet be aware of the political considerations in the United States that make such openness an uncertain proposition. In the second addendum, Sherry Stephenson discusses mode 4 issues in the Latin American context.

APPENDIX—A GUIDE TO SERVICES NEGOTIATIONS BY GEZA FEKETEKUTY

The Appendix examines the negotiating processes that have evolved for negotiating issues on trade in services, how negotiations should be organized and prepared, and good negotiating habits used by successful negotiators. The Appendix focuses first on where negotiations on trade in services take place, why governments negotiate in different venues and how the venues affect the outcome of negotiations, what is negotiated under the rubric of trade in services, how the negotiation on a particular issue moves from one venue to another, and how issues related to trade in services are negotiated. The Appendix then considers that WTO negotiations on trade in services concentrate on specific commitments by individual national governments and the rules that apply to all member countries. Countries negotiate specific national commitments bilaterally, with each country negotiating with every other member of the WTO. Since every country must extend the commitment made to any one country to all other countries that belong to the WTO, however, each country will seek to "sell" the same commitment to as many other member countries as possible. In contrast, countries negotiate rules multilaterally, i.e. collectively. The negotiating dynamics are quite different in the two cases. The bilateral negotiation of specific national commitments takes the form of a bilateral bargaining process based on requests and offers, while the multilateral negotiation of rules involves an effort to build consensus among member countries on broad principles. The practical implications of these differences are discussed.

The Appendix moves on to consider the preparation of negotiations. The face-to-face negotiations are the culmination of a long and extended process of preparation. While many may think that the outcome of negotiations depends largely on the negotiating skills of individual negotiators at the bargaining table, good research and analysis and skillful shaping are often just as important, if not more important. It is essential to identify the objectives and an effective strategy in the negotiations to achieve the desired outcome and, in the process, to build coalitions with stakeholders in support of the objectives.

Success in negotiations, whether on services or any other issue, depends not only on innate bargaining skills and on the power of the countries involved, but also on a detailed and comprehensive analysis of the issues, persuasive oral and written communication skills, and the ability to build alliances. These are skills that can be learned and mastered by any competent professional in the field, and when even a relatively small country has provided the necessary training for its trade negotiators, they are able to have considerable influence on any negotiating outcome.

Successful negotiations follow certain guidelines that create an atmosphere of trust conducive to a search for win-win solutions and an orderly sequence for addressing the full range of outstanding issues in a negotiation. When these guidelines are followed by the participants in a negotiation, they create a positive feed-back loop that adds a dynamic momentum to the negotiating process.

The challenges involved in services negotiations are great, because barriers to trade in services are enmeshed in domestic regulations. In services an orderly process for sorting out the issues is therefore especially important, because such negotiations inevitably touch on issues considered the sovereign prerogative of any national government to protect its consumers and the smooth functioning of its domestic economy. Notwithstanding the challenges, negotiations on services have become extremely important for economic growth because the efficiency of all economic activity and the competitiveness of a country's manufacturing sector in the globalized, information-technology based economy of today depends on the efficiency of a country's services sector.

In an addendum to the Appendix, Flavio Marega discusses the experience of Brazil in trade in services negotiations

References

Alexander, I. and A. Estache. 1999. "The Role of Regulatory Reform and Growth: Lessons from Latin America," paper presented at TIPS Annual Forum, Johannesburg, South Africa (September).

Armstrong, M. 1994. "Competition in Telecommunications," *Oxford Review of Economic Policy* 13(1).

Bös, D. and L. Nett. 1990. "Privatization, Price Regulation, and Market Entry: An Asymmetric Multistage Duopoly Model," *Journal of Economics (Zeitschrift für Nationalökonomie)* 51(3): 221–57.

Chadha, R., D. Brown, A. Deardorff, and R. Stern. 2003. "Computational Analysis of the Impact on India of the Uruguay Round and the Forthcoming WTO Trade Negotiations", in A. Mattoo and R. M. Stern (eds), *India and the WTO*, Washington, D.C.: Oxford University Press and World Bank.

Copeland, B. R. 2001. "Benefits and Costs of Trade and Investment Liberalization in Services: Implications from Trade Theory," a paper prepared for the Department of Foreign Affairs and International Trade, Government of Canada.

Cowhey, P. and M. M. Klimenko. 1999. "The WTO Agreement and Telecommunication Policy Reforms," a draft report for the World Bank, Graduate School of International Relations and Pacific Studies, University of California at San Diego (March).

Estache, A., Q. Wodon and V. Foster. 2001. "Accounting for Poverty in Infrastructure Reform: Learning from Latin America's Experience," Washington, D.C.: World Bank.

Ethier, W. 1982. "National and International Returns to Scale in the Modern Theory of International Trade," *American Economic Review*, June, 72: 492–506.

Fink, C., A. Mattoo, and I. C. Neagu. 2002. "Assessing the Impact of Communication Costs on International Trade," World Bank Policy Research Working Paper No. 2929.

Fink, C., A. Mattoo, and R. Rathindran. 2003. "An Assessment of Telecommunications Reform in Developing Countries," *Information Economics and Policy* 15: 443–66.

Hodge, J. 1999. "Liberalizing Communications Services in South Africa," Trade and Industrial Policy Secretariat, Johannesburg.

Hoekman, B. (ed.). 2006. *Trade in Services at 25: Theory, Policy and Evidence*. Cheltenham: Edward Elgar.

—— and A. Mattoo. 2006. "Services, Economic Development and the Doha Round: Exploiting the Comparative Advantage of the WTO," in process (February 22).

Lamont, J. 2001. "South Africa U-turn on Telecoms Competition," *Financial Times*, August 15.

Markusen, J. R. 1989. "Trade in Producers Services and in Other Specialized Intermediate Inputs," *American Economic Review*, 79: 85–95.

—— T. F. Rutherford, and D. Tarr. 2000. "Foreign Direct Investment in Services and the Domestic Market for Expertise," Policy Research Working Paper #2413. Washington, D.C.: World Bank.

Mattoo, A. 2001. "Shaping Future Rules for Trade in Services: Lessons from the GATS," in T. Ito and A. Krueger (eds), *Trade in Services*, NBER, University of Chicago Press.

—— 2005a. "Economics and Law of Trade in Services," unpublished (February).

—— 2005b. "Services in a Development Round: Three Goals and Three Proposals," *Journal of World Trade*.

—— 2006. "Services in a Development Round: Proposals for Overcoming Inertia," in R. Newfarmer (ed.), *Trade, Doha, and Development: A Window into the Issues*. Washington, D.C.: World Bank.

——, R. Rathindran, and A. Subramanian. 2006. "Measuring Services Trade Liberalization and Its Impact on Economic Growth: An Illustration," *Journal of Economic Integration* 21(1): 64–98.

Petrazzini, B. A. and P. Lovelock. 1996. "Telecommunications in the Region: Comparative Case Studies," paper presented at the International Institute for Communication Telecommunications Forum, Sydney, Australia, April 22–3.

Robinson, S., Z. Wang, and W. Martin. 1999. "Capturing the Implications of Services Trade Liberalization," paper presented at the Second Annual Conference on Global Economic Analysis, GL Avernaes Conference Center, Ebberup, Denmark, June 20–2.

Smith, P. L. and Wellenius, G. 1999. "Mitigating Regulatory Risk in Telecommunications," Public Policy for the Private Sector, Note 189 (July), World Bank.

United Nations Conference on Trade and Development (UNCTAD) and World Bank. 1994. "Liberalizing International Transactions in Services, A Handbook," New York and Geneva: United Nations.

Walmsley, T. L. and L. A. Winters. 2005. "Relaxing the Restrictions on the Temporary Movement of Natural Persons: A Simulation Analysis," *Journal of Economic Integration* 20(4): 688–726.

Wellenius, B. 2000. "Extending Telecommunications beyond the Market: Toward Universal Service in Competitive Environments," Public Policy for the Private Sector, Note 206, Finance, Private Sector, and Infrastructure, World Bank.

World Bank. 2001. *Can Africa Claim the 21st Century?* Washington, D.C.: World Bank.

2 The GATS

Rudolf Adlung and Aaditya Mattoo

Introduction

This chapter seeks to explain the basic structure of the General Agreement on Trade in Services (GATS) and how it applies to measures that affect trade in services.* Although a number of terms and concepts in the GATS have been borrowed from the General Agreement on Tariffs and Trade (GATT), the older agreement covering merchandise trade, there are important differences. It is immediately evident, for example, that the GATS is more comprehensive in coverage. Its definition of trade in services extends beyond the traditional notion of cross-border exchange to cover consumer movements and factor flows (investment and labor) as well, and the scope of relevant disciplines is not confined to the treatment of products, i.e. services, but extends to measures affecting service suppliers (producers, traders and distributors).

The Agreement's breadth in coverage must be seen, however, in the context of a very flexible structure. For example, unlike under the GATT, the use of quantitative restrictions or denials of national treatment are not prohibited *per se*, but may be foregone under negotiable commitments. The application of such commitments to individual service sectors is defined in country-specific schedules; there are no common templates. It is therefore virtually impossible to find two identical schedules of commitments.

The structure of the GATS, as explained in the following section, seeks to accommodate the diversity of sector-related objectives and concerns among WTO Members. While it is comforting for governments that there are virtually no policy interests that cannot be pursued under the GATS, the Agreement's flexibility also implies a formidable challenge: the need to define these domestic interests and translate them, within the existing framework, into a coherent and effective negotiating strategy.[1] A subsequent section provides a brief overview of the achievements to date (or lack thereof) of the current round of services negotiations, while the concluding section discusses key negotiating issues from the perspective of developing countries.

---

* This chapter has been adapted in part from WTO (2002), "Interactive Course: General Agreement on Trade in Services," available at: www.wto.org

[1] See Adlung (2006a).

Basic Concepts: Definitions, Scope, and Coverage

WHAT ARE SERVICES?

Somewhat surprisingly, there is no definition of "services" in the GATS. While skeptics may wonder whether this might give rise to problems of interpretation, others may see an advantage in trade policies not being constrained by a particular concept whose implications are difficult to anticipate. From a merely pragmatic point of view, it was probably wise to leave this point open. Given the multitude of definitions of services developed in the relevant literature—intangible, not storable, simultaneity of production and consumption, etc.—negotiators may have found it extremely difficult to distill any clear language for the purposes of the Agreement. Also, it may have been reassuring that the absence of a definition of "goods" in the GATT had apparently not caused problems in the past.

Instead of worrying about precise terminology, negotiators thus opted for an open-ended classification of services proposed by what was then the GATT Secretariat (see Box 2.1).

The GATS takes a very comprehensive view of trade in services. Article I:2 of the Agreement defines trade in services for the purposes of the Agreement as consisting of four types of transactions or modes of supply:

- Mode 1: supply of a service from the territory of one Member into that of another Member, i.e. supplier and consumer interact across distance (cross-border trade).
- Mode 2: consumption of a service by consumers of one Member who have moved into the territory of the supplying Member (consumption abroad).
- Mode 3: services are provided by foreign suppliers that are commercially established in the territory of another Member (commercial presence).
- Mode 4: services are supplied by foreign natural persons, either employed or self-employed, who currently stay in the territory of another Member (presence of natural persons).

Box 2.1. Classification of Services Proposed by the then GATT Secretariat

1. Business services	7. Financial services
2. Communication services	8. Health-related and social services
3. Construction services	9. Tourism and travel-related services
4. Distribution services	10. Recreational, cultural and sporting services
5. Educational services	11. Transport services
6. Environmental services	12. Other services not elsewhere included

According to this definition, the scope of the GATS is much broader than that of the GATT in merchandise trade. The GATS covers not only traditional trade flows across borders, but also three additional types of transactions where supplier and consumer directly interact by way of the consumer moving abroad (mode 2) or the supplier, either a commercial entity or a natural person, moving into the territory of the consumer (modes 3 and 4, respectively). Although activities under various modes may be closely related in practice, e.g. a U.S.-owned hospital established in Australia (mode 3) may employ foreign doctors and nurses (mode 4) and receive medical advice through the Internet from a U.S.-based specialist (mode 1), the access obligations that the Member (Australia) may want to undertake in the sector could vary widely across the individual modes.

In certain instances, it may prove challenging to determine precisely which modes are actually involved in a particular transaction. For example, problems may arise in the case of electronic transmissions, where it is not necessarily clear whether a service is provided from abroad into the territory of a Member or, vice versa, whether consumers have "moved abroad" via the Internet. An additional element of uncertainty is the Agreement's broad definition of what exactly constitutes the supply of a service. According to Article XXV(a), this may include production, distribution, sale and delivery. However, not all stages necessarily fall under the same mode.

MEASURES COVERED BY THE GATS

An interesting feature of the GATS, partly related to the Agreement's broad modal coverage, is its application to the treatment of both services, i.e. products, and service suppliers, i.e., producers and/or distributors. Again, this marks a significant departure from the GATT, whose disciplines are essentially confined to measures impinging on trade flows or, in other words, cross-border flows of products. The GATS' extension also reflects the peculiar nature of many services, which can be properly defined and assessed only if characteristics of the provider are taken into consideration as well. Typically, quality standards in many service sectors do not focus on the product itself (legal advice, medical intervention, bank deposit), but on the education, qualification, solvency, etc. of the supplier involved (lawyer, surgeon, bank).

What types of measures are actually covered? Articles I:1 and 3 confine the scope of the Agreement to measures affecting trade in services taken by governments and public authorities, at all federal levels, as well as by non-governmental bodies in the exercise of delegated powers (e.g. government-mandated regulators or licensing bodies). In turn, this implies that purely commercial decisions without government interference are beyond the scope of the Agreement.

Table 2.1. Measures that May Affect Services Trade under the Four Modes of Supply

Mode of supply	A. Hotel services	B. Hospital services	C. Insurance services
Cross-border trade (mode 1)	[Feasible?*]	B.1 Hospitals not allowed to contract foreign suppliers of tele-health services	C.1 Car and fire insurance may be provided only by domestic companies
Consumption abroad (mode 2)	A.2 Exit charge for nationals traveling as tourists abroad	B.2 No cover of treatment abroad under public health insurance scheme	C.2 Life insurance policies purchased abroad are subject to a tax of [. . .] %
Commercial presence (mode 3)	A.3(a) Foreign equity ownership limited to X% A.3(b) Investment grants of up to Y% for new constructions A.3(c) Local zoning rules must be respected A.3(d) Foreigners are not allowed to own land	B.3(a) Total number of hospital beds limited to [. . .] until 1.1.07, and [. . .] thereafter B.3(b) Approval of new hospitals only in regions with less than X beds per Y people B.3(c) Obligation to comply with hygiene standards issued by Ministry of Health	C.3 (a) Number of foreign non-life insurers limited to ten C.3(b) Establishment only as a joint-stock company C.3(c) No more than five branches per company C.3(d) Minimum equity: US$1,000,000
Presence of natural persons (mode 4)	A.4(a) Number of work permits for foreign staff limited to [. . .] A.4(b) Skilled foreign employees must provide training to nationals	B.4(a) Doctors must pass a test of competence with the Ministry of Health B.4(b) Foreign degrees are recognized only if issued in countries with whom recognition agreements exist	C.4(a) No more than 10% of staff may be foreign nationals. C.4(b) Language requirement for board members

Notes: * Many Members have not undertaken commitments on hotel services under mode 1 since they considered cross-border trade of such services not to be technically feasible. However, according to Article XXVIII(b) of the GATS, the 'supply' of a service does not comprise only production and delivery, but includes activities such as distribution, marketing and sale. It may be argued that these are tradable across borders.

The concept of measures affecting trade in services is broader than it might appear at first glance. According to Article XXVII(a), a measure could take virtually any form, including that of law, regulation, rule, procedure, decision, or administrative action. Second, the notion of affecting trade indicates a particularly broad scope of application; "affecting" is wider in reach than, for example, "regulating" or "governing" trade in services.[2] In assessing the relevance of the GATS for a particular policy or policy proposal, Governments are thus well advised to use a broad interpretation. For instance, the mere fact that a particular measure is essentially intended to govern product trade does not preclude the possibility that it also affects trade in services. Table 2.1 gives examples of various types of measures that affect services trade under different modes.[3]

[2] WTO document WT/DS27/AB/R of September 9, 1997 (Report of the Appellate Body: European Communities—Regime for the Importation, Sale and Distribution of Bananas).

[3] As discussed below, the legal status of the individual measures under GATS may vary widely.

EXCLUSIONS FROM THE GATS

Nevertheless, the GATS is not omnipresent. It even excludes certain sectors or activities that might be considered mainstays of a country's service economy. The Agreement provides for two deliberate sector- and policy-specific exclusions. First, there is the so-called governmental service carve-out under Article I:3. It stipulates that, for the purpose of the Agreement, services supplied in the exercise of governmental authority are not considered to be services. The definition of such services rests on a twin criterion: they are supplied neither on a commercial basis, nor in competition with one or more suppliers.

It is relatively easy to list examples of "governmental services" that are relevant for virtually all countries, including fire protection, primary education, police and security services, or the operations of central banks. Other cases are less clear, however. For example, while some governments provide basic health services for free via a public monopoly, others rely primarily on private commercial entities, i.e., medical practices and hospitals, among which patients are allowed to choose. (Such systems tend to be complemented by subsidized health insurance schemes to ensure a degree of social equity.) Although there may be little doubt that the former systems are beyond the scope of GATS, as opposed to the latter, questions may arise in countries where free public provision, e.g. through government hospitals, coincides with a commercial market segment. Would such coexistence be deemed to constitute competition within the meaning of Article I:3?

In the absence of common definitions, any answer necessarily entails an element of speculation. Economists normally tend to associate the existence of competition with attempts of rival operators who may use various marketing instruments (advertisements, price and/or quality differentiation) to attract customers. Accordingly, if a "governmental supplier" does not behave like a rival, it might not be deemed to be in competition.[4] Additional questions may arise in cases where the relevant service is not provided for free, but in return for a certain fee or charge. If it is low in comparison to production cost, one might still be inclined to infer that no commercial interest is involved. Again, however, there may be borderline cases. Although a highly profitable telecom monopoly would certainly be considered as operating on a commercial basis, is this equally true for the exclusive provider of local voice services that is kept afloat only through high (cross-) subsidies?

The second full-fledged exclusion from the GATS is sector-specific. Pursuant to the Annex on Air Transport Services, the Agreement does not apply to measures affecting air traffic rights and services directly related to the exercise of these rights. Nevertheless, three sub-segments are explicitly mentioned as being covered: aircraft maintenance and

---

[4] Adlung (2006b).

repair; selling and marketing of air transport services; and computer reservation system services.[5] In addition, the Council for Trade in Services is mandated to review developments in the sector at least every five years with a view to considering the further application of the Agreement.[6] The first such review, terminated in November 2003, did not produce any results. The persistence of the special status of this sector might be attributed, on the one hand, to domestic commercial interests and, on the other hand, to the apparently smooth functioning of the existing system of bilateral air traffic arrangements under the Chicago Convention. Like any bilateral system, it tends to benefit countries with large home markets, which have stronger negotiating leverage than would be the case under conditions of non-discrimination.

DOMESTIC POLICY IMPLICATIONS

The broad reach of the GATS appears breath-taking at first glance. An outside observer might wonder whether Members have any possibilities left—for whatever political, cultural or historical reasons—to pursue non-trade and non-commercial objectives as they see fit. Concerns about undue external encroachment upon national policy makers are a major source of public criticism. However, there is nothing in the GATS that would justify such concerns.

The drafters of the GATS had the option of creating either a broad framework—in terms of sectors and permissible trade measures—that is very flexible in application or, rather, a system of tight disciplines for a limited number of sectors and circumstances. The Agreement that ultimately emerged from the Uruguay Round is clearly based upon the first option: an almost comprehensive system of rules combined with almost unlimited flexibility. There are virtually no policy regimes that would be GATS-inconsistent per se or, at least, that could not be accommodated under exception provisions. Typically, all measures listed in Table 2.1 are perfectly legitimate for WTO Members to maintain or to introduce. Some measures might even prove compatible with the guarantee of unfettered market access and full national treatment under relevant treaty provisions. An indicative list of relevant examples from Table 2.1 includes A.3(c), B.3(c), B.4(a) and (b), and C.3(d).[7]

---

[5] The commitments and MFN exemptions concerning 'air transport services' that are recorded in Figures 2.1 and 2.2 below thus relate exclusively to these three types of ancillary services.

[6] The Council for Trade in Services operates under the guidance of the General Council, which represents the WTO's Ministerial Conference. The Council for Trade in Services meets several times a year in regular session and, for the conduct of the ongoing services negotiations, in Special Session. It is open to all WTO Members. See also WTO (2002).

[7] Depending on their particular design and actual trade effects, some measures may need to be taken from and others be added to that list.

Access Obligations ("Specific Commitments")

MAIN ELEMENTS

All WTO Members are signatories to the GATS and, thus, are legally required to submit a schedule of commitments (Article XX:1). The schedule serves to specify a set of access and other commitments that a Member undertakes in individual sectors. As noted above, given the diversity of the WTO membership and the flexibility of the Agreement, it might be impossible to find Members with identical schedules.

All schedules have a common format, consisting of four columns. The first column is used to indicate the sector covered, while the second and the third columns serve to specify the trade commitments, by mode of supply, assumed by the Member concerned. These relate to two distinct sets of obligations laid down in Part III of the Agreement, market access (Article XVI) and national treatment (Article XVII). Given the existence of four modes of supply, there are at least eight entries per sector, four each in the market access and national treatment column. A fourth column might be used to undertake any additional commitments not falling under these provisions (Table 2.2).

The scheduling of commitments under the GATS is based on a so-called "hybrid approach." Market access and national treatment commitments are undertaken only in those sectors that a Member has listed in its schedule ("bottom–up"). The GATS, in Article XX:1, requires all WTO Members to set out in a schedule the commitments they undertake, but does not further prescribe any particular sector focus. There are no attempts, whatsoever, to ensure a balance in sector coverage. Figure 2.1 shows vast differences in the extent to which individual sectors have been committed. Members' "scheduling preferences" may have been influenced, first, by the degree to which particular segments have traditionally been open to foreign participation. Tourism is a typical example of an area in which virtually all countries have long maintained comparatively liberal investment regimes. Second, there is an apparent concentration on sectors of general infrastructural importance, which provide economy-wide inputs. Openness in such sectors, and the related flows of investment, skills and expertise, may promote growth and efficiency across very many user industries.

Table 2.2. Structure of a Schedule of Commitments

Sector or sub-sector	Limitations on market access	Limitations on national treatment	Additional commitments
Hotels and restaurants	(1)...	(1)...	...
	(2)...	(2)...	
	(3)...	(3)...	
CPC 641-643	(4)...	(4)...	

The legal scope of the commitments, as specified in Articles XVI and XVII respectively, applies in full unless a Member inscribes one or more limitations under a particular mode ("top–down"). The absence of limitations is indicated by the entry "none." However, Members remain free to completely exclude one or more modes in either column from commitments, thus retaining policy discretion. In this case, the entry would read "unbound." The implications are comparable to a situation in which the sector has not been inscribed at all.

Although there is no uniform classification of service sectors, similar to the Harmonized System used for tariff concessions under the GATT, the sector definitions underlying most current schedules of commitments display a large degree of commonality. Quite a number of Members have worked with a Sectoral Classification List that was developed by the previous GATT Secretariat during the Uruguay Round. It consists of 11 broadly defined sectors (plus one residual category), which are further divided into some 160 sub-sectors. Excluding exceptions in financial and telecommunication services, the sub-sectors concord to a considerable degree to categories contained and described in a classification list developed by the UN in the early 1990s for mainly statistical purposes (provisional UN Central Product Classification). To enhance clarity, many Members have added in their schedules the respective CPC numbers to the sector names. A recent dispute case, revolving *inter alia* around the classification of gambling services, suggests that Members are well

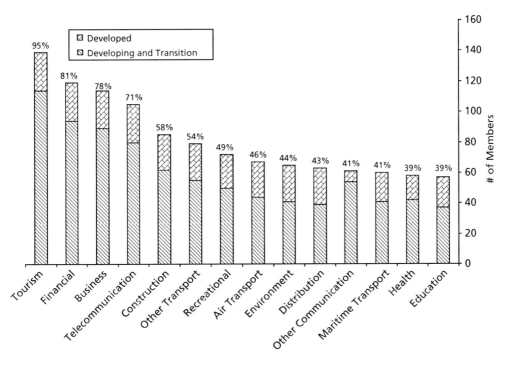

Figure 2.1. Sector focus of current schedules, November 2005

advised either to base themselves explicitly on the relevant CPC categories or, if a CPC category is deemed inappropriate, to specify clearly an alternative definition.[8]

A schedule can be changed only upon the initiative of the Member concerned. The classifications used are thus not affected by revisions of the Central Product Classification (CPC) that have taken place in recent years. To avoid overlaps and other inconsistencies with existing entries, the commitments negotiated in the new round are again based largely on provisional CPC.

Schedules are legal instruments that guarantee, as a minimum, the specified access conditions. Enforceable via dispute settlement, they create an element of transparency and predictability in international services trade that did not previously exist. However, as mentioned before, the number of sectors inscribed and the depth of the commitments undertaken vary widely among Members (Table 2.3). In non-scheduled sectors, governments remain free at any time to grant or withdraw market access and national treatment as defined in the relevant Articles. By the same token, if a sector has been liberalized beyond the scheduled level, nothing in the Agreement would prevent a Member from withdrawing the additional elements. The government concerned is thus able to explore the implications of a more liberal environment, while at the same time retaining the possibility of policy corrections. On the other hand, such non-scheduled liberalization may prove less attractive for potential market entrants, and therefore generate more modest trade and investment effects, than would be the case under corresponding bindings under the GATS.[9]

Table 2.3. Commitments by Country Group, November 2005

Countries	Average number of sectors included in schedules	Range (Lowest/highest number of sectors scheduled by individual countries)
Least-developed economies	24	1–111
Developing & transition economies	52	1–147
	(104)*	(58–147)*
Developed economies	105	86–115
Accessions since 1995	102	37–147
ALL MEMBERS	50	1–147

Notes: Total number of sectors: 160. Total number of Members: 146.
*Transition economies only.

Source: Adapted from WTO.

[8] WTO documents WT/DS285/R of November 14, 2004 and WT/DS285/AB/R of April 7, 2005 (Report of the Panel and Appellate Body: *United States—Measures Affecting the Cross-Border Supply of Gambling and Betting Services*).

[9] A study undertaken in the wake of the extended negotiations on basic telecommunications, terminated in 1997, found that

'controlling for geographical region and income level, countries that have made GATS commitments in basic telecommunications tend to outperform those countries that have not made commitments in basic telecommunications with respect to fixed and mobile penetration as well as sector revenues (as a percentage of GDP).'

See Bressie et al. (2005).

Potentially interested suppliers will consider the risk of policy slippages and reversals, since governments remain more susceptible to pressure from sector incumbents and their lobbies.

MARKET ACCESS (ARTICLE XVI)

Article XVI:2 provides an exhaustive list of six types of restrictions that a Member is not allowed to operate in a scheduled sector unless it has inscribed the relevant limitation. Among the six limitations, four deal with quota-type limits that are placed on the number of suppliers (C.3(a) in Table 2.1), value of transactions or assets (B.1, B.3(a), and C.1(a)), number of operations or quantity of output (C.3(c)), and number of natural persons (A.4(a) and C.4(a)). These limits may also be expressed in the form of an economic needs test (B.3(b)), in which case Members are held to specify the approval criteria that are being applied.[10] The relevant provisions, in Article XVI:2(a) to (d), do not distinguish between restrictions that are non-discriminatory in nature and those targeted only at foreign services or service suppliers seeking access to, or operating within, the relevant market (A.4(a) and C.4(a)). Article XVI can thus be interpreted to cover measures of the type "only five foreign banks (telecom operators, insurance companies, etc.) will be granted licenses" as well as measures relating simply to the number of banks etc. without introducing nationality criteria.

The two remaining limitations, specified in Article XVI:2(e) and (f), are non-quantitative in nature. They relate, respectively, to measures prescribing the form of legal incorporation (C.3(b)), including joint venture requirements, and to limits on foreign capital participation (A.3(a)). Unlike the former four types of restrictions, joint venture requirements and foreign equity ceilings are discriminatory by nature.

One aspect of Article XVI deserves particular attention. The Article's scope of applicability is explicitly limited to the six types of restrictions indicated above, and does not extend to other measures that, from an economic perspective, may be deemed to affect market access as well. Perhaps most significantly, fiscal measures and minimum-size requirements of whatever type (related to equity, capacity, etc.) are not addressed. Thus, a Member could maintain, without being obliged to schedule, a high non-discriminatory tax on a particular service although affected suppliers may consider it as a severe barrier to their trade. Similarly, although minimum capital requirements (C.3(d)) or tight environmental, professional and other standards (A.3(c), B.3(c), and

---

[10] See the so-called Scheduling Guidelines (SG), para. 9 in WTO document S/L/92 of March 28, 2001. The Guidelines have been negotiated by Members with the view to harmonizing scheduling practices and thus, facilitating the interpretation of schedules and promoting precision, clarity and comparability. Although the document notes that "the answers should not be considered as a legal interpretation of the GATS," it has been used by many Members as a basis for drafting their schedules of specific commitments.

B.4(a)) might deter many potential entrants from seeking market access, such measures do not constitute restrictions within the meaning of Article XVI.[11] However, other GATS provisions, in particular Article VI on domestic regulation, may prove relevant.[12]

Furthermore, the limitations must be read as minimum guarantees rather than maximum ceilings. In other words, a country that has limited its commitments to licensing only five foreign banks remains free at any time to accept additional entrants. We shall return to these issues later.

NATIONAL TREATMENT (ARTICLE XVII)

While the GATT (Article III) guarantees full national treatment to duty-paid imports under all trade-related laws and regulations, national treatment under the GATS applies only to the sectors inscribed in schedules and to the extent that no limitations have been attached. The identification of national treatment problems and their proper scheduling may prove challenging, in particular for new and inexperienced WTO Members.

Services schedules may need to be prepared in consultations with far more ministries and agencies (e.g. finance, justice, communication, construction, transport, tourism, education, health) than is the case with tariff concessions on merchandise trade. Coordination thus proves easier, from the perspective of a ministry of trade, if a checklist of relevant measures can be circulated within the government. While Article XVI:2 provides the basis for such a checklist with regard to market access, Article XVII only outlines the national treatment standard in general terms: treatment of foreign services and service suppliers, in respect of all measures affecting the supply of services, that is no less favorable than that accorded to like domestic services and service suppliers. "No less favorable" is defined to mean that the conditions of competition are not biased in favor of domestic services and their suppliers (Article XVII:3).

While the Agreement makes no mention of the measures that might be deemed inconsistent with full national treatment, the Scheduling Guidelines list close to 40 examples of limitations that Members have actually inscribed in their schedules. These include restrictions on foreign land ownership, discriminatory training requirements, and discriminatory tax treatment (A.3(d), A.4(b), and C.2). Additional examples, listed in Table 2.1, are exit visa requirements on tourists traveling abroad under mode 2, exclusion of consumption abroad from domestic support schemes in areas such as health or education, as well as language requirements that are not directly related to the

---

[11] SG, paras. 10 and 11.

[12] The Panel and Appellate Body Rulings on *United States—Gambling Services* (see note 8) have sparked discussions concerning the precise delimitation between Articles XVI and VI in the case of measures that have the effect of banning all trade in a particular service. See, for example, Pauwelyn (2005), Fidler and Correa (2005), and Wunsch-Vincent (2006).

exercise of a profession (A.2, B.2, and C.4(b)). The relevance of the national-treatment obligation may need to be assessed sector-by-sector. For example, while a language requirement for a bank's board members may be deemed to modify the conditions of competition in favor of nationals, a language requirement for interpreters may be considered a core-qualification criterion that all suppliers, regardless of nationality, can reasonably be expected to meet. Accordingly, no Member has scheduled such a requirement for translation and interpretation services.

The national treatment standard hinges on the effects of a measure (modification of conditions of competition), and not on the direct modal context in which the measure is being implemented. For example, domestic subsidies may well be granted regardless of the nationality of the supplier and, thus, would not constitute a national treatment problem under mode 3. However, what is their status if they affect the supply of *like* services under modes 1 or 2? In this context, how can *likeness* be determined under these modes and what are the consequences for scheduling commitments? In general, it would seem appropriate to compare the treatment of services supplied cross-border with those supplied by national providers.[13] Possibly with a view to avoiding unpleasant surprises arising from future interpretations, several Members have elected to inscribe subsidy-related limitations for all four modes in a horizontal section of their schedule (see II.B.3).

The national treatment provision cannot be interpreted to require a government to extend the reach of a particular policy to suppliers established abroad. The Scheduling Guidelines explicitly state (para. 18) that Members are not obliged under the GATS to take measures outside their territorial jurisdiction.[14] They are still, however, bound to provide national treatment for services provided within their territory even if the provider is located outside their territory.[15]

ADDITIONAL COMMITMENTS (ARTICLE XVIII)

Article XVIII provides a framework for undertaking commitments with regard to measures not falling under market access or national treatment. The Article only provides some illustrative examples—qualifications, standards, licensing issues, etc.—to which many more could be added. Additional Commitments currently play a particular role in telecommunications where some 70 Members have inscribed a so-called reference paper in the relevant column. This paper defines a range of regulatory disciplines, competitive safeguards, transparency and institutional obligations (e.g. independence of regulator)

---

[13] See Mattoo (1997). A dispute panel has ruled, against the background of a particular case (wholesale trade of motor vehicles), that like services may be supplied through various modes. WTO document WT/DS139/R of September 11, 2000 (Report of the Panel: *Canada—Certain Measures Affecting the Automotive Industry*). See also Cossy (2006).

[14] SG, para. 15.   [15] Mattoo (1997) and Adlung (2007).

that go beyond relevant provisions in the Agreement.[16] While the reference paper was developed by an informal group of countries and Members remained free to inscribe it, with or without modifications, the ensuing obligations are as legally binding as any other commitments laid down in schedules. Members have also used the relevant column to foreshadow liberalization initiatives—for example the preparation and submission to parliament of a law that would terminate a monopoly regime—where they are able to control only the procedural steps, but not yet a final outcome. The binding undertaking vis-à-vis other Members thus remains confined to undertaking these procedural steps.

OTHER SCHEDULING ISSUES

Horizontal Commitments

Many schedules contain a horizontal section. It specifies limitations and/or additional commitments that apply across all services contained in the sector-specific part that follows. The relevant entries are to be treated as if they had been scheduled sector-by-sector. The sole purpose of this section is to facilitate the readability of schedules and avoid unnecessary repetition. Horizontal limitations may well coincide with a sector-specific "none" which implies, in the absence of additional clarification, that the limitation prevails. In contrast, if a sector entry (e.g. 25 per cent foreign capital ceiling) is more restrictive that the horizontal limitation (e.g. 75 per cent), the former applies.

Overlaps Between Market Access and National Treatment

A number of the measures listed in Table 2.1 are not only inconsistent with full market access, but at the same time with national treatment as well. As mentioned above, some of these cases are explicitly listed and thus need to be scheduled under Article XVI (joint-venture requirements and restrictions on foreign capital participation). All other market-access restrictions may, or may not, be implemented on a discriminatory basis or otherwise modify the conditions of competition within the meaning of Article XVII. Typical cases of discriminatory restrictions are to be found under mode 4, presence of natural persons, where virtually all quantitative barriers are targeted only at foreigners (A.4(a) and C.4(a)). Under mode 3, commercial presence, many schedules also contain quantitative restrictions that exclude nationals (C.3(a)). Article XX:2 provides that the relevant measures need to be inscribed under market access only, the entry also provides cover for any inconsistencies with Article XVII if these are properly specified.[17]

---

[16] See, for example, Bronckers and Larouche (1997).

[17] Questions remain, however. For example, Members were unable to agree on what measures could be taken if a Member had left market access unbound, but undertaken full commitments on national

Phase-in Commitments

Services liberalization may prove more difficult to implement domestically than tariff reductions under the GATT. If a country's applied tariff is to be adjusted, the government may simply need to amend the administrative decree or regulation that specifies the relevant rates. In services, the process is likely to be more resource- and time-consuming, given that many barriers reflect sector-specific circumstances—exclusivity rights and other structural or institutional peculiarities—that defy rapid change. Thus, even if a country is prepared in principle to open a sector such as telecommunications to competition, e.g. in view of expected efficiency effects and budget savings, it may take years for the necessary legal and institutional changes to be implemented in full. And it is not rare for these changes to be staged over time, for example, in the form of an increasing number of licenses being auctioned off in subsequent years.

Nevertheless, a government may want to use external policy bindings as a spur to advance internal reforms and, if assumed during services rounds, as negotiating coinage to prod other Members to move along as well. Again, the GATS offers sufficient flexibility to accommodate such intentions. Commitments must not necessarily be implemented at a stroke when the results of a round enter into force, but may be postponed to specified later dates. Such phase-in commitments (B.3(a) in Table 2.1) are as legally valid and enforceable as any other commitments inscribed in schedules. They have been used for telecommunication services mainly where many countries have adopted more open regimes over the past decade. A number of African, Latin American, and Caribbean countries have bound themselves to introduce competition at precise future dates (Table 2.4).[18] Several Asian countries have also scheduled phase-in commitments to telecom liberalization, although in generally weaker terms. (In many cases, more ambitious bindings have been offered in the ongoing round of negotiations.) Phase-in commitments may be an interesting option in other sectors as well.

Modification or suspension of Commitments

As mentioned before, the very purpose of commitments is to enhance the stability and predictability of trade and investment conditions. The ensuing positive effects on economic expectations may have prompted several Members, including developing countries, to bind autonomously under the GATS liberalization moves undertaken in

treatment. There are essentially three lines of thought concerning the range of permissible market access restrictions: (i) Only those restrictions that can be applied in a non-discriminatory manner, i.e., measures under Article XVI:2(a)–(d); (ii) the former measures plus the limitations that are discriminatory by nature (Article XVI:2(e)–(f); and (iii) all types of market access restrictions, whether applied on a discriminatory or non-discriminatory basis. See Mattoo (1997) and Adlung (2006a: 881).

[18] See Mattoo (2003). For several countries, this would mark the end to the exclusive rights they have granted to foreign carriers for many years.

Table 2.4. Examples of Pre-commitments to Liberalization in Basic Telecommunications (Mode 3)

LATIN AMERICA

Argentina	No restrictions as of November 8, 2000.
Grenada	Reserved for exclusive supply until 2006. No restrictions thereafter.
Venezuela	No restrictions as of November 27, 2000.

AFRICA

Côte d'Ivoire	Monopoly until 2005, no restrictions thereafter.
Mauritius	Monopoly until 2004, no restrictions thereafter.
South Africa	Monopoly until December 31, 2003: thereafter duopoly and authorities will consider the feasibility of more licenses.

ASIA

India	Review the subject of opening up national long-distance services in 1999, and international services in 2004.
Korea, Rep. of	Will raise in stages foreign equity participation in facilities-based supplier.
Pakistan	Proposes to divest 26% to a strategic investor who will have an exclusive license for the operation of basic telephonic services for seven years.
Thailand	Will introduce revised commitments in 2006, conditional upon the passage and coming into force of new communication acts.

Source: Adapted from WTO.

their telecommunication sectors. It would contradict such intentions if commitments could be modified or reversed easily.

This does not imply, however, that governments are locked in for good, should something have gone wrong in the scheduling process or initial expectations fail to materialize. In such cases, Article XXI offers the possibility to modify or withdraw existing commitments. The Member concerned would need to notify the Council for Trade in Services of its intentions and be prepared to negotiate compensatory adjustments with affected Members. Should such attempts fail, Article XXI provides for arbitration. Only once all procedural steps have been exhausted in full, which may take several months, the commitment concerned can be modified or withdrawn.[19]

In addition, Members are allowed to restrict trade, even in circumvention of existing specific commitments, in the event of serious balance-of-payments and other financial difficulties. The relevant conditions—temporary application, avoidance of unnecessary damage, etc.—are laid down in Article XII.

Broader exception clauses, which could provide an override over all provisions of the Agreement, are contained in Article XIV. Modeled on Article XX of the GATT, they provide cover for measures necessary to protect public morals and/or human, animal or plant life and health, and to accommodate some other situations. The measures must

---

[19] The procedures for the implementation of Article XXI, as decided by the Council for Trade in Services, are contained in WTO document S/L/80 of October 29, 1999. Only one such process has been completed to date (February 2007). It had been invoked by the EC following its recent enlargements and served to consolidate the pre-existing Community schedule and those of the new Members.

not be applied so as to constitute "a means of arbitrary or unjustifiable discrimination between countries where like conditions prevail, or a disguised restriction on trade in services." The security exceptions of Article XIV *bis* allow Members, *inter alia*, to take any action considered necessary for the protection of their essential security interests.

Framework Disciplines

Part III of the GATS ("Specific Commitments"), comprising the provisions governing the scheduling of commitments (Articles XVI to XVIII), may be viewed as the centerpiece of the Agreement. All the access and country-specific trade obligations under the GATS are specified in and assumed under these three Articles. Nevertheless, their full implications can only be properly understood in the context of a broader framework of disciplines that are laid down in Part II. These disciplines essentially fall into two groups. First, there are those that must be respected by all Members in all sectors covered by the GATS, regardless of the existence of specific commitments ("unconditional obligations").[20] Second, there are disciplines ("conditional obligations") whose scope is confined to those sectors and modes for which a Member has undertaken specific commitments. Both sets apply as they are and cannot be modified by way of scheduling limitations.

UNCONDITIONAL OBLIGATIONS

The unconditional obligations contained in Part II can be grouped into three broad categories. Accordingly, all Members are required in all sectors under the Agreement:

- *not to discriminate between other WTO Members* (→ most-favored-nation (MFN) treatment pursuant to Article II and related disciplines (e.g. Article VIII:1));
- *to ensure transparency in the use of measures* (→ publication and information requirements, including establishment of enquiry points, under Articles III.1 and 4):[21] and
- *to comply with some additional duties, mostly procedural in nature, vis-à-vis other Members and their suppliers* (→ access to domestic judicial mechanisms (Article VI:2); consultation requirements concerning restrictive business practices (Article IX) and trade-distorting subsidies (Article XV:2)).

---

[20] Thus, only governmental services and core segments of air transport are excluded per se.

[21] Enquiry Points are mandated to inform other Members, upon request, on measures falling under the Agreement. In addition, Article IV:2 requires developed country Members in particular to establish Contact Points that facilitate the access of service suppliers from developing countries to information on commercial, regulatory and technical issues. The Enquiry and Contact Points notified by WTO Members are listed in WTO documents S/ENQ/78/Rev.[. . .].

Given the relatively modest levels of many access commitments, it is probably fair to say that the most immediately palpable result of the Uruguay Round, concluded in 1993, was the entry into force of the MFN requirement.[22] Pursuant to Article II of the GATS, all Members—regardless of economic weight, political affiliation, levels of liberalization, etc.—are automatically entitled to any trade benefits, whether or not covered by specific commitments, that a Member extends in areas falling under the GATS. All like foreign services and service suppliers must be treated on a par.

As in merchandise trade, the MFN requirement is a powerful instrument in particular from the perspective of small countries that do not have the economic leverage and administrative resources to negotiate effectively with large trading partners. It ensures that the "mice" are able to share automatically—"immediately" and "unconditionally" in the terms of Article II:1—any trade benefits that the "elephants" may be able to extract from, or otherwise extend to, each other. If there is a continued disadvantage of small Members, it is not rooted in discriminatory treatment, but unequal agenda-setting power. A Sub-Saharan country will certainly find it far more difficult to make itself heard and articulate its trade interests than a large developed country. Nevertheless, the GATS helps to contain such imbalances insofar as it provides a forum for information exchange, cooperation and coalition-building among all Members, large and small, that does not otherwise exist.[23]

Even for such core obligations as MFN treatment, the GATS offers more scope for accommodating country- and sector-specific peculiarities than is the case with the GATT. This was necessary for mainly two reasons. First, the Agreement's broad policy coverage, including investment-related issues under mode 3, extends its reach into areas with a long tradition of bilateral accords. These had certainly not been drafted in view of an MFN obligation that might be contained in a future multilateral agreement, and it could take years for them to be adjusted. Second, sector-specific reciprocity concepts are particularly widespread in services trade. Since reciprocity alludes to notions of fairness and burden-sharing, governments have found it easier to overcome domestic resistance to foreign competition if access remained confined to countries that offer comparable conditions. Reciprocity considerations are particularly widespread in professional services and transport.

There was thus little alternative for the drafters of the GATS but to include provisions, in Article II:2, that allow for the grandfathering of existing MFN-inconsistent measures. The Annex on Article II Exemptions specifies that relevant exemptions should not exceed a period of ten years in principle and be subject to review, the first to take place five years after the WTO's entry into force (i.e. in 2000), and be negotiated in any

---

[22] For a full discussion of the MFN obligation, see Mattoo (2000), and for an overview of current commitments see Adlung and Roy (2005).

[23] See Adlung (2004).

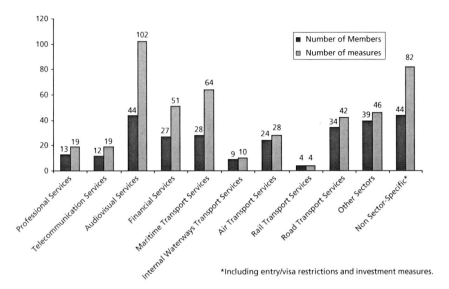

Figure 2.2. Sector policy profile of MFN exemptions, September 2004
Source: Calculations provided by WTO Secretariat.

subsequent trade round. About two-thirds of WTO Members considered it necessary to attach a list of MFN exemptions to their services schedules in order to obtain legal cover.

In total, more than 470 MFN-inconsistent measures have been listed. The relevant lists are in standard format, indicating the sector concerned, the relevant measure and its inconsistency with the MFN obligation, affected countries, intended duration, and the underlying policy needs. In over 90 per cent of all cases, the exemptions are intended to apply for an indefinite or otherwise non-specified period. Figure 2.2 shows their sector focus.

The possibility of listing MFN exemptions still exists for new WTO Members at the time of accession, but not for current Members. The only option for them to obtain cover for additional measures would be a waiver under Article IX:3 of the WTO Agreement. However, no such waivers have not been sought to date for MFN inconsistent measures.[24]

There are additional GATS rules that allow for departures from MFN treatment in specified circumstances, which may have been inspired by precursors in the GATT and certain multilateral trade agreements for goods. Relevant provisions allow Members to facilitate exchanges of locally produced and consumed services in frontier zones (Article II:3); to conclude economic integration agreements (Article V) and labor market integration agreements (Article V*bis*); and to recognize educational degrees, licenses, certificates, etc. from particular countries (Article VII). Unlike the ten-year time frame

---

[24] The only services-related waiver to date was sought by Albania which had encountered difficulties in implementing a phase-in commitment to telecom liberalization. See WTO document WT/L/567 of May 17, 2004 and Adlung (2007).

for MFN exemptions, softened by the insertion of "should" and "in principle," application of the latter provisions is not subject to any time limits. However, there are other constraints to prevent abuse. Article II:3, by its very nature, is strictly limited in its geographic application; Article V requires an economic integration agreement, inter alia, to have "substantial sectoral coverage" and provide for the elimination of "substantially all discrimination" between participants in the relevant sectors; while recognition agreements under Article VII must be open in principle for third countries to join.[25] Unlike Article II:3, whose application is virtually impossible to monitor, Articles V, V*bis* and VII contain notification requirements. However, doubts have been expressed by some WTO Members as to whether these are always properly complied with.[26]

In addition, the general exceptions contained in Article XIV, already referred to before, allow Members to disregard the MFN obligation, if necessary, for the attainment of the specified policy objectives, including protection of life and health.

CONDITIONAL OBLIGATIONS

While unconditional obligations apply across all sectors falling under the Agreement, the scheduling of commitments triggers an additional range of (conditional) obligations that apply only to sectors and modes for which bindings are being assumed. The basic purpose of these obligations is to protect the commercial value of what has been inscribed in schedules and prevent commitments from being gradually undermined, intentionally or otherwise, by ongoing policy changes.

Disciplines on Domestic Regulation

The GATS does not entail any constraints on a government's ability to pursue the regulatory objectives that it deems appropriate. The Preamble explicitly recognizes the right of Members to regulate and introduce new regulations on the supply of services in order to meet national policy objectives. These basic principles have since been reiterated, inter alia, in the Ministerial Declarations of Doha (2001) and Hong Kong (2005).

If there are "regulatory disciplines" in the GATS, they apply to the measures that may be taken in pursuit of any legitimate policy objective, but not to the objective per se. The intention is that Members prefer implementing measures (qualification and licensing

---

[25] In the event of autonomous recognition, other Members must be afforded "adequate opportunity" to demonstrate that their licenses or standards should be recognized as well.

[26] Concerning recognition measures under Article VII, see reports of various meetings of the Services Council in 2003, included in WTO document S/C/M/69 of December 15, 2003. In a similar vein, as early as 2000, the United States noted that a number of economic integration agreements had apparently not been notified to the Council as required under Article V:7(a) (WTO document S/C/W/147 of May 17, 2000).

requirements, technical standards and qualification procedures) that avoid unnecessary trade restrictions. Except for the accountancy sector, the relevant disciplines are, however, rudimentary at present. Article VI:4 merely contains a negotiating mandate to develop disciplines that seek to ensure, inter alia, that regulatory requirements are: based on objective and transparent criteria; not more burdensome than necessary to ensure the quality of the service; and not in themselves a trade restriction (in the case of licensing procedures).

As long as the negotiations are underway, Article VI:5 imposes some relatively soft stand-still obligations. Accordingly, Members should refrain from applying measures (qualification and licensing requirements, etc.) that would nullify or impair a specific commitment, that are incompatible with the above set of criteria, and that could not reasonably have been expected of them at the time when they made the commitment.

The only disciplines developed to date under the mandate of Article VI:4 relate to the accountancy sector. They have been put on hold pending the completion of the ongoing services negotiations. Although not explicitly provided for under Article VI:4, these disciplines apply only to Members that have undertaken specific commitments in accountancy.[27] An important feature is their focus on measures that neither fall under Article XVI (market access) nor are discriminatory within the meaning of Article XVII. In other words, it is impossible under the accountancy disciplines to justify citizenship requirements and similar discriminatory measures.

Negotiations under Article VI:4 are going on within the framework of the Working Party on Domestic Regulation. It is difficult to predict to what extent future disciplines in other sectors will be based on the accountancy model. Discussions in the Working Party have revolved around four core elements and concepts: necessity in view of a specific legitimate objective; transparency of regulatory principles and processes; equivalence (including recognition of relevant foreign qualifications); and international standards and their possible role as benchmarks.

Services trade under the four modes of supply may be affected by a multitude of measures—zoning laws, building regulations, shop opening hours, labor legislation, environmental standards, traffic rules, etc.—that are normally contained in general economy-wide legislation. The impact and scope of such legislation are broader than the Article VI:4 mandate, which is confined to qualification requirements and procedures, licensing requirements, and technical standards. With regard to measures of general application, the GATS adopts an even lighter approach. Rather than specifying requirements in substance, Article VI:1 calls on Members to ensure that such measures be administered in a "reasonable, objective and impartial manner" in sectors where specific commitments exist.

---

[27] WTO document S/L/64 of December 17, 1998 ("Disciplines on Domestic Regulation in the Accountancy Sector").

Table 2.5. Rationale for Regulation in Services and Potentially Relevant GATS Rules

Rationale	Relevant service sectors	Possible GATS disciplines
A. Monopoly/ oligopoly (→prevent abuse of market power, e.g. excessively high prices for access to networks)	Network services, including in telecommunications, transport (terminals and infrastructure), and energy services (distribution networks).	Transparency (Articles III and IV:2) and non-discrimination (Articles II and, in scheduled sectors, XVII); + possible generalization of key disciplines in telecom reference paper to ensure cost-based access to essential facilities + possibly strengthened disciplines to deal with anti-competitive conduct.
B. Information problems (→ protect users from dubious suppliers and low-quality services)	Intermediation and knowledge-based services, e.g. financial and various professional services.	Transparency and non-discrimination (see above); administration of relevant measures in a "reasonable, objective and impartial manner" (Article VI:1)
C. Externalities (→ protect third parties and the 'public interest', e.g. from pollution or congestion)	Transport, tourism, construction, etc.	+ possible generalization of the accountancy disciplines including application of a "necessity" test.
D. Public policy objectives (→ ensure social equity, distributional justice, regional access, etc.)	Health, education, telecommunications, transport, etc.	Transparency and non-discrimination (see above); administration of relevant measures in a "reasonable, objective and impartial manner" (Article VI:1).

Even though services sectors are very diverse, there is similarity in the rationales for regulation and the reasons for multilateral rules. The economic case for regulation arises essentially from market failure attributable to three kinds of problems—natural monopolies or oligopolies, asymmetric information, and externalities—and to government obligations to pursue non-economic objectives for public policy reasons (Table 2.5).

Because of its immediate impact on trade, market failure due to natural monopolies or oligopolies may need to be addressed directly by multilateral disciplines. However, the GATS provisions applying to monopolies, in Article VIII (see below), are limited in scope. They only deal with monopolistic and exclusive suppliers established or enabled under government legislation and only with resulting *domestic* distortions that are inconsistent with the MFN principle or specific commitments in relevant sectors.[28] Other monopoly situations that may be attributable, for example, to the existence of network effects (electricity grids, public transport, etc.) and/or economies of scale in markets of limited size, are not covered. Nor could Article VIII be used to challenge

---

[28] Given the import-related nature of the main GATS disciplines (MFN, market access, and national treatment), there are no effective remedies under the Agreement—apart from requesting consultations with the government concerned (Article IX)—for a Member whose market is distorted by monopolies operating from abroad and capitalizing on an exclusive position in their home country. See, for example, Adlung (2007).

competition-related access problems that affect all potential market entrants, whether domestic or foreign, to the same extent. As a consequence, in the context of the telecom negotiations, negotiators developed the so-called reference paper to ensure that such problems would not undermine market access.[29] The question arises, and may need to be addressed by WTO Members, whether there is a similar rationale for pro-competitive disciplines in other network services, including transport (terminals and infrastructure), environmental services (sewage), and energy services (distribution networks).

In other cases of market failure, multilateral disciplines may not need to target the problem *per se*, but rather to ensure that any domestic regulatory response does not unduly restrict trade. (The same is true for measures designed to achieve social policy objectives.) Such trade-restrictive effects can arise from a variety of technical standards, including prudential regulations, and qualification and licensing requirements in professional, financial and numerous other services. They are to be addressed in the negotiations mandated under Article VI:4.

Other Conditional Obligations: Additional transparency obligations

Article III:3 requires Members to inform the Services Council at least once a year of the introduction of new, or any changes to existing laws, regulations etc. that "significantly affect" trade in services covered by specific commitments. Like other notifications, these are circulated as WTO documents and accessible via the WTO Website. About two-thirds of the 370-odd notifications made between January 1995 and April 2006 fall under Article III:3. Of these, some 12 per cent are recognition measures covered by Article VII.

Competition Disciplines

Article VIII:1 calls on Members to ensure that monopoly suppliers in their territories respect the MFN requirement and, if they compete outside their turf, specific commitments that may exist in the sectors concerned.[30] Extension of monopoly rights into these sectors must be notified to the Council for Trade in Services and may result in the Member being required to modify the relevant commitments against compensation.[31]

In a similar vein, the Annex on Telecommunications aims to ensure that the conditions governing access to and use of basic telecommunications networks and services are not biased against foreign suppliers. Again, this obligation applies only in sectors, possibly including other telecom services, that are covered by specific commitments.

---

[29] See Section II.B.4.

[30] As indicated before, natural and any other monopolies that have emerged without government involvement are not covered by these obligations.

[31] However, such notifications have not been made to date.

Payments, Transfers and Capital Transactions

Apart from the balance-of-payments difficulties referred to in Article XII, Article XI prohibits Members from restricting payments and transfers for transactions falling under specific commitments. Similarly, any restrictions on capital transactions must be consistent with the access conditions that a Member has inscribed in its schedule of commitments.

NEGOTIATIONS ON (OTHER) GATS RULES

In addition to the negotiating mandate on regulatory disciplines under Article VI:4, the GATS contains three further rule-making mandates, namely on emergency safeguard measures (Article X), government procurement (Article XIII), and subsidies (Article XV). The fact that these issues were not solved during the Uruguay Round may not only be attributable to time constraints, but also to the structural peculiarities of the GATS (four modes of supply, right to operate quota-type and other limitations) and lack of empirical experience. Negotiators thus sought to avoid a final decision on the need for, and shape of, particular rules and disciplines. Even after several years of negotiations, in the Working Party on GATS Rules, the current situation in these areas would not allow for a consensus outcome.

The rule-making negotiations are some times referred to as the "built-in agenda," since the respective mandates are self-contained and not directly connected with the new round of services negotiations. A formal link was established only in the Negotiating Guidelines and Procedures adopted by the Council for Trade in Services in March 2001.[32] Accordingly, Members are held to complete all rule-making negotiations, with the exception of those on safeguards, but including those mandated in Article VI:4, prior to concluding the negotiations on specific commitments. The safeguards negotiations were initially subject to an earlier deadline, which since has been revised several times. A Council Decision of 15 March 2004 now provides that, depending on the outcome, the results of the negotiations under Article X shall enter into force not later than the results of the current services round.[33]

Discussions on GATS rules tend to revolve around some broad sets of questions, for which common answers remain to be found:

- The GATS allows Members to omit "sensitive" sectors and modes from their schedules or otherwise to inscribe limitations, including in the form of economic needs test. What (additional) purpose could be served by an emergency safeguard mechanism? What

---

[32] WTO document S/L/93 of March 29, 2001.
[33] WTO document S/L/159 of March 16, 2004.

would be the (remaining) value of a commitment if safeguards could be applied on top of scheduled limitations? In view of various structural differences between GATS and GATT, impinging, inter alia, on Members' use of import-displacing subsidies, can safeguards be expected to play a similar role in services as in merchandise trade?[34] Could the existence of a safeguards mechanism, and the possibility to avoid injury in the event of unforeseen developments, encourage governments to undertake more ambitious commitments? Given the paucity of detailed trade information in services, would it be possible to properly administer and monitor any safeguards action?

- While exempting government procurement of services from the application of the MFN obligation and any market access and national-treatment commitments, Article XIII provides for negotiations under the GATS. What should be their focus? Should it be the potential application of Articles II, XVI, and XVII to government procurement of services and, if so, in which circumstances? How would the new disciplines, if any, interact with other WTO frameworks, including the Plurilateral Agreement on Government Procurement (Annex 4 to the Marrakesh Agreement)? Or should the negotiations under the GATS remain confined to other procurement-related aspects? If so, what should be the focus?

- Acknowledging that subsidies may have trade-distortive effects in certain circumstances, the mandate of Article XV focuses on developing necessary multilateral disciplines. What could be the scope of such disciplines, given that subsidies affecting trade in services are already covered by the MFN requirement in Article II as well as, in scheduled sectors, the national treatment obligation of Article XVII? Are there adverse effects (e.g. via export enhancement) that are not, or not sufficiently, covered by these provisions? Is there any empirical evidence of such effects?

The New Services Round:[35] The Mandate and (Slow) Initial Progress

Unlike the GATT, the GATS explicitly provides for future trade negotiations. This mandate reflects the recognition that while the Uruguay Round proved a milestone in the history of services trade, because it helped create a multilateral framework of rules and disciplines and the architecture for future rounds, it was certainly not a milestone in services liberalization, judging by the breadth and depth of most current

---

[34] See Adlung (2007).

[35] See also the introduction and section III of Hoekman (2006) for a discussion and references on "The GATS: Genesis and State of Play."

commitments.[36] Today virtually all current schedules offer significant scope for improvement even if Members confine themselves to incorporating only the currently prevailing access conditions across a wider range of sectors or extending the benefits exchanged in a recent tide of preferential agreements to all WTO Members.[37]

According to Article XIX:1, WTO Members are committed to enter into successive rounds of such negotiations "with a view to achieving a progressively higher level of liberalization." The first of such rounds was to start "not later than five years from the date of entry into force of the WTO Agreement," that is January 1, 2000. The failure of the Seattle Ministerial Meeting in late 1999 thus did not prevent these negotiations from being launched. Nevertheless, the overall climate had deteriorated, and it took more than one year until delegations in Geneva were able to agree upon a negotiating mandate for services. (The Seattle Draft Ministerial Declaration had contained such a mandate, which initially mustered broad support, but was no longer endorsed by all Members as a basis for single-track negotiations.)

In March 2001, the Council for Trade in Services, in Special Session, finally approved the "Guidelines and Procedures for the Negotiations on Trade in Services." The two-page document, in three parts, builds to a large extent on relevant GATS provisions, in particular Article IV ("Increasing Participation of Developing Countries") and Article XIX ("Negotiation of Specific Commitments"). The Guidelines' content may be summarized as follows:[38]

1. *Objectives and Principles.* Confirmation of the objective of progressive liberalization as enshrined in relevant GATS provisions; appropriate flexibility for developing countries, with special priority to be given to least-developed countries; reference to the needs of small and medium-sized service suppliers, particularly of developing countries; and commitment to respect "the existing structure and principles of the GATS" (e.g., the bottom-up approach to scheduling and the four modes of supply).

2. *Scope.* No sectors or modes are excluded a priori; special attention to be given to export interests of developing countries; (re-)negotiation of existing MFN exemptions.

3. *Modalities and Procedures.* Negotiations shall start from current schedules (rather than actual market conditions); request-offer approach as the main method;[39] negotiating

---

[36] The situation tends to be different for recently acceded countries some of which have not only scheduled more sectors (Table 2.3), but also attached fewer limitations than any other group of Members. Furthermore, the extended negotiations in basic telecommunications (terminated in February 1997) and financial services (December 1997), in which some 70 Members participated, resulted in more meaningful commitments than those that had initially emerged from the Uruguay Round. See also Adlung and Roy (2005).

[37] See Roy et al. (2006).

[38] Elements that go beyond existing GATS provisions are in italics.

[39] Article XIX:4 refers to the possibility of bilateral, plurilateral and multilateral negotiations to advance liberalization without establishing priorities between these approaches. Request–offer negotiations are normally conducted in a bilateral context. (See, however, the additional—plurilateral—element introduced by the Hong Kong Ministerial Declaration).

credit for autonomous liberalization based on common criteria;[40] ongoing assessment of trade in services;[41] mandate for the Services Council to evaluate the results of the negotiations prior to their completion in light of Article IV.

In keeping with another mandate under Article XIX:3, the Negotiating Guidelines were complemented later by the "Modalities for the Special Treatment for Least-Developed Country Members."[42]

In view of the relatively detailed Negotiating Guidelines of March 2001, and Members' attention being absorbed by controversial other issues, the Doha Ministerial Declaration essentially confined itself to endorsing these Guidelines and integrating the services negotiations, including the rule-making parts (Sections II.C.2(i) and II.D), into the framework of the Doha Development Agenda.[43] The Doha Declaration contained target dates for the circulation of initial requests (June 30, 2002) and initial offers (March 31, 2003) of specific commitments, and envisaged all negotiations to be concluded not later than January 1, 2005.

However, the failure of the Ministerial Conference in Cancun, in November 2003, marked a serious setback. It was not until August 2004 that the negotiations were put back on track again. As far as services are concerned, the relevant Decision of the General Council ("July Package") contains a relatively short Annex which essentially confirms existing mandates and decisions and sets a target date of May 2005 for the submission of revised offers.[44]

There are no WTO documents that could be used to trace the requests exchanged between WTO Members. The circulation of requests was essentially a bilateral issue and not subject to any further information or notification requirements, let alone guidelines concerning structure or content. It was left to the individual Members to decide whom to approach and what issues to raise under relevant GATS provisions (Annex on Article II Exemptions, Articles XVI, XVII, and XVIII). Anecdotal evidence suggests that large developed countries circulated requests to almost all other Members, covering a wide range of services, and that most economically advanced developing countries have actively participated in this process as well. With the possible exception of some recently acceded transition economies, every WTO Member appears to have received at least a handful of requests to date.

The initial offers of new or improved commitments were made known to all WTO Members since everybody would be affected by their entry into force. Envisaged

---

[40] These criteria were developed later by the Services Council ('Modalities for the Treatment of Autonomous Liberalization' in WTO document TN/S/6 of March 10, 2003).

[41] Initially, this assessment was not conceived as an ongoing process, but was to be conducted for the purpose of establishing the Negotiating Guidelines (Article XIX:3).

[42] WTO document TN/S/13 of September 4, 2003.

[43] WTO document WT/MIN(01)/DEC/1 of November 20, 2001.

[44] WTO document WT/L/579 of August 2, 2004.

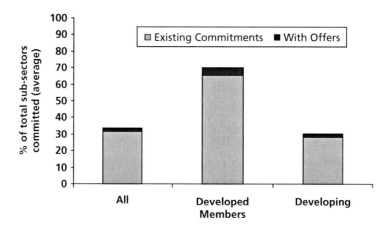

Figure 2.3. The impact of offers on the share of sectors subject to commitments under the GATS, November 2005

Source: Calculations provided by WTO Secretariat.

amendments are inscribed into the existing schedules and made commonly available via the WTO Secretariat.

While the request-and-offer process advanced smoothly, at least in procedural terms, some qualifications may need to be made.

● The overall momentum was not particularly impressive. At the target date of March 31, 2004, only 12 offers were available, to be followed by 26 more submissions prior to the Cancun Ministerial Meeting in early September 2004.[45] Although this number has increased significantly since—by mid-April 2006, 70 initial and 30 revised offers have been tabled—the geographic participation has remained uneven. While a relatively large number of countries from Latin America and, with some gaps, Asia have made contributions, Sub-Saharan Africa has remained largely on the sidelines.

● Possibly more important, there is a sense of disappointment concerning the "quality" of offers, both in terms of new sector inclusions and improvements of existing commitments. On average for all Members, if current offers entered into effect, the share of service sectors subject to commitments would increase by two or three percentage points to reach some 36 per cent (Figure 2.3). The overall emphasis is on the services and modes that already dominate existing schedules, with relatively little innovation in "sensitive" areas (education, health and other social services, as well as mode 4).

● The picture for MFN exemptions does certainly not look brighter either. Less than 7 per cent of the 480-odd exemptions have been earmarked for removal. The situation

---

[45] The EU is counted as one entity.

is disappointing. in particular because many of the proposed changes are only by-products of the Communities' enlargement to EC 25 and the re-organization of preferential relations in Europe.

Hong Kong and a Renewed Impetus

The services-related sections of the Hong Kong Ministerial Declaration, of December 2005, set a new standard.[46] The negotiating objectives contained in the relevant Annex are far more detailed than those listed in any preceding Declaration (see Table 2.6). This is true not only for the definition of mode-specific objectives, but also for the language on MFN exemptions and the proclaimed need to improve the technical quality and accuracy of the schedules. The gains in clarity and focus are combined, however, with relatively soft political language. An introductory sentence provides that "...Members should be guided, to the maximum extent possible, by the following objectives in making their new and improved commitments...".

Other new elements in the Declaration are provisions governing collective exchanges of request and offers (plurilateral request-offer negotiations) and an obligation to develop methods for the implementation of the LDC modalities. At the same time, the Declaration exempts LDCs, in recognition of their "particular economic situation," from the expectation to undertake new commitments. A second round of revised offers was due to be submitted by July 31, 2006, but fell victim to the suspension of the Doha Round negotiations, announced by the WTO's Director General on July 27, 2006 in view of the stalemate in agriculture.

In the aftermath of the Hong Kong Ministerial Conference, many Members have engaged intensively in the plurilateral request-offer process. By mid-April 2006, 22 plurilateral requests had been tabled and discussed in subsequent meetings with the targeted Members.

The general response to this new element in the negotiating process had been positive. However, process must not be equated with substance. It is one thing for delegations to have stimulating meetings in Geneva, and it is quite another thing for them to convince sector ministries at home of the potential benefits of achieving "a progressively higher level of liberalization" (Article XIX:1) in sectors and modes of interest to other Members. Moreover, it is worth keeping in mind that the services negotiations are part of a wider package and, thus, are intertwined with what happens in other areas of the Doha Agenda.

---

[46] See the proposal in Mattoo (2005) and WTO document WT/MIN(05)/DEC of December 22, 2005.

Table 2.6. Overview of Mode-specific Objectives as Contained in the Hong Kong Ministerial Declaration

---

Mode 1

(i) Commitments at existing levels of market access

(ii) Removal of existing requirements of commercial presence

Mode 2

(i) Commitments at existing levels of market access

(ii) Commitments on mode 2 where commitments on mode 1 exist

Mode 3

(i)   Commitments on enhanced levels of foreign equity participation

(ii) Removal or substantial reduction of economic needs tests

(iii) Commitments allowing greater flexibility on the types of legal entity permitted

Mode 4

(i) New or improved commitments on Contractual Services Suppliers, Independent Professionals and Others, delinked from commercial presence [. . .]

(ii) New or improved commitments on Intra-corporate Transferees and Business Visitors [. . .]

These commitments are to reflect, *inter alia*:

   - removal or substantial reduction of economic needs tests

   - indication of prescribed duration of stay and possibility of renewal. if any

---

Source: Adapted from WTO.

BUILDING ON HONG KONG

Once the negotiations are re-launched at full throttle, further thought needs to be given to the negotiating methodology, including in areas of export interest to developing countries, and greater assistance be provided to these countries in the design and implementation of services reform.

FORMULAE vs. REQUEST-AND-OFFER

As countries seek improved access for their exports, they must determine the appropriate approach to international negotiations, and choose in particular between two alternatives. One is a conventional request-and-offer approach; the other is the use of generally applicable negotiating formulae or model schedules. In the sphere of trade in goods, governments have sometimes agreed to a formula on the basis of which they cut tariffs across-the-board by a certain percentage. With a few notable exceptions, formulae have proved difficult to design for services negotiations because many different non-quantifiable instruments affect access to markets.[47] Moreover, developing countries

---

[47] See Adlung (2006a).

have strongly supported the request-and-offer approach because it allows considerable freedom in deciding on the intensity—by sector, mode and measure—of liberalization. There might, however, be a case for a more ambitious approach in modes 1 and 4 where developing countries tend to have a comparative advantage. More specifically, it may be possible to complement the traditional request-and-offer process with concerted or more coordinated approaches to liberalization. There seem to be four broad reasons to favor such approaches:

1. In a world of unequal bargaining power, multilaterally agreed formulae that can be deemed to be equitable and efficient are likely to produce a more favorable outcome for the weaker party (in terms of negotiating leverage or skills and expertise) than bilateral negotiations.

2. Formulae help reduce the transaction costs of negotiations by avoiding the need to barter commitments sector-by-sector, country-by-country. Thus, formulae can help overcome the difficulty in accomplishing an exchange (and balance) of concessions between countries that do not necessarily have a reciprocal interest in each other's markets. This argument is valid, of course, only insofar as agreement on a formula itself does not involve large negotiating costs.

3. Formulae can help overcome the free-rider problem that arises in negotiations conducted under an MFN-based system. The problem arises in bilateral negotiations because each of the beneficiaries of a concession from a trading partner may be tempted to understate their willingness to pay for it, hoping that offers of reciprocal concessions from other Members will be sufficient to induce the concession anyway. If each Member behaved accordingly, mutually beneficial deals might not be struck.

4. The use of multilaterally applied formulae is perhaps the only credible way of granting credit to unilateral liberalizers. It is much more difficult to ensure compensation for the loss of negotiating coinage caused by unilateral liberalization in a bilateral request-and-offer negotiation.

A FRAMEWORK FOR LIBERALIZING MODE 1

In light of the protectionist pressures that are emerging with regard to cross-border trade in services, especially business process outsourcing services, the GATS could help pre-empt the introduction of new restrictions.

Since GATS commitments are undertaken according to a "positive list" approach for specified activities, it is necessary to ensure adequate coverage of schedules. Two problems are evident: the inadequacy of the services sector classification and the paucity of Members' commitments. The existing GATS Service Sectoral Classification list

(W120) does not provide an adequate description of a range of services that are yet being traded today. Many of the "input" or "support services" (e.g. payroll or customer care services) do not have fully corresponding entries in the W120. Furthermore, it is not possible to "infer" commitments on input services from commitments on main service classifications (e.g. a commitment on insurance claims processing cannot be inferred with certainty from a commitment on non-life insurance services).

In order to remedy the inadequate classification and commitment situation, it may be desirable to push for comprehensive horizontal market access and national treatment commitments for GATS modes 1 and 2 that apply to all services and not only to a possibly limited range of scheduled activities. Such a broad forward-looking commitment could exempt particular measures (e.g. domestic support programs for disadvantaged groups or regions) and sectors (e.g. financial services that presuppose the movement of capital, and transport services that necessarily involve the movement of freight and people). If such an approach is not politically acceptable, then a less ambitious alternative could be to push for full commitments on a positive list of sectors, ideally at a high level of aggregation so that new services are more likely to be captured.

A FRAMEWORK FOR NEGOTIATING LIBERALIZING COMMITMENTS ON MODE 4

In previous GATS negotiations, many developing countries were disappointed by the dearth of commitments in an area of comparative advantage—that is, the movement of workers unrelated to a commercial presence abroad (foreign direct investment)—and are now seeking greater openness. At the same time, many multinational firms would like to see more scope for international movement of their personnel. This coincidence of interest could be harnessed to deliver greater openness. Again, a "model schedule" may facilitate an exchange of access commitments and define an acceptable set of multilateral rules that lead to more transparent and less burdensome policies.[48]

The challenge is to define a package that can exempt at least some forms of movement from the prohibitive political difficulties that have prevented any progress on mode 4. To begin with, and in order to harness the coincidence of interest between industrial and developing countries, the package could include both intra-corporate movement and the movement of personnel independent of commercial presence, as envisioned in the Hong Kong Declaration. Secondly, in order to remain politically feasible, the proposed liberalizing commitments may need to be circumscribed in terms of levels of

---

[48] The basic idea has been elaborated in the model schedule approach endorsed by the service industry bodies of the United States and the European Union. See Hatcher (2003).

skills, (maximum) periods of stay, and types of movement. For example, independent movements could remain confined to persons fulfilling services contracts and exclude employment seekers. Countries would be able to adopt more flexible and liberal regimes for other types of movement—within or even beyond the GATS. It might be possible, for example, to make greater progress on the movement of low-skilled persons in specified segments, for example old-age care, through bilateral agreements to which the WTO could acquiesce. The suggested delineation would focus negotiating attention on areas for which there seems to be an emerging international market, and for which multilateral negotiations could help eliminate explicit restrictions and create stream-lined procedures.

Even with this limited ambition, progress on mode 4 may require a more cooperative and less antagonistic approach, drawing upon the experience of a few relatively successful bilateral and regional agreements. The inclusion of labor mobility in the framework of a multilateral trade agreement implies that obligations are assumed by host countries only, to provide market access on an MFN basis regardless of conditions in source countries. The assumption of obligations by *source* countries also is a key element of regional trade agreements (e.g. APEC) that have facilitated mobility of the skilled, and bilateral labor agreements (e.g. between Spain and Ecuador, Canada and the Caribbean, Germany and Eastern Europe) that have to a limited extent improved access for the unskilled. Source-country obligations include pre-movement screening and selection, accepting and facilitating return, and commitments to combat illegal migration. In effect, such cooperation can help address security concerns, ensure temporariness and prevent illegal labor flows in a way that the host is incapable of accomplishing alone—thus conferring benefits for which the host may be willing to pay in the form of increased access.

Can these elements be incorporated in a multilateral agreement? One possibility would be for host countries to commit under the GATS to allow access to nationals of any country that fulfills certain pre-specified conditions—along the lines of mutual recognition agreements in other areas. Even if these conditions were specified unilat-erally and compliance determined unilaterally, they would still constitute a huge improvement over the arbitrariness and lack of transparency in existing visa schemes. Eventually, it would be desirable to negotiate these conditions (and establish a mechanism to monitor compliance) multilaterally rather than in an unequal, non-transparent and potentially labor-diverting bilateral context.

According to the current GATS framework, a country that makes a market access commitment is obliged to grant a fixed level of access regardless of domestic economic conditions. In contrast, bilateral labor agreements allow host countries to vary access depending on the state of the economy. One example is the bilateral agreement between Germany and certain Eastern European countries, under which the quota on temporary migrants increased (decreased) by 5 per cent for every one percentage point decrease (increase) in the level of unemployment. It may be desirable to consider GATS commitments along these lines, which allow necessary flexibility albeit in a transparent, predictable, and objectively verifiable manner, and would be a big improvement over the opaque economic needs tests that infest GATS schedules.

Facilitating Liberalization within Developing Countries

While market access is negotiated within the WTO, policy advice and assistance for regulatory reform are provided by multilateral institutions and other agencies. There is hardly any link between the two processes.

The Doha Declaration contains innumerable references to technical assistance, but they are not binding. There is a risk that the absence of assistance stymies reform—while the persistence of old (poor) policies weakens the case for assistance. A link could lend credibility to both liberalization and assistance programs. In their service schedules, developing countries would commit to phasing-in liberalization over a certain period of time, and developed countries would commit to providing the requisite technical assistance.

Two types of assistance are required in particular, as follows.

MORE POLICY RESEARCH TO HELP DESIGN REFORM PROGRAMS

In goods trade there are (or at least seem to be) straightforward recommendations on desirable changes of trade policy, in terms of the elimination of quotas and the reduction of tariffs. Any commensurate results of trade negotiations can thus be celebrated. In services, not only do we know less about the implications of market-opening, but the sequence of reform matters more. In some circumstances negotiations can lead to sub-optimal sequences, e.g. liberalization may be undertaken without the necessary regulatory improvements.

The challenge is to ensure that international commitments reflect good economic policy, rather than the dictates of political economy or negotiating pressure. An informed judgment will require a thorough analysis of the implications of, and rationale for, the existing barriers. In particular, it is essential to distinguish between the areas where liberalization is prevented solely by the political power of vested interests—to which the WTO's reciprocal market opening is an antidote—and the areas where regulatory or other problems are prevalent and need to be remedied before the full benefits of liberalization can be reaped. If the time frame for reform can be predicted, a government is able to decide whether to undertake phase-in commitments to future liberalization so as to lend credibility to the reform program or obtain a negotiating benefit.

Negotiating deadlines create a desirable sense of urgency about the need to find solutions to reform problems, but negotiating pressure alone is hardly likely to produce the best results. In previous negotiations, most countries erred on the side of caution and made few commitments to genuine liberalization, while some have gone very far. Among those who allowed unrestricted cross-border trade in financial services and, hence, full capital mobility were countries like Guyana and Gambia, but not the United States and the European Communities. Malaysia, Pakistan, the Philippines, and others were persuaded to protect foreign incumbents while they offered inferior conditions of operation to new entrants—thus establishing a new class of privileged suppliers. The 1998 Ministerial Decision on "duty-free" electronic commerce may have created the illusion of a liberated medium, but it has not addressed much more important quantitative and regulatory barriers. The liberalization of maritime and air transport was not even seriously negotiated due to the power of vested interests in the developed world; and yet, Sub-Saharan African countries pay transport costs that are on average more than five times higher than the tariffs they face. While negotiating proposals are seeking further liberalization of financial and telecom services in the current round, barriers in key transport sectors are likely to survive unscathed.

No government can participate meaningfully in international services negotiations without understanding how domestic reform is best implemented. Especially developing countries could benefit from the experience of other countries with these issues—although the experience with electricity in California and rail transport in Britain suggests that there is scope for learning on all sides.

Genuine ownership and understanding of reform strategies can come only through active engagement by national stakeholders—including producers and consumers of services—informed by independent research. Education, motivation and organization may take more time in many cases, however, than has been allocated for the Doha Round. However, negotiations cannot wait for these processes to be concluded in all countries. In the short run, a stock-taking exercise to consider national and cross-country experiences with services reform could help to identify the areas where there is little reason to defer market-opening, given the situation in a particular national market and the potential for economy-wide benefits, and those where there is significant uncertainty and a consequent need for caution in responding to ambitious demands.

MORE TECHNICAL SUPPORT AND RESOURCES TO IMPROVE THE REGULATORY ENVIRONMENT

It is clear that improved regulation—ranging from prudential standards to address informational and stability problems in financial services to pro-competitive regulation to deal with monopoly power in a variety of network-based services (see Table 2.5)—will be critical to the realization of the benefits of services liberalization. Policy intervention will also be necessary to ensure compliance with universal service objectives that seek to achieve, for example, a degree of social or regional equity. However, the necessary institutional underpinning can be expensive and require sophisticated skills. For example, even a bare-bones telecommunications regulatory authority is likely to cost around $2 million each year, or 5 per cent of government budget in a country like Dominica.

The development community is already providing support, but a link may need to be established between market-opening negotiated at the WTO and additional assistance for complementary reform that is vital for successful liberalization, but may not be a priority for national governments.[49] It will be necessary to diagnose regulatory inadequacies in specific countries and assess needs for assistance. Some relevant work is already underway as part of the IMF and World Bank Financial Sector Assessment Programs, for example. It will also be necessary to ensure that such links pertain to additional assistance, and that assistance is provided in a neutral manner, disconnected from the donors' domestic political agendas.

References

Adlung, R. 2004. "GATS and Democratic Legitimacy," *Aussenwirtschaft* 59(2): 127–49.

—— 2006a. "Services Negotiations in the Doha Round: Lost in Flexibility?" *Journal of International Economic Law* 9(4): 865–93.

—— 2006b. "Public Services and the GATS," *Journal of International Economic Law* 9(2): 455–85.

—— 2007. "Negotiations on Safeguards and Subsidies in Services: A Never-Ending Story?" *Journal of International Economic Law* 10(2): 235–65.

—— and M. Roy. 2005. "Turning Hills into Mountains? Current Commitments Under the General Agreement on Trade in Services and Prospects for Change," *Journal of World Trade* 39(6): 1161–94.

[49] There is, of course, a prior need for cost–benefit analyses to establish priorities for regulatory improvements, as has been argued by Finger and Schuler (2002).

Bressie, K., M. Kende, and H. Williams. 2005. "Telecommunications Trade Liberalization and the WTO," *info 7*, 3–24 at 20.

Bronckers, M.C.E.J. and P. Larouche. 1997. "Telecommunications Services and the World Trade Organization," *Journal of World Trade* 31.

Cossy, M. 2006. "Determining 'Likeness' under the GATS: Squaring the Circle?" WTO Staff Working Paper ERSD-2006-08.

Fidler, D. and C. Correa. 2005. "The WTO Decision in US-Gambling: Implications for Health Policy," in World Health Organization (ed.), *Legal Review of the General Agreement on Trade in Services (GATS) from a Health Policy Perspective*. Geneva: WHO.

Finger, J. M. and P. Schuler. 2002. "Implementation of WTO Commitments: The WTO Challenge," Chapter 48 in B. Hoekman, A. Mattoo, and P. English (eds.), *Development, Trade, and the WTO: A Handbook*. Washington, D.C.: World Bank.

Hatcher, M. 2003. "Draft Model Schedule for Mode 4: A Proposal," in A. Mattoo and A. Carzaniga (eds.), *Moving People to Deliver Services*. Washington, D.C.: Oxford University Press and World Bank.

Mattoo, A. 1997. "National Treatment in the GATS: Corner-stone or Pandora's Box?" *Journal of World Trade* 31(1): 107–35.

—— 2000. "MFN and the GATS," in T. Cottier and P.C. Mavroidis (eds.), *Regulatory Barriers and the Principle of Non-Discrimination in World Trade Law: Past, Present and Future*, The World Trade Forum Vol. II. Ann Arbor, MI: University of Michigan Press.

—— 2003. "Shaping Future Rules for Trade in Services: Lessons from the GATS," in T. Ito and A. Krueger (eds.), *Trade in Services in the Asia Pacific Region*. NBER. Chicago: University of Chicago Press.

—— 2005. "Services in a Development Round: Three Goals and Three Proposals," *Journal of World Trade* 39: 1223–38. (Shorter version published as "Services in a Development Round: Proposals for Overcoming Inertia," in R. Newfarmer (ed.), *Trade, Doha, and Development: A Window into the Issues*. Washington, D.C.: World Bank, 2006.)

Pauwelyn, J. 2005. "Rien ne Va Plus? Distinguishing Domestic Regulation from Market Access in GATT and GATS," *World Trade Review* 4(2): 131–70.

Roy, M., J. Marchetti, and H. Lim. 2006. "Services Liberalization in the New Generation of Preferential Trade Agreements (PTAs): How Much Further than the GATS?" WTO Staff Working Paper ERSD-2006–07.

WTO (World Trade Organization). 2002. Interactive Course: General Agreement on Trade in Services, available at: www.wto.org/english/tratop_e/serv_e/cbt_course_e/signin_e.htm

Wunsch-Vincent, S. 2006. "The Internet, Cross-Border Trade in Services, and the GATS: Lessons from US-Gambling?" *World Trade Review* 5(3): 319–55.

3 The Basic Economics of Services Trade

Brian Copeland and Aaditya Mattoo

Introduction

This chapter will review the basic economics of trade in services. Much of the logic behind trade and protection in services is the same as for goods trade. However, there are also a number of issues unique to services that will be highlighted.

Service trade differs from goods trade in two major ways. First, goods trade involves shipping goods from one country to another but cross-border trade is not the most important way of conducting international transactions in services. For services which require personal contact between customers and clients, trade is possible only via sales through a foreign affiliate or if either the customer or producer travels across borders. While foreign investment and labor mobility are also issues affecting goods trade, they are fundamental aspects of trade for some services.

Second, services tend to be highly regulated. Many types of services are publicly provided or are produced by regulated monopolies. In contrast to goods, relatively few services are subject to simple discriminatory taxes on trade. Instead barriers to trade in services arise from domestic regulations that often serve the dual purpose of responding to market failures (such as ensuring quality standards for medical practitioners) and protecting local suppliers from foreign competition. This means that identifying and measuring trade barriers in the service sector is very complex. It also means that simple rules for trade liberalization that have worked for goods trade (such as reducing all tariffs by 30 per cent) are not available as an option for service trade liberalization. Instead service trade liberalization is organized around the notion of non-discrimination and is often linked with domestic regulatory reform.

This chapter is organized as follows. We begin with a brief overview of how services are traded and then review the reasons for trade in services and discuss the sources of potential welfare as well as the effects of liberalization on income distribution. These issues are very similar to the standard analysis of trade in goods and factors. In the next section, we discuss interactions among the different modes of supply. This is important because restrictions on some modes (such as labor mobility) may either render some services non-tradable, or may force service providers to use another (possibly less efficient) mode. Then we analyze the effects of some of the most common barriers to trade in services. We point out via some examples how the effects of trade liberalization cannot be analyzed independently of the domestic regulatory system. The next section contains a discussion of the relative merits of trade agreements versus unilateral liberalization of service trade. We conclude with a summary.

What are Services and How are they Traded?

WHAT ARE SERVICES?

It may be useful to begin by asking: how are services different from goods? Services are often seen as intangible, invisible and perishable, requiring simultaneous production and consumption. Goods, in contrast, are tangible, visible, and storable—and hence do not require direct interaction between producers and consumers. However, there are exceptions to each of these characteristics of services. For example, a software program on a diskette or an architect's design on paper are both tangible and storable, many artistic performances are visible, and automated cash-dispensing machines make face-to-face contact between producers and consumers unnecessary. But these exceptions do not detract from the usefulness of the general definition of services presented above.

Instead of worrying about a precise definition of what a service is, it may be more useful to consider examples of various types of services. Below, we list the range of services covered by the General Agreement on Trade in Services (GATS):

1. Business services
2. Communication services
3. Construction services
4. Distribution services
5. Educational services
6. Environmental services
7. Financial services
8. Health-related and social services
9. Tourism and travel-related services
10. Recreational, cultural, and sporting services
11. Transport services
12. Other services not elsewhere included

HOW ARE SERVICES TRADED?

We can distinguish between services that necessarily require physical proximity between the user and the provider and those that do not. For many services—whose number is growing with the development of electronic means of delivery—proximity is not necessary, though it may enhance the quality of the service. A variety of financial, entertainment, information and communication services can be produced in one country and delivered, either electronically or stored in some medium (paper, disk, cassette), to consumers in another country. Trade in these services is not much different from trade in goods.

A number of services, however, require proximity between the consumer and producer, one of whom must move to make an international transaction possible. Such services include: construction services, where the supplier moves to the location of the consumer; tourism, where the consumer moves to the location of the supplier; and hair cuts or surgical operations, where either the supplier or the consumer moves. The movement of the supplier could involve the flow of capital, i.e. foreign direct investment (FDI), labor, or both. (See Box 3.1).

Thus, there are four ways in which international service transactions take place (four modes of delivery) that can be categorized as follows:

(a) *Cross-border:* services supplied from the territory of one country into the territory of another.

Box 3.1. Some Stylized Facts About Services*

- Services account for a large and growing share of both production and employment in most countries. In developing countries, the average share of services in GDP increased from around 40 per cent in 1965 to around 50 per cent in recent years, while in the OECD countries, the average share increased over the same period from 54 per cent to over 60 per cent. Many of the fastest growing sectors in many countries are services like telecommunications, software, and finance.
- The share of services in world trade and investment has also been increasing. They have been among the fastest growing components of world trade, growing by over 15 per cent per annum since 1980. Services trade, as estimated from balance of payments statistics, was around $2.1 billion in 2004, representing over one-fifth of world trade in goods and services. This value is certainly understated, because much "trade" in services takes place through an established presence, i.e. via FDI, and hence generates local activity and value added that do not appear as exports in balance of payments statistics.
- Today, more than half of annual world FDI flows are in services, and the value of sales abroad by foreign affiliates of US service firms is estimated to be 3.5 times greater than their cross-border exports.

There are two main reasons why trade and investment in services are growing:

- Technological progress, especially in telecommunications and information technology, has greatly enhanced the scope for trade in conventional services, like education and finance, and also created a host of new tradable services, such as software development and internet access.
- There has been a strong trend towards liberalization and regulatory reform in key service industries, creating for the first time scope for private and foreign provision. This trend began with the Thatcherite revolution in the UK in the late 1970s, and pursued also in the US, in areas like air transport, rail and telecommunications. Now most countries around the world are allowing private and foreign provision in increasingly competitive markets for services like telecommunications, transport, and finance.

Note: *See the data sources cited in Chapter 4.

(b) Consumption abroad: services supplied in the territory of one country to the consumers of another.

(c) Commercial presence (foreign direct investment): services supplied through any type of business or professional establishment of one country in the territory of another.

(d) Presence of natural persons (labor movement): services supplied by nationals of one country in the territory of another. This mode includes both independent service suppliers and employees of the services supplier of another country.

Goods production also frequently involves the movement of producers. After all, many multinationals produce cars and shoes in foreign locations for foreign consumers. However, in the case of goods, such movement is a substitute for cross-border trade: the cars and shoes could have been produced at home and shipped across frontiers. The same is true for some services: a legal service can be supplied over the phone or through the movement of the lawyer. But the important difference is that in the case of many services, cross-border trade is either not possible at all, or only possible if complemented by some form of local presence. A nanny must move if there is to be trade in child-care services; some types of software or an insurance company may be able to transmit services long distance provided their representatives are in face-to-face contact with the consumer.

What are the Causes of Trade in Services?

There are two major explanations for trade between countries: comparative advantage, and gains from specialization arising from increasing returns to scale or agglomeration effects. Both of these explanations apply to service trade as well as to goods trade. Moreover, both explanations apply not only to cross-border trade, but also to other modes of trade, including commercial presence and movement of natural persons. The first explanation relies on fundamental differences between countries to generate trade. The second approach can explain trade between similar countries: differences may emerge because of trade, but the differences need not have been present at the outset to generate trade. We will discuss each of these in turn.

COMPARATIVE ADVANTAGE

Consider the following examples of service trade: call centers in India provide customer contact services for US firms; nannies from the Philippines move to Canada temporarily to provide childcare services; and Europeans travel to Peru for a week in the jungle as part of an eco-tourism package. In each of these examples, trade takes place via a different mode: the call center services are sent across border using the telephone; the nannies travel to a foreign country to provide their services (movement of natural persons); and the eco-tourism consumers engage in consumption abroad. However, each of these examples has something in common: trade is driven by differences between countries. The trade in both child care and call center services is driven by differences in labor costs across countries; and the Amazon has unique attributes that are not available at home to the European tourists.

Differences in technology, natural resources, land/labor ratios, government policies, institutions, and other factors can all lead to differences in the prices of both inputs and outputs in the absence of trade. These price differences create incentives to trade.

One of the major sources of differences between countries is in factor supplies; that is, differences in availability of arable land, skilled labor, capital, etc. A country with an abundance of forested land will likely export forest products, a country with an abundance of highly skilled workers will export goods and services that are intensive in their use of skilled labor, and a country with an abundance of labor relative to capital and land will likely have relatively low wages and so export labor-intensive goods and services.

Differences between countries can also arise from a variety of other sources. Technological differences affect trade in both goods and services. For example, countries with access to sophisticated medical technology will export medical services. Differences in institutions and legal systems can also be important. Services such as insurance, for example, require that the client trust that contracts will be honored if a claim is made. Differences in legal and regulatory systems affect the degree of confidence that a foreign client has in a firm, and this can affect its export success. Differences in regulatory systems can also affect the speed and flexibility with which service providers can respond to customers' needs, and this too will generate differences between countries that affect trade patterns.

Some differences, such as skill levels and technological knowledge, are not innate characteristics of countries but evolve over time in response to economic decisions made by policy-makers and individuals within a country. It is therefore useful to distinguish between short-run differences between countries and those that persist in the long run. Knowledge of new technology will diffuse across countries. Hence specific technologically-based differences may only provide short-run explanations of trade in specific goods. However, countries that have institutions that encourage and reward innovation should on average be expected to export innovation-intensive products or processes even in the long run.

GAINS FROM TRADE

Trade driven by differences between countries generates two types of potential benefits. Producers gain from access to a larger market and higher prices, and consumers gain because they get access to both a wider variety of goods and services and to lower-priced imported goods and services.

Standard trade theory predicts that if markets are perfectly competitive, then a country will always gain from trade, in the sense that the country as a whole can consume more goods and services after trading than before. The logic for this result relies on the simple premise that if markets are perfectly competitive, then profit-maximizing firms will end up maximizing the value of national income.

While the gains from trade via export opportunities may seem self-evident, the gains from increased imports may seem less so. As an example, consider a country that imports software programming services and exports clothing, and for clarity, suppose these are the only products. Suppose it costs $100 to import a software package that would have cost $120 to produce at home. If markets are competitive, the $120 represents the opportunity cost to the economy of producing the software program itself. That is, the workers who produced software could produce clothing instead. And the value of the foregone clothing production must be $120 if markets are competitive. So this means that if the economy produces the software package itself, it has to give up $120 worth of clothing; but if it imports it, then it only has to give up $100 worth of clothing. Consequently, importing the software generates real gains to the economy, in the sense that it can consume more of both software and clothing with the same resources.

One of the major differences between service trade and goods trade is that much service trade must take place via movements of factors—such as movement of labor or foreign investment. If trade must take place through the movement of factors, are the basic propositions of trade theory—based on the notion of cross-border trade—put into question? One problem does arise from the point of view of positive theory: if different modes of supply are close substitutes, it is not easy to predict whether comparative advantage will manifest itself as a trade flow, investment flow or labor flow. However, from the point of view of normative theory there is no obvious problem: a country gains from the import of services, irrespective of the choice of mode, if the terms at which international transactions take place are more favorable than those available on the domestic market.

We illustrate this with an analysis of factor mobility, adapted from Bhagwati (1965). Assume a world where there are two countries, "home" and "abroad," and two factors of production, capital and lawyers. Capital and lawyers together produce legal services that can only be traded by the movement of lawyers to the location of the consumers. Capital is assumed to be immobile but the same analysis applies to capital mobility.

In Figure 3.1, the width of the box is equal to the total lawyer endowment of the two countries. Every point along the horizontal axis represents an allocation of lawyers between home and abroad. The number of lawyers at home is measured from the origin 0, and the number of lawyers abroad is measured from the origin 0*. Suppose initially

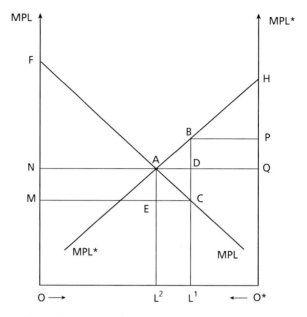

Figure 3.1. Welfare effects of service trade

there are OL^1 lawyers are at home, and the remaining 0^*L^1 lawyers are abroad. The two lines, MPL and MPL*, represent the marginal products of lawyers in each country, holding the amount of other factors and knowhow constant. MPL and MPL* are assumed to be declining in the number of lawyers for the usual reason of diminishing returns.

Now assuming that factors are paid their marginal product, lawyers will be paid L^1C at home and L^1B abroad. By adding up the marginal product of each lawyer in a particular country, we can determine the total product (that is, output or GDP) of that country. This equals the area under the MP curve for that country, up to the number of lawyers it has. For example, the output of home is everything under MPL to the left of point L^1, while the output abroad is everything under the MPL* curve, to the right of point L^1.

Note that with this initial allocation, the return to lawyers is lower at home than abroad. If lawyers can move, some will leave home and go abroad to take advantage of these higher returns. This flow from home to abroad will stop when the return to lawyers is equal in both countries, which will occur where the MP curves cross and L^1L^2 lawyers have moved. At this point, home will have OL^2 lawyers, and abroad will have 0^*L^2 lawyers. The equalized return will be L^2A.

Now consider the impact of the movement of lawyers on aggregate economic welfare and on income distribution, both internationally and nationally.

Table 3.1.A Welfare Economics A: Lawyers that Move Counted in GDP of Abroad

	Capital (home)	Lawyers staying at home	Output (home)	Capital (abroad)	Lawyers: old and new (abroad)	Output (abroad)	World output
Before trade	FCM	$OMEL^2$	FOL^1C	HBP	$BPO*L^1$	$HO*L^1B$	
After trade	FAN	$ANOL^2$	FOL^2A	HAQ	$AQO*L^2$	$HO*L^2A$	
Change	$-ACMN$	$+AEMN$	$-ACL^1L^2$	$+PBAQ$	$+AD\,L^1\,L^2$ $-BPQD$	$+ABL^1L^2$	$+ABD$ $+ADC$

Table 3.1.B Welfare Economics B: Lawyers that Move Counted in GDP of Home

	Capital (home)	Home lawyers	Output (home)	Capital (abroad)	Lawyers: old (abroad)	Output (abroad)	World output
Before trade	FCM	$CMOL^1$	FOL^1C	HBP	$BPO*L^1$	$HO*L^1B$	
After trade	FAN	ADL^1L^2 $+ANOL^2$	ADL^1L^2 $+FOL^2A$	HAQ	$DQO*L^1$	$HO*L^2A-ADL^1L^2$	
Change	$-ACMN$	$+MNDC$	$+ADC$	$+PBAQ$	$-BPQD$	$+ABD$	$+ABD$ $+ADC$

GLOBAL WELFARE

Total world output increases by the area ABD and ADC. Allowing factors to move to their most productive locations has clearly increased global welfare.

INTERNATIONAL INCOME DISTRIBUTION

World welfare improves. But whether welfare improves for home, the country of emigration depends on whether the welfare of moving lawyers is included. If such movement is permanent migration, and excluded from the calculation of national welfare, then welfare of those left at home declines by the amount ACE; welfare of those originally abroad, increases by ABD; and welfare of the migrants increases by ADCE. Thus, unlike in the case of cross-border trade, trade through the movement of factors can lead to a decline in the welfare of the country from which factors move. However, if such movement is temporary, or if migrants make substantial remittances, then welfare can increase at home as well. In the limiting case, if all the income earned abroad is remitted home or is considered part of the welfare of the country from where the lawyers left, total welfare at home increases by the area ADC. In this case, welfare of abroad also increases by the same amount as before—ABD.

NATIONAL INCOME DISTRIBUTION

The lawyers who originally worked in home and remained at home (OL^2) receive higher returns equal to the amount AEMN: their marginal product has increased because each lawyer has more capital to work with than before. By the same token capital at home loses by an amount ACMN because its marginal product declines. Thus there is a redistribution of income at home. Similarly, those who originally worked (O^*L^1) abroad receive lower wages and lose by an amount equal to BPQD. Capital abroad benefits from the increased supply of lawyers by an amount PBAQ. Thus, in both countries there is a significant redistribution of income, which may create political economy problems.

More generally, trade theory predicts that factors that have strong ties to import-competing industries will tend to lose from trade, while factors with strong ties to export industries will tend to gain. This means that it is unlikely that there will ever be unanimity regarding the merits of trade liberalization. It also means that it can be quite rational for individuals and interest groups to oppose trade liberalization. In principle, this opposition can be overcome by taxing the gainers to compensate the losers, but this is rarely done and is likely to be too complex to be practical. It may also delay or hamper the reallocation of factors of production. Consequently, when assessing the impact of trade liberalization, it is important to examine the impacts on income distribution, and to consider what mitigating policies can be put in place to soften the blows to the losers. These effects can be particularly critical for a country that lacks social insurance mechanisms to help those who lose their jobs or whose incomes suffer major reductions during the adjustment to freer trade.

To keep things in perspective, however, it is important to note that trade is only one of many factors that affect the distribution of income. For example, a number of studies on the evolution of income distribution over the past 30 years in the United States have concluded that technological change has been the main driver of increased inequality, dwarfing the effects of increased trade. Although improved technology generates gains to the economy as a whole, the benefits are not evenly spread, and some people lose. A dynamic and growing economy will constantly be subject to innovations, shocks, and entry and exit of firms. Trade is one of many sources of such change.

TRADE IN INPUTS

The argument for gains from trade applies both to goods and services destined directly for final consumers, as well as to those used as an input into production (Markusen, 1989). At one level the issues are very much the same. That is, if goods can be imported at a lower opportunity cost than produced locally, then the country's real consumption possibilities increase. However, there is an important added twist. Imports of producer services can lower costs of firms in the export sector and thereby stimulate exports. An example would be a country with untapped oil reserves. Access to foreign engineering services could lower the cost of developing oil extraction facilities that could then lead to increased exports of oil. That is, the benefits of allowing increased imports of producer services can be potentially magnified via their effects on improving productivity in other sectors of the economy.

Increasing Returns to Scale

While differences between countries are one of the major explanations for trade, particularly between countries with very different income levels, they cannot account for all trade. Much of the world's trade occurs between high-income countries, suggesting that similarities between countries need not deter trade. In fact, there is some evidence that the more similar are countries, the greater is the volume of trade between them. Moreover, much of the trade between similar countries is in similar products. For example, Canadian engineers work on projects in the U.S., and U.S. engineers work on projects in Canada.

There are several theories that explain why trade occurs between similar countries. Although these explanations have been stimulated by a need to explain the large amount of trade between similar countries, these same motives for trade will also be present when countries are different. Hence these additional explanations for trade complement and interact with the standard comparative advantage approach that we have already discussed.

One way to think about how trade can emerge between similar countries is to consider a labor-market example. Think of two students starting university who are equally bright and talented. At this point their productive capacities may seem indistinguishable. However, suppose one chooses to study medicine and the other chooses to study engineering. If we revisit these same students ten years later, they will have very different skills and they can trade with each other via the labor market, with the doctor selling medical services and the engineer selling engineering services.

This example highlights three key processes. First, there are *gains from specialization*. However, specialization did not initially occur because of comparative advantage. The students were assumed to be initially identical so there was no comparative advantage at the outset. Comparative advantage evolved over time because of the opportunity to trade. That is, each student made investments in education to develop his or her productive capacity in a particular field. This brings us to the second key aspect of this example, which is *fixed costs*. Instead of trading with each other, the two students could have each decided to spend part of their time being an engineer and part of their time being a doctor. However, because there are large up-front investments in education and experience required to be good in each of these fields, the students can avoid paying these fixed costs twice if they each specialize in different fields. Finally, because the fixed cost is an up-front investment, there is an element of *lock-in* to this example. At the beginning of university education, each student could have gone down a different path. But once the investments in education and experience have been made, it is very costly to switch fields. History matters, and decisions made in the past (including past government policies) have a large influence on current patterns of trade and apparent comparative advantage.

Let us now consider how increasing returns to scale can explain trade between countries (Krugman, 1980; Helpman and Krugman, 1985). There are at least four different ways that scale effects can generate trade: market niche effect, the development of firm-specific intangible assets, agglomeration, and networks.

MARKET-NICHE EFFECT

Let us come back to our engineering example. Why would engineering services be both exported and imported by the same country? First, if product variety is valued either by producers purchasing services as inputs or by final consumers, then firms have an incentive to carve out their market niche and produce a specialized variety of a good or service. If there are fixed costs to establishing a market niche or developing a new variety, then larger markets will have more product variety.

Examples of product variety in the service sector include entertainment (movies, television programs, music), tourism (consumers gain a wider choice of destinations), restaurants (cities that are open to a lot of foreign visitors can support a wider variety of restaurants), architecture and engineering services (a larger market allows firms or individual producers in these sectors to specialize in different types of projects), and many others. In fact since many types of services are tailored to individual customer needs, product variety is a major aspect of service trade.

The product-variety or market-niche motives for trade are important for producer services as well as for final consumer services. A larger market can support a wider variety of specialized producer services, which can lead to increases in productivity for producers of both final goods and services. As noted above, imports of producer services can lead to increased exports in other sectors.

GAINS FROM TRADE AND EFFECTS ON INCOME DISTRIBUTION

Trade driven by the market-niche effect will potentially generate three types of gains. First, the total variety of products available to consumers in any given market will increase because consumers gain access to both domestic and foreign varieties of the products. Second, each individual producer will have access to a larger market, and this can allow them to expand their output and reduce costs due to scale economies. Third, a specialized service that might not be economically viable in a small country might become viable as a result of the market-expansion effects of trade. That is, a larger market will allow the development of new goods and services that might not have otherwise been available.

The income-distributional effects of trade driven by the market-niche effect are likely to be less significant than when trade is driven by differences between countries. Because product variety is valued, and because trade can increase both imports and exports within the same sector, it provides both increased opportunities at the same time as it increases competition in any given sector. As we will see later, it is possible that trade may squeeze out some specialized local services; we will discuss this possibility when we consider trade policy. It should also be noted that the ability to create market-niche services may itself be a source of comparative advantage. That is, the market-niche motive for trade will interact with country differences, in which case our earlier discussion of the distributional effects of trade liberalization will be relevant here as well.

FIRM-SPECIFIC INTANGIBLE ASSETS

Consider yet another example of service trade. Large European and American financial institutions and insurance companies set up foreign affiliates to provide services to local customers in foreign countries. Foreign-owned firms may also operate local electric power plants or retail outlets. Some types of foreign direct investment (FDI) can be explained either by differences between countries (for example in the costs of capital) or by the market-niche effect (such as McDonald's fast-food franchises). However, the market-niche effect alone cannot explain why a foreign firm might be better able to more profitably operate a retail store or a power plant.

Many firms exist because they have developed specialized firm-specific assets, such as specialized knowledge of organizational and production processes, distribution and supply networks, and reputations for quality and reliability. This can explain the success of large firms in many different industries, such as financial institutions, construction firms, and courier companies.

Successful large firms can potentially provide services to foreign markets via each of the four modes. However the notion of intangible firm-specific assets is particularly helpful in explaining FDI. It is useful to think of two types of fixed costs: firm-specific fixed costs, and plant-level fixed costs. Once the investment in firm-specific assets is made, the firm's knowledge and reputation can then be exploited in each of the plants that a firm sets up (see, for example, Markusen and Venables, 2000). This can create gains from FDI. By setting up branch plants in various countries, the firm-level fixed costs need only be paid once, and each plant can be set up by paying only plant-level fixed costs. This creates gains to the host country as consumers gain access to a wider variety of specialized services at lower prices than otherwise would be available.

AGGLOMERATION EFFECTS

Increasing returns to scale can also lead to agglomeration. Agglomeration can take two forms. A particular industry can concentrate in one area, such as the concentration of financial services in cities like New York and London, and the concentration of the computer industry in Silicon Valley. Or there can be a general concentration of a wider variety of economic activity in cities, regions, or countries. That is, trade can lead to the emergence of "cores" and "peripheries."

Agglomeration can be explained in a couple of ways. One explanation is that there are spillover effects across firms. When a large number of firms locate close to each other, there can be positive externalities. There can be knowledge spillovers, as firms learn from each other. Firms can benefit from access to a common pool of specialized labor. And infrastructure can be set up to address the needs of a specialized industry.

Another explanation is that agglomeration arises from the interaction between scale economies and transportation costs or trade barriers. Suppose producers require intermediate goods and services, and that production costs fall on average when there is access to a wider variety of intermediate goods and services. Then if it is costly to trade intermediate goods and services either because of transport costs or trade barriers, market forces will tend to concentrate production in one place. Why? First, there is an advantage to being in a larger market because it can support a wider variety of specialized producers of goods and services. Second, trading costs segment markets. If it is costly to trade, then there is a cost advantage to being close to all the other producers of intermediate goods and services. But the more producers choose to locate in one market, the larger the demand for intermediate goods and services, and so the larger the effective market size is. Agglomeration can be self-reinforcing.

GAINS AND DISTRIBUTIONAL EFFECTS OF AGGLOMERATION-DRIVEN TRADE

The welfare effects of trade in the presence of agglomeration are complicated. Those who live in the core area gain from trade because the concentration of economic activity in their area leads to benefits from both scale economies and access to a wide variety of goods and services. However, those who live in the periphery may lose from trade if specialized goods and service production migrate to the core.

Whether or not there are gains or losses from trade depend on the magnitude of trading costs. To investigate this issue, Krugman and Venables (1995) consider a simple agglomeration model with two identical countries. There are two sectors, manufacturing and agriculture. Agriculture has constant returns to scale, while manufacturing productivity rises if firms have access to specialized intermediate goods and services. If there is no trade, then both countries are equally well off. As trading costs fall, then initially both countries gain because of access to increased variety of goods and services. However, at some point, the fall in trading costs results in one of the two countries becoming the core. This occurs when trading costs are low enough to make export of final goods cost-effective, but still high enough to create incentives for intermediate goods and services producers to locate close to final good producers. Once the core/periphery production pattern emerges, the periphery becomes worse off because the demand for labor drops, pushing down real wages.

However, as trading costs continue to fall, eventually, the low wages in the periphery lure back some of the manufacturing production, and real income in the periphery starts to rise. Finally, if all trading costs are completely eliminated, distance and location do not matter any more, and the distinction between the core and periphery becomes irrelevant.

This example suggests that while completely free trade could potentially benefit all countries, partial trade liberalization could hurt the periphery. It also suggests that the core does not have an incentive to eliminate all barriers to trade, because then the advantage of being in the core is reduced.

NETWORKS

Another scale-related motive for trade arises from access to networks. This motive for trade is at root driven by economies of scale, but the scale economies are not specific to an individual firm or even a given country. In many sectors, such as telecommunications, shipping, financial services, transportation, the efficiency, quality and benefits to consumers of the services provided depend on access to networks of other consumers and producers. For example, a phone system is only useful if many other people have phones; email became a standard form of communication after a critical mass of people had access to it; and the value of having a debit or credit card increases with the number of places that have access to a network that accepts the card. In such cases, there are gains from trade that arise from increased market size. If two countries of similar size each had their own internet network, then establishing a connection between the two networks would roughly double the number of sites that can be accessed, and double the number of people who can be contacted by email. This scale effect generates gains from trade.

In the case of shipping and transportation, networks develop within countries but regulatory barriers can limit the connection points between domestic and foreign networks. Allowing smooth connection and integration of systems can also generate gains from trade. For example, if three neighboring countries have customers who want to send packages to Peru, each country could have an airplane that carries packages to Peru, or they could all send their packages to a hub in one of the three countries, from which a single airplane would carry the cargo to Peru. Integration of the shipping network generates economies of scale that in turn can generate gains from trade.

The analysis of the benefits of liberalizing trade rules to allow smoother access to international networks is complicated by two important factors. First, because of the economies of scale that arise from having a large integrated network, some networks can come to be dominated by a small number of large firms. Therefore, there can be a tradeoff between the advantages of economies of scale and the costs of the concentration of power. Second, in part because of the issues of concentration of power, many networks are highly regulated. Networks are publicly owned in some countries, run by monopolies in other countries, and subject to various entry and regulatory constraints in still other countries. These differences in regulations across countries lead to barriers to trade that can be difficult to circumvent. These types of policy issues will be discussed later.

Box 3.2. Dynamic Benefits of Services Trade Liberalization

It is not easy to model dynamic gains from trade formally, but there are strong intuitive reasons to believe that well functioning service industries contribute to growth in different ways. An efficient financial sector leads to an efficient transformation of savings to investment, ensuring that resources are deployed where they have the highest returns; increased product variety associated with an efficient financial sector also leads to improved quality of consumer services and better risk-sharing in the economy. In the case of telecommunications, improved efficiency generates economy-wide benefits as telecommunications are a vital intermediate input and are also crucial to the dissemination and diffusion of knowledge—the spread of the internet and the dynamism that that has lent to economies around the world is telling testimony to the importance of telecommunications services. Transport services facilitate both the efficient distribution of goods within a country and a country's participation in global trade, and hence generate benefits in terms of learning and spillovers in knowledge. Although these are the more prominent services, others are also crucial—business services such as accounting and legal services are important in reducing transaction costs. Some believe that the single most important innovation in the history of the American capital markets was the idea of generally accepted accounting principles. Software development is the foundation of the modern knowledge-based economy. Education and health services are necessary in building up the stock of human capital, a key ingredient in long run growth performance.

The growth effects of services liberalization also arise from allowing movement of factors of production. A country that liberalizes its services sector is likely to augment its stock of capital (through increased FDI) and crucially the stock of human capital and technology that is embodied in or associated with such FDI. The impact of this on long-run growth is unambiguously positive. Furthermore, there is evidence that the presence of foreign factors can help enhance the productivity of domestic resources. This is as true for developing country capital importers as for developed country importers of skilled labor services. The contribution of imported skilled labor to the high-technology sectors in the U.S. is now widely recognized.

Modes of Supply

We have reviewed the major different explanations for the pattern of trade. These explanations provide a motive for trade. But they do not always explain why firms choose particular modes to supply services to foreign customers.

The possibility that services may be supplied by more than one mode raises a number of issues. First, if trade in all modes was unconstrained, how would firms choose to supply services to their foreign customers? Second, are different modes substitutes or complements? Third, what is the effect of allowing trade via some modes but not others? The answers to these questions have important implications both for predicting and assessing the implications of trade liberalization in services. Unfortunately, this issue has not received a great deal of study in the academic literature.

Asymmetric Costs Across Modes of Supply

For many types of services, the costs of provision vary substantially across the different modes of supply, and for some services, supply is essentially not feasible via some modes.

Tourism, for example, cannot take place unless consumers are free to travel and spend their money in foreign countries. Fast-food restaurant services cannot be provided without a commercial presence in the country where the food is served; hence this requires FDI or provision for franchising agreements. Construction services require a physical presence as well, so construction workers have to be able to move across borders if their services are to be tradable.

This heterogeneity across services is particularly important because countries have comparative advantages in different types of services. Rules that allow some modes but not others will favor some countries over others. A set of rules that allows FDI, direct cross-border export of services, and movement of customers between countries, but which does not allow labor movement across countries will preclude certain types of services from being traded at all. The services that cannot be traded in such a regime are labor-intensive services that require physical contact between the customer and service provider. Hence countries that have a comparative advantage in such services (labor-abundant countries) will be seriously constrained in their ability to export these types of services. Although there are many potential gains from importing services (especially via increased productivity in goods production), the gains from trade will generally be larger when foreign barriers to exporting services are removed as well. Consequently, the rules affecting different modes of supply can be critically important both in determining which services will be traded, and in determining the distribution of the gains from trade across countries.

Modes of Supply as Substitutes

For some types of services, different modes of supply are substitutes, in the sense that if one mode is not available, firms will use a different mode to supply their service to foreign customers. For example, consider an insurance firm. A foreign customer could buy an insurance contract by mail or electronically. That is, the insurance services could be directly exported. Alternatively, the insurance company could set up a branch office in the foreign country to serve its foreign customers. In that case, the foreign client would deal with the local office of the foreign insurance company. When it comes time to settle claims, the insurance company could send agents from the home office to assess the claim; that is, it could rely on temporary movements of personnel for assessments of claims. Or, if it set up a branch office, then foreign personnel from the foreign office could assess the claims. Another example is medical services. A specialized surgical team could come from a foreign country to perform surgery in the home country; or the patient could go to the foreign country to receive treatment.

If the different modes of supply are substitutes, then in some cases virtually all of the gains from trade can be realized by opening up just one mode of trade. This is the basis of Mundell's (1957) observation that under some conditions, trade in goods and services and trade in factors are perfect substitutes. That is, a country with an abundance of skilled workers can either export goods and services directly produced by these workers; or the workers themselves can move to produce in other countries. In both cases, gains from trade will be realized.

However, even when modes of supply are substitutes, restrictions on which modes are available to firms can have important implications. First, modes are typically not perfect substitutes. In the example of the surgeon above, hospital facilities will differ across countries and so the success rate and cost of the surgery will differ depending on where it is performed. Travel costs for patients and surgeons will differ. The health of a seriously ill patient may be jeopardized by travel; and the opportunity costs of travel for a surgeon may be high because of the needs of other patients. In the case of the insurance company, the reliance on a foreign office may increase managerial overhead expenses; but the presence of a local office might allow the firm to better deal with the needs of local clients. If firms are free to choose their modes of supply, one would expect that they would choose the most cost-effective mix. Restrictions on access to foreign markets via some modes but not others can therefore lead to increased costs of provision of the services and therefore potentially reduce the gains from trade.

Second, different modes of supply will have different effects on income distribution. For example, consider the insurance example again. Suppose a country (North) has a comparative advantage in the provision of insurance services. Suppose also that FDI in insurance services is liberalized but insurance agents are not allowed temporary access to foreign countries to assess claims and serve the local needs of their clients. In this case, insurance firms from North are likely to set up branch offices in foreign countries to serve foreign clients. This will increase the demand for labor in the insurance sector in foreign countries and may push up wages. On the other hand if FDI is not allowed, and Northern insurance personnel are allowed temporary access to foreign countries, this can reduce the demand for labor in the insurance sector in foreign countries and may push down wages.

The effects on income distribution can be more subtle and complicated than this example indicates. Complementarities may also occur across similar types of factors. For example, if a large foreign engineering firm has a contract to build a bridge, then allowing temporary access for foreign engineers can increase the productivity of local engineers who also work on the project (Markusen, Rutherford and Tarr, 2000). That is, allowing temporary access for foreign engineers may increase the incomes of local engineers. As another example, allowing foreign movie stars into a country to make a film can increase the demand for local actors who will work on the film as well. More generally, allowing FDI will have different effects on wages and employment than will policies that allow labor to move across countries. Even if the efficiency effects of the two different modes of supply are not very different, the effects on income distribution may be important in determining political support for the different modes.

In models with agglomeration effects, the choice between FDI and direct exports of services can affect the incentives to agglomerate. If direct trade is the only mode permitted, this tends to favor the country with a larger market because its larger size allows it to take advantage of the agglomeration effects. On the other hand, if direct trade is restricted, and governments require a local presence as a condition for local provision of the service, then the smaller market is favored, because such a policy will encourage FDI, which can increase the demand for local producer services, and thereby transfer some of the agglomeration benefits from the large market to the smaller one.[1]

Modes of Supply as Complements

In many cases the different modes of supply will be complementary. For example, if a firm chooses to have a physical presence in a foreign market, then the effectiveness of

---

[1] See Markusen and Venables (2000) who show how allowing multinationals to set up in smaller countries can erode some of the larger country's advantages.

their operation may be enhanced if personnel are allowed to move between the home and foreign establishments. As well, there will likely be direct intra-firm trade in services, with for example, research services concentrated in one location, accounting services in others, etc. A policy that restricted any of these three modes would affect either the cost or quality of the service provision. In cases where there are strong complementarities across different modes of supply, fully effective liberalization of service trade requires that all modes be opened up.

Services may also be complementary with goods trade. Export of goods requires transportation and insurance services, but it may also require the establishment of distribution networks, facilities to deal with repairs or with training of customers in the use of products, etc. Hence in some cases the potential gains from goods trade cannot be fully realized without liberalization of service trade. Conversely, liberalization

---

Box 3.3 Impact of Restrictions and Substitutability between Modes

---

How much a restriction on a particular mode matters depends on the scope for substitution between modes. At one extreme, if a service (e.g. construction) can only be supplied through one mode (movement of builders), then a prohibitive trade restriction on that mode shuts out foreign supply completely. At the other extreme, if modes (say cross-border and movement of individuals) are substitutes for the supply of a service (e.g. standardized software development), then the impact of a restriction on one mode is diluted. What determines substitutability between modes?

Technology

A few decades ago back-office services had to be performed quite literally in the back of the office. Today, the development of information and communications technology has made it possible for Swiss Air to have its bookkeeping services performed in Mumbai. Even though a surgical operation still requires proximity between the patient and the surgeon, it is conceivable that in a few decades, with the development of remote controlled robots, it will not.

Consumer Preferences

It is possible to conduct almost the entire range of financial services electronically. But while most consumers are happy to borrow long-distance, when it comes to depositing money, many still derive reassurance from the concreteness of local banks. Similarly, while an increasingly large number of consumers buy property insurance long distance, life insurance remains for the most part a face-to-face business.

Regulatory Environment

Sometimes market failures, such as those arising from asymmetric information, may be more difficult to remedy when the supplier is located abroad. For instance, it may be easier to establish that a doctor or lawyer established locally is adequately trained than one located in another country. Some financial services, such as borrowing from abroad, necessarily require capital mobility and governments are sometimes reluctant to allow this for macro-economic reasons. In the case of regulatory restrictions, however, it is important to distinguish between those which are the best instruments to fulfill legitimate objectives and those which serve a protectionist purpose. This is an issue that we consider more fully later.

of goods trade, e.g. in computers, may well be a condition for the realizing the benefits of services trade.

Trade Policy and the Service Sector: The Instruments of Protection

OVERVIEW

In this section, we analyze government policies that affect international trade in services. Although the analysis of barriers to service trade has much in common with the analysis of barriers to goods trade, trade policy in the service sector is much more complex because of the scope of and types of government regulations that inhibit trade in services.

For goods trade, analysts typically distinguish between tariff and non-tariff barriers (NTBs) to trade. Tariffs are discriminatory taxes on trade. An import tax is a tax levied on foreign goods but not domestic goods. Tariffs tend to be easy to measure and are very transparent. It is therefore quite straightforward to design an agreement to liberalize trade via tariff reduction (provided governments have the will to open up their economies to trade). Successive rounds of GATT negotiations were successful in achieving broad-based reductions in trade barriers via across-the-board reductions in trade taxes. Another feature of tariffs is that it is fairly clear what is meant by free trade: zero tariffs. This means there is a clear focal point for negotiations, and this has been exploited in numerous regional free trade agreements such as NAFTA, which have eliminated substantially all taxes on trade flows.

NTBs, on the other hand, are much more complex. An NTB is any government policy that has the effect of favoring local producers over foreign producers or which restricts or raises the cost of access to domestic markets by foreigners. NTBs can include delays at the border, quantitative restrictions on foreign products, government purchasing policies that give preference to local suppliers, subsidies, quality and certification requirements that favor local suppliers, etc. NTBs are more difficult to measure and are less transparent than tariff barriers. Moreover, there is often not an obvious focal point for negotiations because the trade-distorting effects of many policies are intertwined with other government policy objectives, such as protecting health and safety, encouraging regional development, etc.

Most trade barriers in the service sector are NTBs. Tariffs (discriminatory taxes imposed on foreign service providers) are relatively uncommon. There are several reasons for this. First, cross-border trade in services is often in intangible form, and this makes it difficult to monitor and tax. Second, the modes of supply for many services are different than for goods. Many services are exclusively delivered via commercial presence or via temporary labor movement. Barriers to FDI and international labor mobility can therefore result in serious restrictions on service trade and obviate the need for additional discriminatory taxes. Finally, many services are highly regulated or are provided by the public sector. Regulations that either intentionally or unintentionally make it relatively more costly for foreign suppliers to operate are major sources of trade barriers in services.

The pervasiveness of NTBs in the service sector means that trade liberalization in this sector is complex. Moreover, a major reason for the pervasiveness of NTBs is because of market imperfection in service sectors. Many trade barriers in the service sector are a side effect of domestic regulations that have legitimate purposes. For example, because of issues in asymmetric information, doctors must be certified to protect patients, engineers need certification to ensure that bridges they build do not collapse, and insurance companies have to be regulated to ensure their solvency. However, these same rules can be manipulated to protect local suppliers. For example, a rule requiring that an engineer graduate from a domestic university might ensure that quality standards are met, but would prevent consumers from having access to the services of highly qualified foreign engineers. The regulatory apparatus may therefore serve the dual purpose of responding to market failures and protecting local suppliers at the expense of consumers. A challenge for trade-policy analysis is to isolate the protective effect of regulatory policy from the beneficial effects, and to suggest rules for liberalization that provide the benefits of increased trade while ensuring that other legitimate policy objectives are achieved. In many cases, trade liberalization may not be possible or viable unless it is accompanied by domestic regulatory reform.

In what follows, we analyze a few of the common types of trade barriers that affect the service sector. However, because trade protection is often inextricably linked with domestic regulation, our analysis is not exhaustive. The trade-related implications of regulations will depend on the special characteristics of the service industry in question, and the types of market failures the regulations are designed to correct. Some of the later chapters will focus on trade barriers in specific service sectors. Our objective here is to highlight some general principles. Perhaps the most important of these is that the analysis of regulation-induced trade barriers must take place in a framework where the market failures that led to regulations in the first place must be explicitly considered.

We will focus on the following types of trade barriers:

- Tariffs as noted above are relatively uncommon in the service sector. However, we begin by reviewing the standard analysis of the costs of tariff protection because it serves as a useful benchmark to compare with other forms of protection.

- Discriminatory regulations which add to the cost of trading services, but which do not yield any direct benefits to local consumers, are a very common form of trade barrier. Examples include delays in crossing the border, country-specific standards for trucks (such as differing weight and trailer length regulations) that add to the cost of cross-border transport services, preferential government procurement policies, and lack of transparency of domestic regulations.

- Licensing and certification requirements inhibit trade in professional services. Doctors, engineers, architects, lawyers, accountants, and other service providers typically need to satisfy local regulations for certification. In some cases, compliance may be very costly (a domestic residence or graduating from a domestic educational institution may be required). These types of regulations can be justified by the need to protect consumers by ensuring that quality and safety standards are met. However, they can also protect local service providers from foreign competition, which can lead to higher prices and reduced choice for local consumers.

- Quotas are pervasive. On cross-border trade, they are common in the transport sectors. Foreign providers are either completely shut out (i.e. a zero quota) of certain segments, such as transport within a country; or only provided limited access, as in international transport. On consumption abroad, quotas are sometimes implemented through foreign exchange restrictions; e.g. the ability of citizens to consume services, such as tourism and education, abroad is limited by limits on foreign exchange entitlements. On commercial presence, quotas are imposed on the number of foreign suppliers who are allowed to establish in sectors like telecommunications and banking. Quotas on foreign participation also take the form of restrictions on foreign equity ownership in individual enterprises. Finally, quotas are perhaps most stringent in the case of movement of service-providing personnel, and affect trade not only in professional services, but also in a variety of labor-intensive services.

TARIFFS

We begin by reviewing the analysis of a tariff to use as a the benchmark. For those familiar with the analysis of trade barriers on goods, the analysis of the welfare effect of a tariff on services is the same as that for services.

Figure 3.2 illustrates the welfare effects of a tariff for a small country facing a fixed world price p for the imported service. The domestic demand for the service is denoted by D, and domestic supply is S. In free trade, domestic output is x_0 and domestic consumption is c_0. A tariff t on imports raises the domestic price to $p^d = p + t$, which raises output to x_1, but lowers consumption to c_1.

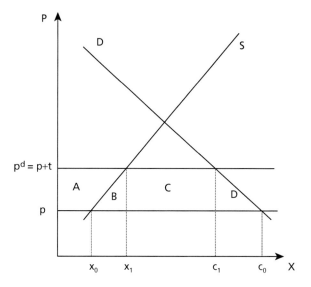

Figure 3.2. Welfare effects of trade taxes

The tariff redistributes income within the economy and also generates inefficiencies. Producers gain from higher prices, consumers lose, and the government collects tax revenue. Using a cost-benefit approach, we can measure the effects on each group by referring to areas in the diagram:

Rise in Producer Surplus:	A
Loss in Consumer Surplus:	A+B+C+D
Gain in Tariff Revenue:	C
Net social *Loss:*	B+D

The social loss is a measure of the inefficiency induced by the tariff; it is the cost of foregone trade. To understand why there is a social loss, first note that part of the loss suffered by consumers (due to higher prices) is offset by the gains to producers (area A) and the government's revenue (area C). However areas B and D do not accrue to anyone in the economy and hence represent a real loss to the economy.

Area B represents the production distortion induced by the trade barrier. The tariff increases output to x_1, but at this point the opportunity cost of X production is $p+t$ (the supply curve measures marginal production costs). If instead, X is imported, the opportunity cost to the economy of acquiring a unit of X is p, which is lower than the marginal production cost. The trade barrier therefore induces excessive production of X, and the area B represents this cost.

Similarly, area D represents the consumption distortion induced by the trade barrier. The demand curve represents the marginal benefit to the economy of consuming X. And at the tariff-induced consumption level, this marginal benefit is above the opportunity cost of acquiring the good from foreigners (p). This means that consumption is too low, and the cost of under-consumption is represented by area D.

RESTRICTIONS THAT DO NOT GENERATE REVENUE

A wide variety of trade barriers includes restrictions on foreigners that raise the costs of serving the domestic market but which do not generate any revenue for the government. This can involve bureaucratic measures that generate delays, restrictions on travel, requirements, inspections, etc.

These types of policies can also be assessed with the aid of Figure 3.2. Suppose that restrictive measures increase foreign costs by t per unit but do not generate revenue. Then domestic price rises to p^d, output rises to x_1, and consumption falls to c_1. So far the policy has effects that look like a tariff. But there is no tariff revenue and so Area C is a deadweight loss in the sense that it imposes costs on the foreign supplier (and which contribute to a domestic price increase) without generating revenue for the importing country. Hence the total social cost of the policy is $B+C+D$. So the loss in welfare is much greater than for a tariff.

QUOTAS

Many types of quantitative restrictions apply to service trade. For example, Canada and Australia have restrictions that require that foreign content in broadcasting (such as popular music or television programs) not exceed some limit. There are also many types of licensing restrictions that put explicit quantitative limits on the number of foreign suppliers who are permitted to compete in a local market.

To analyze the effects of a quota, consider a quota that requires that imports do not exceed M_1. We can represent this in Figure 3.3. The curve RD is the residual demand. It is the amount of domestic demand for X left over after the import quota has been filled. Graphically, it is obtained by shifting the demand curve D to the left by the amount of the quota M_1. The domestic price is determined by the intersection of the residual demand curve and the domestic supply curve, which yields a price p^d. This is the same price that was obtained above when a tariff was imposed. As well, output rises to x_1, and consumption falls to c_1.

A tariff and quota therefore have similar effects. If markets are competitive, as they are in the example so far, producer surplus will rise by the same amount in both cases, and consumer surplus will fall by the same amount. But there are some differences.

The first difference is obviously that a tariff generates tax revenue, while a quota does not. The area $C+D$ in Figure 3.3 is called the quota rents. Since X can be produced in

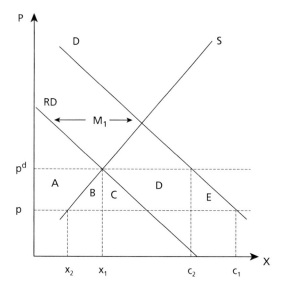

Figure 3.3. Effects of an import quota

foreign markets at a price p, and sold domestically at the higher price p^d, the gap in prices generates a surplus, which is referred to as the quota rents. The quota rents accrue to the individuals who have the right to import services into the domestic economy.

If the government auctioned off the rights for foreigners to provide M_1 units of services to the economy, then the revenue generated would be area $C+D$ (assuming an efficient auction) and the government would collect rents equal to the revenue it would have collected from tariffs. However, such auctions typically do not occur.

In the case of quotas on goods imports, the quota rents typically accrue to domestic agents who have import licenses. In this case area $C+D$ represents a redistribution of consumer surplus to importers. If domestic importers acquire the import licenses costlessly, then a cost/benefit approach treats area $C+D$ as a benefit and so the social costs of the quota are areas $B+E$, which is the same as a tariff.

In practice, however, quota rents are often dissipated by rent-seeking activities. That is, because those who obtain import licenses can earn quota rents, there is an incentive to spend resources on lobbying and other activities (some possibly involving corruption) to try to acquire import licenses. Since these activities consume real resources and are unproductive, they are a cost, and tend to push the social costs of quotas above tariffs.

There is an even more compelling reason to expect that the quota rents will be lost. Because services are provided directly by foreign providers, they are typically not imported by middlemen, as in the case of goods. That is, those foreign service providers who are allowed to operate in the domestic economy will sell their services directly to domestic consumers at a price p^d. Hence the foreign service providers will typically collect the quota rents. In this case, (unless the government auctions off quota licenses for the right to provide services), area C represents a loss in consumer surplus that accrues to foreigners and so counts as a loss to the domestic economy.

Consequently, in the service sector, the social cost of imposing a quota is likely to be area $B+C+D+E$, which is higher than for tariffs.

Quotas fare even worse when markets are not competitive, as was pointed out by Bhagwati (1965). To see this, suppose there is a single domestic firm. In the absence of international trade, the domestic firm would act as a monopolist and unless it is regulated, would charge a price above marginal cost. However, if there is free trade, then the domestic firm cannot charge a price above the import price p. That is, free trade eliminates the domestic monopolist's power.

The key difference between a tariff and quota is that in a tariff regime, the domestic monopolist faces potential foreign competition on every unit of X that it sells. But under a quota, there is competition only for the first M_1 units imported. Once the quota is filled, the monopolist faces no more competition. That is, an import quota gives the monopolist power that it does not have in a tariff regime. This means that quotas are significantly inferior to tariffs in markets where there are not very many local firms.

The other major benefit of tariffs over quotas is the added transparency of tariffs. Consumers may not be aware of the extent to which quotas are pushing up domestic costs. However, if they have to pay a tax on foreign services, then the magnitude of the

---

Box 3.4. Fiscal Instruments: Is the Difficulty of Substitution Between Policy Instruments Overstated?

The difficulty of switching to fiscal instruments of protection in services has probably been exaggerated. As far as cross-border trade is concerned, the imposition of duties is probably most difficult—perhaps impossible, given the current state of technology—when a service is delivered electronically. But in this case, imposing other barriers to trade is also likely to be infeasible. Where quotas are feasible and maintained, as on cross-border trade in transport services, it is easy to conceive of tariff-type instruments: e.g. a tax per passenger or unit of cargo carried by a foreign company. Moreover, the auction of a quota is analogous in economic effect to the imposition of a tariff.

In the case of commercial presence, a number of fiscal instruments are possible, including entry taxes (or auctions of entry licenses), output taxes and profit taxes. An output tax on foreign suppliers increases their marginal cost of providing a service and is similar in effect to a specific tariff. An entry tax increases the fixed costs of firms and their willingness to enter the market: the market structure is therefore likely to be less competitive than in the absence of such a tax. A profit tax is least likely to affect the economic decisions of firms. But if there are any fixed costs of entry that must be covered by future profits, then a profit tax would reduce the number of firms that could recover their costs of entry. One or more of these fiscal instruments could help achieve outcomes superior to quotas from a social welfare point of view. Ironically, the legal systems of many countries allow discrimination against foreigners through outright bans and entry quotas but make it difficult to impose discriminatory taxes. For instance, in the European Union, a locally established foreign firm is treated in all respects like a European firm and cannot be subject to any form of discrimination.

tax is a useful index of the stringency of protection. Moreover tariffs can simplify negotiations over trade liberalization, in part because of the added transparency. An agreement to reduce tariffs by 30 per cent is easier to implement that one that requires the import quotas be relaxed.

Are there any cases where a quota might be better than a tariff? If the government wants to completely exclude foreigners, then an import ban (a prohibitive quota) and a prohibitively high tariff will have the same effect, except that the ban will be more certain in its effects. Also, producers often prefer quotas. Quotas help to insulate the domestic market from price changes occurring in foreign markets. This can reduce uncertainty for domestic producers. However, as discussed above, this added benefit for producers can come at a high cost to consumers.

Restrictions on FDI in Competitive Markets

If markets are competitive, the benefits of FDI are similar to the standard gains from trade. Figure 3.4 illustrates a case where a service (X) can be provided only via commercial presence. Domestic supply is S^D and demand is D. In the absence of foreign investment, output is x_0 and price is p_0. If FDI is allowed, the supply of service providers

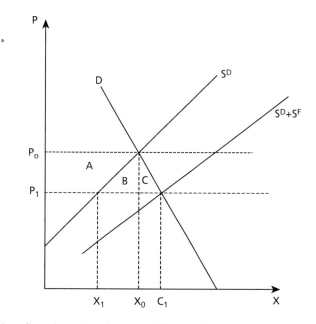

Figure 3.4. Foreign direct investment: competitive market

will shift out. We denote the expanded supply as the sum of supply from domestic and foreign firms: $S^D + S^F$. With the foreign presence in the local market, price falls to P_1 and output increases to X_1. There is a gain in consumer surplus (A+B+C), and a loss in producer surplus (A), which yields a net social gain of B+C. FDI increases welfare by increasing competition, lowering prices and increasing consumer choice. Conversely, restricting FDI would shift in the foreign supply curve and lead to social costs as the area B+C is eroded.

There are also many other potential benefits from FDI—through joint ventures, local firms may gain access to improved technology and financing. For some services such as insurance and finance, there can be increased risk pooling. There may also be spillover effects: local workers employed in foreign owned firms may receive knowledge, experience and training that might otherwise be unattainable. Taking these effects into account would increase the measure of social costs of restricting FDI.

Trade Restrictions vs. Subsidies

The relative merits of different instruments of protection depend in part on why the trade barrier is there in the first place. In many cases, the purpose of the trade barrier is to increase local output in certain sectors. It may be seen as desirable to have more domestic engineers, or to have a domestic airline, or a domestic banking sector. Restrictions on foreign service providers give domestic providers an advantage and so their output expands.

However, a domestic production subsidy will also increase the output of local producers, and will do so without increasing consumption distortions. To see this, refer to Figure 3.2 again. Suppose the government's objective is to increase the output of local service providers to X_1, which is above the free trade level of X_0. We saw above that a tariff or quota will do this. But suppose instead the government provides a subsidy s to producers for each unit that they sell. Moreover, suppose the subsidy s is set equal to t in the figure. Then producers get $p+s = p+t$ for each unit that they sell and so output rises to x_1 as desired. Consumers still get to buy at world prices, and so consumption stays at c_0.

The subsidy has to be financed. Total subsidy payments are represented by the amount A+B in the diagram. This will have to come out of tax revenue. Let us now do a cost/benefit analysis of the subsidy:

Rise in Producer Surplus: A
Loss in Consumer Surplus: none

Subsidy financing cost: A + B
Net social *Loss:*   B

The subsidy creates a production distortion measured by area B (which is unavoidable because the purpose of the policy is to raise output), but does not generate a consumption distortion. Consequently, the subsidy is more socially efficient than either a tariff or an import quota. Intuitively, the problem with trade barriers as a means to raise local output is that they also lower local consumption. A subsidy can raise output without distorting consumption and so generates lower social costs, even when we take into account the fact that the subsidy has to be financed.

A couple of factors can weaken the case for subsidies. First, a subsidy needs to be financed, which means that taxes must be raised. The implementation of taxes can create other distortions in the economy that have to be weighed against the distortions caused by tariffs and quotas. However, it should be noted that a tariff on X is essentially a production subsidy for X producers financed by a consumption tax on X consumers. It is highly unlikely that a tax on X consumers is the optimal way to raise revenue.

Second, a more significant problem with subsidies is that money has to be paid out to domestic producers, which can increase administrative costs and open up opportunities for corruption. If subsidies get diverted away from their intended purpose, the social costs of the policy would be higher and could possibly exceed the costs of tariffs.

Interaction Between Trade Policy and Domestic Regulation

Our analysis of trade policy so far has been based on the premise that markets work well and that trade barriers are in place only to protect local producers. However, many service industries are in imperfect markets. For example financial services, electric power, telecommunications, and air transport are all sectors in which there are large firms that have market power. This market power often arises from barriers to entry arising from domestic regulations. Other service industries, especially in the professional service sector, are plagued with problems of asymmetric information—the service provider knows more than the consumer about the quality of service dispensed and the appropriate level of care needed.

In this section, we consider several examples to illustrate the interaction between trade policy reform and domestic regulation.

Barriers to Entry and the Impact of FDI Restrictions on Welfare

Restrictions on FDI assume particular significance in the case of services where cross-border delivery is not possible, so that consumer prices depend completely on the domestic market structure. In many service sectors, such as in communications and financial services, there are restrictions both on entry and on foreign ownership. A basic conclusion from the literature on privatization is that larger welfare gains arise from an increase in competition than from simply a change in ownership from public to private hands. What are the implications of alternative policies vis-à-vis FDI for welfare?

If FDI comes simply because the returns to investment are artificially raised by restrictions on competition, the net returns to the host country may be negative (returns to the investor may exceed the true social productivity of the investment). To some extent the rent appropriation may be prevented by profit taxation or by holding competitive auctions of licenses or equity, but the static and dynamic inefficiencies from lack of competition would still exist.

This situation is depicted in Figure 3.5. Consider a country in which the domestic market is initially monopolized. Domestic demand is denoted by Demand, and MR is the corresponding marginal revenue curve. The constant marginal costs of the monopolist are denoted by MC. The monopoly produces Q_M and charges a price P_M. National welfare is equal to the area HAEJ, i.e., the sum of consumer surplus, HAP_M, and producer surplus, P_MAEJ.

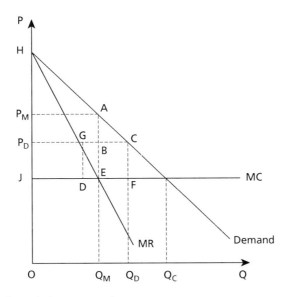

Figure 3.5. Impact of restrictions on market structure

Now suppose one foreign firm is allowed to enter the market, converting it from a monopoly to a duopoly. For simplicity we assume that the foreign firm's marginal costs are identical to those of the national firm. It is also reasonable to assume that the duopolists neither collude nor indulge in cut-throat competition, so that the outcome is between a monopoly and competitive one—and results in aggregate output Q_D and price P_D. Since marginal costs are identical, each firm produces half the aggregate output and makes half the aggregate profits. Aggregate national welfare is equal to the area HCGDJ, as before the sum of the consumer surplus HCP_D, and the producer surplus, $P_D GDJ$. Note the former has increased while the latter has declined: consumers benefit from foreign competition but the national firm loses. An examination of national welfare in the two situations reveals that national welfare could decline with entry if area GBDE were greater than area ACB. This is an empirical question, but is clearly possible: the national firm could lose more than consumers gain. However, it is important to remember that the main reason for a decline in welfare would be the appropriation of rents by a foreign firm. If there were no restrictions on entry, and a perfectly competitive outcome resulted, then national welfare would necessarily increase. To summarize, full liberalization in terms of removal of all barriers to entry leads to an increase in social welfare. Partial liberalization, in terms of limited entry or only change of ownership, could lead to a decline in national welfare.

Foreign Investment with Regulated Pricing

In many cases, services (such as electricity, water, and telecommunications) are provided by regulated monopolies. In this case, allowing foreign owned firms to provide the service can generate benefits provided that the monopoly is efficiently regulated. However, if the service provider extracts some rents via the regulation process, then the benefits of foreign provision are not so clear.

Consider Figure 3.6. Let AC denote the average cost of the domestic firm, and D denote domestic demand. Then if the regulator enforces average cost pricing, output would be X_0 and price would be P_0. Now consider a foreign-owned firm which could provide the service locally with an average cost $AC^* < AC$. With average cost pricing, output increases to X_1 and price falls to P_1 yielding social benefits equal to area A (reflecting an increase in consumer surplus). Allowing foreign provision leads to increased productivity, benefiting consumers.

Regulation is not always perfect, however. Suppose that the regulator is not able to extract all average costs, so that the price charged is average cost plus a markup, π. The markup could result either from asymmetric information about the cost function, or from corruption. This is illustrated in Figure 3.7. With domestic production (with average cost AC), output is X_0 and price is P_0. Now compare this with the effects of

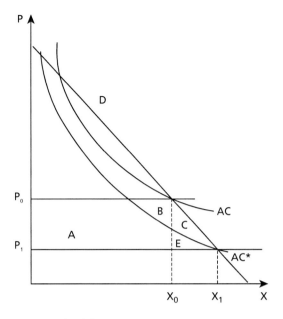

Figure 3.6. FDI with average cost pricing

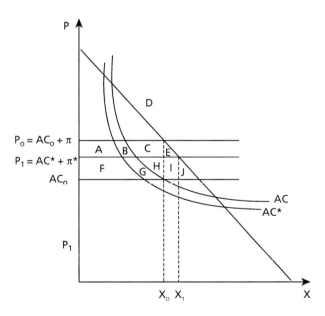

Figure 3.7. FDI with markup pricing

allowing a foreign firm to provide the service. The foreign average cost AC* is lower and so potentially there are gains from trade. If the foreign firm is able to achieve the same markup $\pi^* = \pi$, then the new price is P_1 and output rises to X_1. Domestic consumers benefit from the higher productivity of the foreign service provider.

However, it is not obvious that this is beneficial to the economy. The gain in consumer surplus is $A+B+C+E$. But the loss in rents (via markups) accruing to the domestic producer is $A+B+C+F+G+H$. The net social gain is $E - (F+G+H)$, which is negative in the example illustrated. Even though the foreign firm is more productive and charges a lower price, the economy is worse off by allowing foreign ownership of the local utility in this case. Why? Rents from the previous markup accruing to the local firm now go to the foreign firm. This leakage of rents can more than offset the increased benefits to consumers.

Box 3.5. Are there Good Reasons to Limit Entry?

As discussed in Chapter 1, entry restrictions are becoming harder to justify in the face of growing evidence of the benefits of competition. In Latin America, for example, countries that granted monopoly privileges to telecom operators of six to ten years to the privatized state enterprises saw connections grow at 1.5 times the rate achieved under state monopolies but only half the rate in Chile, where the government retained the right to issue competing licenses at any time. Why then do we observe such widespread restrictions on entry? While it is possible to construct special models of market and/or regulatory failure where entry barriers enhance welfare, there are usually more prosaic reasons for the barriers. First, restrictions generally aim to protect the incumbent suppliers from immediate competition for infant-industry type reasons, to facilitate "orderly exit" or simply due to political economy pressures. And the result is protection not only of national firms but also foreign incumbents—as in the case of foreign insurance companies in Malaysia, and, most strikingly, the bilateral agreements in air transport. Other instruments, such as discriminatory subsidies or taxes could be better targeted.

Monopolistic or oligopolistic rents are also sometimes seen as a means to help firms to fulfill universal service obligations through cross-subsidization (When South Africa partially privatized its telecommunications utility, it conferred a limited monopoly in return for which it required that the utility increase the number of rural connections). However, governments are increasingly devising means of achieving these objectives without sacrificing the benefits of competition: e.g. by imposing universal services obligations on new entrants or asking for competitive bids for subsidies to serve unprofitable areas. In some cases, a form of "investment pessimism" exists, leading to the belief that promises of oligopoly rents are necessary to attract new investment. However, it is not clear why the market structure needs to be determined by policy, unless there are some initial investments the benefits of which may be appropriated by rivals. Finally, governments may seek to raise revenue (or rents for politicians/bureaucrats) by auctioning monopoly or oligopoly rights. This amounts to indirect appropriation of consumer surplus. But the static and dynamic inefficiencies consequent upon lack of competition would still exist.

Ideally, governments should not resort to trade restrictions to pursue objectives that are better achieved through other means. In each of the cases mentioned above, entry restrictions are at best a second or third-best instrument to achieve the objective in question, but are chosen because of constraints such as the inability to raise revenue without economic or political cost. It will probably be difficult and not necessarily desirable to outlaw completely barriers to entry. But it may be possible to create a legal presumption against such barriers by requiring that a country that imposes them demonstrate that they are necessary—in the sense that more appropriate instruments are not feasible.

Opening up to foreign provision need not necessarily be harmful, however. If the foreign average cost is sufficiently lower than domestic average cost, then the price fall will be higher, area E will be larger, and there will be net benefits. Alternatively, even in the case illustrated, the domestic government may be able to avoid rent leakage by auctioning off the rights to provide the local service. If auctioning is competitive, then in principle, the foreign firm's markup could be extracted, and true average-cost price could be implemented, yielding unambiguous social gains.

However, matters could also be worse than illustrated if it is more difficult for the regulator to monitor costs of a foreign firm than a domestic firm. If the foreign firm imports parts and management skills and pays royalties for proprietary process to the parent firm, then because of familiar issues of transfer pricing, the foreign firm may be able to inflate its reported costs and push up the effective markup π^*. This would increase rent leakage and further reduce the benefits (or increase the costs) of foreign provision.

Regulation of Professional Services

Most professional service providers, such as doctors, engineers, and lawyers, have to be certified in order to practice their profession. The certification requirements can serve as barriers to trade because they raise entry costs for foreign service providers. Foreigners often have to take courses, exams, and sometimes establish a residence to meet local certification requirements. In some cases, such as in law, foreigners are sometimes completely shut out of the market.

Certification requirements, however, cannot simply be dismissed as a trade barrier because they are a response to problems of asymmetric information in these markets. The client often does not have enough information to judge the safety and quality of the service. Even if the client could determine quality and safety at some cost, it can be more efficient to require certification to economize on screening costs.

To illustrate the interaction between trade policy and regulation of professional services, we consider an example where low-quality service providers generate externalities. For example, if a bridge collapses or if a public building is not constructed safely, then there will be costs to society at large, not just to the contractor. Similarly, in countries with public medical systems, the costs of bad medical treatment will fall not just on the patient but also on taxpayers.

We consider two scenarios. First we consider a case where the domestic regulatory system is initially inadequate. That is, screening is imperfect and there is a mix of good and bad service providers in practice. In this case, we show that trade liberalization without reforms of the domestic certification system can lower welfare. Next we consider the effects of trade under a well-functioning certification system. In this case, trade will be welfare-improving. However, the magnitude of the gains depends on the way in which foreigners are screened.

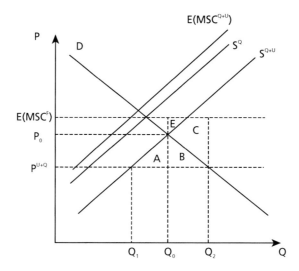

Figure 3.8. Trade in professional services with imperfect screening

Figure 3.8 illustrates a market for professional services. There are two types of service providers: qualified (Q) and unqualified (U). Unqualified providers make mistakes that cause external harm. The demand for services is denoted by D. S^Q is the (long run) domestic supply of qualified personnel (this takes into account training costs). These providers do not generate external harm. S^{Q+U} is the combined domestic supply of qualified and unqualified personnel. The curve $E(MSC^{Q+U})$ measures the expected average social cost of service provision by the mix of qualified and unqualified personnel.

If initially there is no trade, the price is P_o and output is Q_o. Now consider the effects of allowing foreigners to provide services under the same rules affecting local providers. For simplicity, we have assumed that the mix of qualified and unqualified personnel is the same among foreigners as among domestic suppliers, so that the expected external costs are the same.

When trade opens up, price falls to P^{U+Q}, and consumption rises to Q_2. Domestic output falls to Q_1 because of increased competition from foreigners. Consumers gain from lower prices and domestic producers lose. The net gain in consumer and producer surplus (ignoring the external harm caused by bad screening) is A + B. However, the increase in service provision caused by trade also generates more harm as more mistakes are made by unqualified service providers. The increase in external harm is measured by B + C + E.[2] Hence the net social gain from trade is A—(E + C). Welfare could rise or fall: in the example here it falls.

---

[2] Recall that we have assumed that the domestic and foreign providers generate on average the same external harm. Consequently, there is no change in the harm generated by the displacement of domestic providers—it is only the increase in output beyond the initial output level that generates more harm. If foreigners are on average less qualified than domestic agents, this would generate additional costs; if they are better qualified, this would generate some offsetting gains.

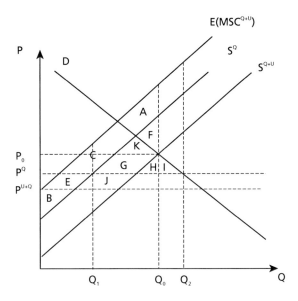

Figure 3.9. Trade in professional services with reform of screening

The point of this example is similar to the point raised in the discussion of entry barriers above. If the domestic regulatory system is initially inadequate, then liberalizing trade can exacerbate the problems arising from imperfect regulation. The ensuing costs can potentially more than offset the gains from trade liberalization.

This does not mean, however, that trade liberalization is a bad policy; however. On the contrary, if domestic regulatory reform accompanies trade liberalization, then gains can be assured. To see this, consider Figure 3.9. Now suppose that the government introduces a certification requirement that fully screens both domestic and foreign personnel. Let P^Q be the price of services provided by qualified foreign service personnel. If trade opens, price falls from P_o to P^Q, consumption rises to Q_2, and domestic output falls to Q_1 (since now only qualified domestic agents supply output). In this case in addition to the net gain in consumer and producer surplus, there are additional gains as the external harm from mistakes is eliminated. Social gains are therefore $B+E+C+A+F+K+G+H+I$; these are unambiguously positive. Trade liberalization, accompanied by domestic regulatory reform raises welfare.

A final issue is how foreigners should be screened. Trade liberalization in many service industries and especially in professional services requires both that foreigners be given market access, and that they not be subject to discriminatory barriers. There are several ways of implementing non-discrimination rules.

In a National Treatment regime, governments have the flexibility to implement their own regulations subject to the requirement that the same regulations apply to domestic and foreign suppliers. That is, a national treatment regime essentially requires non-discrimination. Such a rule does not completely eliminate discrimination, however.

For example, an insurance company might be required to establish a local office before it can sell insurance. While both domestic and foreign firms are subject to the same requirement, it may be much easier for local firms to meet the requirement—such a rule imposes a fixed cost that excludes foreign firms who might want to do only a small amount of business locally. Similarly, a requirement that engineers, doctors, or truck drivers obtain domestic licensing and certification can impose additional costs on foreigners who have already gone through a similar certification process in their own country.

In a mutual recognition regime, each country agrees to accept service providers who meet the certification requirements of their home country. For example, under a mutual recognition regime, a U.S. resident can be permitted to drive in Canada as long as he holds a valid U.S. driver's license. Under a national treatment rule, the U.S. resident could be permitted to drive in Canada only if a Canadian drivers license is obtained. The advantage of mutual recognition regimes is that they can economize on regulatory costs. The disadvantage is that it can be more difficult for a government to meet its regulatory objectives. If the trading partner has weaker certification requirements, then the average quality of service provision may fall when imports increase. For this reason, mutual recognition is not appropriate for many types of services, and may also only be feasible for countries with very similar approaches to regulation. However, in countries with very different standards, the country with the weak standard can agree to recognize certification from the country with the high standard, but not vice versa.

Harmonization of regulatory standards is another option. In this case, countries agree on common regulatory standards. For example, countries may agree on a common set of rules to regulate insurance companies, and this then may facilitate easy access by insurers to markets in each country. The advantage of harmonization is that it removes the ability of governments to unilaterally adjust standards to favor local suppliers. The disadvantage is that it can add inflexibilities into the system that make it more difficult to change regulations when conditions merit changes. As well, harmonization by its nature eliminates diversity in regulatory approaches. Regulations appropriate for one country need not be the best solution for other countries.

Each of these approaches constrains government flexibility in some ways, and so may raise regulatory costs. They may also conflict with other government objectives. For example, a government may choose to have an exclusively public education or health system. In cases of cultural services, a government pay prefer to explicitly favor local providers. For some types of services, governments may see value in having them provided by producers with a long-term vested interest in a local community. The literature on social capital suggests that this can strengthen communities and provide both economic and non-economic benefits. Consequently, for some types of services the conflicts between regulatory objectives and trade liberalization may be difficult to circumvent.

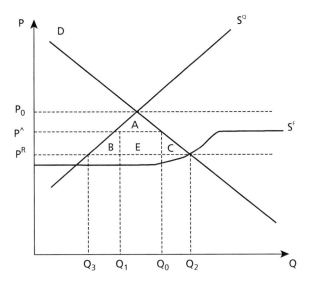

Figure 3.10. National treatment vs. recognition

We consider here just one simple example to illustrate how the choice of rules for market access may affect trade and welfare. Consider Figure 3.10. Suppose the domestic government fully screens professionals, so the domestic supply is S^Q. There is no external harm generated. Under a national treatment regime, foreigners could be required to undergo the same (costly) certification procedures as domestic agents. Let $P^\wedge$ be the price foreigners would charge under these rules. Opening up to trade (allowing foreigners market access) under this rule would generate gains from trade to area A, reflecting a fall in price and increased consumption. Suppose, however, that there are three types of foreign service providers: those who have evidence that they are fully qualified because of the certification they have received in their own countries; those who need some retraining to adapt the local market; and those who must undergo the same full certification process as local professionals. Let S^F denote the sum of the domestic and foreign supply curve when the domestic government fully recognizes foreign credentials, and requires just enough retraining to meet the local standard. The initial flat part of the curve corresponds to the supply of professionals certified in countries that clearly meet the standard; the later flat part (at level $P^\wedge$ corresponds to supply from those that need full retraining), and the upward sloping part in the middle reflects those that need only partial retraining.

Under this regime, output is higher and price is lower. The gains from trade are given by $A+B+E+C$. The gains from trade will be larger if the government chooses the most efficient screening regime.

Protection to Preserve Local Product Variety

Much of the above analysis of trade barriers assumed that local and foreign products are essentially the same. However, in some cases, local and foreign products may be very different. This is particularly true in the cultural sector, where a foreign movie or television program is often very different from a local production. Hence while foreigners may object to local content rules in broadcasting and other media as protectionist, the motivation for such policies may be to preserve distinctly local cultural products. The issue of the preservation of distinctly local services arises in other contexts as well: for example, allowing foreign restaurant franchises (such as fast-food chains) may squeeze out local restaurants selling indigenous cuisine.

There are two ways to analyze protective policies in the case where locally-produced services are distinct from foreign-produced services: the first allows for externalities in service provision, and the second is to confront the larger issue of optimum product variety.

Let us first consider the case where there are externalities. This is illustrated in Figure 3.11. Let D denote demand for television programming and let S denote local supply. Suppose that viewing of locally-produced programs has spillover effects—it might promote a sense of community or preserve and enhance social capital. Since all local production is consumed locally in the example presented here, the spillover benefits of local consumption of local products can be represented as a positive externality from

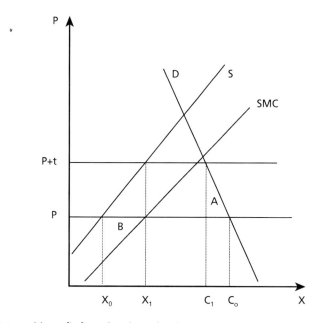

Figure 3.11. External benefit from local production

local production—hence the social marginal cost of production (private costs less spillover benefits) is given by SMC, which is lower than the supply curve (which represents private marginal costs). In free trade, domestic production is X_0. However, because of the externality, this is too low: the socially efficient level of domestic consumption is X_1. A tax t on foreign programs (or an auctioned quota) will implement the efficient domestic output level. However, it does so at the cost of creating a consumption distortion (consumer prices rise). The social cost of the tariff is $A - B$. Area A is the cost of the consumption distortion. Area B represents the external benefits of increased local programming. Note that if the external benefits (B) are sufficiently high, trade restrictions can improve local welfare.

The analysis in the previous section suggests that a better policy than a tariff or quota would be a production subsidy for local programs. This would indeed achieve the first best: a production subsidy set equal to t would increase output to X_1 but would not affect total consumption, and so would achieve net social benefits of B, even after the financing cost is considered. It should be noted, however, that a production subsidy discriminates in favor of local suppliers and hence would violate some notions of free trade in services.

An argument for preferential treatment of local suppliers can also be made without resort to the externality argument. Consider Figure 3.12, which is based on Snape (1977). Let AC denote the average cost of providing a local service (such as a weekly television show, a local restaurant, or local music). We assume there is a fixed cost of production; this leads to downward sloping average costs. MC denotes the marginal cost. Suppose there are initially trade barriers that reduce the number of foreign

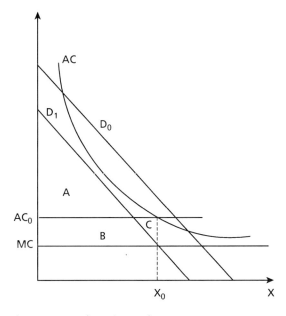

Figure 3.12. Local product squeezed out by trade

products that are close substitutes for the domestic service in the domestic market. Given this initial level of protection, the domestic demand for the domestic service is D_0. Since the demand curve is above average cost for some levels of output, the local service is viable and will be produced.

Now suppose that a trade agreement eliminates local-content preferences, and more foreign firms enter the local market. Because foreign services are imperfect substitutes for the domestic service, the local demand curve shifts in. Let D_1 denote the free trade domestic demand for the domestic service. Since D_1 is below average cost, the domestic production shuts down. Foreign movies, television programs and music squeeze out domestic products.

Now it might be thought that these products *should* be squeezed out because domestic demand is below average cost. However, this is not necessarily correct. To see this, suppose that (in free trade) X_0 units of the domestic service were supplied at price $p = MC$. Consumer surplus would be $A + B$, and the loss to producers would be $B + C$ (this reflects the costs that are not recovered by charging p). The net social gain from provision of the domestic service is $A - C$, which is clearly positive in the example illustrated. That is, even though foreign competition squeezes the domestic service out of the market, it would nevertheless still be socially efficient for the domestic service to be supplied. When there are fixed costs, there is no presumption that free markets will provide optimal product variety. Either trade barriers or domestic subsidies could be superior to free trade in this case.

Trade Policy Substitution Between Modes of Delivery

We conclude our analysis of the interaction between trade policy and regulation with an example in which different types of trade barriers apply to different modes.

The exemption of one mode of delivery from taxation while others continue to be taxed is analogous to a preferential trading arrangement. And as in the case of such arrangements there is a positive trade-creating aspect and a negative trade-diverting aspect. The latter arises when the tax-exempt mode is chosen simply to avoid the tax, even though it is less efficient than the taxed alternative.

This is illustrated with Figure 3.13. D and S are domestic demands and supplies for a service X. Suppose that foreigners can provide the service directly to local customers through temporary movement of personnel. This would cost w^* per unit. Alternatively, the service can be provided at higher cost through cross-border trade at price p per unit.

With free trade in all modes, price is w^*, domestic output is x_0 and consumption is c_0. Now suppose that a tax t is imposed on temporary movement of personnel. First suppose this was the only way to provide the service (that is, first suppose cross-border

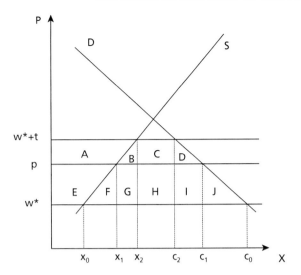

Figure 3.13. Substitution between modes of supply

trade is not feasible). Then the price would rise to $w^* + t$, consumption would fall to c_2 and output would rise to x_2. Domestic producers gain, consumers lose, and the social cost of the tariff is $B + F + G + D + I + J$ as usual.

Now suppose that cross-border trade *is* feasible at price p. Then the imposition of the tax on temporary movement of personnel leads to a switch from this mode to direct trade because direct trade is now cheaper $(p < w^* + t)$. At first glance, it may appear that this is a good thing. Because of the option of cross-border trade, the tariff causes price to rise only to p (instead of $w^* + t$), and consumption to fall to c_1 (instead of c_2). The switch to the alternative mode has resulted in less of a price increase, and more consumption than in the case where this option was not available. That is, the availability of multiple modes of service provision means that providers can respond to trade barriers by finding alternative modes, and this can help to keep prices down and reduce the impact of the trade barriers on consumers.

However, there is another effect. Let us consider a cost/benefit analysis of the tariff in the presence of mode switching.

Rise in Producer Surplus	E
Loss in Consumer Surplus	$E + F + G + H + I + J$
Tariff revenue	none
Net social *Loss*	$F + G + H + I + J$

Recall that if cross-border trade was not feasible, the tariff would have led to a social loss of $B + F + G + D + I + J$. With mode-switching, the loss from the tariff is $F + G + H + I + J$. The option of switching to cross-border trade in response to the tariff on temporary labor movement will generate welfare gains if $B + D > H$. However, this need not hold in general, and note that in the case illustrated in Figure 3.13 we have the reverse: $H > B + D$.

Area H represents the cost of trade diversion. In this example, cross-border trade is less efficient than direct provision by temporary movement of personnel. A switch to cross-border trade therefore induces an increase in the cost to the economy of acquiring the service. This increased cost has to be balanced against the lower price that results from mode-switching. If the trade-diversion effect dominates, then mode-switching contributes to a decline in welfare.

The point of this example is that the analysis of the effects of trade barriers in services can be complicated by the possibility of mode-switching induced by trade barriers. Even though mode-switching generates some benefits, it also creates costs via the trade-diversion effect. If the trade-diversion effect is not accounted for, then the costs of protection may be underestimated.

Trade Agreements vs. Unilateral Liberalization

Although it is only recently that trade agreements have begun to focus on liberalizing trade in services, governments have been opening up their markets to foreign service providers for a long time. Moreover, as technology changes and as global markets evolve, governments have responded to pressures from both producers and consumers to change their rules to allow increased access to their markets. This raises the issue of why governments need to be constrained by trade agreements in services. If designing trade agreements is going to raise complicated issues involving trade-offs between internal regulatory flexibility and trade, why not just let each government decide on its own rules regarding foreign access and avoid the complexity of trade agreements?

There are three major reasons for signing a trade agreement rather than simply liberalizing trade unilaterally.

There are benefits from reciprocity. That is, a major advantage of trade agreements is that they can ensure that each country gains increased access to the other's market. If governments are under pressure to protect jobs for engineers in their country, then an agreement to allow foreign engineers into the country may well benefit local consumers, but is likely to encounter resistance from producers. But if it is coupled with an agreement that includes increased access for domestic producers in the foreign market, then the gains from increased trade will be greater and domestic resistance will be lessened.

A second aspect of reciprocity is that it can help avoid trade wars. It is well known that governments can get into self-defeating trade wars, as for example happened during the Great Depression in the 1930s. Each government may face pressure to protect local firms. But if all governments do this, then overall economic activity falls and all countries can be worse off. The situation is much like a prisoners' dilemma. The optimal strategy for an individual government may be to protect, but if they all do it, they are all worse off. Coordinated liberalization can circumvent the problem.

Trade agreements also have important commitment advantages, in both a local and international context. In the local context, the advantage of signing a trade agreement is that it helps a domestic government stand up to local protectionist interest groups. Producers stand to gain from trade barriers, and although the barriers may lower social welfare as discussed above, the costs are widely dispersed across consumers. Consequently producer lobbies for protection will often be stronger than consumer lobbies for free trade. Governments may therefore face considerable pressure to cave into producers and raise trade barriers that ultimately harm the country. If the government signs a trade agreement, then the costs of caving in are increased. This commitment effect would then have two advantages: trade barriers will stay lower because the government caves in less often; and fewer resources are wasted on lobbying because the lobbyists know the payoff to lobbying has fallen.

The second commitment effect is in the international context. Service providers often have to invest in fixed costs to serve a foreign market, either through direct investment or in obtaining certification or developing local knowledge. Because the investment will be worthless if firms are later shut out of the foreign market, firms may be reluctant to make such investments and a country that wants to attract foreign service providers may fail to do so. Even if foreign providers are not shut out, they may feel vulnerable because of what is known as the hold-up problem. Once foreigners have invested in country-specific skills, they may be concerned that the foreign government will try to extract rents from them by imposing discriminatory taxes or other requirements. Signing a trade agreement can help to increase the credibility of a commitment either to not cut off access once investments have been made, or to not arbitrarily change the rules to extract rents.

Finally, a commitment to a trade agreement allows the development of a rules-based system that helps facilitate trade. Much of the success of internal trade within a country relies on confidence that contracts will be enforced and rules will be applied in a predictable manner. International governments do not exist to fill this role; but trade agreements lead to the development of institutions that can help settle disputes and increase the consistency with which rules are applied.

On the other hand, although trade agreements have their advantages, whether any given trade agreement is better than unilateralism depends on the terms of the agreement. Trade agreements in services cannot avoid intruding on what used to be thought of as internal domestic policy. Trade agreements require trade-offs involving flexibility, domestic sovereignty and international trade. These trade-offs are much more complex and intrusive than in the case of goods trade. Different countries will have different approaches to these trade-offs, and it is not even clear what freer trade means in some cases. So although there are a number of reasons to pursue trade liberalization via trade agreements rather than unilaterally; it may also be very difficult to design trade agreements that are both effective and acceptable to a wide range of countries.

Summary

Trade in services is in some important ways different from trade in goods. First, many services require proximity between the supplier and the consumer, and hence factor mobility is necessary for many international service transactions. Second, the limited scope for "border" restrictions implies that domestic regulations have a much stronger influence on trade in services.

However, while interesting twists arise because of the way services are traded and regulated, the basic insights from the theory of trade in goods apply to trade in services. There are likely to be substantial gains from liberalizing trade in services, immediately and in the longer term provided the regulatory framework is adequate.

NOTES ON THE LITERATURE

For an in-depth treatment of the motives for trade and trade policy, with a focus on goods trade, see any standard trade theory textbook, such as Krugman and Obstfeld (2005). For an early application of trade theory to services, see Hindley and Smith (1984) and Deardorff (1985). Sapir and Winter (1994) and Copeland (2002) provide reviews of the literature on the economics of trade in services. See also Hoekman (2006), Introduction and Section I, "Determinants and Patterns of Trade in Services," for further discussion and references to pertinent literature.

References

Bhagwati, J. N. 1965. "On the Equivalence of Tariffs and Quotas," in R. E. Baldwin et al. (eds.), *Trade, Growth and the Balance of Payments—Essays in Honor of Gottfried Haberler.* Chicago: Rand-McNally.

Copeland, B. R. 2002. "Benefits and Costs of Trade and Investment Liberalization in Services," in J. M. Curtis and D. Ciuriak (eds.), *Trade Policy Research 2002.* Government of Canada, pp. 107–218.

Deardorff, A. V. 1985. "Comparative Advantage and International Trade and Investment in Services," in R. M. Stern (ed.), *Trade and Investment in Services: Canada/US Perspectives*, Toronto: Ontario Economic Council.

Helpman, E. and P. Krugman. 1985. *Market Structure and Foreign Trade*. Cambridge, M.A.: MIT Press.

Hindley, B. and Smith, A. (1984). "Comparative Advantage and Trade in Services," *World Economy* 7: 369–89.

Hoekman, B. (ed.). 2006. *Trade in Services at 25: Theory, Policy and Evidence*. Cheltenham: Edward Elgar (forthcoming).

Krugman, P. 1980. "Scale Economies, Product Differentiation, and the Pattern of Trade," *American Economic Review* 70: 950–9.

—— and M. Obstfeld. 2005. *International Economics: Theory and Policy*, 7th edn. Addison Wesley.

—— and A. J. Venables. 1995. "Globalization and the Inequality of Nations," *Quarterly Journal of Economics* 110(14): 857–80.

Markusen, J. R. 1989. "Trade in Producer Services and in Other Specialized Intermediate Inputs," *American Economic Review* 79: 85–95.

——, T. F. Rutherford, and D. Tarr. 2000. "Foreign Direct Investments in Services and the Domestic Market for Expertise," NBER Working Paper No. W7700 (May).

Markusen, J. R. and A. J. Venables. 2000. "The Theory of Endowment, Intra-industry and Multi-national Trade," *Journal of International Economics* 52: 209–34.

Mundell, R. 1957. "International Trade and Factor Mobility," *American Economic Review* 67: 321–35.

Sapir, A. and C. Winter. 1994. "Services Trade," in D. Greenaway and L. A. Winters (eds.), *Surveys in International Trade*. Oxford: Basil Blackwell.

Snape, R. H. 1977. "Trade Policy in the Presence of Economies of Scale and Product Variety," *Economic Record* 53: 525–34.

Part II
Analyzing Trade in Services

4 Measuring Trade in Services*

Andreas Maurer, Yann Marcus, Joscelyn Magdeleine, and Barbara d'Andrea

Services and Trade in Services in the Economy

Services covers a wide range of intangible and heterogeneous products and activities. Services have a significant impact on growth and efficiency across a wide range of user industries and overall economic performance. For instance, sectors such as transport, telecommunications, and financial services are key determinants of the conditions in which persons, merchandises, services, and capital flow. Also important are environmental services, which contribute to sustainable development by alleviating negative impacts of economic activities.

Box 4.1. Measuring Services Production

Statistics on Domestic Activity

National Accounts constitute the statistical framework out of which main macro-economic aggregates are calculated (production, GDP, Gross National Income, consumption...). Value added broken down by industry, permits the measurement of the contribution of the services sector and its sub-sectors to GDP. A majority of countries have adopted the international guidelines of the 1993 System of National Accounts (1993 SNA), which facilitates international data comparability.

Employment statistics provide the total number of people employed in various sectors of activity. They allow us to identify the number of people employed in the services sector, and their distribution among different sub-sectors (it should be noted that such statistics also form part of the central framework of National Accounts).

Other information such as business statistics (available from regional and international organizations) as well as data provided by business federations may also be useful for assessing the activity of specific services sectors.

Quantitative Indicators on Specific Sectors

Quantitative indicators on specific sectors (international number of students enrolled in basic education, arrivals of tourists, number of letters mailed, kilometers flown by planes, number of phone calls, etc.) also provide valuable information for assessing services production and performance, which enables more meaningful analysis of services sectors. However, quantitative indicators do not permit comparisons across sectors.

---

* This chapter is adapted from the WTO (2006) training module, "Measuring Trade in Services," which was produced by the Economic Research and Statistics Division of the World Trade Organization. The WTO Secretariat is very grateful to the participants of the Inter-agency Task Force on Statistics of International Trade in Services as well as Nelly Ahouilihoua who provided material for the training module. The views expressed in this document are those of the authors and do not represent a position of the WTO Secretariat or WTO Members.

Box 4.2. Different Types of Movement of Persons, Viewpoint of the Recipient Country

Categories	Assessing GATS mode 4	Statistical coverage
I. Service contracts, delivered in the host country by independent foreign supplier, or its employee(s)	X	BOP: Service transactions between resident and non-residents, major BPM5 services components
II. Employment contracts (non-permanent), for foreigners, in all domestic firms		BOP: compensation of employees, with adjustments: sectoral breakdown and duration. Employment/migration statistics: short-term migrants working. Would need adjustments for short-term but more than one year. Provide sectoral breakdown.
(a) of which: foreign-owned or controlled resident services companies	X	A subset of the above; could be derived using the FATS register

TRADE IN COMMERCIAL SERVICES[1]

As shown in Figure 4.1, world exports of commercial services amounted to US$2,100 billion in 2004, after growing on average at around 7.6 per cent per year in value terms since 1980. Trade in commercial services grew faster than trade in goods (6.6 per cent on average) during this period, increasing its share in total world trade by three percentage points. In 2004, *services* accounted for approximately 19 per cent of total world trade.

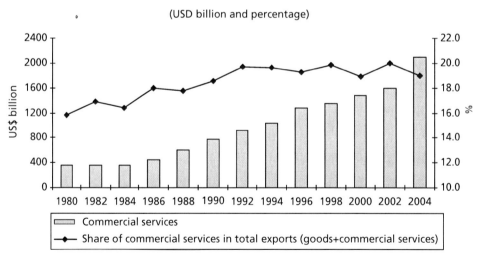

Figure 4.1. World trade in commercial services, total exports, 1980–2004

Source: Adapted from WTO.

[1] A more detailed overview of international trade in commercial services and activities of foreign affiliates is provided in WTO (2006).

Box 4.3. Patterns of Trade in Services Expansion

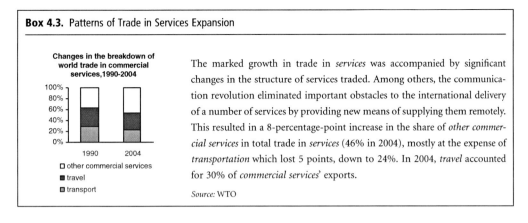

Changes in the breakdown of world trade in commercial services, 1990-2004

□ other commercial services
■ travel
□ transport

The marked growth in trade in *services* was accompanied by significant changes in the structure of services traded. Among others, the communication revolution eliminated important obstacles to the international delivery of a number of services by providing new means of supplying them remotely. This resulted in a 8-percentage-point increase in the share of *other commercial services* in total trade in *services* (46% in 2004), mostly at the expense of *transportation* which lost 5 points, down to 24%. In 2004, *travel* accounted for 30% of *commercial services'* exports.

Source: WTO

The share of services in world trade contrasts with the central contribution of services production in domestic economies. As a matter of fact, due to their intangible nature, trade in services is inherently subject to more constraints than trade in goods. While a (tangible) good may be produced, stored, moved and consumed at different places and times, the delivery of a (intangible) service is seldom dissociated from its production and its consumption, requiring the proximity of the supplier and the customer. For instance, hairdressers and their clients need to be physically close to each other.

The need for proximity for supplying many services has led providers to deliver their products through a commercial presence abroad, i.e., the establishment of foreign affiliates. This form of international trade in services is considered as important as "conventional" international trade in services between residents and non-residents.

GATS and Modes of Supply

One of the most important achievements of the Uruguay Round trade negotiations (1986–93) was to bring international trade in services under common multilateral rules. Entering into force on January 1, 1995, the WTO General Agreement on Trade in Services (GATS) is the first set of multilaterally negotiated and legally enforceable rules covering international trade in commercial services (i.e. excluding government services). As stressed in GATS, international trade in services can take place through four modes of supply:

- Mode 1, cross-border supply, only the service crosses the border.
- Mode 2, consumption abroad, occurs when consumers consume services while outside their country.

- Mode 3, in which the service supplier establishes its commercial presence in another country.

- Mode 4, presence of natural persons, when an individual has moved temporarily into the territory of the consumer to provide a service.

The GATS includes a set of general obligations, applying to all WTO members and all services, such as the Most-Favored-Nation treatment (MFN) ensuring non-discrimination between trading partners; countries' schedules of specific commitments resulting from negotiations; and several annexes on specific sectors and on the movement of natural persons.

The Manual on Statistics of International Trade in Services

Following the entry into force of GATS, there has been an increasing demand for detailed, relevant and internationally comparable statistical information on trade in services. Trade negotiators require statistics, possibly by mode of supply, as a guide to negotiate specific commitments and to monitor their economic impact for each type of service. Among others, statistics are necessary to evaluate market access opportunities, compare liberalization commitments, assess the extent of liberalization reached in specific sectors/markets, and provide statistical background for the settlement of disputes.

As a first step to respond to these needs, the recently published *Manual on Statistics of International Trade in Services* (MSITS) was produced. Building upon internationally agreed standards, it provides guidelines and recommendations on how to use and develop sources to measure trade in services. Two building blocks are identified:

- Balance of payments (BOP) statistics, which conform to the fifth edition of the IMF Balance of Payments Manual (BPM5), summarizes transactions of an economy with the rest of the world into the components of the current account and the capital and financial account. BOP statistics under BPM5 display data on trade in services between residents and non-residents (within the current account) into 11 items. MSITS proposes further breakdowns of these items to respond to needs for more detailed information. Furthermore, although BOP statistics do not allow a comprehensive measurement of services delivered through mode 3, they support the measurement of supplementary indicators, e.g. Foreign Direct Investment (FDI) under mode 3.

- MSITS expands the statistical definition of international trade in services by recommending the measurement of services supplied by foreign affiliates, within the new framework of Foreign Affiliates Trade in Services (FATS) statistics. This framework provides for the compilation of a number of indicators aimed at describing the operations of foreign affiliates, with a particular—but not exclusive—focus on services.

The guidelines of MSITS—once implemented by a large number of countries—will provide statisticians, economists and trade negotiators with data on trade in services that would enable more pertinent statistical and economic analyses and improved information for negotiations.[2] MSITS recommendations for developing these two sources should indeed provide a set of statistics covering most services delivered through all modes of supply.

MSITS identifies needs for further methodological work in two main areas:

1. As highlighted in Table 4.1, a satisfactory linkage of statistics with GATS modes of supply is not feasible at present. As a first step, MSITS proposes a simplified approach, based on the overall good correspondence between: (1) FATS statistics and mode 3, and (2) BOP statistics and the three other modes of supply, (as described further below).

Table 4.1. Correspondence Between Modes of Supply and Statistical Domains

Mode of supply	Relevant statistical domains	Inadequacies
Mode 1: Cross-border supply	BOP: commercial services (excluding travel and construction services)	BOP does not allow a separation between modes 1 and 4
Mode 2: Consumption abroad	BOP: Travel	• Travel also contains goods and is not subdivided into the different categories of services consumed by travelers • Some transactions related to this mode of supply are also in other BOP categories
Mode 3: Commercial presence	• FATS statistics • BOP: FDI data (supplementary information) • BOP: construction services	• Very few countries produce FATS data • FDI statistics cover a larger subset, not only (majority) controlled companies • Not distributed between modes 3 and 4
Mode 4: Presence of natural persons	BOP: commercial services (excluding travel)	BOP does not allow a separation between modes 1 (3 for construction services) and 4
Labor mobility	BOP statistics: compensation of employees and workers' remittances (supplementary information)	Of interest for labor mobility

---

[2] See also Box 4.3 for a discussion of U.S. statistical practices.

2. The supply of services through mode 4 is currently not well measured in existing statistics. MSITS opens the way to the creation of a statistical framework in an annex on the movement of natural persons supplying services under GATS.

Statistics of Trade in Services Between Residents and Non-residents of an Economy

Balance of payments (BOP) statistics on services transactions between residents and non-residents provide a sound basis for the measurement of trade in services in the conventional sense. Recommendations made in the MSITS for the development of such statistics are made with the underlying concern to build upon existing principles and classifications.

In what follows, there is an overview of the fundamental concepts of the fifth edition of the IMF *Balance of Payments Manual* (BPM5) that underpin the measurement of trade in services. While keeping full consistency with the BPM5 concepts and classification, MSITS provides a more detailed classification of trade in services statistics (the Extended Balance of Payments Services Classification—EBOPS), which is presented below. MSITS also makes recommendations for the production of a geographical breakdown of trade in services data and proposes a simplified approach to allocate services transactions statistics to the four modes of supply.

PRINCIPLES OF RECORDING SUCH TRADE

The residence concept is a key concept for the measurement of services transactions between residents and non-residents. Other essential concepts relate to the valuation and time of recording transactions.

Transactions and Residence of Transactors

A country's BOP is a balanced statistical statement that summarizes the economic transactions of its residents with the rest of the world. A transaction is an economic flow that involves change of ownership of goods and/or financial assets, the provision of services, or the provision of labor or capital. Services international transactions are in practice referred to as trade in services. These transactions are in general to be recorded gross, with each service item displaying a credit and a debit value, representing respectively exports and imports of that service.

The residence concept is not based on nationality or legal criteria but on a transactor's center of economic interest. Further, because territorial boundaries recognized for political purposes may not always be appropriate for economic purposes, the economic territory of a country is used as the relevant geographical area to which the concept of residence is applied.

The economic territory of a country consists of the geographic territory administered by a government. It also includes territorial enclaves such as embassies, consulates, and military bases located in foreign countries.

It is not always straightforward to determine precisely whether an institutional unit has a center of economic interest within a country, and thus is resident in this country. It is deemed that an enterprise has a center of economic interest in an economy when it engages or intends to engage in economic activities on a significant scale, and over a long time period, within the economic territory of that country. A household has a center of economic interest where it maintains one or more dwellings within the country that members of the household use as their principal residence.[3]

A period of one year or more is suggested as a flexible guideline (the "one-year rule") for determining residence (center of economic interest).

Other Principles of Recording

Market price (i.e. the price at which buyers and sellers trade the item in an open marketplace) should be used as the basis for valuation of international transactions in services. In certain circumstances, such as exchanges between affiliated enterprises (related enterprises integrated under the same management), the pricing adopted for bookkeeping purposes ("transfer pricing") may not always be based closely on market considerations. Because it may be very difficult to evaluate a market price for the recording of such transactions, BPM5 acknowledges that in most cases such an evaluation or imputation would not be applied. In practice, if certain transfer prices are so divorced from those of similar transactions that they significantly distort measurement, they should either be replaced by market-price equivalents or be separately identified for analytical purposes.

The appropriate time to record transactions in services is the time at which they are rendered (that is, when they are delivered or received). This may differ from the time at which payment is made or received, which may be either before or after the transaction takes place. Thus transactions should be recorded, whenever possible, on an accrual rather than a cash-accounting basis.

---

[3] Civil servants and military personnel employed abroad in government enclaves, and their dependents, continue to have centers of economic interest (i.e. they are residents) in their home countries.

Transactions may take place in a range of currencies, including the domestic currency of either the provider or the consumer of the service. To produce meaningful statistics, however, it is necessary for the compiler to convert all transaction values to a common unit of account. Most often, the common unit will be the national currency; this will facilitate the use of such statistics in conjunction with other economic statistics relating to the domestic economy. However, in some cases such as a significant depreciation of the national currency or hyperinflation, it may analytically be more useful to express transactions in another, more stable currency. The most appropriate exchange rate to be used in converting transaction values from the currency of transaction to the currency of compilation is the market rate prevailing at the time the transaction takes place.

THE EXTENDED BALANCE OF PAYMENTS SERVICES CLASSIFICATION

Main Principles

EBOPS provides for the production of statistical information at a level of detail that, among others, meets needs for information in the framework of GATS negotiations. It builds upon the BPM5 classification of services. In BPM5 the 11 main items are also broken down into a list of standard and supplementary components. EBOPS consists of a further breakdown of these components into more detailed sub-items, and is therefore consistent with BPM5. EBOPS also contains several "memorandum items" for the recording of useful additional information regarding transactions in various services sectors such as freight transportation, travel, or insurance services.

Like the BPM5 services classification, EBOPS is primarily a product-based classification. Items of these classifications may be described in terms of the Central Product Classification Version 1.0 (CPC Ver. 1.0), which is the standard international product classification.[4] In order to facilitate the use of statistics based on EBOPS for GATS purposes, MSITS provides, as an annex, tables of correspondence between EBOPS, CPC Ver. 1.0, and GNS/W/120 (the list of service sectors that is generally used as a basis for GATS negotiations).

MSITS recognizes that it will not be possible for all compilers to immediately develop statistics at the detailed component level specified in EBOPS, and puts the highest

---

[4] However, correspondences cannot be established in the areas of travel, construction services, and government services, n.i.e., which focus on the mode of consumption of goods and services, rather than on the type of product consumed.

priority on the development of statistics on international trade in services at the level described in BPM5. Where the breakdown of the main EBOPS components is developed, it should be carried out in stages. Compilers should commence with the disaggregation of services of major economic importance to their own economies and data on related memorandum items should also be produced if these are immediately available as a result of the data compilation process.

EBOPS Components

EBOPS, like BPM5, includes eleven main services components which are listed below. The entire classification is provided in WTO (2006), and complete definitions of the components are given in MSITS.

- Transportation covers all transportation services performed by residents of one economy for those of another and that involve the carriage of passengers, the movement of goods (freight), rentals (charters) of carriers with crew, and related supporting and auxiliary services. In addition, EBOPS distinguishes eight modes of transportation—sea, air, space, rail, road, internal waterway, pipeline, and other supporting and auxiliary transportation services.

- Travel differs from most other internationally traded services in that it is the consumer of these services that gives travel its distinctive characterization. Thus travel does not refer to a particular product and covers expenses for goods and services (including accommodation, food, souvenirs, etc.) acquired by the traveler during his visit abroad. In line with the concept of residence, only persons staying in the visited country for less than one year are regarded as travelers. If they stay more than one year, they are considered to be residents of the visited country. This guideline does not apply to students and patients receiving health care abroad, who remain residents of their economies of origin even if they stay longer than one year.

    With respect to the purpose of the trip, travel is subdivided into business travel, and personal travel. The latter can be further divided into—health-related expenditure, education-related expenditure, and all other personal travel expenditure.[5]

- Communications services can be further disaggregated into two sub-components, postal and courier services, and telecommunication services.

---

[5] An alternative disaggregation of travel services is included in the EBOPS memorandum items distinguishing between expenditure on goods, expenditure on accommodation and food and beverage serving services, and all other travel expenditure. It allows the allocation of expenditure on services to mode 2.

- Construction services covers work performed on construction projects and installation by employees of an enterprise in locations outside the territory of an enterprise. Construction services is further disaggregated into construction abroad and construction in the compiling economy.

- Insurance services covers the provision of various types of insurance to non-residents by resident insurance enterprises, and vice versa. Insurance services are further subdivided into five components—life insurance and pension funding, freight insurance, other direct insurance, reinsurance, and auxiliary services to insurance. Information on gross premiums and gross claims, which may be the basis for estimating the service charge, is included in the memorandum items.

- Financial services covers financial intermediation and auxiliary services, provided by banks, stock exchanges, factoring enterprises, credit card enterprises, and other enterprises.

- Computer and information services are subdivided into computer services (hardware and software related services and data processing services), news agency services (provision of news, photographs, and feature articles to the media), and other information provision services (database services and web search portals).

- Royalties and license fees are divided into franchises and similar rights and other royalties and license fees. The former comprises international payments and receipts of franchising fees and the royalties paid for the use of registered trademarks. Other royalties and license fees include transactions for the authorized use of patents, copyrights, and industrial processes and designs and the use, through licenses of produced originals or prototypes (such as manuscripts and computer programs).

- The coverage of other business services is identical to that of BPM5 but it provides much more detail. This category includes merchanting; other trade-related services; operational leasing services; and miscellaneous business, professional, and technical services, including legal services; accounting, auditing; business and management consulting and public relations services; etc.

- Personal, cultural, and recreational services comprises audiovisual and related services and other personal, cultural, and recreational services. The first component includes services and fees related to the production of motion pictures, radio and television programs, and musical recordings. Other personal, cultural, and recreational services includes services such as those associated with museums, libraries, archives, and other cultural, sporting, and recreational activities. EBOPS provides for the production of additional information within the latter item among two separate sub-components: education services and health services that are important for trade negotiating purposes.

- Government services, n.i.e., covers all government and international organizations transactions not contained in other EBOPS items. It can be subdivided into services transacted by embassies and consulates, by military units and agencies, and all other transactors. Note that GATS does not cover services supplied in the exercise of governmental authority.

For various analytical purposes, compilers may wish to aggregate service and non-service transactions to provide information on areas of particular interest or concern to users, such as all transactions relating to health care, educational, environmental or audiovisual activities. As an example, MSITS provides a suggested aggregation of transactions, the memorandum item audiovisual transactions, which includes transactions that relate to audiovisual activities (audiovisual services, royalties and license fees, and also the acquisition and disposal of non-produced, non-financial assets such as patents, copyrights, trademarks, and franchises). Compilation of this item is recommended for its analytical usefulness, and for its particular relevance to GATS negotiations.

STATISTICS BY TRADING PARTNER

There is a need for detailed geographical allocations of the statistics on the various types of services supplied and consumed by each economy according to the country of residence of trading partners. Such statistics give a firm basis for the multilateral and bilateral trade in services negotiations, and are important for a variety of analytical purposes. For instance, bilateral comparisons of a country's data with those of a trading partner, through the use of "mirror statistics," are an important tool for investigating and improving data quality.

One of the core recommendations of MSITS is that countries should compile statistics on international trade in services on an individual trading partner basis, at least at the level of services trade as a whole and the 11 main components of the BPM5 classification of services, and where possible at the more detailed EBOPS level. However, it may be very resource-intensive and difficult (disclosure or incomplete information) for compilers to develop statistics on trade in services by trading partner. Thus, it is suggested that countries start compiling these statistics at least for their main partners and in their most important services sectors. It is also recommended that, to the extent possible, compilers use an identical geographical basis for all related sets of international trade in services statistics (including FATS statistics).

ALLOCATION OF BOP/EBOPS ITEMS TO MODES OF SUPPLY[6]

A country's exports of computer services may be well measured overall. However how much of these sales relate to cross-border supply (mode 1, e.g. electronic transmission of a specific software developed in the country of the provider), and how much relate to the presence of natural persons (mode 4, e.g. a programmer developing a specific application in the premises of the foreign customer)? MSITS acknowledges that compilers will not be able to allocate each EBOPS type of service by GATS modes of supply in the near future. As a first step, it proposes a simplified approach, operational in the current statistical context, for producing approximations. Based on the determination of the location of the supplier at the time of the service transaction, it is assumed that a given service category in the BOP accounts corresponds to only one or two dominant mode(s) of supply.

According to this methodology, the following EBOPS services, when exchanged between residents and non-residents, are deemed to be predominantly delivered through mode 1 (cross-border supply): transportation (except supporting and auxiliary services to carriers in foreign ports, which should be allocated to mode 2), communications, insurance, and financial services, and royalties and license fees. All services recorded under item travel (i.e. excluding goods) should be allocated to mode 2 (consumption abroad).

The picture is more complex for the remaining commercial services, which may involve significant elements of two modes of supply: computer and information services; other business services; and personal, cultural, and recreational services may be delivered through mode 1 and mode 4; construction services may be provided through mode 3 and mode 4. Further work is necessary to determine an allocation of these statistics to modes of supply.

Foreign Affiliates Trade in Services Statistics

The international delivery of a number of services requires close and continuous contact between producers and consumers, which can often only be achieved through locally established affiliates (i.e. GATS mode 3, commercial presence). To allow the measurement of this particularly important channel of delivery,[7] MSITS recommends the

---

[6] Note that mode 3 (commercial presence) is primarily concerned with FATS and that a number of other additional indicators are used to assess mode 4 (presence of natural persons).

[7] Although only fragmentary data are available, we have noted that the value of services delivered through foreign affiliates is substantially higher than the value of services traded on a BOP basis.

implementation of the Foreign Affiliates Trade in Services (FATS) statistical framework. It provides guidelines for the production of indicators on the operations of both resident affiliates of foreign firms (inward FATS), and affiliates abroad of resident firms (outward FATS). Apart from providing indicators on mode 3 trade in services, FATS statistics provide general indicators that help understand the phenomenon of globalization.[8]

In what follows, criteria are presented for determining the population of foreign producers for consideration in FATS statistics as well as indications for choosing the statistical unit within that population. Also discussed are the time of recording statistics, the variables of most interest for economic and policy analysis, and how to break down the variables in order to draw a complete picture of foreign affiliate activities.

PRINCIPLES FOR RECORDING FATS STATISTICS

Principles for recording FATS statistics are in line with international statistical standards, especially those governing the measurement of foreign direct investment (FDI) within BPM5 and the *OECD Benchmark Definition of FDI,* third edition (BD3). The FDI universe is introduced in the first subsection below as it enables the understanding of the universe of FATS statistics. Furthermore, FDI statistics may provide interim indicators of commercial presence for those countries that have not yet begun to compile FATS statistics.[9]

The FDI Universe

FDI is the category of international investment that reflects the objective of a resident entity in one economy (the direct investor) to obtain a lasting interest in an enterprise resident in another economy (the direct investment enterprise). The lasting interest implies the existence of a long-term relationship between the direct investor and the enterprise, and a significant degree of influence of the investor on the management of the enterprise.

The direct investment enterprise is an incorporated or unincorporated enterprise in which a direct investor owns 10 per cent or more of the ordinary shares or voting power

[8] Guidance in the OECD *Handbook on Economic Globalisation* indicators (2005: chapter III, The economic activity of multinational enterprises) is fully consistent with guidelines of MSITS.

[9] FDI statistics comprise initial investments and subsequent transactions between related enterprises. They cover direct investment financial transactions (recorded primarily on a directional basis), direct investment income (accruing to the direct investor) and direct investment positions (value of the stock of direct investment at the end of the reference period).

(for an incorporated enterprise) or the equivalent (for an unincorporated enterprise). It may be (1) a subsidiary (a majority-owned corporation), (2) an associate (a corporation owned at 10–50 per cent), or (3) a branch (wholly or jointly owned unincorporated enterprises) of the foreign direct investor.

Direct investors may be individuals, incorporated or unincorporated public or private enterprises, associated groups of individuals or enterprises, Governments or government agencies, or other organizations that own direct investment enterprises in economies other than those in which the direct investor resides.

Firms Covered in FATS Statistics

FATS statistics generally cover only those affiliates controlled by a foreign direct investor. For statistical purposes, the relevant population for FATS statistics comprises affiliates that are majority-owned by a single direct investor[10] holding more than 50 per cent of ordinary shares or voting power.[11] Thus, the statistical population of FATS statistics is a subset of the FDI universe, which comprises subsidiaries and branches, but excludes associates. It should be noted that FATS statistics reflect all operations of the affiliates concerned rather than being prorated according to the ownership share of the foreign parent firms.

FATS statistics cover producers of goods and services alike. Some firms produce both goods and services, and it is only by the coverage of all producers that the activities of firms producing services as a secondary activity will be reflected in the statistics. In addition, coverage of all producers allows for the activities of services producers to be seen in the context of statistics covering all firms.

Statistical Units

FATS statistics may be collected either at the enterprise (company) level, or at the individual business location or establishment level. The units employed can strongly influence the interpretation of the statistics (see example below), and either basis has its strengths and weaknesses (difficult allocation of some variables among establishments of an enterprise, different costs for data collection, etc.). As these statistics are often derived from existing statistical systems in which the units are already defined, MSITS

---

[10] In this respect, an associated group of investors acting in concert is considered as a single investor.

[11] Some firms other than those majority-owned by a foreign investor are recognized to be of interest, either in the context of the GATS or in studies of globalization (e.g. firms that are exactly 50 per cent owned by a foreign investor, firms in which there is collective majority ownership by multiple foreign investors). MSITS encourages compilers to provide separately identified supplemental statistics, along with appropriate explanatory notes, covering such cases of interest.

makes no recommendation on which statistical units should be used, but recommends that FATS statistics disclose the units used in explanatory notes.

For example, suppose an enterprise has two establishments—one that provides financial services and one that provides information services. Suppose further that the financial services establishment accounts for 60 per cent of the enterprise's sales, and that the information services establishment accounts for the remaining 40 per cent. In establishment-level statistics, the sales would be recorded in the two industries in the proportions indicated. In enterprise-level statistics, by contrast, the entire enterprise would be classified under a single industry (financial services, if the distribution of sales were used as the basis for classification), in which case all the sales would be recorded in that industry and none in the other one. However it is more costly to collect the information from establishments than at the enterprise level.

Time of Recording

As for other economic statistics, guidelines for FATS statistics recommend that variables be measured and recorded on an accrual basis (i.e. in the period in which the transaction occurs rather than, for example, under the period in which the related payments are made). Flow variables, such as output and value added, should refer to a reference year, while stock variables, such as assets and net worth, should refer to the end of a reference year.

The basis should be the calendar year. However, for some countries, only fiscal or accounting year data are likely to be available. These countries are encouraged to provide explanatory notes indicating this and providing any information on the extent to which fiscal and calendar years deviate in their FATS universe.

ECONOMIC VARIABLES FOR FATS

A wide range of economic data or variables—operational or financial—regarding FATS may be pertinent for analytical and policy purposes. MSITS recommends that the FATS variables to be collected include at least the following basic measures of foreign affiliate activity: sales (turnover) and/or output, employment, value added, exports and imports of goods and services, and number of enterprises. Details and examples of these measures are given in MSITS.

Although these variables constitute a basic set that can provide answers to a variety of questions, additional measures of foreign affiliate activities may prove useful in addressing specific issues. MSITS suggests that the following additional variables be considered for collection in a second stage by countries able to compile them: assets, compensation of employees, net worth, net operating surplus, gross fixed capital formation, taxes on income, and research and development expenditures.

Most of both the "basic" and the "additional" variables are drawn from 1993 SNA.

ATTRIBUTION (CLASSIFICATION) OF FATS VARIABLES

FATS variables may be distributed following two main breakdowns. The geographical breakdown indicates where the production took place, and where the owner of the producing affiliate is located. The primary industrial activity breakdown of the producer indicates which sector of activity is concerned. Moreover, some variables may be classified by product. The recommendations of MSITS on each of these breakdowns are given below.

By Country

In breaking down variables by country, the issues to be addressed depend on whether the statistics are on inward FATS or outward FATS.

For inward FATS, the question is either to attribute the transaction to the immediate investing country or to the ultimate investing country. MSITS recommends that the country of the ultimate beneficial owner (UBO) of the affiliate be the primary basis of the geographical breakdown. The country of the UBO is the country that ultimately owns or controls—and that derives the primary benefits from owning or controlling—the affiliate. For example, if a French company indirectly owns an affiliate in Russia, through its wholly owned subsidiary in the Netherlands, then in inward FATS statistics compiled by Russia, France should be the owner country. However, considering that information on immediate owners (or "first foreign parents") may be available as a by-product of FDI data, and to facilitate comparisons with those data, MSITS encourages countries to also compile data broken down according to the country of the immediate owners.

For outward FATS, there are two options. The variables could be attributed to the country of location of the affiliate (immediate host country) or—if the ownership is through a directly held affiliate located in another country—to the country of that affiliate (ultimate host country). MSITS recommends attributing them to the country of the affiliate whose operations are described by the variables.[12] This treatment is indeed the most relevant for revealing the country of location of the affiliate in which the direct investor's commercial presence exists. For example, if a British company owned an

---

[12] It should be noted that FDI transactions recorded in the BOP framework are attributed to the immediate host country, which is appropriate for tracking financial flows and positions.

affiliate in the United States through a holding company located in Bermuda, then in British outward FATS statistics the affiliate should be classified in the United States rather than in Bermuda.

By Activity (Industry) and by Services Product

All FATS variables should be allocated to the industrial activities of the producers. MSITS provides an activity classification for FATS variables drawn from the International Standard Industrial Classification of All Economic Activities, Revision 3 (ISIC Rev.3). This classification, termed ISIC Categories for Foreign Affiliates (ICFA) is given in the MSITS.

The data recorded against any given ICFA category must be interpreted as an indication of the principal activity of firms rather than as a precise measure of the activity itself. The industry where a given firm is classified only reflects the most important activity carried out. For example, computer services may be provided not only by firms classified in the computer services industry but also by firms classified in computer manufacturing and computer wholesale trading. Similarly (though in reality less commonly), computer services firms may engage in manufacturing or wholesale trade as secondary activities. Statistics shown for the activity "computer services" would thus misstate the value of the activity, both by excluding the computer services provided by manufacturers and wholesale traders and by including the manufacturing and wholesale trade activities of computer services firms.

For this reason, as well as because of differences in the classifications themselves, the extent to which data on resident/non-resident trade classified according to EBOPS can be aligned with data on FATS variables classified according to ICFA is inherently limited. Nonetheless, a correspondence between the two bases of classification (provided in MSITS) may be useful for some purposes, especially in sectors where firms are specialized and do not tend to have significant secondary activities. For example, if legal services were performed only by law firms and law firms tended to perform legal services alone, then sales recorded under the activity "legal services" would correspond closely to sales of legal services, as they would be recorded under a product classification.

Although MSITS recommends as a first priority to break down FATS statistics by activity, it encourages countries, as a longer term goal, to work towards breaking down a number of variables such as sales, exports and imports, by types of services produced and sold.[13] Data on a product basis would allow the identification of specific types of services delivered through commercial presence. Any product detail for FATS that is available or can be developed should be broken down on a basis compatible with

---

[13] Other variables such as value added and employment cannot be classified by product.

EBOPS. If this level of specificity cannot be achieved, countries may wish to disaggregate sales in each industry as between sales of goods and sales of services, as a first step toward a product breakdown.

Box 4.4 Measuring Trade in Services: The U.S. Statistical Practices

---

Obie G. Whichard

Services account for a significant share of the international trade of the United States. In 2006, U.S. exports of services amounted to $423 billion, or 29 per cent of total U.S. exports of goods and services. U.S. imports of services were $343 billion, or 16 per cent of total U.S. imports of goods and services. The balance on trade in services—a surplus of $80 billion—lay in sharp contrast to the $838 billion deficit on trade in goods recorded in the U.S. international transactions accounts for 2006.

In 2004 (as of this writing, the latest year available), the values of services delivered to foreign markets by foreign affiliates of U.S. companies, and to the U.S. market by U.S. affiliates of foreign companies, exceeded the respective values of U.S. exports and imports of private services. In that year, sales of services to foreign (non-U.S.) persons by majority-owned foreign affiliates of U.S. companies, at $490 billion, were 48 per cent higher than the $333 billion in U.S. exports of private services. Sales of services in the United States by majority-owned U.S. affiliates of foreign companies totaled $383 billion, 48 per cent higher than the $259 billion in private services imports.

To meet the needs associated with growth in the value of trade in services, trade negotiations, and the development of new and more detailed international statistical guidelines, the United States has taken a variety of steps to improve the coverage, specificity, and international comparability of its statistics on international trade in services. These steps have included improvements in data on both trade in the conventional sense of transactions between residents and nonresidents and services delivered through locally established affiliates, the latter corresponding broadly to the General Agreement on Trade in Services commercial presence mode of supply and commonly referred to as "foreign affiliates' trade in services," or FATS.

The data on both channels of services delivery are compiled—and for the most part are collected—by the Bureau of Economic Analysis (BEA), a statistical agency within the U.S. Department of Commerce. Most of the data on international services are collected by BEA in a system of mandatory surveys conducted under legislation known as the International Investment and Trade in Services Survey Act. This act requires the periodic collection of data on trade in services, makes reporting mandatory for U.S. businesses that engage in international services trade, and stipulates that the data reported will be held confidential and used for statistical purposes only. A second law governing the collection of data on trade in services (as well as other topics) is the Paperwork Reduction Act of 1995. Under this act, the surveys must undergo an approval process in which BEA is required to demonstrate that the data are necessary, that they cannot be obtained from other sources, and that their collection does not place an unreasonable burden on respondents.

BEA conducts several surveys, each of which is targeted to a particular group of services or type of transactions. Other sources are used as well, sometimes in conjunction with the survey data. In some instances, one source is used to obtain a unit value or per capita amount, which is then multiplied by an independently derived volume measure to produce an estimate of the total dollar value of the transactions. For some types of transportation services, for example, sample data on carriers' revenues collected in BEA surveys are expanded to universe estimates by multiplying the sample data by the ratio of the total shipping weights tabulated from export and import declarations to the corresponding sample data on shipping weights obtained from the BEA surveys. As another example of this methodology, estimates of expenditures by air travelers are derived by multiplying a sample-based estimate of expenditures per traveler, obtained from an in-flight survey conducted by the International Trade Administration of the Department of Commerce, by figures on the total number of travelers obtained from the U.S. Citizenship and

Immigration Services. Estimates for education services are similarly derived through multiplication of per capita figures on tuition and student living expenses by figures on the total number of U.S. students studying abroad or foreign students studying in the United States.

For the most part, the U.S. data on exports and imports of services are compiled in conformity with the fifth edition of the International Monetary Fund's *Balance of Payments Manual* (*BPM5*). The breakdown by type of service is in fact somewhat more detailed than that suggested by the *BPM5* standard components for services and includes several items needed to meet the recommendations of the Extended Balance of Payments Services Classification (EBOPS) of the international *Manual on Statistics of International Trade in Services (MSITS)*. Since the appearance of these guidelines—or, in some cases, in anticipation of their appearance—several changes have been made to improve conformity. In addition, BEA has taken a number of steps to improve the accuracy, comprehensiveness, timeliness, and detail of its data on trade in services. These not only have improved conformity with international guidelines, but also have improved the general quality of the data and added to BEA's ability to meet the detailed needs of data users.

Among the most important of these steps have been those to improve the coverage of trade in services. In 1986, a new survey was instituted to collect data on trade in variety of "selected" services—mainly, business, professional, and technical services. Benchmark surveys have been conducted at five-year intervals, with less detailed annual surveys conducted in the interim years. In 2004, a new quarterly survey was introduced to improve the timeliness of the data. In 1994, a new survey of trade in financial services was introduced. Initially, benchmark and annual surveys were conducted; in 2004, a quarterly survey was instituted.

While the most significant improvements in coverage have resulted from the new surveys, BEA has increased its use of outside source data to develop estimates of services that are not covered by its own surveys. In addition, the quality of data on some services was improved in the late 1980s, when previously voluntary surveys were made mandatory under the International Investment and Trade in Services Survey Act. Finally, a number of methodological and presentational changes have been made to improve the usefulness of the data and to meet current international guidelines. Examples of methodological and presentational changes include the following:

- A change from a net method of recording trade in services between domestic and foreign units of multinational companies to a gross method. The net method had tended to mask the two-way flow of services trade between related parties and to cause an understatement of total exports and total imports of services.
- Better integration of data on intrafirm trade with data on trade between unrelated parties. This improvement has given a more complete picture of total U.S. trade in particular types of services. The existing data have been brought together from separate surveys covering intrafirm transactions and transactions with unrelated parties. In 2007, this integration is being carried a step further by collecting both types of transactions on the same surveys.
- Reclassification of certain categories of transactions to improve alignment with international classifications (*BPM5* standard components and EBOPS). Recent changes have included the reclassification of operational leasing and computer software royalties and license fees.
- Introduction of new measures of insurance, which provide an economically more meaningful measure of the services provided. Previously, insurance had been measured as the net of current-period premiums and losses. Recently, a new measure was introduced that views insurance as the sum of (1) premiums less "normal" losses, where normal losses are inferred from the historical relationship between premiums and losses, (2) "premium supplements," which represent the returns on reserves held by insurance companies on behalf of policyholders, and (3) services auxiliary to insurance, such as agents' commissions and actuarial services.

While it cannot be described as a specific problem or data improvement, treatment of these topics cannot be considered complete without some mention of the challenge and the necessity of keeping abreast of new services that come into existence and of new ways of delivering services. The most obvious examples involve the Internet. In recent years, as surveys have come up for renewal, instructions have been added to indicate that the criteria for reporting are based on whom the transactions are between, not on the location of the buyer or seller at the time of the transaction. Thus, the instructions indicate, transactions conducted over the Internet or other computer-mediated networks are to be reported if they otherwise meet the criteria for reporting. In addition, where new Internet-related services fall within the scope of existing services categories, definitions are revised to mention them specifically.

Measuring commercial presence.—For information on services delivered through foreign affiliates—"FATS" statistics—BEA relies entirely on its own surveys. As explained above in Chapter 4, FATS statistics encompass a variety of indicators of affiliate operations, organized in a way that highlights the role of services. Although the initial data were collected without any particular regard for services, BEA has collected statistics that could qualify as FATS statistics since 1950. As interest in services grew and as it became apparent that services would be included in negotiations, a few key adjustments were made to accommodate this new emphasis. In particular, existing questions on sales were expanded to request that this item be broken down into sales of goods and sales of services, and definitions were provided to distinguish between the two. In addition, when industry classifications were revised, additional detail was provided for services industries.

Perhaps the most important change has been requesting that sales of services be reported separately from sales of goods. Because the data on affiliate operations are (with minor exceptions) classified according to the primary industry of the affiliate, all of an affiliate's sales are recorded in a single industry, even if the affiliate has operations in multiple industries. Many manufacturing firms and other goods producers have secondary operations in services, but these operations would not be recognized as services in a breakdown by primary industry alone, thus leading to an understatement in the role and importance of services. The breakdown of sales into separate goods and services components avoids this understatement. It would be better still if sales could be broken down by product—that is, by type of good or service—but from the standpoints of respondent burden and processing costs, BEA did not feel justified in requesting this. Disaggregating sales as between goods and services thus served as a compromise solution, which avoided misstatement without imposing a large increase in reporting burden or processing costs.

In its annual detailed article on international services, published in the *Survey of Current Business*, BEA presents the following two items: (1) sales of services to foreign persons by majority-owned nonbank foreign affiliates of U.S. companies, and (2) sales of services to U.S. persons by majority-owned nonbank U.S. affiliates of foreign companies. The foreign affiliates' sales to U.S. customers, and U.S. affiliates' sales to foreign customers, are excluded from this integrated presentation because they are already reflected in the data on trade between residents and non-residents of the United States. (However, they are made available separately.) Except in benchmark years, the data are for non-bank affiliates only, because the annual surveys used in deriving the data currently exclude banks from coverage. The coverage is restricted to majority-owned affiliates, consistent with the guidelines of the *MSITS* for compiling FATS statistics.

In addition to sales, BEA data on affiliate operations include a variety of other indicators of affiliate operations, including balance sheets, income statements, employment and employee compensation, research and development expenditures, taxes, and sources of external financing. Although sometimes presented using different nomenclature, the variables covered include both the "basic" and the optional "additional" FATS variables suggested by the *MSITS*.

In addition to being broken down by industry of affiliate (and, for foreign affiliates, also by industry of U.S. parent), all of the variables collected are disaggregated geographically. For foreign affiliates, the disaggregation is based on the location of the affiliate whose operations are being described. For U.S. affiliates of foreign companies, it is based on the location of the ultimate beneficial owner of the affiliate.

The Movement of Natural Persons

MSITS recognizes that a comprehensive statistical framework for the measurement of mode 4 still needs to be developed. As a first step an annex on the movement of natural persons (MSITS Annex) was included in the manual. Progress has been made since MSITS was prepared, but at present, it is difficult to define the coverage of mode 4 delivery of services. There is a need to discuss statistical sources that could be used to help assess this mode of supply and also present possible ways for improving its measurement.

THE MOVEMENT OF NATURAL PERSONS IN GATS

GATS does not provide a precise definition of mode 4 that could be immediately used for statistical purposes. GATS qualifies mode 4 as being "the supply of a service . . . by a service supplier of one Member, through presence of natural persons of a Member in the territory of any other Member." Mode 4 can generally be described as follows:

- It covers both foreign natural persons who are service suppliers (self-employed) and foreign natural persons employed by a foreign service supplier;
- The GATS Annex on Movement of Natural Persons Supplying Services Under the Agreement (GATS Annex) further specifies the temporary nature of the movement: measures regarding citizenship, residence and employment on a permanent basis are excluded from the Agreement. In addition, GATS does "not apply to measures affecting natural persons seeking access to the employment market of a Member."

Mode 4 can therefore be described in terms of purpose of stay and duration. The supplier gains entry to fulfill a service contract, or as an employee, with respect to the supply of a service under GATS. When the service has been delivered, the natural person should leave the country.

Mode 4 Service Suppliers

From the point of view of recipient/importing countries according to the GATS, it is generally understood that mode 4 comprises independent service suppliers (i.e. self-employed) or employees of a foreign service supplier entering the host country of the client to supply a service (contractual service supplier) and employees of foreign service suppliers established in the host country (intra-corporate transferees). It also covers service sellers and persons responsible for setting up commercial presence. However there are areas where it may be difficult to define the coverage with respect to the supply of services under mode 4 as for instance:

- it is not always easy to determine what constitutes a service: for example, should fruit-pickers be viewed as temporary agricultural laborers (outside the scope of mode 4) or as suppliers of fruit-picking services?

- although mode 4 applies to service suppliers whatever their skills, for the time being many WTO members' commitments are generally focusing on highly skilled workers;

- The difference between a service contract and an employment contract may be difficult to establish.

"Temporary": A Key Issue in the Measurement of Mode 4

GATS does not define temporary presence. As stated above, the Agreement only specifically excludes measures regarding citizenship, migration, residence and employment on a permanent basis. In practice, when defined in countries' schedules of commitments, the length of stay related to mode 4 varies between about three months for business visitors up to between two to five years for intra-corporate transferees.

Within international statistical standards (BPM5, 1993 SNA and UN *Recommendations on Statistics of International Migration, Revision 1*), the distinction between temporary and permanent presence is generally determined by the one-year rule, which distinguishes residents of an economy from non-residents. The MSITS Annex notes the divergence between the definition given to "temporary" by statistical standards and GATS and concludes that available statistical information on economic activities of residents (i.e. more than one year) also contains elements related to the temporary presence in the GATS sense.

Mode 4 and Relations to Existing Classifications

The MSITS Annex stresses the relevance of a number of existing international classifications for GATS negotiations and for measuring mode 4: CPC Ver. 1.0 (which is also relevant for other modes of supply); the ILO International Standard Classification of Occupations (ISCO-88) distinguishing between the different categories of employment; ISIC Rev. 3 which could be relevant in the context of lack of statistical information on the distribution of foreign employment according to occupation; and the International Classification of Status in Employment (ICSE-93) relevant for instance to identify "independent service providers" which are often subject to GATS-specific commitments.

STATISTICS FOR MEASURING MODE 4

Various indicators are of interest for assessing mode 4. Most of them relate to the different types of movement of natural persons identified in previous sections. These indicators concern the value of services traded or the number and types of persons moving across borders. Box 4.4 provides a picture of how different types of mode 4 service suppliers can be linked to existing statistical areas.

BOP Statistics

The BOP statistical framework comprises several items that may prove useful in approximating the value of trade in services supplied through mode 4. In addition, supplementing information may be provided by BOP labor-related items.

- Services components in BPM5/EBOPS include transactions relating to service contracts and are thus the most relevant indicators for measuring mode 4 supply of services. As stated above, in many cases a single service transaction may cover more than one mode of supply. For a number of service categories the mode 4 component is believed to be relatively marginal. However, a number of BPM5/EBOPS services items are thought to include significant elements of mode 4: computer and information services; other business services; personal, cultural and recreational services; and construction services.

- BOP labor-related flows provide information on the general temporary movements of persons. Compensation of employees refers to transactions received from/paid to non-residents in the context of employment contracts, generally of less than one year. It comprises not only compensation of foreigners employed in services foreign affiliates established in the host country (intra-corporate transferees where mode 4 movement is instrumental to the supply of services trough commercial presence—mode 3) but includes also the compensation of other employees working in services industries and employees working in other industries (labor migration), local employees of embassies abroad, seasonal workers and longer-term employees such as border workers. Workers' remittances (within BOP current transfers) provide information that complements compensation of employees. They refer to current transfers by migrant workers who are employed in a foreign economy where they are considered to be residents (i.e. more than one year). Workers' remittances refer to the part of the migrants' earning that they forward to their home country.

FATS Statistics

Supplementary indicators on movements related to mode 4 could also be obtained from the FATS statistical framework (number of employees). A number of commitments taken on mode 4 concern directly intra-corporate transferees (their right to move facilitates the provision of services through mode 3). It could prove useful to identify separately foreign non-permanent employment in FATS statistics.

Migration Statistics

Information on numbers of temporary workers moving across borders may be found in the migration/employment statistics. Elements related to the presence of natural persons and more generally labor mobility are identified in the UN *Recommendations on Statistics of International Migration, Revision 1*, which includes, for example, temporary migrations for the purpose of work.[14]

Other Possible Sources

A number of other sources of information could be of interest:

- statistics on the number and type of work permits granted and currently valid (e.g. by duration and by occupation);
- if available, information from government-run social security systems and national health insurance schemes where foreigners may be distinguished;
- statistics on arrivals and departures monitored by immigration or tourism authorities may provide information about foreign nationals concerning their origin/destination, length of stay, purpose of visit, etc.;
- household surveys and population censuses could also provide information on migrants, although they are frequently limited to the resident population, and therefore do not cover short-term visitors involved in trade in services. In addition population censuses are produced at too long intervals and available too late to monitor recent developments related to the presence of foreign workers.

Improving Mode 4 Related Statistics

Trade-related statistics and migration/labor statistics, which may help approximate mode 4 trade in services, diverge widely in terms of concepts, definitions, classifications, etc. The indicators presented above are often readily available, but for a much wider population than that relevant for mode 4. The major difficulty in the measurement of mode 4 is to identify the subset of services contracts that should be measured.

At present, little seems feasible for an accurate estimation of the value of services supplied through mode 4. Much remains to be done in developing the compilation of BOP and FATS statistics so that they fulfill needs for information on trade in services.

---

[14] In practice, the coverage of countries' migration statistics might differ to some extent from the UN recommendations. For instance, some countries may use two years or longer periods as the borderline between short-term and long-term migration; detailed information available may not necessarily enable identifying UN categories of migrants.

Identifying separately mode 4 components within the services sub-items is currently not a priority when compared to other possible improvements.

It is believed that migration/labor statistics could respond to the need for measuring the number of persons moving under mode 4. Improvement of migration statistical concepts, e.g. duration of stay, and categories of migrants and non-migrants, could be very helpful for trade-policy needs. It should also be noted that it is unlikely that trade-policy needs be duly taken into account in migration statistics in the short-term, and GATS mode 4 has not been translated into precise statistical requirements.

Data Availability and Dissemination by International Organizations

An essential element of the quality of BOP and FATS statistics is the public access to the data. International and regional organizations collect and disseminate trade in services statistics compiled by individual countries, which enables users to have an immediate access to a wide range of data and also allows the dissemination of statistics that are internationally comparable. Moreover, international and regional organizations encourage national compilers to produce statistics at the highest useful level of detail. The following discussion reviews the type of trade in services indicators and breakdowns disseminated, the availability and international dissemination of BOP trade in services statistics, and characteristics of the FATS and FDI data.

BOP TRADE IN SERVICES DATA AVAILABILITY AND DISSEMINATION

BOP/EBOPS Trade in Services Data

BOP trade in services data collection is relatively well established and widespread according to the principles and framework of BPM5. An overview of the number of countries that report components and supplementary items of BPM5, as of June 2005, is given in WTO (2006). Between 120 and 152 countries reported export data for transport, travel, communications services, insurance services, and other business services; and between 76 and 95 countries reported export data for construction services, financial services, computer and information services, and royalties and license fees.

Table 4.2 shows the recent developments with respect to export statistics of a number of BPM5 major services components. For most of the components, the number of reporting countries has more than doubled between October 1997 and June 2005. For example, in

Table 4.2. Countries Reporting Exports of Selected BPM5 Services Components (As a Percentage of Countries Reporting Total Services)

	Reporting countries in October 1997 %	Reporting countries in June 2005 %
Communications services	39	78
Construction services	21	51
Insurance services	61	81
Financial services	26	61
Computer and information services	11	55
Royalties and license fees	32	57
Other business services	92	90
Miscellaneous business, professional, and technical services	44	73
Legal, accounting, management, consulting, public relations serv.	8	35
Advertising, market research, and public opinion polling services	10	33
Research and development services	7	20
Architectural, engineering, and other technical services	8	27
Agricultural, mining, and on-site processing services	4	17
Other services	28	54
Personal, cultural, and recreational services	14	53

Sources: Adapted from WTO (October 1997) and IMF monthly CD-ROM on BOP statistics (June 2005).

June 2005, 61 per cent of countries reporting total services exports also reported exports of financial services, compared to only 26 per cent in October 1997. When looking at more detailed services items, for instance the breakdown of miscellaneous business, professional, and technical services, the number of countries reporting this breakdown, although lower than those reporting BPM5 standard items, has also significantly increased.[15]

Concerning services items according to EBOPS, it is currently difficult to evaluate the capacity of countries to report statistics according to this new classification. According to the information available, an increasing number of countries is able to provide trade in services data according to part or all of this classification (up to 50 countries for a number of items). An increasing number of countries also began breaking down their BOP trade in services statistics by partner countries (including non-OECD countries).

International Dissemination of BOP Statistics

As may be seen in Table 4.3, which summarizes the dissemination of statistics by international organizations, Eurostat, the OECD, and the IMF currently collect and disseminate BOP data by type of service for their respective member countries (Eurostat is also responsible for information concerning E.U. candidate countries). They use the IMF's internationally agreed BOP coding system that facilitates common reporting of data.

---

[15] BPM5 supplementary items are reported on a voluntary basis by countries. These items are present in the IMF BOP questionnaire mainly due to the fact that they are part of EBOPS.

Table 4.3. Summary of BOP Trade in Services Data Dissemination by International Organizations

Publication	Country coverage	By type of service	By partner country
IMF Balance of Payments Statistics Database (book and CD-ROM)	IMF members	Yes BPM5 and EBOPS (provided to IMF on voluntary basis)	No
Eurostat New Cronos Database (on-line and CD-ROM)	EU members, total EU, euro area, EU candidate countries	Yes EBOPS	Yes 70 partner countries and partner regions (250 for total services)
OECD Statistics on International Trade in Services, Volume 1, Detailed Tables by Service Category (a joint publication of OECD and Eurostat) (book, on-line and CD-ROM)	OECD members	Yes EBCPS	No
OECD Statistics on International Trade in Services, Volume 2, Detailed Tables by Partner Country (book, on-line and CD-ROM)	29 OECD members, Hong Kong, and Russian Federation	Total services Transportation Travel Other commercial serv. n.i.e. Government serv. n.i.e.	Yes 70 partner countries and partner regions
WTO's International Trade Statistics (book, on-line and CD-ROM)	All countries	Yes Summary data and analysis	Yes Summary data

With respect to geographical breakdown, Eurostat and the OECD collect and disseminate data broken down by partner country for their members (the OECD publication also contains data for Hong Kong as a declaring country). These data sets make it possible to partially estimate non-reporting countries' exports and imports by partner on the basis of bilateral ("mirror") data. No worldwide collection of data broken down geographically is currently available, but the United Nations Statistics Division is currently conducting feasibility studies for possible data collection.

COMMERCIAL PRESENCE: INFORMATION AVAILABLE

Compared with trade in services in BOP, FATS statistics are at an early stage of development. Nevertheless, their collection and dissemination are taking an increasing importance at Eurostat, the OECD and the UNCTAD, fuelled by the growth in national activity in this area. When countries do not yet collect FATS data, FDI statistics can provide "an alternative interim indicator of commercial presence." The international and regional organizations are working together to coordinate data collection, improve consistency of data, avoid duplication of effort, and reduce reporting burdens on countries.

Availability and Dissemination of FATS Statistics

Eurostat and the OECD use a common FATS questionnaire requesting their member countries to provide both inward and outward FATS information, by activity (37 categories of the ISIC Rev.3 classification) and by country of origin/destination of investment. Table 4.4, derived from OECD (2001), shows the relatively good coverage of inward FATS statistics compared to the outward situation, which is due to the difficulty for national agencies to collect statistics on operations performed outside the country territory or jurisdiction.[16]

The OECD conducted two surveys relating to 1995 and 1998 (or 1997). Many countries could not provide all requested data but about 20 of them provided some. The results of these two surveys were published in 2002 in *Measuring Globalization: The*

Table 4.4. Availability of Inward and Outward FATS Statistics in OECD Countries

	Inward			Outward		
	Number of employees	Turnover	Value added	Number of employees	Turnover	Value added
Australia	X		X	X	X	
Austria	X	X		X	X	
Belgium	X	X		X	X	
Canada					X	X
Czech Republic	X	X	X			
Denmark	X	X	X			
Finland	X	X	X			
France	X	X	X		X	
Germany	X	X		X	X	
Hungary	X	X	X			
Ireland	X		X			
Italy	X	X		X	X	
Japan	X	X	X			
Luxembourg	X	X		X	X	
Netherlands	X	X	X			
Norway	X	X	X			
Poland	X	X				
Portugal	X	X	X	X	X	X
Sweden	X	X	X	X		
Turkey	X	X	X			
U.K.	X	X	X			
U.S.	X	X	X	X	X	X

Source: Adapted from OECD (2001) and national sources.

[16] It should be noted that FATS figures, at the detailed activity/geographical breakdown level, are not disseminated due to the requirement in most countries to protect the confidentiality of individual firms' data (e.g. when it only concerns a small number of firms or when a small number of firms account for a significant part (e.g. 75 per cent) of the figure).

Role of Multinationals in OECD Economies: 2001 Edition, Volume II: Services. Eurostat has also several publications in the Statistics in Focus series, and publishes available FATS statistics in the reference database New Cronos. These data are provided to UNCTAD that also collects data on FDI (see below) and conducts a direct survey of multinationals. The UNCTAD publishes combined results including estimates in the *World Investment Report.*

FDI Statistics

The state of implementation regarding the collection of FDI statistics by activity of the ISIC Rev. 3 and by origin and destination is well described in periodic reports on the joint OECD/IMF Survey of Implementation of Methodological Standards for Direct Investment (SIMSDI). The report of the 2001 SIMSDI update showed a significant improvement of data on availability for the 61 countries participating in the update exercise.[17] Fifty-three countries collect inward flows with geographic break-downs (43 countries for outward flows) and 49 collect inward flows with an activity breakdown (36 for outward flows). Corresponding figures for FDI income flows and FDI positions are lower. More than 90 per cent of OECD countries were able to provide geographic disaggregations of FDI financial flows and disaggregations by economic activity were almost as commonly available. Around 80 per cent of non-OECD countries participating in the update exercise were also able to provide geographic and activity disaggregations.

The main collectors and disseminators of FDI data are Eurostat, the IMF, the OECD, and the UNCTAD. Eurostat and the OECD use a common questionnaire to collect FDI inward and outward stocks, flows and income data, broken down by industry and by country of origin or destination. The IMF collects FDI positions, flows and income according to the components set out in BPM5, but without any industry and partner country breakdowns.

Current State and Prospects

As already noted, international and regional organizations have been very active in the area of trade in services statistics over the past years. The Interagency Task Force on Statistics of International Trade in Services[18] (Task Force) developed the MSITS, which

---

[17] Thirty OECD members and 31 of the 84 non-OECD countries participating in the 1999 SIMSDI.

[18] The six international organizations that have jointly developed and published the *MSITS* are the Organization for Economic Co-operation and Development (OECD), the Statistical Office of the European Communities (Eurostat), the International Monetary Fund (IMF), the United Nations Statistical Division

was completed in 2002. The tasks of the group are multiple and concentrate in the short term on the promotion—and assistance in the implementation—of MSITS, which is a first step towards the MSITS' phased implementation. Some results achieved to date in the measurement of trade in services, as well as ongoing work are reviewed below, and there is a discussion of the areas in which improvements are necessary and medium-term plans of the Task Force.

THE PHASED APPROACH OF MSITS TO IMPLEMENTATION

MSITS proposes a phased approach to the implementation of its recommendations so that countries, including those that are starting to develop statistics on international trade in services, can gradually structure the available information in line with this new international standard framework. This phased approach is reflected in a set of ten recommended elements, of which the first five are designated as core elements. Their sequence takes into account the relative ease that many compilers may find in their implementation. However, the order is quite flexible, so that countries can meet the priority needs of their own institutions.

The implementation of the core elements would provide a basis for internationally comparable basic data sets. These core elements are:

- the implementation of BPM5 recommendations on service transactions between residents and non-residents;
- the compilation of BOP data according to items in the EBOPS classification (beginning with items of major economic importance to the country and available related memorandum items should also be provided);
- the collection of FDI statistics by activities of ISIC Rev. 3;
- the compilation of basic FATS variables, broken down by activity according to ICFA; and
- the compilation of statistics on trade in services by partner country for each of the main types of services in BPM5. (Also for FATS and FDI).

The implementation of other elements—generally seen as a long-term goal—would represent a considerable increase in the detail of information available on trade in services. These elements relate to:

(UNSD), the United Nations Conference on Trade and Development (UNCTAD), and the World Trade Organization (WTO). The task force also benefits from expertise in other international organizations (World Tourism Organization—UNWTO) and in national organizations, particularly the U.S. Bureau of Economic Analysis, Statistics Canada, the Deustche Bundesbank, Bank of Japan, Ufficio Italiano dei Cambi, and Central Bank of the Philippines.

- the full implementation of EBOPS, to the extent relevant to the compiling economy;
- the additional details in FATS statistics;
- the collection of statistics on the presence of natural persons;
- the subdivision of trade in services between residents and non-residents: separate trade with related parties from that with unrelated parties; and
- the allocation of transactions between residents and non-residents over GATS modes of supply.

RECENT PROGRESS AND SHORT-TERM PLANS

The quality and quantity of statistics on international trade in services has dramatically improved over the past years. Before 1995, with the exception of travel and transport, services in BOP statistics were all lumped together in one category named "other goods, services, and income." The detail provided has progressively improved. Thanks to the detail asked for in BPM5, there is now a multi-country data set on statistics for major services categories.

As described above, for most of the major BPM5 service components, the number of reporting countries has more than doubled since 1997. The number of countries reporting BPM5 supplementary items has also significantly increased between 1997 and 2003. Even though MSITS is still relatively recent, an increasing number of countries are now able to provide trade in services data according to part or all of the EBOPS classification (up to 50 countries for a number of items), and provide statistics broken down by partner countries.

Until recently, the United States was the only country compiling FATS statistics. It was therefore not possible to determine the magnitude of mode 3: commercial presence. On a wider context, using new FATS data from the OECD together with BOP statistics, it has been estimated that trade through commercial presence surpasses the three other modes of supply together. Despite its limitations, such an estimate shows the importance of FATS trade, which had been neglected for so long in the economic/statistics literature. The importance of FATS statistics is now well recognized, and data collection has started in many OECD countries as well as other countries.

According to information reported by countries participating in the 2001 update of the joint OECD/IMF Survey of Implementation of Methodological Standards for Direct Investment, between 1997 and 2001 there has been a significant incr-ease in the number of countries compiling FDI data with geographic and activity breakdowns.[19]

---

[19] Available individual country information with respect to the 2003 SIMSDI is provided at www.imf.org

Eurostat has prepared two regulations that require from EU member states a more detailed reporting of trade in services, using MSITS as the benchmark. One of these regulations, which was adopted in June 2004 by the European Parliament and the Council of Community Statistics, covers BOP statistics—trade in services and FDI, which embodies the EBOPS classification. EBOPS has thus become binding for EU member states. The other regulation which is under consideration for adoption at the time of writing will cover the compilation of FATS statistics. A recommendations manual on the production of foreign affiliates statistics (FATS) is being developed by the Eurostat Joint Working Group on Foreign Affiliates Statistics.

The IMF and OECD collect data according to EBOPS including memorandum items (on a voluntary basis for the IMF), which generates hopes that EBOPS reporting will substantially increase. The OECD is progressively expanding its collection of BOP trade in services by partner country as well as of FATS statistics as recommended in MSITS. The latter is part of a wider OECD work on developing indicators of economic globalization. The United Nations Statistics Division is investigating the feasibility of collecting BOP trade in services data by partner country from non-OECD countries and of developing a database to store and disseminate trade in services statistics which follow the recommendations of MSITS. The UNCTAD will expand data collection on activities of foreign affiliates.

Eurostat and OECD are also working together to monitor the implementation of MSITS and data quality. The results of the joint Methodological Soundness Questionnaire on Measurement of Trade in Services in the Balance of Payments, published in 2006, provide useful information for around 30 countries.

Finally international agencies have organized/participated in a number of regional/country workshops in order to present the concepts and methodologies of MSITS (e.g. south-eastern European countries, UN ESCWA, UN ECLAC). Moreover joint projects (e.g. Caribbean Community/USAID or Andean Community/EU) have been established, which cover the improvement and introduction of common guidelines for the compilation of trade in services statistics.

PROSPECTS FOR TRADE IN SERVICES STATISTICS

Areas Where Improvements are Needed

Statistics on international trade in services still need important improvements. Only a few countries report the full BPM5 requested detail, and the reported data often lack reliability. In addition, documentation is rarely available on data coverage and deviations from standards. Due to the infancy stage of FATS statistics, the lack of data reliability and inter-country comparability is almost a general rule. According to available information outside the OECD area, countries have rarely started collecting FATS statistics. In the FATS context, confidentiality issues severely limit the amount of detail countries are able to provide.

At present, non-OECD countries are not encouraged to collect BOP statistics by origin and destination or FATS statistics, since no international organizations collect and disseminate such data. This adds to the inherent difficulties and cost to engage in such an exercise.

Even if the recommendations of MSITS related to BOP and FATS statistics were fully implemented, it would only be a first step in providing information by modes of supply, for two major reasons. First, the simplified rules provided in MSITS only lead to a rough approximation of trade in services by modes of supply. Second, a true assessment of services provided through the movement of natural persons would require more detailed information provided by the BPM5 and FATS domains and a coherent statistical framework for this mode still needs to be completed.

It is important to note that in 2004 and 2005 activity intensified on the coordinated revision of the SNA (to be updated in 2008), the balance of payments manual (2008), ISIC and CPC (2007), which set out the fundamental frameworks that serve as a base for reliable and comparable services statistics (including trade). As a consequence an updated version of MSITS is under preparation. However changes not reflected in the revision of other international guidelines will be limited in scope.

Future Work

In the framework of the phased approach adopted for the implementation of MSITS, the Interagency Task Force on Statistics of International Trade in Services identified the need to further develop technical assistance to develop statistical capacities on measuring trade in services. In addition, the preparation of a compilation guide is under way, but this task might take some time, as MSITS covers new areas such as the movement of natural persons and FATS statistics.

The Task Force also concentrates on further methodological work, for instance the movement of natural persons and modes of supply, or trade in software.

The work of the Task Force will provide helpful tools for improving statistics on trade in services. This is however a long term process and the success of this challenge depends on a number of factors:

- efforts by national agencies to employ the appropriate methodologies;
- governments' willingness to allocate the necessary resources;
- cooperation and coordination between national institutions, such as Central Banks, National Statistical Offices and Ministries of Trade;

- cooperation between international and regional institutions, and their support to national initiatives;

- effective technical assistance, i.e. transfer of knowledge and resources from countries having advanced statistical systems to the other countries, especially developing and least developed ones; and

- ability of international and regional institutions to provide effective compilation guidance.

References

European Commission; IMF; OECD; UN; UNCTAD; WTO (unstats.un.org/unsd/tradeserv). 2002. *Manual on Statistics of International Trade in Services* (MSITS). New York: United Nations.

European Commission, IMF, OECD, UN and World Bank. 1993. *System of National Accounts.* New York: United Nations.

Eurostat. *Asymmetries of Current Account in the Intra-EU Balance of Payments*, Working Papers and Studies. Available at: europa.eu.int/comm./eurostat

Eurostat. *EU International transactions*, detailed tables. Available at: europa.eu.int/comm./eurostat

Eurostat. *European Union Foreign Direct Investment Yearbook*, Panorama of the European Union, annual.

Eurostat. 2003. *Foreign-controlled Enterprises*, Statistics in Focus—Theme 4 (Industry, Trade and Services). Available at: europa.eu.int/comm./eurostat

Eurostat. 2002. *Sales and Employment of Affiliates Abroad—1998 Outward FATS Data for Eight Member States*, Statistics in Focus—Theme 2 (Economy and Finances). Available at: europa. eu.int/comm./eurostat

Eurostat. 2001. *Foreign-Owned Enterprises*, Statistics in Focus—Theme 4 (Industry, Trade and Services). Available at: europa.eu.int/comm./eurostat

Eurostat. 2005. *New Cronos Database.* Available at: europa.eu.int/comm./eurostat

Eurostat—UNECE (United Nations Economic Commission for Europe) joint meeting on migration statistics. 2003. *GATS, Modes of Supply and the MSITS: The Case of the Movement of Natural Persons* (WTO). Available at: www.unece.org/stats/documents/ 2003.04. migration

Eurostat—UNECE (United Nations Economic Commission for Europe) joint meeting on migration statistics. 2003. *A Needle in a Haystack: Migration Statistics and GATS Mode 4.* New York: OECD.

ILO. 1990. *International Standard Classification of Occupations (ISCO-88)*. Available at: www.ilo.org

ILO. 1993. *International Classification of Status in Employment (ICSE-93)*. Available at: www.ilo.org

ILO. Annual. *Yearbook of Labor Statistics.* Available at: www.ilo.org

ILO. 2003. *International Labour Migration Database.* Available at: www.ilo.org

IMF (International Monetary Fund). 1995. *Balance of Payments Manual*, 5th edn. Available at: www.imf.org

IMF (International Monetary Fund). 1995. *Balance of Payments Compilation Guide.* International Monetary Fund. 1995. "IMF Committee on Balance of Payments Statistics," *Annual Report.*

IMF (International Monetary Fund). 1995. Dissemination Standards Bulletin Board. Available at: dsbb.imf.org/

IMF (International Monetary Fund). 1995. *Balance of Payments Statistics*, annual (also published in monthly CD-ROMs).

OECD/IMF. 2000. *Report on the Survey of Implementation of Methodological Standards for Direct Investment*, March.

OECD/IMF. 2003. *Foreign Direct Investment Statistics: How Countries Measure FDI*, October.

OECD (Organization for Economic Co-operation and Development). 1996. *Benchmark Definition of Foreign Direct Investment*, 3rd edn.

OECD (Organization for Economic Co-operation and Development). 2001. *Measuring Globalization: The role of multinational in OECD countries. Volume II—Services.*

OECD (Organization for Economic Co-operation and Development). Annual. *International Direct Investment Statistics Yearbook.*

OECD (Organization for Economic Co-operation and Development). 2005. *OECD Handbook on Economic Globalisation Indicators.*

OECD (Organization for Economic Co-operation and Development). Annual. *OECD Statistics on International Trade in Services (Vol. 1), Detailed Tables by Service Category.*

OECD (Organization for Economic Co-operation and Development). annual. *OECD Statistics on International Trade in Services (Vol. 2), Detailed Tables by Partner Country.*

United Nations. *Central Product Classification, Version 1.0* (CPC Ver. 1.0).

United Nations. *International Standard Industrial Classification of All Economic Activities*, Revision 3 (ISIC Rev.3).

United Nations. *Recommendations on Statistics of International Migration, Revision 1.*

United Nations. 2006. *Background Note on GATS Mode 4 Measurement (WTO).*

UNCTAD (United Nations Conference on Trade and Development). Annual. *World Investment Report.* Available at: www.unctad.org

World Bank. Annual. *World Development Indicators.* Available at: www.worldbank.org

WTO (World Trade Organization). 1995. "General Agreement on Trade in Services." *The Results of the Uruguay Round of Multilateral Negotiations: The Legal Text*, appendix IB. Available at: www.wto.org

WTO (World Trade Organization). Annual. *International Trade Statistics.*

WTO (World Trade Organization). 1997. S/C/W/27. "A Review of Statistics on Trade Flows in Services: Note by the Secretariat," November 10.

WTO (World Trade Organization). 2000. S/C/W/27/Add1. "A Review of Statistics on Trade Flows in Services: Note by the Secretariat," Addendum, October 30.

WTO (World Trade Organization). 2006a. S/C/W/27/Add2. "A Review of Statistics on Trade Flows in Services: Note by the Secretariat," Addendum, June 30.

WTO (World Trade Organization). 2006b. *Measuring Trade in Services.* Available at: http://wto.org/english/res_r?/statis_?/services_training_module_?.pdf

5 Empirical Analysis of Barriers to International Services Transactions and the Consequences of Liberalization

Alan V. Deardorff and Robert M. Stern

Introduction

Barriers to trade interfere with the ability of firms from one country to compete with firms from another. This is true of trade in goods, where a tariff or nontariff barrier (NTB) typically drives a wedge between the price of the good on the world market and its domestic price. This wedge, or "tariff equivalent," provides a convenient and often observable measurement of the size of the impediment. In the case of services, however, no such simple measurement is often observable. It remains true, though, that the concept of a tariff equivalent—now thought of as the equivalent tax on foreign suppliers in their competition with domestic suppliers—is a useful way of quantifying a barrier to trade even though it may be much harder to observe. Both the role of barriers to trade in services and the possible meaning of a tariff equivalent can be better understood in the context of each of the standard four "modes of supply" that arise for traded services and are shown in Table 5.1 for 1997. The four modes of supply, for which examples are given in Chapter 1, are:

- Mode 1—services that are traded internationally across borders.
- Mode 2—services that require the consumer to be in the location of the producer.
- Mode 3—services that require commercial presence in the form of foreign direct investment.
- Mode 4—services that require the temporary cross-border movement of worker.

For all four modes of the supply of services, a central objective of empirical measurement is to deduce some sort of tariff equivalent of the barrier to trade in particular services. Since direct price comparisons seldom serve that purpose, however, researchers have pursued other means of inferring the presence and size of barriers to trade. Some of these methods have been quite direct: they simply ask governments or participants in

Table 5.1. International Services Transactions by Modes of Supply, 1997

Mode of supply[a]	Category	Value ($bn)	Cumulative share (%)
Mode 1	Commercial services (excl. travel)	890	41.0
Mode 2	Travel/Tourism	430	19.8
Mode 3	Gross output of foreign affiliates	820	37.8
Mode 4	Compensation of employees	30	1.4
Total		2,170	100.0

Notes: [a] Modes 1, 2, and 4 are derived from balance-of-payments accounts. Mode 3 is derived from data on the operations of foreign affiliates in host countries.
Source: Adapted from Karsenty (2000).

markets what barriers they impose or face. The answers are usually only qualitative, indicating the presence or absence of a particular type of barrier, but not its quantitative size or effect. Such qualitative information takes on a quantitative dimension, however, when it is tabulated by sector, perhaps with subjective weights to indicate severity. The result is a set of "frequency measures" of barriers to trade, recording what the barriers are and where, and perhaps also the fraction of trade within a sector or country that is subject to them. Frequency measures do not directly imply anything like the tariff equivalents of trade barriers, but in order to use them for quantitative analysis, analysts have often converted them to that form in rather ad hoc ways that we will indicate below.

Other, more indirect, measurements of trade barriers in service industries have also been used, alone or in combination with frequency measures. These may be divided into two types: measurements that use information about prices and/or costs; and measurements that observe quantities of trade or production and attempt to infer how trade barriers have affected these quantities. In both cases, as we will discuss, if one can also measure or assume an appropriate elasticity reflecting the response of quantity to price, a measured effect on either can be translated into an effect on the other. Thus both price and quantity measurements are also often converted into, and reported as, tariff equivalents.

In what follows, we begin with a conceptual framework for understanding international services transactions and the barriers that may affect them. We then turn to a discussion of the characteristics of services barriers, and we provide some examples of barriers for the banking sector and for foreign direct investment in services sectors. This is followed with a discussion of methods of measurement of services barriers, including frequency measures and indexes of restrictiveness, price-effect and quantity-effect measurements, gravity-model estimates, and financial-based measurements. In each case, we provide information and examples of how the measurements are constructed and an evaluation of their merits and limitations. We also provide in Annex 5.A brief summaries of studies that have used these methods. We consider thereafter how the various measurements can be used in assessing the economic consequences of the liberalization of services barriers. We conclude the chapter with a presentation of guideline principles and recommended procedures for measuring services barriers and assessing the consequences of their liberalization.[1] Finally, we include an annex containing discussion of selected technical issues and summaries of literature pertinent to methods of measurement of services barriers.

Following the chapter, Box 5.1 addresses the macro-economic, sector, labor market, and household effects of Russia's WTO accession.

Box 5.1. Russia's WTO Accession: What Are the Macro-economic, Sector, Labor Market, and Household Effects?*

Thomas F. Rutherford and David Tarr

Introduction

It is widely believed that WTO accession will have important effects on the Russian economy, and a growing majority of Russians believe that WTO accession will benefit the country. But many questions about the impact of WTO accession remain, including the nature of the macro-economic impact; how different sectors and regions of the economy will be affected; and the impact on incomes of the population and poverty. Some observers are also asking for clearer explanations of why the WTO will bring about any of the claimed impacts. In this Box, we reflect on the probable sources of gains and losses for the Russian economy.[1]

To analyze the impact of WTO accession, we have constructed a 35 sector computable general equilibrium, comparative static model of the Russian economy, based on the Russian input–output table. Primary factors include capital, skilled and unskilled labor, and sector-specific workers. The model contains the 49,000 households of the Russian Household Budget Survey. The principal effects of WTO accession that are modeled include: (1) significant liberalization of barriers to foreign direct investment (FDI) in business services sectors; (2) an across-the-board reduction in tariff barriers by 50 per cent (exact cuts are unknown); and (3) reduced application of antidumping duties against Russian exporters.[2]

WTO Accession Will Have Significant Aggregate Benefits

Liberalization of the barriers to FDI in the services sectors is the most important source of gains from WTO accession. About 73 per cent of the gains follow from liberalization of the barriers to multinational providers of services. Examples of the barriers that are under negotiation as part of the WTO accession are: the Rostelekom monopoly on long distance telephone services; the restraints on multinational banks opening affiliates in Russia; and the quotas on multinational providers of insurance services. Russian commitments to multinational service providers would encourage more FDI in Russia. This would give Russian businesses improved access to the services of multinational service providers in such sectors as telecommunications, banking, insurance, and transportation. This should lower the cost of doing business and should also lead to productivity gains for firms using these services. It should also encourage Russian exports in a wide variety of sectors.

Tariff reduction will lead to significant gains but is not the most important source of benefits from WTO accession, yielding 18 per cent of the gains. Tariff reduction should lead to improved allocation of resources in Russia, as resources will shift to sectors where they are more highly valued at world prices. More important, tariff reduction would more readily permit Russian businesses to import products that contain new and diverse technologies. This

---

[1] These issues are also addressed in an earlier, abridged version of this chapter in Dee and Ferrantino (2005). See also Dee (2005).

would lead to productivity gains and is likely to expand exports. But the Russian tariff rate is at present not very high (1.6 per cent of GDP, or about 7 per cent of the value of imports).[3] Therefore, this would not yield the largest macroeconomic effect, although it would be important for a few sectors.

Improved market access is valuable but is the least important of the three key changes from WTO accession, accounting for only 9 per cent of the gains. Russia has already attained either bilateral Most Favored Nation (MFN) status or preferential status in the Commonwealth of Independent States (CIS) from almost all of its trading partners. Hence, the MFN status accorded to WTO members will not significantly help Russian exporters to obtain better market access. Russian exporters subject to antidumping cases, however, will obtain improved legal status to challenge the application of duties. Yet this is not likely to lower duties significantly on average.

The potential long-term growth effects resulting from improvements in the investment climate could result in much larger gains, but estimates are subject to a large margin of error. Although we do not use an explicit dynamic model, we conduct a long-term analysis that allows the capital stock to change. The improvement of the investment climate in the long-term should expand the capital stock. Hence, we estimated that the long-term gains could be three or four times larger than the medium term gains.

Aspects of WTO accession that are not modeled are likely to provide additional gains to Russia. WTO accession will have numerous other impacts that not modeled. WTO accession will encourage modernization of standards and customs clearance, and requires implementation of intellectual property law. And as a member of the WTO, Russia will have a voice in establishing the rules of the WTO in the future. These other aspects will, on balance, be positive for Russia. Consequently, the gains to Russia from WTO accession are not being overestimated.

Impact on the Sectors and Employment

Export-intensive manufacturing sectors are likely to experience the largest expansion. Outside of services, the sectors that will experience the greatest expansion in employment are non-ferrous metals, ferrous metals, and chemicals. These sectors are among those that export the highest percentage of their output, and thus they will benefit most from a lower real value of the ruble that should accompany the tariff reduction. In addition, these sectors are among the seven sectors that will benefit from improved treatment in antidumping cases. The expansion of these sectors is beneficial for the economy, since these sectors will attract labor from the less internationally competitive sectors of the economy and this will push up wages overall.

Overall employment will not change. International experience indicates that there is no aggregate change in employment in the medium term from trade liberalization, and this is what will likely occur in the Russian economy following WTO accession. Labor market institutions and other structural factors that determine the long run level of unemployment and macroeconomic policy are most relevant for unemployment in the short- to medium-term.

Protected manufacturing sectors that export little are likely to contract. Despite overall gains to the economy, some sectors will contract in the medium run. In manufacturing, the greatest fall in employment will be in the food industry, light industry, construction materials, and machinery and equipment. Exports as a share of output are quite low in these sectors, and the first three sectors are the only ones with tariff rates at about 10 per cent. In the longer run, however, many of these sectors will expand due to the expansion of the capital stock.

Wage Payments and the Returns to Capital

It is estimated that the wage rate of skilled labor will rise by 5.5 per cent, the wage rate of unskilled labor will rise by 3.8 per cent and the rate of return on capital will increase by 1.7 per cent. Although the returns to all factors of production should increase, the impact on Russian "specific" capital owners in sectors that compete with FDI will depend on their ability to participate in joint ventures. It is estimated that there would be a significant increase in FDI and an increase in multinational firms operating in the business services sectors in Russia, which would result in a more competitive environment for Russian capital owners in these sectors. The Russian firms that become part of a joint venture with foreign investors are likely to increase the value of their investments. Russian capital owners in business services who remain wholly independent of multinational firms, either because they avoid joint ventures or because they are not desired as joint venture partners, are likely to see the value of their investments decline. The concentration of losers in a few sectors could create significant political lobbying against measures associated with WTO accession, despite the fact that gains will be widespread throughout the economy.

Distribution of Gains at the Household Level

The vast majority of households are expected to gain from WTO accession. Some 99 per cent of the households fall within a range of gains 2–18 per cent of household consumption in the medium-term. In the long run, when the positive impact on the investment climate and productivity materializes, the gains will be larger.

Government safety nets are very important in helping with the transition, and especially for the poorest members of society that can ill afford a harsh transition. Despite gains in the medium- to long-term, it is possible that many households will be worse off during a short-run transition period during which the economy is adjusting to the new incentives. There will be unskilled workers who will suffer losses from transitional unemployment and are likely to incur expenses related to retraining or relocation. Thus, despite a likely substantial improvement in the standard of living for almost all households after accession to the WTO (and after adjustment to a new equilibrium), there is a strong role for public policy especially in helping the poorest members of society to adjust to the transition.

Broader Impact

WTO accession is an important step toward an open economy model of development. The modeling results are consistent with international experience of the past 20–30 years that shows that rapid and sustained economic growth has occurred only in countries that progressively liberalized import protection, and that provided incentives to exporters that offset the tax that import protection imposes on exports. This is true for Chile, Hong Kong, and Singapore who pursued classical free market principles; it is true for Mauritius, which used export processing zones to encourage exports and provide exporters with equivalent incentives as importers; and it is even true for South Korea and Taiwan, who started with significant import protection, but progressively lowered protection. Moreover, since import protection implicitly imposes a tax on exports, South Korea and Taiwan implemented complicated programs (like indirect duty drawback) to provide exporters with incentives equivalent to sectors that received import protection. Their programs required a very competent and non-corrupt government bureaucracy, something that most developing and transition countries do not possess. Diverse and rapid export growth characterized the experience of all these countries and appears crucial for sustained rapid economic growth. Since import protection penalizes exporters, it appears that lowering protection is a crucial necessary (but not sufficient) condition for sustained rapid economic development.

WTO accession can galvanize domestic support for liberalization of trade and FDI, and represents an opportunity to "lock-in" reforms of the trade and FDI regimes in the direction of an open economy model of economic development. Lobbying and political economy considerations often allow special interests to strongly influence policy of a particular ministry, thereby slowing reforms.. WTO accession, however, requires across-the-board reform in many sectors, and the pressure of WTO negotiations engages policy-makers at the highest levels of government. As a result, WTO accession provides an opportunity for a quicker realization of key reforms. Moreover, commitments at the WTO "lock-in" reforms under international treaty. Consequently, unlike reforms unilaterally undertaken, WTO commitments cannot easily be reversed by a later government that is less inclined to offer a liberal trade and foreign direct investment regime.

Notes: * Adapted from David Tarr, "Services Trade Barriers in Russia," World Bank, 2004.
  [1] Unless otherwise stated, the gains reported are annual gains from a medium-term computational model, where in the medium-term the economy has adjusted to the new incentives and reached equilibrium. Results from a long-run version of the model are also reported with allowance for the capital stock to adjust to an improved investment climate; these results are called long-term gains. The detailed papers containing the modeling framework and computational results may be found at: www.worldbank.org/trade/russia-wto
  [2] Tariff data and trade data are taken from the Customs Committee. Barriers to FDI in key sectors have been estimated based on data provided by Russian experts.
  [3] Seven per cent is an effective tariff rate (i.e. value of collected import duties divided by imports) which is different from an average statutory rate of 11 per cent, owing to application of various preferential customs regimes.

Conceptual Framework

In this section, we use demand-and-supply analysis to show how the introduction of a services barrier will affect the domestic price of a service, the quantity demanded, and the quantity supplied by domestic and foreign firms. We show, using diagrammatic analysis, how the service barrier can be measured as a tariff equivalent. Three cases are presented:

- Figure 5.1—domestic and foreign firms are highly competitive and their services are highly substitutable.
- Figure 5.2—the services of the domestic and foreign firms are not readily substitutable and have distinctive prices.
- Figure 5.3—there is a single domestic firm with monopoly power and the entry of foreign firms is restricted.

The effects of a service barrier, and thus the tariff equivalent, in these various cases will depend on the competitiveness of domestic and foreign firms and the degree of substitution between the services that they provide.

Figure 5.1 illustrates the functioning of a domestic market for a service when there are domestic and foreign suppliers present. It is assumed here that the suppliers are highly competitive and that their services are readily substitutable. Other cases will be considered below. The foreign suppliers may be serving the domestic market through any of the four modes of supply already discussed, although the degree of substitution between the foreign and domestic services may vary for the different modes.

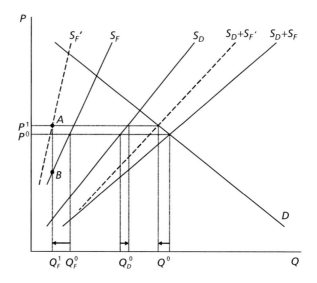

Figure 5.1. Perfect competition and perfect substitution between domestic and foreign services firms

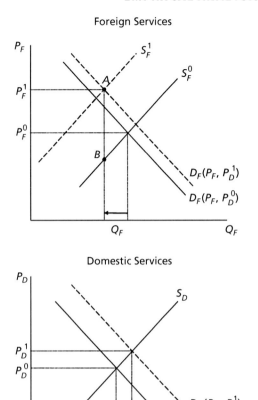

Figure 5.2. Imperfect competition and substitution between domestic and foreign services firms

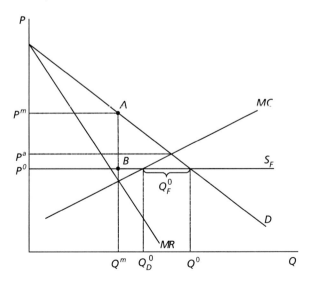

Figure 5.3. Domestic services firm with monopoly power and restrictions on foreign firms

The horizontal axis in Figure 5.1 measures the quantity of the service supplied to and demanded by domestic purchasers. This could include amounts purchased abroad, as in the case of mode 2, which are nonetheless regarded here as competing with domestic supplies. The demand schedule for the service is downward sloping with respect to the price, P, which is the same for all suppliers. The supply schedules for the two sets of suppliers, domestic and foreign, are upward sloping and shown by S_D for domestic firms and S_F for foreign firms.[2] In the absence of any impediments to trade, the relevant total supply schedule in this market is the horizontal sum, labeled $S_D + S_F$. Price is determined where the total supply schedule intersects the demand schedule at P^0, with the quantity Q^0 divided between domestic firms, Q_D^0, and foreign firms, Q_F^0.

Let us suppose now that a barrier is introduced that inhibits the ability of the foreign firms to serve this market. This may raise foreign firms' costs, shifting their supply schedule upward, or it may reduce or constrain the quantity that they supply, shifting the schedule to the left. Either way, S_F is shifted up and to the left, as is the total supply schedule, $S_D + S_F$, to the positions shown as S_F' and $S_D + S_F'$. The effect is to raise the price of the service to P^1, reduce the total quantity purchased, and increase the quantity sold by domestic firms. Sales by the foreign firms fall from Q_F^0 to Q_F^1, which is the decline in imports of the service due to the barrier.

The tariff equivalent of this barrier may be defined as the *ad valorem* tax on foreign service providers that would have caused the same effects as this barrier. Such a tax, by increasing the cost of sales by foreign firms, would cause their supply schedule to shift up by the amount of the tax. Therefore, a tax that shifts S_F up so as to pass through point A is the tariff equivalent. That is, the tariff equivalent is the percentage by which point A lies above point B. What should be noted in the case of Figure 5.1 is that the tariff equivalent is not measurable from any observable price or price change. That is, the increase in the price of the service on the domestic market is considerably smaller than the tariff equivalent of the barrier that caused it.

There is, however, one special case in which the tariff equivalent would equal the price change. This occurs when the foreign supply schedule is horizontal (i.e., infinitely elastic) at some price P^0 so that the effect of the barrier is to raise foreign firms' cost to P^1. Then the two foreign supply schedules are horizontal at these prices, and the tariff equivalent would be just the amount by which they are shifted upward. To the extent that empirical measurements of tariff equivalents are based on observed prices, a horizontal foreign supply schedule will represent a special case that may exist for a small country that faces a given world price for the service.

Figure 5.2 shows a case in which the services provided by domestic and foreign firms are not readily substitutable and can therefore have different prices. In this case we must

---

[2] Domestic supply is shown as further to the right (larger quantity for given price) than foreign supply, but this is not needed for any of the implications of the analysis.

consider markets for the two services separately, as is done in the two panels of Figure 5.2, and we must also allow for the two services being imperfect substitutes. This is done by having each of the two demand schedules depend on the price in the other market, as indicated. Once again, the figure shows supply and demand schedules, quantities, and prices without any trade barrier with superscript 0, and those in the presence of a trade barrier with superscript 1. The introduction of a barrier shifts the foreign supply schedule to the left and up, as before, to S_F^1 and leads to higher prices in both markets, P_F^1 and P_D^1, which now cause both demand schedules to shift somewhat to the right. As in the case of Figure 5.1, with close substitution of the services, the domestic quantity supplied increases while the foreign quantity supplied declines. And here again, the tariff equivalent can be observed in the figure as the percentage by which S_F^1 lies above S_F^0, that is, the percentage by which point A is above point B.

So far we have assumed that markets are highly competitive. But this is clearly inappropriate in many service markets where an incumbent domestic firm may have a monopoly or only a very limited number of competitors. In such markets, a barrier to service trade may be a limit on entry by new firms that, though not explicitly discriminatory, favors the domestic incumbent firm and implicitly limits trade more than domestic supply. We therefore now consider, in Figure 5.3, the case in which there is a single domestic incumbent firm together with competing foreign suppliers. If there is unimpeded entry of firms, the market price will be P^0. In this case, the single domestic firm whose costs are increasing along MC will produce Q_D^0. Total sales are Q^0, and the foreign firms will sell $Q_F^0 = Q^0 - Q_D^0$ in the domestic market. Let us now suppose that a barrier is introduced that raises the cost of the foreign firms when they sell in the domestic market. This would cause the domestic firm's sales to rise along MC and foreign sales to decline. If the foreign cost rises above P^a (the intersection of domestic MC and demand), however, then foreign sales will fall to zero. The domestic firm can thus charge a price that just barely undercuts the foreign cost, so that the domestic firm will be able to monopolize the market. The tariff equivalent of the barrier in the case of Figure 5.3 is therefore the amount by which it increases foreign cost, up to the limit of $P^m - P^0$. However, if the foreign supply schedule were instead upward sloping rather than horizontal, then both the analysis and the identification of the tariff equivalent would be accordingly more difficult to measure. But the general conclusion is that the tariff equivalent of an entry restriction will be measured by the excess of the monopoly price over the competitive price that would have obtained if both trade and entry were free.

Figures 5.1 to 5.3 clearly do not exhaust all of the possible cases. The real world is bound to involve further mixtures of imperfect substitution between the products of domestic and foreign services firms and the degree of competition between these firms that have not been considered here. Also, many service industries have numerous special features, both in the ways that they operate and in their amenability to measurement, and simple theoretical models do not take these factors into account. Empirical work is therefore essential to address the measurement of the various services barriers that impede international services transactions. In what follows, we review and summarize many of the studies that have been done.

Characteristics of Services Barriers

As noted by Hoekman and Primo Braga (1997: 288), border measures such as tariffs are generally difficult to apply to services because customs agents cannot readily observe services as they cross the border. It is also the case, as discussed above, that many services are provided in the country of consumption rather than cross-border. Typically, therefore, services restrictions are designed in the form of government regulations applied to the different modes of services transactions. Thus, for example, regulations may affect the entry and operations of both domestic and foreign suppliers of services and in turn increase the price or the cost of the services involved. Services barriers are therefore more akin to NTBs than to tariffs, and their impact will depend on how the government regulation is designed and administered.

These regulations can take many forms, and are usually specific to the type of service being regulated. Therefore, since services themselves are so diverse, services barriers are also diverse, making them somewhat difficult to classify in general terms. There are, however, two distinctions that that tend to apply across many types of services and service barriers: regulations that apply to entry or establishment of firms *versus* their operations; and regulations that are nondiscriminatory *versus* discriminatory.[3] That is, most barriers to trade in services can be placed in one of the four cells of the following simple 2×2 classification:

	Entry/Establishment	Operations
Non-discriminatory		
Discriminatory		

For example, a limit on the number of firms that may be licensed without regard to their nationality would fall into the upper left cell, while such a limit that favors domestically owned firms would be in the lower left. Likewise, a regulation that all service providers in an industry to perform certain extra tasks would raise cost or operations in a

---

[3] These distinctions are suggested by the Australian Productivity Commission, whose website can be consulted for more details (www.pc.gov.au/research/memoranda/ servicesrestriction/index.html). See also Hoekman and Primo Braga (1997: 288), who classify and provide examples of services barriers as follows: (1) quotas, local content, and prohibitions; (2) price-based instruments; (3) standards, licensing, and procurement; and (4) discriminatory access to distribution networks.

nondiscriminatory fashion and lie in the upper right cell, while a regulation that requires special performance by foreign providers that is not expected of domestic firms would be in the lower right. Of course a policy could in principle be discriminatory in favor of foreign firms rather than against them, but that would not be typical.

In terms of our conceptual framework, the entry vs. operations distinction may be thought of as determining whether the regulation shifts the supply schedules of services to the left or up. That is, regulations that restrict or impede the establishment of service providers within a market will usually reduce their numbers and therefore the quantity supplied at any given price. Regulations of ongoing operations, on the other hand, may not reduce the number of suppliers, but they will increase their costs, causing them to supply a given quantity only at a higher price. This distinction is not perfect, however, and in any case it does not need to be, since as long as the supply schedules are upward sloping, shifts to the left and up have the same qualitative effects, as we have seen. The distinction is useful mainly for classifying different types of barriers.

Likewise, the nondiscriminatory vs. discriminatory distinction above determines whether a regulation shifts the supply curve of only foreign service providers (when it is discriminatory), or instead raises costs and shifts supply for both foreign and domestic suppliers. As we have noted, however, a regulation that impedes establishment of all new service providers, in spite of being nondiscriminatory, can nonetheless limit trade and competition by favoring a domestic incumbent. It is also important to note that some regulations may be designed to achieve certain social objectives, such as health and safety or environmental requirements, and may not be protectionist in intent.

Of course, actual regulations differ greatly across service industries and are often based on characteristics of the particular service being provided. Thus, within each cell of the table above we may think of additional distinctions being made, usually distinctions that are peculiar to the service sector under consideration.

To illustrate, we use the case of banking services based on a study by McGuire and Schuele (2000) done under the auspices of the Australian Productivity Commission. Table 5.2 lists groupings of restrictions that apply especially to modes 3 and 4 of international banking services transactions. These restrictions relate to commercial presence and "other restrictions" applied to banking services, together with a brief indication of what these restrictions represent and how an index of them has been constructed.[4] As McGuire and Schuele note (p. 206):

The commercial presence grouping covers restrictions on licensing, direct investment, joint venture arrangements, and the movement of people. The "other restrictions" grouping covers

---

[4] See the Productivity Commission website for detailed listings by country of the categories of domestic and foreign restrictions on establishment and ongoing operations for some selected services sectors, including: accountancy, architectural, and engineering services; banking; distribution; and maritime services.

Table 5.2. Restriction Categories for Banking Services

Restriction category	Relevant for foreign index	Total weight	Relevant for domestic index	Total weight
Restrictions on commercial presence				
Licensing of banks Based inversely on the maximum number of new banking licenses issued with only prudential requirements	Yes	0.200	Yes	0.190
Direct investment Based inversely on the maximum equity participation permitted in an existing domestic bank	Yes	0.200	Yes	0.190
Joint venture arrangements New bank entry only through joint venture with a domestic bank	Yes	0.100	No	n.a.
Movement of people Based inversely on years that executives, specialists and/or senior managers can stay	Yes	0.020	No	n.a.
Other restrictions				
Raising funds by banks Banks are restricted from accepting deposits from the public and/or raising funds from domestic capital markets	Yes	0.100	Yes	0.143
Lending funds by banks Banks are restricted in types or sizes of loans and/or are directed to lend to housing and small business	Yes	0.100	Yes	0.143
Other business of banks—insurance and securities services Banks are excluded from insurance and/or securities services	Yes	0.200	Yes	0.095
Expanding the number of banking outlets Based inversely on the number of outlets permitted	Yes	0.050	Yes	0.048
Composition of the board of directors Based inversely on the percentage of the board that can comprise foreigners	Yes	0.020	No	n.a.
Temporary movement of people Based inversely on the number of days temporary entry permitted to executives, specialists and/or senior managers	Yes	0.010	No	n.a.
Total weighting or highest possible score		1.000		0.808

Source: Adapted from McGuire and Schuele (2000: tables 12.1 and 12.3, pp. 204–5, 208.

restrictions on raising funds, lending funds, providing other lines of business (insurance and securities services), expanding banking outlets, the composition of the board of directors and the temporary movement of people.

Thus the top half of Table 5.2 corresponds roughly to regulations of entry/establishment in the small table above, while the bottom half corresponds to roughly to regulations of operations. For each type of restriction, separate columns also indicate whether they apply to foreign and domestic firms, hence being discriminatory if they apply only to the former. An indication of the restrictiveness of these regulations is also provided in Table 5.2 and will be discussed below.

Just as different sub-classifications may be needed for different types of services, so too may the appropriate classification depend on the purpose for which the classification will be used. This point is made especially by Hardin and Holmes (1997) in their discussion of barriers affecting FDI (mode 3). Focusing, in effect, on the lower left cell of our table above—the establishment of a commercial presence in many sectors in host countries—they define (p. 24) an FDI barrier as "... any government policy measure which distorts decisions about where to invest and in what form." In considering ways of classifying such FDI barriers, they note (pp. 33–4):[5]

The appropriate classification system may vary, depending on the purpose of the exercise. For example, if the purpose is to check and monitor compliance with some policy commitment, then the categories should reflect the key element of the commitment ... If the primary interest is instead the resource allocation implications of the barriers, some additional or different information may be useful.

Barriers to FDI may distort international patterns and modes of ... trade. They may also distort allocation of capital between different economies, between foreign and domestic investment, between different sectors, and between portfolio and direct investment ... the classification system ... should highlight the key characteristics of the barriers that will determine their size and impact. Market access and national treatment are ... relevant categories from a resource allocation perspective.... national treatment is generally taken to refer to measures affecting firms after establishment. A ... way to classify barriers is therefore ... according to what aspect of the investment they most affect: establishment, ownership and control; or operations. In addition ... some further information may be useful ... on distinctions ... between direct versus indirect restrictions on foreign controlled firms; and rules versus case-by-case decisions.[6]

The main types of FDI barriers that have been identified by UNCTAD (1996) are noted in Table 5.3, which divides barriers into three groups, the first of which concerns entry and the last operations. The middle group—ownership and control restrictions—illustrates the weakness of any simple classification system since it seems to include elements of both. Further information on the barriers most commonly used to restrict FDI especially in the APEC economies is provided in Hardin and Holmes (1997, esp. pp. 37–40 and 45–55). As they note (p. 40), some common characteristics appear to be:[7]

---

[5] See also Holmes and Hardin (2000).

[6] Direct restrictions include limitations on the total size or share of investment in a sector and requirements on inputs used (e.g. local content). Indirect restrictions include net benefit or national interest criteria and limitations on membership of company boards. The distinction between rules and case-by-case decisions relates to issues of clarity in specification and transparency as compared to the exercise of administrative discretion.

[7] Hardin and Holmes (pp. 40–3) also provide information on investment incentives, which are widely used and for the most part are not subject to multilateral disciplines.

Table 5.3. Barriers to FDI

Restrictions on market entry	Bans on foreign investment in certain sectors
	Quantitative restrictions (e.g. limit of 25 per cent foreign ownership in a sector)
	Screening and approval (sometimes involving national interest or net economic benefits tests)
	Restrictions on the legal form of the foreign entity
	Minimum capital requirements
	Conditions on subsequent investment
	Conditions on location
	Admission taxes
Ownership and control restrictions	Compulsory joint ventures with domestic investors
	Limits on the number of foreign board members
	Government appointed board members
	Government approval required for certain decisions
	Restrictions on foreign shareholders' rights
	Mandatory transfer of some ownership to locals within a specified time (e.g. 15 years)
Operational restrictions	Performance requirements (e.g. export requirements)
	Local content restrictions
	Restrictions on imports of labor, capital, and raw materials
	Operational permits or licenses
	Ceilings on royalties
	Restrictions on repatriation of capital and profits

Source: Adapted from UNCTAD (1996).

application of some form of screening or registration process involving various degrees of burden for the foreign investor; restrictions on the level or share of foreign ownership, particularly in some service sectors, and often in the context of privatizations; widespread use of case-by-case judgments, often based on national interest criteria; widespread use of restrictions on ownership and control (e.g. restrictions on board membership), particularly in sectors such as telecommunications, broadcasting, banking; and relatively limited use of performance requirements on input controls in services sectors.

It is evident from the foregoing discussion that services barriers exist in a variety of forms, depending on the types of services involved, the country imposing the barriers, and the sectors to which the barriers are applied. To help further the understanding of the different services barriers, it would be useful accordingly to organize the available information by country and sector, according to the four modes of international services transactions and whether or not they are protectionist in intent. As already noted, these modes cover: cross-border services (mode 1); consumption abroad (mode 2); FDI (mode 3); and the temporary movement of workers (mode 4). Using this information, the next and difficult step will be to devise methods of measurement of the various barriers and to integrate these measures within a framework designed to assess their economic effects.

It should be emphasized, finally, that not all regulations of services should be viewed as protectionist, even when they do serve to reduce service imports. Many regulations serve legitimate purposes, such as protecting health and safety or preventing fraud and other misconduct. Such a regulation, if applied in a nondiscriminatory manner, is not protectionist and should not be viewed as a barrier to service trade, even though it may maintain a higher standard than prevails abroad and thus reduce imports compared to what they would be without the regulation. On the other hand, nondiscrimination is not by itself enough to absolve a regulation from being protectionist if it, say, enforces a standard that has no legitimate purpose but happens to be met by domestic providers and not by foreign ones. Distinguishing legitimate from illegitimate regulations may not be easy, especially since it usually requires the sort of detailed knowledge of the industry that can only be gotten from industry insiders who are unlikely to be disinterested.

Methods of Measurement of Services Barriers

Measurements of trade barriers, in markets for both goods and services, can be either direct or indirect. Direct measurements start from the observation of an explicit policy or practice, such as an import quota or a regulation of a foreign provider of services, and then attempt in some fashion to measure its economic importance. Indirect measurements try instead to infer the existence of barriers using observed discrepancies between actual economic performance and what would be expected if trade were free. Direct measurements have the advantage that one knows what one is measuring, and the disadvantage that they can only include those barriers that are in fact explicit and recognized. Indirect measurements have the advantage that their quantitative importance is known, at least in the dimension used to identify them, but the disadvantage that they may incorporate unrecognized frictions other than the policy impediments that one seeks to identify.

In the case of trade in goods, direct measurements of NTBs typically take the form of inventories of identified trade restrictions, such as those compiled in the United Nations Conference on Trade and Development (UNCTAD) TRade Analysis and INformation System (TRAINS).[8] Since NTBs usually cover only some industries or products, a first step in quantifying them is often to measure the fraction of trade that they cover in different sectors and countries. These fractions may then be used directly in empirical work, even though they do not themselves say anything about how effective the NTBs have been in restricting trade.[9] Indirect measurements, on the other hand, can be fairly

---

[8] TRAINS is available on-line at www.unctad.org.
[9] In fact, they are somewhat perverse for this purpose, since the more restrictive is an NTB, the less will be the trade that it permits.

straightforward in the case of goods, based either on their observed prices before and after they cross an international border or on the quantities that cross it. For example, one can often infer both the presence of an import barrier and its effect on price by simply comparing the price of a good inside a country to that outside, since in the absence of any barrier one would expect competitive market forces to cause these prices to be the same. Indirect measurements based on quantities are more difficult, since they depend on a theoretical benchmark for comparability that is likely to be much less certain. Nonetheless, as we note in our discussion below, such quantity-based measurements of NTBs have been used with some success.

For trade in services, direct measurements must be carefully done since regulation in service industries is so common that merely to document its presence would not be informative. A common approach is therefore to complement the documentation of regulations by incorporating information about the restrictiveness of the regulations, and then use this information to construct an index of restrictiveness that can be compared across countries. We will provide further detail of how this may be done below, together with examples from the literature.

Indirect measurements of restrictiveness are also possible with traded services, although simple price comparisons are seldom of much use. This is because many services are differentiated by location in a way that renders comparison of their prices inside and outside of a country meaningless. For example, the cost of providing telephone service to consumers on the Texas side of the U.S.–Mexican border need bear no particular relationship to the cost, for the same firm, of providing it across the border in Mexico, where wages are much lower but costs of infrastructure may be much higher. So even if trade in the service were completely unimpeded, we would not expect these prices to be the same, and we therefore cannot infer a trade barrier in either direction from the fact that they are not. Similar arguments can be made about most traded services.

Indirect measurements of barriers to trade in services are therefore less common than for trade in goods, although they do exist. As we will discuss below, there has been some success using the so-called gravity model as a benchmark for quantities of trade in services, and the results of these models have therefore been the basis for indirect measurement of barriers in the quantity dimension. Financial data have also been the basis for inferring barriers from differences in the markups of price over cost, as we will also discuss.

With indirect measurements of the presence of services barriers less common, however, there is therefore the need for some other approach to quantifying the effects of barriers that have been identified. In this connection, indexes of restrictiveness can be constructed that are typically measured on a scale of zero to one, and they do not purport to say how much a barrier either raises price or reduces quantity. To get such information, another step is needed. Commonly, this step involves using econometric analysis to relate an index of restrictiveness to observed prices or quantities, thus translating the measures of the presence of barriers into an estimate of their economic effect in particular services markets.

In what follows, then, we first discuss the construction of measures of the presence of barriers, commonly referred to as frequency-based measurements, and the use of these measurements to construct indexes of restrictiveness. This is followed by a discussion of how the effects on prices and quantities can be derived. We then turn to methods that attempt to infer the presence of services barriers indirectly, first from a gravity model of the quantities of trade, and second from financial data within service firms.[10]

Frequency Studies and Indexes of Restrictiveness

Studies of frequency-based measures start by identifying the kinds of restriction that apply to a particular service industry or to services in general. For particular industries, this requires considerable industry-specific knowledge, since each industry has, at a minimum, its own terminology, and often also its own distinctive reasons for regulatory concern. Regulations often serve an ostensibly valid purpose—protecting health and safety, for example—and knowledge of the industry is also necessary to distinguish such valid regulations from those that primarily offer protection. Thus, a frequency study is best carried out by an industry specialist, or it must draw upon documents that have been prepared by such specialists. Industry studies therefore often build upon the documentation provided by industry trade groups, such as the International Telecommunications Union in the case of telecoms, bilateral air service arrangements in the case of passenger air travel, or the TradePort website in the case of maritime services.

For broader studies of restrictions in services, covering multiple industries, some source must be found that incorporates such expertise across sectors. An early approach to doing this was in the studies by PECC (1995) and Hoekman (1995, 1996) that we discuss below. These studies used information that countries had submitted to the General Agreement on Trade in Services (GATS), to be used as the basis for commitments to be made for services liberalization in the Uruguay Round negotiations. Such measures are therefore not ideally suited for documenting trade barriers. Better information requires that someone deliberately collect the details of actual barriers and regulatory practices, as in the data collected by Asia Pacific Economic Cooperation (APEC) and used by Hardin and Holmes (1997), whose study we also discuss below. In all cases, the goal is not just to assemble a complete list of barriers, but also to know the restrictiveness of these barriers in terms such as the numbers of firms or countries to

---

[10] Interested readers may also consult Warren and Findlay (2000), Whalley (2004), and Dee (2005), which cover many of the same issues of measurement and services as we do.

which they apply and other characteristics. This latter information is then used to construct an Index of Restrictiveness. Typically, each barrier is assigned a score between zero and one, with a score of one being the most restrictive and a score of zero being the least restrictive. These scores are then averaged, using weights that are intended to reflect the relative importance of each type of barrier.

There are several ways in which the weights on different barriers in a restrictiveness index may be assigned. Most commonly, these reflect the judgments of knowledgeable investigators as to the importance of each type of barrier. This may well be the best approach if the investigator really is knowledgeable, as in the case when an index is being constructed for a specific, narrowly defined industry.

An alternative that has been used by Nicoletti et al. (2000) and subsequently by Doove et al. (2001) is to apply factor analysis to the data once they are assembled. This enables them to distinguish those barriers that vary most independently among their data, and then to apply the largest weights to them. This is a purely statistical technique that is not, in our view, necessarily an improvement on the use of judgmental weights.

A third approach is not to construct an index at all, but rather to use the scores or proxy measures for each barrier separately in an empirical analysis. The difficulty here is that these scores may be interrelated, so that their independent influence on any variable of interest may be impossible to ascertain using standard statistical methods. If this can be done, however, the advantage is that it allows for the fact that barriers may differ in their importance for different aspects of economic performance, and this approach allows these differences to make themselves known. Ideally, one would prefer an approach that allows the weights in an index of restrictiveness to be estimated simultaneously with the importance of that index for a particular economic outcome. Thus the construction of the index would be interlinked with its use for estimating effects on prices and quantities, for example, which we will discuss below.

First, however, we discuss a few of the main studies that have constructed frequency measurements and indexes of restrictiveness.

PECC AND HOEKMAN

PECC (1995) and Hoekman (1995, 1996) use information contained in the country schedules of the GATS, referring to all four modes of supply of services, to construct frequency ratios that measure the extent of liberalization promised by countries in their commitments to the GATS, as part of the Uruguay Round negotiations completed in 1993–4. The frequency ratios are constructed based on the number of commitments that were scheduled by individual countries designating sectors or sub-sectors as unrestricted or partially restricted. The ratios that are calculated equal the number of actual commitments in relation to the maximum possible number of commitments.[11] Hoekman focused on commitments relating to market access and national treatment. As he notes (1996: 101), there were 155 sectors and sub-sectors and four modes of supply specified in the GATS. This yields $620 \times 2 = 1,440$ total commitments on market access and national treatment for each of 97 countries.[12] The frequency ratio for a country or a sector is then defined as the fraction of these possible commitments that were in fact made, implying an index of trade restrictiveness equal to one minus this fraction.

There are some important limitations to these calculations that are worth mentioning. Thus, as Holmes and Hardin (2000: 58–9) note, Hoekman's method may be misleading or biased because it assumes that the absence of positive country commitments in the GATS schedules can be interpreted as indicating the presence of restrictions, which may not be the case in fact. Also, the different types of restrictions are given equal weight.[13]

HARDIN AND HOLMES

Hardin and Holmes (1997) and Holmes and Hardin (2000) have attempted to build on and improve Hoekman's methodology, though focusing only on restrictions on FDI in services (mode 3). In particular, they use information on the actual FDI restrictions taken from Asia Pacific Economic Cooperation (APEC), rather than just the GATS commitments. Rather than treating all restrictions equally, they devise a judgmental system of weighting that is designed, as in the case of the banking restrictions noted in Table 5.2 above, to reflect the efficiency costs of the different barriers. The components of their index and the weights assigned to the different sub-categories are given in Table 5.4. It can be seen, for example, that foreign equity limits are given greater weights than the other barriers noted. Their results for 15 APEC countries for the period 1996–98 are summarized in Table 5.5.[14] It is evident that communications and financial services are most subject to FDI restrictions, while business, distribution, environmental, and recreational services are the least restricted. Korea, Indonesia, China, Thailand, and the

---

[11] In counting commitments, the commitment for a sector or sub-sector to be unrestricted is counted as one, whereas a listing of the restrictions that will continue to apply, so that the commitment to liberalization is only partial, is counted as one-half.

[12] As noted in Hardin and Holmes (1997: 70), the GATS commitments are based on a "positive list" approach and therefore do not take into account sectors and restrictions that are unscheduled. In PECC (1995), it is assumed that all unscheduled sectors and commitments are unrestricted, which will then significantly raise the calculated frequency ratios compared to Hoekman (1996), who treats unscheduled sectors as fully restricted.

[13] More information is needed accordingly on the restrictions that may apply to both scheduled and unscheduled services sectors in order to obtain a comprehensive measure of all existing restrictions.

[14] Details on the construction of the indexes and their sensitivity to variations in the restrictiveness weights are discussed in Hardin and Holmes (1997, esp. pp. 103–11).

Table 5.4. Components of an Index of FDI Restrictions

Type of restriction	Weight
Foreign equity limits on all firms	
No foreign equity permitted	1.000
Less than 50 per cent foreign equity permitted	0.500
More than 50 per cent and less than 100 per cent foreign equity permitted	0.250
Foreign equity limits on existing firms, none on greenfield	
No foreign equity permitted	0.500
Less than 50 per cent foreign equity permitted	0.250
More than 50 per cent and less than 100 per cent foreign equity permitted	0.125
Screening and approval	
Investor required to demonstrate net economic benefits	0.100
Approval unless contrary to national interest	0.075
Notification (pre or post)	0.050
Control and management restrictions	
All firms	0.200
Existing firms, none for greenfield	0.100
Input and operational restrictions	
All firms	0.200
Existing firms, none for greenfield	0.100

Source: Adapted from Holmes and Hardin (2000: 62).

Table 5.5. FDI Restrictiveness Indexes for Selected APEC Economies and Selected Sectors, 1996–98 (Percentage)

Sectors	Australia	Canada	China	Hong Kong	Indonesia	Japan	Korea	Malaysia
Business	0.183	0.225	0.360	0.015	0.560	0.062	0.565	0.316
Communications	0.443	0.514	0.819	0.350	0.644	0.350	0.685	0.416
Postal	1.000	1.000	1.000	1.000	1.000	1.000	1.000	1.000
Courier	0.175	0.200	0.275	0.000	0.525	0.050	0.550	0.075
Telecommunications	0.300	0.325	1.000	0.200	0.525	0.100	0.550	0.375
Audiovisual	0.295	0.530	1.000	0.200	0.525	0.250	0.640	0.215
Construction	0.175	0.200	0.400	0.000	0.525	0.050	0.750	0.775
Distribution	0.175	0.200	0.275	0.050	0.525	0.050	0.625	0.075
Education	0.175	0.200	0.525	0.000	0.525	0.200	0.550	0.075
Environmental	0.175	0.200	0.275	0.000	0.525	0.117	0.700	0.075
Financial	0.450	0.375	0.450	0.233	0.550	0.358	0.875	0.608
Insurance and related	0.275	0.425	0.475	0.400	0.575	0.450	0.838	0.600
Banking and other	0.625	0.325	0.425	0.067	0.525	0.267	0.913	0.617
Health	0.175	0.200	0.275	0.000	0.525	0.050	0.550	0.317
Tourism	0.175	0.200	0.283	0.000	0.525	0.050	0.617	0.542
Recreation	0.175	0.200	0.275	0.000	0.525	0.050	0.550	0.175
Transport	0.204	0.235	0.455	0.093	0.525	0.114	0.573	0.122

	Mexico	New Zealand	Papua New Guinea	Philippines	Singapore	Thailand	United States
Business	0.289	0.086	0.300	0.479	0.261	0.775	0.005
Communications	0.739	0.434	0.475	0.758	0.518	0.838	0.345
Postal	1.000	1.000	1.000	1.000	1.000	1.000	1.000
Courier	0.775	0.075	0.300	0.475	0.250	0.775	0.000
Telecommunications	0.705	0.425	0.300	0.975	0.571	0.804	0.200
Audiovisual	0.475	0.235	0.300	0.580	0.250	0.775	0.180
Construction	0.450	0.075	0.300	0.475	0.250	0.775	0.000
Distribution	0.325	0.075	0.300	0.475	0.250	0.775	0.000
Education	0.450	0.075	0.300	0.475	0.250	0.775	0.000
Environmental	0.075	0.075	0.300	0.475	0.250	0.775	0.000
Financial	0.554	0.200	0.300	0.954	0.378	0.875	0.200
Insurance and related	0.575	0.125	0.300	0.975	0.250	0.775	0.000
Banking and other	0.533	0.275	0.300	0.933	0.506	0.975	0.400
Health	0.408	0.075	0.300	0.475	0.250	0.775	0.000
Tourism	0.275	0.075	0.300	0.808	0.317	0.775	0.000
Recreational	0.075	0.075	0.300	0.475	0.250	0.775	0.000
Transport	0.283	0.131	0.300	0.975	0.250	0.780	0.025

Note: The higher the score, the greater the degree to which an industry is restricted. The maximum score is 100%. Because of data constraints on the value of output by sector, the indexes shown are based on simple averages of the sub-sectors involved in the individual countries.

Source: Adapted from Holmes and Hardin (2000: 63–4).

Philippines have relatively high restrictiveness indexes, while the United States and Hong Kong have the lowest indexes.

MCGUIRE AND SCHUELE

Table 5.2 above indicated the restriction categories and weights applied to banking services in the study by McGuire and Schuele (2000), which is based on a variety of data sources (pp. 202–3), including the GATS schedules of commitments and a number of other reports and documentation pertaining to actual financial-sector restrictions in 38 economies for the period 1995–8. McGuire and Schuele (pp. 204–5) have assigned scores for different degrees of restriction, ranging between 0 (least restrictive) and 1 (most restrictive). The various categories are weighted judgmentally in terms of how great the costs involved are assumed to be with respect to the effect on economic efficiency. Thus, it can be seen in Table 5.2 that restrictions on the licensing of banks are taken to be more burdensome than restrictions on the movement of people. Also, the scores are given separately for the restrictions applicable only to foreign banks and the "domestic" restrictions applicable to all banks. The differences between the foreign and domestic measures can then be interpreted as indicating the discrimination imposed on foreign banks. Finally, it will be noted that the foreign scores sum to a maximum of 1 and the domestic scores to a maximum of 0.808, because some of the restrictions noted apply only to foreign banks and not to domestic banks.

Based on detailed information available, the scores for banking restrictions in individual countries can be constructed. Using the category weights in Table 5.2, it is then possible to calculate "indexes of restrictiveness" of the foreign and domestic regulations by country. These indexes are depicted graphically for selected Asia-Pacific countries, South Africa, and Turkey in Figure 5.4 and for Western Hemisphere countries in Figure 5.5. India, Indonesia, Malaysia, and the Philippines can be seen to have relatively high foreign index scores, Korea, Singapore, Thailand, and Turkey have moderate foreign index scores, and Australia, Hong Kong, Japan, New Zealand, and South Africa have the lowest foreign index scores. The domestic index scores are indicative of the restrictions applied both to domestic and foreign banks, and it appears that the domestic index scores are highest for Japan, Korea, Malaysia, and the Philippines.

While the absolute values of the foreign and domestic index scores are not reported, the differences in the scores can be interpreted visually as a measurement of the discrimination applied to foreign banks. Thus, in Figure 5.4, India, Indonesia, Korea, Malaysia, the Philippines, Singapore, Thailand, and Turkey appear to have the highest discrimination against foreign banks. In Figure 5.5, Brazil, Chile, and Uruguay have the

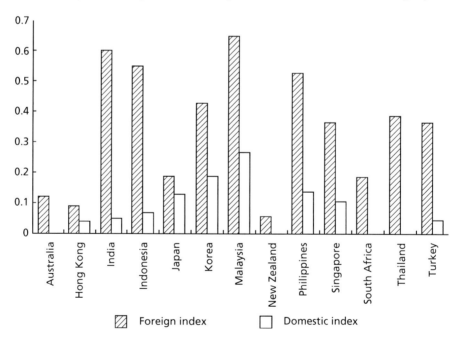

Figure 5.4. Restrictiveness indexes for banking services for selected Asia-Pacific economies, South Africa, and Turkey

Note: The higher the score the more restrictive an economy; scores range from 0 to 1.

Source: Adapted from McGuire and Schuele (2000: 211).

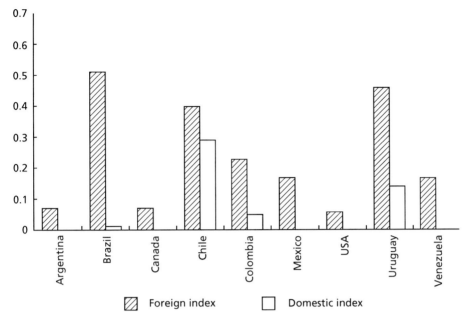

Figure 5.5. Restrictiveness indexes for banking services for selected Western Hemisphere economies
Note: The higher the score the more restrictive an economy; scores range from 0 to 1.
Source: Adapted from McGuire and Schuele (2000: 211).

highest foreign index scores, Colombia, Mexico, and Venezuela have moderate scores, and Argentina, Canada, and the United States have the lowest scores. Chile and Uruguay have the highest domestic index scores, while Argentina, Canada, Mexico, the United States, and Venezuela have domestic index scores of zero. Brazil, Colombia, and Uruguay have the most discriminatory regimes against foreign banks.[15] McGuire and Schuele (2000, pp. 212–13) further found that countries with less restricted banking sectors tended to have higher GNP per capita.

The frequency measures and indexes of restriction that we have discussed thus far are especially useful in identifying the types of barriers and the relative degrees of protection afforded to particular services sectors across countries. In Annex 5.A, we review briefly some other studies that are based on measurements of this type. It is evident accordingly that there exists a considerable amount of information on barriers covering a wide variety of services sectors, including financial services, telecommunications, accountancy, distribution, air transport, and electricity supply. As such, the compilation of such measurements and construction of such indexes are important first steps that can provide the basis for the next step, which involves using available methodologies to assess the economic effects of maintaining or eliminating the barriers.

---

[15] The detailed scores for the components of the domestic and foreign banking restrictions are broken down by individual countries and are available on the Productivity Commission website.

Price-Impact Measurements[16]

As discussed above, the nature of services tends to prevent the use of price and quantity differences across borders to measure their presence or size. Therefore, in order to construct measurements of the price and/or quantity effects of barriers to trade in services, some other approach is needed.

The simplest is just to make an informed guess. For example, having constructed a frequency ratio for offers to liberalize services trade in the GATS as discussed above, Hoekman (1995, 1996) then assumed that failure to liberalize in a sector would be equivalent to some particular tariff level that he selected using knowledge of the sector. These maximum tariff equivalents ranged from a high of 200 percent for sectors in which market access was essentially prohibited in most countries (e.g. maritime cabotage, air transport, postal services, voice telecommunications, and life insurance) to 20–50 per cent for sectors in which market access was less constrained. He then applied his frequency-ratio measurements of liberalization to these maximum tariffs to construct tariff equivalents that differed by country based on their offers in the GATS. Thus, for example, assuming a benchmark tariff equivalent of, say, 200 per cent for postal services, and a frequency ratio of 40 per cent to reflect a country's scheduled market access commitments, the tariff equivalent for that sector and country is set at $200 - 0.4(200) = 120$ per cent.

Using the value of output by sector for a representative industrialized country, it is then possible to construct weighted average measurements by sector and country. The resulting weighted-average tariff equivalent "guesstimates" for 1-digit International Standard Industrial Classification (ISIC) sectors for selected countries are indicated in Table 5.6. It can be seen that the tariff equivalents are highest for ISIC 7, Transportation, Storage & Communication, reflecting the significant constraints applied within this sector. There is also considerable variation within the individual sectors for the relatively highly industrialized countries listed in Table 5.6.

It should be emphasized that Hoekman's measurements are designed to indicate only the *relative* degree of restriction. We refer to them as "guesstimates," which are not to be taken literally as indicators of absolute ad valorem tariff equivalents. That is, the tariff equivalent benchmarks are just judgmental and are not distinguished according to their economic impact. Further, the benchmarks include only market-access restrictions and cover all of the different modes of service delivery.

An improved approach that has been used in more recent studies is to combine other data together with an index or proxy measures of restrictiveness in order to estimate econometrically the effects of barriers. For example, suppose that an index of restrictiveness has been constructed for a group of countries, and that price data are also available for the services involved in this same group. Using knowledge and data on the

---

[16] See Bosworth et al. (2000) for a useful methodological discussion of the construction and interpretation of price-impact measurements of impediments to services trade.

Table 5.6. Constructed Ad Valorem Tariff Equivalent "Guesstimates" by 1-Digit ISIC Services Sectors for Selected Countries (Percentage)

Country	ISIC 5 Construction	ISIC 6 Wholesale & Retail Distr.	ISIC 7 Transp., Storage & Communic.	ISIC 8 Business & Fin. Services	ISIC 9 Social & Personal Services
Australia	12.0	7.4	183.4	24.8	25.4
Austria	5.0	4.6	98.7	20.1	13.9
Canada	6.0	9.0	117.7	25.9	40.2
Chile	40.0	34.4	182.2	45.2	42.9
E.U.	10.0	10.0	182.0	27.2	23.6
Finland	19.0	14.6	181.0	23.8	31.7
Hong Kong	32.0	31.5	149.8	39.0	42.9
Japan	5.0	4.6	142.0	28.9	32.3
Korea	16.0	21.4	164.9	36.3	40.7
Mexico	24.0	21.3	152.3	40.9	29.8
New Zealand	5.0	13.4	181.5	30.5	36.1
Norway	5.0	13.4	122.2	25.7	24.0
Singapore	12.0	34.4	138.8	35.9	33.7
Sweden	12.0	13.4	184.2	22.5	26.9
Switzerland	5.0	8.0	178.1	27.7	32.3
Turkey	5.0	34.4	31.6	35.4	35.9
U.S.	5.0	4.6	111.4	21.7	31.7

Source: Adapted from Hoekman (1995: 355–6).

economic determinants of these prices, an econometric model can be formulated to explain them. Then, if the restrictiveness index and/or proxy measures of restrictiveness are included in this equation as additional explanatory variables, the estimated coefficient(s) will measure the effect of the trade restrictions on prices, controlling for the other determinants of prices that have been included in the model.

Use of this method of course requires data on more than just the barriers themselves, including prices and other relevant determinants of prices. However, these additional data may be needed for only a subset of the countries for which the restrictiveness measures have been constructed, so long as one can assume that the effects of restrictions may be common across countries. The coefficients relating restrictiveness to prices can be estimated for a subset of countries for which the requisite data are available, and the estimated coefficients can then be applied to the other countries as well.

An example of this approach may be found in the study of the international air passenger transport industry by Doove et al. (2001: chapter 2), which is summarized in Annex 5.A. They built on work by Gonenc and Nicoletti (2001), who had constructed an index of restrictiveness for this industry in the manner already discussed, and who had also used an econometric model to estimate the effects of restrictiveness for a group of 13 OECD countries. Doove et al. extended the index of restrictiveness to a larger set of 35 OECD and non-OECD countries and applied this estimated coefficient to calculate price effects.

The estimating equation used for this was the following:

$$\dot{p} = \alpha + \beta BRI + \gamma E + \epsilon \tag{1}$$

Table 5.7. International Air Passenger Transport: Bilateral Restriction Indexes and Price Impacts

	Number of agreements/routes	Bilateral Restriction Index[a]	Price impacts[b]		
			Business	Economy	Discount
Asia Pacific economies					
Australia	24	0.62	146.0	54.8	14.6
India	20	0.77	164.4	81.3	21.8
Indonesia	16	0.73	139.7	53.0	20.4
Japan	29	0.73	121.1	41.4	18.1
Korea	18	0.72	181.5	89.9	20.4
Malaysia	22	0.71	199.1	95.6	18.4
New Zealand	15	0.39	82.1	66.8	11.7
Philippines	20	0.79	207.5	70.1	20.9
Singapore	30	0.70	141.5	57.5	16.8
Thailand	25	0.68	124.5	71.3	16.2
Americas economies					
Argentina	12	0.74	161.7	62.0	17.5
Brazil	19	0.70	195.5	63.9	15.5
Canada	29	0.60	114.5	56.9	11.4
Chile	17	0.61	125.2	49.5	12.9
Mexico	19	0.82	224.7	92.2	18.4
Uruguay	32	0.52	96.9	38.5	12.3
U.S.	32	0.40	52.9	33.2	8.9
European economies					
Austria	28	0.32	47.2	20.6	6.1
Belgium	31	0.36	63.3	22.0	6.9
Denmark	30	0.34	53.1	21.1	7.0
Finland	22	0.23	33.6	11.5	3.8
France	32	0.35	57.0	20.8	8.3
Germany	32	0.37	56.5	20.3	8.1
Greece	26	0.31	72.1	24.9	7.2
Ireland	23	0.21	32.2	20.1	4.5
Italy	25	0.29	49.9	18.5	6.4
Luxembourg	23	0.24	36.9	15.0	4.2
Netherlands	31	0.39	104.0	20.0	10.0
Norway	28	0.32	62.1	16.4	4.4
Portugal	21	0.14	45.5	20.3	6.1
Spain	31	0.36	68.0	25.4	8.9
Sweden	29	0.32	45.5	20.3	6.1
Switzerland	32	0.75	102.5	42.6	13.8
Turkey	20	0.56	98.8	32.2	10.7
U.K.	32	0.30	46.3	21.5	7.6

Notes: [a] Unweighted average of the route-level bilateral restriction indexes for each economy based on the number of agreements/routes shown in the preceding column. Ranges from 0 to 0.97, with a higher score indicating more restrictions. [b] Percentage increase in airfares compared to the benchmark regime.

Source: Adapted from Doove et al. (2001: 39).

where $\dot{p}$ represents the price of air travel over a particular route, *BRI* is the index of restrictiveness for that route, and *E* is a vector of variables for the determinants of prices, including indexes of market structure both for the route and at the route ends, measurements of airport conditions, government control, and propensity for air travel. The coefficients, α, β, and γ, are to be estimated econometrically, while ϵ is the disturbance term. The price variable $\dot{p}$ in this equation is of some interest, since it demonstrates the not uncommon need to model particular features of a service industry. It is based on a separate analysis of international airfares, relating them to distance and to other route-specific variables. The price that is entered in equation (1) is then the percentage that the actual airfare lies above the price predicted from this analysis.

Thus, holding this predicted price constant as unaffected by a particular trade restriction, the estimated coefficient measures the percentage by which the price—air fare in this case—is increased by a restrictiveness of one, compared to the price at a restrictiveness of zero. Applying this estimated coefficient to the values of the index of restrictiveness for the larger set of countries, Doove et al. (2001) produced the price-effect estimates reported in Table 5.7. As can be seen, these tend to be largest for developing economies and for business travel.

Other studies have been done using variations on this technique. These variations include the use of separate indexes of restrictiveness or proxy measures for different types of trade barriers, including individual modes of supply. A number of these other studies of price impacts of services restrictions are summarized in Annex 5.A. These studies cover several sectors, including international air services, wholesale and retail food distributors, banks, maritime services, engineering services, telecommunications, and industrial electricity supply in both developed and developing countries. These various sectors are evidently distinctive in terms of their economic characteristics and the regulatory measures that affect their operations. Specialized knowledge of the sectors is thus essential in designing the conceptual framework and adapting the available data to calculate the price impacts of the regulatory measures involved.

Quantity-Impact Measurements

Another approach, appropriate for some service industries, is to model the determination of quantity rather than price, and then to include the trade restrictiveness index in a quantity equation. The result, analogous to that for prices above, is an estimate of effects of trade barriers on quantities. This can in turn be converted into an effect on prices by use of an assumed or an estimated price elasticity of demand.[17]

For example, Warren (2000b) has assessed the quantitative impact of barriers in telecommunications services, chiefly mobile telephony and fixed network services, for

---

[17] That is, having estimated that barriers reduce the quantity of a service by some percentage, this is divided by the elasticity of demand to obtain the percentage price increase to which it corresponds.

136 countries. For this purpose he estimated equations such as the following, which was for mobile telephony:

$$Q_i^m = a + \beta_1 Y_i + \beta_2 Y_i^2 + \beta_3 PD_i + \beta_4 [P_i^m] + \epsilon_i \qquad (2)$$

Here, for each country i, Q_i^m is the number of cellular telephone subscribers per 100 inhabitants, Y_i is GDP per capita, and PD_i is population density. $[P_i^m]$ is a policy variable, which for mobile telephony took two forms: an index of market access for investment in the industry based on number of competitors, privatization, and policies towards competition; and a broader average of several trade and investment-related indexes.

Combining these quantitative estimates of the effects of removing existing barriers with an estimate of the price elasticity of demand for the telecommunications services involved, tariff equivalents in the form of price wedges were calculated. The tariff equivalents for domestic and for foreign providers of telecommunication services in the major nations are shown in Table 5.8. The estimates for the advanced industrialized

Table 5.8. Tariff Equivalents of Barriers to Telecommunication Services in Major Nations (Percentage)

	Domestic	Foreign
Australia	0.31	0.31
Austria	0.85	0.85
Belgium	0.65	1.31
Brazil	3.81	5.68
Canada	1.07	3.37
Chile	1.68	1.68
Hong Kong	1.26	1.26
Colombia	10.55	24.27
Denmark	0.20	0.20
Finland	0.00	0.00
France	0.34	1.43
Germany	0.32	0.32
Ireland	1.46	2.67
Italy	1.00	1.00
Japan	0.26	0.26
Korea	4.30	8.43
Mexico	6.24	14.43
Netherlands	0.20	0.20
New Zealand	0.27	0.27
Singapore	2.10	2.72
Spain	2.03	3.93
Sweden	0.65	0.65
Switzerland	1.23	1.23
Turkey	19.59	33.53
U.K.	0.00	0.00
U.S.	0.20	0.20

Source: Adapted from Warren (2000b).

countries are relatively low in comparison to the much higher estimates for the newly industrializing countries shown. There are cases of developing countries (not shown) that in some cases have very large tariff equivalents, including some with several hundred per cent, e.g. China (804 and 1,000 per cent), Colombia (11 per cent and 24 per cent), India (861 and 1,000 per cent), Indonesia (71 and 128 per cent), South Africa (14 and 21 per cent), and Venezuela (10 and 15 per cent).

Gravity-Model Estimates

Because the modeling of prices that is needed to estimate a price effect above is necessarily very sector specific, the techniques described so far have limited use for quantifying barriers across sectors. Likewise, they are not useful for comparing the overall levels of service trade barriers across countries. For that, one needs a more general model of trade to use as a benchmark, and the natural choice is the so-called gravity model. This model relates bilateral trade volumes positively to the incomes of both trading partners, and also negatively to the distance between them.[18] It has become a very popular tool in recent years for eliciting the effects of a wide variety of policy and structural influences on trade in a manner that controls for the obvious importance of income and distance.

Francois (1999) has fit a gravity model to bilateral services trade for the United States and its major trading partners, taking Hong Kong and Singapore to be free trade benchmarks. The independent variables, in addition to distance between trading partners, included per capita income, gross domestic product (GDP), and a Western Hemisphere dummy variable. The differences between actual and predicted imports were taken to be indicative of trade barriers and were then normalized relative to the free trade benchmarks for Hong Kong and Singapore. Combining this with an as-sumed demand elasticity of 4, tariff equivalents can be estimated. The results for business/financial services and for construction are indicated in Table 5.9. Brazil has the highest estimated tariff equivalent for business/financial services (35.7 per cent), followed by Japan, China, Other South Asia, and Turkey at about 20 per cent. The estimated tariff equivalents are considerably higher for construction services, in the 40–60 per cent range for China, South Asia, Brazil, Turkey, Central Europe, Russia, and South Africa, and in the 10–30 per cent range for the industrialized countries. Further details are given in Annex 5.A on the limitations of the use and interpretation of gravity models.

---

[18] Typically, the log of the volume of total bilateral trade between two countries is regressed on the logs of their national incomes, the log of distance between them, and other variables such as per capita income and dummy variables to reflect a common border, common language, etc.

Table 5.9. Estimated Tariff Equivalents in Traded Services: Gravity-Model Based Regression Method (Percentage)

Countries/regions	Business/financial services	Construction
North America[+]	8.2	9.8
Western Europe	8.5	18.3
Australia and New Zealand	6.9	24.4
Japan	19.7	29.7
China	18.8	40.9
Taiwan	2.6	5.3
Other Newly Industrialized Countries	2.1	10.3
Indonesia	6.8	9.6
Other South East Asia	5.0	17.7
India	13.1	61.6
Other South Asia*	20.4	46.3
Brazil	35.7	57.2
Other Latin America	4.7	26.0
Turkey*	20.4	46.3
Other Middle East and North Africa	4.0	9.5
CEECs & Russia	18.4	51.9
South Africa	15.7	42.1
Other Sub-Saharan Africa	0.3	11.1
Rest of World (ROW)	20.4	46.3

Notes: *Turkey and Other South Asia are not available, separately, in the U.S. data, and have been assigned estimated ROW values. [+]North America values involve assigning Canada/Mexico numbers to the United States.

Source: Adapted from Francois (1999).

Financial-based Measurements

Hoekman (2000) has suggested that financial data on gross operating margins calculated by sector and country may provide information about the effects of government policies on firm entry and conditions of competition.[19] As he notes (p. 36):

In general, a large number of factors will determine the ability of firms to generate high margins, including market size (number of firms), the business cycle, the state of competition, policy enforcement, the substitutability of products, fixed costs, etc. Notwithstanding the impossibility of inferring that high margins are due to high barriers, there should be a correlation between the two across countries for any given sector. Data on operating margins provide some sense of the relative profitability of activities, and therefore, the relative magnitude (restrictiveness) of barriers to entry/exit that may exist.

The country-region results of Hoekman's analysis, averaged over firms and sectors for 1994–96, are indicated for agriculture, manufacturing, and services in Table 5.10. Sectoral results for services only are given in Table 5.11. Services margins are generally

---

[19] Gross operating margins are defined as total sales revenue minus total average costs divided by total average costs.

Table 5.10. Average Gross Operating Margins of Firms Listed on National Stock Exchanges, 1994–96 by Country/Region (Percentage)

Country/Region	Agriculture	Manufacturing	Services
Australia	8.4	15.5	16.6
Canada	32.1	22.6	32.9
Chile	39.1	40.8	44.0
China	30.6	28.1	49.5
E.U.	22.9	23.8	31.6
Hong Kong	25.9	12.8	18.1
Indonesia	41.8	34.3	41.3
Japan	38.4	26.4	28.7
Republic of Korea	11.2	25.7	25.8
Malaysia	22.6	6.0	21.6
Mexico	38.4	39.3	37.2
New Zealand	33.3	16.6	26.8
Philippines	18.1	28.6	42.3
Singapore	0.0	11.1	22.0
Taiwan	19.6	25.1	41.3
Thailand	38.2	27.3	52.6
U.S.	36.6	21.2	42.3
Rest of Cairns Group[a]	36.3	31.1	39.0

Note: [a] Includes Argentina, Brazil, and Colombia.

Source: Adapted from Hoekman (2000). Based on calculations using Disclosure, *Worldscope* (1998) data.

Table 5.11. Average Gross Operating Margins of Services Firms Listed on National Stock Exchanges, 1994–96, by Country/Region and by Sector (Percentage)

Country/Region	Recreation	Business Services	Construction	Consulting	Finance	Health	Hotels	Retail Trade	Wholesale	Transport/ Utilities
Australia	17.9	13.8	15.3	7.0	41.0	B	27.3	7.9	9.1	C
Canada	60.1	51.7	14.4	19.2	44.5	2.3	67.8	12.0	16.0	36.5
Chile	b	b	68.7	b	55.2	B	b	21.3	27.9	46.8
China	b	b	45.9	67.1	34.0	B	77.5	24.4	25.5	46.9
E.U.	42.5	32.1	19.3	22.1	51.6	22.3	23.7	23.6	19.9	32.6
Hong Kong	b	6.5	12.9	11.5	25.4	B	31.3	10.1	6.9	31.0
Indonesia	b	81.1	22.9	25.3	53.6	B	68.2	26.4	24.8	45.3
Japan	28.1	31.6	14.2	28.6	40.5	40.1	27.2	32.9	15.6	20.6
Republic of Korea	b	41.2	15.3	b	b	B	b	26.7	14.9	31.2
Malaysia	13.3	c	18.3	14.7	28.3	24.3	38.7	11.2	10.8	30.7
Mexico	19.6	b	25.7	37.3	33.3	B	49.6	28.4	25.0	51.0
New Zealand	b	b	13.8	b	57.6	B	26.9	6.6	19.7	35.6
Philippines	19.9	b	40.2	b	53.9	b	55.8	43.9	40.3	42.3
Singapore	46.7	8.6	10.6	7.7	46.3	29.2	28.2	5.4	7.9	28.0
Taiwan	79.9	36.3	21.6	11.1	64.8	b	74.5	21.5	23.2	38.9
Thailand	85.4	35.8	38.1	c	60.3	40.6	55.5	44.2	25.6	56.7
U.S.	46.8	56.2	20.2	c	56.3	37.0	48.5	34.6	27.0	43.4
Other Cairns[a]	b	b	28.9	26.2	69.8	29.3	64.6	24.2	22.9	52.4

Note: [a] Includes Argentina, Brazil, and Colombia. [b] Data not available. [c] Reflects negative gross operating margin.

Source: Adapted from Hoekman (2000). Based on calculations using Disclosure, *Worldscope* (1998) data.

higher than manufacturing margins by 10–15 percentage points, and the services margins vary considerably across countries. Australia, Hong Kong, and Singapore have the lowest services margins—in the neighborhood of 20 per cent—while Chile, China, Indonesia, Philippines, Taiwan, Thailand, and the United States have services margins in excess of 40 per cent. The sectoral results indicate that the margins for hotels and financial services are relatively high, and the margins for wholesale and retail trade are lower. The margins for several developing countries appear to be relatively high in a number of sectors. Overall, as Hoekman suggests (p. 39):

...business services, consultancy, and distribution do not appear to be among the most protected sectors...barriers to competition are higher in transportation, finance, and telecommunications. These are also basic "backbone" imports that are crucial for the ability of enterprises to compete internationally.

Diversity of Methods

As should be clear from the foregoing, studies of services barriers have used a wide variety of approaches. This is not surprising given the wide variety of the service industries themselves and the variation across them in the data that may be available. In our concluding section, below, we will outline the steps that seem to have been most commonly used and/or successful in the largest number of studies, as a guide to those who intend to replicate their work in other industries and countries. However, it will often be the case that one or more of these steps cannot be followed in particular cases. Research on services barriers must therefore often make do with whatever information may be available. As illustrated by the studies discussed here, this may require creative exploitation of seemingly heroic assumptions in order to extract any information at all.

Measuring the Economic Consequences of Liberalizing Services Barriers

While the various measurements of services barriers that we have reviewed are of interest in themselves, they need to be incorporated into an explicit economic modeling framework in order to determine how the existence or removal of the barriers will affect conditions of competition, productivity, the allocation of resources, and economic welfare within or between sectors and countries. In this regard, a modeling framework can be devised for individual sectors or on an economy-wide basis using computable general equilibrium (CGE) modeling.

Sectoral Modeling

An example of sectoral modeling is provided by Fink et al. (2003), who analyze the impact of policy reform on sectoral performance in basic telecommunications. Their data cover 86 developing countries globally for the period, 1985–99. They address three questions, covering the impact of: (1) policy changes relating to ownership, competition, and regulation; (2) any one policy reform coupled with the implementation of complementary reforms; and (3) the sequencing of reforms.

Their findings are: (1) privatization and the introduction of competition significantly increase labor productivity and the density of telecommunication mainlines; (2) privatization and competition work best through their interactions; and (3) there are more favorable effects from introducing competition before privatization. They further conclude that autonomous technological progress outweighs the effects of policy reforms in increasing the growth of teledensity.

What is especially noteworthy about this type of study is its focus on both the policy and market structure of the sector and the econometric framework that is designed to measure the determinants of teledensity and telecommunications productivity. The assessment of particular services barriers may therefore be most effectively addressed when incorporated into a sectoral modeling framework.[20]

Computational General Equilibrium (CGE) Modeling

In contrast to sectoral modeling, CGE modeling provides a framework for multi-sectoral and multi-country analysis of the economic effects of services barriers and related policies. Most CGE modeling research to date has been focused on barriers to international trade in goods rather than trade in services and FDI. The reasons for this stem in large part from the lack of comprehensive data on cross-border services trade and FDI and the associated barriers, together with the difficult conceptual problems of modeling that are encountered. Some indication of pertinent CGE modeling work relating to services is provided in Hardin and Holmes (1997), Brown and Stern (2001: 272–4), and Stern (2002: 254–6). The approaches to modeling can be divided as follows: (1) analysis of cross-border services trade liberalization in response to reductions in services barriers; (2) modeling in which FDI is assumed to result from trade liberalization or other exogenous changes that generate international capital flows in the form of FDI in response to changes in rates of return; and (3) modeling of links between

---

[20] See also Fink et al. (2002) and Annex 5.A for a summary of their study of the importance of restrictive trade policies and private anti-competitive practices relating to international maritime services.

multinational corporations' (MNCs) parents and affiliates and distinctions between foreign and domestic firms in a given country/region.

The third type of CGE modeling study just noted comes closest to capturing the important role played especially by MNCs and their foreign affiliates in providing mode 3-type services. This, for example, is the focus of the study by Brown and Stern (2001), some details of which are presented in Annex 5.A. Brown and Stern analyze the effects of removal of services barriers under alternative conditions of international capital mobility and changes in the world capital stock due to increased investment. Their results, presented in Table 5.A.7, suggest that the welfare effects of removing services barriers are sizable and vary across countries depending on how international capital movements and changes in domestic investment respond to changes in rates of return. The largest potential benefits are realized for all of the major developed and developing countries when allowance is made for changes in investment that augment the stock of capital.

Guideline Principles and Recommended Procedures for Measuring Services Barriers and for Assessing the Consequences of their Liberalization

As a summary of what we have reported in detail here about the methodologies for measuring services barriers and using these measurements to assess the consequences of liberalization in services, we conclude first with several principles to be kept in mind during this process and then with more detailed procedural steps that we recommend should be followed:

PRINCIPLES

1. Most barriers to trade and investment in services take the form of domestic regulations, rather than measures at the border.
2. No single methodology is sufficient for documenting and measuring barriers to trade in services. Instead, investigators need to draw upon all available information, including both direct observation of particular barriers and indirect inference of barriers using data on prices and quantities.
3. Because of the special role of incumbent firms in many service industries, regulations do not need to be explicitly discriminatory against foreign firms in order to have discriminatory effects.

PROCEDURES

1. Collect the details of domestic regulations and related policies affecting services firms in the countries and/or sectors being examined, including the manner in which they apply to foreign vs. domestic firms, plus quantitative details of their application, such as any percentage or dollar limits that they impose.

2. Ideally, this information should be collected by systematic surveys of governments and/or firms. However, it may also be possible to infer it less directly from documents prepared for other purposes, such as the commitments that governments made to the GATS in the Uruguay Round and subsequent negotiations.

3. For each type of regulation or policy, define degrees of restrictiveness and assign scores to each, ranging from zero for least restrictive to one for most restrictive.

4. Construct a measure of restrictiveness by: weighting the scores from step 3 based on judgments of the relative importance of each policy; using a statistical methodology such as factor analysis that will serve to identify the weights; or designing proxy measures, such as dummy variables, to represent particular restrictions. The resulting measures can then be used directly for reporting the presence and importance of barriers across industries and countries, as well as for providing an input to subsequent analysis.

5. Convert the measures of restrictiveness from step 4 into a set of tariff equivalents by one or more of the following methods. Depending on the quality of information that goes into their construction, these tariff equivalents may be superior to the measures themselves for reporting about barriers and analyzing their effects.
   a. Assign judgmental tariff-equivalent values to each of the component measures, representing the percentage taxes on foreign suppliers to which each component is thought to correspond at their most restrictive levels (index = 1).
   b. Use data on prices and their determinants as the basis for a regression model that includes an index or other measures of restrictiveness and that estimates the effect on prices.
   c. Use data on quantities produced or traded as the basis for a regression model that includes an index or other measures of restrictiveness and that estimates the effect on quantities. This estimate can then be converted to tariff equivalents using an assumed or estimated price elasticity of demand.

6. Use an index or other measures of restrictiveness or the tariff equivalents constructed above as inputs into a model of production and trade in order to ascertain the effects of changes in the barriers to which they correspond. The appropriate model for this purpose depends on whether sectoral or economy-wide policy changes are to be analyzed. For economy-wide policy changes, the model should be a general equilibrium one, incorporating the full effects of barriers across sectors and countries.

Ideally, too, the model should be designed to capture the effects of service regulations in the form that they have been observed and quantified as above.

Annex 5.A

LITERATURE SUMMARIES OF METHODS OF MEASUREMENT[21]

In this Annex, we provide a somewhat more technical discussion of the various methods of measurement of services barriers, focusing especially on available studies that have been completed and that can be consulted for more information on methodology and data and possible adaptation in further research.

FREQUENCY STUDIES AND INDEXES OF RESTRICTIVENESS

In what follows, we summarize several studies that complement our discussion in the main text:

- Mattoo (1998) analyzed market access commitments in *financial services*, covering direct insurance and banking. His results indicated that Latin America was the most restricted in direct insurance and Asia the most restricted in banking services.

- Marko (1998) constructed frequency measures for the basic *telecommunications* markets, using Hoekman's (1995) methodology. Marko found that 58 per cent of the basic telecommunications services market for the 69 signatories of the February 1997 Agreement on Basic Telecommunications was covered by partial or full GATS commitments.

- McGuire (1998) showed that Australia's impediments in *financial services*, including banking, securities, and insurance, were much lower as compared to other economies in Asia.

- Colecchia (2000) provided a methodological, pilot study of the barriers on *accountancy services* for Australia, France, the United Kingdom, and the United States, using OECD information on regulatory regimes for 1997. The United Kingdom was found to be the most liberal, the United States the least liberal.

- Kalirajan (2000) constructed restrictiveness indexes for 38 economies, using GATS schedules and a variety of other information on barriers to *distribution services* as of June 1999. The indexes covered the services of commission agents, wholesalers,

---

[21] See also Whalley (2004) and Dee (2005), who cover much of this same literature and some additional studies as well.

retailers, and franchisers. The findings were that: (1) Belgium, India, Indonesia, France, Korea, Malaysia, the Philippines, Switzerland, and Thailand were the most restrictive economies and Singapore and Hong Kong the most open; and (2) the countries that were the most discriminatory against foreign firms included Malaysia, the Philippines, Venezuela, Brazil, the United States, and Greece. The detailed domestic and foreign restrictiveness indexes were broken down by country and are available on the Productivity Commission website.

- Kemp (2000) constructed restrictiveness indexes for the four modes of providing *educational services*, using GATS data on commitments for market access and national treatment for the five sub-sectors of educational services and covering 29 countries. While only a quarter of GATS member countries scheduled commitments, the evidence suggested that consumption abroad, which is the major mode of educational trade in terms of foreign-student tuition, fees, and expenditures, was comparatively the least restricted mode.

- McGuire, Schuele, and Smith (2000) developed indexes for restrictions on foreign *maritime service* suppliers and all maritime service suppliers covering 35 economies during the period 1994–8, using a variety of GATS and other data sources. They found that: (1) Brazil, Chile, India, Indonesia, Korea, Malaysia, the Philippines, and the United States had the most restricted markets against foreign maritime suppliers; and (2) Chile, the Philippines, Thailand, Turkey, and the United States were the most discriminatory in favoring domestic suppliers. The detailed domestic and foreign indexes of restrictiveness were broken down by country and are available on the Productivity Commission website.

- Nguyen-Hong (2000) constructed restrictiveness indexes for *accountancy, architectural, and engineering services* for 34 economies and legal services for 29 economies. The indexes were compiled from WTO, OECD, APEC, and a variety of other sources. The findings were that: (1) legal and accounting were the most highly restricted services; (2) Indonesia, Malaysia, Austria, Mexico, and Turkey were the most restrictive for the four professions, and Finland and the Netherlands the most open; (3) nationality requirements were the most extensive in legal and accountancy services; (4) residency requirements were common in accountancy services; (5) partnerships and practices between accountants and lawyers were commonly restricted; and (6) recognition of foreign qualifications and licenses was subject to a variety of restrictions among countries. The detailed domestic and foreign restrictiveness indexes were broken down and are available on the Productivity Commission website.

- Warren (2000a) used data for 136 countries from the International Telecommunications Union (ITU) to construct five indexes for the regulation of *telecommunications* policies that discriminate against: (1) all potential providers of cross-border telecommunications services; (2) foreign providers of cross-border services; (3) all potential providers of fixed network services; (4) all potential providers of cellular services via FDI; and (5) foreign providers of mobile services via FDI. He found: (1) significant variation across countries in all five indexes; (2) most countries relied only on foreign carriers to provide competition in mobile markets; (3) countries were less prepared to use majority-owned foreign carriers in their fixed network markets; (4) countries that liberalized their mobile networks were more likely to liberalize their fixed networks; (5) countries that limited commercial presence via FDI were more liberal in permitting cross-border entry; and (6) GATS-based indexes that tended to reflect legal conditions, as calculated by Marko (1998), were not altogether well correlated with ITU-based indexes that were designed to reflect economic conditions. The detailed domestic and foreign indexes by country are available on the Productivity Commission website.

• Doove et al. (2001) constructed restrictiveness indexes for international air passenger transport, telecommunications, and electricity supply. The index for *air transport* was an average of the bilateral restrictiveness indexes applicable to pairs of countries. The data covered 875 airline routes for 35 economies and referred to the late 1990s. The bilateral restrictions included designation, capacity, fares, and charter services, with weights derived using factor analysis in an OECD study by Gonenc and Nicoletti (2001). The bilateral restrictions were generally not covered under the GATS, so that discriminatory restrictions on third countries may have been applied. The results are shown in column (2) of Table 5.7 and indicate substantial variation across countries as a consequence of the agreement-specific bilateral restrictions.

The restrictiveness index for *telecommunications* covered 24 OECD member countries and 23 non-OECD countries, using data for 1997. The telecommunications industry has been undergoing rapid technological change in recent decades, and there has been widespread regulatory reform and structural reform undertaken in many countries. Doove et al. built upon the OECD study by Boylaud and Nicoletti (2000), who focused on the four major telecommunications sectors: trunk (domestic long distance); international (international long distance); mobile (cellular); and leased-line services. The regulatory measures covered include: market share of new entrants; index of governmental control of the public telecommunications operators (PTOs); degree of internationalization of domestic markets; time to liberalization; and time to privatization. These measurements were incorporated into an econometric framework for the individual sectors in order to estimate the price impacts involved that are noted in Table 5.A.1.

Electricity supply has also been undergoing significant deregulation and structural reform. Building upon OECD work by Steiner (2000), Doove et al. assembled data for 50 economies for 1996. The regulatory measures covered were: unbundling of electricity generation from transmission; third party access; presence of a wholesale electricity market; degree of private/public ownership; time to liberalization; and

Table 5.A.1. Price Impact of Regulation on Telecommunications Prices, 1997

Economy	Trunk	International	Mobile	Leasing	Industry-wide
OECD					
Australia	21	33	23	4	19
Austria	10	51	17	11	20
Belgium	41	207	18	5	52
Canada	33	95	8	0	27
Denmark	63	12	16	3	39
Finland	5	34	50	17	22
France	41	95	16	9	34
Germany	40	176	17	8	38
Greece	37	35	10	19	27
Iceland	31	199	96	11	54
Ireland	17	56	16	10	22
Italy	32	41	10	3	21
Japan	39	34	14	5	23
Luxembourg	17	108	105	22	59
Netherlands	32	30	13	5	23
New Zealand	30	24	15	1	21
Norway	26	67	42	14	31
Portugal	22	15	8	6	15
Spain	28	30	7	4	18
Sweden	53	b	54	15	b
Switzerland	13	165	49	16	40
Turkey	35	b	17	24	b
U.K.	78	63	6	2	47
U.S.	61	32	8	1	38
Unweighted mean	34	73	26	9	31
Standard deviation	17	61	27	7	13
Economy	Trunk	International	Mobile	Leasing	Industry-wide
Additional OECD[a]					
Czech Republic	36	20	6	ne	22
Hungary	69	44	2	ne	38
Korea	18	16	9	ne	14
Mexico	54	16	7	ne	40
Poland	18	30	9	ne	17
Unweighted mean	39	25	7	na	26
Standard deviation	23	12	3	na	12
NON-OECD					
Argentina	64	21	6	ne	45
Brazil	27	15	16	ne	23
Chile	41	35	7	ne	32
China	b	b	b	ne	b
Colombia	28	22	20	ne	25
Hong Kong	49	47	24	ne	43
India	68	41	b	ne	b
Indonesia	41	52	56	ne	46
Malaysia	23	34	23	ne	24
Peru	32	12	7	ne	24
Philippines	30	23	8	ne	23

(Continued)

Table 5.A.1. *(Continued)*

Economy	Trunk	International	Mobile	Leasing	Industry-wide
Russia	63	b	b	ne	b
Singapore	25	196	35	ne	44
South Africa	35	26	b	ne	b
Taiwan	25	54	40	ne	32
Thailand	41	111	18	ne	42
Uruguay	42	37	8	ne	33
Vietnam	b	b	b	ne	b
Unweighted mean	40	48	21	na	34
Standard deviation	15	47	15	na	9
All 47 Economies					
Minimum	5	12	2	0	14
Maximum	78	207	105	24	59
Unweighted mean	36	58	22	9	31
Standard deviation	17	54	22	7	12

Notes: ne: not estimated. na: not applicable. [a] OECD economies not included in Boylaud and Nicoletti (2000). [b] Excluded. *Source*: Adapted from Doove et al. (2001: 72–3).

time to privatization. The price impacts of regulation were estimated and are indicated in Table 5.A.2.

Price-impact Studies

We summarize below a number of other pertinent studies of price-impacts that may be consulted for further technical details and results:

- Johnson et al. (2000) noted that *international air services* are regulated by means of bilateral agreements and are largely excluded from the GATS. They developed a partial-equilibrium, spatial econometric model that was used to analyze the effects on prices, quantities, and economic welfare, in Australia and foreign countries, of the entry of a new airline (Ansett) into the Australian market, as well as plurilateral reform for an "open club" for airlines among Australia, China, Hong Kong, and Japan. They showed that there were significant benefits realized from the entry of new competitors into the airline markets. Also, members of an open club gained, but at the expense of non-members.

- Kalirajan (2000) used firm-level accounting data for wholesale and retail *food distributors* in 18 economies to indicate the relationship between trade restrictiveness and distributors' price-cost margins. The results suggested that the restrictions were primarily cost creating rather than rent creating and were accounted for mainly by

Table 5.A.2. Price Impacts of Regulation on Industrial Electricity Prices, 1996[a]

Economies in Original Study	Per cent	Extended Coverage	Per cent
Australia	0.0	Argentina	0.0
Belgium	15.4	Austria	13.2
Canada	8.8	Bolivia	16.5
Denmark	8.5	Brazil	15.6
Finland	0.0	Chile	0.0
France	16.0	China	17.2
Germany	8.3	Colombia	0.0
Greece	16.6	Czech Republic	13.6
Ireland	13.9	Hong Kong	15.6
Italy	17.1	Hungary	13.3
Japan	10.2	Iceland	35.3
Netherlands	15.5	India	17.2
New Zealand	0.0	Indonesia	16.8
Norway	0.0	Korea	15.4
Portugal	17.9	Luxembourg	13.8
Spain	9.5	Malaysia	16.6
Sweden	0.0	Mexico	17.3
U.K.	0.0	Peru	0.0
U.S.	7.5	Philippines	17.6
		Poland	13.6
		Russia	17.1
		Slovak Republic	14.8
		Singapore	15.6
		South Africa	15.6
		Switzerland	21.9
		Taiwan	16.1
		Thailand	16.3
		Turkey	20.7
		Uruguay	32.2
		Venezuela	27.2
		Vietnam	32.0

Notes: [a] Percentage increase in pre-tax industrial electricity prices relative to the estimated price under the benchmark regulatory regime.

Source: Adapted from Doove et al. (2001: 105).

restrictions on establishment. Using the restrictiveness indexes, coefficient estimates, and sample means, the estimated cost impacts noted in Table 5.A.3 range between 0 and 8 per cent.

- Kalirajan et al. (2000) developed and estimated a model applied to 694 banks in 27 economies for 1996–97 to assess the impact of non-prudential restrictions on the interest margins of *banks*. The net interest margin is the difference between a bank's lending and deposit rates. A two-stage procedure was used for estimation purposes. In the first stage, bank-specific variables were used to explain the interest margins in all the economies, and, in a second stage, cross-country estimation was used to take economy-wide variables into account. The foreign and domestic restrictiveness

Table 5.A.3. Estimated Cost Impacts of Foreign and Domestic Barriers to Establishment in Wholesale and Retail Food Distributors (Per cent)

Economy	Cost impact of foreign barriers to establishment	Cost impact of domestic barriers to establishment
Australia	0.57	—
Belgium	4.87	6.69
Canada	3.09	0.98
Chile	1.32	1.92
France	5.16	7.10
Greece	0.25	—
Hong Kong	0.06	—
Indonesia	3.66	—
Ireland	2.70	—
Japan	2.26	6.79
Malaysia	8.23	3.97
Netherlands	2.73	—
New Zealand	0.77	—
Singapore	0.03	—
South Africa	0.47	—
Switzerland	5.24	8.32
U.K.	2.76	—
U.S.	2.26	—

Note: - Zero.

Source: Adapted from Kalirajan (2000: 52).

indexes calculated in McGuire and Schuele (2000) entered into the second-stage estimation. The foreign restrictiveness index was found to be a significant determinant of interest rate spreads, while the domestic restrictiveness index was not significant. The price impacts of the restrictions were calculated from the second-stage results and are presented in Table 5.A.4. Chile, Indonesia, Malaysia, the Philippines, Singapore, South Korea, and Thailand have the highest price impacts due to the restrictions on foreign banks.

- Kang (2000) investigated the impact of restrictions on *maritime services*, using a partial-equilibrium econometric model that incorporated cross-country and bilateral trade data as determinants of demand for these services. Shipping margins for manufactured goods were derived from FOB/CIF value differentials and were used as a proxy for price. The shipping margins were to be explained by bilateral restrictions, distance, and the scale of bilateral trade. Indexes for 23 countries were adapted from McGuire et al. (2000), and the remaining data were from the 1995 database of the Global Trade Analysis Project (GTAP). The foreign index of restrictiveness was decomposed into measures affecting commercial presence and into other restrictions such as on cabotage and port services. Allowance was also made for different bilateral relationships as between industrialized and developing economies. The most important conclusion reached was that a low degree of restrictions in any trading partner

Table 5.A.4. Estimated Price Impacts of Foreign and Domestic Trade Restrictiveness Indexes (TRI) on Net Interest Margins of Banks (Per cent)

Economy	Price effect using the foreign TRI$_i$	Price effect using the domestic TRI$_i^b$
Argentina	5.34	0.00
Australia	9.30	0.00
Canada	5.34	0.00
Chile	34.00	23.67
Colombia	18.35	3.73
European Union[a]	5.32	0.00
Hong Kong	6.91	2.97
Indonesia	49.32	5.26
Japan	15.26	9.99
Malaysia	60.61	21.86
Philippines	47.36	10.79
Singapore	31.45	8.39
South Korea	36.72	14.93
Switzerland	5.95	0.00
Thailand	33.06	0.00
U.S.	4.75	0.00

Notes: [a] The European Union grouping excludes Finland, Ireland, and Luxembourg. [b] Uses the coefficient estimate for the foreign trade restrictiveness index as a proxy.

Source: Adapted from Kalirajan et al. (2000: 229).

was necessary in order to have low shipping charges. Further, low-income countries stood to gain the most from eliminating restrictions on shipping services.

- Nguyen-Hong (2000) estimated the influences of restrictions on the price–cost margins of 84 *engineering service* firms in 20 economies, using 1996 company accounting data compiled from a variety of private and official sources. A model of firm behavior was developed to include the determinants of the observed price–cost margins, and a linear version using ordinary least squares was implemented with cross-section data. The index of foreign barriers to establishment was highly significant and had a positive and statistically significant impact on price–cost margins. The index of domestic barriers to establishment had a negative and significant impact. The price and cost impacts of the restrictions were calculated, using the actual indexes of restrictiveness, estimated coefficients, and the sample means of the independent variables. The price impacts, which are summarized by country in Table 5.A.5, exceed 10 per cent for Austria, Mexico, Malaysia, Indonesia, and Germany. The cost impacts are relatively small, ranging between 0.7 and 6.8 per cent. The price and cost impacts were also calculated by types of barriers.

- Trewin (2000) used time-series data on the total costs of providing *telecommunications services* for 37 countries obtained from the International Telecommunications Union (ITU) for the period 1982–92. He used a frontier cost method as a means of estimating the minimum possible costs that are expended from a given combination

Table 5.A.5. Estimated Price and Cost Impacts of Restrictions on Engineering Services (Per Cent)

	Price impact			Cost impact
	Foreign barriers to establishment	Foreign barriers to ongoing operations	All foreign barriers	Domestic barriers to establishment
Austria	11.1	3.5	14.5	6.8
Mexico	13.9	0.2	14.2	1.9
Malaysia	11.3	0.7	12.0	5.3
Indonesia	9.9	0.3	10.2	3.2
Germany	4.7	5.5	10.2	2.9
Spain	5.1	3.7	8.7	3.9
U.S.	5.1	2.2	7.4	3.8
Sweden	5.9	0.9	6.8	0.7
Japan	3.1	3.4	6.6	2.2
Canada	3.1	2.2	5.3	2.7
Singapore	4.9	0.2	5.0	0.8
Hong Kong	3.6	1.5	5.1	2.3
South Africa	3.5	0.2	3.7	0.7
Netherlands	3.5	0.2	3.7	5.2
Australia	2.1	0.7	2.8	2.1
U.K.	2.3	0.2	2.5	1.4
Finland	1.8	0.5	2.3	0.7
Denmark	0.3	0.8	1.1	0.7
France	0.3	0.6	0.9	0.7
Belgium	0.3	0.2	0.5	0.7

Note: [a] The price impact for all foreign barriers is the sum of the price impacts for foreign barriers to establishment and ongoing operations, respectively.

Source: Adapted from Nguyen-Hong (2000: 63).

of inputs. The distance of an observation above the cost frontier is a measurement of the degree of technical inefficiency. The measurements of restrictiveness calculated by Marko (1998) and Warren (2000a) were used in the estimation process. The results suggested that countries that provide higher levels of FDI face lower costs. Making allowance for the quality–cost aspects of telecommunication services reinforced the importance of the cost impacts of restrictions. When the sample was divided between low and high income countries, the average efficiency of the high income set was more than three times better than the low income set. The results are listed in Table 5.A.6. It can be seen, in the high income set, that Luxembourg is close to the efficiency frontier whereas Portugal and Korea are relatively high cost countries.

• Doove et al. (2001) constructed restrictiveness indexes and estimates of price impacts for international air passenger transport, telecommunications, and electricity supply. Their indexes of bilateral restrictions on *international air passenger transport* referred to 35 economies in the Asia-Pacific, Americas, and European regions. Focusing on the discount segment of the air passenger market, they implement a procedure for estimating the price effects of the applicable restrictions, using fare data primarily

Table 5.A.6. Coefficient Estimates of Technical Efficiency in Telecommunications Services

Low income	Technical efficiency	High income	Technical efficiency
Chile	3.82	Australia	1.67
China	6.31	Austria	1.31
Hungary	2.61	Belgium	1.55
Iceland	1.16	Canada	1.34
Indonesia	11.96	Denmark	1.43
Ireland	3.22	Finland	1.24
Malaysia	4.31	France	1.74
Mexico	15.41	Germany	1.66
PNG	7.75	Greece	1.11
Philippines	3.06	Hong Kong	1.44
Poland	2.30	Italy	1.71
Thailand	5.25	Japan	1.21
Turkey	4.07	Korea	1.98
		Luxembourg	1.03
		Netherlands	1.43
		New Zealand	1.83
		Norway	1.75
		Portugal	2.08
		Singapore	1.57
		Spain	1.75
		Sweden	1.40
		Switzerland	1.42
		U.K.	1.67
		U.S.	1.48
Mean	5.48	Mean	1.54

Note: A coefficient estimate equal to 1.00 indicates full technical efficiency in relation to the minimum-cost frontier.
Source: Adapted from Trewin (2000: 112).

for the end years of the 1990s. The results, which are shown above in Table 5.7, indicated that the higher price effects range from 12 to 22 per cent in the Asia-Pacific economies, 9 to 18 per cent in the Americas, and generally below 10 per cent in the European economies. The price impacts for business and economy airfares were considerably higher but should be interpreted tentatively due to data constraints.

Measurements of the impact of *telecommunications* regulations were derived for 24 OECD and 23 other countries, using data for 1997. Price-impact measurements of regulation were calculated for four major sectors of telecommunications, including trunk, international, mobile, and leasing services and are listed by country and type of service in Table 5.A.1. While the results suggested that countries with more stringent regulatory regimes tended to have higher telecommunications prices, the authors noted that there were several cases in which the results appeared to be counter intuitive and sensitive to small changes in the data. The reported results should therefore be treated with caution, pending further clarification and improvement of the model and data that were used.

Measurements of regulation and impacts on *industrial electricity* prices for 50 economies, using 1996 data, were developed. The estimated price impacts are listed by country in Table 5.A.2. The impacts ranged from 0 to 35 per cent, with a mean of 13 per cent and a standard deviation of 13 per cent. The authors noted, however, that the estimated price impacts were quite sensitive to the methodology and data used and therefore should be treated as ordinal rankings rather than absolute values.

- Fink et al. (2002) analyzed the importance of restrictive trade policies and private anti-competitive practices for *international maritime services*. For this purpose, they used data on U.S. imports carried by liners from 59 countries that accounted for about 65 per cent of the total value of U.S. maritime imports in 1998. While restrictions on the provision of port services were found to be significant, private anti-competitive practices involving collusion among international maritime cartels were shown to have a considerably greater influence on maritime transport prices.

Gravity-Model Estimates

Deardorff and Stern (1998: 24) have noted that measurements based on the gravity model are useful mainly in identifying *relative* levels of protection across sectors and countries. But gravity models have some important drawbacks. That is, by attributing to trade barriers all departures of trade from what the included variables can explain, there is a great burden on the model being used. Thus, the worse the model, the more likely it is that trade barrier estimates will have an upward bias.

An additional problem exists when this technique is used to infer barriers for separate industries. The theoretical basis for the gravity equation, as in Anderson (1979) and Deardorff (1998), applies to total trade, not to trade in individual sectors. The gravity equation makes sense at the sectoral level only if all countries are equal in their capacity to produce in a sector, which of course would be a denial of the role of comparative advantage. Thus, if a country were in fact to have a comparative advantage in a particular service sector, so that its output would be high and its cost of serving its domestic market itself would be low, then it will import less from abroad than would be expected based on income and distance alone. Thus comparative advantage may show up as an implicit barrier to trade, when in fact none exists.

Computable General Equilibrium (CGE) Modeling

In the study by Brown and Stern (2001), each MNC is assumed to produce a differentiated product and to allocate production to its various host-country locations.

The monopolistically competitive firms employ capital, labor, and intermediate inputs in their production, and they set prices as an optimal mark-up of price over marginal cost. The number of firms is permitted to vary to hold MNC profits at zero. Consumers are assumed to allocate their expenditure between goods and services that are produced by firms domestically and varieties that are imported from each national source. Labor is taken to be freely mobile among domestic sectors but not across borders. Capital, however, is mobile internationally, although not perfectly so, because there is a risk premium that will vary depending on the size of a country's capital stock.

Barriers to FDI are assumed to take the form of an increased cost of locating investment in a host country. For this purpose, Brown and Stern use the cost–price margins estimated by Hoekman (2000), which have been discussed above and are listed in Tables 5.10 and 5.11, as indicative of barriers to FDI. Since the cost–price gap is smallest in most sectors in Hong Kong, a country thought to be freely open to foreign firms, the excess in any other country above the Hong Kong figure is taken to be due to barriers to the establishment of foreign firms.

Using the aforementioned modeling structure with three sectors (agriculture, manufactures, and services) and 18 countries/regions, Brown and Stern calculate the economic effects of removal of services barriers according to the following three scenarios:[22]

- *Scenario A:* Removal of services barriers, with perfect international capital mobility and fixed world capital stock.
- *Scenario B:* Removal of services barriers, with risk-premium elasticity = 0.1 to allow for imperfect capital mobility, and fixed world capital stock.
- *Scenario C:* Removal of services barriers, with risk-premium elasticity = 0.1 to allow for imperfect capital mobility, and world capital stock increased by 3 per cent.

When barriers are lowered, international capital in the form of FDI will then be attracted to countries with the relatively highest rates of return and away from other countries.

The welfare effects, as a percentage of GNP and in billions of dollars, resulting from the assumed removal of the services barriers for each of the three scenarios are listed in Table 5.A.7 for the countries/regions covered by the model.[23] When services barriers are lowered, international capital in the form of FDI will then be attracted to countries with the highest rates of return and away from other countries.

---

[22] See also studies undertaken at the Australian Productivity Commission by Dee and Hanslow (2001) and Verikios and Zhang (2001) for computational results based on a related modeling framework and with estimates of services barriers taken from Kalirajan et al. (2000) and Warren (2000 a, b).

[23] See Brown and Stern (2001: 277–8) for the results for the absolute changes in imports and exports, the percentage change in the terms of trade, and the percentage change in the real wage. The sectoral results for the three aggregated sectors for Scenario C are reported in Brown and Stern (pp. 281–2). They show that output increases economy-wide in just about every sector in all countries/regions, and there is a wide prevalence of the realization of economies of scale. There are also generally significant increases in activity by foreign-owned affiliates, especially in the countries that record large increases in output.

Table 5.A.7. Welfare Effects of Elimination of Services (Per cent and Billions of Dollars)

Country	Scenario A Perfect int'l capital mobility and fixed world capital stock		Scenario B Risk-premium elasticity=0.1 and fixed world capital stock		Scenario C Risk-premium elasticity=0.1 and world capital stock increased by 3%	
	% GNP	$Bill.	% GNP	$Bill.	% GNP	$Bill.
Industrialized countries						
Australia	1.8	6.0	1.5	5.0	4.9	16.8
Canada	14.8	84.0	12.9	73.7	14.9	85.0
E.U.	0.5	42.4	0.5	38.0	2.5	202.4
Japan	−2.0	−103.7	−1.7	−88.4	0.5	25.7
New Zealand	9.1	5.2	7.5	4.3	10.5	6.0
U.S.	0.5	35.0	0.3	23.2	3.1	222.5
Developing countries						
Asia						
China	3.8	26.9	3.2	22.9	6.0	42.8
Hong Kong	6.6	6.6	5.4	5.5	13.4	13.5
Indonesia	15.6	30.8	13.1	25.8	16.9	33.3
Korea	−2.8	−12.3	−2.3	−10.1	1.4	6.4
Malaysia	2.3	2.1	1.9	1.8	4.7	4.4
Philippines	2.3	1.6	1.9	1.3	8.3	5.7
Singapore	1.7	1.0	1.3	0.7	4.3	2.5
Taiwan	7.6	20.7	6.8	18.5	7.7	21.2
Thailand	−2.2	−3.6	−1.8	−2.9	4.4	7.1
Other						
Chile	−2.0	−1.3	−1.6	−1.0	2.7	1.7
Mexico	−4.3	−11.7	−3.2	−8.8	0.2	0.5
Rest of Cairns	−3.7	−39.6	−3.2	−34.1	0.6	6.2
Total		**90.3**		**75.6**		**703.7**

Source: Adapted from Brown and Stern (2001: 277–78).

It is evident in Table 5.A.7 that the welfare effects of removing the services barriers are sizable and that they vary markedly across countries. For the industrialized countries in Scenario A with perfect international capital mobility, the largest increases are for Canada, $84.0 billion (14.8 per cent of GNP), the European Union (EU), $42.4 billion (0.5 per cent of GNP), and the United States, $35.0 billion (0.5 per cent of GNP). Because it loses capital, Japan has a decline of $103.7 billion (2.0 per cent of GNP). Among the developing countries, the largest increases are for Indonesia, $30.8 billion (15.6 per cent of GNP), China, $26.9 billion (3.8 per cent of GNP), and Taiwan, $20.7 billion, $7.6 per cent of GNP). It is also evident that there are declines in welfare for a number of developing countries, in particular, Korea, Thailand, Chile, Mexico, and the Rest of Cairns Group. What is reflected in the results is that welfare is affected by whether or not a country attracts or loses capital as a result of services liberalization. Countries that lose capital become "smaller" in the economic sense of the word. As the economy contracts, surviving firms produce less than before. The fall in firm output generally occurs in order to avoid a large loss in variety of domestically produced goods. The subsequent economy-wide reduction in scale economies is usually the source of the welfare loss.

The results in Scenario A are sensitive to the assumption of perfect capital mobility. As noted above, countries that import capital are assumed to pay a risk premium that is a function of capital imports. The elasticity of the risk premium with respect to the volume of capital imports can be set exogenously in the model. Thus, in Scenario B, Brown and Stern assume that capital imports that result in a 1 per cent increase in the capital stock generate an interest-rate risk premium of 0.1 per cent. That is, the risk-premium elasticity is 0.1 per cent. It is apparent from the results for Scenario B in Table 5.A.7 that the introduction of a risk premium that reflects a decrease in international capital mobility has the effect of reducing the welfare effects of services liberalization as compared to Scenario A, in which there was perfect capital mobility.

In both Scenarios A and B, there is a rise in the real return to capital. Therefore, it is likely that, over time, there will be an increase in the world's capital stock as savers and investors respond to the increased incentive to accumulate capital. To take this into account, in Scenario C, with the risk premium elasticity remaining at 0.1 per cent, Brown and Stern allow for an increase in the world's capital stock by 3 per cent. This is the amount necessary to hold the real return to capital equal to the level in the base period. As can be seen in Table 5.A.7, the welfare effects of services liberalization are now positive for all of the countries shown. For the world as a whole, welfare rises by $703.7 billion. Canada's welfare increases by $85.0 billion (14.9 per cent of GNP), the EU by $202.4 billion (2.5 per cent of GNP), and the United States, $222.5 billion (3.1 per cent of GNP). There are also sizable absolute and percentage increases for the developing countries, in particular China, Indonesia, Taiwan, and Hong Kong. It is further note-worthy that welfare increases for all of the countries/regions shown.

It is evident accordingly that these welfare effects associated with an increase in the world's capital stock in response to an increase in the rate of return to capital are consid-erably larger than what is commonly seen in CGE models in which capital is assumed to be internationally immobile.[24] This may not be surprising because it has been apparent from previous CGE analyses of trade liberalization that have made allowance for international capital flows that the largest welfare gains stem from these flows rather than from the removal of tariffs and other trade barriers that distort consumer choice in goods trade.[25]

The understanding of the consequences of liberalizing services barriers thus is enhanced when allowance is made for the behavior of multinational firms whose foreign affiliates are already located in or attracted to host countries. When services liberaliza-tion occurs and the real return to capital is increased, so that there are FDI (Mode 3)

[24] Compare, for example, the results of the Michigan Model reported in Brown et al. (2003).
[25] See Brown et al. (1992) and Dee and Hanslow (2001).

international capital flows and the world capital stock expands, most countries stand to gain significantly in terms of economic welfare.

References

Anderson, J. E. 1979. "A Theoretical Foundation for the Gravity Equation," *American Economic Review* 69: 106–16.

Bosworth, M., C. Findlay, R. Trewin, and T. Warren. 2000. "Price-impact Measures of Impediments to Services Trade," in C. Findlay and T. Warren (eds.), *Impediments to Trade in Services: Measurement and Policy Implications*. London and New York: Routledge.

Boylaud, O. and G. Nicoletti. 2000. "Regulation, Market Structure and Performance in Telecommunications," Working Paper No. 237ECO/WKP (2000), 10, Economics Department, OECD, Paris, April 12.

Brown, D. and R. M. Stern. 2001. "Measurement and Modeling of the Economic Effects of Trade and Investment Barriers in Services," *Review of International Economics* 9: 262–86.

Brown, D. K., A. V. Deardorff, and R. M. Stern. 1992. "Estimates of a North American Free Trade Agreement: Analytical Issues and a Computational Assessment," *The World Economy* 15(1): 11–29.

—— —— —— 2003. "Multilateral, Regional, and Bilateral Trade-Policy Options for the United States and Japan," *The World Economy* 26(6): 803–28.

Colecchia, A. 2000. "Measuring Barriers to Market Access for Services: A Pilot Study on Accountancy Services," in C. Findlay and T. Warren (eds.), *Impediments to Trade in Services: Measurement and Policy Implications*. London and New York: Routledge.

Deardorff, A. V. 1998. "Determinants of Bilateral Trade: Does Gravity Work in a Neoclassical World?" in Jeffrey A. Frankel (ed.), *The Regionalization of the World Economy*. Chicago: University of Chicago Press.

—— and R. M. Stern. 1998. *Measurement of Nontariff Barriers*. Ann Arbor: University of Michigan Press.

Dee, P. 2005. "A Compendium of Barriers to Services Trade," World Bank, unpublished.

—— and M. Ferrantino (eds.) 2005. *Quantitative Methods for Assession, the Effects of Non-tariff Measures and Trade Facilitation*. Singapore: World Scientific.

—— and K. Hanslow. 2001. "Multilateral Liberalization of Services Trade," in R. M. Stern (ed.), *Services in the International Economy*. Ann Arbor: University of Michigan Press.

Dee, Philippa, Alexis Hardin, and Leanne Holmes. 2000. "Issues in the Application of CGE Models to Services Trade Liberalization," in C. Findlay and T. Warren (eds.), *Impediments to Trade in Services: Measurement and Policy Implications*. London and New York: Routledge.

Disclosure. 1998. *Global Researcher—Worldscope Database*. Bethesda, M.D.: Disclosure.

Doove, S., O. Gaabbitas, D. Nguyen-Hong, and J. Owen. 2001. "Price Effects of Regulation: Telecommunications, Air Passenger Transport and Electricity Supply," Productivity Commission Staff Research Paper, AusInfo, Canberra (October).

Fink, C., A. Mattoo, and I. C. Neagu. 2002. "Trade in International Maritime Services: How Much Does Policy Matter?" *World Bank Economic Review* 16: 81–108.

—— ——, and R. Rathindran. 2003. "An Assessment of Telecommunications Reform in Developing Countries," *Information Economics and Policy* 15: 443–66.

François, J. 1999. "Estimates of Barriers to Trade in Services," Erasmus University, unpublished manuscript.

Gonenc, R. and G. Nicoletti. 2001. "Regulation, Market Structure and Performance in Air Passenger Transportation," OECD Economic Studies, No. 32, OECD, Paris.

Hardin, A. and L. Holmes. 1997. *Services Trade and Foreign Direct Investment.* Staff Research Paper, Industry Commission. Canberra: Australian Government Publishing Services.

Hoekman, B. 1995, 1996. "Assessing the General Agreement on Trade in Services," in W. Martin and L. A. Winters (eds.), *The Uruguay Round and the Developing Countries*, World Bank Discussion Paper No. 307. Washington, D.C.: The World Bank. (Revised version published in W. Martin and L. A. Winters (eds.), Cambridge University Press, 1996).

—— 2000. "The Next Round of Services Negotiations: Identifying Priorities and Options," *Federal Reserve Bank of St. Louis Review* 82: 31–47.

—— and C. A. Primo Braga. 1997. "Protection and Trade in Services: A Survey," *Open Economies Review* 8: 285–308.

Holmes, L. and A. Hardin. 2000. "Assessing Barriers to Services Sector Investment," in C. Findlay and T. Warren (eds.), *Impediments to Trade in Services: Measurement and Policy Implications.* London and New York: Routledge.

Johnson, M., T. Gregan, G. Gentle, and P. Belin. 2000. "Modeling the Benefits of Increasing Competition in International Air Services," in C. Findlay and T. Warren (eds.), *Impediments to Trade in Services: Measurement and Policy Implications.* London and New York: Routledge.

Kalirajan, K. 2000. "Restrictions on Trade in Distribution Services," Productivity Commission Staff Research Paper, AusInfo, Canberra (August).

—— G. McGuire, D. Nguyen-Hong, and M. Schuele. 2000. "The Price Impact of Restrictions on Banking Services," in C. Findlay and T. Warren (eds.), *Impediments to Trade in Services: Measurement and Policy Implications.* London and New York: Routledge.

Kang, J-S. 2000. "Price Impact of Restrictions on Maritime Transport Services," in C. Findlay and T. Warren (eds.), *Impediments to Trade in Services: Measurement and Policy Implications.* London and New York: Routledge.

Karsenty, G. 2000. "Just How Big Are the Stakes? An Assessment of Trade in Services by Mode of Supply," in P. Sauvé and R. M. Stern (eds.), *Services 2000: New Directions in Services Trade Liberalization.* Washington, D.C.: Brookings Institution.

Kemp, S. 2000. "Trade in Education Services and the Impacts of Barriers on Trade," in C. Findlay and T. Warren (eds.), *Impediments to Trade in Services: Measurement and Policy Implications.* London and New York: Routledge.

McGuire, G. 1998. *Australia's Restrictions on Trade in Financial Services.* Staff Research Paper, Productivity Commission, Canberra.

—— and M. Schuele. 2000. "Restrictiveness of International Trade in Banking Services," in C. Findlay and T. Warren (eds.), *Impediments to Trade in Services: Measurement and Policy Implications.* London and New York: Routledge.

McGuire, G., M. Schuele and T. Smith. 2000.. "Restrictiveness of International Trade in Maritime Services," in C. Findlay and T. Warren (eds.), *Impediments to Trade in Services: Measurement and Policy Implication*. London and New York: Routledge.

Marko, M. 1998. "An Evaluation of the Basic Telecommunications Services Agreement," CIES Policy Discussion Paper 98/09, Centre for International Economic Studies, University of Adelaide.

Mattoo, A. 1998. "Financial Services and the WTO: Liberalization in the Developing and Transition Economies," for presentation at the Workshop, "Measuring Impediments to Trade in Services," Productivity Commission, Canberra, April 30–May 1, 1998.

Nguyen-Hong, D. 2000. "Restrictions on Trade in Professional Services," Productivity Commission, Staff Research Paper, AusInfo, Canberra, (August).

Nicoletti, G., S. Scarpetta, and O. Boylaud. 2000. "Summary Indicators of Product Market Regulation with an Extension to Employment Protection Legislation," Working Paper No. 226, Economics Department, ECO/WKP(99)18, OECD, Paris, April 13 (revised).

PECC (Pacific Economic Cooperation Council). 1995. *Survey of Impediments to Trade and Investment in the APEC Region*. Singapore: PECC.

Steiner, F. 2000. "Regulation, Industry Structure and Performance in the Electricity Supply Industry," Working Paper No. 238, ECO/WKP (2000), Economics Department, OECD, Paris, April 12.

Stern, R. M. 2002. "Quantifying Barriers to Trade in Services," in B. Hoekman, A. Mattoo, and P. English (eds.) *Development, Trade, and the WTO: A Handbook*. Washington, D.C: The World Bank.

Trewin, R. 2000. "A Price-Impact Measure of Impediments to Trade in Telecommunications Services," in C. Findlay and T. Warren (eds.), *Impediments to Trade in Services: Measurement and Policy Implications*. London and New York: Routledge.

UNCTAD (United Nations Conference on Trade and Development). 1996. *World Investment Report 1996: Investment, Trade and International Policy Arrangements*. New York and Geneva: UNCTAD.

Verikios, G. and X.-g. Zhang. 2001. "Global Gains from Liberalizing Trade in Telecommunications and Financial Services," Productivity Commission Staff Research Paper, AusInfo, Canberra (October).

Warren, T. 2000a. The Identification of Impediments to Trade and Investment in Telecommunications Services," in C. Findlay and T. Warren (eds.), *Impediments to Trade in Services: Measurement and Policy Implications*. London and New York: Routledge.

—— 2000b. "The Impact on Output of Impediments to Trade and Investment in Telecommunications Services," in C. Findlay and T. Warren (eds.), *Impediments to Trade in Services: Measurement and Policy Implications*. London and New York: Routledge.

—— and C. Findlay. 2000. "How Significant Are the Barriers? Measuring Impediments to Trade in Services," in P. Sauvé and R. M. Stern (eds.), *Services 2000: New Directions in Services Trade Liberalization*. Washington, D.C.: Brookings Institution.

Whalley, J. 2004. "Assessing the Benefits to Developing Countries of Liberalization in Services Trade," *The World Economy* 27(8): 1123–53.

6 Regionalism in Services Trade

Aaditya Mattoo and Pierre Sauvé[1]

Introduction

There is a large literature on the costs and benefits of integration agreements on trade in goods, but hardly any analysis of the implications of such agreements in services. Such a gap is surprising given the strong growth witnessed in the last decade and a half in the number of regional trade agreements featuring detailed disciplines on trade and investment in services. The recent proliferation of trade agreements covering services is evidence of heightened policy interest in the contribution of efficient service sectors to economic development and a growing appreciation of the gains likely to flow from the progressive dismantling of impediments to trade and investment in services.

Regional attempts at developing trade rules for services have paralleled efforts at framing similar disciplines in the WTO, under the aegis of the GATS. Because they have typically been negotiated in a concurrent fashion, regional and multilateral efforts at services rule-making have tended to be closely intertwined processes, with much iterative learning by doing, imitation, and reverse engineering. Experience gained in developing the services provisions of regional trade agreements (RTAs) has built up negotiating capacity in participating countries, providing expertise available for deployment in a multilateral setting. Since the GATS itself remains incomplete, with negotiations pending in a number of key areas (e.g. emergency safeguards, subsidies, government procurement, domestic regulation), regional experimentation has generated a number of useful policy lessons in comparative negotiating and rule-making dynamics.

The efforts that countries have devoted to developing rules governing the process of services-trade liberalization at the regional level have typically come in the wake of far reaching changes in many countries' services and investment policy frameworks over the last decade. For many countries, regional negotiations offer the opportunity to pursue, deepen or lock in some (or much) of the policy reforms put in place domestically in

[1] The authors are grateful to E. Philip English and Gianni Zanini for their guidance throughout this project and to Carsten Fink and other colleagues at the World Bank for helpful comments and discussions on the first draft of this chapter.

recent years and to reap the benefits, notably in terms of improved investment climates, likely to flow from such policy consolidation.

This chapter aims to take stock of the more recent wave of RTAs with a view to informing some of the policy choices developing countries will typically confront in negotiating regional regimes for services trade and investment. While a country's choice of integration strategy will in most instances be dictated by political considerations, there remains a need for a careful assessment of the economic benefits and costs of alternative approaches to services liberalization.

The chapter focuses on three core issues. The first sub-section considers the economics of regional integration in services, asking whether services trade differs sufficiently from trade in goods as to require different policy instruments and approaches in the context of preferential liberalization. Also discussed is whether and how RTAs may allow deeper forms of regulatory cooperation to occur. It highlights the importance for third countries of multilateral disciplines on regional agreements and the criteria for regional agreements not to be detrimental to non-members.

The second section addresses the political economy of regionalism in services trade, identifying a number of lessons arising from the practice of preferential liberalization in services. Based on a comparison of the GATS and a sample of 25 RTAs featuring services provisions, it is asked whether and how regional approaches to services trade and investment liberalization differ from the GATS, both in terms of market access (liberalization) and rule design. It also asks whether such differences matter in policy terms.

The third section addresses the legal dimension of this policy interface, focusing on a number of issues of rule design, including the strengths and weaknesses of existing multilateral disciplines on regional approaches to services trade and investment liberalization. The section briefly summarizes the major provisions of Article V (Economic Integration) of the GATS, which governs the relationship between RTAs and the WTO system (in a manner analogous to Article 24 of GATT for trade in goods) and discusses the extent to which its disciplines are likely to allow third countries to object to provisions in proposed agreements that are detrimental to their interests. Where relevant, GATS provisions are contrasted with those of Article 24 of GATT, and the experience to date of Working Parties that have investigated the compatibility of customs unions and free trade areas with GATT rules.

Each section is prefaced with a summary of key findings. The chapter concludes with a brief discussion of issue areas that parties to prospective RTAs in services will likely need to confront and seek novel solutions to in advancing the process of services liberalization and rule making at the regional level.

In the first addendum to this chapter, Carsten Fink discusses liberalizing trade in the ASEAN region, and Sherry Stephenson discusses liberalization in the Latin American region.

Preferential Liberalization of Services Trade: Economic Considerations[2]

KEY FINDINGS

- The analysis of preferential agreements in services trade requires an extension of conventional trade theory in two ways, both of which relate to core-distinguishing features of services: first, the manner in which trade in services occurs and, second, the form that trade protection takes in the sector.

- A common effect of many restrictive measures in services trade is to increase the variable costs of operation faced by foreign providers without necessarily generating equivalent rents. Under such circumstances, which characterize much of services trade (given the regulatory nature of impediments), there may be little or no cost to granting preferential access because there is little or no revenue to lose. In such circumstances, preferential liberalization will necessarily be welfare-enhancing. However, countries outside the preferential arrangement may lose.

- A country is likely to benefit from eliminating, even on a preferential basis, any excessive fixed costs of entry by removing unnecessary or needlessly burdensome qualification, licensing and local establishment requirements. The presumption that a country will benefit from such initiatives is greater if agreements are not exclusionary but rather open to all parties able to satisfy the regulatory requirements maintained within the integrating area. The greatest benefits arise if recognition agreements include all countries that have comparable regulation.

- Allowing limited new entry by foreign firms, irrespective of whether this is done preferentially or on an MFN treatment basis, may not necessarily be welfare enhancing. The main reason is that even though consumers may benefit from the increased level of competition, such a gain may be offset by the transfer of rents from domestic to foreign oligopolists.

- Absent liberal rules of origin on investment, the establishment of preferences may result in entry by inferior suppliers. Because the most efficient suppliers may also generate the greatest positive externalities, the downside risks of preferential liberalization may be greater—especially in crucial infrastructural services.

- Location-specific sunk costs are arguably higher in a number of service sectors in which suppliers need to establish a presence close to consumers. One consequence is that preferential liberalization may exert more durable effects on the nature of competition than in the case of goods. For instance, concluding an agreement that allows second-best

---

[2] This section draws on work by Mattoo and Fink (2002) and Hoekman and Sauvé (1994).

providers to obtain a first-mover advantages may imply that a country could be stuck with such providers even if it subsequently liberalizes on an MFN basis.

- "South-South" RTAs covering services can be looked at as a variant of the infant-industry argument. Exposure to competition first in the more sheltered confines of a regional market may help firms prepare for global competition. Firms that have gained competitiveness at the regional level may also be less likely to resist broader-based liberalization. The risk does exist, however, that regional liberalization might create a new constellation of vested interests that could resist further market opening. The GATS offers a way out of this dilemma by allowing Member countries to pre-commit to future multilateral liberalization, signaling a time-frame over which regional preferences may be progressively eroded and/or eliminated.

- The gains from preferential agreements are likely to be significant in areas where there is scope for more fully reaping economies of scale. In principle, these gains can also be reaped through MFN liberalization, but in practice the full integration of markets may require a deeper convergence of regulatory regimes. Regulatory cooperation may be more desirable—and likely more feasible—among a subset of countries than if pursued on a global scale.

- If national standards are not optimal or insufficiently developed, then regional and/or international harmonization or standardization can be a way of improving such standards. In such situations, the best partners for regulatory cooperation are likely to be those with the soundest regulatory frameworks. Such partners may not always be found within regional compacts.

- There are gains from regulatory cooperation but also costs. The former will dominate where national regulation can be improved. The costs are likely to be smallest when foreign regulatory preferences are similar and regulatory institutions are broadly compatible.

- Whether an individual country benefits from regulatory convergence or harmonization, its willingness to participate in such an area may depend on where the standard is set, the level at which it is set, and the regulatory environment to which such a standard responds.

While the economic effects of preferential tariff arrangements are generally well under-stood (see Box 6.1) and form the core of conventional trade theory, such is hardly the case of services. The analysis of preferential agreements in services trade requires an extension of conventional trade theory in two ways, both of which relate to core distinguishing features of services: first, the manner in which trade in services occurs and, second, the form that trade protection takes in the sector.

Since services trade often requires proximity between the supplier and the consumer, we need to consider preferences extended not just to cross-border trade, but also to foreign direct investment (FDI) and foreign individual service providers. Moreover, preferential

---

Box 6.1. The Standard Economics of Preferences

The conventional analysis of regional agreements focuses on goods trade and emphasizes two main types of effects.[3] The first are "trade and location" effects. The preferential reduction in tariffs within a regional agreement will induce purchasers to switch demand towards supply from partner countries, at the expense of both domestic production and imports from non-members. This is trade creation and trade diversion. The former is beneficial, but the latter may be costly. In particular, governments will lose tariff revenue, and the overall effect on national income may be positive or negative, depending on the costs of alternative sources of supply and on trade policy towards non-member countries.

Furthermore, changes in trade flows induce changes in the location of production between member countries of a regional agreement. These relocations are determined by the comparative advantage of member countries, and by agglomeration or clustering effects. In some circumstances, they can be a force for convergence of income levels between countries. For example, labor-intensive production activities may move towards lower-wage countries, raising wages there. In other circumstances they can be a force for divergence, for instance if industry is pulled towards a country with a head start or some natural advantage. This may drive up incomes in the country attracting new production while other countries lag.

The second source of economic change induced by preferences in goods trade relates to "scale and competition" effects. The removal of trade barriers can be likened to a market enlargement, as separate national markets move towards integration into a bigger, regional, market. Such expansion allows firms to take advantage of greater scale, and attracts investment projects for which market size is a central determinant. Removing barriers also induces heightened intra-firm competition, possibly inducing them to make efficiency-enhancing improvements. In sum, enlarging the market shifts the trade-off between scale and competition, making it possible to have both larger firms and more competition.

Source: Adapted from World Bank (2000).

---

treatment in services is granted not through tariffs but through discriminatory restrictions on the movement of labor and capital (e.g. in terms of the quantity or share of foreign ownership), and a variety of domestic regulations, such as technical standards, licensing and qualification requirements.

Given such differences, can one say that trade in services differs enough from trade in goods that we need to modify the conclusions reached so far as regards the economic effects of preferential liberalization? In particular, what would happen if a country liberalized services trade faster in the regional context than at the multilateral level? To answer such questions, we need to look at the various sources of trade preferences arising in services trade and determine whether and how their economic effects differ from those observed for goods trade.

SOURCES OF PREFERENTIAL TREATMENT IN SERVICES TRADE

The manner in which privileged access can be granted in services markets depends on the instrument of protection in use. By imposing a quantitative restriction on services output

---

[3] This discussion draws on World Bank (2000). See Panagariya (2000) for a cogent review of the economics of preferential trade agreements.

or on the number of service providers, a country can allocate a larger proportion of the quota to a preferred source. Examples of the former abound in air, land and maritime transport, where countries often allocate freight and passenger quotas on a preferential basis, and in audiovisual services, where preferential quotas exist on airtime allocated to foreign broadcasts. Examples of the latter include restrictions on the number of telecommunications operators, banks or professionals that may be allowed to operate.

Another common means of restricting access to service markets that lends itself to preferential treatment concerns limitations on foreign ownership, on the type of allowed legal entity, on branching rights, etc. While most host country governments provide foreign investors with post-establishment national treatment, such treatment rarely applies in the pre-establishment phase. This allows host countries to impose a range of performance requirements on foreign services providers, for instance in terms of training or employment in managerial level positions. These can easily be waived for members of a preferential arrangement.

Preferences can also be granted through taxes and subsidies. Foreign providers can be subject to different taxes and may be denied access to certain subsidy programs. Again, these forms of discrimination can be waived selectively, as is the case, for example, in co-production agreements in audiovisual services.

Another much practiced form of preferential treatment occurs through domestic regulations pertaining to technical regulations, licensing and qualification requirements. Countries can and do impose qualification and licensing requirements on foreign providers that may be more burdensome than necessary to satisfy otherwise legitimate public policy objectives. Where these are waived selectively in favor of members of an RTA, and denied to others who would otherwise qualify for the benefits, de facto preferences result. While regulatory preferences may arise in all sectors, they are especially prevalent in professional and financial services, where domestic regulatory requirements and licensing regimes respond to information asymmetries.

MEASURES AFFECTING VARIABLE COSTS

A common effect of many restrictive measures in services trade is to increase the variable costs of operation faced by foreign providers without necessarily generating equivalent rents. In such cases, the analysis of discriminatory regulation can proceed in a manner analogous to tariffs. When tariffs are the instruments of protection, the costs of trade diversion can be an important disincentive to concluding preferential liberalization agreements. Despite the increase in consumer surplus from any liberalization, there may still be an aversion to such agreements because the displacement of high tariff imports from third countries by low or zero-tariff imports from preferential sources implies lost revenue.

The situation may differ when the protectionist instrument is a regulatory barrier that imposes a cost on the exporter without necessarily yielding a corresponding revenue for the government or any other domestic entity. Under such circumstances, which characterize much of services trade (given the regulatory nature of impediments), there may be little or no cost to granting preferential access because there is little or no revenue to lose.[4] In such circumstances, preferential liberalization will necessarily be welfare-enhancing.

However, countries outside the preferential arrangement may lose. Exemption from a needlessly burdensome regulation implies reduced costs for a class of suppliers and hence a decline in prices in the importing countries. This decline in prices may hurt third-country suppliers who may suffer reduced sales and a decline in producer surplus.

The analysis of discriminatory regulation is also relevant to quantitative restrictions on the sale of services. In the case of goods, the quota rents can be appropriated by domestic intermediaries like the importer rather than the foreign exporter. However, in many services, intermediation is difficult because the service is not always storable and directly supplied by producers to consumers. Rents are, therefore, usually appropriated by exporters rather than domestic importers. As in the case of frictional measures that increase variable costs, there is typically no cost of trade diversion to the preference-granting country.

The main policy implication one can draw from the above discussion is that where a country maintains regulations that impose a cost on foreign providers, without generating any benefit (such as improved quality) or revenue for the government or other domestic entities, welfare would necessarily be enhanced by preferential liberalization. However, it bears noting that non-preferential liberalization would yield an even greater increase in welfare, both nationally and globally, because the service would then be supplied by the most efficient providers.

MEASURES AFFECTING FIXED COSTS

A number of measures that countries maintain can have the effect of increasing the fixed costs of entry or establishment in services markets. Examples include requirements to establish a local presence, license fees for entry into the market, or the need to re-qualify for purposes of providing professional services. As with measures affecting variable costs, a country is likely to benefit from eliminating, even on a preferential basis, any excessive fixed costs of entry by removing unnecessary or needlessly burdensome qualification, licensing and local establishment requirements in professional and financial services.

Regardless of the chosen partners, the presumption that a country will benefit from such initiatives is greater if agreements are not exclusionary but rather open to all parties

---

[4] It should be noted, however, that there may be sectors where new entry pursuant to preferential liberalization may have implications for government revenue, such as in the case of public telecommunications operators.

able to satisfy the regulatory requirements maintained within the integrating area. The greatest benefits arise if recognition agreements include all countries that have comparable regulation. The benefits in such instances come from both increased competition and greater diversity of services.

MEASURES RESTRICTING THE NUMBER OF SERVICE PROVIDERS

The norm in many service industries is for the quantum (level) of competition to be restricted by government regulation. There may be legitimate reasons to do so, such as the existence of significant economies of scale or in industry segments characterized by natural monopoly features (the case of a number of network-based industries in energy, water distribution or transportation/railways). In such circumstances, the question of the manner in which entry is allowed—by mergers and acquisitions or through green-field (i.e. *de novo*) investments, can assume considerable significance.

Interestingly, allowing limited new entry by foreign firms, irrespective of whether this is done preferentially or on a most-favored-nation (MFN) treatment basis, may not be welfare-enhancing. The main reason is that even though consumers may benefit from the increased level of competition, such a gain may be offset by the transfer of rents from domestic to foreign oligopolists.

Restrictions on de novo entry are often imposed with a view to channeling new foreign capital into weak or undercapitalized domestic financial institutions (a common occurrence in financial services for example) to help the restructuring process in the context of progressive liberalization. The above considerations may affect the preferred mode of entry: entry, that is, through acquisition implies less competition than greenfield entry, but it allows domestic firms to extract some rents through the disposal of their assets.

Liberalization tends to generate gains when all barriers to entry are removed.[5] But if only limited entry is allowed, then open, non-discriminatory access—for instance through the global auctioning of licenses—would predominate preferential access, which cannot guarantee that preferential (i.e. insider) investors will be the most efficient ones. Absent liberal rules of origin on investment, the establishment of preferences may indeed result in entry by inferior suppliers.[6] Because the most efficient suppliers (in terms of costs and/or quality) may also generate the greatest positive externalities (including the dynamic learning properties associated with knowledge flows and the associated rise of total factor productivity), the downside risks of preferential liberalization may be greater. The ability of non-preferential liberalization

---

[5] However, the existence of significant economies of scale implies that free entry may not lead to socially optimal outcomes (Tirole, 1998).

[6] Much recent emphasis has been laid in the growth literature on the scope for trade and especially FDI to promote knowledge flows between countries (see Coe et al., 1997, and Lumenga-Neso et al., 2001).

to more readily secure access to the most efficient suppliers of services is a matter of some importance given the crucial infrastructural role many services perform and the strong influence such intermediate inputs can exert on economy-wide performance.

Preferential liberalization of entry barriers may also bring higher prices for consumers, lower takeover prices for domestic assets or lower license fees for the government (by limiting the pool of potential buyers). These concerns are likely to be compounded in concentrated markets, a common occurrence in many service industries in the developing world.

SUNK COSTS AND THE SEQUENCE OF LIBERALIZATION

Sunk costs are important in goods and services industries alike. However, location-specific sunk costs—those incurred in supplying a particular market—are arguably higher in a number of service sectors to the extent that their provision requires proximity between suppliers and consumers. One consequence (which is closely related to the above discussion on barriers to new entrants) is that preferential liberalization may exert more durable effects on the nature of competition than in the case of goods. For instance, concluding an agreement that allows inferior providers to establish may mean that a country could be stuck with such providers even if it subsequently liberalizes on an MFN basis.

Sunk costs matter because they have commitment value and can be used strategically by first movers to deter new entrants (Tirole, 1998). A firm that establishes a telecommunications or transport network signals that it will be around tomorrow if it cannot easily dispose of its assets. The commitment value is stronger the more slowly capital depreciates and the more firm-specific it is.

Firms allowed early entry into such types of markets may accumulate a quantity of capital sufficient to limit the entry of new rivals. Such incumbency effects may be stronger in services with network externalities, such as telecommunications, where new entrants must match the technical standards of the incumbent (standards that the latter may have also played a large part in defining). The incumbent may also succeed in assuring itself of the services of the best franchisees by selecting them early on and imposing exclusivity arrangements on them. Each of these forms of capital accumulation enhances first-mover advantages and allows the established firm(s) to prevent, restrict or retard competition.

Because of the importance of sunk costs in many service industries, sequential entry (which preferential liberalization with restrictive rules of origin may entail) can produce very different results from simultaneous entry. If entry is costly, an incumbent may be able to completely deter entry, leading to greater market concentration.

Second, and perhaps more important, the first-mover advantage may be conferred on an inferior supplier. The latter may naturally use such advantages to establish a position of market dominance, insulated from more efficient third-country competitors. How durable such a position may be in practice will depend on the importance of sunk costs relative to differences in price and quality.

Two important qualifications to the above reasoning can nonetheless be made. First, subsequent entry by a more efficient firm can take place through the acquisition route, thus circumventing some of the problems linked to first-mover advantages. This has notably been the experience of a number of countries in the financial sector, especially those where first movers may have overbid or sunk excessive costs in setting up their operations in the early stages of liberalization. Second, in certain service sectors, firms could learn by doing: the experience acquired by established operators during a previous period may reduce their current costs, enhancing their profitability and discouraging others from entering.[7] Caveats aside, a country needs to carefully evaluate not just the static costs of granting preferential access to a particular partner country, but also how the eventual benefits from multilateral liberalization are likely to be affected.

STATIC AND DYNAMIC ECONOMIES OF SCALE

Combining of services markets through a regional integration agreement can lead to gains arising from a combination of scale effects and changes in the intensity of competition. In a market of a given size, there is a trade-off between scale economies and competition: if firms are larger, there are fewer of them and the market is less competitive. Enlarging the market shifts this trade-off, as it becomes possible to have both larger firms and more competition (World Bank, 2000).

Regional liberalization can also act as an inducement to FDI. Apart from changing the organization of local industry, if regional agreements create large markets and do not impose stringent ownership-related rules of origin, they may also assist in attracting foreign investment when economies of scale matter. For example, a foreign transport service provider might not find it worthwhile to establish in Latin America if each country market were segmented, but might find Latin America attractive with a continent-wide integrated market.

One rationale for RTAs covering services is a variant of dynamic economies of scale or the infant-industry argument. "South-South" RTAs, in particular, are seen as a form of gradual liberalization. Exposure to competition first in the more sheltered confines of a regional market may help firms prepare for global competition. This approach improves on traditional infant-industry protection because some degree of international competition is fostered as a result of the integration process. There is also the possibility that firms that have gained competitiveness at the regional level are less likely to resist broader-based liberalization. They may even champion subsequent MFN liberalization as they begin to

---

[7] In such circumstances, entry deterrence may actually promote welfare.

reap the benefits of open markets and run up against the constraints of a regional market. In this sense, RTAs can be seen as "building blocks" towards multilateral liberalization (Bhagwati, 1990; Lawrence, 1991). The risk does exist, however, that regional liberalization might create a new constellation of vested interests that could resist further market opening, raising the concern that regionalism can become a "stumbling block" to further multilateral liberalization. The GATS offers a way out of this dilemma by allowing Member countries to pre-commit to future multilateral liberalization, signaling a time frame over which regional preferences may be progressively eroded and/or eliminated.

REGIONALISM AND REGULATORY COOPERATION

The gains from preferential agreements are likely to be significant in areas where there is scope for more fully reaping economies of scale, as in certain international transport and financial services, and for securing increased competition, as in business or professional services. In principle, these gains can also be reaped through MFN liberalization, but in practice the full integration of markets may require a deeper convergence of regulatory regimes. Such convergence might well be more feasible in a regional context, for instance when "proximity" (be it geographic or in terms of income levels or legal traditions) implies greater pre-integration institutional ties and regulatory dialogue. The regulatory intensity of services trade make it necessary to consider whether and how regional trade agreements can be conduits for trade- and investment-facilitating convergence in domestic regulatory practices. Simply put, under what circumstances is a country more likely to benefit from cooperation in a plurilateral or regional forum than in a multilateral one?

ADDRESSING THE REGULATORY INTENSITY OF SERVICES TRADE

The economic case for regulation in services arises essentially from market failure attributable to four kinds of problems: (1) asymmetric information (especially in knowledge-intensive industries, such as financial or professional services); (2) externalities (tourism, transport, water distribution); and (3) natural monopoly/oligopolies (especially in network-based services where access to essential facilities is a critical ingredient).

In the first two cases, national remedial problems can themselves become an impediment to trade if domestic regulatory requirements are needlessly burdensome or framed with a view to tilt competitive conditions in favor of domestic suppliers.

The institution of some variant of a necessity test in services agreements (the purpose of which, as in goods trade, is to ensure some broad measure of proportionality between regulatory objectives and the means of pursuing them), together with strengthened disciplines on transparency, would enable exporters to challenge needlessly burdensome regulatory impediments abroad.[8] Doing so would help to ensure that domestic regulations serve legitimate objectives rather than mask protectionist interests, and hence create benefits for domestic consumers/users of services.

In the third case (natural monopoly/oligopoly), it is the absence of regulation (typically pro-competitive regulation) that can lead to trade problems and directly inhibit and or nullify negotiated market access. As negotiations in basic telecommunications services have shown already, international rules on access to essential facilities and on means of ensuring that dominant suppliers do not abuse their market advantages to deter entry and stifle competition, can provide significant benefits to consumers and users of telecommunications services.

In order to ensure that domestic regulations at home and abroad support trade, a country must decide on the appropriate forum (multilateral, regional, bilateral) and the approach (international rules or standards, mutual recognition or harmonization) to pursue in individual service sectors.[9]

International rules can do little to address impediments to trade arising from fundamental differences across countries in regulatory standards. In such circumstances, two approaches can be envisaged: harmonization and mutual recognition. Even though these approaches are often presented as alternatives, the former tends to be either a precondition or a result of the latter. Where differences in mandatory quality standards matter, mutual recognition may be feasible only when there is a certain degree of prior harmonization of mutually acceptable minimum standards. A similar logic applies to compatibility standards, though there may be no alternative to full harmonization if differences matter, as for instance in the case of road-safety standards, railway gauges or legal procedures.

Regulatory cooperation may be more desirable—and likely more feasible—among a subset of countries than if pursued on a global scale. However, there is little, if any, empirical guidance on the payoffs to regulatory cooperation. What are the costs and benefits of deeper harmonization of regulatory standards and/or the establishment of mutual recognition agreements? The lack of empirical evidence complicates the task of deciding on the scope and depth, as well as the geographical reach and the optimal institutional forms, of regulatory cooperation.

If national standards are not optimal or insufficiently developed, then regional and/or international harmonization or standardization can be a way of improving such standards, as has happened in the financial services field with the Basle accord on capital

---

[8] See the papers by Keyia Iida and Julia Nielson, David Leebron, and Joel Trachtman in Mattoo and Sauvé (2003) for a fuller discussion of strengthened disciplines on transparency and some of the policy challenges flowing from the adoption of a necessity test for services trade.

[9] For a fuller discussion of the challenges arising at the interface of domestic regulatory sovereignty and services trade liberalization, see Mattoo and Sauvé (2003).

adequacy. In such situations, the best partners for regulatory cooperation are likely to be those with the soundest regulatory frameworks. Such partners may not always be found within regional compacts. Moreover, the standard-setting process can at times be captured by protectionist interests, in which case convergence around "best" regulatory practice can serve a useful liberalizing purpose.

There are gains from regulatory cooperation but also costs. The former will dominate where national regulation can be improved. The aggregate adjustment cost of regulatory convergence depends on the level of differences between the policy-related standards of the countries involved in an integration area. The costs are likely to be smallest when foreign regulatory preferences are similar and regulatory institutions are broadly compatible. The benefits of eliminating policy differences through harmonization depend on the prospects of creating a truly integrated market, which depends on the "natural distance" between countries, and that in turn depends on levels of development, physical distance, legal systems, language, etc.

If national standards optimally serve national objectives, there is a trade-off between the gains from integrated markets and the costs of transition and of departing from optimal domestic standards. For instance, a poor country may prefer to maintain a low mandatory standard for certain services because that reflects the socially optimal trade-off between price, quality and implementation capacities whereas the socially optimal trade-off in a rich country may lead to the adoption of—and a preference for—a higher standard. Under such circumstances, a harmonization of standards could create benefits in terms of increased competition in integrated markets, but would necessarily impose a social cost in at least one country. This matter may be non-trivial in the growing number of integration agreements concluded along "North-South" lines.[10]

RTAS AS OPTIMUM REGULATORY AREAS FOR SERVICES

Optimum regulatory areas can be taught of as defining the set of countries for which aggregate welfare would be maximized by regulatory convergence. Such an area would balance the benefits and costs of participation. The benefits of eliminating policy differences through harmonization depend on the prospects of creating truly integrated markets, which depends on natural ties between countries and factors such as geographic and linguistic proximity. The costs depend on the ex ante similarity of regulatory preferences and compatibility of regulatory institutions.

---

[10] The issue can also arise at the WTO level, where one could describe the TRIPs Agreement as illustrative of upward harmonization. Similar claims have been voiced with regard to other aspects of the Marrakech Agreement and are being heard today in respect of some of the so-called Singapore Issues, most notably with regard to competition policy.

In the definition of an optimal regulatory area, it must also be recognized that cooperation can be a vehicle to exchange information on different experiences with regulatory reform and to identify good regulatory practices. This form of cooperation can be especially useful for regulating new services in sectors characterized by continuous technical change. Developing countries may have a particular interest in cooperating with advanced industrial countries that have the longest experience with regulatory reform and where the newest technologies and their regulatory implications are often first introduced.

However, whether an individual country benefits from regulatory convergence or harmonization, its willingness to participate in such an area may depend on where the standard is set, the level at which it is set, and the regulatory environment to which such a standard responds. The latter factors will in turn determine who will bear the costs of transition towards the adoption of such a standard. The incentive to make regulations converge may depend on the relative size of markets, with small countries often having more to gain. This may explain why small countries acceding to the European Union (EU) accept to bear the full cost of transition.[11]

It should be noted that the process of regulatory convergence can itself involve sunk costs of transition. The sequence in which a country chooses to harmonize (or progressively converge) its regulations with different trading partners is thus a relevant consideration. One reason is that the sequence of harmonization may influence the bargaining power of different country groupings in the negotiation over the level at which the harmonized standard should be set. For example, the countries in Eastern Europe that acceded to the EU on an individual basis could arguably have had a greater say in the EU-wide standard in specific areas if they had either been original members, negotiated collectively, or both. Similarly, harmonization first conducted at the MERCOSUR level, and then at the Free Trade Area of the Americas (FTAA) or WTO level, could imply different costs and produce a different outcome from direct harmonization at the broader level.

A final consideration to note in regard to preferential regulatory convergence relates to the possible administrative burden implied by the maintenance—and administration—of distinct regulatory requirements and procedures as between members and non-members of an RTA. Such costs may be sufficiently acute for a number of developing countries as to tilt negotiating incentives in favor of multilateral undertakings. It may also encourage the multilateralization of norms first brokered at the regional level or incite countries to simply extend to all third countries treatment similar to that afforded to RTA members, bearing in mind the limits - widely acknowledged under GATS[12]—of MFN-based outcomes on regulatory issues.

---

[11] At the same time, smaller countries may stand a greater chance of being "rule-takers", as they are likely to be hampered by their lesser ability to influence the choice, nature or level of regulatory standards vis-à-vis larger countries. The concomitant lack of strong domestic corporate voices may further lessen the standard-setting influence of smaller countries.

[12] Departures from MFN treatment on regulatory matters are foreseen, for instance, under Articles II (MFN), VI (Domestic Regulation) and VII (Recognition) of the GATS, as well as under the Financial Services Agreement in matters of recognition of prudential standards.

THIRD-COUNTRY EFFECTS

Regional agreements between countries that are (or will be) WTO members can be potentially harmful to non-member countries as they imply preferential liberalization in favor of certain member states. Such discrimination violates one of the central obligations imposed by both the GATT and the GATS—the MFN treatment rule. The GATS is similar to the GATT in permitting signatories to pursue preferential liberalization arrangements, subject however to a number of conditions that are intended to minimize potential adverse effects on non-members as well as on the multilateral trading system as a whole (these conditions are discussed in greater depth below).

In the context of agreements liberalizing trade in goods, a sufficient condition for preferential liberalization to be deemed multilaterally acceptable is that it not have detrimental impacts on third countries. That is, the volume of imports by member countries from the rest of the world should not decline on a product-by-product basis after the implementation of the agreement (Kemp and Wan, 1976; McMillan, 1993). While in principle a simple enough criterion, it is not straightforward to implement in practice given that the focus is on trade flows at the individual product level.

The liberalization of services trade implies not only that measures restricting the ability of foreign suppliers to engage in cross-border trade are reduced or eliminated, but also that factor mobility (and especially the establishment of a commercial presence) is allowed.

In determining the welfare implications for third parties of regional integration agreements covering services, account therefore needs to be taken of the impact on trade *and* factor flows. Both of these flows are endogenous and interdependent. Simple prescriptions or criteria along Kemp-Wan lines therefore can no longer be applied. If, for example, trade and factor flows are substitutes, a decline in trade in products need not necessarily be detrimental to an outside country, as greater factor flows substitute for trade. This is the standard case in neoclassical trade theory assuming constant-returns-to-scale technology. If, conversely, there are increasing returns, the relationship between factor movements and product-trade flows may well be complementary, i.e. an increase in one may be associated with an increase in the other.[13] Although the presumption is that by liberalizing both product and factor markets, the aggregate benefits for participants will increase, and this in turn will be beneficial to the rest of the world as a whole (partly through induced growth and investment effects), straight-forward criteria with which to evaluate such integration effects *ex ante* do not exist. These problems are compounded by the difficulty of establishing clear-cut criteria of product likeness in services, given the far greater degree of product differentiation and customer tailoring arising in services markets.

---

[13] See, e.g., Markusen (1983).

The Practice of Services Liberalization at the Regional Level[14]

KEY FINDINGS[15]

- RTAs tend to show broad commonality, both among each other and vis-à-vis the GATS, as regards the standard panoply of disciplines directed towards the progressive opening of services markets. In some instances, however (e.g. non-discriminatory quantitative restrictions, domestic regulation), GATS disciplines go further than those found in a number of RTAs.

- Starting with the NAFTA in 1994, an increasing number of RTAs have in recent years sought to complement disciplines on cross-border trade in services (modes 1 and 2 of the GATS) with a more comprehensive set of parallel disciplines on investment (both investment protection and liberalization of investment in goods- and services-producing activities) and the temporary movement of business people (related to goods and services trade and investment in a generic manner).[16]

- RTAs featuring comprehensive or generic investment disciplines typically provide for a right of non-establishment (i.e. no local presence requirement as a pre-condition to supply services) as a means of securing the right to cross-border trade in services. Such a provision, for which no GATS equivalent exists, might prove particularly well suited to promoting e-commerce.

- With generally few exceptions (of a mainly sectoral nature), RTAs covering services typically feature a liberal "rule of origin"/denial of benefits clause, i.e. extend preferential treatment to all legal persons conducting substantial business operations in a member country. In practice, the adoption of a liberal stance in this regard implies that the post-establishment treatment of what in many instances represents the most important mode of supplying services in foreign markets—investment—may be largely akin to non-preferential treatment insofar as third country investors are concerned.

- RTAs covering services tend to follow two broad approaches as regards the modalities of services trade and investment liberalization. A number of RTAs tend to replicate

---

[14] This section draws on the work by OECD (2002e), Stephenson (2001, 2002), Sauvé (2002), and Mattoo and Sauvé (2003). See Annex II for a statement of GATS Article XXXI: Modification of Schedules.

[15] The stylized facts summarized in this section depict very broad trends. These may obtain even as the treatment of specific rule-making issues and/or the degree of liberalization achieved in specific agreements and sectors or with regard to particular modes of supplying services may show greater variance. The large number of RTAs covering services and the even greater number of individual sectors such agreements encompass obviously complicate attempts at making broad analytical generalizations.

[16] For a fuller account of the treatment of investment and the movement of labor in RTAs, see OECD (2002d).

the use, found in GATS, of a hybrid approach to market opening, whereas others pursue a negative-list approach. While both approaches can in theory generate broadly equivalent outcomes in liberalization terms, a negative-list approach tends to generate liberalization commitments that lock-in the regulatory status quo. The process of preparing (domestically) and exchanging a negative list with trading partners may also generate gains useful gains in governance and transparency terms. It may, however, deprive countries of some measure of policy flexibility as regards the introduction of future regulatory measures.

- A number of governments participating in RTAs have shown a readiness to subsequently extend regional preferences on an MFN basis under the GATS. This may reflect both a realization that preferential treatment may be harder to confer in services trade (and is indeed perhaps economically undesirable with regard to investment) and the growing acknowledgment that multilateral liberalization may offer greater opportunities of securing access to the most efficient suppliers, particularly of infrastructural services likely to exert significant effects on economy-wide performance.

- RTAs have generally made little progress in developing disciplines on non-discriminatory domestic regulation potentially affecting trade in services. Indeed, many RTAs feature provisions in this area that are no more fleshed out and, in some instances, weaker or more narrowly drawn (i.e. focusing solely on professional services) than those arising under Article VI of the GATS (including the Article VI:4 work program).

- RTAs tend to be viewed as offering greater scope for making speedier headway on matters relating to regulatory cooperation in services trade, notably in areas such as services-related standards and the recognition of licenses and professional or educational qualifications. Despite the greater initial similarities in approaches to regulation and greater cross-border contact between regulators that geographical proximity can afford, progress in the area of domestic regulation has been slow and generally disappointing even at the regional level.

- With a few exceptions, RTAs have similarly made little headway in tackling the key "unfinished" rule-making items on the GATS agenda. This is most notably the case of disciplines on emergency safeguards and subsidies for services, where governments confront the same technical challenges or political sensitivities at the regional level as they do on the multilateral front. More progress has however been made at the regional level in opening up procurement markets for services, though such advances have tended to be made in procurement negotiations rather than in the services field.

- With the notable exception of land-transportation issues, where physical proximity stands out as a determinative facilitating feature, RTAs have generally made little progress in opening up those service sectors that have to date proven particularly difficult to address at the multilateral level (e.g., air and maritime transport;

audio-visual services;[17] movement of service suppliers; energy services). In the key infrastructural areas of basic telecommunications and financial services, the GATS has in fact achieved a higher level of bound liberalization than that on offer in most RTAs. The latter result suggests that, in some sectors, the political economy of multilateral bargaining, with its attendant gains in critical mass, may help overcome the resistance to liberalization arising in the narrower or asymmetrical confines of regional negotiations.

In addressing questions of rule design and choosing the most appropriate level at which to conduct negotiations, policy officials must begin by asking: what should be expected from an international agreement governing services trade? Even though the main challenges in services liberalization are domestic in nature, and despite the fact that, as with goods trade, unilateral reform efforts carry the greatest potential payoffs, international agreements can assist in three important ways. They can help achieve: (1) greater transparency through rules that require mutual openness; (2) heightened credibility of policy through legally binding commitments; (3) and efficient protection and regulation through rules that favor the choice of superior policy instruments.

This section investigates the manner in—and degree to—which RTAs covering services achieve the above objectives. It does so by comparing substantive provisions and negotiated outcomes under the GATS with progress made under a broad range of RTAs featuring disciplines on trade in services. In doing so, the section seeks answers to the question of whether the regional route to services trade and investment liberalization offers significant prospects for speedier and/or deeper liberalization and more comprehensive rule-making than that on offer multilaterally.

KEY DISCIPLINES: CONVERGENCE AND DIVERGENCE

While RTAs covering services come in many different shapes and sizes, they tend to feature a common set of key disciplines governing trade and investment in services that are also found in the GATS, albeit with differing burdens of obligation (see Table 6.1). Areas of greatest rule-making convergence between the multilateral and regional levels relate to: the agreements' scope of coverage, depending on carve-outs in respect of air-traffic rights and public services tend to define the norm; disciplines on transparency; national treatment; MFN treatment; disciplines on payments and transfers; monopolies and exclusive service providers; general exceptions and state-to-state dispute settlement.[18] Considerable

---

[17] While such a result obtains within the great majority of RTAs, some agreements, notably the Chile–Mexico FTA, the Chile–MERCOSUR FTA or the U.S.–Jordan FTA, did achieve some measure of liberalization in audio-visual services.

[18] With the exception of the recently concluded FTA between the United States and Australia, RTAs featuring comprehensive chapters on investment tend to allow investors direct recourse to dispute settlement procedures (so-called investor-state arbitration).

similarities also exist between the multilateral and regional levels as regards the need for sectoral specificity (i.e. sectors requiring special treatment in dedicated annexes).

Lesser convergence (and more limited regional progress) can be observed in areas of rule-making that have posed recurring difficulties in a GATS setting. This includes issues such as non-discriminatory quantitative restrictions (or "market access" in GATS-speak), domestic regulation, emergency safeguards and subsidies.

The principles of MFN and national treatment constitute two of the most basic building blocks to any agreement on services, just as they do in the goods area. As with the GATS, very few RTAs set out such principles in unqualified form,[19] regardless of whether they are framed as general obligations (which is the case for MFN in virtually all agreements and for national treatment in agreements pursuing a negative list approach to liberalization) or as obligations that apply solely in sectors where liberalization commitments are positively undertaken.

As may be expected given the regulatory intensity of services trade, transparency disciplines are common to all RTAs covering services. These typically stipulate, as is the case under GATS, an obligation to publish relevant measures and notify new (or changes to existing) measures affecting trade in services and to establish national enquiry points to provide information on measures affecting services trade upon request. One innovation over the GATS is the provision that some RTAs, particularly in the Western Hemisphere, make for members to afford the opportunity (to the extent possible, i.e., on a "best endeavors" basis) for prior comment on proposed changes to services regulations. Two recent RTAs, the U.S.–Chile and U.S.–Singapore FTAs have gone one step further by making such provisions legally binding.

While RTAs covering services typically address non-discriminatory quantitative restrictions that impede access to services markets (addressed under Article XVI of the GATS), many agreements, particularly those concluded in the Western Hemisphere and modeled on the NAFTA, are weaker than the GATS, committing parties solely to making such measures fully transparent in annexes listing non-conforming measures and to a best endeavors approach as regards their progressive dismantling in the future. In contrast, under GATS, WTO members undertake policy bindings in sectors, sub-sectors and modes of supply against which market access commitments are scheduled. Many other RTAs, such as MERCOSUR and the various RTAs to which EU Members are party, introduce a prohibition on the introduction of new non-discriminatory Quantitative Restrictions (QRs) on any scheduled commitment and sector, mirroring a similar requirement under the GATS.

The argument has been made that RTAs in the services field provide scope for creating so-called "optimum regulatory areas" (see discussion above), the presumption being that the aggregate adjustment costs of regulatory convergence and policy

---

[19] Only the Mercosur Protocol and Decision 439 of the Andean Community provide that no deviation from MFN and national treatment be allowed among members to the two integration groupings.

Table 6.1. Key Disciplines in RTAs Covering Services

Agreements	MFN treatment	National treatment	Market access (N-D QRs)+	Domestic regulation	Emergency safeguards	Subsidy disciplines	Government procurement	Rule of origin (denial of benefits)
GATS	Yes	Yes	Yes	Yes	Future	Future negotiations	Future negotiations	Yes
NAFTA	Yes	Yes	Yes	Yes*	No	No	Separate chapter	Yes
Canada–Chile	Yes	Yes	Yes	Yes*	No	No	No	Yes
Chile–México	Yes	Yes	Yes	Yes*	No	No	No	Yes
Bolivia–Mexico	Yes	Yes	Yes	Yes*	Future	No	Separate chapter	Yes
Costa Rica–México	Yes	Yes	Yes	Yes*	Future	No	Separate chapter	Yes
Mexico–Nicaragua	Yes	Yes	Yes	Yes*	No	No	Future negotiations	Yes
Mexico–Northern Triangle[1]	Yes	Yes	Yes	Yes*	Future	No	No	Yes
Central America–Dominican Republic	Yes	Yes	Yes	Yes*	Future	Future negotiations	Separate chapter	Yes
Central America–Chile	Yes	Yes	Yes	Yes*	No	No	Separate chapter	Yes
Group of Three	Yes	Yes	Yes	Yes*	No	No	Separate chapter	Yes
MERCOSUR	Yes	Yes	Yes	Yes	No	Future negotiations	Future negotiations	Yes
Andean Community	Yes	Yes	Yes	Yes*	No	No	No	Yes
CARICOM	Not specified	Yes	Not specified	Yes*	Yes	No	No	Yes
CARICOM–Dominican Republic	Yes	Yes	Yes	Yes*	Future	No	Separate chapter	Yes
Central American Economic Integration	Not specified	No general article	No	No	No	No	No	Not specified
E.U.	Yes	Yes	Yes	Yes	No	Yes (covered under competition disciplines)	Yes	Yes
Europe Agreements	Yes	Yes	No	Yes	No	Yes (covered under competition disciplines)	No	Beneficiaries specified through definition of "undertakings"
E.U.–Mexico	Yes	Yes	Yes	No (provisions on regulatory	No	No	Separate chapter	Yes

Agreement				carve-out and recognition)				
EFTA–Mexico	Yes	Yes	Yes	Yes	No	No	No	Not specified
EFTA–Singapore	Yes	Yes	Yes	Yes	No	Requests for consultations to be given sympathetic consideration	Separate chapter	Yes
Japan–Singapore	No	Yes	Yes	Yes	No	No	Separate chapter	Yes
ASEAN Framework Agreement on Services	Yes	Yes	Yes	Not specified	Yes	No	No	Yes
Australia–New Zealand Closer Economic Relations trade Agreement	MFN for excluded sectors	Yes	Yes	Yes	No	Export subsidies prohibited Other subsidies excluded	No	Yes
U.S.–Jordan	Yes	Yes	Yes	Yes	No	Future negotiations	Yes	Yes
U.S.–Singapore	Yes	Yes	Yes	Yes*	No	No	Separate chapter	Yes
U.S.–Chile	Yes	Yes	Yes	Yes*	No	No	Separate chapter	Yes

Notes: + Non-discriminatory quantitative restrictions. * Rules on domestic regulation are set out more narrowly (in most cases they apply only to the licensing and certification of professional services suppliers). ¹ Honduras, Guatemala and El Salvador harmonization are likely to be smaller when foreign regulatory preferences are similar and regulatory institutions broadly compatible (Mattoo and Fink, 2002).

In practice, however, it is notable how the broad intersect between domestic regulation and services trade has tended to prove intractable (just as it has under the GATS) even among the smaller subset of countries engaging in RTAs. In many instances, RTAs address domestic regulation in a manner analogous to that found in Article VI of the GATS, i.e. with a focus on procedural transparency and ensuring that regulatory activity does not lead to disguised restrictions to trade or investment in services.

With the exception of the E.U. itself and agreements reached between the E.U. and countries in Central and Eastern Europe in pre-E.U. accession mode, no RTA has to date made tangible progress in delineating the possible elements of a necessity test aimed at ensuring broad proportionality between regulatory means and objectives (as is potentially foreseen under the GATS Article VI:4 mandate, but where progress at the negotiating table has also been limited to date, with the exception of accountancy disciplines agreed by WTO Members in 1999).

As noted above, two recent RTAs, the U.S.–Chile and U.S.–Singapore FTAs, have nonetheless gone beyond the WTO in adopting transparency provisions that mandate prior notification requirements, an issue long championed by a number of OECD countries but that has proven controversial in the WTO context (Iida and Nielson, 2003). The latter development offers an interesting example of what could be described as "demonstration effect" regionalism, with regional advances creating precedents that proponents hope will be replicated at the multilateral level.[20]

Similarly, with a few exceptions (mostly in the E.U. context as well as under the Australia–New Zealand Closer Economic Relations Trade Agreement or ANZCERTA), it is notable how progress has tended to prove difficult even at the regional level in matters of regulatory harmonization or mutual recognition (see Box 6.2). Neither the NAFTA nor the many NAFTA-type agreements reached in the Western Hemisphere contain an article on domestic regulation *per se* in their services chapters. Rather, such agreements feature more narrowly drawn disciplines relating to the licensing and certification of professionals. Whereas similar GATS language states that the measures in question should not be a restriction to the supply of a service under any of the four GATS modes, the NAFTA-type agreements narrow this requirement to the cross-border supply of a service. No comparable provision can be found in these agreements' investment chapters. Meanwhile, in the ANZCERTA, language on licensing and certification is not legally binding but rather hortatory in nature.

---

[20] Other examples of demonstration effect/precedent-setting regionalism are the provisions on the linkage between trade and labor standards inserted by the Clinton administration into the U.S.–Jordan FTA and the recurring tendency of the European Commission to insert disciplines on trade and competition policy into the E.U.'s RTAs with developing countries.

Box 6.2 Harmonization and Mutual Recognition in Services: Promise and Pitfalls

Difficulties encountered in heeding calls for regulatory harmonization may in part be traced to the absence of widely accepted international standards in services. Where such standards do exist, as in financial services or maritime transport, meeting them tends to be seen as a first step towards acceptability, rather than as a sufficient condition for market access. The GATS, like the GATT, does not specifically require the use of international standards. It generally provides weaker incentives for the use of such standards than the Sanitary and Phytosanitary Standards (SPS) or the Technical Barriers to Trade (TBT) Agreements, and does not provide a presumption of compliance as do the latter two agreements.[21]

It is unlikely that meaningful international standards for most services will be developed soon. Still, it bears noting that in those areas where global standards do exist, one may presume that the likelihood of disguised or needlessly restrictive impediments to trade and investment may be significantly lower, even as overtly discriminatory regulatory barriers or market access impediments subject to Articles XVI (Market Access) and XVII (National Treatment) (and typically "reserved" in scheduled sectors) may remain in place. The presumption must also be that the existence of such standards may significantly facilitate trade. This may be particularly true of cross-border trade in services in as much as agreed standards may help overcome the various forms of information asymmetries that hold such trade—and its commensurate liberalization under GATS—back.

Accordingly, calls are frequently made for trade agreements to create a stronger presumption in favor of genuinely international standards in services trade. As with recognition agreements, efforts at developing international standards for services trade will likely require greater technical assistance and capacity building. This may be usefully done at the national and regional levels, particularly as proximity, both geographic historical, and cultural, may be expected to facilitate regulatory convergence.

It is important to note that efforts to promote the adoption of international standards will invariably be carried out outside a trade-policy framework. Be they regional or multilateral in scope, trade agreements are not in the business of making regulatory standards. Rather, their remit lies in how such standards are implemented if they impact on trade. The relevant institutions for promoting international standards for services are to be found in various specialized regulatory institutions, such as the Bank for International Settlements for banking standards, the International Telecommunications Union for telecommunications or the International Standardization Organization (ISO) for various categories of services (including the means of producing and supplying them).[22]

As regards mutual recognition agreements (MRAs), three observations seem in order in the light of realities on the ground. First, they cannot be mandated, i.e. made to happen, under trade agreements. Second, MRAs do not seem to be occurring on any major trade-influencing scale. Often touted as a desirable transaction cost-reducing alternative to regulatory harmonization, there are in practice relatively few examples of successful, operative MRAs in services trade.[23] Third, even if MRAs were to happen in greater numbers, it is unclear whether they would always be desirable.

---

[21] Such a presumption can be found in Article 2.5 of the TBT Agreement and Article 3.2 of the SPS Agreement.

[22] One concrete example of forward movement in international standardization involving developing countries is provided by the IMF–World Bank Comprehensive Financial Sector Adjustment Programs, which are helping many jurisdictions to assess their compliance with international standards in the financial sector with the aim to help them address any underlying weaknesses. Carried out on a voluntary basis outside of the trade-policy framework, such regulatory cooperation may nonetheless be expected to facilitate the progressive, orderly, pursuit of liberalization of trade and investment in financial services.

[23] For a detailed and candid analysis of problems encountered in realizing the E.U. single market program for services, see Beviglia-Zampetti (2000); and Nicolaidis and Trachtman (2000); Commission of the European Communities (2002).

A multilateral agreement like the GATS cannot mandate countries to conclude MRAs—just as any provision such as Article V of GATS (Economic Integration) or Article XXIV of GATT cannot make regional integration agreements happen. As in the case of regional agreements, multilateral disciplines can be more or less permissive with regard to mutual recognition.

This in turn raises a key question: where and how strong are the incentives to conclude MRAs? The practice of MRAs suggests that their scope is quite limited; they are invariably concluded between very similar countries. Even in a region with as strong (and institutionalized) an integrationist dynamic as Europe, and despite a significant level of prior and/or complimentary (minimal) regulatory harmonization, the effect of MRAs has been limited by the unwillingness of many host country regulators to cede full control (Beviglia-Zampetti (2000)).

Such an outcome in turn raises the question of the benefits and costs of MRAs. The analogy with regional integration agreements is here again useful, as MRAs can be likened to sector-specific preferential arrangements. In instances where regulatory barriers are prohibitively high—one can imagine autarky as the ultimate example—then recognition can only be trade-creating. But if they are not, then selective recognition can have discriminatory effects and lead to trade diversion. The result may well be to create trade according to a pattern of mutual trust rather than on the basis of the forces of comparative advantage. For instance, one can readily observe industrial countries making some limited headway towards MRAs in professional services, but avoiding such agreements with countries such as India, Egypt or the Philippines.

Article VII (Recognition) of the GATS strikes a delicate balance by allowing such agreements, provided third countries have the opportunity to accede or demonstrate equivalence. Thus, Article VII has a desirable open-ended aspect that Article V (dealing with integration agreements) does not. This makes it particularly worrisome that many MRAs have been notified by WTO Members under Article V rather than VII.

An important concern for any multilateral agreement should be not how those who enjoy preferential access are treated, but how those who do not enjoy such access are treated. Ironically, the only line of defense of the rights of third countries could well come from a necessity test aimed at ensuring that such countries would not be subject to unnecessarily burdensome regulation even if they were not parties to an MRA.

Given the potential of MRAs to create trade and investment distortions, it has been noted that bilateral or plurilateral recognition agreements should respect the non-discrimination principle, as mandated by Article VII of GATS. In pursuance of this logic, the point has been made that such agreements should not, as a rule, be notified under Article V of GATS (Economic Integration) but rather be open to all eligible participants under the terms of Article VII.

Source: Adapted from Mattoo and Sauvé (2003).

Moreover, even though a number of RTAs, notably those concluded in the Western Hemisphere, call on Members to recognize, at times on the basis of explicit timetables (as in the NAFTA in the case of foreign legal consultants and the temporary licensing of engineers), foreign educational credentials and professional qualifications in selected professions, progress in concluding mutual recognition agreements has proven slow and difficult, particularly when pursued between countries with federal political systems and systems of delegated authority to licensing bodies at the sub-national level.

The experience to date with regulatory convergence and cooperation at the regional level does not provide clear-cut evidence in support of the argument that RTAs can more readily be likened to optimum regulatory areas. There is, admittedly, little evidence of substantial regulatory cooperation in services trade outside of RTAs.

Given however that any attempt at reaching MRAs in the services area (as with goods-related MRAs) is almost by definition likely to involve a limited number of participating countries, it is not altogether clear that RTAs offer a superior alternative to that available to WTO Members under Article VII of the GATS.

Indeed, Article VII of GATS arguably allows greater initial selectivity in the choice of partners for regulatory harmonization, whereas RTAs allow for convergence between countries whose regulatory fit may not always be optimal. There is, of course, one important difference between RTAs and the GATS insofar as preferential treatment (including in regulatory matters) can be fully protected under Article V of the GATS; whereas WTO Members must be prepared under Article VII to extend recognition privileges to all Members willing and able to satisfy national regulatory requirements.

With few exceptions, RTAs have similarly made little headway in tackling the key "unfinished" rule-making items on the GATS agenda. This is most notably the case for disciplines on an emergency safeguard mechanism (ESM) and subsidies for services, where governments confront the same conceptual challenges, data limitations and political sensitivities at the regional level as they do on the multilateral front. It is interesting to note for instance that the countries of Southeast Asia, which have been among the most vocal proponents of an emergency safeguard mechanism in the GATS, have not adopted such a provision within the ASEAN Framework Agreement on Services (AFAS). To date, only members of CARICOM (in Protocol II) in the Western Hemisphere, have adopted (but not yet used) such an instrument, and questions remain as to the operational feasibility of an ESM in services trade. Elsewhere, the NAFTA has provided one example of sectoral experimentation (in financial services) with measures, framed essentially in the context of transitional (or phase-in) liberalization measures, that nonetheless feature safeguard-type characteristics.[24]

On subsidies, with the exception of the EU (including its pre-accession agreements with countries in Central and Eastern Europe) and of ANZCERTA, the adoption of regional disciplines in the services area has proven elusive, particularly in countries with federal political systems, given the extent of sub-national policy activism (and the concomitant reluctance to take on binding obligations) in this area. Whereas a number of RTAs (e.g., MERCOSUR) replicate the call made in GATS to develop future disciplines on subsidies in services trade, others, notably the NAFTA and numerous NAFTA-type agreements in the Western Hemisphere, specifically exclude subsidy practices from coverage. The EFTA-Singapore FTA requires that sympathetic consideration be given to requests by a

---

[24] Under the terms of the NAFTA's chapter on financial services, Mexico was allowed to impose market-share caps if the specific foreign ownership thresholds agreed to—25 per cent and 30 per cent respectively for banks and securities firms—were reached before 2004. Mexico can only have recourse to such market-share limitations once during the 2000–04 period and can only impose them for a three-year period. Under no circumstances may such measures be maintained after 2007. It bears noting that Mexico has not to date made use of such provisions even as the aggregate share of foreign participation in its financial system is today significantly higher than the thresholds described above. See Sauvé (2002); Sauvé and Gonzalez-Hermosillo (1993).

party for consultations in instances where subsidy practices affecting trade in services may be deemed to have injurious effects. The Japan–Singapore New Partnership Agreement features generic provisions on subsidies applicable to both goods and services trade.

More progress has been made at the regional level in opening up government procurement markets for services, though this has tended to be achieved through negotiations in the area of government procurement *per se* (as with the WTO's Government Procurement Agreement or GPA) rather than addressed in services negotiations.[25] The approach taken in RTAs is for the most part very similar to that adopted in the WTO, i.e., non-discrimination among members within the scope of scheduled commitments and procedures to enhance transparency and due process. RTAs whose members are all parties to the GPA, such as EFTA and the Singapore–Japan FTA, specifically mention that the relevant GPA articles apply and most agreements concluded in the Western Hemisphere basically replicate GPA disciplines at the regional level. However, it bears noting that unlike the GPA, which applies in principle to purchases by both state and sub-national governments, many RTAs provide for binding government-procurement disciplines at the national level only (OECD, 2002a).

THE TREATMENT OF INVESTMENT IN SERVICES: ESTABLISHMENT AND NON-ESTABLISHMENT RIGHTS

Starting with the NAFTA in 1994, an increasing number of RTAs have in recent years sought to complement disciplines on cross-border trade in services (modes 1 and 2 of the GATS) with a more comprehensive set of parallel disciplines on investment (rules governing both the protection and liberalization of investors and their investments in goods—and services-producing activities) and the temporary movement of business people (related to goods and services trade and investment in a generic manner; see OECD, 2002b and c).[26]

One important difference in approaches to services trade as between (and among) RTAs and the GATS concerns the interplay between cross-border trade and investment in services. At the multilateral level, the GATS (and the WTO more broadly) does not yet contain a comprehensive body of investment disciplines (the GATS is silent for instance on

---

[25] Still, it bears recalling that despite notable progress in RTAs, government procurement-practices continue in most instances to be the province of discriminatory practices. In the case of NAFTA, for instance, despite the fact that the scope of covered purchases was quadrupled when compared to the outcome of the 1987 Canada–United States FTA, covered entities only represented a tenth of North America's civilian procurement market at the time of the Agreement's entry into force. See Hart and Sauvé (1997).

[26] Many RTAs have innovated over the multilateral approach by integrating a full set of generic disciplines for goods and services. While the WTO is fragmented into three parts, with disciplines applying to trade in goods in Part I in (the GATT 1994), Part II on services under the GATS and disciplines on trade-related intellectual property rights under Part III (TRIPs), a growing number of RTAs have followed an integrated approach. Starting with the NAFTA in 1994, several RTAs (more than a dozen in the Western Hemisphere alone) feature disciplines on cross-border trade in services together with provisions on

matters of investment protection) but incorporates investment in services ("commercial presence" in GATS-speak) as one of the four modes of service delivery (see Table 6.2).

A GATS-like approach has been followed in a number of RTAs, notably by MERCO-SUR members and many RTAs concluded outside the Western Hemisphere (e.g. ASEAN Framework Agreement on Services, U.S.–Jordan FTA, E.U.-Chile FTA, E.U.–Mexico). This approach contrasts with that taken by NAFTA and the NAFTA-type RTAs, where investment rules and disciplines covering both matters of investment protection (as typically treated under bilateral investment treaties (BITs)) and liberalization (typically with respect to both pre- and post-establishment matters), combined with investor-state and state-to-state dispute settlement provisions, apply in a generic manner to goods and services in a separate chapter.

The latter agreements thus feature services chapters that focus solely on cross-border delivery (modes 1 and 2 of GATS), complemented by separate chapters governing the movement of capital (investment) on the one hand, and the temporary entry of business people on the other. Such labor movement is usually defined as comprising four distinct categories of business people (and not "workers") to which preferential temporary entry privileges are bestowed: business visitors, traders and investors, intra-company transferees, and professionals.

A number of RTAs, such as the Japan–Singapore FTA, CARICOM as well as the EFTA–Mexico and EFTA–Singapore FTAs, address investment in services both under the commercial presence mode of supply (in their services chapters) as well as in separate chapters dealing with investment, the right of establishment or the movement of capital (See Table 6.2).

As Table 6.3 indicates, RTAs featuring generic investment disciplines typically provide for a right of non-establishment (i.e. no local presence requirement as a pre-condition to supply a service, subject to the right to reserve and list existing non-conforming measures) as a means of encouraging greater volumes of cross-border trade in services. While such an obligation, for which no GATS equivalent exists,[27] was initially crafted (starting with the NAFTA) before the Internet became a tangible commercial reality, they may nonetheless prove particularly well suited to promoting e-commerce and encouraging countries to adopt less onerous restrictions on cross-border trade whilst achieving legitimate public policy objectives (e.g. prudential supervision, consumer protection).

---

investment, government procurement, labor mobility, monopolies, intellectual property rights (IPRs), and technical barriers to trade that apply to both goods and services. This has allowed for greater coherence in rule-design, resulting in trade rules that bear a greater resemblance to the integrated manner in which global commerce unfolds in world markets (Stephenson, 2002).

[27] It could be argued that such a provision is somewhat implicit in the GATS insofar as the Agreement only allows Member countries to maintain local presence requirements in scheduled sectors (under modes 1 and 2) to the extent that such non-conforming measures are explicitly inscribed in their schedules. No such discipline, however, applies to sectors that do not appear in Members' GATS schedules or in those modes of supply where WTO Members remain unbound. In contrast, the right to non-establishment is a general obligation under the NAFTA and in agreements modeled on the NAFTA, against which reservations to preserve existing non-conforming measures can be lodged.

Table 6.2. Key Features of RTAs Covering Services

Agreements	Scope/ coverage	Negotiating modality	Treatment of investment in services	Right of non-establishment	Ratchet mechanism
GATS	Universal*	Positive list approach	Covered as "commercial presence" (mode 3)	No	No
NAFTA	Universal*	Negative list approach	Separate chapter	Yes	Yes
Canada–Chile	Universal*	Negative list approach	Separate chapter	Yes	Yes
Chile–Mexico	Universal*	Negative list approach	Separate chapter	Yes	Yes
Bolivia–Mexico	Universal*	Negative list approach	Separate chapter	Yes	Yes
Costa Rica–Mexico	Universal*	Negative list approach	Separate chapter	Yes	Yes
Mexico–Nicaragua	Universal*	Negative list approach	Separate chapter	Yes	Yes
Mexico–Northern Triangle[1]	Universal*	Negative list approach	Separate chapter	Yes	Yes
Central America–Dominican Republic	Universal*	Negative list approach	Separate chapter	Yes	Yes
Central America–Chile	Universal*	Negative list approach	Separate chapter	Yes	Yes
Group of Three	Universal*	Negative list approach	Separate chapter	Yes	Yes
MERCOSUR	Universal*	Positive list approach	Separate Protocols	No	No
Andean Community	Universal*	Negative list approach	Covered as "commercial presence"	No	No
CARICOM	Universal*	Negative list approach	Covered as "commercial presence" and in separate chapters (on right of establishment and movement of capital)	No	No
CARICOM–Dominican Republic	Universal*	Negative list approach	Separate chapter	Yes	No
Central American Common Market	Construction services	Positive list approach	Not specified	No	No
EU	Universal*	Negative list approach	Treated as freedom to establish	Yes	No
Europe Agreements	Universal*	Negative list approach	Separate chapter	Yes	No
E.U.–Mexico	Universal* (audio-visual services explicitly excluded)	Standstill (+ future negotiation of commitments à la GATS)	Covered as "commercial presence" and under a separate investment chapter	No	No
EFTA–Mexico	Universal *	Positive list approach	Covered as "commercial presence" and under a separate investment chapter	No	No
EFTA–Singapore	Universal*	Positive list approach	Covered as "commercial presence" and under a separate investment chapter	No	No

(cont'd)

Table 6.2. *(Continued)*

Agreements	Scope/ coverage	Negotiating modality	Treatment of investment in services	Right of non-establishment	Ratchet mechanism
Japan–Singapore	Universal *	Positive list approach	Covered as "commercial presence" and under a separate investment chapter	No	No
ASEAN Framework Agreement on Services	Universal*	Positive list approach	Covered as "commercial presence" and under a separate investment chapter	No	No
Australia–New Zealand Closer Economic Relations Trade Agreement	Universal*	Negative list approach	Covered as "commercial presence" but no common disciplines on investment	Yes	No
U.S.–Jordan	Universal*	Positive list approach	Covered as "commercial presence"	No	No
U.S.–Singapore	Universal*	Negative list approach	Separate chapter	Yes	Yes
U.S.–Chile	Universal*	Negative list approach	Separate chapter	Yes	Yes

Notes: * Air transport and in certain cases cabotage in maritime services is excluded. ¹ Honduras, Guatemala and El Salvador

With generally few exceptions (often of a sectoral nature), most RTAs covering services tend to adopt a liberal "rule of origin" (via a provision on denial of benefits), whereby the benefits of RTA treatment are typically only denied to juridical persons that do not conduct substantial business operations in a member country. In practice, the adoption of a liberal rule of origin implies that the post-establishment treatment of what in many instances represents the most important mode of supplying services in foreign markets—investment—is in large measure non-preferential for third country investors as regards liberalization commitments.[28] Stated differently, under a liberal rule of origin for services and investment, third country investors can in most instances take full advantage of the expanded market opportunities afforded by the creation of a RTA by establishing within the region (see Box 6.3).[29]

[28] It bears recalling, however, that a number of economic factors (e.g. the scale economies arising from a larger regional market) and policy variables (e.g. the maintenance of discriminatory sectoral rules of origin within an RTA), can affect global patterns of investment, as discussed in TD/TC/WP(2002)18.

[29] Indeed, the aim of attracting greater volumes of FDI, including from third-country sources, is often a central objective of RTAs. For this reason, there are generally few instances in which the benefits of an RTA in the investment field are restricted to juridical persons that are owned or controlled by nationals of a member country. Among the RTAs reviewed in this note, only the MERCOSUL and the Andean Pact feature such restrictions.

Table 6.3. Key Provisions of GATS Article V (and V *bis*)[40]

SCOPE	Economic integration agreements (EIAs).liberalizing trade in services
BASIC PRINCIPLES (ARTICLE V:4)	The purpose of an EIA is to facilitate trade between the parties and not to raise the overall level of barriers to trade in services *vis-à-vis* third parties.
CONSISTENCY CRITERIA (ARTICLE V:1)	An EIA must have "substantial sectoral coverage" (number of sectors, volume of trade affected and modes of supply), with no a priori exclusion of any mode of supply. An EIA must also provide for "the absence or elimination of substantially all discrimination, in the sense of [GATS] Article XVII" (national treatment), between or among the parties, in the sectors covered by the Agreement.[41]
CONSISTENCY CRITERIA (ARTICLE V:4 AND 5)	The EIA must not, in respect of any Member outside the agreement, raise the overall level of barriers to trade in services within the respective sectors or sub-sectors, compared to the level applicable prior to such an agreement. Any significant modification or withdrawal of a specific commitment, in a manner inconsistent with the terms and conditions set out in a Member's schedule, resulting from its affiliation with an EIA, must be notified at least 90 days in advance. The procedure set out in paragraphs 2, 3 and 4 of GATS Article XXI is applicable for this purpose.
CONSISTENCY CRITERIA (ARTICLE V:6)	Any service supplier of a country not party to an EIA, if recognized as a juridical person under the laws of a party to the EIA, is entitled to receive the treatment granted under the EIA. However, it is necessary for the supplier concerned to engage in "substantive business operations in the territory of the parties to such agreement".
DEVELOPING COUNTRIES: FLEXIBILITY REGARDING THE CONSISTENCY CRITERIA (ARTICLE V:3)	Developing country Members of the WTO which are parties to an EIA for the liberalization of trade in services benefit from flexibility with regard to two of the above criteria, "in accordance with the level of development of the countries concerned, both overall and in individual sectors and sub-sectors", in relation to the consistency criteria set out in Article V:1 and V:6.
OBLIGATION TO NOTIFY AND POSSIBLE REVIEW (ARTICLE V:7)	Any EIA, or any enlargement of modification thereof, must be promptly notified to the Council for Trade in Services. In addition, WTO Members that are parties to an EIA must make available to the Council such relevant information as may be requested by it. The Council for Trade in Services decides whether a notified agreement should be examined by the Committee on Regional Trade Agreements, which will be required to report on its consistency with the provisions of Article V. Agreements providing for an implementation time frame for the elimination of "substantially all discrimination between or among the parties" must be the subject of periodic reports to the Council on their implementation.
LABOR MARKET EIAS (ARTICLE V *BIS*)	These are EIAs concerned with labor markets, i.e. agreements that grant a right of free access to the employment markets of the parties and include measures concerning conditions of pay, other conditions of employment and social benefits. In order to be consistent with the GATS, such agreements must exempt citizens of parties thereto from requirements concerning residency and work permits. Article V *bis* does not provide for any review of the consistency of this type of agreement.

[40] This table is reproduced from WTO (2000), *Regional Integration: Synopsis of WTO Agreements and Related Provisions*, Paper prepared for Libreville 2000, Meeting of African Trade Ministers, MM/LIB/SYN14, (23 October), Geneva: World Trade Organization.

[41] Article V states that the latter condition must be fulfilled through '(i) elimination of existing discriminatory measures, and/or (ii) prohibition of new or more discriminatory measures', either at the entry into force of the agreement concerned or on the basis of a time frame. Measures taken under GATS Articles XI, XII, XIV and XIV *bis* do not fall within the scope of the latter obligation.

The above considerations may to some extent explain the observed readiness that a number of governments participating in RTAs have shown to subsequently extend (either immediately or in a progressive manner) regional preferences on an MFN basis under the GATS. This may reflect both a realization that preferential treatment may be harder to confer in services trade (and may indeed be economically undesirable with regard to investment/mode 3) and that multilateral liberalization may offer greater opportunities of securing access to the most efficient suppliers, particularly of infrastructural services likely to exert significant effects on economy-wide performance.

A readiness to extend RTA preferences on an MFN basis in GATS (or to extend such preferences in RTAs concluded with other countries) is most noticeable amongst countries of the Western hemisphere, the majority of which have tended to lock-in the regulatory *status quo* prevailing in their investment regimes by virtue of adopting a negative list approach to liberalization in the RTAs to which they are party (See below).

Box 6.3. Liberal Rules of Origin Can Minimize Investment Diversion

As with goods trade, and despite their greater uniformity across sectors, experience shows that rules of origin for services (and investment) can play a significant role in determining the degree to which RTAs discriminate against non-member countries, and hence the extent of potentially costly trade and investment diversion. When levels of protection differ between participating countries, the effective preference granted to a trading partner may ultimately depend on how restrictive the applied rule of origin is. In the extreme, if one participant has a fully liberalized market, the adoption of a liberal rule of origin by the other participants can be likened to MFN liberalization, as services and service suppliers can enter or establish themselves in the liberal jurisdiction and from there move to—or service—the other partner countries. Not surprisingly, participants who seek to benefit from preferential access to a protected market and deny benefits to third country competitors are likely to argue for the adoption of restrictive rules of origin, based on criteria such as ownership or control considerations. This could be the attitude, in particular, of regionally dominant but non-globally competitive service providers towards third-country competition within a regionally integrating area. Examples of restrictive rules of origin for services and investment can be found in Mercosur, the Andean Pact, both of which limit benefits to juridical persons that are owned and controlled by natural persons of a member country, as well as in the Hong Kong–China Free Trade Agreement, which features a detailed annex spelling out the set of criteria by which Hong Kong service suppliers may benefit from the terms of the agreement.[30]

The experience of the Mexican banking market in the decade that has elapsed since the signing of the NAFTA suggests that the adoption of a liberal rule of origin played an important role in mitigating any strong preferences that U.S. and Canadian owned banks received from Mexico under NAFTA.

Trade Preferences Under NAFTA and the E.U.–Mexico FTA

Prior to the negotiation of the NAFTA, Mexico's financial markets were all but closed to foreign competition. The NAFTA saw Mexico extend market access preferences to U.S.- and Canadian-based banks over third country foreign

---

[30] These include: incorporation and possession of a valid operating license; substantive business operations for three years or more (and up to five in some sectors); the need to have pay profit taxes in Hong Kong and the obligation that more than 50 per cent of employed staff be local residents. For a more comprehensive discussion of rules of origin regimes for services and investment, see Beviglia-Zampetti and Sauvé (2004).

banks in the form of unrestricted foreign equity participation: banks based in the US and Canada could set up wholly-owned subsidiaries in Mexico, being subject only to transitional aggregate market share limits.

Mexico chose an incorporation test in connection with the admission of foreign banks, where a bank's nationality was determined by its country of incorporation, provided it conducted substantial business operations in that country. Thus, even European or Asian banks based in the US could set up wholly-owned subsidiaries in Mexico under NAFTA. Since the gradual opening of Mexico's financial markets involved the maintenance of foreign market-share limitations, there was concern that Mexico might give precedence to Canadian or U.S. financial institutions over non-NAFTA applicants during the transition period when the aggregate ceilings might be close to being met. Language contained in Mexico's financial services reservations under NAFTA (Annex VII) suggested that, in administering license applications, the Mexican authorities would attempt to ensure, *inter alia*, that benefits were not denied to enterprises controlled by U.S. or Canadian nationals because of expansion in Mexico of institutions controlled by non-NAFTA Parties.

In 2000, Mexico concluded another regional agreement: the E.U.–Mexico FTA, which extended the right to establish fully-owned and controlled financial affiliates in Mexico to European based banks. The degree of liberalization between the EU and Mexico became almost equivalent to the degree of liberalization achieved between Mexico and its NAFTA partners.

Did Mexico's NAFTA Commitment Lead to Preferential Treatment of U.S. and Canadian Banks?

The experience of several European banks suggests that the liberal rules of origin adopted under NAFTA prevented the occurrence of significant trade and investment diversion. For example, in 1994, Spain's Banco Santander established a financial group in Mexico as a subsidiary of Santander's American subsidiary in Puerto Rico, using the NAFTA benefits. Once established, in 1997, Santander acquired Invermexico, and formed Grupo Financiero Santander Mexicano. Further, in 2000, Santander acquired Banco Serfin and formed Grupo Financiero Santander-Serfin. In the second half of 2001, after the E.U.–Mexico FTA entered into effect, Grupo Financiero Santander Serfin's ownership was transferred from the American (Puerto Rican) subsidiary to Banco Santander Central Hispano of Spain.

Similarly, ING Barings (Mexico) was established in November 1995 as a subsidiary of the American subsidiary of ING Bank NV (Netherlands). However, in 2001, after the entry into force of the E.U.–Mexico FTA, ownership of ING Barings (Mexico) was transferred from ING Barings (USA) to ING Bank NV (Netherlands) as it was more efficient from a tax standpoint to be directly owned by the parent rather than by a holding company in a third jurisdiction. In a slightly different fashion, HSBC Bank Mexico S.A. was established in August 1995 when HSBC USA Inc (an American holding company of the Hong Kong and Shanghai Banking Corporation) took over Republic National Bank of New York, which had already established a subsidiary in Mexico. The name Republic National Bank was changed to HSBC Bank Mexico S.A. HSBC Bank Mexico is owned entirely by HSBC USA Inc, which is in turn owned by HSBC Holdings PLC of Great Britain.

Foreign institutions have come to occupy a central place in the Mexican banking market in recent years. In 2000, besides controlling the largest and third largest financial groups (both under Spanish control), they managed 48 per cent of the banking system assets, 46 per cent of the outstanding loans, and held roughly half (48 per cent) of the banking system capital. In July of 2001, Citibank and Banamex merged to create the largest bank in Mexico, which today comprises the operations of Banamex, Citibank Mexico, and Banca Confia. Foreign banks have made significant inroads in retail banking. Citibank, Canada's Bank of Nova Scotia, and Spain's BBVA and BSCH, after initially operating with a relatively small presence, have all recently acquired control of Mexican banks with a sizeable participation in retail banking. As a result, the share of assets managed by foreign banks is around 80 per cent today, a remarkable spectacular transformation when one considers that foreign banks were absent from the Mexican financial sector at the time of NAFTA's negotiation a mere decade ago.

Sources: Adapted from Mattoo and Fink (2002); Beviglia-Zampetti and Sauvé (2004).

MODALITIES OF LIBERALIZATION: NEGATIVE VS. POSITIVE LIST APPROACHES

Two major approaches towards the liberalization of trade and investment in services have been manifest in RTAs and in the WTO: the positive list or "bottom-up" approach (which in reality should be described as a hybrid approach featuring a voluntary, positive, choice of sectors, sub-sectors and/or modes of supply in which governments are willing to make binding commitments together with a negative list of non-conforming measures to be retained in scheduled areas), and the negative list or "top-down/list it or lose it" approach. While both negotiating modalities can produce (and indeed have in some instances produced) broadly equivalent outcomes in liberalization terms, the two approaches can be argued to generate a number of qualitative differences of potential significance from both a domestic and international governance point of view.[31]

While the debate over these competing approaches appears settled in the GATS context (where reliance on the hybrid approach shows no sign of being modified), it is useful to recall these differences as the issue is still very much alive in a regional context and as WTO Members contemplate the scope that may exist in the current negotiations for making possible improvements to the GATS architecture even while keeping with its current foundations.

Under a GATS-like, hybrid approach to scheduling liberalization commitments, countries agree to undertake national treatment and market access commitments specifying (through reservations in scheduled areas) the nature of treatment or access offered to foreign services or foreign-service suppliers.[32] Under such an approach, countries retain the full right to undertake no commitments. In such instances, they are under no legal obligation to supply information to their trading partners on the nature of discriminatory or access-impeding regulations maintained at the domestic level.

A related feature of the GATS that tends to be replicated in RTAs that espouse a bottom-up approach to liberalization is to afford countries the possibility of making commitments that do not necessarily reflect or lock-in (i.e., are made below) the regulatory status quo (a long-standing practice in tariff negotiations that was replicated in a GATS setting).

---

[31] The purpose of the ensuing discussion is to note such differences without advocating any implicit hierarchy of policy desirability. Both approaches have strengths and weaknesses. The governance-enhancing aspects of negative listing have, however, been noted by several observers. See, in particular: Sauvé (1996); Snape and Bosworth (1996); World Trade Organization (2001); and Stephenson (2002).

[32] Members of MERCOSUR adopted one slightly different version of the positive-list approach with a view to liberalizing services trade within the region. According to MERCOSUR's Protocol of Montevideo on Trade in Services, annual rounds of negotiations based on the scheduling of increasing numbers of commitments in all sectors (with no exclusions) are to result in the elimination of all restrictions to services trade among the members of the group within ten years of the entry into force of the Protocol. The latter has yet to enter into force. See Stephenson (2001a) and Pena (2000).

The alternative, "top-down" approach to services trade and investment liberalization is based upon the concept of negative listing, whereby all sectors and non-conforming measures are to be liberalized unless otherwise specified in reservation lists appended to an agreement. Non-conforming measures contained in reservation lists are then usually liberalized through consultations or, as in the GATS, periodic negotiations. It bears noting however that most RTAs that employ a negative list approach to liberalization feature so-called "unbound" reservations, listing sectors in which Members wish to preserve the right to introduce new non-conforming measures in the future. In many RTAs, particularly those modeled on the NAFTA, such reservations nonetheless oblige member countries to list existing discriminatory or access-impairing measures whose effect on foreign services or service suppliers might in the future be made more burdensome.

It is interesting to note that despite the strong opposition that such an approach generated when first mooted by a few GATT Contracting Parties during the Uruguay Round, the negative-list approach to services liberalization has in recent years been adopted in a large number of RTAs covering services. Canada, Mexico and the United States pioneered this approach in the NAFTA in 1994. Since the NAFTA took effect, Mexico played a pivotal role in extending this liberalization approach and similar types of disciplines (i.e. right of non-establishment) on services to other RTAs it has signed with countries in South and Central America.[33]

A number of distinguishing features of negative listing can be identified. For one, such an approach signals adherence (subject to reservations) to an overarching set of general obligations. This is currently the case under the GATS primarily with respect to the Agreement's provisions on MFN treatment (Article II, with scope for one-time exceptions) and transparency (Article III), with virtually all other disciplines applying to sectors and modes of supply on those terms inscribed in members' schedules of commitments.

A second, and perhaps more immediately operational, defining characteristic of negative listing lies in its ability to generate a standstill, i.e., to establish a stronger floor of liberalization by locking-in the statutory or regulatory *status quo*. Such an approach therefore avoids the GATS practice of allowing a wedge to arise between applied and bound regulatory or statutory practices. The suggestion has been made that WTO Members could address this issue in GATS without revisiting the Agreement's negotiating modality by agreeing to a new framework provision whose purpose would

---

[33] The Andean community has adopted a somewhat different version of the negative list approach. Decision 439 on Trade in Services specifies that the process of liberalization is to begin when comprehensive (non-binding) national inventories of measures affecting trade in services for all members of the Andean Community are finalized. Discriminatory restrictions listed in these inventories are to be lifted gradually through a series of negotiations, ultimately resulting in a common market free of barriers to services trade within a five-year set out to conclude in 2005.

be to encourage governments to reflect the statutory or regulatory status quo in their scheduled commitments while keeping with the voluntary nature of such commitments (Sauvé and Wilkie, 2000).

Another governance-enhancing feature arising from the adoption of a negative list approach is the greater level of transparency it generates. The information contained in reservation lists may be important to prospective traders and investors, who will likely value the one-stop shopping attributes of a comprehensive inventory of potential restrictions in foreign markets. They are also likely to benefit home-country negotiators, assisting them in establishing a hierarchy of impediments to tackle in future negotiations. Such information can in turn lend itself more easily to formula-based liberalization, for instance by encouraging members to agree to reduce or progressively phase out "revealed" non-conforming measures that may be similar across countries (e.g. quantitative limitations on foreign ownership in airlines).

The practice of producing a negative list has also been shown to help generate a useful domestic policy dialogue between the trade-negotiating and regulatory communities, thereby encouraging countries to perform a comprehensive audit of existing trade- and investment-restrictive measures, benchmark domestic-regulatory regimes against best international practices, and revisit the rationale for, and most efficient means of satisfying, domestic policy objectives.

A further liberalizing feature found in a number of RTAs using a negative list approach to liberalization consists of a ratchet mechanism (See Table 6.2), whereby any autonomous liberalization measure undertaken by an RTA member between periodic negotiating rounds is automatically reflected in that member's schedule of commitments or lists of reservations. Such a provision typically aims at preventing countries from backsliding with respect to autonomously decreed policy changes. It may however need to be complemented by an arrangement to grant negotiating credit for autonomous liberalization in order to eliminate any incentive to refrain from unilateral liberalization in order to retain negotiating coinange.

Such provisions are found in many RTAs concluded in the Western Hemisphere where, besides the NAFTA, it has been adopted in several RTAs covering services and concluded *between* developing countries. For instance, Article 10 of Andean Community Decision 439 on Services applies to all new measures affecting trade in services adopted by member countries and does not allow for the establishment of new measures that would increase the degree of non-conformity or fail to comply with the commitments contained in Article 6 (market access) and Article 8 (national treatment) of the Decision. Article 36 of the CARICOM Protocol is also a *status quo* or standstill provision, prohibiting members from introducing any new restrictions on the provision of services in the Community by CARICOM nationals.

A provision of this type can exert positive effects on the investment climate of host countries by signaling to foreign suppliers the latter countries' commitment not to reverse the liberalizing course of policy change. Such credibility-enhancing provisions may be especially important for smaller countries that often find it difficult to attract larger doses of FDI.

Two potential pitfalls arising from the use of negative listing can however be identified. First, that such an approach may be administratively burdensome, particularly for developing countries. Such a burden may however be mitigated by allowing progressively in the completion of members' negative lists of non-conforming measures. In the NAFTA, for instance, sub-national governments were initially given an extra two years to complete their lists of non-conforming measures pertaining to services and investment. The NAFTA parties subsequently decided not to complete the lists at the sub-national level, opting instead for a standstill on existing non-conforming measures. Compliance with the production of negative lists has similarly been problematic elsewhere in the Western Hemisphere, as a number of agreements were concluded without such lists being finalized and without firm deadlines for doing so. The inability of "users" to access the information contained in the negative lists to such agreements deprives the latter of an important good-governance promoting feature.

A second, more substantive, concern relates to the fact that the adoption of a negative list implies that governments ultimately forgo the right to introduce discriminatory or access-impairing measures in future, including in sectors that do not exist or are not regulated at the time of an agreement's entry into force.

To assuage the latter concerns while promoting the transparency-enhancing properties associated with the use of negative listing, the suggestion has been made to encourage countries (including possibly in the WTO context) to exchange (as they have in the Andean Community and are considering doing within MERCOSUR) comprehensive (and non-binding) lists of non-conforming measures (Sauvé and Wilkie, 2000).

THE TREATMENT OF LABOR MOBILITY[34]

Regional agreements take a range of approaches to labor mobility. Some provide a relatively high degree of freedom of movement with few special procedures (e.g., the EEA and Europe Agreements, CARICOM). Others provide for some regulated mobility and involve relatively detailed special procedures implemented among few parties (e.g., NAFTA, U.S.–Chile, U.S.–Singapore, Canada–Chile). Others are aimed more at facilitating existing mobility, involving some special procedures, but with maximum flexibility for continuing existing national practices (e.g. APEC).

Coverage ranges from essentially only intra-corporate transferees and business visitors to the free movement of labor. A key consideration is the extent to which any of

---

[34] The discussion is this section is based on OECD (2002d).

these models could inform the future development of GATS disciplines. The scale of any potential labor movements may be more manageable at the regional level; and the ability to put in place any mitigating programs may be greater. Indeed, the larger and more diverse the membership of an RTA, the greater the flexibility provided for continuance of existing national migration practices. Administrative capacity is also an important factor, in particular for developing countries.

The differing approaches in RTAs to labor mobility reflect a range of factors, including the degree of geographical proximity of the parties and the extent of similarities in their levels of development, as well as other cultural and historical ties. While agreements among countries enjoying geographic proximity and similar levels of development generally adopt a more liberal approach to labor mobility (e.g. EU, EFTA, EEA, Trans-Tasman Travel Arrangement) as compared to agreements comprising geographically distant members of differing levels of development (e.g. APEC, U.S.–Jordan), this is not always the case (e.g. MERCOSUL, SAARC).

With very few exceptions, progress in facilitating the temporary movement of less skilled workers has not been extensive at the regional level. Indeed, RTAs tend to replicate the two key biases found in GATS favoring highly skilled (mostly professional) workers and the close links between investment and specialist categories the establishment and operation of such investment entails.

Observations regarding whether particular RTAs contain additional provisions to the GATS are thus generally made on the basis of whether the agreements include elements that are not covered by the general GATS provisions, rather than the specific commitments of WTO Members. For example, additional elements can include: access to the labor market (EU, EFTA, EEA, Trans-Tasman Travel Arrangement); full national treatment and market access for service suppliers (ANZCERTA); commitments on visas (NAFTA, U.S.–Singapore, U.S.–Chile, Canada–Chile), including for groups beyond service suppliers (U.S.–Jordan); special market access or facilitated access for certain groups, including beyond service suppliers (CARICOM, NAFTA, Canada–Chile, Europe Agreements, APEC); separate chapters dealing with all temporary movement, including that related to investment (Japan–Singapore) or to trade in goods or investment (Group of Three); specific reference to key personnel in relation to investment (E.U.–Mexico, FTAA); extension of WTO treatment to non-WTO Members (AFTA); or non discriminatory conditions for workers, including beyond service suppliers (Euro-Med).

Additionally, for the purposes of assessing the degree of liberalization offered in an RTA and for comparison with the GATS, provisions related to labor mobility in RTAs should be read in conjunction with provisions in the same agreements related to the supply of services. Facilitated movement of people does not always automatically entail the right to provide specific services; actual opportunities will also depend upon the degree of liberalization in particular service sectors. This is true not simply of agreements where labor mobility is covered only by mode 4 in the services chapter (e.g., MERCOSUR, E.U.–Mexico, U.S.–Jordan), but also of agreements that provide for broad freedom of movement (e.g., the E.U.) or where movement of natural persons related to services and investment is the subject of a separate chapter (Japan–Singapore).

Additionally, a number of agreements exclude certain service sectors from coverage (e.g. ANZCERTA, E.U.–Mexico, Europe Agreements) or apply special rules to certain sectors (e.g. E.U., E.U.–Mexico). Generally, the right to labor mobility does not automatically entail the right to practice a certain profession. National regulations regarding licensing and recognition of qualifications are still applied and candidates must meet all criteria and conditions.[35]

While some agreements allow for general mobility of people and confer immigration rights (e.g. E.U.), the majority of agreements provide only special access or facilitation of existing access within existing immigration arrangements. In most agreements, labor mobility does not over-ride general migration legislation and parties retain broad discretion to grant, refuse and administer residence permits and visas. Additionally, some agreements (e.g. Euro-Med) specify that liberalizing provisions of the agreement cannot be used to challenge immigration decisions refusing entry, or that dispute settlement under the agreement can only be invoked in cases where the matter involves a pattern of practice and local remedies have been exhausted (e.g. Canada–Chile, NAFTA).

ASSESSING THE DEPTH OF REGIONAL VS. MULTILATERAL LIBERALIZATION IN SERVICES TRADE

With the notable exception of land-transportation issues, where physical proximity stands out as a determinative facilitating feature, RTAs have on the whole made little tangible progress in opening up those service sectors that have to date proven particularly difficult to address at the multilateral level.

With the notable exception of the E.U. for intra-E.U. traffic and ASEAN, whose Members are currently considering the scope for an open-skies agreement for air-cargo transport), the vast majority of RTAs concluded to date have tended to exclude the bulk of air-transportation services from their coverage in a manner analogous to that found in GATS, where only a handful of commercially marginal aviation-related activities are covered.[36]

---

[35] Provisions facilitating mutual recognition are included in some agreements (e.g., EFTA) and others have complementary arrangements (e.g. the ANZCERTA Services Protocol, the Trans-Tasman Travel Arrangement and the Trans-Tasman Mutual Recognition Arrangement together provide that persons registered to practice an occupation in one country can practice an equivalent profession in the other country).

[36] Political and regulatory realities in civil aviation would appear to suggest, however, that air transport may in the future lend itself more readily to regional rather than multilateral liberalization (as may be evidenced by ongoing talks to create a Transatlantic aviation space as well as by strides made within ASEAN and APEC in the sector).

Relatively limited progress has similarly been achieved at the regional level in sectors where particular policy sensitivities arise, such as maritime transport and audio-visual services (and, to some extent, on the movement of service suppliers as discussed above). The same result obtains in sectors where the scope for meaningful liberalization was limited by technology or market structure and state ownership considerations at the time of the Uruguay Round and in the many RTAs negotiated during the Round or shortly thereafter. This is notably the case of energy services or of environmental services such as waste disposal or water distribution and/or treatment services.

More recently, however, regional advances have been made in market segments characterized by rapid technological and commercial change. The area of e-commerce, which was not yet a commercial reality at the time of either the Uruguay Round or the NAFTA, is one prominent example, with significant, precedent-setting progress made in the U.S.–Chile and U.S.–Singapore FTAs (See Box 6.4).

Advances are also notable in sectors where new, pro-liberalization, constituencies have emerged seeking to use trade agreements to secure expanded opportunities in world markets. This is notably the case of express delivery and courier services, which also feature prominently in the most recent FTAs concluded by the United States. Similarly, new areas of financial services, such as asset management or financial services delivered through electronic means, trade in higher education and related (e.g. educational testing) services, as well as the electronic delivery of health-related services, have received greater attention in a number of recent RTAs. It is possible that many such regional commitments could be replicated at the WTO level in the Doha Round (most of them are actively being discussed in ongoing request-offer negotiations under the GATS).

Just as RTAs may advance liberalization and rule-making over and above what may be possible in any given multilateral round, so too have RTAs tended in some circumstances to be simply overtaken by events at the multilateral level. Such a trend reveals the iterative and incremental nature of service-sector liberalization, where both regional and multilateral advances can reinforce each other over time. Thus, in the key infrastructural areas of basic telecommunications and financial services, the GATS has achieved a higher level of bound liberalization than that on offer in most RTAs.[37] In part, this may simply reflect timing issues. For instance, the conditions required to contemplate far-reaching liberalization in basic telecommunications services were generally not ripe at the time that the NAFTA was completed in 1993,[38] whereas the required constellation of forces—in political, regulatory, and technological terms—

---

[37] Negotiations in the GATS on financial services, and notably the development of the GATS Understanding on Commitments in Financial Services, took advantage of insights gained in addressing financial-market opening at the regional level. This was particularly the case under the NAFTA, whose chapter 14 addressed (in 1993) a range of issues that would feature prominently in negotiations of the WTO's 1997 Financial Services Agreement. See Sauvé and Gonzalez-Hermosillo (1993); Leroux (1995); and Sauvé and Steinfatt (2001).

[38] For instance, E.U. member countries had not yet put in place the pro-competitive regulatory framework required to achieve an integrated market for telecommunication services.

Box 6.4. Demonstration Effect Regionalism: The Digital Trade Agenda and RTAs

---

A central innovation of the current US Trade Promotion Authority (TPA) is its instruction to the USTR to conclude trade agreements that anticipate and prevent the creation of new trade barriers that may surface in the digital trade environment. Apart from the greater specificity of negotiating objectives on issues like the protection of U.S. trade remedy rules and the inclusion of labor and environmental standards that stand out vis-à-vis prior fast track authorities, the TPA posits a set of ambitious negotiating goals that in effect formalize a new U.S. digital trade policy. Under this negotiating agenda, a set of rules and trade concessions is called for that concerns the elimination of tariffs on physical media carrier, the liberalization of trade in telecommunications, computer, entertainment and other electronically deliverable services, free trade chapters on e-commerce, and a strong protection of intellectual property rights, especially copyrights, in an online environment. The digital-trade agenda is thus tailored to the objective of securing free trade in so-called digital products like music, software or movies that derive their value from "content" produced by the information technology and entertainment industries, and that were previously—in the offline world—delivered on physical carrier media like CDs. The new U.S. digital-trade policy also targets the trade liberalization of other services that can be delivered electronically across borders, such as financial, educational or health-related services.

The recent FTAs that the United States concluded with the governments of Chile and Singapore provide vivid illustrations of the above policy in practice. Both agreements have been described by the U.S. Industry Sector Advisory Committee (ISAC) on Services as featuring "groundbreaking" provisions on e-commerce that introduce the concept of digital products in trade agreements for the first time. The agreements' chapters on e-commerce prevent the application of customs duties on electronically-delivered digital products, assure the non-discriminatory treatment of digital products, address the valuation of physically delivered digital products and provide commitments to cooperate on e-commerce policy (on issues such as small and medium-sized enterprises, consumer confidence, cyber security, electronic signatures, IPR issues, and electronic government).

Sources: Adapted from Wunsch-Vincent (2003); U.S. Coalition of Service Industries (2003).

---

obtained at the time the GATS Agreement on Basic Telecommunications (ABT) was concluded in 1997.

Experience under both the ABT and the Financial Services Agreement (FSA) also suggests that, in some sectors, the political economy of multilateral bargaining, with its attendant gains in critical mass, may help overcome the resistance to liberalization arising in the narrower or asymmetrical confines of regional agreements.

Multilateral Constraints on Preferential Services Liberalization: Article V of the GATS

KEY FINDINGS

- The need for clarity in respect of the relationship between regional and multilateral disciplines on services has assumed heightened importance given the large number of regional trading agreements that have been signed or extended to the services area since the conclusion of the Uruguay Round.

- As with goods trade under Article 24 of the GATT, Article V of GATS imposes three conditions on economic integration agreements between WTO members for the latter to be deemed WTO-compatible. First, such agreements must have "substantial sectoral coverage" (Art. V:1(a)). Second, regional agreements are to provide for the absence or elimination of substantially all discrimination between or among the parties to the agreement in sectors subject to multilateral commitments. Third, such agreements are not to result in higher trade and investment barriers against third countries.

- The greater policy flexibility shown by WTO members towards preferential liberalization in services may in part reflect the novelty of the subject matter at the time of the Uruguay Round as well as the policy preferences of a number of important WTO members that were negotiating (or contemplating future) RTAs in services at the time that GATS Article V was being drafted.

- As with the GATT, compensation of non-members is only foreseen for increases in *explicit* discrimination under GATS (i.e. the raising of external barriers), and not for rises in implicit discrimination.

- Article V of GATS features a number of loopholes for the formation of agreements that do not fully comply with multilateral disciplines. In particular, Article V:3(b) allows developing countries particular flexibility in according more favorable treatment to firms and services that originate in parties to an integration agreement.

- Implementation of Article V of the GATS is likely to be more straightforward than that of Article 24 of the GATT. In large part this conclusion stems from the fact that GATS disciplines are both weaker with respect to internal liberalization and somewhat less ambiguous with respect to external protection.

Article V of the GATS provides for WTO Members to participate in regional trade arrangements that discriminate against the services or service providers of other countries. Thus Article V grants coverage for preferential treatment extended to services trade in derogation of the MFN obligation of GATS Article II. The underlying rationale behind this derogation is that preferential arrangements can contribute to the further liberalization of the multilateral trading system. The exemption from the MFN obligation, however, is based on a number of requirements set out in GATS Article V. Some of these requirements are similar to those of GATT Article 24, which governs the interface between the WTO and preferential agreements in goods trade, while others differ. Table 6.3 sets out the key provisions of Article V and of Article V *bis* governing labor market arrangements brokered at the regional level (the full text of both Articles is set out in Annexes to this module).

The need for clarity in respect of the relationship between regional and multilateral disciplines on services has assumed heightened importance given the large number of regional trading agreements that have been signed or extended to the services area since the conclusion of the Uruguay Round. For countries that are members to several integration agreements, the consistency of these agreements, as between each other, is also an important question. A further source of potential concern arises from the fact that several sectoral 'stand-alone' agreements on services have been concluded that may have no legal cover under the GATS if they have not been notified under the list of MFN Exemptions or if they have yet to be woven into broader integration arrangements.

Understanding Article V (Economic Integration) of GATS

Article V of the GATS is entitled "Economic Integration," not "Free Trade Areas and Customs Unions" (as in Article 24 of the GATT), reflecting the fact that the GATS covers not only cross-border trade in services, but also three other "modes of supply": (1) provision implying movement of the consumer to the location of the supplier; (2) services sold in the territory of a member country by entities originating in other contracting parties through a commercial presence; and (3) provision of services requiring the *temporary* movement of service suppliers who are nationals of a contracting party.

Analogous to Article 24 of the GATT, Article V of the GATS imposes three conditions on economic integration agreements between signatories of the GATS for the latter to be deemed WTO-compatible.[39] First, such agreements must have "substantial sectoral coverage" (Art. V:1(a)). An interpretive note states that this should be understood in terms of the number of sectors, volume of trade affected, and modes of supply. With respect to the latter, economic integration agreements should not provide for the *a priori* exclusion of any mode of supply.

Second, regional agreements are to provide for the absence or elimination of substantially all discrimination (which is defined as measures violating national treatment) between or among the parties to the agreement in sectors subject to multilateral commitments. This is to consist of the elimination of existing discriminatory measures *and/or* the prohibition of new or more discriminatory measures, and is to be achieved at the entry into force of the agreement or on the basis of a reasonable time frame (Art. V:1(b)). Third, such agreements are not to result in higher trade and investment barriers against third countries.

The above conditions constitute the "price" to be paid for the MFN obligation and specific commitments to be waived by WTO Members, i.e. for the implicit discrimination against non-members resulting from the agreement to be found multilaterally acceptable.

---

[39] The complete text of the Article is reproduced in Annex 1.

The first condition (Art. V:1(a)) pertains to the internal dimension of economic integration and is analogous to the "substantially all trade" criterion contained in Article 24 of the GATT. The rationale underlying this requirement is no doubt also similar: the goal is to "raise the cost" for GATS signatories to violate the MFN obligation. That is, regional integration is to be tolerated so long as it clearly constitutes an attempt to go (substantially) beyond GATS disciplines and coverage (i.e. is not intended to selectively circumvent the MFN obligation). However, the term "substantial sectoral coverage" is not the same as "substantially all" sectors, suggesting that the intention of the drafters of Article V of the GATS was perhaps to be more permissive than that of those drafting Article 24 of the GATT.

The above conclusion is reinforced when Art. V:1(b) is taken into account, which concerns the magnitude of required liberalization at the regional level. While Article 24 of the GATT requires that "duties and other restrictive regulations of commerce" be eliminated on substantially all intra-area trade, Article V:1(b) of the GATS posits that a mere standstill may be deemed sufficient in the services context. The GATS requirement is not elimination of existing discriminatory measures and prohibition of new measures, but elimination of existing discriminatory measures and/or a prohibition on new measures (see Article V:1.b(ii) in Annex 1).

The third condition—pertaining to the external dimension of integration agreements-is also analogous to language found in GATT Article 24. GATS Article V:4 states that economic integration agreements are not to raise the overall level of barriers to trade in services originating in other GATS members within the respective sectors or sub-sectors compared to the level applicable prior to such an agreement. Thus, average levels of protection against the rest of the world should not increase.

As a result of the more disaggregated (i.e. sub-sectoral) focus taken in Article V, a contracting party cannot argue—in contrast to GATT—that the average level or "general incidence" of protection has not changed, regardless of what might occur at the level of individual products (sub-sectors). Averaging has proven to be a difficult issue in the GATT, starting with the creation of the European Economic Community. As discussed in the next section, notwithstanding the apparent greater precision of the GATS in this regard, similar problems are likely to arise in the services context.

No distinctions are made between customs unions and free trade areas in GATS Article V. The absence of such a distinction, which appears to have been quite deliberate, may however turn out to be of some significance. For one, it implies that countries participating in an FTA may be permitted to raise some barriers against non-members, so long as the overall level of barriers of all the members of the agreement vis-à-vis non-members, for each of the relevant sectors or sub-sectors, does not increase. This is an important departure from the practice of GATT Article 24, which prohibits such "re-balancing" for members of a free trade area, unless compensation is offered to affected WTO Members.

There are a number of possible explanations for why this approach was not followed in the GATS context. One may be that negotiators felt that the distinction between FTAs and customs unions was not relevant in a services context. Currently the European Union is the only common market in existence where services markets are substantially liberalized, a process that has only just begun, somewhat unevenly, within the MERCOSUR.

Another possible explanation is the belief that integration agreements in services, even if not formally seeking to put in place a common external policy, will often involve some degree of harmonization of regulatory policies pertaining to specific sectors. This may then imply that some countries might have to increase the "restrictiveness" of their policies, while others become more "liberal". Any such harmonization is unlikely to allow the balancing requirement of Article V to be met (i.e. overall level of barriers is not to rise on a sectoral basis).

Under both the GATT and GATS, compensation of non-members is only foreseen for increases in explicit discrimination (i.e. the raising of external barriers), and not for rises in implicit discrimination. As noted earlier, the latter is a central—and inherent— feature of regional integration agreements and is "tolerated" by WTO Members so long as the necessary conditions noted above are met. Increases in explicit discrimination are not prohibited per se, but if imposed must be accompanied with compensation of negatively affected parties.

As stated in Article V:5, WTO members engaged in economic integration efforts intending to withdraw or modify specific commitments (i.e. raise external barriers) must follow the procedures set out in GATS Article XXI (Modification of Schedules), which is reproduced in Annex 2.

GATS Article XXI applies to any WTO member that is negatively affected by an increase in external barriers that violates a specific commitment. Members intending to alter previously negotiated concessions are required to notify the Council of the GATS at least three months before implementing contemplated changes. This is to be followed by consultations and negotiations with affected parties regarding compensation. Any such compensation is to be applied on an MFN basis. Such language contrasts with an equivalent GATT provision, Article 28 (Modification of Schedules), which pertains only to contracting parties with an initial negotiating interest or to those with a "principal supplying interest." In practice this excludes many smaller countries from the compensation negotiations. The GATS language is much broader and allows *any* affected signatory to participate.[40] GATS disciplines also differ from those of the GATT in that there is no provision made for "balancing." Article 24 of the GATT specifies that due account be taken of reductions of duties on the same tariff line made by other members of a customs union.

---

[40] The Uruguay Round's Final Act contained some modifications to Article 28 of the GATT, giving smaller countries greater access to such negotiations.

The GATS allows affected Members to request binding arbitration in instances where members cannot agree on the level of compensation required when renegotiating concessions. If the findings of the arbitration panel are not implemented by the country modifying or withdrawing a concession, affected countries that participated in the arbitration may retaliate through the withdrawal of substantially equivalent benefits. There is no need for authorization by the GATS Council. In this respect Article XXI of the GATS also goes beyond GATT Article 24, which only provides for countries concerned to refer disagreements regarding compensation to WTO Members, who may in turn "submit their views."

Both the GATT and GATS contain provisions relating to transparency and surveillance matters. Countries intending to form, join or modify a preferential agreement must notify the relevant multilateral bodies, make available relevant information that may be requested by non-members, and may be subjected to the scrutiny of a Working Party to determine the consistency of the agreement with multilateral rules. In both the GATT and GATS, a Working Party's report on the consistency of an agreement may lead to members acting jointly to make "recommendations" to member countries "as they deem appropriate."[41]

Article XXIV of GATT and Article V of GATS both contain loopholes allowing for the formation of agreements that do not fully comply with multilateral disciplines. As regards preferential agreements in the area of goods trade, WTO members may by a two-thirds majority approve a proposed regional trade agreement that does not fully comply with Article 24, provided that such proposals lead to the formation of a customs union or free trade area in the sense of Article 24.

Articles V:2 and V:3(a) of the GATS respectively allow for consideration to be given to the relationship between a particular regional agreement and the wider process of economic integration among member countries, and give developing countries flexibility regarding the realization of the internal liberalization requirements (i.e. Art. V:1). Given that a standstill may already be sufficient, presumably this flexibility will be invoked with respect to sectoral coverage.

It is also worth noting that Article V:3(a) does not speak of agreements *between* developing countries, but of agreements that have developing countries as parties. Thus, in principle, this 'flexibility' extends to agreements that have both developed and developing country signatories, such as the NAFTA or the EU–Chile FTA. Moreover, Article V:3(b) allows developing countries negotiating integration agreements among themselves to give more favorable treatment to firms, services and suppliers that

---

[41] The GATT differs from the GATS, however, in that Article 24 contains stronger language than GATS Article V on the 'conditionality' attached to the time frame for implementation. Article 24 requires that if a Working Party finds that the plan or schedule for an interim agreement is not likely to result in a GATT-consistent customs union or FTA, its members "shall not maintain or put into force ... [an] agreement if they are not prepared to modify it in accordance with ... the recommendations." No such provision is found in Article V of the GATS.

originate in parties to the agreement. That is, it allows for discrimination against firms originating (incorporated or headquartered) in non-members, even if the latter are established within the integrating area.

It is debatable whether such "special and differential treatment" type of provisions can be effective in building up world efficient domestic suppliers of services and in attracting the inward FDI (investment creation) that is often sought by participants in integration agreements.[42] The GATS' provisions are thus arguably weaker than those of the GATT in both substantive and procedural terms with respect to loopholes.

Implementing Article V

The Working Parties that have been established to determine the multilateral consistency of preferential liberalization agreements notified to the GATT and WTO have been singularly unsuccessful in reaching unanimous conclusions. The relevant question in the present context is whether GATT-like problems can be expected to arise in the GATS context.

As noted earlier, apart from notification and transparency requirements, the GATS, like the GATT, imposes two broad conditions on economic integration agreements: (1) external barriers may not be increased unless affected parties are compensated; and (2) internal (preferential) liberalization must have substantial sectoral coverage. With respect to both dimensions, one can surmise that GATS Working Parties might face fewer difficulties in reaching unanimous conclusions than those formed under GATT auspices. In part, this is a result of the introduction under the GATS of binding arbitration. It may also reflect, somewhat paradoxically, the fact that Article V disciplines are in some respects weaker.

As far as the internal dimension of integration agreements is concerned, the minimum that is required under the GATS is a standstill commitment.[43] This condition should be easily met by most regional agreements, as the only binding condition is that the standstill have substantial sectoral coverage.

Moreover, as noted earlier, the requirement under the GATS is not for preferential agreements to cover substantially *all* sectors, as under the GATT but rather to satisfy the

---

[42] Such language was introduced in the final stages of Uruguay Round negotiations in order to meet the concerns of countries that were parties to agreements containing similar provisions. This was also the reason for the inclusion of Article V *bis* on common labor markets, which was required in order to safeguard agreements such as those between Australia and New Zealand, and between the Nordic countries.

[43] It can be speculated that the drafting of this rather minimalistic requirement was in no small measure linked to the outcome of the 1989 Canada–United States Free Trade Agreement, which largely consisted of a standstill agreement applied to a finite list of covered services. The need to "protect" the services outcome of the North American Free Trade Agreement, which at the time of drafting GATS Article V was in the midst of being negotiated and whose outcome in terms of both sectoral coverage and liberalization was quite unclear, also influenced the drafting of GATS Article V.

more flexible notion of substantial sectoral coverage. And, to the extent that members of a regional integration agreement seek to go beyond a standstill (i.e. achieve some degree of rollback of protective measures), the drafting of Article V suggests that a mix of standstill and liberalization will be enough, so long as an agreement does indeed coverage a substantial number of sectors.

In those instances where this may not clearly obtain, GATS Article V:2 allows parties to integration arrangements to argue that such an agreement should nonetheless be accepted insofar as it is part of a wider process of economic integration or trade liberalization among member countries. Existing regional agreements among OECD countries—such as the European Union, the European Economic Area, the NAFTA, or the Australia–New Zealand Closer Economic Relations Agreement, all easily satisfy Article V requirements regarding internal liberalization.

Taking into account the additional flexibility foreseen for developing countries under GATS Article V, a similar conclusion most likely applies to arrangements between developing countries—e.g. the MERCOSUR, ASEAN/AFTA, Chile–Mexico FTA, etc.

Turning to disciplines against the raising of external barriers towards non-members, the GATS is more clear-cut than the GATT in that the constraint applies on a sectoral/sub-sectoral basis. This language improves upon the GATT insofar as there is less scope for WTO members to argue that the overall or average level of protection has *not* increased. Nonetheless, "averaging" problems still remain as the constraint imposed by Article V is that the *overall* level of barriers to services trade *within* sectors and sub-sectors not increase subsequent to the implementation of a regional integration agreement.

While the scope of the problem may have narrowed insofar as the focus of what needs to be investigated is clearer under GATS, the magnitude of the problem has arguably not declined, as investigations will have to determine the impact of services integration on a sector-by-sector basis. Moreover, the number of regional agreements that may involve GATS members changing their external policies may well be much greater than in the GATT context, as under the GATS all types of agreements may lead to some "re-balancing." Under the GATT, only customs unions are concerned by such re-balancing.

The simplification associated with the GATS requirement that the focus of attention should be on sectors and sub-sectors is likely to be offset by the ambiguity and complexity associated with the fact that the service sector barriers concerned are non-tariff—i.e. regulatory—in nature. Consequently, in many instances, determining—and measuring changes in—the overall level of barriers, whether ex post or ex ante, will remain difficult as these consist of regulatory and other measures affect the contestability of services markets.

Given that the services negotiators were clearly aware of the above problem, one can speculate that this was an important factor leading to the introduction of binding arbitration for disputes relating to the modification and/or re-negotiation of country schedules. The binding nature of arbitration should facilitate the implementation of the procedures contained in Article V.

Although implementation problems may be fewer under the GATS than those experienced in the GATT context, a key question from a policy perspective is whether the conditions imposed by Article V (i.e. the substance of the disciplines) are adequate to safeguard the interests of non-members. The relatively weak requirements regarding the extent of internal liberalization that must occur under Article V imply only a limited constraint on "strategic" violations of the MFN obligation and specific commitments made under the GATS.

As discussed above, in relation to third country effects, one desirable safeguard for WTO members could be to have the option of joining any economic integration agreement that is initially established between other WTO members. The absence of any requirement in Article V that integration agreements be "open" in principle—that is, contain an accession clause—can be regarded as an important shortcoming. Given the difficulty of determining simple, quantifiable criteria with which to ensure that integration agreements liberalizing both trade and factor flows are not detrimental to non-members, a requirement to incorporate such a provision would help ensure that the systemic effects of economic integration agreements remain positive overall. The likelihood of seeing the WTO Committee on Regional Agreements formulate such a recommendation to the General Council remains, however, an open question.

Final Thoughts: Advancing Services Rules and Liberalization at the Regional Level

Our discussion of progress made to date in services liberalization at the regional level suggests that expectations of significant forward momentum and path-breaking results in a regional context probably need to be tempered. Because of the sheer diversity of sectors and the complexity of regulations and institutions it brings into play, experience shows that services-trade liberalization tends to occur in small increments, consisting more often of policy consolidation (and, at times, even less) than *de novo* market opening. This appears to be the case regardless of the negotiating setting.

Another reason for tempering expectations is that most regional attempts at crafting a regime for services trade and investment can be expected to confront the same difficulties—conceptual and practical—encountered at the multilateral level. This is true both in market access terms (e.g. air and maritime transport, audio-visual services, education and health services, labor mobility) as well in terms of outstanding rule-making challenges (e.g. domestic regulation, emergency safeguards, subsidies). It is also true politically, as opposition to services liberalization (especially in sectors displaying public goods properties) have recently shown.

Despite the challenges posed by the above political economy considerations, RTAs afford services negotiators the opportunity to harness more fully the potential of service sector reforms while achieving a GATS+ outcome in both liberalization (market access) and rule-making terms. This closing section draws attention to an illustrative list of policy issues that services negotiators may wish to devote policy attention to at the regional level.

AGREEING ON THE ARCHITECTURE OF RULES ON SERVICES AND INVESTMENT

A central challenge of any RTA addressing services remains how to structure the agreement's services provisions and how to link disciplines on services and investment. Where parties to an integration agreement choose to pursue a GATS-based approach, this issue becomes largely moot. Yet, as has been shown, a large number of RTAs covering services, including those currently under negotiation, must contend with important policy choices regarding the best means of addressing the links between cross-border trade in services, investment (both within and outside services) and the movement of labor. None of these issues are easily resolved, and they have tended in practice to elicit significant policy divergences in a number of regional settings. Issues that can nonetheless usefully be considered in making architectural choices include the following:

- The pros and cons, including in terms of negotiating leverage, of separate rules on cross-border trade in services (modes 1 and 2), complemented by generic (i.e. horizontal) disciplines on investment (services and non-services) and the movement of people.

- The pros and cons, including on governance grounds, of preparing, even on a non-binding basis, a complete inventory of non-conforming measures maintained in service sectors (allowing a domestic audit of service sector regulation to be effected and promoting dialogue between trade and regulatory officials).[44]

- The pros and cons (including in terms of FDI signaling effects) of locking in the regulatory status quo in bound-liberalization commitments vs. binding below the status quo.

- The pros and cons, including in bargaining terms, of adopting a ratcheting mechanism.

- The desirability of providing for a right of non-establishment (i.e. a regulatory presumption in favor of cross-border supply whenever feasible, subject to reservations and limitations).

---

[44] One desirable approach to be considered in a regional context is the one taken by the Andean Community and currently contemplated under MERCOSUR, whereby each Member produces comprehensive lists of restrictive measures that are made available to all other Members.

- The pros and cons of protecting the acquired rights of foreign suppliers established prior to the completion of an RTA by host countries.

PROMOTING GREATER INTRA-REGIONAL LABOR MOBILITY

Developing countries have a strong interest in the movement of labor, their relatively abundant factor of production. And there is good reason to believe that the liberalization of such movement even on a temporary basis could produce substantial welfare gains for all countries. Such large potential gains justify a comprehensive coverage of this mode in international negotiations despite the significant political difficulties in facilitating greater labor mobility.[45]

It is desirable that international agreements be comprehensive in their coverage of the temporary movement of natural persons and endeavor not to exclude any category of skill or type of employment. Comprehensiveness of coverage does not, of course, prejudge the depth of liberalizing commitments and rules, which would be the subject of negotiations.

Consideration should be given to the issue of how best to afford facilitated temporary entry privileges and dedicated visa procedures (i.e. regional trade-related visas) to five categories of natural persons: (1) business visitors; (2) traders and investors; (3) intra-company transferees; (4) professionals; and (5) non professional essential personnel. The last category, which has not received significant attention to date in RTAs, would appear to hold potentially significant promise for developing country exporters, particularly in sectors (such as construction) where the ability to deploy workers with various skill categories holds the key to effective access in foreign markets.

Starting with the FTA it concluded with Australia in 2004, the United States has not incorporated a stand-alone chapter on labor mobility in its FTAs (even though Australian professionals were granted improved access through a separate piece of legislation). The E.U. too is under strong domestic political pressure to exclude labor mobility from its bilateral and regional agreements. Such exclusions do not bode well for significant

---

[45] Inventories of trade restrictive measures affecting services were finalized and adopted in Decision 510 of the Commission of the Andean Community on Adoption of the *Inventory of Measures Restricting Trade in Services* on 31 October 2001. The Decision, which is publicly available, allows for citizens of an Andean member to provide any services without restraint, except for those listed in the inventory. Restrictions are to be phased out gradually by the year 2005 through annual negotiations. Reliance on citizenship amounts to a restrictive rule of origin for third country suppliers. Members of CARICOM finalized their inventories of measures affecting services trade on March 1, 2002 and have made them publicly available on the CARICOM Secretariat's website. The removal of such restrictions in the context of implementation of Protocol II on Establishment, Services and Capital will take place on the basis of these inventories. Restrictions contained in the inventories are those measures that would impede or infringe upon the rights of CARICOM nationals to provide services, move capital and establish service enterprises within the region and which CARICOM members have committed to rescind over the 2003–5 period.

advances on mode 4 under the Doha Development Agenda, and raise questions about the WTO compatibility of these FTAs, particularly as Article V of GATS stipulates that RTAs cannot exclude a mode of supply on an a priori basis. All countries need to take greater advantage of the bilateral and regional fora to cooperate more broadly on labor mobility in order to provide the necessary reassurance to host countries, including by source countries assuming obligations to screen service providers and undertaking to facilitate their return.

STRENGTHENING REGULATORY TRANSPARENCY

Transparency is desirable because it helps to reduce transaction costs for private actors, promotes accountability and good governance and facilitates international trade negotiations. Its importance to services is especially critical given the regulatory nature of impediments to trade in the sector. Transparency has two dimensions. One is with regard to existing policies, and the other with regard to future changes in policy as well as processes leading to such changes.

Most agreements promote transparency on the first dimension by obliging countries to make public all measures of general application. Less progress has been made to date on the latter dimension, though as noted above, some advances have been made recently in a number of RTAs. Strengthened transparency obligations are not without costs. Because of the administrative burden such obligations can entail, any such provisions would need to be either couched in hortatory (i.e. best endeavor) language or, if legally binding, be phased in progressively according to countries' level of development and on the basis of greater doses of technical assistance from major donors (who typically happen to be from demandeur countries).

One approach to consider in this regard could be for RTA signatories to seek agreement on a Transparency Understanding dealing with various aspects of transparency in government regulatory processes and procedures, to which countries could subscribe, in whole or in part, on a voluntary basis. A model for such a flexible approach was provided by the WTO's Understanding on Commitments in Financial Services.

ADDRESSING REGULATORY IMPEDIMENTS

The diversity of services sectors and the difficulty in making certain policy-relevant generalizations have tended to favor sector-specific approaches to the interface between domestic regulation and services trade. However, even though services sectors differ greatly, our earlier discussion has recalled that the underlying economic and social reasons for regulatory intervention do not. Directing rule-making efforts on these reasons may provide the basis for the creation of meaningful disciplines on domestic regulation. Such a route may be particularly attractive at the regional level given the lesser likelihood and feasibility of pursuing harmonization and mutual recognition at the multilateral level.

As the practice of regionalism to date suggests, there is little doubt that progress in this area is likely to be difficult, fraught as it is with political and bureaucratic sensitivities. In today's environment of considerably heightened civil society activism, domestic regulators are becoming increasingly reluctant to seeing sovereign regulatory conduct subjected to a market access/trade prism. Yet greater efforts could be directed in the context of RTAs to introducing disciplines on non-discriminatory regulatory conduct. Doing so would ensure some measure of proportionality between regulatory objectives and the means to achieve them and would likely lessen adverse effects on trade and investment.

Negotiation of liberalization commitments in highly-regulated sectors or in sectors subject to particular types of market failure (e.g. network-based industries prone to monopolistic or oligopolistic market structures and the risk of abuse of dominance by major suppliers) will require the adoption of additional (pro-competitive) regulatory principles and greater regulatory cooperation. Such sectoral experimentation should be encouraged in a regional setting and supported once again through dedicated technical assistance activities. Addressing such issues is indeed likely to be a key component of any future attempt to secure deeper market integration in sectors such as energy (electricity, oil and gas pipelines), environmental services (water distribution), or transport (especially air transport). Cooperation in these areas is both more feasible and desirable in the regional context with proximate countries at a similar level of development than in the multilateral context.

GOVERNMENT PROCUREMENT OF SERVICES

There are many good governance reasons to liberalize government procurement, though experience, both in the WTO and in regional agreements, shows that most countries (developed and developing) are reluctant to immediately accept full liberalization of procurement of services (the same holds for goods procurement). Still, procurement liberalization holds the key to meaningful access for many service-providing firms that are otherwise subject to few other formal barriers to entry and operation. If countries are unwilling to give up the right to protect, they could nonetheless consider the scope for binding the margins of preference granted to national suppliers, and make these margins subject to unilateral or negotiated reductions—in a manner analogous to tariffs. Government procurement stands out as one of the areas where the chances of securing a WTO+ outcome at the regional level is greatest, given the limited membership of the WTO's Government Procurement Agreement (GPA).

One of the most important services sectors in the context of government procurement, and one in which several developing countries have a significant stake, is construction. All signatories to the GPA have accepted its disciplines in this sector above a certain threshold value. Yet in the GATS, Members have usually not bound themselves to grant market access to the supply of construction services through the presence of natural persons, except for certain limited categories of intra-corporate transferees. The assurance that workers can be temporarily moved to construction sites would greatly increase the benefit of non-discriminatory government procurement for developing countries. The same applies to procurement of other services, such as software and maritime transport. RTA negotiations could thus usefully consider the pros and cons of seeing any agreed market-access package in a particular services market feature a procurement complement (either as additional commitments in the services chapter) or as separate commitments under a generic procurement chapter. Moreover, because meaningfully contesting local-procurement markets typically implies a local presence on the part of foreign bidders, the liberalization of investment regimes can usefully underpin procurement liberalization.

RULES OF ORIGIN FOR SERVICES AND INVESTMENT

Under international law the nationality of a company is typically determined by its country of incorporation. However, the criterion of incorporation has been deemed to be inadequate for certain purposes. For example, it may accord nationality to corporations that are incorporated in a country for tax avoidance or related purposes, but do no business or have no assets in that country. This perceived inadequacy is reflected in many bilateral and plurilateral trade and investment agreements and in bilateral tax treaties.

Article V of the GATS states that a juridical person constituted under the laws of a party to a regional agreement shall be entitled to treatment granted under such an agreement provided it engages in substantive business operations in the territory of the parties to such an agreement. But, as noted above, in an RTA involving only developing countries, more favorable treatment may be granted to juridical persons owned or controlled by natural persons of the parties to such an agreement.

As discussed earlier, rules of origin can play a critical role in determining the degree to which RTAs discriminate against non-member countries, and hence the extent of potentially costly trade and investment diversion. When levels of protection differ between participating countries, the effective preference granted to a trading partner may depend on the restrictiveness of the rule of origin. In the extreme, if one participant has a completely open market, the adoption of a liberal rule of origin (one that confers the benefits of regional integration to all firms that can be shown to engage in substantial business activities in any one of the parties to an integration scheme) by the other participants will approximate MFN liberalization. While suffering from the bargaining handicaps of the MFN principle—it lessens the incentive to negotiate a preferential agreement and potentially reduces negotiating leverage vis-à-vis third countries—a liberal rule of origin nonetheless minimizes the costs of trade and investment diversion and is economically efficient, since it more readily affords access to world efficient suppliers.

Because a number of key service sectors—particularly the core infrastructural sectors of telecommunications, energy, finance, transport, water supply, distribution services—possess dynamic, growth-enhancing properties, securing access to the most efficient provider of such services may be of considerable importance to a country's longer-term growth and development prospects.[46] The policy stance taken with regard to rules of origin for services and investment in an RTA can thus play in important role promoting or inhibiting access to the most efficient suppliers of services. Adoption of rules of origin that restrict benefits to firms that are owned and controlled by nationals of member states can exert detrimental effects by potentially locking in integrating partners into sub-optimal patterns of production and consumption. Accordingly, RTA negotiators need to carefully weigh the pros and cons of adopting more or less restrictive rules of origin in services.

Box 6.5. Liberalizing Services Trade in the ASEAN Region

Carsten Fink

Introduction

At their Ninth Summit Meeting in Bali in 2003, Governments of the Association of South East Asian Nations (ASEAN) reaffirmed their pledge to free the flow of trade in services by earlier than 2020.[1] ASEAN's efforts to liberalize services trade had started eight years earlier. In 1995, ASEAN members concluded the ASEAN Framework Agreement on Services, which established the foundation for the scheduling of progressively more liberal trade commitments in the services domain. However, despite several rounds of negotiations, little progress was made in promoting the regional liberalization of services trade. The Bali Summit Meeting sought to reinvigorate the political imperative of integrating regional services markets and inject new life into a stalled negotiating process.

This Box briefly outlines where ASEAN negotiations in services stand, and the main factors that explain the lack of progress in these negotiations. It also offers several recommendations on how negotiations could be moved forward.

Where do ASEAN Negotiations in Services Stand?

The ASEAN Framework Agreement on Services (AFAS) is intended to be a 'GATS plus' agreement. The architecture of AFAS follows closely the GATS structure. The Agreement distinguishes between the four modes of service supply:

---

[46] See chapter 4 of World Bank (2003) for a fuller discussion of prospects for promoting greater labor mobility under trade agreements.

(1) cross-border supply; (2) consumption abroad; (3) commercial presence; and (4) movement of natural persons. Commitments are made according to a positive list of services sub-sectors and a negative list of remaining trade-restrictive measures. That is, countries choose the sub-sectors in which they wish to make binding market opening commitments and, in those sectors and for each mode of supply, identify all measures that limit the provision of services by foreigners. However, there is no obligation that commitments reflect applied policies.

The intended 'plus' element of AFAS is that ASEAN members are expected to schedule commitments that are wider and deeper than those under the GATS—at least for those ASEAN economies that are also members of the WTO. The final aim is to realize a free trade area in services by earlier than 2020. Since its inception, there have been three rounds of negotiations, with the third round to be completed by the end of 2004. However, these negotiations have not produced substantive liberalization. Most AFAS commitments do not go substantially beyond those scheduled under the GATS. And where they do, domestic policy is usually more liberal on an MFN basis, such that there seem to be no preferences given to ASEAN members.

As an illustration, Indonesia's AFAS commitment in maritime transport allows for 60 per cent foreign equity ownership in a joint venture shipping company, whereas Indonesia's (horizontal) GATS commitment only allows for 49 per cent foreign equity ownership. However, Indonesia's latest negative investment list allows a 95 per cent share ownership by foreigners—regardless of the country of origin of the foreign firm.

Dissatisfied with the slow progress, ASEAN members have launched several initiatives designed to encourage wider and deeper liberalization. First, under the so-called 'modified common sub-sector approach,' a particular sub-sector would be identified as a common sub-sector if three or more members make commitments in this particular sector under the GATS or the AFAS. The identified common sub-sector would be subjected to removal of all limitations for modes 1 and 2 and to progressive liberalization for mode 3 and mode 4. The idea behind this approach is "to pick low-hanging fruits"—that is, to promote the scheduling of commitments in sectors where there are few sensitivities about opening up.

Second, under the ASEAN-X formula, two or more members may conduct negotiations and agree to liberalize trade in services for specific sectors or sub-sectors, while other countries may join at a later stage whenever they are ready. The rationale for this approach is to expand and deepen negotiations in all sectors and sub-sectors among member countries who are ready and willing to do so. It can be seen as a form of ASEAN special and differential treatment, whereby poorer member states are not expected to schedule commitments as wide and deep as richer member states.

Third, with a view to facilitate the free flow of professional services in the ASEAN region, ASEAN members commenced negotiations on mutual recognition agreements (MRAs) for professional qualifications. These negotiations would seek to come up with modalities (or guidelines) for concluding MRAs for each professional service. However, MRAs would not necessarily be ASEAN-wide, but could be concluded on a bilateral basis. Substantial work has been conducted in the accountancy sub-sector, involving the professional bodies of member states. However, no modalities for concluding MRAs have been issued, so far. Notwithstanding this lack of progress, one of the recommendations coming out of the Bali summit in 2003 was to complete MRAs for qualifications in major professional services by 2008.[2]

Fourth and also as an outcome of the 2003 Bali Summit, ASEAN Economic Ministers identified eleven priority sectors for integration and nominated a member country as the champion (or coordinator) for each priority sector. Four of these eleven sectors have a substantial services component. These are e-ASEAN and healthcare (led by Singapore) as well as air travel and tourism (led by Thailand). Each coordinating country is in the process of developing a roadmap for integration. Proposed measures to promote deeper integration include accelerated services liberalization in these priority sectors by 2010, accelerated development of MRAs, visa exemptions for intra-ASEAN travel by 2005, facilitated movement of business persons and skilled labor by 2005. One of the rationales for the priority sector approach is to promote tangible progress on a limited range of sectors, which—if successful—could show the way for other sectors in the future.

Challenges in Moving Forward

The lack of progress in ASEAN services negotiations can be attributed to a large number of factors. Five challenges seem paramount in explaining why little has been achieved to date.

Challenge 1: Making the Case for Open Service Markets

Trade agreements are of limited use if governments are not convinced of the benefits of open service markets. Perceptions across ASEAN economies vary significantly. Singapore, which is host to competitive service industries, is unsurprisingly a more natural advocate of services liberalization than, say, Indonesia, which fears domestic service suppliers would mainly lose out from greater foreign competition. The economic pain brought by the Asian financial crisis has also created lingering skepticism about the gains from freeing services trade. Perceptions on the merits of open service markets can also vary across sectors within one country. For example, Vietnam welcomes greater foreign participation in the provision of health services to improve the quality and reach of services, but is reluctant to open up distribution services, fearing the displacement of traditional domestic retailers.

Uneasiness about the consequences of services liberalization translates into a defensive position in services negotiations. This leads policymakers to be reluctant in making binding commitments, because they wish to maintain a certain 'policy space,' in which market opening can be pursued gradually.[3] A related aspect is that export interests in services—which exist in all ASEAN economies—tend to be poorly understood. Services statistics are unreliable and sparse. Exporters themselves are not well organized. And foreign trade barriers mostly take the form of opaque regulatory measures. In addition, poorer economies usually have a comparative advantage in mode 4 trade, in which trade agreements have achieved the least to date. The limited prospects of improving market access for own exports tend to reinforce the defensive negotiating position of some countries in the region.

Challenge 2: Coordinating Trade Negotiations and Making Decisions

The conduct of trade negotiations in services requires careful coordination among various government agencies. Sectoral ministries—say for communications or transport—usually formulate and implement sectoral policies. Depending on the sector and country in question, Ministries of Finance and Prime Minister's Offices may also have a say on key reform questions. Trade negotiations may be conducted by the Ministry of Foreign Affairs, the Ministry of Trade, and/or the Ministry of Finance. Preparing for trade negotiations can be information and time-intensive. Insufficient inter-ministerial coordination in a number of ASEAN countries has arguably contributed to the slow progress in services negotiations. The fact that most countries also negotiate various bilateral trade agreements at the same time has not made the life of trade negotiators any easier.

A related problem is that trade negotiators often do not have the authority to take decisions on service sectors that are under the purview of specialized ministries. And the unwillingness of governments to commit to changes in laws that still need parliamentary approval adds to the lack of decision power during negotiations.

These institutional stumbling blocks are by no means particular to countries in the ASEAN region. Indeed, similar problems in other parts of the world explain why services agreements have achieved relatively little—both at the regional and multilateral level. Nonetheless, if ASEAN members are to move forward as set out in their vision, these obstacles need to be confronted.

Challenge 3: Trade Preferences and the Sequence of Negotiations

ASEAN's efforts to liberalize trade in services cannot be seen in isolation. Nine ASEAN countries (Brunei, Cambodia, Indonesia, Malaysia, Myanmar, the Philippines, Singapore, Thailand, and Vietnam) are members of the World Trade Organization (WTO). Thus, except Laos, ASEAN countries face simultaneous services negotiations at the multilateral level.

AFAS has opted for a liberal rule of origin. Any foreign-owned firm that is established and has substantial business interest in an ASEAN economy benefits from market-access conditions committed to under AFAS.[4] From an economic perspective, a liberal rule of origin should be seen as positive, because it lessens distortions due to trade diversion. However, it raises an important issue. If the margin of preference of AFAS commitments is small, ASEAN governments may not be willing to commit at the regional level in the first place, in order to sustain negotiating coinage at the WTO.

Even under a more restrictive rule of origin, ASEAN governments may be unwilling to enter into regional commitments that are substantially more liberal than the corresponding multilateral commitments. By signaling to other WTO members that a government can go further, a regional commitment may increase the pressure on ASEAN governments at the multilateral level. This may be a cause of concern for those ASEAN members, which have taken a defensive negotiating stance in the Doha negotiations. The sequence of regional and multilateral negotiations therefore has bearing on the outcome of ASEAN-wide negotiations. In particular, ASEAN governments may be reluctant to schedule wider and deeper regional commitments until the ongoing Doha round has come to closure.

Challenge 5: Promoting Regulatory Cooperation Among a Diverse Group of Countries

Regional trade agreements can play an important role in fostering trade-creating regulatory cooperation. Indeed, the conclusion of MRAs for professional services is seen as an important element in ASEAN services negotiations. At the same time, negotiations in the accountancy sub-sector have revealed the difficulties of bridging differences in national regulatory regimes. For example, certain ASEAN countries have not adopted international accounting standards, but rely on own standards (Malaysia, Indonesia) or the U.S. Generally Accepted Accounting Principles (Philippines). Language barriers, differences in legal regimes and disparities in the sophistication of regulatory institution add to the complexities encountered in making regulatory systems compatible.

As an alternative to promoting outright harmonization and mutual recognition, ASEAN countries could agree on regulatory guidelines or principles, on which two or more member countries could base deeper regulatory cooperation. Yet such a role for ASEAN has not yet crystallized.

How Could Negotiations be Moved Forward?

Recommendation 1: Developing a National Vision for the Service Sector For governments to productively engage in services negotiations, they need to have a clear idea where policy should go in a particular sector. Many ASEAN countries still lack a national vision for their service sector. Where should performance be 10 or 20 years from now? What will be the roles of the public and private sectors and of domestic and foreign service suppliers?

A second step is to develop a roadmap of how this vision is to be achieved. This requires a detailed diagnosis of current constraints. What motivates current barriers to services trade? Are they purely protectionist? Or are they motivated by weak institutions to regulate open and competitive markets, by concerns for the poor, by infant industry arguments, or by non-economic considerations? Such a diagnosis sets the stage for timing the opening of service markets to foreign providers, strengthening regulatory capacity, and managing the orderly exit of inefficient service suppliers.

The sharing of reform experiences and regulatory best practices at the ASEAN level could be supportive of this process. It would help in rooting services negotiations in domestic reform priorities.

Recommendation 2: Exchanging Services Commitments that Reflect the Status Quo A strong case can be made for the exchange of services commitments that truly reflect current policies in ASEAN economies. Such an exercise would not imply any actual liberalization. Still, in light of the limited progress over the past several years, it would seem an ambitious goal. Yet it would be a small step in light of where ASEAN economies want to be in 2010 and in 2020. The increased transparency of comprehensive commitments could provide benefits to interested traders and investors. It would also place future negotiations on a firmer footing by putting all trade restrictive measures that governments currently maintain on the table.

Some governments may have reservations about such an exercise. They may fear reduced "policy space" and increased pressure to make wider and deeper commitments at the WTO. Such concerns could be accommodated by initially allowing these commitments to not be legally binding. Similar exercises have been undertaken by other regional agreements in services (e.g. the Andean Community, MERCOSUR).

Recommendation 3: Identifying Export Interests in Services ASEAN governments would be more willing to engage in services negotiations if they saw the prospects of advancing own export interests. All ASEAN economies have some export interest in services. Arguably the most easily identifiable export interests are outside the region—for example, the exports of medical personnel from the Philippines or Indonesia to the U.S., U.K., Japan, and the Middle East.

Greater efforts need to be made in better understanding within ASEAN export interests as well as the foreign trade barriers that inhibit export expansion. Mobilizing the private sector could support such efforts.

A related aspect concerns the extent to which negotiating modalities allow for 'quid pro quos.' ASEAN members would be more likely to make commitments if they see that there are gains for everyone. The challenge here is to engage the poorer countries in the region that feel they have little offensive interests in services. Greater coverage of mode 4—in particular for unskilled workers—by richer ASEAN members could allow for greater reciprocity in services.[5] Another possibility may be to link negotiations in services to negotiations in other areas, notably trade in goods.

Recommendation 4: Strengthening Regulatory Cooperation Efforts of ASEAN members to conclude MRAs for professional services are worthwhile and should be strengthened. The scope and possible form of regulatory cooperation in other sectors need to be carefully studied. In some areas, differences in legal regimes and historical backgrounds may render outright regulatory harmonization at the ASEAN level infeasible. However, in these cases ASEAN regulatory initiatives may still be useful in setting the framework in which bilateral or plurilateral regulatory harmonization can be pursued.

Notes: ¨Adapted from Carsten Fink, "How to Analyze a Country's Services Trade Barriers," World Bank, September 30, 2004, based on preliminary findings of a World Bank Institute-supported research program on trade in services undertaken by the ASEAN Economic Forum. The views expressed here are personal and should not be attributed to the World Bank.
  [1] See Recommendations of the High-Level Task Force on ASEAN Economic Integration, available at: www.aseansec.org/hltf.htm
  [2] See Recommendations of the High-Level Task Force on ASEAN Economic Integration, available at: www.aseansec.org/hltf.htm
  [3] Reflecting the perceived need for "policy space," ASEAN countries have been among the strongest proponents for the establishment of an emergency safeguard mechanism under the WTO (as foreseen under GATS Article X), arguing that countries may be more willing to enter into commitments if these can be reversed in the case of unanticipated emergencies. Interestingly, the establishment of such a mechanism has not been pursued under AFAS.
  [4] See AFAS Article VI on the denial of benefits.
  [5] While an important phenomenon in the ASEAN region, temporary labor movement has so far been governed by arrangements outside the scope of trade agreements. Malaysia, for example, carefully manages worker inflows through quotas that are negotiated bilaterally with governments in the sending countries.

Box 6.6. Regionalism and Trade in Services in the Americas

Sherry Stephenson

The countries of the Western Hemisphere have been at the vanguard of the negotiation of regional trade agreements (RTAs), a proliferation of which has occurred in the region since the mid-1990s. Salient characteristics of these recently concluded RTAs are their ambitious nature and their comprehensive approach to the disciplining of trade.

Since the entry into force of the North American Free Trade Agreement (NAFTA) on January 1, 1994 all of the countries in the Western Hemisphere have become a member of one or more of the 20 regional agreements containing disciplines on trade in services or have deepened previous agreements to incorporate these. Countries in this region have gone further than the WTO GATS in accepting deeper integration as well as more comprehensive disciplines for services through the adoption of the "negative list" approach to services liberalization. In contrast to the GATS or "positive list" approach where WTO Members undertake national treatment and market access commitments specifying the type of access or treatment offered to foreign services or foreign service suppliers only in sectors that they choose to schedule, the negative list approach obliges members of those agreements to liberalize all measures affecting foreign services and service suppliers in all sectors unless otherwise specified in annexes containing reservations, or non-conforming measures. This is the so-called "list-or-lose" obligation.

Services negotiations carried out under the positive listing modality focus on the inclusion of commitments in national schedules and on the need to determine their broad equivalency for the purpose of reciprocity. This is much more difficult to do for services than for goods, because barriers to foreign service providers are not quantifiable border measures such as tariffs and quotas, but rather discriminatory elements contained in national laws, decrees, and regulations. Under the negative listing modality, negotiations focus on the content of the lists of reservations, or non-conforming measures, to ensure that these do not excessively compromise the liberalizing objective of the agreement.

In reality neither of the two negotiating modalities guarantees full liberalization and is not presumed to do so unless this objective is explicitly set out by members to any given integration agreement. The top-down agreements provide a great deal of information in a transparent form on the existing barriers to trade in services (non-conforming measures set out in the annexes), thus giving national service providers precise knowledge of foreign markets. In the bottom-up agreements the sectoral coverage of commitments as well as the type and comprehensiveness of information provided on the commitments may vary significantly between the members. Moreover, the type of conditions and limitations on market access and national treatment in national schedules are often listed as ceilings on or minimum levels of treatment and thus do not necessarily reflect actual practice. This possibility results in less transparency for service providers and less legal and economic certainty regarding market access.

Modality: Contrasting Approaches to Liberalization in RTAs

Positive List or "bottom up"	**Negative List or "top down"**
Characteristics	*Characteristics*
• Specific commitments by choice for sectors and modes of supply with national treatment and market access limitations	• Obligatory comprehensive sectoral coverage
• MFN treatment (with temporary exemptions)	• Unconditional MFN treatment and national treatment (reservations allowed)
	• No local presence requirement
	• Listing of non-discriminatory quantitative restrictions

Members of all but one of the regional agreements on services in the Western Hemisphere have opted for the more ambitious and more transparent approach to services liberalization constituted by the negative list approach.

Choice of Liberalization Modality in the Western Hemisphere

Choice of Liberalization Modality in the Western Hemisphere	
Negative list approach	
NAFTA	1994
Group of Three (now Colombia-Mexico	1995
Mexico–Costa Rica	1995
Mexico–Bolivia	1995
Chile–Canada	1997
CARICOM	1997
Andean Community	1998
CARICOM–Dominican Republic	1998
Central American Common Market–Dominican Republic	1999
Chile–Mexico	1999
Mexico–Nicaragua	1999
Chile–Central American Common Market	1999
Mexico–Northern Triangle	2001
Central American Common Market-Panama (signed)	2002
Chile–United States	2004
DR-CAFTA–U.S. (in force for U.S., El Salvador, Honduras, Nicaragua, and Guatemala)	2004
Peru–U.S. (signed)	2006
Colombia–U.S. (signed)	2006
Panama–U.S. (negotiations completed)	2006
Only Agreement following a Positive List Approach	
MERCOSUR	1998

The table illustrates the structure of most FTAs in the Americas as regards the treatment of services within the agreements which are set forth their texts in a horizontal or cross-cutting manner. The Cross-Border Services chapter covers modes 1, 2, and 4 (the latter to a limited extent) and often contains an Annex on Professional Services to facilitate this exchange. It contains the basic disciplines of most favored nation treatment, national treatment, market access, no local presence, and denial of benefits. Recent agreements also include disciplines on transparency and domestic regulation applying to both cross-border trade and investment in services. The chapter on Investment is based on three pillars: protection by means of legal security through clear and transparent rules; market access through maintenance of status quo or liberalization of barriers to investment; and dispute settlement provisions. This chapter covers both trade in goods and services. The chapter on Temporary Entry for Business Persons contains a set of provisions to facilitate administrative and legal procedures for temporary entry. These provisions do not include obligations for visas or employment considerations. Generally, there is no market access component in this chapter, although specific quotas may be specified separately, for example through side letters. The Financial Services chapter covers cross-border trade and a broad definition of investment—financial services. It contains specific disciplines for the liberalization of trade in financial services and includes trade-related aspects of regulatory disciplines but does not include specific types of regulations. Prudential requirements are outside the scope of this chapter. The Telecommunication Chapter contains specific disciplines for the telecommunications sector which are of a "pro-regulatory" nature and a part of competition policy. This chapter further elaborates disciplines based on the WTO Reference Paper for Telecom 1997 but does not provide for an explicit market access component. Finally, agreements in the Americas provide for Lists of Existing and Future Non-Conforming Measures which set out all of those laws by national (and state) governments that violate the core disciplines of the agreement. Since these lists are meant to be comprehensive in coverage and as they are based by legal requirement on specific laws or administrative decrees, they provide for an extremely high degree of transparency to service providers, the ultimate users and beneficiaries of these trade agreements.

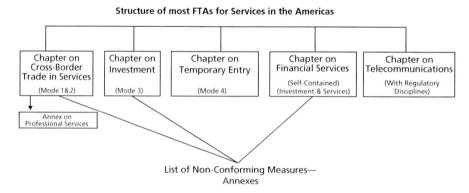

Figure 6.B.6.1. Regionalism and trade in services in the Americas

   Regional agreements on services in the Americas have pushed the envelope of liberalization by opening services markets in some key sectors of Latin American countries that were previously under monopoly control or resistant to creating more market access opportunities. They have also served as catalysts to foster advancements in regulatory reforms. Under the NAFTA Mexico opened its banking sector to majority control by foreign investors from the U.S. and Canada for existing financial institutions, a policy that was soon after further liberalized to allow for majority ownership by all trading partners. Also in the financial services sector, the U.S.–Chile Free Trade Agreement resulted in significant new liberalization by allowing the consumption abroad (mode 2) of all financial services by Chilean nationals and by liberalizing the cross-border management of collective investment schemes. Under the DR-CAFTA the entrenched domestic monopolies in telecoms and insurance will be gradually liberalized in Costa Rica for certain services as a result of the trade agreement with the U.S. And for the members of the Andean Community, their regional integration agreement has served to promote a far-reaching liberalization agenda in telecoms, through the enactment of comprehensive community legislation setting forth provisions on promotion of competition, market access, common definitions, and regulatory harmonization towards the creation of the Andean common market for telecommunications.

Annex 1: GATS Article V—Economic Integration

1. This Agreement shall not prevent any of its Members from being a party to or entering into an agreement liberalizing trade in services between or among the parties to such an agreement, provided that such an agreement:
   (a) has substantial sectoral coverage,[47] and
   (b) provides for the absence or elimination of substantially all discrimination, in the sense of Article XVII, between or among the parties, in the sectors covered under sub-paragraph (a), through:
      (i) elimination of existing discriminatory measures, and/or
      (ii) prohibition of new or more discriminatory measures,
         either at the entry into force of that agreement or on the basis of a reasonable time-frame, except for measures permitted under Articles XI, XII, XIV and XIV bis.

2. In evaluating whether the conditions under paragraph 1(b) are met, consideration may be given to the relationship of the agreement to a wider process of economic integration or trade liberalization among the countries concerned.

3. (a) Where developing countries are parties to an agreement of the type referred to in paragraph 1, flexibility shall be provided for regarding the conditions set out in paragraph 1, in particular sub-paragraph (b), in accordance with the level of development of the countries concerned, both overall and in individual sectors and sub-sectors.
   (b) Notwithstanding paragraph 6 below, in the case of an agreement of the type referred to in paragraph 1 involving only developing countries, more favorable treatment may be granted to juridical persons owned or controlled by natural persons of the parties to such an agreement.

---

[47] This condition is understood in terms of number of sectors, volume of trade affected, and modes of supply. In order to meet this condition, agreements should not provide for the *a priori* exclusion of any mode of supply.

4. Any agreement referred to in paragraph 1 shall be designed to facilitate trade between the parties to the agreement and shall not in respect of any Member outside the agreement raise the overall level of barriers to trade in services within the respective sectors or sub-sectors compared to the level applicable prior to such an agreement.

5. If, in the conclusion, enlargement or any significant modification of any agreement under paragraph 1, a Member intends to withdraw or modify a specific commitment inconsistently with the terms and conditions set out in its schedule, it shall provide at least 90 days advance notice of such modification or withdrawal and the procedure set forth in paragraphs 2–4 of Article XXI shall apply.

6. A service supplier of any other Member that is a juridical person constituted under the laws of a party to an agreement referred to in paragraph 1 shall be entitled to treatment granted under such agreement, provided that it engages in substantive business operations in the territory of the parties to such agreement.

7. (a) Members which are parties to any agreement referred to in paragraph 1 shall promptly notify any such agreement and any enlargement or any significant modification thereto the Council for Trade in Services. They shall also make available to the Council such relevant information as may be requested by it. The Council may establish a working party to examine such an agreement or enlargement or modification thereto and to report to the Council on its consistency with this Article.

   (b) Members which are parties to any agreement referred to in paragraph 1 which is implemented on the basis of a time-frame shall report periodically to the Council for Trade in Services on its implementation. The Council may establish a working party to examine such reports if it deems it necessary.

   (c) Based on the reports of the working parties referred to in paragraphs (a) and (b), the Council may make recommendations to the parties as it deems appropriate.

8. A Member which is a party to any agreement referred to in paragraph 1 may not seek compensation for trade benefits that may accrue to any other Member from such agreement.

Article V*bis*: Labor Markets Integration Agreements

This Agreement shall not prevent any of its Members from being a party to an agreement establishing full integration[48] of the labor markets between or among the parties to such an agreement, provided that such an agreement:

---

[48] Typically, such integration provides citizens of the parties concerned with a right of free entry to the employment markets of the parties and includes measures concerning conditions of pay, other conditions of employment and social benefits.

(a) exempts citizens of parties to the agreement from requirements concerning residency and work permits;

(b) is notified to the Council for Trade in Services.

Annex 2: GATS Article XXI: Modification of Schedules

1. (a) A Member (hereafter in this Article referred to as the "modifying Member") may modify or withdraw any commitment in its schedule, at any time after three years have elapsed from the date on which that commitment entered into force, in accordance with the provisions of this Article.

   (b) A modifying Member shall notify its intent to modify or withdraw a commitment pursuant to this Article to the Council for Trade in Services no later than three months before the intended date of implementation of the modification or withdrawal.

2. (a) At the request of any Member whose benefits under this Agreement may be affected (hereafter "an affected Member") by a proposed modification or withdrawal notified under paragraph 1(b), the modifying Member shall enter into negotiations with a view to reaching agreement on any necessary compensatory adjustment. In such negotiations and agreement, the Members concerned shall endeavor to maintain a general level of mutually advantageous commitments not less favorable to trade than that provided for in schedules of specific commitments prior to such negotiations.

   (b) Compensatory adjustments shall be made on a most-favored-nation basis.

3. (a) If agreement is not reached between the modifying Member and any affected Member before the end of the period provided for negotiations, such affected Member may refer the matter to arbitration. Any affected Member that wishes to enforce a right that it may have to compensation must participate in the arbitration.

   (b) If no affected Member has requested arbitration, the modifying Member shall be free to implement the proposed modification or withdrawal.

4. (a) The modifying Member may not modify or withdraw its commitment until it has made compensatory adjustments in conformity with the findings of the arbitration.

   (b) If the modifying Member implements its proposed modification or withdrawal and does not comply with the findings of the arbitration, any affected Member that participated in the arbitration may modify or withdraw substantially equivalent benefits in conformity with those findings. Notwithstanding Article II, such a modification or withdrawal may be implemented solely with respect to the modifying Member.

5. The Council for Trade in Services shall establish procedures for rectification or modification of schedules of commitments. Any Member which has modified or withdrawn scheduled commitments under this Article shall modify its schedule according to such procedures.

References

Beviglia-Zampetti, A. 2000. "Mutual Recognition Agreements and Services Trade: Promise and Pitfalls," in P. Sauvé and R.M. Stern (eds.), *GATS 2000: New Directions in Services Trade Liberalization*. Washington, D.C.: The Brookings Institution.

—— and P. Sauvé. 2004. "Rules of Origin for Services: A Review of Current Practice." Paper prepared for a conference on *Rules of Origin in the Americas* (February 20–1). Washington, D.C.: Inter-American Development Bank.

Bhagwati, Jagdish. 1990. "Multilateralism at Risk: The GATT is Dead, Long Live the GATT," *The World Economy*, 13(2): 149–69.

Coe, D.T., E. Helpman, and A.W. Hoffmaister. 1997. "North–South R&D Spillovers," *The Economic Journal*, 107.

Commission of the European Communities. 2002. "The State of the Internal Market for Services—Report from the Commission to the Council and the European Parliament." Presented under the first stage of the Internal Market Strategy for Services, COM(2002)41 Final, Brussels (July 30).

Hart, M. and P. Sauvé. 1997. "Does Size Matter? Canadian Perspectives on the Development of Government Procurement Disciplines in North America," in B. Hoekman and P. Mavroidis (eds.), *Law and Policy in Public Purchasing*. Ann Arbor: University of Michigan Press, pp. 203–21.

Hoekman, B. M. and P. Sauvé. 1994. "Liberalizing Trade in Services," World Bank Discussion Paper 243. Washington, D.C.: World Bank.

Iida, K. and J. Nielson. 2003. "Strengthening Regulatory Transparency," in A. Mattoo and P. Sauvé (eds.), *Domestic Regulation and Service Trade Liberalization*. Washington, D.C.: Oxford University Press for the World Bank.

Kemp, M. and H. Wan. 1976. "An Elementary Proposition Concerning the Formation of Customs Unions," *Journal of International Economics* 6: 95–7.

Lawrence, R. Z. 1991. "Regional Trade Agreements: Building Blocks or Stumbling Blocks?," in R. O'Brien (ed.), *Finance and the International Economy: 5*. London: Oxford University Press.

Leebron, D. 2003. "Title," in A. Mattoo and P. Sauvé (eds.), *Domestic Regulation and Service Trade Liberalization*. Washington, D.C.: Oxford University Press for the World Bank.

Leroux, E. 1995. *Le libre-échange nord-américain et les services financiers*. Collection Minerve, Montréal: Editions Yvon Blais.

Lumengo-Neso, O., M. Olarreaga, and M. Schiff 2001. "On Indirect Trade-Related Research and Development Spillovers," World Bank Policy Research Working Paper No. 2580, Washington, D.C.: World Bank.

McMillan, J. 1993. "Does Regional Integration Foster Open Trade? Economic Theory and GATT's Article XXIV," in K. Anderson and R. Blackhurst (eds.), *Regional Integration and the Global Trading System*. London: Harvester-Wheatsheaf.

Markusen, J. 1983. "Factor Movements and Commodity Trade as Complements," *Journal of International Economics* 14: 341–56.

Mattoo, A. and C. Fink. 2002. "Regional Agreements and Trade in Services: Policy Issues," World Bank Policy Research Working Paper No. 2852, (June), Washington, D.C.: World Bank.

—— R. Rathindran, and A. Subramanian. 2006. "Measuring Services Trade Liberalization and Its Impact on Economic Growth: An Illustration," *Journal of Economic Integration*, 21(1): 64–98.

—— and P. Sauvé 2003. "Domestic Regulation and the GATS: Looking Ahead," in A. Mattoo and P. Sauvé (eds.), *Domestic Regulation and Service Trade Liberalization*. Washington, D.C.: Oxford University Press for the World Bank.

Monge-Narango. 2003. "Lessons from the NAFTA for Latin America and the Caribbean," Background Paper for World Bank, mimeo. Washington, D.C.: World Bank.

Nicolaïdis, K. and J. P. Trachtman. 2000. "From Policed National Treatment to...," in P. Sauvé and R. M. Stern (eds.) *GATS 2000: New Directions in Services Trade Liberalization*. Washington, D.C.: Brookings Institution Press.

OECD. 2002a. "The Relationship Between the Multilateral Trade System and Regional Trade Agreements: Government Procurement," TD/TC/WP(2002)24 (April 15).

OECD. 2002b. "The Relationship Between Regional Trade Agreements and the Multilateral Trading System: Investment," TD/TC/WP(2002)18.

OECD. 2002c. "Labor Mobility in RTAs," TD/TC/WP(2002)16.

OECD. 2002d. *Service Providers on the Move: Taking a Closer Look at Labor Mobility and the GATS*. Paris: OECD Trade Directorate.

OECD. 2002e. "The Relationship Between Regional Trade Agreements and the Multilateral Trading System: Services," TD/TC/WP(2002)21.

Panagariya, A. 2000. "Preferential Trade Liberalization: The Traditional Theory and New Developments," *Journal of Economic Literature* 38(2): 287–331.

Pena, M.-A. 2000. "Services in MERCOSUR: The Protocol of Montevideo," in S. M. Stephenson (ed.), *Services Trade in the Western Hemisphere: Liberalization, Integration and Reform*. Washington, D.C.: Trade Unit of the Organization of American States and Brookings Institution Press, pp. 154–68.

Primo-Braga, C. 1992. "NAFTA and the Rest of the World," in N. Lustig, B. Bosworth, and R. Lawrence (eds.), *North American Free Trade: Assessing the Impact*. Washington, D.C.: Brookings Institution.

Sauvé, P. 1996. "Services and the International Contestability of Markets," *Transnational Corporations* 5(1): 37–56.

—— 2000. "Making Progress on Trade and Investment: Multilateral vs. Regional Perspectives," in S. M. Stephenson (ed.), *Services Trade in the Western Hemisphere: Liberalization, Integration and Reform*. Washington, D.C.: Trade Unit of the Organization of American States and Brookings Institution Press, pp. 72–85.

Sauvé, P. 2002. "Completing the GATS Framework: Safeguards, Subsidies and Government Procurement," in B. Hoekman, A. Mattoo, and P. English (eds.), *Development, Trade and the WTO: A Handbook*. Washington, D.C.: World Bank, pp. 326–35.

—— and B. Gonzalez-Hermosillo. 1993. "Implications of the NAFTA for Canadian Financial Institutions," in C.D. Howe Institute Commentary, No. 44 (April). Toronto: C.D. Howe Institute.

—— and K. Steinfatt. 2001. "Financial Services and the WTO: What Next?," in R. E. Litan, P. Masson, and M. Pomerleano (eds.), *Open Doors: Foreign Participation in Financial Systems in Developing Countries*. Washington, D.C.: The World Bank Group, International Monetary Fund, and Brookings Institution Press, pp. 351–86.

—— and C. Wilkie. 2000. "Investment Liberalization in GATS," in P. Sauvé and R. M. Stern (eds.), *GATS 2000: New Directions in Services Trade Liberalization*, Washington, D.C.: Center for Business and Government, Harvard University and the Brookings Institution Press, pp. 331–63.

Snape, R. and M. Bosworth. 1996. "Advancing Services Negotiations," in J. Schott (ed.), *The World Trading System: Challenges Ahead*. Washington, D.C.: Institute for International Economics, pp. 185–203.

Stephenson, S.M. 2001a. "Deepening Disciplines for Trade in Services," OAS Trade Unit Studies: Analyses on Trade and Integration in the Americas (March). Washington, D.C.: Organization of American States.

—— 2002. "Regional Versus Multilateral Liberalization of Services," *World Trade Review* (July) 1(2): 187–209.

Tirole, J. 1998. *The Theory of Industrial Organization*. Cambridge, M.A.: MIT Press.

Trachtman, J. P. 2003. "Title", in A. Mattoo and P. Sauvé (eds.), *Domestic Regulation and Service Trade Liberalization*. Washington, D.C.: Oxford University Press for the World Bank.

United States Coalition of Service Industries. 2003. "Reports of ISAC 13 on the U.S.–Chile and U.S.–Singapore Free Trade Agreements." Available at: www.uscsi.org

World Bank. 2000. *Trade Blocs*. New York: Oxford University Press.

World Bank 2001. *Global Economic Prospects and the Developing Countries 2002: Making Trade Work for the Poor*, Washington, D.C.: World Bank.

World Bank 2003. *Global Economic Prospects and the Developing Countries 2004: Realizing the Promise of the Doha Round*. Washington, D.C.: World Bank.

World Trade Organization. 2000. "Regional Integration: Synopsis of WTO Agreements and Related Provisions," paper prepared for Libreville 2000, Meeting of African Trade Ministers, MM/LIB/SYN 14 (October 23). Geneva: WTO.

World Trade Organization. 2001. *Market Access: Unfinished Business—Post Uruguay Round Issues*, Special Study No. 6. Geneva: World Trade Organization.

Wunsch-Vincent, S. 2003. "The Digital Trade Agenda of the U.S.: Parallel Tracks of Bilateral, Regional and Multilateral Liberalization." *Aussenwirtschaft* 58: 7–46.

Part III

Sectoral and Modal Analysis

7 Financial Services and International Trade Agreements: The Development Dimension

Wendy Dobson

This chapter begins with an introduction to financial services and their special role in an economy, and distinguishes trade policy reform in financial services, domestic deregulation, and capital account liberalization. The second section examines the impact of trade policy reform drawing on empirical evidence. The third section defines the elements of successful trade policy reform, while the final section explores how financial services liberalization in the WTO negotiations can contribute constructively to development goals. In the addenda to the chapter, Patricio Contreras reviews in Box 7.1 the experiences of financial liberalization in the Western Hemisphere, and, in Box 7.2, Yan Wang reviews China's pre- and post-WTO accession involving financial services liberalization.

Introduction, Definitions, and GATS Overview

The questions to be addressed are as follows: What are financial services? What is financial services trade liberalization? How does it differ from capital account liberalization? How does it relate to the GATS framework?

At the outset, a number of definitions are necessary to clarify terms common in industrial, empirical and trade policy usage.

The financial services sector is composed of users and providers of financial services and the government agencies that regulate them. Users of financial services are households, firms and governments. Households save, invest and finance purchases through personal loans from banks and other financial services providers (FSPs); corporations use the services of banks in the form of secured and unsecured loans and revolving credit facilities or through the sale of debt obligations. Governments also borrow from banks and issue securities.

FSPs are of two main types:

- Financial intermediaries (institutions that create or acquire financial assets and obtain the funding for those assets by issuing liabilities) including deposit-taking intermediaries (commercial banks, savings institutions), and nonbank financial intermediaries (NBFIs) such as insurance, finance, credit, leasing and investment companies; and

- Direct finance institutions in capital markets such as brokerages and securities firms that facilitate transactions undertaken directly between the providers and users of funds, such as underwriting and selling bonds and equities. These firms may operate in both the primary (original issue) and secondary (resale) markets for these securities.

Financial services are defined in the GATS Annex on Financial Services as "…any service of a financial nature offered by a financial service supplier of a Member." Financial service suppliers do not include state-owned or -controlled entities. Financial services include insurance and insurance related services, banking, financial trading, asset management, brokerages, settlement and clearing services, provision of financial information and advisory services.

Financial institutions refer to the FSPs and the regulatory agencies that enforce the rules governing what FSPs may do and how they do it. Financial institutions mobilize an economy's resources and facilitate the transactions necessary for economic exchange. One of the central problems that financial institutions address is that of information asymmetry between the providers and users of funds, that is, the unequal knowledge on the parts of providers of funds about the ability of users of funds (i.e. the performance of firms or individuals' ability) to repay. Because of this "leap in the dark" (Caprio, 2002) characteristic of many financial transactions (will the borrower or issuer be able to repay in full at a later date?), the financial sector is inherently unstable.

On the asset side, financial institutions take on risk in valuing projects and funding borrowers whose ability to repay is uncertain. On the liability side, creditors and depositors have imperfect information on the actual position of financial institutions and must have confidence in those institutions. When these institutions are highly leveraged, lack liquidity or provide little information on their assets, they are vulnerable to losses in confidence and depositors have an incentive to flee when confidence erodes.

Financial institutions play a critical role in managing risks and closing information gaps. They reduce the risks faced by investors by pooling their savings and distributing them among many users, so diversifying risk. They also collect and evaluate the information necessary to make prudent and productive investment decisions. And they participate in corporate governance by evaluating the performance of corporate borrowers and, when necessary, compelling them to act in the best interests of the firm – and therefore of its providers of funds.

The domestic banking industry can be a particular source of fragility in all countries, but more so in developing countries and transition economies. Why? Because many of these economies are relatively small and domestic economic activity is concentrated in particular industries or commodities, making it difficult to diversify risk and absorb shocks to the financial system. Immature financial systems (ones that rely exclusively on banking services and debt instruments, or on state-owned banks, for example) can add to the problems. Empirical evidence confirms that state ownership is generally negatively related to financial sector development and growth. "Greater state ownership of banks tends to be associated with higher interest rate spreads, less private credit, less activity on the stock exchange, and less non-bank credit even after controlling for many other factors."[1]

Domestic financial reform refers to the process of deregulation of domestic financial services. Deregulation has several dimensions: the withdrawal of government intervention through, for example, privatizing state-owned banks; freeing key prices like interest rates to be market-determined; and removal of restrictions on intra-sectoral activities so that, for example, banks can offer insurance. A third dimension is the strengthening of domestic financial institutions and markets to increase the efficiency with which finance is channeled from depositors and investors to borrowers and issuers.

Financial services liberalization, the most commonly used term for trade policy reform in financial services refers to the removal of discriminatory regulation, that is, either quantitative or qualitative regulations that discriminate against foreign FSPs and domestic FSPs with respect to market entry or commercial presence, that is, the opening of domestic financial markets to allow cross-border trade in financial services and the entry of foreign FSPs under mode 3 of providing services via foreign direct investment (FDI) transactions under modes 1, 2, and 4, with specific reference to financial services.[2]

Trade in financial services entails as well certain GATS obligations:

- Transparency requires each Member to publish promptly "all relevant measures of general application" affecting trade in services.

- Most-favored-nation (MFN) principle prevents Members from discriminating among their trading partners. The Agreement, however, permits Members to list temporary exemptions to MFN.[3] In the case of financial services, a number of MFN exemptions had been maintained when the preceding round of negotiations were concluded in mid-1995, some of which reserved the right to apply reciprocity as a basis for granting market access.[4] One of the key objectives of the extended negotiations was to achieve the removal of such exemptions and reach a full MFN-based result.

---

[1] See Caprio (2002: 15).   [2] This section draws on Mattoo (2000).

[3] The exemptions are subject to review and should, in principle, not last more than ten years.

[4] Among them was the MFN exemption of the United States, which reserved the right to discriminate between trading partners with respect to new entry or the expansion of existing activities, in order to "protect existing activities of United States service suppliers abroad and to ensure substantially full market access and national treatment in international financial markets." See Key (1997).

- Market access (Article XVI) and national treatment (Article XVII). The liberalizing content of the GATS depends on the extent and nature of sector-specific commitments assumed by individual Members with respect to these two provisions. These provisions apply only to sectors explicitly included by a Member in its schedule of commitments and there too are subject to the limitations that a Member has scheduled. GATS commitments are guarantees but the absence of such guarantees need not mean that access to a particular market is denied. In fact, there are several markets where conditions of access are more liberal than those bound under the GATS.

The market access provision prohibits six types of limitations, unless they have been inscribed by a Member in its schedule. These are: (a) limitations on the number of suppliers; (b) limitations on the total value of service transactions or assets; (c) limitations on the total number of service operations or on the total quantity of service output; (d) limitations on the total number of natural persons that may be employed; (e) measures that restrict or require specific types of legal entity or joint venture; and (f) limitations on the participation of foreign capital. In scheduled sectors, the existence of any of these limitations has to be indicated with respect to each of the four modes of supply, described above.

National treatment is defined as treatment no less favorable than that accorded to domestic services and service suppliers. Members may inscribe limitations on national treatment in their schedules—with respect to each of the four modes of supply, as in the case of the market access provision.[5]

THE IMPLICATIONS OF GATS COMMITMENTS FOR NATIONAL POLICIES

Frequently the question is asked about Members' GATS commitments in relation to national policy objectives. GATS commitments are not intended to compromise governments' ability to pursue sound regulatory and macro-economic policies. Indeed GATS commitments allow considerable freedom to achieve such domestic economic objectives as *prudential regulation and macro-economic policy.*

In financial services, specific commitments are made in accordance with the Annex on financial services that complements the basic rules and definitions of the GATS taking into account the specific characteristics of financial services. Paragraph 2(a) states that:

Notwithstanding any other provisions of the Agreement, a Member shall not be prevented from taking measures for prudential reasons, including for the protection of investors, depositors, policy holders or persons to whom a fiduciary duty is owed by a financial service supplier, or to ensure the integrity and stability of the financial system.

---

[5] Negotiators rejected the traditional GATT approach of making national treatment an overarching principle of general application. Granting market access with full national treatment would have been the equivalent of establishing free trade, whereas governments wanted the option of adopting a more gradual and conditioned approach to opening up their markets. Some have suggested that it may be desirable to replicate a goods-like regime in services with full national treatment and bound taxes on foreign providers that would be progressively negotiated down.

However, the same paragraph notes that prudential measures that do not conform with other provisions of the GATS, must not be used as a means of avoiding commitments or obligations under the Agreement.[6] Even so, regulators have discretion in their choice of prudential measures—especially since no definition or indicative list of such measures is provided in the Annex.[7]

In conducting macro-economic policy, for example, when a central bank conducts open market operations, conditions in the financial sector could be affected through the impact of such interventions on the money supply, interest rates or exchange rates. Services supplied in the exercise of governmental authority, including activities conducted by a central bank or monetary authority or by any other public entity in pursuit of monetary or exchange rate policies, are excluded from the scope of the GATS.[8] As well, such macro-economic management measures as reserve requirements on banks could presumably be justified as measures to ensure the soundness and stability of the financial system under the terms of the Annex on Financial Services.

Of course, governments may also wish to maintain other rules and regulations that influence the operations of markets and competition in a market, such as for example, a requirement to lend to certain sectors or individuals, or lending mandated on the basis of preferential interest rates for certain types of lending. Even though such measures may not be the most efficient means of achieving particular objectives, these policies are not necessarily subject to GATS commitments. If they are neither discriminatory nor intended to restrict the access of foreign suppliers to a market, then such domestic regulatory measures would be permitted provided they met certain basic criteria, such as impartiality and objectivity (specified in Article VI of the GATS).

FINANCIAL SERVICES LIBERALIZATION AND POLICY COHERENCE

Policy coherence is a term that applies to these three complementary activities: trade policy reform; domestic financial reform; and capital account opening. The mutually reinforcing relationships among trade policy reform in GATS negotiations and domestic reform are emphasized in the extensive international programs conducted by the IMF, World Bank, Bank for International Settlements and other institutions to strengthen the domestic financial systems of their members (Key, 2004). Trade policy reforms that free

---

[6] This language differs from and is weaker than that in Article XIV dealing with General Exceptions in that it does not require that the measures be *necessary* to achieve the stated objectives.

[7] Such measures presumably include capital adequacy requirements, restrictions on credit concentration or portfolio allocation, and disclosure and reporting requirements, as well as licensing criteria imposed on financial institutions to ensure the solvency and healthy operation of those institutions. As Kono et al. (1997) argue, the continuing process of regulatory harmonization and enhanced cooperation among financial regulators and supervisors at the BIS (Bank for International Settlements) and in IOSCO (International Organization of Securities Commissions) and elsewhere maintain discipline in the introduction and implementation of prudential measures.

[8] Under Article I:3 of the GATS and the Annex on Financial Services.

up cross-border supply of services and market entry for foreign FSPs eventually require loosening of restrictions on at least some forms of capital flows. This inter-relationship sometimes raises fears about the impact of increased competition, loss of autonomy and increased volatility of capital flows, each of which is discussed below.

The interaction between capital controls and opening the market to foreign financial services providers arises when domestic financial services transactions involve international capital account transactions. While it is possible for some international trade in financial services to take place without cross-border capital flows, controls such as exchange controls substantially reduce users' freedom to buy financial services directly from foreign FSPs and may discourage the FSPs from entering an economy. Arrangements for delivering financial services across borders without affecting capital flows will also be costly. Opening the capital account, therefore, although a distinct issue from that of trade policy reform in financial services, sooner or later becomes an issue that countries must face.

In principle, domestic reform and trade policy reform can be seen as precursors of capital account liberalization. A sound and diverse financial system will better intermediate volatile international capital flows. But there is no one-size-fits-all approach to sequencing, as a variety of sequences seen in various countries will demonstrate. For example, Taiwan has not fully deregulated its domestic financial markets and still imposes some restrictions on the capital account, but it permits market access by foreign FSPs. South Korea restricted both market access and capital flows, yet in 1997 still experienced a severe balance of payments crisis related in part to a weak record of domestic reform.

Systematic studies of country experience demonstrate successful interactions among these three dimensions of policy. Brazil, Chile, New Zealand, Hungary, Portugal, and Spain are all countries that have had successful experiences in opening up to foreign firms. They are also examples of countries that have engaged in domestic reforms to strengthen prudential supervision of their domestic financial systems (World Bank, 2002: 85). Other studies show that diversity in ownership contributes to greater stability of credit in times of crisis (Barth et al., 2000a b; and LaPorta et al., 2000). Several countries with significant foreign presence, such as Argentina and Mexico, have benefited from the access of these institutions to foreign capital in times of crisis (Dages et al., 2000). Foreign presence also encourages a stronger more transparent regulatory and supervisory framework to ensure understanding of and compliance with local rules.

The record on foreign entry, domestic reform and removal of capital account restrictions is more mixed. Chile's experience is one example. Chile reformed its domestic financial market in the late 1970s, opened its capital account in 1980, experienced a financial crisis, re-imposed restrictions on capital flows and later resumed domestic reform and opening. Chile has also had successful experience with controlling capital inflows. [9] China and India,

---

[9] Chile's requirements that a percentage of the value of new lending and investments into the country be placed in an interest-free deposit with the central bank for one year (this requirement has been 0 per cent since 1998) and that foreign investors keep their investments in Chile for at least one year are associated with a change in the mix of foreign borrowing and reducing volatile short-term debt.

two large economies where domestic reform is still work-in-progress, restrict both capital account transactions and market entry by foreign FSPs.[10]

It is important to note, however, that GATS commitments do not oblige a Member to allow international capital mobility. But if a Member undertakes a market-access commitment in relation to the cross-border supply of a service and if the cross-border movement of capital is an essential part of the service itself, that Member is committed to allow such movement of capital. Further, if a Member undertakes a market-access commitment in relation to the supply of a service through commercial presence, that Member is committed to allow related inflows of capital. But Members do not have any obligations with respect to capital flows related to consumption abroad, and with respect to capital outflows related to commercial presence.[11] The imposition of restrictions on current or capital transactions in the event of serious balance-of-payments and external financial difficulties or the threat thereof (Article XII) is permitted.[12]

The Impact of Trade Policy Reform in Financial Services

The following questions are considered in this section. What are the social and economic impacts of trade policy reform? What are the benefits and risks of trade policy reform for broader financial sector development, growth, income distribution and poverty?

ECONOMIC IMPACTS OF TRADE POLICY REFORM

Recent work traces the linkages between financial development, trade policy reform and economic growth.[13] Levine (1996, 2004) traces the channels by which foreign bank entry influences domestic financial development. Conceptually, it is argued that foreign banks can provide high-quality banking services at lower cost, spur quality improvements and

---

[10] As part of its WTO accession agreement in 2001, China's undertakings included permission for foreign bank entry into domestic currency businesses in December 2006. By that time, capital account restrictions, particularly on outward FDI by Chinese firms, had been relaxed. Bit many observers argue that China should not open its capital account more extensively until reform of the banking system is further advanced and the high level of non-performing loans has been reduced. Further details on China's financial sector reforms are noted in Box 7.2.

[11] This can be inferred by reading Article XI, the provision on international payments and transfers together with footnote 8 to Article XVI, the market-access provision.

[12] Article XII stipulates that the restrictions shall not discriminate among Members, shall be consistent with the Articles of Agreement of the Fund, and shall be temporary and be phased out progressively as the situation improves.

[13] See, for example, King and Levine (1993 a, b, c); Levine (1996, 2004); Levine et al. (2000); Baekert et al. (2001); and Caprio (2002).

cost-cutting in the domestic banking industry; promote better accounting, auditing, and rating institutions; and increase the pressure on governments for greater transparency in prudential regulation.

Enhanced market access for foreign insurers will also allow local markets to diversify risk more effectively and to benefit from the foreign companies' know-how and resources (Skipper, 1996). Such changes will increase the efficiency with which capital is allocated and spur economic growth over what would otherwise have been the case.

These arguments illustrate some of the economic impacts of trade policy reform. At least six impacts can be identified, beginning with the effect on domestic competition provided by FSPs, and the associated benefits to households, firms and governments as users of financial services.

Increased Domestic Competition

Users benefit from increased competition and access to foreign expertise in a number of intangible ways such as improved quality of services and wider choice. These benefits take the form of: (1) access to new service channels (credit cards and electronic banking being obvious examples); (2) faster access to services; (3) better credit assessment procedures and information-gathering techniques, and (4) wider choice of products and vendors. Users also benefit from easier and more effective diversification of risk.

Households, businesses and governments are the main users of financial services, and they benefit from domestic reform and liberalization by realizing cost savings and quality improvements in financial services.[14] In the industrialized countries it has been demonstrated that as financial institutions face stiffer competition from both domestic competitors and foreign entrants they learn to exploit economies of scale and scope, reduce managerial inefficiency, and make better use of advanced technology. Savers and investors earn higher rates of return; they have wider choice of savings instruments and opportunities to diversify risk, as well as easier access to financial products. Those seeking funds benefit from better risk appraisal, reduced waiting times, a wider range of lending instruments, a wider range of maturities and expanded access to funds.

In Europe, the Cecchini Commission Report (Ceccini, 1988) predicted that opening trade in financial services would reduce unit costs by facilitating economies of scale, increasing competition, reducing price markups and increasing managerial efficiency. More recent studies broadly confirm these claims (Kono et al., 1997).

---

[14] For a summary of research and research results, see Berger et al. (1993). Claessens et al. (1998) using bank level data for 80 countries show that foreign ownership reduces the profitability and overall expenses of domestic banks, suggesting positive welfare gains for consumers.

Catalysts for Domestic Reform

Because foreign entry is likely to make some domestic financial restrictions redundant, it may play a catalytic role in domestic reform (Edey and Hviding, 1995). The experience of countries acceding to the EU suggests that increased foreign entry bolstered the domestic financial sector framework by creating a constituency for improved regulation and supervision, better disclosure rules and an improved legal and regulatory framework (World Bank, 2002: 85).

Anticipating the arrival of foreign entrants can also be a powerful catalyst for domestic reform, as the 2001 Chinese WTO accession agreement illustrates. During the subsequent phase in period which ended in December 2006, designed to allow domestic firms and individuals to adjust to increasing competition, the PRC has gradually removed geographic and regulatory restrictions on foreign FSPs and liberalized the scope of permitted business. The final commitments fully opened the sector to foreign access at the end of 2006 while maintaining some limitation on cross-border supply and foreign ownership. In insurance services, foreign non-life insurers were immediately permitted to establish a branch or joint venture with 51 percent foreign ownership, and to establish wholly owned subsidiaries in two years. Life insurers were permitted 50 percent ownership of joint ventures immediately.

Catalysts for Great Regulatory Transparency

The participation of foreign financial institutions tends to require greater transparency of domestic regulations and practices. Information about laws, regulations, and administrative guidelines must become available to all market participants to ensure that they are fully aware of their rights and obligations arising from trade-related rules. Implicitly, entry of foreign financial institutions allows a country to import strong prudential supervision for that portion of the financial system, since, for example, the foreign affiliates of banks are supervised on a consolidated basis by regulators in the home country. The branches and subsidiaries of foreign financial institutions are also likely to have disclosure, accounting and reporting requirements that are closely aligned with best international practice.

Enhance Robustness of the Domestic
Financial System to Shocks

Foreign banks can provide a more stable source of credit, in that they can call upon their parents for additional funding and capital if needed, which can make the banking system more resilient in the face of shocks. The parents are better able to provide such funds because they hold internationally diversified portfolios. Several countries with significant foreign presence, such as Argentina and Mexico, have benefited from the access of these institutions to foreign capital during times of crisis (Dages et al., 2000).

Suppliers of New Skills, Products, Technologies

FSPs can provide new skills, new products and technology that eventually diffuse into the domestic financial system, assisting its modernization, as the president of a leading Indonesian insurance firm commented:

> It is common knowledge that the foreign banks operating in Indonesia are the source of banking expertise. They have trained a great many Indonesian men who later have become managers of national private banks. The number is so great that almost every national private bank has one of its managers originating from foreign banks...It is noteworthy that the foreign banks who are operating in Indonesia have played a major role in improving the know-how and expertise of our Indonesian bankers.[15]

Facilitate Access to International Capital

Mode 3 reforms can facilitate access to international capital markets and augment the amount of saving available for productive investment. For example, the Thai trade policy regime lifted restrictions on foreign entry and foreign equity participation for ten years to help recapitalize the financial system following the 1997 crisis. One hundred per cent foreign ownership is now permitted of Thailand's commercial banks and finance companies. This permission extends only until 2007, when any new foreign equity will then be limited to a 49 per cent share. The rationale for this temporary reform is that foreign firms willing to assist in recapitalizing and modernizing the financial sector at a time of great crisis should be rewarded, but not indefinitely.

Economic Risks and Uncertainties

More recent work on the impact of foreign bank entry debates some of these general observations.

While empirical evidence confirms that foreign bank entry is most beneficial when it is part of a more general liberalization of trade and production of financial services, foreign entry is not without risks. Foreign FSPs with more diversified portfolios help to increase efficiency. Offsetting this benefit, however, is the risk that liberalization may not yield a more stable source of credit for domestic borrowers. If foreign bank entry is

---

[15] Munir Sjamsoeddin, President and Director of TP Asuransi Bintang, at the XVth Conference of the East Asian Insurance Congress, Jakarta, September 15–20, 1990.

accompanied by reduced barriers to capital outflows, banks may use funds raised in the domestic market to undertake external lending. In such a case, domestic borrowers may not have the same degree of access to domestic savings as before liberalization. Another risk is that foreign banks might shift funds abruptly from one market to another as they perceive changes in risk-adjusted returns.

Governments make differing stability—efficiency tradeoffs, however. In Central Europe, for example, the need to build institutions quickly combined with the cost of bank recapitalization programs, persuaded authorities to liberalize foreign entry. In Mexico and Venezuela in the mid-1990s, the scale of domestic banking problems created incentives to allow more foreign entry to access new sources of capital and financial expertise. Thailand's case cited above is another example.

More generally, anecdotal explanations for slow increases in foreign participation suggest a number of concerns, real and perceived, particularly about foreign banks. Some of the arguments are as follows:

- Foreign banks "cherry pick" the most desirable markets and customers, leaving the domestic banks with higher-risk assets and customers. This phenomenon was most likely to occur in the early stages of liberalization when domestic institutions still hold loans carried at fixed rates while foreign competitors are able to set higher rates for loans and deposits. The disadvantaged institutions then attempt to compensate by taking high-return, but high-risk activities, especially if their deposits are insured. There are also concerns about the potential for selective servicing by foreigner suppliers. It is feared that the latter will only service profitable market segments and that the resulting under-provision of retail banking in rural areas, for example, could then have detrimental effects on the economy.

- Foreign banks are more likely to "cut and run" during crises.

- Foreign banks' contribution to efficient credit allocation has to be seen in the context of small and concentrated industrial structures in which credit risk evaluation methods, such as centralized credit scoring (widely used in mature markets), facing informational constraints in emerging markets will lead to reduced credit to small firms. The resulting impact can be to encourage the development of oligopolistic, rather than competitive, industrial structures.

- Foreign "names" may not guarantee safety and soundness. Banks operating in industrial economies and with ownership links with reputable foreign entities may be a source of fragility, as with BCCI. Supervisory authorities have learned from such incidents and are increasing their attention to cross-border operations.

Empirical evidence for these propositions is limited. IMF (2002) summarizes the findings of several studies. This evidence indicates the beneficial impact on local banks of more competition. For example, a cross-national study of the behavior of 80 banks in mature and emerging market economies in the 1988–95 period shows that significant foreign bank entry was associated with the reduction of profitability and overall expenses of domestic banks (i.e. efficiency as well as profitability effects). Another study cited by IMF (2002) shows that foreign banks operating in a sample of emerging markets are relatively more efficient than domestic banks. But other evidence shows that domestic banks can improve their performance. For example, a study of Chile shows that local banks are more profitable for two reasons: one is that Chile developed a strong banking system after its banking crisis in the early 1980s; the second is that foreign banks performance was impaired during the execution of mergers with local banks. Another study of Latin American banks in 1999 shows, further, that local banks were able to overcome competitive disadvantages with foreign FSPs by developing new sources of international funding, resorting to international consultants, and selective association with foreign and local companies to improve their systems and products.

Other work studies the differential economic impacts of foreign bank lending. Clarke, Cull and Peria (2001) and Clarke, Cull, Peria, and Sanchez (2001) conclude that small firms obtain credit from foreign banks as much as they do from domestic banks and that firms' access to credit eases when foreign banks enter the market. Giannetti and Ongena (2005) study the impact of foreign bank lending on firm growth and financing. They find that such lending stimulates growth in firm sales, assets and leverage, but that this effect is muted for smaller firms.

Available evidence also confirms the stabilizing impact of foreign bank participation, i.e., reducing the probability of a banking crisis, and evidence of a long term commitment to markets once entered. Unfortunately there are very few studies of these factors (IMF, 2000:168–70).

The sharp rise in foreign bank participation in a number of emerging market economies suggests that authorities in these countries seem to see entry as having an overall positive effect on efficiency and stability of national banking systems. New Zealand's banks are almost entirely foreign-owned, albeit by Australians, located next door; in Chile foreign banks account for 54 per cent of bank assets; the Latin America average, excluding Brazil and Mexico, was 40 per cent in 1999; and in the Czech Republic, Hungary, and Poland, foreign ownership averaged over 44 per cent (IMF, 2000: table 7.1).

These conclusions need some qualification with respect to African economies. While Africans were among the major liberalizers of core banking and insurance services in the FSA, more recent analyses of African financial sectors indicate that small domestic market size constrains financial system development in many of these countries. Thus, trade policy reforms that permit foreign bank entry, for example, may simply increase the concentration of banks in a small economy and reduce the marginal returns to foreign entry. Instead, a more desirable objective of such a small economy may be to increase market size (by liberalizing the cross-border supply of services by existing FSPs) and to diversify the sector by encouraging capital market institutions (World Bank, 2000: 160–9).

SOCIAL IMPACTS

How should governments view the potential contribution of foreign FSPs to addressing issues of poverty alleviation and the access of low-income and rural-based savers and borrowers to financial services? Traditionally governments have assigned this task to government-owned savings banks and cooperatives or thrifts—institutions that provide basic savings services and invest in low risk assets that provide low returns and few credit services.

Very few examples of foreign FSP activities are available. One example can be found in the Philippines where the insurance industry plays a significant role in mobilizing capital and channeling it to development requirements. A US firm, which established a presence in the Philippines in 1947, has developed a series of products to channel savings into investment projects. The first product was an endowment policy for farmers and small merchants, which helped them to build savings in rural areas where banks were scarce. Their savings were invested in roads and water facilities. In the 1950s a product was developed to channel funds into middle-income housing at a time of shortage. Later this firm developed the Philippines' first public mutual fund (Financial Leaders Group, 1997).

Conversely, some evidence is available indicating that financial services liberalization had an adverse effect on access to credit for rural areas and the poor. Mosely (1999) uses sample survey data on households in Uganda, Kenya, Malawi, and Lesotho for the 1992–7 period and reports that the share of households with access to rural credit rose in Kenya and Uganda, but declined in Malawi and Lesotho. This study indicates that domestic financial reforms targeted to rural areas and the poor had more positive impact.

This finding is consistent with the growing number of examples of domestic programs that target finance to rural areas and the poor through micro-credit lending institutions, such as the Grameen Bank in Bangladesh and the Bank Rakyat Indonesia (BRI) in Indonesia. Grameen Bank demonstrates that peer pressure from other small savers and borrowers helps to operate successful credit programs involving modest individual credits. BRI has built a business of lending to small enterprises, both rural and urban. It began as a state-owned enterprise, was troubled by non-performing loans (NPLs) and then was overhauled to introduce lending expertise and appropriate incentive systems. Nearly one-third of all Indonesian households hold accounts with the bank (McCawley, 2003). In 2003 the Indonesian government sold 30 per cent of its shares in an initial public offering.[16]

---

[16] See BRI website (http://www.ir-bri.com).

It is also useful to note, in conclusion, that governments can under the GATS impose requirements that address concerns about the provision of financial services in rural areas. For example, universal service obligations might be considered as part of licensing requirements, provided these do not discriminate between foreign and domestic financial institutions. Social objectives could then be met without sacrificing the efficiency benefits of competition. But this conclusion should be balanced by the fact that foreign FSPs often consider themselves at a distinct disadvantage in providing retail services (i.e., to individual savers and borrowers) because they lack local knowledge necessary to observe the "know your customer" rule.

The Elements of Successful Trade Policy Reform

The questions to be considered in this section are the following. What can we say with confidence about the elements of successful trade policy reform? Where is there agreement? Where is more research required? Is there anything special about trade policy reform in financial services?

WHAT CAN WE SAY WITH CONFIDENCE ABOUT SUCCESSFUL APPROACHES?

The basic rationales for trade policy reform to allow cross-border supply and commercial presence are (1) to enhance domestic competition among producers thereby promoting efficiency and lower costs to users and (2) to contribute to the creation of stable and transparent policy regimes.

Foreign entry can be designed in various ways. Among the choices available to Members, particular attention should be paid to the distinction between foreign entry and permitted equity participation by foreign FSPs. As described below, a Member may liberalize foreign entry to introduce more competition in the domestic market. As noted below, China is following this route using precommitment as the instrument to allow domestic firms to prepare for future competition. In the 1997 FSA Thailand selected a different route, permitting foreign entry and full equity participation in banking for a ten-year period. Latin American Members have selected a combination of restricted entry and free equity participation.

- China: (pre-commitment to expanded national treatment; reduced ownership restrictions).[17]

---

[17] For further details, see Box 7.2.

In banking, China's WTO accession agreement permits the hundreds of foreign FSPs already in the market to provide the following services over the first five years. Foreign currency business was opened immediately with no geographic restrictions. Local currency services to Chinese enterprises, only permitted in some major cities, will then be extended geographically after two years, with all restrictions to be phased out in December 2006, a commitment that has been fulfilled.

In insurance, non-life insurers will be permitted to establish as branches or joint ventures with 51 per cent ownership, rising to 100 per cent foreign ownership within two years. Life insurers are permitted 50 per cent ownership with a partner immediately. Companies offering large scale commercial risks, reinsurance, and international marine, aviation, and transport insurance and reinsurance are allowed immediately to form joint ventures with no more than 50 per cent foreign equity, rising to 51 per cent in three years and 100 per cent after five years. Geographic restrictions confining operations to large cities are to be phased out over three years.

- *Thailand (liberalization of foreign entry and equity participation, but for ten years)*. The Thai government, after weighing the costs of foreign entry against more general economic benefits in the wake of the financial crisis, lifted restrictions on both foreign entry and foreign equity participation for ten years. Permitted services and foreign labor are still restricted. The rationale is political-economic: it is believed that these services are best owned and controlled by domestic interests. Domestic interest groups successfully exert political pressure to protect their interests, but with considerable public support.

  New entrants must be approved by the relevant minister (the Minister of Commerce approves insurance and the Minister of Finance approves banks) and the Cabinet. Foreign banks are also restricted from participating in national ATM networks in Thailand. They are allowed only three branches, with one outside the capital city, Bangkok. ATMs are regarded as a branch.

  Foreign equity in domestic insurance and finance companies is limited to 25 per cent; and to 49 per cent in services auxiliary to insurance. Since 1992, foreign insurance branches have been permitted, but no licenses have been granted. Thailand also uses mode 4 restrictions: foreigners are not permitted to work as insurance brokers; and foreigners are prohibited from being brokers, dealers, traders, or underwriters in the securities industry.

- *Latin America (restricted foreign entry but unconstrained equity participation)*. Another option is to restrict foreign entry but allow unconstrained foreign equity participation, a practice often followed in Latin America. Restricting entry but allowing for equity participation will help strengthen weak financial institutions, promote technological transfer, improve products and raise skill levels. Some of these changes will benefit consumers through lower costs and more choice. Other benefits come in the form of technological innovations, such as new methods of electronic banking and improved management and credit assessment techniques, but also as higher standards of transparency and self-regulation.

These benefits must be compared to their costs, however. If FDI is attracted simply because the returns to investment are artificially raised by restrictions on competition, then the cost to the host country may exceed the benefits. Lack of competition will influence the extent to which these benefits are passed to consumers. With restricted competition, producers have few incentives to do so, and more incentives to collect "rents." To some extent rent appropriation can be prevented by taxing profits, but such taxes are prevented if there is a commitment to provide national treatment. If, however, a Member decides to restrict licenses or equity, these should be allocated by holding competitive auctions of licenses or equity. Even then, the rents accrue to government or existing domestic shareholders.

WHAT ISSUES REQUIRE MORE RESEARCH?

- *The impact on domestic financial performance of foreign equity participation.* Two issues might usefully be the subject of further research. First, it is frequently argued that finance is special because of the important services the financial sector provides to a growing and developing economy. These services, in this view, are therefore best owned and controlled by domestic interests. More sophisticated foreign entrants, pursuing different objectives, could come to dominate the industry to the detriment of national objectives. In this regard, with the current GATS focus on freer cross-border trade and foreign entry in financial services, and the fact that many standard policy interventions in the financial sector are untouched by commitments within the GATS, are there generalizations that can be made about the impact of foreign entry on Member economies? Members retain the scope for macro-economic policy through the "carve-out provision" in the GATS designed to protect prudential regulation. To the extent that they are compatible with broad market access, national treatment, and scheduled commitments to liberalize, other government financial policies can still be maintained, but in a more open context, under the GATS.

A second argument that merits further investigation is the argument, made in relation to African economies, that small market size is more of a problem in developing a modern financial sector than lack of foreign competition. By this argument, regionalization and diversification of existing services (on a national treatment basis) is the priority. The question that follows is whether future trade policy reform should emphasize cross-border supply rather than foreign entry and permitted activities.

- *Improve available data on and transparency of barriers to cross-border transactions and foreign entry.* Lack of comparable cross-country data is a general problem in the service sectors. Many services originate as non-tradables; thus, measures, if they are developed, tend to serve domestic purposes. The variety of measures therefore makes it difficult to aggregate across countries the existing information on parameters of services production and trade. Comparable information would have several benefits. First, it would help advance negotiations in that bargaining would be based on more reliable information. Second, it would assist researchers analyzing the effects of liberalization. Third, it would help regulators and foreign FSPs managing across borders to aggregate information on risks and therefore to anticipate and better manage the concentration of risk. Indices of openness in the financial services industries in key emerging market economies are included in Table 7.1 summarizing commitments on the degree of financial liberalization at the end of 1996.[18]

- *Measures used to moderate unanticipated impacts of liberalization.* Many developing country Members must respond to pressures from incumbent producers opposed to or anxious about intensified competitive pressures from the entry of foreign FSPs. These pressures should be distinguished from difficulties that might arise unexpectedly during the liberalization process once committed to in GATS negotiations. If it is accepted that consumers will benefit from modernizing and competitive pressures from new entrants, foreign entry can be managed by phasing in commitments to increase market access for foreign FSPs.

Table 7.1. An Index of Openness in Financial Services, 1997

	Banking		Securities		Insurance	
	Commitment	Practice	Commitment	Practice	Commitment	Practice
Hong Kong	4.20	4.75	4.00	4.40	4.40	4.00
Indonesia	3.15	3.20	3.50	3.00	3.10	2.60
South Korea	1.10	1.70	1.70	2.10	1.20	2.60
Malaysia	2.40	2.40	2.50	2.50	2.10	2.10
Philippines	2.80	3.35	2.40	2.40	2.90	2.80
Singapore	2.25	2.50	2.70	2.70	4.10	4.10
Thailand	2.95	2.85	2.00	2.00	2.80	2.80
India	2.70	2.25	2.50	2.10	1.00	1.00
Average	2.69	2.88	2.66	2.65	2.70	2.75

Notes: 1= most closed, 5= most open.

Source: Adapted from Claessens and Glaessner (1998).

[18] Figures 7.1 and 7.2 summarize the changes made in the 1997 FSA.

The Chinese example described above illustrates such an approach. With respect to managing difficulties during the liberalization process, discussion is underway in GATS of the question of whether to include an emergency safeguard mechanism (ESM) that can be used by governments, under specified conditions, to impose or increase protection to provide temporary relief when difficulties or pressures arise as a result of liberalization commitments and obligations. The main features of an ESM would be that it target a specific product or industry in which "injury" to domestic producers can be demonstrated; be applied on MFN basis; be of limited duration; and be progressively liberalized over the period of its application (Sauvé, 2002). The other option is to not make a negotiated commitment. Further research would be desirable to determine whether the absence of a mechanism to address difficulties, real or imagined, is one of the reasons why actual liberalization has been modest.

- *Further elucidation of the rationales for Members' FSA commitments.* What were the rationales for Members' commitments (or lack thereof) in the FSA? In particular, when a service is not listed in a Member's schedule or a specific mode is unbound, schedules provide no clue as to what actual policies may be. Further empirical research is needed to obtain a more comprehensive picture of the policies governments actually pursue with respect to the financial sector. It should then be possible to examine more thoroughly not only the determinants of trade policy (such as the conditions in the domestic financial sector, the adequacy of regulatory mechanisms, and political economy aspects), but also what influences the relationship between actual policy and GATS commitments (benefits of binding versus the costs of giving up policy flexibility or negotiating currency).

More research is also desirable to study the impact of trade policy choices (both national and in terms of international commitments) on the performance of the financial sector and the economy more generally.[19]

IS THERE ANYTHING SPECIAL ABOUT TRADE POLICY REFORM IN FINANCIAL SERVICES?[20]

One reason for the willingness of governments to make liberalization commitments may be the realization that liberalization is a good idea and that the WTO offers a useful instrument for consolidating and promoting liberalization, as well as defining and formalizing future liberalization plans. Yet the use of the GATS as a mechanism for lending credibility to liberalization programs has been somewhat disappointing. The result in the 1997 FSA compares unfavorably with the experience in the basic telecommunication negotiations (Low and Mattoo, 2000)—although financial markets are

---

[19] An example of recent research along these lines is the paper by Claessens and Glaessner (1998).
[20] See Mattoo (2000).

generally much more competitive than those in basic telecommunications. Again it is possible that many governments were reluctant to tie their hands in the environment of financial instability in which the negotiations were concluded.

At the other end of the spectrum, however, some governments have undertaken unilateral liberalization of financial services regimes to signal their interest in attracting foreign investors and strategic partners in the cross-border supply of services. For example, Japan and Singapore have unilaterally accelerated foreign-entry provisions because they fear being bypassed for other international financial centers.

DOES THE ROLE OF FINANCIAL SERVICES IN THE ECONOMY RAISE ISSUES FOR TRADE POLICY?

Several points that have been made in previous discussion help to answer this question. First, the fact that financial institutions are characterized by asymmetric information differentiates financial services from other services because they are crisis-prone. Second, the emphasis on strengthening domestic financial systems following the crises of the 1990s, points to the mutually reinforcing nature of trade policy reform and strengthening of the domestic financial system. Third, as pointed out above, the economics literature provides growing evidence that a well-functioning financial system contributes to an economy's long-term prosperity. Well-functioning financial services promote growth and reduce volatility. A fully developed range of financial services in an economy with a reasonable degree of competition among financial service providers can be expected to allocate capital more efficiently, promote higher-quality services and provide lower cost of capital to households, business and government users than would be the case in an immature financial system.[21] The full range of financial institutions will mobilize savings, finance productive investments, ensure that borrowers spend their funds as promised, and pool risks of lending through the aggregation by institutions of those risks and also enabling those that carry risk are also willing to bear it.

Trade policy reforms can assist this process by removing discrimination and market access barriers to foreign FSPs that may provide more competition, access to new technologies, products, and skills that bolster the sector's contribution to overall efficiency in the host economy. Strengthened GATS disciplines on regulatory transparency and procedural fairness can also contribute to stronger domestic financial systems. Measures to promote the stability and integrity of a country's financial system or to protect consumers are still possible under the prudential carve-out.[22]

---

[21] For a full development of these arguments and summary of the evidence, see Caprio (2002).
[22] See Key (2004) for arguments along these lines.

The Role of International Negotiations

The questions to be considered below are the following. How can international negotiations help? What can we learn from how international rules have been designed and commitments undertaken? Is there scope for improvement? Do existing commitments promote desirable policies? Are there reasons for refraining from commitments? Is there need for more research?

This section contains an analysis and interpretation of the negotiating results of the 1997 FSA to illustrate the negotiating approaches that were taken; it also looks forward, suggesting areas for improvement in the Doha Round and other financial services negotiations.[23]

In general, few developing countries made sweeping commitments to market access and national treatment in the 1997 FSA negotiation.[24] Latin American and Asian economies were among the most reluctant to open their insurance and core banking sectors (Figures 7.1 and 7.2), with Eastern Europeans and Africans ahead of them in their commitments.

The negotiations were atypical in that they were a single-sector negotiation following the failure to complete the negotiations before the end of the Uruguay Round. This sectoral focus tended to divide participants into countries looking for export gains and those whose focus could only be the conditions of competition in the domestic market. Despite the absence of any possibility for cross-sectoral trade-offs, or for improvements in the policy environment facing exports for those without export potential in financial services, many governments did make new commitments.[25]

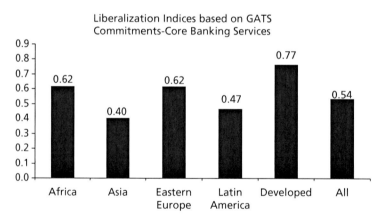

Figure 7.1. Liberalization indices based on GATS commitments—core banking services
Source: Adapted from Hoekman and Mattoo (2002).

---

[23] See Box 7.1 for an assessment of liberalization of trade in financial services in the context of Western Hemisphere regional and bilateral free trade agreements.

[24] For summaries and interpretations, see Kono et al. (1997); Dobson and Jacquet (1998); Mattoo (2000); Low and Mattoo (2000); and Key (2004).

[25] But several countries, including Hungary, Mauritius, Pakistan, Peru, Philippines, and Venezuela, maintained MFN exemptions in their schedules that state that access may be granted on a reciprocal

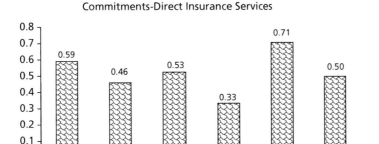

Figure 7.2. Liberalization indices based on GATS commitments—direct insurance services

Source: Adapted from Hoekman and Mattoo (2002).

In the banking sector, more participants made commitments on the acceptance of deposits and lending. Country participation was again highest in Eastern Europe and Africa. African participation was greater than in insurance. Full liberalization was rare and provided only by very small economies such as Gabon and Gambia that made full mode 1 and 2 commitments. Other countries, including Egypt, Ghana, Kenya, Nigeria, and Tunisia made more limited commitments. South Africa, Sierra Leone, Senegal, Lesotho, Nigeria, and Gambia made full mode 3 commitments while Kenya and Ghana imposed foreign equity limitations. On the whole, African countries guaranteed more openness to foreign entry, followed by Latin America and Asia. But again, Latin American reluctance was on free entry while Asian reluctance was foreign ownership. Asians were also more likely to restrict foreign branching (although India allows entry only in the form of branches licensed and supervised in their home countries).

In the insurance sector, country participation was highest in Eastern Europe and Africa. But only four small countries (Bahrain, Gambia, Guyana, and the Solomon Islands) committed to remove all barriers. Participation in opening to insurance services was lowest in Africa (although the large countries were all included), but participants were willing to allow foreign entry. Ghana and Kenya already allow majority foreign ownership. Egypt limits foreign equity to 49 per cent but is committed to raising the limit to 51 per cent by 2003. Asian economies were more likely than Latin Americans to provide assurances of fully open markets for foreign investors, but more reluctant to assure full foreign ownership. Latin Americans, in contrast, were more ready to allow full foreign ownership but also more likely to restrict permitted activities.[26]

basis. Given the structure of the GATS, regardless of the MFN exemption, the benefits of specific commitments made by these Members must be extended to all other Members on a non-discriminatory basis. Thus the exemption has meaning only where commitments have not been made, or where it is used to provide better treatment to some Members than specified in their schedules.

[26] This section draws on Mattoo (2000).

Lessons from the 1997 FSA[27]

In broad terms, governments that participated in the FSA adopted three different approaches: (1) binding the status quo, arrived at after liberalization, either unilateral or in the context of the negotiations; (2) binding commitments that represent less than the status quo in policy terms; and (3) pre-committing to future liberalization, which may or may not have been planned prior to the negotiations. These categories are not necessarily mutually exclusive when the set of a country's commitments is taken as a whole, nor is it always easy to determine the precise category in which a policy position should fall. The distinctions are useful, however, in thinking about the relationship between WTO negotiations and domestic liberalization processes.

(1) BINDING THE STATUS QUO

Governments binding at the status quo signaled that existing market conditions are guaranteed in the future. Even though much greater knowledge of national regimes than is available would be required to make a definitive judgment, most of the FSA commitments were of the status quo variety. Such consolidation is positive in that it is the easiest thing for governments to do but also signals a positive intent and a commitment to the trading system. It is also important to recognize that in many cases, the status quo itself was reached after recent liberalization, either unilateral or during the course of negotiations.

The improvements in commitments by countries since the last round of negotiations ended in mid-1995 provide some idea of the extent of recent liberalization.[28] The clearest evidence exists for the Eastern European countries. Several (like the Czech Republic, Slovak Republic, and Slovenia) gave up the possibility of discretionary licensing in banking based on economic needs, while others (like the Czech Republic in air transport insurance) eliminated monopolies in certain areas of insurance. Several countries (like Bulgaria in insurance) allowed commercial presence through branches while others liberalized cross-border trade and consumption abroad (like Poland with respect to insurance of goods in international trade). Liberalizing trends were also visible in other regions: some countries (like Brazil) replaced prohibitions on foreign establishment with a case-by-case authorization requirement and some liberalized cross-border trade (for instance, the Philippines with respect to marine hull and cargo insurance).

---

[27] See Mattoo (2000).

[28] Unless, of course, there was significant binding below the status quo in 1995, which Sorsa (1997) argues was the case.

It is notable that many of the improvements pertained to relaxation of foreign equity limitations. For instance, Malaysia agreed to raise foreign equity limits in insurance on incorporation of existing branches (and for original owners who had been forced to divest) from 49 per cent to 51 per cent. Mexico raised its limits on foreign participation from 30 per cent of common stock to 40 per cent of common stock (plus 30 per cent and 40 per cent of non-voting common stock in insurance and banking, respectively), Kuwait allowed up to 40 per cent foreign participation in banks and Singapore up to 49 per cent in local insurance companies. Egypt and El Salvador completely removed the limits on foreign ownership of shares in banks (previously at 51 per cent and 50 per cent, respectively). Ghana removed the requirement that at least 20 per cent of the capital of insurance companies be owned by the government and allowed foreign partners to obtain management control of local firms. Hong Kong removed a requirement that made eligibility for new full banking licenses contingent on Hong Kong ownership; and Kenya removed the requirement that one-third of the equity in non-life insurance companies be held by Kenyan citizens.

(2) BINDING BELOW THE STATUS QUO

Several countries bound at less than status quo, in some areas. The Philippines, for example, did so with respect to foreign-equity participation in commercial banks: binding at 51 per cent when domestic law allows 60 per cent.[29] Korea's FSA offer did not include all its OECD liberalization commitments: for instance, in the FSA offer foreign portfolio investment in listed companies is bound at 23 per cent (compared to an OECD commitment to raising this ceiling progressively and eliminating it by the end of the year 2000).[30] While any binding at all provides an identifiable measure of security of market access, the value of a binding at below status quo is attenuated by the scope it gives a government to worsen existing conditions of market access without violating a GATS commitment.

Why would countries choose to bind less than the status quo? Mattoo and Schuknecht (2000) suggest two reasons: domestic macro-economic instability and regulatory weaknesses appear to have had a negative impact on the level of commitments; and

---

[29] Where a binding involving foreign equity limitations is less than the level actually allowed to any investor subsequent to the entry into force of the commitments, the MFN principle will have the practical effect of "ratcheting up" the equity-limitation commitment. This is because a new entrant could demand the same level of equity participation on MFN grounds as that granted to another supplier.

[30] Furthermore, under the terms of the IMF agreement, the de facto regime with respect to foreign capital is already more liberal than the GATS offer. For instance, the new president Kim Dae-Jung was quoted as saying that "From now on there is no need for discrimination between indigenous and foreign capital. We are living in an era where foreign investment is more important than foreign trade" (*Financial Times*, December 29, 1997).

membership of international trade coalitions, such as the groups of agricultural and textile and clothing exporters, was in general associated with a lower level of commitments.[31] This suggests that even small countries that do not have much bargaining power on their own in negotiations, may nevertheless have chosen to retain bargaining chips for future multi-sectoral negotiations when they were part of trade coalitions. Even though such mercantilistic bargaining, and concern with reciprocity, are often judged inappropriate and damaging, it is nevertheless true that countries could benefit additionally if their trading partners were also to liberalize. From a political standpoint, governments may also generate more domestic support for liberalization from interest groups in the sector and in others, if other governments are liberalizing in areas of their export interest at the same time.

(3) PRECOMMITMENT TO FUTURE LIBERALIZATION

GATS is also a vehicle for promoting future liberalization. One reason governments may be reluctant to liberalize immediately is the perceived need to protect the incumbent public/national suppliers from immediate competition, either because of the infant industry type of argument or to facilitate "orderly exit." In the financial sector, the vulnerability of domestic suppliers is related to a larger concern about the stability of the financial system. The fear is that inefficient or otherwise handicapped domestic banks, if exposed to competition, may fail and set off a chain reaction affecting other financial institutions.[32]

Infant industries have either failed in the past or remained infants because governments have been unable to commit credibly to liberalize at some future date, either because they have taken stakes in national firms, or because of vulnerability to the pressures from the interest groups that are being protected from competition. The GATS offers a valuable mechanism to overcome the difficulty of making credible commitments to liberalize, that is, provided market access and national treatment at a future date are binding under WTO law. Failure to honor these commitments would create an obligation to compensate those who are deprived of benefits. This need to compensate does in fact make the commitment more credible than a mere announcement of liberalizing intent in the national context. A precommitment to liberalize can also instill

---

[31] This is probably not true of the developed country members of the Cairns Group.

[32] For instance, the presence of too many financial institutions is sometimes cited as an argument against liberalization in financial services trade. To the extent that this reflects concern about the viability of individual financial institutions, it is best addressed through prudential measures and measures to facilitate orderly exit from the market. In Argentina, for instance, one-quarter of the country's 200 banks were liquidated in 1995 and 1996. See also Kono et al. (1997).

a sense of urgency in domestic reform, and in efforts to develop the necessary regulatory and supervision mechanisms.

Scope for Future Improvements

Looking to the future, several issues can be identified for improvement in the Doha Round. A notable improvement would be to see countries commit to subjecting all service sectors to national treatment and market-access disciplines, with target dates and transition periods. Surprising as it may seem, aiming to bind the status quo for only a specified share of all commitments is a moderately ambitious starting point.

Another improvement to complement such commitments would be efforts on rules to increase the impact of multilateral disciplines for certain modes of supply, particularly national treatment for FDI.

In addition, at least two mechanisms used in the 1997 FSA can be applied to future negotiations: precommitments and grandfathering.

- *Precommitment.* Several governments took advantage of the precommitment mechanism to strike a balance between, on the one hand, their reluctance to unleash competition immediately on protected national suppliers, and, on the other hand, their desire not to be held hostage to the weakness of domestic industry in perpetuity. For example, India and the Philippines committed in the FSA to allow an increased number of branches rather than to change the existing regime. The Czech and Slovak Republics committed to endeavor to remove or reduce the scope of monopolies in certain areas in which insurance is compulsory.[33] Egypt and Slovenia committed to relax certain elements of discretionary licensing, whereas Hungary, Poland and Slovenia will allow branches of financial institutions to operate. Bulgaria and Egypt committed to allow majority foreign ownership in insurance in the near future, while Thailand has created a ten-year window of opportunity for foreign investors to acquire higher equity shares than the maximum 25 per cent normally permitted, as discussed earlier. The commitments by Hungary, Slovenia, and Brazil are interesting in that they have been made contingent on parliamentary approval of new legislation. This approval is not certain, but the current commitment has value because there is an obligation immediately to translate future domestic law into an international commitment.

- *Grandfathering, a scheduling innovation.* A central problem in the FSA negotiations was solved by a scheduling innovation. The conflict arose because certain countries

---

[33] This is by virtue of their subscription to the Understanding on Commitments on Financial Services.

were unwilling to make status quo commitments on commercial presence. Thus, they were either inclined to bind foreign ownership levels below current levels, or to insist on legal forms (local incorporation) other than those currently in the market (branches), or both. The problem arose because policy regimes had become more restrictive than those that prevailed when the incumbent foreign firms first entered, e.g. in Malaysia, where the indigenization policy was being implemented after the establishment of many foreign firms. The negotiated solution was to drive a wedge between the conditions facing firms that were already present and those that would enter when the commitments came into effect. In effect, the privileged situation of existing firms was "grandfathered." This innovation was employed mainly by Asians.

Three types of grandfathering provisions were employed: foreign equity-related, legal form-related and general. The grandfathering provisions reflect the relative emphasis in these negotiations on guaranteeing the rights of incumbents. They provide the benefits of security to investors who are already present in the market rather than to new investors. But they may even place new entrants at a competitive disadvantage where differences in ownership and legal form affect firm performance.

Future Research

The foregoing discussion suggests the following three areas for research:

- *What were the main reasons for liberalization commitments in the 1997 FSA?* The discussion in this chapter has been based on analysis of actual commitments in a single sector negotiation. One of the outstanding questions arising from the record is why countries that liberalized in 1997 did so when so many others simply bound at or below the status quo. Research into specific cases would be useful to understand more precisely the impulses for further liberalization. For most members there were no immediate benefits in terms of improved access to foreign markets. Was foreign pressure a major impetus? If so, how did this compare as a determining factor with domestic policy considerations?

- *What are the rationales for the goals of OECD countries in financial services negotiations?* Another potential focus of research is to identify more precisely the rationales for the negotiating goals of OECD countries and to provide greater understanding of the role of business strategies in these objectives. Further research is desirable to confirm several rationales that have been advanced.

For example, it has been argued that OECD firms' decisions to enter foreign markets are driven more by reputational concerns than market share. If problems arise in foreign markets, these are likely to undermine the reputation of their global brands. Reputational factors determine the desire for full control of local operations to ensure that rigorous operational standards are met. Furthermore, their interests are also served by being subject to regulatory treatment that is identical to that for domestic companies. Current practices, such as countries' limits on foreign bank ATM offerings, deny foreign FSPs the network externalities that are increasingly relevant to the provision of modern financial services. Restrictions on cross-border trade in services limit the ability to monitor and manage risk concentrations; beyond an obvious interest in limited and transparent exemptions, grandfathering is also desirable to protect existing investments from any new exemptions to established principles.[34]

Investment decisions are also influenced by evidence of best practice regulation in host economies. In the insurance industry, for example, representatives of industry associations in OECD countries have prepared a model schedule for use by WTO members in scheduling commitments in the Doha Round (Financial Leaders Working Group (FLG), 2002). The model schedule has two aims: to promote some uniformity in insurance commitments and to help increase regulators' awareness of what is internationally regarded as best practice. The FLG propose a text for use in scheduling commitments within the existing GATS framework on market access and national treatment using existing methods. But they encourage time frames for staging obligations to encourage greater clarity and predictability to commitments since foreign investors take these into account in investment decisions. The model schedule goes beyond market access and national treatment to address certain aspects of domestic regulation by outlining best practices with respect to transparency of regulations, solvency and prudential focus, rules and rights with respect to insurance monopolies and independence of the regulatory authority.

- *What is the record of financial services liberalization outside the WTO, i.e., in regional trade agreements (RTAs)? Through unilateral liberalization commitments?* A recent partial analysis (covering East Asian, Latin American and North American agreements) of financial services liberalization in RTAs shows that participating countries broadened the levels bound in the FSA, with the exception of mode 1 supply of core banking, core insurance and securities services (see Contreras and Yi, 2004). A global analysis along these lines would be desirable.

---

[34] See, for example, Dobson (2002).

Box 7.1. Liberalization of Trade in Financial Services: New Trends in the Western Hemisphere

---

Patricio Contreras[1]

Introduction

In spite of the large number of trade agreements negotiated in past years throughout the world, the actual level of bound market opening of financial services continues to be rather limited. This is particularly evident in developing countries, which for the most part have committed to fairly open regimes on foreign investment and very restrictive regimes on cross-border trade, both in regional trade agreements and in the Financial Services Agreement of the World Trade Organization's General Agreement on Trade in Services (GATS) (Contreras and Yi, 2003).

A new wave of trade agreements involving the participation of Western Hemisphere countries and promoted by developed countries, in particular the European Community (EC) and the United States, seems to have triggered a renewed interest to commit to enhanced bound liberalization of trade in financial services. The purpose of this paper is to analyze these agreements with a view to determining the extent to which they have fostered enhanced liberalization of trade in financial services with respect to previous regional attempts or the multilateral option.

The paper focuses on the agreements concluded between the E.C. with Chile and with Mexico, as well as those recently negotiated between the United States with regional and extra-regional partners (i.e. Australia, Chile, Central American countries and the Dominican Republic (DR-CAFTA), Morocco and Singapore). Common to all these trade pacts is that they acknowledge the special characteristics of financial services through the development of sector-specific text in a separate chapter. In analyzing these agreements, it is recognized that progress need not be exclusively found in bound commitments, but also in whether the agreements developed new or deepened existing rules and disciplines or innovated with respect to the approaches followed to liberalize trade in financial services.

The paper is organized as follows. The following three sections present comparative analyses of the approaches to liberalization, rules and disciplines and commitments adopted by each member country; and the final section concludes.

Liberalization Approach

Significant improvements were introduced in the recent Western Hemisphere free trade agreements (FTAs) with respect to the liberalization approach adopted for financial services. Before the implementation of the agreements between the E.C. with Chile and Mexico, trade pacts in the region had predominantly followed the North American FTA (NAFTA) model or negative list approach, although with more limited commitments. Under this approach, trade in services (including in financial services) distinguishes between cross-border trade and investment and is liberalized unless otherwise specified by reservations or non-conforming measures. The Chapter on financial services of the Chile-EC FTA adopted a positive list (or GATS) approach,[2] whereby trade in financial services can take place through four different modes of supply and commitments, rather than reservations, are listed with respect to each service and mode of supply. The Mexico-EC FTA, on the other hand, combined a modal definition of trade in financial services with a negative list approach, thereby eliminating the possibility provided in GATS-type agreements on services of making commitments more restrictive than the status quo.

A new template for financial services trade liberalization was developed in the parallel Singapore–U.S. and Chile–U.S. negotiations and provided the core elements for subsequent U.S. agreements. It draws from a combination of elements in the GATS, GATS Understanding on Commitments on Financial Services (from hereon the Understanding), and NAFTA. The new template permits countries to more effectively reflect the special sensitivity of financial services, as it more accurately specializes general investment and cross-border trade rules and permits countries to make selective commitments on the different financial services subsectors. As a general rule and in similar fashion to the Understanding, countries agree to open the cross-border supply of a specified list of financial services and consumption abroad. In the case of investment, countries agree to apply the financial services obligations to financial institutions subject to a negotiated list of non-conforming measures (a la NAFTA). A ratcheting clause that applies to investment ensures that any future liberalization of existing non-conforming measures is automatically bound.

Rules and Disciplines

Table 7.B.1.1 presents a summarized list of the main provisions contained (not necessarily in a separate article) in the financial services chapters/annexes of Western Hemisphere agreements. The main innovations found in the more recent agreements with respect to rules and disciplines relate to market access, transparency, domestic regulation and capital flows liberalization. These are analyzed in turn below.

Market Access: For the first time in Western Hemisphere trade agreements, the Chile–E.C. and Mexico–E.C. FTAs specialized for financial services a GATS Article XVI-type prohibition to impose market-access limitations,[3] such as certain quantitative restrictions or form-of-establishment requirements.[4] A similar provision was later adopted in all recent U.S. FTAs.[5] The obligation applies to the four modes of supply in the Chile–E.C. FTA and to investment in the Mexico–E.C. FTA, whereas a modified version applies to investment in financial institutions in the recent U.S. FTAs. A key contribution of the market access obligation is that it forces member countries to explicitly acknowledge in their schedules remaining non-discriminatory quantitative restrictions. This is in contrast to NAFTA, which provides an absolute right of establishment by permitting an investor of another Party that does not own or control a financial institution in a Party's territory to establish one. More importantly, the market-access obligation helped countries to focus on providing a very liberal regime for investment, while being more selective as regards market access in cross-border trade. A distinctive feature of the Chile–U.S. agreement is that instead of the market-access article for banking and other non-insurance financial services, it incorporated a separate provision, which explicitly grants the right of establishment to foreign providers of these services and the right to choose the type of legal entity.[6] Thus, this obligation substitutes the market-access provision as regards investment in banking and other non-insurance financial services (similar to NAFTA but with a choice of legal entity), while investment in insurance services remain subject to the market access article.

Transparency

The main objective of this provision, found in most trade agreements, is to promote the prompt notification or publication of laws and regulations and make the application process to obtain authorization to supply financial services transparent and not excessively burdensome. A key innovation with respect to this provision introduced in the recent U.S. agreements, is the explicit recognition of the importance of transparent regulations in facilitating both the operations and market access of foreign providers. CAFTA-DR members, except the U.S., complement this obligation by listing in a separate annex measures that although affecting financial services are not inconsistent with their obligations. A similar provision developed for self-regulatory organizations recognizes the importance of these institutions and ensures transparency in the rules of general application adopted by them. The provision hence looks to increase the transparency of a set of rules that may potentially constitute barriers to trade in financial services.[7] Other significant innovations included in the more recent agreements negotiated by the U.S. are the *explicit* acknowledgement of the need to address in *writing* substantive comments received with respect to laws and regulations that a Party proposes to adopt; the potential trade-inhibiting impact of non-transparent regulations; and the need to inform applicants that so request of the reasons for denial of their application to supply a financial service.[8]

Domestic Regulation

All Western Hemisphere arrangements containing specialized text on financial services recognize a Party's right to regulate its financial markets, so long as these regulations are not discriminatory and not more burdensome than necessary to achieve their aim. They all incorporate GATS and/or NAFTA carve-outs for prudential, monetary and

Table 7.B.1.1. Main Provisions on Financial Services—Regional and Extra-Regional Agreements of the Western Hemisphere

Main provisions/agreement	NAFTA[1]	Mexico–E.C.	Chile–E.C.	Recent U.S. agreements	MERCOSUR	GATS (Annex and understanding
Trade liberalization						
Commercial presence/establishment	X			X[2]		X
Market access		X	X	X	X*	X
Cross-border trade	X	X		X		X
Senior management and board of directors/key personnel	X	X		X		
New financial services	X	X	X	X		X
Non-discrimination						
National treatment	X	X	X	X	X*	X
Most-favored nation treatment	X	X	X*	X	X*	X*
Domestic regulation						
Transparency	X	X	X	X	X	X
Domestic regulation		X		X[3]	X*	X*
Recognition of prudential regulations	X	X	X	X	X	X
Harmonization					X	
Self-regulatory organizations	X		X	X		X
Prudential carve-out	X	X	X	X	X	X
Exceptions relative to the dissemination of confidential information	X*	X	X	X	X	X
Payment and clearing systems (national treatment)				X		X*
Expedited availability of insurance services			X	X		
Capital flows						
Transfers (investment)	X*	X*	X*	X	X*	X*
Transfers and payments (cross-border trade)	X*		X*	X[4]	X*	X*
Limitations on capital flows			X*	X[5]		
Exceptions for monetary policy, exchange rate reasons or balance of payments difficulties	X	X*	X	X	X*	X*
Other						
Financial services committee	X	X	X	X		
State–state disputes	X	X	X	X	X*	X
Investor–state disputes	X			X[6]		

Notes:* The provision applies to financial services; however, it is not contained in the financial services chapter/annex.

[1] Most of the provisions in this column were also included in the NAFTA-type agreements signed by Mexico with Central and South American countries, as well as by Central American countries with the Dominican Republic.

[2] A Right of Establishment Provision is contained in the Chile–U.S. FTA and in CAFTA-DR for Costa Rica only.

[3] Except the Chile–U.S. FTA.

[4] The Chile–U.S. and Singapore–U.S. FTAs only.

[5] The Chile–U.S. and Singapore–U.S. FTAs only.

[6] Except the Australia–U.S. FTA.

exchange rate reasons. One of the most significant innovations with respect to domestic regulation is contained in a separate article in the agreements negotiated by the U.S. with Central American Countries and the Dominican Republic, Morocco and Singapore. Under the new obligation, member countries commit to administer all laws, regulations and administrative rules and procedures in a "reasonable, objective and impartial manner." However, since none of the agreements define any of these terms the applicability of the provision is questionable. Although the obligation is not new in the area of services trade, its contribution is that for the first time it is made specific to financial services. A similar provision is contained in the Chile–U.S. FTA. However, it is not stated as an obligation, but rather as a best endeavour clause aimed at enhancing regulatory transparency. The Australia–U.S. FTA excludes this provision completely. Another innovation of the recent U.S. agreements is the recognition of the importance of the expedited availability of insurance services. On behalf of this provision, member countries to the Chile–U.S. FTA and CAFTA-DR made a best endeavour commitment not to require prior regulatory approval for insurance sold to individuals or compulsory insurance. Expedited procedures are available in other cases when prior product approval is necessary. The recent U.S. agreements also recognize the right of member countries to adopt or enforce measures such as those relating to the prevention of deceptive and fraudulent practices or to deal with the effects of a default on financial services contracts. This obligation is intended to reaffirm the right of countries to preserve the stability of their financial system through the use of a broader set of non-discriminatory measures than those covered by the prudential carve-out above.

Exchange and Capital Flows Liberalization

A common principle contained in most trade arrangements is to secure rights with regard to expropriation and the transfer, in and out of each country, of capital and funds related to an investment, as well as the right to resolve disputes with a host government through binding international arbitration for these obligations.[9] Except for the Mexico–E.C. and Chile–U.S. FTAs, all Western Hemisphere agreements in our sample also secure rights with respect to transfers and payments related to cross-border trade in financial services. A number of exceptions permit countries to limit transfers and payments, such as those relating to bankruptcy laws, prudential regulation, balance-of-payment difficulties and measures taken in pursuit of monetary or exchange-rate policy. In lieu of these exceptions, countries may impose restrictions on financial flows that horizontally affect international transactions, such as exchange restrictions and capital controls.[10] This type of restriction was severely limited in the Chile–U.S. and Singapore–U.S. FTAs. Under the new provision, Chile and Singapore are permitted to impose restrictions on outward payments and transfers related to an investment for 12 months, as long as such restrictions do not "substantially impede transfers." If countries impose restrictions for longer than 12 months, they may be required to compensate the investors for the extent and loss of asset value beginning in the second year (United States Trade Representative). Chile is also permitted to impose restrictions on capital inflows for 12 months, such as its well known *encaje*,[11] in which case losses or damages arising from the imposition of such restrictions are limited to the reduction in value of the transfers.

Commitments

An analysis of the commitments bound by Western Hemisphere countries members to the above agreements shows that Latin American countries significantly deepened regional and extra regional market opening in financial services. This is particularly the case for countries that concluded trade agreements with the United States. It is also the case for Chile, and to a lesser extent Mexico, in their agreements with the E.C. The United States basically extended its very liberal GATS (and in most part NAFTA) commitments to its bilateral and plurilateral agreements. The main GATS plus commitments made by these countries are analyzed below and summarized in Table 7.B.1.2.

Banking and Other Non-insurance Financial Services

Latin American countries made significant commitments on cross-border supply and foreign investment in banking at the regional level. Perhaps the most remarkable commitment was made by most Central American countries, Chile, and the Dominican Republic, which bound for the first time the cross-border supply (including through the

Table 7.B.1.2. Main GATS plus Component in Financial Services Commitments of Selected Western Hemisphere Countries

	Investment[1]		Cross-Border Trade	
	Banking and non-insurance services	Insurances and related services	Banking and non-insurance services	Insurances and related services
Chile (GATS+ in FTAs with the E.C. and U.S.)	• Allows the establishment of foreign providers of mandatory pension savings plans (AFPs) (U.S.) • Allows established banks to provide voluntary pension savings plans (E.C. and U.S., by March 1 2005) • Eliminates economic needs test (E.C., U.S.) • Ratcheting with respect to national treatment, most-favored nation treatment, senior management and board of directors and annex on right of establishment (U.S.)	• Limited branching (U.S., 4yrs) • Eliminates economic needs test (E.C., U.S.) • Ratcheting with respect to national treatment, most-favored nation treatment, senior management and board of directors, excludes market access (U.S.)	• Provision and transfer of financial information, data processing and related software (U.S.) • Investment, portfolio and corporate advice services (U.S.) • Credit reference and analysis in the future[2] (U.S.) • Investment advice and portfolio management services to a collective investment scheme located in Chile (U.S.) • Consumption abroad (subject to exchange rate regulations) of banking and non-insurance services (U.S.)	• MAT Insurance (E.C., 1 yr; U.S.) • Brokerage of MAT insurance (E.C., 1 yr; U.S., 1yr or when Chile has implemented amendments to its legislation) • Consultancy, actuarial and risk assessment services (U.S.) • Consumption abroad (subject to exchange rate regulations) of insurance services (U.S.) • Consumption abroad (subject to exchange rate regulations) of sales and brokerage of MAT insurance (E.C., 1yr)

Central America and the Dominican Republic
 	
(GATS+ in DR-CAFTA)
CR = Costa Rica
DR = Dominican Republic
ES = El
	• Bank deposit and lending [ES; GA; HA (expands to mortgage credit and financial leasing)]
	• Savings and credit institutions [ES]
	• Bureaux de Change [DR; HA]
	• Investment, portfolio and corporate advisory services [CR; DR; ES; HA; NA]
	• Credit reference and
		• Establishment in all lines of insurance through:
		  ○ Subsidiaries, joint-ventures [CR (by January 2008); ES; GA]
		  ○ Branches [CR (by January 2008),[3] DR (4 ys); ES (3 ys); GA (4 ys); NA (4 ys, for U.S. providers)]
		• Removes foreign equity limitations [DR, HA]
		• Removes economic needs test [HA]
		• Eliminates local employment
			• Provision and transfer of financial information, data processing [ES, NA] and related software [DR, HA]
			• Investment, portfolio and corporate advisory services [CR; DR; ES; HA; NA]
			• Credit reference and analysis [CR; DR; ES; HA]
				• MAT insurance [GA] and reinsurance and retrocession, [CR; DR; ES; HA; NA]
				• Services necessary to support global accounts [CR]
				• Brokerage and agency of MAT insurance, reinsurance and retrocession [CR; DR;

Salvador
GA = Guatemala
HA = Honduras
NA = Nicaragua

analysis [CR; DR; ES; HA; NA]
● Provision and transfer of financial information, data processing and related software [DR; ES; NA]
● Asset management:
  ○ [GA; HA]
  ○ excluding management of mandatory employee-employer contributions [CR]
  ○ including the establishment by a foreign investor of a pension fund manager (AFP) [DR, NA]
  ○ including foreign investments in a pension fund manager (AFP) [ES]
● Securities [CR, GA, HA, NA]
● Eliminates local employment limitations for senior management and board of directors [GA]
● Removes economic needs test [HA]
● Removes or reduces foreign equity limitations [DR, ES]
● Branching [GA]
● Salvadorian banks may establish branches in the U.S. (subject to the development of prudential measures and other requirements in El Salvador)
● Ratcheting with respect to national treatment, most-favored nation treatment, senior management and board of directors and market access

limitations for senior management and board of directors [GA]
● Independent regulator by January 2007 [CR]
● Ratcheting with respect to national treatment, most-favored nation treatment, senior management and board of directors and market access

● Portfolio management services to a collective investment scheme located in the country [CR; HA; DR, ES, GA and NA (subject to the adoption of necessary laws - within 4 years in the DR and ES)]
● Consumption abroad (without reservations) of banking and non-insurance services [CR; DR; ES; HA; NA; GA4]5

ES and NA (excluding agency); GA; HA] and
● Brokerage and agency of services necessary to support global accounts [CR (all other lines of insurance by July 2007)]
● Consultancy, actuarial, risk assessment and claim settlement services [CR, as relate to the insurance services above (all other lines of insurance by July 2007); DR; ES; GA; HA; NA]
● Provision of surplus lines of insurance (by July 2007) [CR]
● Consumption abroad of all lines of insurance [CR (except compulsory automobile insurance and occupational risk insurance), DR; ES; GA (limited to the services listed above); HA; NA]
● Movement of persons in all insurance services [CR; DR; ES; GA; HA; NA]

Mexico[6] (GATS+ in FTA with the E.C.. Mexico and the E.C. commit to eliminate "substantially all remaining discrimination" three years after entry into force of the agreement. This has not yet taken place.)	• Removes or reduces foreign equity limitations for establishing banking institutions (E.C.) • Removes limitations on equity and ownership (NAFTA, E.C.), as well as on aggregate capital and assets for foreign financial affiliates (NAFTA, after a transition period; E.C., as of entry into force) • Allows foreign investments in foreign exchange firms (GATS, subject to equity limitation and E.C., 100% equity ownership) • Ratcheting with respect to national treatment, most-favored nation treatment, establishment, cross-border provision and: ○ key personnel (E.C., on a voluntary basis) ○ and new financial services (NAFTA)	• Removes or reduces foreign equity limitations for foreign insurance providers (NAFTA, E.C.) • No limitations on equity holdings in casualty and health insurance companies (NAFTA, E.C.) and aggregate capital by foreign financial affiliates (NAFTA, after a transition period; E.C., from entry into force) • Eliminates the possibility in NAFTA of limiting the eligibility to establish a foreign financial affiliate in Mexico to an investor of another Party that is directly or through any of its affiliates, engaged in the same general type of financial services in the territory of the other Party (E.C.) • Ratcheting with respect to national treatment, most-favored nation treatment, establishment, cross-border provision and: ○ key personnel (E.C., on a voluntary basis) ○ and new financial services (NAFTA)	The following cross-border transactions as long as they are not denominated in Mexican pesos: • Cross-border provision and purchase of banking services (NAFTA) • Cross-border provision and purchase of non-insurance and non-deposit banking services (NAFTA, E.C.) • Ratcheting (see first column)	The following cross-border transactions as long as they are not denominated in Mexican pesos: • Consumption abroad in life and health insurance (NAFTA) • Tourist and MAT insurance provided the vehicle is licensed outside Mexico (NAFTA, E.C.) • Intermediary services incidental to tourist and MAT insurance (NAFTA, E.C.) • Reinsurance and retrocession (GATS, E.C.) • Ratcheting (see second column)
United States[7]	• Ratcheting with respect to national treatment, most-favored nation treatment, senior management and board of directors and: ○ market access or right of establishment, excluding juridical form of establishment (Australia, DR-CAFTA, Chile Morocco, Singapore) ○ establishment and cross-border	• Ratcheting with respect to national treatment, most-favored nation treatment, senior management and board of directors [Chile, CAFTA and Singapore] plus market access or right of establishment (Australia, Morocco) and cross-border trade (NAFTA) • Commits to review regulations that do not allow branching of	• Ratcheting (see first column) • Investment advice and portfolio management services to a collective investment scheme located in the U.S. (Australia, CAFTA, Chile, Morocco, Singapore)	• Ratcheting (see second column) • Life insurance (NAFTA) • Mode 4 in all lines of insurance (Australia, CAFTA, Chile, NAFTA, Morocco, Singapore)

trade (NAFTA)

- Allows citizenship exception for a minority of directors (Australia, Chile, DR-CAFTA, Morocco, Singapore)
- Extended the right to intersate expansion through merger to all states by adding Montana and Texas (Australia, Chile, DR-CAFTA, Morocco, Singapore)
- The U.S. Government may grant advantages to Government-Sponsored Enterprises (Australia, CAFTA, Chile, Morocco, Singapore)

non-U.S. providers in certain states (Chile)

Notes:[1] It is important to note that since the recent U.S. FTAs adopted a negative list approach for investment, the entire financial services sector is covered by the investment provisions of the FTAs unless otherwise specified. This important GATS plus element is not reflected in the Table.

[2] Chile reserves the right to allow credit reference and analysis as long as it is provided on a cross-border basis. Should Chile decide to allow the provision of such services, it is entitled to reverse this measure in the future.

[3] For third party auto liability insurance and workman's compensation, Costa Rica will allow establishment through any juridical form by January, 2011.

[4] The Dominican Republic allows consumption abroad of financial information and data processing in GATS.

[5] The Dominican Republic also bound mode 1 in mortgage loan services, personal instalment services, and credit card services in GATS.

[6] The table is not intended to identify the GATS plus component of Mexico's or the U.S.' commitments in NAFTA. NAFTA commitments are shown in selected cases to highlight differences with respect to the more recent commitments.

[7] See footnote 23.

movement of persons) of financial advisory services, excluding intermediation, and financial information, data processing and related software upon entry into force of their agreements with the U.S. The commitments also allow, without reservations, citizens to consume banking and securities services abroad. Only Costa Rica and Guatemala had previously committed the opening of cross-border trade on a limited basis in GATS. Mexico, on the other hand, significantly limits all cross-border transactions through a prohibition to operate in Mexican pesos, whereas the Dominican Republic is the only country in the sample that permits cross-border transactions of certain core-banking services (mortgage loans, personal installment loans and credit cards) with regional and multilateral partners. DR-CAFTA and Chile–U.S. FTA member countries reciprocally permit the cross-border supply of portfolio management services by asset managers abroad to a collective investment scheme located in their territories. The application of this commitment is subject to the adoption of necessary laws and regulations in the Dominican Republic, El Salvador, Guatemala, and Nicaragua. The Dominican Republic and El Salvador will adopt such laws and regulations within four years of entry into force of DR-CAFTA and Guatemala and Nicaragua will take on these commitments as soon as the appropriate laws and regulations are passed.

With respect to investment, foreign establishment with choice of juridical form (branch, subsidiary, joint venture) is permitted in all countries with very few restrictions upon entry into force of the respective FTAs. Branching is permitted for the first time in Guatemala and remains restricted only in Costa Rica, whereas El Salvador committed to allowing its own banks to branch abroad. Economic needs tests and domestic employment requirements for senior management and board of directors were eliminated, and equity limitations were either eliminated or substantially reduced in countries where these remained. With respect to specific subsectors, Costa Rica, Guatemala, Honduras, and Nicaragua committed for the first time to permit foreign investment in the securities sector, although the four countries reserved the right to maintain or adopt incorporation requirements for foreign investors. El Salvador, the Dominican Republic, Chile, and Mexico simply extended their *limited* GATS (or NAFTA) commitments, without any changes in laws or regulations. Asset-management services were also opened at the regional level in Central American countries and the Dominican Republic, as well as by NAFTA partners and Mexico in its agreement with the E.C. In addition, for the first time, Chile, the Dominican Republic, El Salvador, and Nicaragua permit foreign investment in financial institutions serving as pension-fund managers. Chile, however, distinguishes between foreign investment in mandatory pension-savings plans (allowed for U.S. investors only) and voluntary savings plans (allowed for E.C. and U.S. investors).

The United States bound very liberal commitments in banking and securities services under GATS and NAFTA, which in most part were extended to its FTAs with Australia, Chile, Central American countries and the Dominican Republic, Morocco, and Singapore. U.S. commitments on cross-border supply, which in some cases do not reflect the status quo, are limited to the provision and transfer of financial information, data processing and related software, as well as advisory services (excluding intermediation). The U.S. also undertook commitments without reservations on cross-border consumption of banking and securities services. Investment with choice of juridical form is permitted for commercial banks and securities firms, although bank branching is prohibited in a few states. With respect to interstate expansion by branching, foreign-owned banks are generally subject to the same rules as domestically owned banks. The United States also extended to the recent FTAs the ratchet clause developed in NAFTA and absent in GATS. This implies that any liberalization of an existing non-conforming measure related to investment automatically creates a new commitment to that level of openness. All five FTAs exclude from the ratchet measures that restrict or require a specific (non-discriminatory) type of juridical form of establishment and cross-border trade.

Insurance

Improvements in regional and extra-regional market opening of the insurance sector have also been substantial. On the cross-border trade front, except for Guatemala which committed reinsurance services under GATS, all remaining Latin American members of DR-CAFTA will allow for the first time the cross-border supply of maritime and transport (MAT) insurance, reinsurance, intermediation, services auxiliary to insurance and, Costa Rica, services necessary to support global accounts also. Chile too extended a similar commitment to U.S. and E.C. providers, although it excludes the cross-border supply through the movement of persons. In addition, the cross-border supply commitments of Chile and DR-CAFTA members permit citizens to consume abroad all lines of insurance, with very few exceptions and limitations. These commitments apply upon entry into force of the respective FTAs, except for Chile with the EC (one year) and for Costa Rica (July 2007) with respect to intermediation, services auxiliary to insurance and provision of surplus lines in DR-CAFTA. As before, Mexico's cross-border commitments are limited to transactions in foreign exchange in both NAFTA and the Mexico–E.C. FTA.

As regards investment, establishment with choice of juridical form in all major lines of insurance is (or will be) permitted by all countries in our sample. El Salvador made no commitments on insurance under GATS, whereas Guatemala bound reinsurance services only. Significant liberalization was achieved with the removal of economic needs tests in Chile, Honduras, and Mexico and with the removal or reduction of foreign equity limitations in the Dominican Republic, Honduras, and Mexico. Guatemala also eliminated domestic employment limitations for senior management and board of directors. No country except Honduras made commitments on branching in insurance in GATS. Regionally, however, Chile and DR-CAFTA members committed to phase-in branching in this sector in three to four years (except Honduras, where the commitment applies upon entry into force).

Probably the most significant market opening will take place in Costa Rica, where insurance services are currently dominated by a state monopoly. Costa Rica committed in DR-CAFTA to phase-in through January 2011 virtually full liberalization of both establishment and cross-border trade in insurance services and to establish and independent regulator by January 2007.

Given that the U.S. had bound a very liberal regime for foreign investment and cross-border trade in most lines of insurance in GATS and NAFTA, its new regional commitments do not seem significant. The main contribution of the FTAs (and also NAFTA) with respect to GATS are the opening of foreign supply through the movement of persons of all lines of insurance and a U.S. commitment with Chile to review regulations that do not allow branching in insurance in certain states. More significantly, NAFTA and the FTAs introduced a ratcheting clause for insurance similar to that for banking and securities services. It applies with respect to investment, except for market access in the FTAs with Chile, Central American countries and the Dominican Republic and Singapore. The U.S. opened cross-border trade in life insurance only in NAFTA.

Conclusion

The analysis here shows that Latin American countries have favored regional (and extra-regional), rather than multilateral opening of financial services markets. Except for NAFTA, the arrangements signed before the Mexico–E.C. FTA were successful in developing a framework of rules and disciplines for financial services internationalization, but have not yet been effective in substantially opening domestic financial markets to international competition (see Contreras and Yi, 2003). Only the arrangements signed after and including the Mexico–E.C. FTA have deepened at the regional level the degree of market opening granted by these countries at the multilateral level.[12]

Clearly, the most significant contribution of the more recent agreements of the Western Hemisphere, in particular the U.S. agreements, is the opening of the cross-border supply of a limited set of financial services. With few exceptions, cross-border trade in deposit and lending services and life-insurance services remains virtually completely closed throughout the Americas. However, this reality is likely to change once the common markets of the Western Hemisphere are fully implemented. Another important value added of these agreements is that countries bound very liberal regimes on investment in financial services.

Three main elements explain the more liberalizing nature of the recent regional agreements, namely: (1) a more comprehensive coverage of the financial services sector implicit in the negative list approach adopted for investment; (2) the formula approach adopted for the liberalization of cross-border trade, which allowed countries to focus their liberalization efforts in the least sensitive financial services; and (3) the relaxation of many of the limitations that countries still maintain in GATS.

Although not in itself liberalizing, another key contribution of the above agreements is that member countries both locked-in their legal and regulatory regimes affecting the financial services sector and committed to much needed regulatory reform. The most significant example of the latter is the introduction of competition in the Costa Rican insurance sector.

Finally, regional agreements have also helped to deepen a number of provisions governing financial services trade liberalization present in previous agreements. These comprise mainly disciplines on transparency in the rules and procedures set forth by domestic regulators and self-regulatory institutions, as well as disciplines that recognize the right of governments to regulate domestic markets in a non-discriminatory manner. New disciplines, such as regulatory procedures to expedite the supply of insurance services and limitations to the imposition of capital controls, were also introduced for the first time. In addition, an obligation to limit quantitative restrictions was borrowed from GATS and introduced in the most recent agreements.

Notes:

[1] The ideas, views and opinions expressed in this paper are the exclusive responsibility of the author and do not necessarily reflect the views of the OAS General Secretariat or the World Bank.

[2] The Montevideo Protocol of the South Cone Common Market (MERCOSUR) was the first Western Hemisphere agreement to adopt a positive list approach for services.

[3] A similar provision was also incorporated in MERCOSUR's Protocol of Montevideo and the Andean Community's Decision 439 on Services, both of which cover financial services.

[4] The market access provision of the financial services chapter of the Mexico–EC FTA excludes the GATS Article XVI prohibition to restrict or require specific types of legal entity or joint venture.

[5] These agreements exclude from the market-access obligation a limitation on the participation of foreign capital found in GATS Article XVI, as it constitutes a violation of the national treatment obligation.

[6] A limited right-of-establishment provision for insurance providers is also contained in CAFTA–DR for U.S. investors in Costa Rica.

[7] An important distinction between most Western Hemisphere agreements and the Understanding with respect to self-regulatory organizations is that the former require that these organizations afford national treatment to both investments and cross-border suppliers of financial services. The Understanding, on the other hand, does not require self-regulatory organizations to afford national treatment to cross-border suppliers of financial services.

[8] The U.S. also agreed to consult with Australia, Morocco, and Singapore with the goal of promoting objective and transparent regulatory processes in each Party.

[9] Most Western Hemisphere trade agreements follow the NAFTA dispute settlement provision, which permits both state-state and investor-state disputes relating to financial services. The only exception is the Australia–U.S. FTA, which provides for state-state disputes exclusively.

[10] Controls on current payments and transfers refer to exchange controls over current account transactions, whereas capital controls refer to restrictions over capital account transactions.

[11] Chile's *encaje* consists of a non-remunerated reserve requirement on external borrowing. This tax on short-term capital inflows was set to zero in 1998 and eliminated it in 2001.

[12] Although in most areas Mexico's commitments in NAFTA are currently more liberal than those in GATS, this does not necessarily hold for its initial NAFTA commitments given that Mexico phased-out a number of restrictions during a transition period.

Bibliography

Contreras, P. and S. Yi. 2003. "Internationalization of Financial Services in Asia-Pacific and the Western Hemisphere," Pacific Economic Cooperation Council. OAS Foreign Trade Information System (www.sice.oas.org). United States Trade Representative (www.ustr.gov). World Trade Organization (www.wto.org).

Box 7.2. China's Financial Sector: Pre- and Post-WTO Reforms

Yan Wang[1]

Restructuring the domestic financial sector is difficult everywhere, as it could be blocked by vested interest groups. Implementing GATS commitments can become a positive driving force for domestic restructuring in the financial sector, and China is an example. This Box focuses on the interaction between openness and restructuring, especially in the banking sector. The pre-WTO financial-sector reform was first initiated by the government, independent of the WTO accession process. Only in later stages were reform measures linked to the WTO or GATS commitments. China took the approach of introducing competition before privatizing the state financial institutions, which was similar to their approach in restructuring other monopolistic industries. Unlike some other countries that first opened their capital account or stock market, China adopted a different reform sequence, namely, to gradually open its financial sector to domestic and foreign competition, and leave the capital account liberalization to a later stage. The jury is still out on whether these unique features in sequencing will have significantly affected the end result.

Pre-WTO Reforms: Introducing Limited Competition

China's financial-sector reform was slow and gradual with no specific blueprint or roadmaps. It lagged behind reforms of other competitive industries due to many factors, including its links with the reforms of state enterprise and constraints related to regulatory capacity. The pre-WTO reforms focused on introducing limited competition from domestic and foreign-service providers with the latter subjected to strict geographical constraints. This period can be roughly divided into four stages:

1979-1986: breaking up the mono-bank system and revitalizing the specialized state banks.

1987-1991: introducing limited domestic competition. This period saw a rapid growth of non-bank financial intermediaries and the emergence of a joint stock universal bank (Bank of Communications) and Credit Cooperatives.

1991-1996: diversifying the financial sector. Two stock exchanges and the inter-bank market were established; and life and non-life insurance licenses were extended to foreign firms. A number of shareholding banks were established. In 1996, the People's Bank of China (PBoC) licensed nine foreign banks to conduct Renminbi (RMB) business in the Pudong Development Zone in Shanghai.

1997-2001: addressing the portfolio problems of the commercial banks. The preparations for WTO accession started in this period and attempts were made to strengthen State Owned Banks, including recapitalization, and establishment of Asset Management Companies (AMCs). A few foreign banks were allowed to operate in a limited number of cities to provide services to foreign residents and foreign and joint-venture enterprises. Their business with Chinese corporations and individuals was generally limited to foreign currency transactions and international settlement services for Chinese enterprises. Their local currency operations were constrained (For details see Lardy (1998), Bhattasali (2004), Holz and Zhu (2000), Lo (2001), and Tong (2002)).

Post WTO Reforms: Restructuring and Consolidation

"China's GATS commitments represent the most radical services reform program negotiated in the WTO. China promised to eliminate in a few years most restrictions on foreign entry and ownership, as well as most forms of discrimination against foreign firms." (Mattoo, 2004). The committed schedule has indeed "locked in" some proposed reform steps and provided pressure for implementing the reform agenda in the financial sector, which had been blocked by interest groups.

Five years after China joined the WTO, a series of changes have taken place.

Strengthening Supervision and Regulation.

New regulation was passed by the State Council in December 2001 to give legal guidance to revoke problematic financial institutions. In 2002, the PBoC started the liquidation of Everbright International Trust and Investment Corporation. In May 2002, the PBoC published regulations requiring financial institutions to improve their information disclosure system. In April 2003, The China Bank Regulation Commission (CBRC) was established in charge of bank regulation. The People's Bank Law and Commercial Banks Law were both re-drafted, and together with the first Bank Supervisory Law that empowers the CBRC, came into effect on February 1, 2004.

Accelerating the Structural Reform in the Domestic financial Sector

In October 2002, the government announced preliminary regulations governing mergers and acquisitions (M&A). Foreign banks have started to negotiate with Chinese banks for M&A deals. And foreign financial institutions have been invited to form joint ventures and to dispose of Non-performing Loans (NPLs). In December 2003, CBRC Chairman Liu Mingkang outlined plans for future reform of the banking sector, "to improve retail banks' badly damaged balance sheets, provide them with new capital, introduce better corporate governance, and foster competition through more foreign bank operations." "Once the State-owned commercial banks have conditions in place for restructuring or issuing stocks, the central government will encourage them to accept overseas funding as well as domestic capital" (*China Daily*, January 7, 2004). Several commercial banks have been restructured by attracting foreign strategic investors. Goldman Sachs, Allianz and American Express bought 8.89% of Industrial and Commercial Bank of China (ICBC). A consortium led by Royal Bank of Scotland, Asia Financial Holding, UBS, Asian Development Bank is holding 8.25%, 4.64%, 1.33% and 0.20% Bank of China (BOC)'s shares respectively. Bank of America and Asia Financial Holding acquired 8.52% and 6.04% of China Construction Bank (CCB). Other deals include HSBC investing 19.9% of The Bank of Communications, Standard Chartered Bank investing 19.9% of Bohai Bank, and Commonwealth Bank of Australia investing 11% of Jinan City Commercial Bank. (See Table 7.B.2.1).

On January 6, 2004, the State Council completed capital injection into the BOC and CCB-two of the "big four" state-owned commercial banks, using 45 billion US dollars of the nation's foreign exchange reserves. In 2005, another 15 billion US dollars were injected into ICBC-the largest bank in China. The capital infusion gave these state commercial banks a strong push in the process of their ongoing reforms, with all of these 3 Banks having successful Initial Public Offerings (IPOs) in 2005 and 2006. ICBC's IPO raised about US$20 billion, and was the largest IPO in history. According to Tier One capital strength, they are now among the strongest banks in the world-CCB, ICBC and BOC ranked 11th, 16th and 17th respectively in the world (*The Banker*, July 2006). Other commercial banks also had some improvement in their capital strength. With the recent Industrial Bank (Fujian)'s IPO in January 2007, there are

Table 7.B.2.1: Foreign Ownership in China's Local Banks

Local banks	Investing foreign banks	% of shares
Industrial and Commercial Bank of China	Goldman Sachs, Allianz and American Express	9.9
Bank of China	Royal Bank of Scotland-Li Ka-shing-Merrill Lynch/ Temasek Holding/ UBS/ADB	10 / 10 / 1.68 /0.2
China Construction Bank	Bank of America/Temasek Holding	9.1 / 5.1
Bohai Bank (Tianjin)	Standard Chartered Bank	19.9
Jinan City Commercial Bank	Commonwealth Bank of Australia	11
Bank of Communications	HSBC (Shanghai)	19.9
Shenzhen Development Bank	New Bridge Capital	17.89
Shanghai Pudong Development Bank	Citi Bank	4.6
China Minsheng Banking Corp.	Temasek Holding / IFC	5 / 1.6
Industrial Bank Co.(Fujian)	Hang-Seng Bank/ Tetrad Ventures /IFC	16 / 5 / 4
China Everbright Bank	China Everbright Group (Hong Kong) /ADB	20.1 / 3
Bank of Shanghai	HSBC/IFC/Shanghai Commercial Bank	8 / 7 / 3
Nanjing City Commercial Bank	IFC	15
Fujian Asia Bank(a joint venture bank)	HSBC/Ping An Insurance Group	50 / 50
Xi'An City Commercial Bank	IFC/ Scotia Bank	12.5 / 12.4
Dalian City Commercial Bank	SHK Financial Group	10

Source: Updated based on *Securities Market Weekly*, July 2004, *Oxford Analytica*, various issues, Directors and Boards, April 2006

Table 7.B.2.2 Non-performing Loans and Capital Adequacy of Banks

	2004	2003	2002	2001
	Five part classification		Old classification	
	Per cent			
Non-performing loans ratio (NPL)				
State owned commercial banks	15.6	20.4	26.1	31
Joint stock banks	4.9	7.9	11.9	..
City commercial banks	14.1[1]	15.0[2]	..	..
	Per cent			
Memorandum:				
Capital adequacy ratio				
State owned commercial banks	6.8[1]	6.7	5.2	5.4
Joint stock banks	7.6[2]	7.4	..	..
City commercial banks	..	6.1	..	..

Note: 1. End-June. 2. End-September.
Source: Adapted from *OECD Economic Survey: China*.

8 Chinese Banks publicly listed domestically or internationally. By September 2006, 66 Chinese banks (44.3% of total, accounting for 73.6% of total bank assets) had met the Basel I requirement of an 8% capital-adequacy ratio. Asset quality also improved (see Table 7.B.2.2). However, more than half of the commercial banks and credit cooperatives still face problems of under-capitalization and large amount of NPLs.

Encouraging Domestic Competition by Establishing More Shareholding Banks

The pace of opening the market to the domestic private sector has been rather slow. After the approval of the new banking laws, several new share-holding banks with private shares were already under preparation. Bohai Bank with headquarters in Tianjin was approved in November 2003, Northeast Reconstruction Bank, Guangdong Nanhua Bank, and some other inter-provincial banks with private shares are expected to emerge in the near future. However, all of these banks still have strong government backing-with the central or local government being the biggest shareholder, which inevitably will bring some constraints on the banks' independent management.

Introduce International Competition to the Financial Sector

Opening further to foreign bank entry

In February 2002, the PBoC published detailed implementation rules of Regulations on the Administration of Foreign Financial Institutions; in March, the PBoC unified the regulations on deposit and loan interest rates on domestic banks and foreign banks. In March 2002, the PBoC began issuing licenses to allow banks to extend foreign exchange services to domestic companies and individuals. Citibank Shanghai HSBC, the Bank of East Asia, Hang Seng Bank and Standard Chartered received licenses in 2002. In June 2003, the Closer Economic Partnership Arrangement (CEPA) was signed between the mainland and Hong Kong, with the services sector benefiting most from it. A wide range of professions enjoyed freer access to the mainland market and, in particular, the entry requirements for banks were relaxed, and the mainland implemented some of the commitments made to the WTO members ahead of schedule for the benefit of Hong Kong.

In December 2003, the ceiling on foreign ownership in local banks was raised from 15% to 20% for single shareholders and 25% overall, to encourage foreign banks to take a strategic stake in domestic banks. Foreign banks would benefit by gaining immediate market access and the right to undertake limited local-currency operations ahead of competitors who must wait until geographical restrictions are lifted in 2006. Many foreign financial institutions have since become important shareholders in China's banks (See Table 7B.2.1).

In December 2006, five years after China's WTO accession, the new Regulations on Administration of Foreign-Funded Banks came into effect. Non-prudential measures regarding the ownership, operation and establishment of foreign banks as well as geographic restrictions were eliminated. "Qualified" oversea banks were allowed to deal with Renminbi business across China. To become "qualified," however, foreign banks need to meet minimum capital requirements, have a consecutive earnings record, and have to be incorporated locally-that is, to set up a China-registered legal entity. Otherwise, they will have to set aside two times as much capital (200 million yuan-US$25.4 million), and can take only large deposits (1 million yuan or above), limiting their ability to amass funds and grow through lending. Still they cannot issue bank cards. These rules aim to ensure that only "high quality" banks can enter China. Encouraging foreign banks to incorporate locally enables the government to better monitor banking institutions. Although some foreign banks complained that these requirements constrain market access by smaller banks and are de facto discriminatory, many of them already started the process to transform their branches into locally registered legal entities. On December 24, 2006, CBRC approved nine foreign banks' application, all to be registered in Shanghai, including the Standard Chartered Bank, the Bank of East Asia, the Hong Kong and Shanghai Banking Corp. (HSBC), the Hang Seng Bank, the Mizuho Corporate Bank, the Bank of Tokyo-Mitsubishi UFJ, the DBS Group, Citibank and the ABN Amro Bank.

Significant steps have been taken to open stock market

In late 2001, the China Securities Regulatory Commission (CSRC) issued regulations on the public listing of foreign-invested enterprises. In December 2002, China launched the Qualified Foreign Institutional Investors (QFII) scheme, enabling eligible foreign investors to invest in "A" shares (which were previously only open to domestic investors) under certain limitations. These funds are to be transferred and converted into domestic currency, deposited in special accounts and invested in equities and bonds. By the end of 2005, the ceiling on foreign investment in the stock markets was increased from US$4 billion to US$10 billion, By the end of 2006, CSRC had approved 52 QFIIs with an accumulated quota of US$9.045 billion. (See Table 7.B.2.3 for a series of important events in China's QFII development.)

Insurance market was opened gradually according to the accession schedule

By the end of 2004, The China Insurance Regulatory Commission (CIRC) announced further easing of restrictions on foreign participation in the insurance sector, including: elimination of geographical restrictions on foreign insurers, who were previously confined to 15 cities; opening of health insurance, group insurance and annuity sectors (foreign insurers had been limited to selling individual life policies); abolition of compulsory reinsurance requirements; and raising the cap on foreign insurance brokers' ownership share from 50% to 51%. By the end of 2004, more than 100 foreign insurers had established offices in China, of which 32 have business licenses. Of these, 19 are life-insurance joint ventures, and 13 have licenses that apply to property and casual insurance. By the end of 2005, foreign Insurers had a 6.92% (RMB34.12 billion) market share of the total premium in China, a considerable increase compared to around 2% in 2004. By the end of 2006, 41 foreign insurers had obtained a business license in China, and 133 foreign insurance companies from 20 countries had opened 195 representative offices in China.

Unfinished Reform Agenda

It is clear from the above that implementing the GATS agreement has become a positive driving force for domestic restructuring in the financial sector. Although China's banking industry has gone through many changes, some important challenges remain to be resolved.

- *Non-performing loans remain a big issue* and new NPLs are being created each day due to perverse incentives in a largely state owned monopolistic system. NPLs were estimated at about 25-30 percent of the total loans outstanding for the state commercial banks and higher for the rural credit cooperatives, city commercial banks and policy banks (World

Table 7.B.2.3 Important Events Related to the Qualified Foreign Institutional Investors (QFII)

Nov. 7, 2003	CSRC and PBC jointly issued Administration Rules on Qualified Foreign Institutional Investors (QFII)'s Security Investment, which were implemented from Dec. 1.
Nov. 28, 2003	State Administration of Foreign Exchange(SAFE) issued Foreign Exchanges Administration Rules on QFII's Security Investment, effective from Dec. 1.
Dec. 1, 2003	QFII Scheme was officially launched. The scheme stipulates that in order to be eligible for QFII a foreign investing institution must have at least US$10 billion in assets and foreign banks must be in the top-100 globally. And their investment in A shares is limited to only 10% of any one company. There are restrictions for repatriation: investments in closed-end funds are not allow to repatriate for three years, other funds must wait a year and money can only be repatriated in small trenches.
Mid-Jan., 2003	PBC announced that 6 domestic banks (ICBC, ABC, BOC, CCB, Bank of Communications, China Merchants Bank) and 3 foreign banks' branches in Shanghai (Standard Charted Bank, HSBC, Citi Bank) have been allowed to open custodial services for domestic securities investment by QFIIs.
May 26, 2003	CSRC awarded QFII license to UBS Warburg and Nomura Securities. They became the first foreign institutions to receive approval to invest directly in RMB-denominated "A" shares and government bonds.
May 30, 2003	SAFE authorized investment quotas of US$300 million and US$50 million respectively to UBS Warburg and Nomura Securities.
Jun. 24, 2003	SAFE authorized UBS Warburg to open an special QFII RMB account in its custodial service provider—Citi Bank's Shanghai Branch. This is the first QFII RMB account.
Jul. 9, 2003	Through Shenyin & Wanguo Securities, UBS Warburg bought stocks of Baoshan Iron & Steel, Shanghai Port Container, SinoTrans Development, and ZTE, completed the first QFII transaction.
Oct. 23, 2003	Deutsche Bank was allowed to open custodial service for domestic securities investment by QFIIs. The total number of such banks reached 12.
Dec. 12, 2003	CSRC awarded QFII license to Standard Charted Bank(Hong Kong), Nikko Cordial Securities, brought the total QFII number to 12, total investment amount US$1.7 billion.
Mar. 30, 2004	Nikko Cordial Securities made their first investment in China's capital market. By setting up the first foreign fund to invest in China's Government bond market, it became the first foreign institution enter the QFII scheme in the form of fund. It also represented Chinese Government's RMB-denominated bond entered the international investment stage.
May 9, 2004	CSRC awarded QFII license to Merrill Lynch.
May 12, 2004	CSRC awarded QFII licenses to HSBC Co. Ltd, and Daiwa Securities SMBC Co. Ltd. Till then, a total of 15 QFIIs have entered China's security market.
Jul. 12, 2004	SAFE authorized Daiwa Securities SMBC Co. Ltd an investment quota of US$50 million. Till then 15 foreign investment institutions have received a cumulative investment quota of US$1.875 billion.
Dec 2004	24 QFIIs had received a cumulative quota of US3.42 billion.
July, 2005	The US$4 billion quota has been used up, and CSRC is to "expand the pilot QFII program and steadily increase the investment quota," according to Shang Fulin, Chairman of CSRC. The ceiling on foreign investment in the stock markets is to be increased from US$4 billion to US$10 billion.
By April 2006	There are 6 joint venture securities companies (China International Capital, BOC International (China), China Euro Securities, Changjiang BNP Paribas Peregrine Securities, Haiji Daiwa Securities, and Goldman Sachs Gaohua Securities), 34 QFIIs, and 18 joint venture fund management companies in China.

| September 2006 | CSRC adopted revised rules concerning QFII, reduced the threshold for foreign investor to qualify as investors in the Chinese A-Share markets. Requirement of minimum securities assets managed by a QFII applicant was reduced by half to $5 billion; Insurance companies must exist for at least five years before becoming eligible for QFII, a much shorter period than the 30 years in the previous rules. |
| By December 2006 | CSRC approved 52 QFIIs, allocated quota US$9.045 billion. |

Source: Adapted from *Securities Market Weekly*, July 2004; People's Bank of China, *China Monetary Policy Report 2004*; *China Daily*, June 28, 2005; *Oxford Analytica*, July 12, 2005, Directors & Boards, April 2006.

Table 7.B.2.4 Comparison of Some Indicators between China's Banks and Top Banks in the World

	Tier one capital $m	Return on assets %	Profit/ employee US$000	Basel capital adequacy ratio %	NPL to total loans %
Citi-Group(12/04)	74,415	1.63	84.26	11.85	2.06
HSBC(12/04)	67,259	1.38	72.36	12.00	1.94
Industrial & Commercial - Bank of China (ICBC) (12/04)	20,170	0.05	0.94	5.52[*]	18.99
Agricultural Bank of China (12/03)	16,670	0.19	1.60	n.a	30.07[*]
Bank of China (BoC) (12/04)	27,602	0.81	22.97	10.04	5.12
China Construction Bank (12/04)	23,530	1.29	19.55	11.29	3.92

Note: [*]*The Banker*, July, 2004, before capital injections of US$15 billion in early 2005.
Source: Adapted from *The Banker*, July and August 2005.

Bank, 2003). Even though the state-owned commercial banks' NPL ratio dropped from 31% at the end of 2001 to 9.3% in 2006 (CBRC statistics), the ratio is still higher than the international level (see Table 7.B.2.4). Furthermore, the reduction in the NPL ratio may be misleading since it may be the result of a rapid increase in new loans.

The government's capital injection may worsen the problem of perverse incentives. A second round of re-capitalization would help to clean up balance sheets of some existing banks such as the Agricultural Bank of China, as some have suggested, but will not address the fundamental incentive problems in the governance system of the largely state-owned banks. On the contrary it may foster moral hazard - more risk taking by these banks.

- *Problems of access to credit by the poor and regional disparity.* With the state banks engaging in credit rationing and retreating from lagging regions, it is becoming more difficult for the poor to access credit. As mentioned earlier, the consolidation of domestic state-owned banks led to a reduction of 44,000 branches in rural and remote regions. Just as Mattoo (2004) pointed out: "Initial restrictions on the geographical scope of services liberalization could encourage the further agglomeration of economic activity in certain regions - to an extent that is unlikely to be reversed completely by subsequent country-wide liberalization." Complementary measures (including reforming rural credit cooperatives and developing micro-finance institutions) must be taken to ensure the poor's access to credit. The government has started to attach more importance to this issue. The recent third National Financial Work Conference listed rural financial reforms as one of the priorities.. Several measures were taken to reduce the barriers for market access by financial institutions entering the rural market, to encourage the establishment of diversified rural credit organizations including those engaged in micro-credit, and to move forward on agricultural insurance. CBRC has also approved the launching of the China Postal Saving Bank in January 2007, which is expected to maintain a strong rural focus. It is hoped that this bank will strengthen the provision of financial services in the countryside. However, it remains to be seen whether the bank will become just another channel for capital to flow from the poor to the rich regions.

- A broader reform agenda includes liberalizing interest rates, developing the domestic bond market, and gradually opening the capital account. After many years of tightly controlled interest rates, they have been deregulated to some extent. Since January 1 2004, banks and urban credit co-operatives are allowed to set lending rates at 1.7 times the central bank's basic, or benchmark rate (*China Business Weekly*, December 16, 2003). However, to have a well defined yield curve and better risk diversification, it is crucial to develop a deeper domestic bond market as many developing countries such as Korea and India have done. China's bond market expanded in the recent years, and several new products were introduced, including asset-backed securitizations (ABSs), Mortgage-backed Securitizations (MBSs), Panda bonds issued by International Financial Institutions, financial bonds for commercial banks and finance companies, and short term financing bills for enterprises on the inter-bank bond market. (See World Bank, 2006.)

In summary, China has made significant inroads in its financial-sector reforms but faces many challenges. Risk in the financial sector arises from the accumulation of NPLs, weak internal control, regulation and supervision, outright fraud, and an ambiguous exit/bankruptcy mechanism. Without major restructuring, the state commercial banks alone are unlikely to be able to grow out of their NPL problems. The injection of capital is likely to be effective only if accompanied by structural and regulatory reforms in the banking system. Eliminating ambiguities in the objectives and performance measures of bank managers may not be possible "without a greater role for the private sector in bank ownership and operation" (World Bank, 2003).

Table 7.B.2.5 China: A Summary of Implementing GATS Commitments in the Financial Sector

Sectors	Accession commitments	Progress in implementation as of January 2007
Banking	Location: Upon accession, foreign currency business allowed without geographical restriction. Geographical restrictions on local currency business of foreign banks will be phased out over five years; four cities opened upon accession, four additional cities thereafter. Products: Within two years after accession, China will permit foreign banks to provide local currency services to Chinese enterprises; within five years to all Chinese individuals. Investment: Within five years after accession, all current non-prudential measures regarding the ownership, operation and establishment of foreign banks, as well as those concerning their branches and restrictions on issuing licenses, will be eliminated (national treatment).	Foreign currency banking business was fully opened in 2001; From December 2003, foreign banks were allowed to provide local currency service to Chinese enterprises. By 2006, 25 cities have been opened for foreign bank on local currency business. By the end of 2006, non-prudential practices regarding the ownership, operation and establishment of foreign banks were removed, retail RMB business was opened to qualified foreign banks in China (but foreign banks need to register as Chinese legal entities to offer bank cards and mass-market banking services in Yuan). Nine foreign banks have been approved by CBRC to transform their local branches into legalized entities in China. Implementation: ceiling on foreign ownership in local banks was raised from 15% to 20% for single shareholders; the requirement on the working capital of foreign bank's branch was lowered; foreign banks were allowed to engage in derivatives and insurance companies' cross-border foreign currency custodial services. 6 commercial banks have had partial foreign ownership. In 2004, marked by the RMB45 billion ($5.4 billion) capital injection, Bank of China and China Construction Bank started their comprehensive reforms. By the end of 2005, 25 foreign banks have invested in 20 China's domestic banks (some of them invested in more than one).

Insurance	Location: All geographical restrictions will be lifted in three years after the entry. Product: Upon accession, foreign life insurers will be permitted to provide individual (non-group) life insurance services. Two years after entry, they will be permitted to provide health insurance, group insurance, pension insurance and annuities to Chinese and foreign customers. Reinsurance is completely open upon accession, with no restrictions. Investment: Upon accession, foreign life insurers will be allowed to hold 50% ownership in joint ventures. They may choose their own joint-venture partners. For non-life, China will allow branching or 51% foreign ownership upon accession and wholly owned subsidiaries in two years after the entry (i.e. no restriction on the form of enterprise establishment). Licenses will be granted solely on the basis of prudential criteria with no economic needs test or quantitative limits on the number of licenses granted.	In January 2002, Generali China Life Insurance became the first joint-venture insurance company in China after WTO accession. Later on, similar joint-venture life insurance companies such as Sino-French Life Insurance, MetLife China, etc. were established. Air China and Korean Samsung Life, China Eastern Airline and Taiwan Cathay Life have been working on cooperation procedures. Major international insurance companies have already entered China's insurance market. Till the end of 2003, 39 foreign insurance companies had opened 70 branches, and 124 foreign insurance companies had established representative office in China. On supervision, China accelerated its steps on approaching international standards. The supervision principal based on Solvency Supervision was adopted. Major national insurance companies reformed their ownership structure, and were successfully listed in stock market. The market cap of the 3 national insurance companies which was listed abroad accounts more than half of the total domestic market. In the first half of 2004, China Insurance Regulatory Commission approved the establishment of 18 new Chinese Insurance Company of different kinds. According to CIRC, by the end of 2005, 40 foreign insurers have got business license in China. Foreign Insurers have a 6.92% (RMB34.12 billion) market share of the total premium in China, increased considerably compared to around 2% in 2004. By the end of 2006, 41 foreign insurers have got business license in China, 133 foreign insurance companies from 20 countries opened 195 representative offices in China.
Securities	Product: Foreign securities companies may engage directly in B share business. Investment: Within three years, foreign investment banks will be permitted to establish joint ventures, with foreign ownership not exceeding 33%, to engage (without Chinese intermediary) in underwriting domestic shares (A shares) and underwriting and trading in foreign currency denominated securities (B and H shares, government and corporate debts). Representative offices of foreign securities companies may become special members of Chinese stock exchanges.	By 2006, 34 foreign financial institutes have been granted Qualified Financial Institutional Investor (QFII) qualification to enter China's securities market. Joint-venture securities companies also emerged. Newly established China-Euro Securities Limited and Changjiang BNP Paribas Peregrine Securities both have 33% foreign shares. Currently (April 2006), there are 6 joint venture securities companies (China International Capital, BOC International (China), China Euro Securities, Changjiang BNP Paribas Peregrine Securities, Haiji Daiwa Securities, and Goldman Sachs Gaohua Securities), 34 QFIIs, and 18 joint venture fund management companies in China.

Source: Updated by the author based on *Caijing Magazine*, 2004 (23).

Opening wider to foreign (and Hong Kong) bank entry and establishing new shareholding banks with private stakes are steps in the right direction. However, opening to foreign bank entry alone will not solve the above mentioned problems. It must be combined with measures of restructuring the financially nonviable state-owned banks. One of the options was to break up the existing state banks into smaller commercial banks and allow qualified foreign banks to take a large controlling stake in them through M&As (Wang, 1997). However, there has been increased political sensitivity recently over foreign ownership of domestic banks. China's Premier Wen Jiabao said in March 2006 that the state should retain a controlling interest in commercial banks. The Central Huijin Company holds more than half of the shares of the three largest listed state commercial banks, and for the foreseeable future these banks will remain under central government control. Even for other commercial banks, it will be difficult for foreign banks to take a controlling stake and conduct structural reforms. The current regulation limits single foreign ownership of domestic banks to 20%, and total foreign ownership to 25%. Citigroup's investment in Guangdong Development Bank was delayed for almost a year on issues regarding non-compliance with this rule. Even in the rare case of being the largest shareholder, should foreign shareholders move to carry out reforms that the authority deems detrimental, it would have been easy for the authority to block the move by coordinating with other state shareholders.

China's financial sector is at a critical juncture in which opening/internationalization and restructuring can be combined to reinforce each other. Here, implementing the GATS agreement has been a positive driving force for domestic restructuring-largely consistent with the Government's reform agenda. This is a unique opportunity where trade in financial services is likely to become the engine of reform and growth. The jury is still out, however, on whether the current trend of restructuring the state-owned financial institutions through attracting foreign strategic investors will continue, and whether corporate governance issues will be resolved in these hybrid financial institutions.

Note

[1] This box focuses on China's openness and domestic financial-sector reforms. On openness, bank performance and growth, see Bayraktar and Wang (2006, 2004). The author thanks Bintao Wang for his excellent research assistance. Errors and omissions are entirely the author's own responsibility.

References

Bayraktar, Nihal and Yan Wang. 2006. "Banking Sector Openness and Economic Growth: Evidence from Bank level data." World Bank Policy Research Working papers 4019.

—— 2004. "Foreign Bank Entry, Performance of Domestic Banks, and Sequence of Financial Liberalization." World Bank Policy Working Papers 3416.

Bhattasali, Deepak. 2004. Accelerating Financial Market Restructuring in China," Ch. 11 in Deepak Bhattasali, Shantong Li and Will Martin (eds.), *China and the WTO: Accession, Policy Reform, and Poverty Reduction Strategies*. New York: Oxford University Press.

Branstetter, Lee and Nicholas Lardy. 2006. "China's Embrace of Globalization." NBER Working Paper 12373, June.

Greene, Malory, Nora Dihel, Przemyslaw Kowalski, and Douglas Lippoldt. 2006. "China's Trade and Growth: Impact on Selected OECD Countries." OECD Trade Policy Working Paper no. 44.

Holz, Carsten and Zhu, Tian. 2000. "Banking and Enterprise Reform in the People's Republic of China after the Asian Financial Crisis: An Appraisal."

Lardy, Nicholas R. 1998. *China's Unfinished Economic Revolution*, Washington DC: Brookings Institution Press.

Lo, Wai Chung 2001. "A Retrospect on China's Banking Reform," *The Chinese Economy* 34(1):15-28 (January-February).

Mattoo, Aaditya. 2004. "The Services Dimension of China's Accession to the WTO," Ch. 8 in Deepak Bhattasali, Shantong Li and Will Martin (eds.), *China and the WTO: Accession, Policy Reform, and Poverty Reduction Strategies*. New York: Oxford University Press

Tong, Donald D. 2002. The Heart of Economic Reform-China's Banking Reform and State Enterprise Restructuring. Ashgate Publishing Limited.

Wang, Yan. 1997. "Transforming Specialized Banks to Commercial Banks via Foreign Direct Investment: Feasibility in Guangzhou," in Chun Zhang, Decheng Zheng, and Yijiang Wang (eds.), *Bank-Enterprise Reforms and Strategies to Develop Regional Financial Centers*. China Economic Press.

World Bank, 2003, "China: Promoting Growth with Equity," Country Economic Memorandum. Report no. 24169-CHA. October 15, 2003

World Bank. 2006. *China Quarterly Update*. Beijing: World Bank Office.

World Trade Organization. Various Documents and *Trade Policy Review on China*.

References

Baekert, G., C. Harvey, and C. Lundblad. 2001. "Does Financial Liberalization Spur Growth?" NBER Working paper No. 8245.

Barth, J. R., G. Caprio, Jr., and R. Levine. 2000a. "The Regulation and Supervision of Banks around the World: A New Database." *World Bank Policy Research Working Paper* No. 2588. Washington, D.C.: World Bank.

——2000b. "Banking Systems around the Globe: Do Regulation and Ownership Affect Performance and Stability?" Washington, D.C.: World Bank.

Berger, A. N., W. G. Hunter, and S. G. Timme. 1993. "The Efficiency of Financial Institutions: A Review of Research, Present, Past and Future," *Journal of Banking and Finance* 17: 221–49.

Caprio, G. 2002. *Finance for Growth: Policy Choices in a Volatile World.* Washington, D.C.: World Bank.

Ceccini, P. 1988. *The European Challenge in 1992: The Benefits of a Single Market.* Aldershot: Gower.

Claessens, S. and T. Glaessner. 1998. *Internationalization of Financial Services in Asia.* Available at: www.worldbank.org (accessed July 2003).

——A. Demirguc-Kunt, and H. Huizinga. 1998. "How Does Foreign Entry Affect the Domestic Banking Sector?" Manuscript available at www.worldbank.org (accessed November 2003).

Clarke, G., R. Cull, and M. Soledad Martinez Peria. 2001. *Does Forcing Bank Penetration Reduce Access to Credit in Developing Countries? Evidence from Asking the Borrowers.* Washington, D.C.: World Bank.

——and S. M. Sanchez. 2001. "Foreign Bank Entry: Experience, Implications for Developing Economies, and Agenda for Further Research." *World Bank Research Observer* 18: 25–9.

Contreras, P. and S. Yi. 2004. "Internationalization of Financial Services in Asia-Pacific and the Western Hemisphere." Available at: http://sice.oas.org/tunit (accessed January 2007).

Dages, G. B., L. Goldberg, and D. Kinney. 2000. "Foreign and Domestic Bank Participation in Emerging Markets: Lessons from Mexico and Argentina," *Economic Policy Review* 6/3: 17–36. (Federal Reserve Bank of New York. September.)

Dobson, W. 2002. "Further Financial Services Liberalization in the Doha Round?" International Economics Policy Briefs. PB02-8. Washington, D.C.: Institute for International Economics (August).

——and P. Jacquet. 1998. *Financial Services Liberalization in the WTO.* Washington, D.C.: Institute for International Economics.

Edey, M. and K. Hviding. 1995. *An Assessment of Financial Reform in OECD Countries.* Economics Department Working Papers 154. Paris: Organization for Economic Cooperation and Development.

Financial Leaders Group. 1997. *Barriers to Trade in Financial Services: Case Studies.* London: Barclays.

FLWG (Financial Leaders Working Group). 2002. "Insurance: Proposed Model Schedule and Best Practices." Washington, D.C.: FLWG.

Giannetti, M. and S. Ongena. 2005. "Financial Integration and Entrepreneurial Activity: Evidence from Foreign Bank Entry in Emerging Markets," unpublished.

Hoekman, B. and A. Mattoo. 2002. "Financial Services and the GATS." Paper presented at a conference on "Further Liberalization of Global Financial Markets?" Washington, D.C: Institute for International Economics. June 5.

IMF (International Monetary Fund). 2000. *International Capital Markets.* Washington, D.C.: IMF (September).

Key, S. 2004. *The Doha Round and Financial Services Negotiations.* Washington, D.C.: American Enterprise Institute.

King, R. G., and R. Levine. 1993a. "Finance and Growth: Schumpeter May Be Right," *Quarterly Journal of Economics* 108: 717–37.

—— 1993b. "Finance, Entrepreneurship, and Growth: Theory and Evidence," *Journal of Monetary Economics* 32: 513–42.

King, R. G., and R. Levine. 1993c. "Financial Intermediation and Economic Growth," in C. Mayer and X. Vives (eds.), *Capital Markets and Financial Intermediation,* 156–89. Cambridge, United Kingdom: Cambridge University Press for the Centre for Economic Policy Research.

Kono, M., P. Low, M. Luanaga, A. Mattoo, M. Oshidawa, and L. Schuknecht. 1997. "Opening Markets in Financial Services and the Role of the GATS." Geneva: World Trade Organization.

LaPorta, R., F. López-de-Silanes, and A. Shleifer. 2000. "Government Ownership of Banks." Harvard Institute of Economic Research Discussion Paper Series (U.S.). 1890: 1–55 (March).

Levine, R. 1996. "Foreign Banks, Financial Development, and Economic Growth," in C. Barfield (ed.), *International Financial Markets.* Washington, D.C.: American Enterprise Institute Press.

—— 2004. *Finance and Growth: Theory and Evidence.* Cambridge, MA: National Bureau of Economic Research.

—— N. Loayza, and T. Beck. 2000. "Financial Intermediation and Growth: Causality and Causes," *Journal of Monetary Economics* 46(1): 31–77.

Low, P. and A. Mattoo. 2000. "Is There a Better Way? Alternative Approaches to Liberalization under the GATS," in P. Sauvé and R. M. Stern (eds.), *GATS 2000: New Directions in Services Trade Liberalization.* Washington, D.C.: Brookings Institution.

McCawley, T. 2003. "Lend a Little," *Far Eastern Economic Review* August 7.

Mattoo, A. 2000. "Developing Countries in the New Round of GATS Negotiations: Towards a Proactive Role," *World Economy* 23(4): 471–89.

—— and L. Schuknecht. 2000. "Trade Policies for Electronic Commerce," *World Bank Policy Research Working Paper* no. 2380. Washington, D.C.: World Bank.

Mosely, P. 1999. "Micro-macro Linkages in Financial Markets: The Impact of Financial Liberalization on Access to Rural Credit in Four African Countries," *Journal of International Development* 11: 367–84.

Sauvé, P. 2002. "Completing the GATS Framework: Safeguards, Subsidies and Government Procurement," in B. Hoekman, A. Mattoo, and P. English (eds.), *Development, Trade and the WTO: A Handbook.* Washington, D.C.: World Bank.

Skipper, H. D. 1996. "International Trade in Insurance," in C. Barfield (ed.), *International Financial Markets.* Washington, D.C.: American Enterprise Institute Press.

Sorsa, P. 1997. "The GATS Agreement on Financial Services: A Modest Start to Multilateral Liberalization." IMF Working Paper WP/97/55. Washington, D.C.: IMF.

World Bank. 2000. *Can Africa Claim the 21st Century?* Washington, D.C.: World Bank.

World Bank. 2002. "Trade in Services: Using Openness to Grow," *Global Economic Prospects 2002-2003.* Washington, D.C.: World Bank.

8 Trade in Infrastructure Services: A Conceptual Framework

Philippa Dee and Christopher Findlay

Introduction

A well-functioning and open infrastructure sector is an important determinant of economic growth and improving living standards. Limao and Venables (2001) show that infrastructure is a significant and qualitatively important determinant of transport costs and bilateral trade flows. For example, improving destination infrastructure by one standard deviation reduces transport costs by an amount equivalent to a reduction of 6,500 sea kilometers or 1,000 kilometers of overland travel. Mattoo et al. (2001) show that openness in two key infrastructure services—telecommunications and finance—influences long-run growth performance. Countries with fully open telecommunications and financial services sectors grow up to 1.5 percentage points faster than other countries. Fay et al. (2003) show how infrastructure affects three child-health outcomes related to the Millennium Development Goals—the infant mortality rate, the child mortality rate, and the prevalence of malnutrition. They show that apart from the traditional determinants (income, assets, education, and direct health interventions), better access to basic infrastructure services has an important role in improving health outcomes.

The purpose of this chapter is to focus on one key attribute that many infrastructure industries have in common—economies of scale or scope—and to show how this poses some significant policy challenges for successful trade-policy reform. These conditions can lead to natural monopoly in which costs of provision are minimized with only one supplier in the market, but the problem is that the single producer may abuse its monopoly power by restricting the quantity or quality of output and pricing above costs. Opening this market to trade creates opportunity for introducing alternative suppliers but also creates challenges of arranging the transition to a new provider and regulating them appropriately. The chapter then discusses in general terms how international trade negotiations can contribute to ensuring successful outcomes. More specific suggestions for the design of international trade agreements are left to the individual chapters elsewhere in the volume on each type of infrastructure. So too is detailed evidence of the impact of trade policy reform, since the experience differs significantly across different types of infrastructure.

Key messages here are that while natural monopoly is a common feature of the infrastructure sector, care should be taken not to exaggerate its importance. There are circumstances in which no policy problem arises. Further, even if there is an apparent natural monopoly, it is important to separate that part of the chain of supply from other elements in which competition can develop. However, even so, natural monopoly elements remain. The GATS is relevant to natural monopoly markets and contains some disciplines on policy in those markets. Trade-policy reform can contribute to performance in markets in which natural monopolies have some influence, both in markets for services of the natural monopoly component of a longer chain of supply or in competitive markets for related services. However, market opening has to be complemented by the appropriate regulatory structures to capture these benefits, for example, related to the terms on which competitive firms have access to bottleneck facilities. Commitments made through international trade negotiations can facilitate the necessary regulatory reform.

Economies of Scale and Scope, the Natural Monopoly Problem and the GATS

Economies of scale occur when costs continue to fall as output rises, and as firms are able to adjust their capacity to meet the higher levels of output. These economies are sometimes exhausted beyond particular levels of output. But given the scale of demand, they can also lead to a situation of natural monopoly in which a single firm can produce all the output the market requires. They can pose the following policy dilemma:

- By definition, they mean that a single firm can produce all the output that the market requires more cheaply than could two or more firms. Introducing competition by having more than one firm may lead to technical inefficiency, meaning that total costs per unit of service are not at their lowest.

- But in the absence of competition (actual or threatened), the incumbent firm will maximize profits by restricting output and inflating prices above costs. The consumers and users of the infrastructure service will face distorted price signals in making their usage decisions. This leads to allocative inefficiency, meaning that prices exceed costs at the margin, so that from society's point of view there is too little output.

Many infrastructure industries have economies of scale in some or all parts of their operation because some production costs are fixed, that is, independent of usage. For example, the costs of providing and maintaining the copper-wire connection that connects a household to the public-switched telecommunications network does not depend on the number of calls the household makes. However, the costs of installing and maintaining the switching at the nearest telephone exchange will depend on their usage. Another example is that some of the costs of running an individual airplane (e.g. labor costs, costs of running a reservations system, costs of using the airport runway slot) will not depend on how many passengers the aircraft carries. Some of the costs of running an airline (costs of running a reservations system) will not even depend on the number of airplanes used. Some airline costs (fuel costs) will depend both on the number of airplanes and the number of passengers per plane. A further example is that the costs of installing and maintaining long-distance electricity transmission lines are largely independent of the amount of electricity transmitted. Similarly, the cost of installing and maintaining rail lines or water reticulation systems is largely independent of use.

Wherever there are some fixed costs of delivering a service, there will likely be at least some output levels over which the costs incurred per unit of service fall as the number of units delivered increase. Further, when fixed costs are important, it is also often the case that as output increases and producers move to larger facility sizes (bigger airports or larger exchanges), the costs of those facilities do not increase as fast as output. Total costs will be lowest when there is only one producer.

A related concept is economies of scope. This occurs where there are cost savings from bundling together the production of more than one service, so that it is cheaper for one firm to produce all the different services than it is for more than one firm. It is often claimed that there are economies of scope in the production of local and long distance calls, so it is cheaper for one firm to produce both products than for two separate firms. The cost savings come because both local and long distance calls use some parts of the public-switched telecommunications network in common. Similarly, it may be cheaper to bundle together the provision of air-passenger and air-freight services into one firm than to split them among more than one firm, since both services use the same fixed costs elements.

A final source of economies of scale is network economies. Some services are provided through networks—telecommunications and transport being two examples.

Network economies sometimes mean that from a user perspective, the benefits of the service increase with the size of the network. The benefit to a person of connecting to a telephone network that includes all the people in their city is greater than the benefit of connecting to a network that includes only half the city. This aspect of network economies is sometimes used as a rationale for consumer subsidies to encourage more users to connect to the network. Each user will recognize the benefits to themselves from connecting, but not the additional benefit to other users from having them connect. Subsidies can help to internalize this externality. The same argument does not apply as strongly to transport, water or electricity networks.

Critical for the current purpose is not what network economies mean for consumers but what they mean from a producer perspective. The switching costs of running a telecommunications network depend in complex ways on the pattern of usage through the network, but can be optimized according to particular patterns of use. Similarly, the switching costs and transmission losses through an electricity grid depend on usage patterns, but can be optimized to any particular pattern. Network economies in production can arise where operating costs can be optimized (relative to usage patterns) more successfully in large networks than in small. This is because larger networks often provide more flexibility to manage particular bottlenecks. For this reason, operating costs may be lower in a single large network than in two or more smaller ones.

Economies of scale or scope are a feature of many infrastructure services, particularly telecommunications and various modes of transport—road, rail, maritime, and air transport. This chapter focuses on the problem of natural monopoly that can arise from economies of scale or scope, and the implications for successful trade policy reform in the affected industries.

When is there *not* a Policy Problem?

As noted, there may be a significant policy problem associated with a natural monopoly—technical efficiency may require only one producer, but that producer may abuse its monopoly power by restricting the quantity or quality of output and pricing above what is required to achieve allocative efficiency.

There is a huge literature that discusses the conditions under which this is a policy problem in practice, and what it means for good economic policy design. A flavor of some of that literature is given later, when discussing the elements of successful trade policy reform. But at the outset, it is useful to identify some situations when there is not a policy problem.

First, the definition of natural monopoly refers to the boundaries of a particular market. In some cases, the likelihood of natural monopoly is increased by policy. For example, in markets where network effects are important, regulation might exclude a segment of a domestic market, for transport services for example, from the international networks. If this barrier is removed, there may be competition in the market for those services, as international operators take the domestic sectors into their networks. This situation is of special advantage to small economies. Restrictions on foreign entry may actually increase the likelihood of a natural monopoly problem, but opening the market to trade converts it into a component of a larger market in which competition can be sustained.

The definitions of economies of scale and scope apply to a given technology, but if there is sufficient competition from alternative technologies, there is not necessarily a policy problem. For example, a rail network may constitute a natural monopoly in a technical cost sense, but if there is sufficient competition from a road transport network that can provide a close substitute service, this can limit the ability of a single rail operator to engage in monopoly pricing. In this case, the question is how to define the market, as the land transport market or the rail transport market. Similarly, there is some evidence that competition from mobile-phone operators is limiting the ability of incumbent providers of fixed-line telecommunications services to monopoly price their services.

A related point is that natural monopoly only requires a policy response if it is a long-run problem, i.e. once all firms involved have had sufficient time to choose their scale of plant to minimize costs per unit of service delivered. A single provider with an inefficient scale of plant may face sufficient competitive discipline from a rival with a more appropriate scale of plant. And in infrastructure industries such as telecommunications where technology has been changing very rapidly, the minimum efficient scale of operation has also been falling rapidly over time, providing technological solutions in areas such as long distance telephony, which are no longer regarded as natural monopolies.

Finally, a natural monopolist may, under certain circumstances, be effectively disciplined by the threat of competition. This is an important consideration for many smaller developing economies. The size of their market may be small relative to prevailing technologies, meaning that lowest unit cost may come from having one producer. But if that producer is subject to the credible threat of replacement by a rival, this may provide enough discipline for the monopolist to keep prices close to costs. A credible threat requires there to be no legislative or regulatory barriers to such entry. It also requires that the rival not have to incur any costs that they could not recoup if they were unsuccessful. The absence of sunk costs—costs that cannot be recovered once committed—is an important precondition for the threat of 'hit and run' entry to work. If it does work, the market is said to be contestable. Examples of sunk costs include the costs of market research and advertising, which can be significant even if other fixed costs associated with production are not. But in many parts of infrastructure services, investments are lumpy and location-specific, and this often ensures that their costs are sunk.

Where sunk costs are prevalent, rivals are likely to be reluctant to commit resources, and the incumbent will have a strong incentive to lower prices if necessary to deter entry. The problem of inefficient duplication of infrastructure is therefore unlikely, but the problem of monopoly pricing continues to be important.

Natural Monopoly and the GATS

The General Agreement on Trade in Services contains some disciplines on natural monopolies. Article VIII requires:

- that Members ensure that monopoly providers act consistently with the Member's general most-favored-nation commitment and its specific commitments, these being:
  1. market-access commitments to avoid non-discriminatory limitations on entry or on service production levels, except where specified otherwise;

2. national treatment commitments to avoid discrimination against foreign suppliers, except where specified otherwise; and
3. where a monopoly supplier competes in the supply of a service outside the scope of its monopoly rights and subject to specific commitments, the Members ensure that the supplier does not abuse its monopoly position to act in a manner inconsistent with such commitments.

Thus monopolists are to be bound by specific commitments where they apply to either the monopoly service, or to a service outside the scope of its monopoly rights but produced by the monopolist.

Article VI of the GATS provides for additional disciplines on domestic regulation in sectors in which specific commitments are undertaken. These disciplines cover qualification procedures and requirements, technical standards and licensing requirements. They would therefore cover the licensing requirements applied to a natural monopolist. They require these to be based on objective and transparent criteria, to be no more burdensome than necessary to ensure the quality of the service, and not be in themselves a restriction on the supply of the service.

There is one additional situation, not covered by these provisions, in which a monopolist could act anti-competitively to thwart the intent of a Member's specific commitments to liberalize trade in services. This is when the monopolist owns a bottleneck facility with natural monopoly characteristics, access to which is required as an input to a subsequent (or "downstream") service that is subject to specific commitments, for example, a value added telecommunications services or mobile telephony (in these cases, the provision of the bottleneck facility is an "upstream" service). These commitments may have a liberalizing intent, but if the monopolist denies access to the bottleneck facility, or prices access to the facility on unreasonable terms, the liberalizing intent of the commitments made concerning the downstream services may be thwarted. Gamberale and Mattoo (2002) argue that because incumbents can impede access to markets in the absence of appropriate regulation, and because this has a direct impact on trade, natural monopoly is the one form of market failure that needs to be addressed directly by multilateral disciplines.

The Elements of Successful Trade-Policy Reform for Infrastructure Services

There are at least two dimensions to the problem of natural monopoly—in the provision of the monopoly service per se, and where the monopoly service is a necessary input to downstream services that could be supplied competitively.

TRADE-POLICY REFORM AND PROVISION OF MONOPOLY SERVICES

There is a potential role for trade-policy reform even in the provision of a monopoly service per se. This is because a foreign provider may provide advantages in terms of cost or quality of service over a domestic provider. Foreign providers of transport or telecommunications networks can bring new technologies that have been tried and tested in offshore markets. This can allow them to offer a better quality and/or lower cost service than a local provider. They can also bring new business practices that lower costs. They may have greater access to financial capital, or greater ability to bear risks. In these cases, there can be significant advantages in allowing foreign operators the option of becoming the incumbent monopolist. There is a growing body of empirical literature that identifies where actual and/or potential entry by foreign providers can offer improvements in economic performance in particular infrastructure industries (e.g. Barth et al., 2002). In some circumstances, the threat of foreign entry may be sufficient to discipline the costs of a domestic provider.

There are at least three offsetting considerations. One is whether there is a case for protecting a domestic incumbent from foreign competition in the expectation that the domestic provider will eventually become as efficient as a foreign provider. In some service industries, e.g. some professional services, domestic firms may have a comparative advantage in any event in tailoring their services to meet local language or other needs. In infrastructure services, this is less likely to be the case. But then there is a series of questions about the incentives that the less efficient domestic provider will have to become more efficient over time.

A second consideration is whether it is easier to apply pro-competitive regulation to guard against monopoly pricing when the incumbent is government owned, and therefore by definition domestic. As will be argued later, there is mounting evidence that the traditional methods of regulating a traditional integrated public monopoly are not conducive to promoting competition in those parts of an infrastructure industry that are amenable to competition. New regulatory methods are emerging to guard against monopoly pricing, while promoting competition in those market segments where competition is sustainable and desirable.

A final consideration in deciding whether a domestic or foreign operator should provide a monopoly service is that, in the presence of location-specific sunk costs, any incumbent will have a 'first mover' advantage that can protect it from being displaced by a lower cost rival in the future. First movers can have an advantage over potential entrants because of the costs which they have already sunk into the project, and which are therefore not recoverable, but those costs are associated with investments about which the entrant has yet to commit. While this argues for making the right choice in the first place, few countries have the luxury of making such a 'greenfield' decision, that is, a decision in which there is no existing project or infrastructure—they are stuck with the incumbent (and its cost structure) that they have inherited.

But there are other techniques that can be used to ensure that an incumbent keeps costs low (separate regulation may still be required to guard against monopoly pricing).

One option is to allow competition for the market, that is, by encouraging firms to bid for the right to be the sole supplier (competition in the market occurs when firms compete against each other within the same market, which cannot be sustained in the presence of the conditions for natural monopoly). Competition for the market could be arranged, for example by allocating the license to be the incumbent operator through a competitive process. This can be done on a once-off basis or regularly, every few years. Foreign operators can be invited to make bids for the license. The specifications for the license could include:

- provision of specific services, such as information technology or vehicle maintenance (service contract);
- management of the relevant infrastructure but without any exposure to commercial risk (management contract);
- inclusion in a contract of not only responsibility for managing some components of the system but also for collecting revenue, which implies taking a share of commercial risk, although without any responsibility for capital spending (lease);
- the inclusion of responsibility for financing and managing capital works (concession); or
- complete privatization.

Policy makers are not necessarily converging on any one model. The choice depends on a number of considerations, including:

- the extent of stakeholder support;
- whether infrastructure prices are set to recover costs;
- whether the bidders and/or those seeking the bids have extensive knowledge of the system;
- whether those seeking the bids have good regulatory capacity; and
- whether the country has a low risk rating.

Brook Cowen (1997) discusses how these factors affect the choice of model in the water sector, for example.

Where natural monopolies are regional rather than national, another mechanism to discipline costs and prices is to use 'benchmarking' or 'yardstick' competition by comparing estimates of technical efficiency across the regional operators. Estache et al. (2001) show the potential for this form of competition across ports, for example.

TRADE-POLICY REFORM AND THE PROVISION OF MONOPOLY INPUTS INTO COMPETITIVE SERVICES

There is growing realization that not all segments of infrastructure industries are natural monopolies. Empirical estimation of the extent of economies of scale is frustratingly imprecise, but a priori consideration of whether costs are fixed (i.e. do not vary with usage) can also help to provide some generalizations. For example:

- electricity transmission may be a natural monopoly but generation and retail distribution are generally regarded as not;

- in telecommunications, the "local loop" (the copper wire that connects each subscriber to the network) is generally regarded as a natural monopoly, there is less agreement on whether network economies and economies of scope mean that the remainder of the fixed network is a natural monopoly, but cellular services are generally regarded as being not;

- the provision of core airport services, such as runways and landing rights, may be a natural monopoly (although in some locations there may be sufficient competition from airports nearby), while the provision of ground-handling services may not be, and the provision of airline services is not likely to be.

However, cost patterns vary greatly across countries. In part this is because technologies differ—an important consideration in electricity generation is whether the technology is hydro, coal-fired or nuclear, and airline costs depend on the sizes of aircraft used. Differences in country size and population density can also have an important bearing on cost structures—long-distance telecommunications may be a natural monopoly in a small or sparsely populated country, but highly competitive in a larger or more densely populated one. These factors mean that it is important for each country to make its own assessment of which parts of its infrastructure industries may be natural monopolies.

Having done so, there can be significant advantages in ensuring that those parts of the industry that are capable of sustaining competition are opened up to it. Estache and de Rus (2000) illustrate the resulting decision tree in Figure 8.1.

As before, there is a case for including foreign operators in competition *in* the competitive segments of the market.

A country needs to consider two types of supporting domestic regulatory reform. The first is measures to contain monopoly pricing in the monopoly segment of the market. Trade-policy commitments may help to facilitate competition for the market and thus help to contain costs and ensure technical efficiency. Regulation to control monopoly pricing, and thus ensure allocative efficiency, is an additional measure that can be considered independently of a country's trade policy decision on market access (with an important proviso noted below).

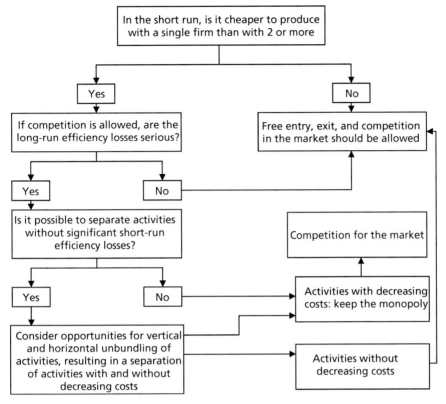

Figure 8.1. Separating the natural monopoly and competitive elements of infrastructure industries
Source: Adapted from Estache and de Rus (2000).

The second element of domestic regulatory reform is measures to ensure that the monopoly operator does not abuse its monopoly power over the monopoly bottleneck facility to thwart competition in competitive upstream or downstream activities. Where a country has made liberalizing commitments in the competitive activities, it will be a necessary adjunct to that trade-policy reform to ensure that competitive suppliers, including foreign suppliers, can gain access to the bottleneck facility on reasonable terms. It is beyond the scope of this chapter to go into detail on the appropriate design of such access regulation, since the details will vary from one type of infrastructure to the next. It is nevertheless useful to outline some of the main considerations.

There are two dimensions to the problem. One is where the competitive segment is downstream of the bottleneck facility. Telecommunications is an example. The other is where competition is upstream of the bottleneck facility. Electricity generation is an example.

Competition Downstream of the Bottleneck Facility

Here the incumbent monopolist is selling an input to competitive suppliers. The problem is whether the competitive suppliers can get access to the monopoly input on reasonable terms. Gamberale and Mattoo (2002) argue that from a trade-policy perspective, there is a case for pro-competitive access regulation to ensure access to a bottleneck facility, irrespective of whether it is a natural monopoly.

But if it is a natural monopoly, the issue of what constitutes 'reasonable terms' is somewhat complicated. In developing economies with limited or weak regulatory capacity, there are also clear advantages in designing a system so that the incumbent has the incentive to offer reasonable terms through commercial negotiation, without there needing to be regulatory oversight. Both the definition of reasonable terms, and whether they are likely to be offered through commercial negotiation, depend on how other aspects of the monopoly problem have been regulated, the key aspects being retail price control over the monopoly facility, and universal service obligations (USOs) to meet equity objectives. Thus, indirectly, trade negotiators will need to have some appreciation of these domestic regulatory issues, because they are connected to the problem of access regulation.

The fundamental problem with pricing the services of a natural monopoly facility, be it for retail sale or as an input to downstream competitive industry, is that 'first best' pricing to ensure allocative efficiency involves pricing the facility at marginal cost—this is the real resource cost of producing an extra unit, once the fixed costs have already been incurred. The problem with marginal cost pricing is that it will not recover those fixed costs, only the operating costs of producing the extra units.

There are several alternative methods for recovering fixed costs that do least damage to allocative efficiency. One is so-called Ramsey pricing—where contributions to fixed costs are graded according to the price sensitivity of demand. Allocative efficiency requires that contributions be greatest from those customers of those services whose demands are relatively price-insensitive, so their quantities demanded remain relatively unaffected by the contribution they make. Another solution is two-part pricing, with an access charge used to recover fixed costs, and a usage charge to recover variable costs (another form of two-part pricing is quantity discounts).

It is not always appreciated by regulators that a profit-maximizing monopolist has the right incentives to introduce pricing structures of this form on its own account. In addition, the monopolist will typically be more aware than the regulator of its own cost structures, and of the price sensitivities of its own demands, and may therefore be better placed than regulators to decide their form. The only problem is that in the absence of any pricing regulation, the level of those pricing structures will be too high.

If the policy concern is only for technical efficiency, with no concern about allocative efficiency (or alternatively, if allocative efficiency concerns are met in other ways), then it may be appropriate to have access charges that follow the so-called efficient component pricing rule (ECPR). These charges include an element that compensates the monopolist for a loss of monopoly profits in the downstream market.

The issue is further complicated by whether the monopolist is vertically integrated, meaning that they also produce for and compete in the downstream market, or whether there has been structural separation of the monopoly and competitive elements of the monopolist's business. With vertical integration, there is the opportunity for the monopolist to use its monopoly position in the upstream market to distort competition in the downstream market. The appropriate access charges also depend on whether competition in the downstream market is sufficiently fragile for there to be a case for retail price regulation in the downstream market. Finally, it depends on how universal service obligations to meet equity objectives have been implemented.

Valletti and Estache (1998) discuss the details of the appropriate access pricing schemes in these and other situations. A flavor of their conclusions is given in Tables 8.1 and 8.2.

Several general observations can be made. This is clearly a situation in which there are multiple objectives—a need for allocative efficiency in both retail prices and (wholesale) access charges in the upstream market, a need for allocative efficiency in the downstream market, a need for full cost recovery of the monopolist's fixed costs, a need to ensure universal service, and other possible objectives besides. If the access charge is used as the single instrument to meet all these objectives simultaneously, it is unlikely that any of them will be met with any precision. The more separate instruments that can be brought to bear, the better. Two key additional instruments are separate retail price

Table 8.1. Access Charges with Structural Separation

Objective	Access charge	Comment
First best	Marginal cost	Fixed costs not recovered so that a subsidy is required
Second best (one final good)	Average cost	
Second best (many final goods)	Ramsey prices	
Dealing with imperfect downstream competition	Lower prices than above to avoid the effect on final service prices of extra margins imposed downstream	Fixed costs not recovered so that a subsidy is required
Dealing with downstream entry costs	Higher prices than above to discourage the entry of too many firms	The problem is less significant if entry brings product variety

Source: Adapted from Valletti and Estache (1998).

Table 8.2. Access Charges with Vertical Integration

Objective	Access charge	Potential problems	Eventual remedies
First best	Marginal cost	Requires lump sums, otherwise fixed costs not covered	Tariff rebalancing USO funds
Second best	Ramsey	High information content, may not be sustainable	Price cap
Productivity efficiency	ECPR	Partial rule	
Entry promotion for - product variety - entry barriers - learning-by-doing	Lower than above	Fixed costs may not be covered	Direct subsidies, equal access
Dealing with bypass, cost duplication	Higher than above	Small entrants disadvantaged	Quantity discounts
Dealing with risk and hold-up by the incumbent	Higher than above		Long-term contracts, spot and forward market, capacity charges
Dealing with asymmetric information	Incentive regulation	Predatory behavior	Accounting separation, price floors and ceilings
Dealing with market power	Lower than above	Fixed costs may not be recovered	Price regulation

Source: Adapted from Valletti and Estache (1998).

regulation,[1] and separate instruments for meeting universal services obligations. In these circumstances, Valletti and Estache (1998) show how the solution to the problem of regulating access prices may be particularly simple—a single global price cap to be applied to an average of the monopolist's retail prices and access charges, leaving it up to the monopolist to choose the appropriate Ramsey or two-part structure for the individual prices within the overall cap.

Second, it is worth considering one common situation in which the monopolist is unlikely to be willing to offer access to the bottleneck facility at reasonable terms, even if access is mandated by regulation. In the past it was common for telecommunications services (in both developed and developing countries) to be provided by a single, often publicly owned monopoly. The goal of restraining monopoly pricing was met by a detailed system of retail price regulation, while universal service obligations were met by cross-subsidies built into the monopolist's retail pricing structure. Typically, access charges were kept low for all users to encourage participation by the poor, and usage

---

[1] It is now generally recognized that price-cap regulation is superior to rate-of-return regulation in controlling monopoly pricing. This is because rate-of-return regulation controls the total return to capital, not just the super-normal profit component. So the monopolist's choice of capital inputs will be distorted, with the monopolist choosing either too much or too little capital, depending on whether they are charged with maximizing profits or maximizing welfare more generally. See, for example, Beesley and Littlechild (1989).

charges were too high, to compensate. This typically did not follow Ramsey or two-part pricing principles, since the demand for access, especially by businesses, is typically far less price sensitive than the demand for (especially long-distance) usage. If competition is then introduced into downstream markets and the monopolist is required to offer cost-based access to downstream competitors on commercial terms, the access charges the monopolist will demand will typically be too high. This is because, in the absence of being able to recover the fixed costs of subscriber access through retail charges, the monopolist will seek to recover them from downstream competitors, and will have an apparently legitimate cost-based reason for doing so.

The failure of some developing countries to 'rebalance' their retail pricing structures, and to find ways other than cross-subsidization to fund USOs, is currently thwarting the development of effective downstream competition in telecommunications, even where the countries have made commitments to provide access according to the WTO's Reference Paper on telecommunications.

As noted in the introduction, there is mounting evidence that access to infrastructure is a key component of an effective poverty reduction strategy. But there are two distinct but related aspects to the problem of universal service—one is whether the physical infrastructure is available, and on what terms, and the other is whether the prices of using the infrastructure are prohibitive. An effective method of providing for the poor requires an accurate assessment of the problem. Subsidizing usage by the poor may not be effective if the primary problem is physical access. Foster and Araujo (2004) give an example of such inappropriate subsidization of electricity prices in Guatemala. Foster and Irusta (2003) give an example in which the access charge for fixed line telephony in Bolivia was prohibitive. Effective mechanisms for ensuring access by the poor may involve subsidies for either access or usage, other than through blanket cross-subsidization, plus establishing a USO fund to which all providers (not just the incumbent) contribute to cover the investment required for new connections in poor and remote areas.

Competition Upstream of the Bottleneck Facility

Here the monopolist is buying from the competitive suppliers. The main problem is the one of hold-up and refusal to deal, which is also noted in Table 8.2. In electricity generation, there is also a series of technical issues—electricity is completely non-storable, so that supply and demand have to be matched on a second-by-second basis, and sudden surges in supply from competitive suppliers could result in short-circuiting the entire system.

The thinking on how to deal with these issues in electricity has changed somewhat recently. It is still generally agreed that if competition in electricity generation is to be encouraged, then regulated or negotiated third-party access is necessary and structural separation of the generation and transmission facilities is desirable. Long-term contracts have often been used as a mechanism to handle the technical problems with integrating competitive generators into a transmission system, but these were seen as having the disadvantage of locking in particular suppliers and protecting them from more competitive new entrants.

One solution to the problem of lock-in was to establish a wholesale pricing pool. Under this arrangement, competitive suppliers would make bids to supply blocks of electricity for certain future time slots, and an independent grid-management authority would choose best bids and arrange them in increasing order of cost to stand ready to meet whatever demand eventuated in those time slots. There is a huge literature on how to design the auction to minimize the problems of collusion or 'gaming' by dominant providers.[2] In this connection, see Milgrom (1989) or Chan et al. (2003) for non-technical overviews.

Until recently, the United Kingdom was viewed as having gone furthest and most successfully in implementing the necessary regulatory regimes to promote competition in electricity generation, while California was seen as an example of regulatory failure. But in March 2001, the United Kingdom suspended the operation of its wholesale pricing pool and returned to a system of bilateral contracts, because of the problem of gaming by dominant players.

The Role of Competition Policy

A residual policy question is whether, having allowed entry and competition in the potentially competitive parts of an infrastructure industry, and established an access regime to endure access to bottleneck facilities, a country can afford to rely on a general competition policy regime to discipline any remaining problems of anti-competitive conduct, either by the monopolist, or where competition in the competitive segment is fragile. Or does a country need to establish industry-specific rules on anti-competitive conduct?

In the first instance, the answer depends on whether a country has a general regulatory regime to protect against anti-competitive behavior. And if it does not, a key question is what the priority should be—establishing a general regime, or regulating on an industry-specific basis.

But even countries that have reasonably sophisticated competition policy regimes have judged it necessary to retain industry-specific regulation against anti-competitive conduct in certain infrastructure industries. In Australia, for example, there are telecommunications-specific provisions of the Trade Practices Act that are speedier and less costly to implement than the general provisions (See PC 2001a and 2001b for a review of the issues).

---

[2] There is similar literature on how to auction scarce radio spectrum for use by competitive cellular and broadband service providers.

Consider again the case of electricity generation. Because electricity is completely non-storable and both demand and supply are volatile, the market-clearing price can spike dramatically at certain times, reducing the price sensitivity of demand. In these circumstances, individual generators may have considerable market power to further increase prices and profits by withholding generating capacity, even when there is no collusion among them. This was found to be a factor (along with underlying supply and demand conditions) contributing to the tenfold rise in wholesale electricity prices in California in 2000. Among the regulatory failures were wholesale-market design rules that prevented a smoothing of the wholesale prices, and the maintenance of retail price caps that prevented the signals about market conditions being passed on to consumers and also led to bankruptcy of major suppliers (Joskow 2001). There is evidence of similar anti-competitive conduct in the United Kingdom (e.g. Fabra and Toro 2003).

These physical characteristics of electricity generation mean that there can be considerable residual problems of anti-competitive conduct. They also make it unlikely that general competition policy regimes can respond quickly and strongly enough to the anti-competitive conduct where it occurs. The issues are well summarized by Newbery (2002: 16), expressing concern about the direction of liberalization in Europe:

All of this suggests that workable electricity liberalization is very different from deregulation. If anything, the regulatory requirements to ensure security and quality of supply, not just in surplus but also tight markets, are far more demanding than for other utilities, as the speed with which system-wide problems can emerge is considerably faster… The European ideal that potentially competitive markets like generation and supply can be left to the competition authorities is in contrast to this apparent need for more sophisticated, informed and possibly interventionist regulatory power to ensure satisfactory wholesale market performance.

In this context, promoting trade in electricity by establishing interconnection across national borders can help alleviate the supply constraints that are conducive to the exercise of market power. On the other hand, it makes it more difficult for national regulatory authorities to monitor the behavior of suppliers that may engage in anti-competitive conduct outside their jurisdiction. This jurisdictional problem is common to many traded services, and calls for cooperation and communication among national regulatory authorities.

Conclusion: The Role of International Negotiations

It is now recognized that infrastructure industries are typically not natural monopolies throughout. There is scope for separating the competitive and natural monopoly elements, and domestic benefits from introducing competition for the market in the monopoly segments, and in the market in the competitive segments. However, reaping the benefits fully requires regulation to control monopoly pricing in the monopoly segment, and to mediate the interactions between the monopoly and competitive segments.

Commitments made through international trade negotiations can facilitate this process of domestic regulatory reform.

First, as noted, widening the scope of competition in or for the market to include foreign operators widens a country's choice set, and can offer advantages in terms of economic performance. This need not cause undue adjustment costs. Granting market access to foreigners in conventional cross-border goods trade may put pressure on the output and employment levels in domestic import-competing industries. By comparison, granting market access and national treatment to foreign operators in the competitive segments of an infrastructure industry could lead to higher output and employment across the whole competitive segment. This has typically been the case in telecommunications, for example, with an overall expansion in the quantity and variety of services offered. However, foreign establishment may still impose pressure on the output and employment levels of the domestic incumbent that must therefore absorb some costs of adjustment.

Second, making liberalizing commitments through international trade negotiations can enhance the credibility of domestic policy reforms. Where the policy reforms are made today, international commitments can insure investors against the risk of policy reversal in the future. Where the domestic reforms are to be phased in over time, international commitments can add credibility to those future plans. The value of such credibility is particularly important in infrastructure sectors, in which new operators may need to make large sunk investments in advance.

Third, making international trade commitments can allow countries to tap into the regulatory expertise of their trading partners, bolstering domestic regulatory capacity where this is weak. Regulators who seek to design reform programs for regulatory structures, following for example the directions indicated by 'principles of good regulation' (Coghlan, 2003), may take a more active interest in trade negotiations, and use those negotiations as vehicles for pursuing regulatory harmonization and the elimination of unnecessary regulatory barriers. There is also emerging evidence of international trade in regulatory expertise. One example is the Caribbean initiative to establish a single regional prudential regulator, staffed with international expertise.

Finally, the international negotiating framework may sometimes, but not always, generate a model schedule for domestic regulatory reform. As noted, there are no requirements in the body of the GATS agreement for countries to establish an access regime to ensure that foreign operators in competitive segments can get access to a bottleneck facility on reasonable terms. But there has been one instance, namely in the Reference Paper in Telecommunications, where international negotiations have resulted in a framework of principles for such a regime. This example may be repeated in other infrastructure industries.

References

Barth, J., G. Caprio, and R. Levine. 2002. "Bank Regulation and Supervision: What Works Best?" Mimeo, World Bank (January).

Beesley, M. and S. Littlechild. 1989. "The Regulation of Privatized Monopolies in the United Kingdom," *Rand Journal of Economics* 20(3): 454–72.

Brook Cowen, P. 1997. "The Private Sector in Water and Sanitation—How to Get Started," Public Policy for the Private Sector, Note No. 126. Washington, D.C.: World Bank.

Chan, C., P. Laplagne, and D. Appels. 2003. *The Role of Auctions in Allocating Public Resources.* Melbourne: Productivity Commission Staff Research Paper, Productivity Commission.

Coghlan, P. 2003. "The Principles of Good Regulation," in A. Sidorenko and C. Findlay (eds.), *Regulation and Market Access.* Canberra: Asia Pacific Press.

Estache, A. and G. de Rus. 2000. *Privatization and Regulation of Transport Infrastructure: Guidelines for Policymakers and Regulators.* Washington, D.C.: World Bank.

Estache, A., M. Gonzalez, and L. Trujillo. 2001. "Technical Efficiency Gains from Port Reform: The Potential for Yardstick Competition in Mexico," Policy Research Working Paper No. 2637. Washington, D.C.: World Bank.

Fabra, N. and J. Toro. 2003. "The Fall in British Electricity Prices: Market Rules, Market Structure, or Both?" Mimeo, available at: http://econwpa.wustl.edu/eps/io/papers/0309/-309001.pdf (accessed April 1, 2004).

Fay, M., D. Leipziger, Q. Wodon, and T. Yepes. 2003. "Achieving the Millennium Development Goals," World Bank Working Paper No. 3163. Washington, D.C.: World Bank.

Foster, V. and M.C. Araujo. 2004. "Does Infrastructure Reform Work for the Poor? A Case Study from Guatemala," World Bank Working Paper No. 3185. Washington, D.C.: World Bank.

Foster, V. and O. Irusta. 2003. "Does Infrastructure Reform Work for the Poor? A Case Study on the Cities of La Paz and El Alto in Bolivia," World Bank Working Paper No. 3177. Washington, D.C.: World Bank.

Gamberale, C. and A. Mattoo. 2002. "Domestic Regulations and Liberalization of Trade in Services," in B. Hoekman, A. Mattoo, and P. English (eds.), *Development, Trade and the WTO.* Washington, D.C.: World Bank, pp. 290–303.

Joskow, P. 2001. "California's Electricity Crisis," NBER Working Paper No. 8442 (August).

Limao, N. and A. Venables. 2001. "Infrastructure, Geographical Disadvantage and Transport Costs," *World Bank Economic Review* 15: 315–43.

Mattoo, A., R. Rathindran, and A. Subramanian. 2001. "Measuring Services Trade Liberalization and Its Impact on Economic Growth: An Illustration," World Bank Working Paper No. 2655. Washington, D.C.: World Bank.

Milgrom, P. 1989. "Auctions and Bidding: A Primer," *Journal of Economic Perspectives* 3(3): 3–22.

Newbery, D. 2002. "Regulatory Challenges to European Electricity Liberalization," DAE Working Paper WP 0230, Department of Applied Economics, University of Cambridge.

PC (Productivity Commission). 2001a. *Telecommunications Competition Regulation*, Inquiry Report No. 16. Canberra: Ausinfo.

PC. 2001b. *Review of the National Access Regime*, Inquiry Report No. 17. Canberra: Ausinfo.

Valletti, T. and A. Estache. 1998. "The Theory of Access Pricing: An Overview for Infrastructure Regulators." Mimeo, Washington, D.C.: World Bank (March).

9 Transport Services

Christopher Findlay

Introduction: Transport and Development[1]

The accessibility, quality and cost of transport and distribution services determine how efficiently goods move from producers to final consumers. Free movement of people facilitates trade in services, thereby increasing business transactions. It also makes labor markets more flexible. The performance of transport and distribution services is therefore an important determinant of productivity growth and can have a marked impact on economic growth.

For a small economy for which world prices of traded goods are largely given, higher costs of transportation feed in one for one into import and export prices. To remain competitive, exporting firms that face higher shipping costs must pay lower wages to workers, accept lower returns on capital, or be more productive.

Export competitiveness for example hinges on the costs of international transport services. Shipping costs are often a more important inhibitor to participation in the world economy than are policy barriers to entry into export markets. For example, the World Bank (2002a) finds that

- *A doubling of shipping costs is associated with slower growth of more than half a percentage point.*
- *Potential access to foreign markets, of which transport costs are a determinant, explains up to 70 per cent of variations in country GDP.*

The pressure on factor prices and productivity from high transport costs is even higher for industries with a high share of imported inputs. Small differences in transport costs thus can easily determine whether or not export ventures are at all profitable. For labor-intensive manufacturing industries in developing countries such as textiles, high transport costs most likely translate into lower wages, directly affecting standards of living of workers and their dependents (see Radelet and Sachs, 1998).

If services are unreliable and infrequent or if a country lacks third-party logistics providers who efficiently handle small shipments, firms are likely to maintain higher inventory holdings—at every stage of the production chain. The costs of financing large inventories can be significant, especially in countries with high real interest rates. Long

---

[1] This section draws in part on Findlay and Fink (2005).

travel journeys have a similar effect. They delay payments if goods are exported on a c.i.f. basis (cost, insurance and freight) or importers may demand a time discount if goods are delivered f.o.b. (free on board). If products are perishable or subject to frequent changes in consumer preferences such as high-fashion textiles, longer travel journeys lead to additional losses in terms of a product's shortened lifetime in the export market.[2]

High transport costs also restrain the growth of trade in services (World Bank, 2002a). The tourism sector depends on the costs of international travel, and for some types of tourism given the substitutability of destinations for travelers, small changes in transport costs can lead to large changes in travel volumes. The provision of professional services through the movement of providers also depends on costs of transport. Services businesses are furthermore complementary to the growth of merchandise trade, for example, through the contribution of business trips to the development of production networks or the provision of after-sales service.

Within an economy, lower costs of transport help to integrate isolated and poor areas into the national economy. But when transport costs are high, economic activity tends to become more concentrated. China provides an important example. The World Bank (2002a: box 9.1) argues that an inefficient internal transport system has contributed to the concentration of China's export industries in its coastal region. The corollary of this observation is that internal transport costs also affect the extent to which markets are

---

Box 9.1. Inefficient Internal Transport System Contributes to the Concentration of China's Export Industries in Coastal Regions

---

A remarkable feature of China's dramatic expansion in international trade over the past two decades has been the concentration of export-oriented industries in coastal regions. The four main coastal provinces (Guangdong, Jiangsu, Fujian, and Shangkai) have been the main recipients of outward-oriented foreign investment, with the remaining portion going to either other coastal provinces or regions adjoining coastal areas. The provinces in the central core—usually referred to as lagging provinces—barely benefited from the incoming investment. While dispersion of export-oriented units has narrowed coastal income disparities—with the south coast regions catching up with the hitherto affluent east coast—the export boom has exacerbated the coastal-inland gap. Thus, while China's economic reforms have been successful in raising living standards for a considerable share of the population, a large number of Chinese people in inland provinces still live below the poverty line.

---

[2] One interesting recent estimate, based on comparisons between air and ocean freight rates for U.S. imports, puts the per day cost for shipping delays at 0.8 per cent of the value of trade. Only a small fraction of these costs can be attributed to the capital costs for the goods during the time they are onboard the ship. In addition, delivery time is found to have little impact on trade in homogenous commodities, while its effect is more pronounced for trade in manufactured goods, especially imports of intermediate products (Hummels, 2001). This latter result suggests that the fast delivery of goods is crucial for the maintenance of multinational vertical product chains. Quality aspects of transportation are thus likely to be an important factor in the location decisions of multinational companies.

Another contributing factor to coastal agglomeration has been various inefficiencies in China's internal transport systems. Transport infrastructure disparities between the coastal and inland provinces narrowed considerably following policies aimed at promoting more regionally balanced economic development since 1990. However, indications of increasing inter-provincial trade between inland regions, and between inland and coastal regions, suggests that it is not the availability of transport infrastructure per se that has precluded inland provinces from actively participating in foreign trade. Rather the inadequacies associated with transport services are the more binding constraint to better integrating China's hinterland economy.

The compositional shift of exports from low-value raw materials to high-value manufactured goods has made transport increasingly suitable for containerization. Though there has been a significant increase in the volume of container traffic in China since 1990, the increase is largely confined to coastal regions, and associated with the oceangoing leg of travel. Container traffic in inland areas is much less, with no significant change in the percentage of sea-borne containers traveling beyond port cities and coastal provinces. Truck rates for moving a container 500 kilometers inland are estimated to be about three times more, and the trip time five times longer, than they would be in Europe or the United States. China's railways still charge what is, in effect, a penalty rate for moving containers. Priority on the congested rail network is still given to low-value bulk freight (mostly coal), rather than to high-value freight, such as containers.

Surveys based on major foreign shippers, shipping lines, and freight forwarders based in the United States, Japan, and Hong Kong (China) indicate that China's transport systems, particularly inland transport, are well below international standards. First, respondents pointed to the lack of container freight stations, yards, and trucks in inland regions. Second, border procedures were perceived to be cumbersome and time-consuming, due to the many certification requirements and duplication of documents—in part, a consequence of the lack of coordination between the different government agencies involved in the various modes of transport. Third, container-tracking capability was particularly poor, with shippers often unaware of their containers' whereabouts. Shippers attributed this to poorly trained staff, the lack of a reliable recovery system, and the poor accountability system in government agencies. Fourth, the intermodal transport system was found to be poorly integrated, with no streamlined procedures to support the continuous movement of containers between the coast and inland.

Another source of inefficiencies is the dominance of state-owned enterprises and the lack of competition in transport service markets. Since pricing in many of the intermediate transport service activities is controlled, the companies have little incentive for aggressively pursuing cost-cutting methods. Due to a lack of competition, intermediate service providers represent the interests of transport operators. Hence value added service and reliability, hallmarks of winning business confidence in a modern economy, are not practiced by most participants. Investment by foreign enterprises or joint ventures between foreign and domestic enterprises in intermediate transport services is limited in inland regions. Though foreign investment is not prohibited, there are restrictions on investors' activities.

Source: Reproduced from box 4.2 in World Bank (2002c), which was adapted from Atinc (1997); Graham and Wada (2001); Naughton (2002); and World Bank (1996).

integrated. Access to markets is an important determinant of the level of income and the rate of development in rural areas.

Transport costs are determined partly by geography and by economic variables. A more widely dispersed economy clearly incurs higher transport costs. Also economic variables determine traffic volumes and are related to infrastructure quality, both of which in turn affect transport costs. Higher traffic volumes tend to lower the per unit/per kilometer cost of transport.

Reform that reduces transport costs also generates extensive real gains. The impacts on real incomes are greater than those of the removal of a tax, the impact of which includes transfers of income, from taxpayers to the government, for example. But when transport costs are reduced, resources are saved (Deardorff, 2001).

Reductions in transport costs can also lead to significant increases in trade orientation. Limao and Venables (2001) find relatively high elasticities of trade volumes in response to reductions in transport costs. Transport costs also depend on policy parameters and on the presence or absence of competition in transport markets. Port performance is directly related to the policy environment, and handling costs in port are in many cases just as important as costs associated with physical distance (Clark et al., 2001).

In summary, lower transport costs are associated with integration of markets within an economy and with the integration of those domestic markets with the rest of the world. These linkages support economic development and contribute to the growth of income. Important determinants of transport costs include policy choices by government.

A wide set of policies affects the performance of the transport sector. But the focus in this chapter is the contribution of trade policy and its reform. The key points are the following.[3]

The GATS provides a structure in which policy makers can commit to sets of policy changes in the transport sector, including policy with respect to entry by domestic as well as foreign participants. A significant number of WTO Members have already made commitments to policy applied to transport services. However there are some important exemptions that remain to be negotiated or reviewed, including in maritime transport and air transport.

Foreign participation in the sector offers gains from specialization and trade, from competition and from making available a wider variety of services. Trade reform in the service sector, including in the transport services sector, can lead foreign suppliers to establish local operations. Local incumbent suppliers may still lose market share after reform, but the foreign presence adds to the options available to suppliers of labor in this sector.

Special features of the transport sector complicate the application of trade-policy reform. These are the tendency to natural monopoly, at least in some parts of the sector. Another set of policy issues relates to the sector's contribution to congestion and to environmental problems. The trade-policy interest in the former problem is to ensure that there is sufficient domestic regulation in place to avoid these natural monopoly elements becoming a barrier to entry of new suppliers in other parts of the sector, and to avoid them being captured and exploited by new entrants into the sector. The trade-policy interest in the latter problems of congestion and pollution are to avoid the policy responses being more restrictive of trade than necessary to solve the problems. These complications indicate that successful trade policy reform in this sector will demand a

---

[3] For some additional commentary, see Box 9.6.

high level of capacity in government to design a trade-policy reform strategy, and to construct the necessary regulatory institutions. Support in the development of this capacity is an item for economic cooperation between developed and developing countries with interests in these fields. A further concern linked to policy reform in this sector will be its impact on poor areas. Research has highlighted the elements of efficient solutions for meeting this concern, including the design of subsidy policies.

The contribution of international negotiations and the related commitments made through the GATS is to add credibility to domestic policy. That is important because of the nature of the investment necessary in the transport sector, to suggest direction of changes in regulatory reform, and perhaps to offer additional market access opportunities that ease the adjustment costs in domestic markets that are becoming more open. At the same time, the GATS offers sufficient flexibility to policy makers who want to fix a timetable for their reform programs and pursue social objectives while seeking the gains from foreign participation.

Definitions and GATS Overview

The first step for a policy maker considering the use of the GATS to make international commitments on services policy is to decide in which sectors those commitments are to be documented. Within the GATS structure members can choose from a set of classifications of service activities. The coverage of transport services in the GATS is shown in Box 9.2; it covers all the transport modes, and includes a number of activities that are complementary to transport services. The willingness to commit in these and other sectors is then recorded in a national schedule and the commitments refer to the various principles and rules of the GATS that WTO Members have adopted.

The GATS is built on general principles and rules (such as Most-Favored-Nation (MFN) and transparency), and on specific commitments to the principle of national treatment and to the terms of market access. The Agreement applies to four modes of supply of services, all of which are relevant to transport services:

1. Provision of maritime services from a home base in one economy to consumers in another (whether on routes between the two countries or not) is cross border supply.
2. Provision of air transport services to consumers of one country when they buy tickets in a foreign country is consumption abroad.
3. A road transport operator from one country setting up a business to supply services in another is supply through commercial establishment.
4. Movement of natural persons includes the employment of foreign crews on ships.

Box 9.2. Transport Services Categories in the GATS[1]

11.	**TRANSPORT SERVICES**	**CPC code**[2]
A.	*Maritime Transport Services*	
a.	Passenger transportation	7211
b.	Freight transportation	7212
c.	Rental of vessels with crew	7213
d.	Maintenance and repair of vessels	8868**
e.	Pushing and towing services	7214
f.	Supporting services for maritime transport	745**
B.	*Internal Waterways Transport*	
a.	Passenger transportation	7221
b.	Freight transportation	7222
c.	Rental of vessels with crew	7223
d.	Maintenance and repair of vessels	8868**
e.	Pushing and towing services	7224
f.	Supporting services for internal waterway transport	745**
C.	*Air Transport Services*	
a.	Passenger transportation	731
b.	Freight transportation	732
c.	Rental of aircraft with crew	734
d.	Maintenance and repair of aircraft	8868**
e.	Supporting services for air transport	746
D.	*Space Transport*	*733*
E.	*Rail Transport Services*	
a.	Passenger transportation	7111
b.	Freight transportation	7112
c.	Pushing and towing services	7113
d.	Maintenance and repair of rail transport equipment	
e.	Supporting services for rail transport services	743
F.	*Road Transport Services*	
a.	Passenger transportation	7121 + 7122
b.	Freight transportation	7123
c.	Rental of commercial vehicles with operator	7124
d.	Maintenance and repair of road transport equipment	6112 + 8867
e.	Supporting services for road transport services	
G.	*Pipeline Transport*	
a.	Transportation of fuels	7131
b.	Transportation of other goods	7139
H.	*Services auxiliary to all modes of transport*	
a.	Cargo-handling services	741
b.	Storage and warehouse services	742
c.	Freight transport agency services	748
d.	Other	
I.	*Other Transport Services*	

Notes:
  [1] From http://www.wto.org/english/tratop_e/serv_e/mtn_gns_w_120_e.doc
  [2] UN Central Product Classification code. See http://unstats.un.org/unsd/cr/family2.asp?Cl=16: **Indicates that the service specified constitutes only a part of the total range of activities covered by the CPC concordance.

The MFN principle is that "Each Member shall accord immediately and unconditionally to services and service suppliers of any other Member treatment no less favorable than it accords to like services and service suppliers of any other country." The GATS allows for exemptions for this principle and in transport services these exemptions are important. Transport services attracted more exemptions than any other sector (147 in total as of March 2000), mainly in maritime transport and road transport. A special Annex on air transport exempts flying operations from coverage in the GATS. These exemptions are subject to a regular review.

The principles of national treatment and market access apply only when a sector is listed in the member's GATS schedule (Positive list). Even then, conditions or qualifications may be made to the application of these principles and these too are shown in the schedule.

According to the national treatment principle,

In the sectors inscribed in its Schedule, and subject to any conditions and qualifications therein, each Member shall accord to services and service suppliers of any Member, in respect of all measures affecting the supply of services, treatment no less favorable than it accords to its own services and service suppliers.

The treatment of transport services contravenes this principle when foreign operators are not permitted to operate on domestic routes. However, this situation can arise under the GATS since a WTO member may not have scheduled the relevant services or when even if they have done so they note the exception in their schedules.

The terms of market access in the GATS refers to a list of measures that cannot be used in a scheduled sector, unless a Member records their application as a qualification or condition. The list includes quantitative restrictions, such as limits on the number of suppliers, on the value of transactions, on the total quantity of output, on the number of people that can be employed, or on the shares of or values of foreign equity in a business. The list also includes restrictions on the business form in which services are supplied. Market access commitments apply to restrictions on entry by all potential suppliers, that is, both local and foreign firms. A licensing scheme that capped the number of licenses available to applicants of any origin is an example of an item on this list. However, even in a scheduled sector a Member could retain its use by listing that arrangement as a limitation on market access in their schedule.

The terms of market access in the GATS refers to a list of measures that cannot be used unless specified in a Member's schedule. The list mainly includes quantitative restrictions, such as limits on the number of suppliers, the value of transactions, the total quantity of output, the number of people that can be employed, or the shares of or values of foreign equity. The list also includes restrictions on the business form in which the services are supplied. Market-access commitments apply to restrictions on entry by both local and foreign suppliers. This principle would be contravened, for example, by a licensing scheme that capped the number available to applicants of any origin.

Members may also make horizontal commitments that apply across sectors to a particular mode of supply. For example, rules on employment of professional staff may apply to employment of skilled labor in transport operations.

Members can make additional commitments that do not fall under market access or national treatment commitments. They may for example commit to move to adopt international standards (in place of a unique set of domestic standards) on safety, security or other operational matters in transport systems.

In summary, the process of making commitments under the GATS involves two steps:

1. select the sectors in which commitments are to be made; and
2. list any qualification or conditions that apply to measures that contravene GATS principles and rules but which are to be kept in place.

Table 9.1 shows some examples of the forms of trade in transport services and the measures which might be applied in those modes of supply.

Table 9.2 provides examples of commitments that might be made in a particular sector.

The commitments allow for cross-border delivery of services but also insist that some commercial presence is required; this might be sought in order to support the application of domestic regulation to the service provider.

National treatment as applied to cross-border trade is unbound, meaning that the government has reserved the right to apply different policies to foreign providers in this mode, compared to domestic providers (such policies may already be in place, but their detail is not available in the GATS schedule when commitments are made in this manner, and an additional research effort is required to uncover the detail of the policy actually applied).

There are no conditions or limitations on consumption abroad, so this mode is bound (in practice it is almost impossible to apply restrictions to this mode).

Market access via commercial presence is limited by a cap on foreign entry (though this measure only applies to foreigners, the definition of market access in the GATS requires that it be listed in this column).

Table 9.1. Trade in Transport Services: Some Examples

Modes	Service	Measures
Mode 1: Cross border supply	International air, road, maritime or rail transport; cabotage services	Quotas, safety standards
Mode 2: Consumption abroad	Tourist travel by air, rail, or bus within a foreign country	Foreign exchange restrictions
Mode 3: Commercial presence	Establishment of a subsidiary or branch of a foreign transport operator	Foreign equity limitations; joint venture requirements
Mode 4: Movement of individual service providers	Entry of foreign bus drivers, pilots, sailors; managers of transport operators	Quotas on temporary workers; visa requirements

Source: Adapted from Findlay and Fink (2005).

Table 9.2. Example of GATS Commitments

GATS mode of supply	Conditions and limitations on *market access*	Conditions and qualifications on *national treatment*
1. Cross border	Commercial presence required	Unbound
2. Consumption abroad	None	None
3. Commercial presence	Maximum equity stake of 49 per cent	Approval required for any equity stake over 25 per cent
4. Temporary entry of natural persons	Unbound, except for intra-corporate transfers of senior managers	Unbound, except for categories included in the market access column

The national treatment column shows the more general limitation that investments accounting for over 25 per cent of a local company must be approved.

The government of this economy has not bound itself on policy with respect to movement of people, except on the movement of managers within companies.

In summary, WTO members could make three types of commitments with reference to market access or national treatment. They could:

• Bind their policy to adhere to the principle without qualification (denoted by 'none' with respect to a mode of supply in their schedule).
• Make a partial commitment (and the sector is scheduled but a condition is noted against a mode of supply).
• Make no commitment at all (and therefore show 'unbound').

Adlung et al. (2002) report that the transport-services sector attracted a relatively high level of commitment. The sector ranked fifth in terms of member coverage after tourism, financial services, business services, and communications. Mattoo (2002) shows that common conditions on market access in transport services refer to rules on the type of legal entity to be used and caps on participation of foreign capital.

By mode across all service sectors, there tend to be fewer commitments on mode 4, while consumption abroad is the most liberal and the treatment of modes 1 and 3 is mixed (mode 3 generally attracts more total commitments but also with more qualifications than mode 1).

Figure 9.1 shows the number of Members scheduling commitments in selected transport sectors in all modes. A relatively small share of the total Membership included these sectors in their schedules. Developing and transition economies have made more commitments in maritime transport, though two-thirds of these involve some qualification on market access in mode 1 and 90 per cent in mode 3. Very few economies made commitments in rail transport. Road transport attracted commitments from both developing and developed economies, but with high rates of qualifications or limitations in all modes.

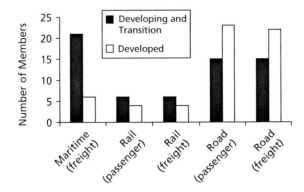

Figure 9.1. Number of WTO members scheduling transport services
Source: Adapted from WTO (1999).

The assessment of these commitments made during the Uruguay Round is that they reflected the status quo of policies or even less. Findlay and Fink (2005) indicate that negotiations did not lead to any liberalization of actual trade policies. This has been different in the case of WTO accession negotiations since the end of the Uruguay Round, which led to services commitments that—at least over time—imply the actual dismantling of trade barriers. Notably, China committed to a schedule of reforms in the transport sector, including some complementary services with the exception of air transport (see Mattoo, 2003).

There are two key sectors in which there are important exceptions to MFN in the GATS, maritime services (especially for developed economies) and air transport.

As evident in Figure 9.1, a number of WTO members have made commitments on maritime services, but two key members have not, namely the U.S. and the E.U. Negotiations on maritime services continued past the end of the Uruguay Round, but they were eventually suspended. Members were unable to agree on the application of the MFN principle to maritime transport. The U.S. for example argued that it needed to retain the capacity to discriminate in order to bargain away the restrictions that other countries imposed, through the threat of retaliation.

The focus of the maritime negotiations was on international shipping, access to and use of port facilities and auxiliary maritime services, including the multi-modal services discussed above (Choi et al., 1997). The international shipping sector is relatively open, especially in bulk shipping. Market forces and unilateral changes in policy in many countries are undoing remaining restrictions affecting liner shipping. The most important remaining restrictions are cabotage (coastal shipping), which was actually excluded from the negotiations, and access to port services. A target for the current Doha round of negotiations will be to bind the unilateral policy reforms already made and seek to make progress in the remaining restricted areas, which is possible by using the opportunities for trade-offs in the negotiations across sectors.

There is some coverage of air transport services in the GATS but mainly those complementary to the flying operations, such as computer reservation systems, aircraft repair and maintenance, and selling and marketing. The core flying operations are excluded in a special Annex to the GATS on air transport. The Annex was designed to quarantine the current regulation of international trade in air transport services. It involves an elaborate structure of bilateral agreements (there are over 3,500 such agreements) that fix a set of rules to identify the airlines of the contracting parties with the rights to fly on each route, determine the capacity that can be provided by each of those designated airlines and limit the capacity that can be offered by airlines from third countries (Nikomborirak and Findlay, 2003). The system therefore imposes a set of country-specific quotas in each market, where markets are defined in terms of routes between pairs of countries and in terms of the two-way traffic flow. A rule has to be specified to decide which airlines are able to take up the quotas negotiated, and the traditional approach has been to specify that effective ownership and control of the designated carriers must rest in the countries negotiating the agreement. These arrangements are discriminatory and clearly contravene the MFN principle. The exclusion of foreign carriers from domestic markets, a common regulation, also contravenes the national treatment principle.

The Annex therefore isolates these aspects of air transport regulation from the disciplines of the GATS. A review of the Annex began in 2001 but little progress was made (Goldstein and Findlay, 2003) and a new review was to begin in 2006. Apart from resistance to change from protected interests in this sector, a further complication to the treatment of air transport in the GATS is that there is another international organization with jurisdiction in this field, namely the International Civil Aviation Organization—ICAO. The WTO and ICAO have yet to resolve their respective roles. Meanwhile, Members with strong interests in aviation matters could also pursue them in the general negotiations now in progress, for example, through the introduction of other complementary services such as ground handling into the set of sectors in which commitments are made (Goldstein and Findlay, 2003).

Commitments in the GATS are made according to the categories of services that the members have adopted. This set of categories does not always match the scope of activities used by businesses operating in the transport sector. An important example of this problem arises in the logistics sector. Luo and Findlay (2004) provide a concordance between the GATS categories and the coverage usually required by business for establishing a successful logistics operation, including different modes of transport as well as warehousing services. It is important for logistics companies to have access not only to international services, either sea or air, but also to internal transport services, which might be forms of land transport. Many economies retain restraints on the ability of foreign service providers to operate within their domestic networks.

Other examples of gaps between business models and GATS services categories will emerge as new ideas about the organization of business change, and as new forms of contracting out develop. One response to these issues is to produce sets of model commitments that show how the GATS categories can be used to match business structures. A business perspective on commitments is important to avoid a situation in which substantial liberalization occurs but in which rents are also retained by incumbents. For example, a transport chain is often made up of a series of related services. If all but one sector is liberalized, the incumbents in the remaining restricted sector will capture even more rents than they might have before the policy change.

The GATS does not apply to 'services supplied in the exercise of government functions', that is, services supplied neither on a commercial basis nor in competition with one or more service suppliers. Therefore the GATS does not force WTO members to privatize or allow competition in these areas. However debate continues about the specification of these areas, and in which instances such a form of supply is legitimate.

Impact of Trade Policy Reform

Impacts of reform include:

- *Comparative advantage-based efficiency gains.*
- *Attraction of foreign investment and relaxation of a capacity constraint.*
- *More intense competition.*
- *Greater choice for consumers.*
- *Transfers of skills and technologies.*

The following provides some illustrations of these effects.

Transport services differ in the mix of factors of production required in their delivery, and economies differ therefore in their competitiveness to supply those services from their home base (that is, in cross-border supply). Trade policy reform allows transport service providers to take advantage of commercial opportunities in their areas of competitiveness.

Air transport is an example. The empirical evidence is that there is a wide variation in the costs of the provision of the service between countries (Oum and Yu, 1998). Low-wage countries with access to sufficient management skill (which itself might be provided via commercial establishment of a foreign airline or through mode 4 movements) can compete in international markets. An illustration is the ability of the airlines of the ASEAN economies to compete on routes outside their own region.

Further, many services comprise not just one activity but involve a combination of activities. Some developing countries will be competitive in a number of 'back office' activities rather than the whole bundle of services. For example, data processing is an important component of all transport services, including recording reservations and monitoring movements of people and cargo. The application of this technology is the basis of the development of new business models in transport, including the logistics specialists. The extent of this information demand has increased in some economies as a result of new security requirements applied to international freight transport. There is scope for developing economies to become providers of information services.

Developing economies therefore have interests in transport services as both consumers and as suppliers. As noted earlier, global-quality transport services are critical for the competitiveness of other export services. In addition developing economies have interests in the role of supplier of those services.

The entry of foreign providers not only contributes to the reallocation of resources according to international competitiveness but also adds to capacity and to competition in the market.

Foreign entry through commercial presence may be associated with substantial inflows of foreign investment, which may help to relax a domestic capital constraint.

Box 9.3 illustrates the positive impact of reform in Argentina's ports that made possible greater private investment in port capacity, including from foreign port operators. It also provided a stronger institutional environment in which to assess the effects on competition of foreign participation, as well as subsequent consolidation among the operators. As a consequence, port performance improved significantly.

Foreign entry adds to the number of operators in the market, which contributes to competition. Competition could also develop as a result of the incorporation of a previously closed domestic network, which supported only one operator, into an international route structure in which a larger number of suppliers are operating.

A greater role of foreign providers in the trucking sector in Africa has been reported. Partly this shift was stimulated by the liberalization of trade in goods, which led companies that were previous vertically integrated to outsource some services. This has led in

---

Box 9.3. Argentina's Experience in Port Reform

Before reform, cargo volumes through the ports had been declining especially for domestic freight that had switched to other modes. There had been a big rise in stevedoring fees in real terms (250 per cent from 1980 to 1991). Despite the rise in fees, cross subsidies between ports continued. Investment was not sufficient and in the ports of Rosario, Buenos Aires, and La Plata, for example, 'docks collapsed into the water' (Trujillo and Serebrisky, 2004).

In the early 1990s, most port responsibilities were devolved to the provinces, alongside greater private-sector participation and promotion of service competition. Provinces were given the freedom to operate, concession or close ports. Independent autonomous companies were established for some large ports, and six terminals were competitively concessioned to the private sector in Buenos Aires. An international company (P&O) was awarded two of the terminals, and since then another (Maersk) has purchased one of the winning bidders. All now compete against each other, plus there is free entry into the sector by allowing any operator to build, manage, and operate a port for public or private use. A new regulatory agency was created under the Ministry of the Economy, which was not allowed to be an operator. In addition, general anti-trust laws, such as those on mergers of operators, were applied to the port sector.

The effects of reform were significant. The average period of stay of a container fell from 72 to 15 hours (between 1991 and 2002), the system capacity increased by a factor of 5 and productivity per worker by more than that. Charges per container fell to world benchmark levels. (Traffic volumes however have been affected adversely by the macro-economic crisis.)

The remaining challenges are the following:

- The risk of collusion, due to horizontal mergers (there is also some debate about vertical mergers—e.g. between ports and shipping companies).
- Improved monitoring and benchmarking mechanisms (across ports) so that services continue to be provided on a cost-efficient basis.
- Inefficient customs operations which now pose a key constraint towards further productivity gains
- Restraints on intermodal integration, such as the quality of land transport access.
- Maintaining credibility of regulation, for example in the assessment of merger proposals.

Source: Adapted from Findlay and Fink (2005).

turn to evidence of greater movement of trucks to neighboring countries and beyond. South African trucks are observed as far north as Malawi, and trucks from Kenya and Zimbabwe are observed working in neighboring countries (Pedersen, 2000). The growth of longer-distance trucking has focused attention on road quality, and governments have responded by reconsidering their road investments as well as their enforcement of regulation of vehicle-axle loads (enforcement of this regulation on the one hand reduces payloads but also increases vehicle speed and reduces maintenance costs).

Foreign providers also offer service variety and new technologies. Consumers value variety and foreign providers may provide a different quality service as they attempt to enter the market is competition with incumbents. An example is the entry of low-cost carriers, such as those managed by the Virgin group, into various air transport markets: the low cost model is now also proliferating in Asia (for example, Air Asia), following the experience in Europe and the U.S. (Ergas and Findlay, 2003; Rose, 2004).

Foreign providers are likely to enter new markets through the provision of a differentiated service. That could leave space for home suppliers to establish positions for different bundles of price and service quality. Domestic suppliers may also have some advantage with local consumers because of their immediate familiarity (available without substantial investments in research) with local preferences for service quality and product mixes.

New technologies include not just the hardware required, but also the ways of doing things. Luo and Findlay (2004) offer the example of the logistics sector in China, which had already undergone substantial domestic deregulation before WTO accession. Foreign entrants, however, brought new methods of managing logistics businesses which through quality improvements were expected to lead to significant reductions in the costs of delivery. These were mainly associated with lower damage rates and lower warehousing costs.

The impact of trade-policy reform varies between modes of supply. Cross-border supply (mode 1) displaces local producers, but provision of the service through establishment (mode 3) does not, since it involves investment in new facilities and the employment of local staff. A foreign shipping company that provides cross-border services might displace a local provider in open markets, which adds to the costs of adjustment in the local economy and perhaps to the resistance to reform of policy that leads to this outcome.

However, services are also provided through commercial establishment. A foreign land-transport company would have to establish a local business, investing capital and employing local staff. The adjustment process is different in this case compared to cross-border supply. While the incumbent supplier may lose market share, new employment opportunities are created. The distribution of adjustment costs shifts, which may affect the political resistance to policy reform. Furthermore, the organization of transport businesses is changing. A foreign shipping company could also be part of a multimodal operation so that it too could seek to establish local networks in its new market.

Elements of Successful Trade Policy Reform

There are three key elements of successful trade policy—an emphasis on competition, the development of effective domestic regulation and attention to sequencing. The significance of these topics in transport is linked to some important features of this sector. Also discussed in this section is the importance of capacity building and taking into account the impact of liberalization on the poor.

COMPETITION, REGULATION, AND SEQUENCING

The link to competition policy arises because of key characteristics of transport services that are provided in a network structure. There are variations on this model, but most have in common the use of local collection systems congregated around a hub point where traffic is consolidated, with the transfer between the hubs points of the aggregated traffic, then the distribution of traffic after arrival at another hub in local systems to final destinations. The collection and distribution systems may use different modes to that operating between the hub points.[4]

---

[4] The following paragraphs apply to transport services some of the material presented in more general terms in the module on Infrastructure Services in Chapter 8.

The use of hubs has many advantages, including capturing the economies from the integration/concentration of various functions or activities, for example, the links between local and long-distance transport services, the point of transfer between modes, provision of related services (e.g. maintenance, finance, communications, and coordination, as required). A transport structure built on hubs and a series of spokes from each hub can lower transport costs, since even though trip time between two points is longer, the frequencies of service are higher. There might also be gains from the economies of density in vehicle size on all services.

Some services will continue to operate point-to-point. The choice depends on traffic volumes and vehicle technology as well as the length of the trip and the extent of congestion at both the hubs and the final destinations and origins. Smaller communities are likely to receive a higher level of service in a hub and spoke structure compared to the alternative of point-to-point operations.

In other cases, for example road systems, the traffic does not change vehicles in the course of the journey (the passengers remain in the same cars or buses), but the infrastructure does change its form, for example, vehicles more from local feeder roads to a freeway. The hub point is then less well defined, but the technological differences between the feeder system and the longer distance connection remain significant.

There are likely to be economies of scale in the operation of the hub or in the infrastructure that connects the hub points. There are also likely to be economies in vehicle sizes operating the higher volume services between the hub points (also called economies of density). The presence of these economies means that it is likely to be efficient for only one firm to supply at least sections of the package of transport services. Even if competition for the provision of these critical services were possible, only one firm would be expected to survive.

The notion of economies of scale has two important dimensions. First, the concept applies in the long run, that is, when all the firms involved have sufficient time to choose the scale of plant that minimizes their average total costs. Second, the economies may be exhausted if the market is big enough. The nature of the technology in the context of the parameters of the market determines whether one or more firms are likely to survive a competitive process. While it appears to be efficient to have a single supplier of a particular service in one market, it may in others be appropriate to have more than one.

These advantages of the incumbent in markets of this type may be reinforced by the presence of economies of scope in which case costs are lower because of a bundling of services to different markets. Examples include the carriage of both passengers and freight in aircraft, the combination of passengers bound for different final destinations along a hub-to-hub service, or the provision of land transport by an international air-freight-service supplier.

Sometimes the threat of entry may be sufficient to constrain an incumbent and even with only one firm, prices may be close to costs. However, the capital investments involved in the activities with which those economies of scale are associated also tend to be highly specific. They are not easily recovered once committed, in other words they are sunk. The presence of large sunk costs makes it difficult to constrain an incumbent through the threat of entry. In that case, the market is classified as a 'natural monopoly'. In this case, only one firm survives the competitive process, and that firm may be able to raise prices without inducing a response from other potential entrants into the market.

Assessments of whether there is 'a competition policy problem' depend on the definition of the market. For example, a road operator can provide competition for a rail operator. Whether the rail operator has market power depends on whether the relevant market is the rail-transport market or the land-transport market. A single rail operator may be the lowest cost provider of rail services, but this may not rule out effective competition to discipline prices in the broader market for land transport.

Not all the segments of the transport chain necessarily have these features of natural monopoly. Local collection or distribution systems might for example be able to sustain competition. The various modes that feed into a city airport could sustain a large number of operators, even if it is appropriate to have only one airport. Firms supplying services between airports could also compete with each other, even though at each end of a route, they all use one airport.

The policy maker can take advantage of competition when the market supports more than one firm. When only one firm might be expected to survive, the policy maker can still obtain the benefits of competition by arranging competition for the right to be the sole supplier in the market place. It is possible in these cases to arrange competition for the market rather than competition in the market.

The presence of scale economies in some parts of the transport chain complicates the strategies of opening markets to foreign participation. For example, foreign providers offer a new source of competition in previously closed markets; however their entry will not be effective, or will not even occur, when incumbents continue to dominate the essential infrastructure. Foreign airlines will not enter local markets if incumbents dominate access to airports. Foreign shipping lines will not enter if they cannot obtain port services.

In circumstances of natural monopoly, a significant barrier to entry into that market or related markets is the lack of regulation of the terms of access to essential facilities. The experience of the telecommunications sector in which a Reference Paper set out the core regulatory principles provides some guidance. Adlung et al. (2002) suggest that the GATS offers a "small step forward" in this respect. The Paper makes reference to issues relevant to transport such as access to essential facilities, but it also refers to competitive safeguards, universal service policy, transparency, independent regulators, and the allocation of scarce resources (such as landing rights at congested airports).

The key to implementing this approach is to separate the components of the transport chain that are natural monopolies and those that are not. In rail for example, one model has been to separate the ownership and control of the essential infrastructure (of the tracks) from the operation of the trains themselves. The aim was to introduce competition into the provision of the rail-transport services. The World Bank (2002b) suggests, however, that, according to the experience of this approach particularly in the UK, it may be preferable to retain a vertically integrated model (see Box 9.4). In large economies, competition can then take place between different routes connecting any two points. This model was adopted by Brazil and Mexico. In other cases, and especially in smaller or less densely settled economies, some attempt to develop approaches to sharing a common facility will be important.

The priority is therefore to make markets more competitive, and that perspective has implications for the focus on the question of national treatment compared to market access. The appropriate first step in the reform process from this perspective is to focus on market access barriers that apply to all potential entrants, including foreign providers. This sequence is likely to lead to more significant benefits so that taking a first step in which discrimination against foreign suppliers is reduced. This does not mean that entry opportunities should favor domestic suppliers while increasing the degree of discrimination against foreigners. This case might be presented and based on the argument that eventually the domestic firms so advantaged will become internationally competitive. But this approach faces some problems. The questions are what incentives does this situation provide for the domestic firm to develop in that way, and does the domestic firm have access to the technologies that are regarded as 'best practice' in infrastructure management?

Box 9.4. Derailed British Railway Reforms

Privatization of the rail sector in the U.K. led to separation of the track from the operators of trains. Initial effects of the reform were positive, particularly in terms of volumes of services. Pollitt and Smith (2002) report that the reforms led to improvements in operating efficiency. A major accident and subsequent speed restrictions suggest that investment in the infrastructure may not have been efficient. In October 2002, the private-track operator went into administration, and operation of the network was taken over by a company that was limited by guarantee and run on a commercial basis but without shareholders. A White Paper on the organization of the rail sector (U.K. Department for Transport, 2004) refers to the "flawed structure" put in place at the time of privatization. It refers to the features that led to the track operator's loss of understanding of the quality of the track, to the absence of linkages between prices paid for access to the rail infrastructure and the costs of its provision, and to the lack of incentives of train operators to respond to any changes in access prices. Neither the track operators nor the train operators had incentives to control costs. A re-specification of the roles of the track and train operators, and clarity over their responsibilities for their financial performance, alongside a process of regulation of track access prices, would be one solution. It would link the demand side of the market for track services more closely with the supplier. However, the White Paper appears to propose what is in effect the re-nationalization of the track by re-instating the Government as the 'client' of the track management company.

Source: Adapted from Findlay and Fink (2005).

Another example of a problem in the management of reform arises when a government decides to encourage foreign participation by a reallocation of licenses, perhaps as a result of a competitive tendering process. But even after the new license has been allocated, effective domestic regulation is important if the license applies to the provision of the services of essential infrastructure. Otherwise the new entrant's pricing behavior will not be constrained, and the result will be the replacement of a previously domestically-owned monopoly with a foreign-owned monopoly. The latter can bring advantages in terms of lower costs of operations or new technologies—monopolists, at least privately owned ones, are generally cost minimizers—but the host economy could be worse off since the rents created are transferred offshore. The sequence of reform, in other words, is not correct. This example reinforces the point made earlier about the priority to be given to market access over national treatment.

The main gains from liberalization depend on its contribution to competition, as a result of which the benefits of foreign entry are more widely distributed. However, the design of access arrangements is not the only important contribution to a competitive outcome. Adlung et al. (2002) for example stress that any reform route in air transport has to be accompanied by arrangements that can be used to respond to anti-competitive behavior, especially the abuse of market power that might be associated with the domination of particular hubs, the use of loyalty programs or predatory pricing.

Competition policy issues also arise in markets for shipping services. Fink et al. (2002) conclude that while unilateral policy action in the maritime sector can remove trade restrictions, and while the GATS can be used to bind those commitments, "there is also a need to deal with the possible private anti-competitive practices of international maritime cartels." They observe that large states can probably deal with these issues through their own competition laws, but that small states without enforcement capacity will be at a disadvantage. These conclusions are based on an analysis of transport charges for imports into the United States. They find that the liberalization of port services would reduce transport prices by 35 per cent, whereas the breakup of private carrier agreements would lower prices by 44 per cent. But removing the price-fixing agreements between carriers would reduce prices by 38 per cent.

Francois and Wooton (1999) also report striking results with respect to shipping services. They build a model in which they simulate both tariff cuts on goods shipped (agricultural exports from developing economies, for instance) and changes in the extent of competition in the shipping sector. They examine the effects of a reduction in tariffs and find that when tariffs are cut, shippers with market power can replace the trade-tax to some extent with a higher mark-up of their own. They also examine some numerical examples. At one extreme, they find that "approximately one-half of the gains from full and unconditional market access can be lost by producers to the shipping industry when the latter is concentrated and fully exploits its market power."

Structures in some markets will be the result of competition policy choices made in others. This issue provides another area for discussion, at least, among regulators. For example, a competition authority may permit two land-transport services operators to merge without a substantial reduction in competition in a market in its jurisdiction. But in a smaller foreign market, where both are established, the consequence could be a reduction in the number of suppliers. The smaller market might re-examine its entry policy, but at its size, and in spite of its GATS commitments, further credible entry (at least, within the existing technology) may be unlikely. Depending on the behavior of the incumbents, prices may rise. There is a possibility that the extent of market power of incumbents in one market need not be independent of policy choices applying to others. A forum for discussion of these linkages would be valuable.

Gamberale and Mattoo (2002) suggest (a) an end to the exemption from national competitive law of collusive agreements that affect only foreign markets and (b) create the right for foreign consumers to take action in the courts of countries whose citizens own companies that abuse their market power. These procedures could also be added to the GATS provisions.

Competition issues are not the only reason for applying regulation to the transport sector. Its operations are also associated with problems of congestion and environmental pollution. In connection with regulation to deal with those problems, the trade-policy concern is generally to avoid the forms of intervention being more restrictive of trade than necessary to achieve their target (Gamberale and Mattoo, 2002).

Estache and Gomez-Lobo (2004) explain that in the presence of lack of ownership rights in the common property resources in the urban bus sector, namely the rights to pick up at the curb side, the service can attract excessive entry, which exaggerates the existing congestion and environmental problems. Vigorous competition between operators can also lead to high accident rates and high casualty rates. Estache and Gomez-Lobo illustrate their argument using the experience of services in Santiago, Chile.

There are regulatory solutions to these problems. Free entry as Estache and Gomez-Lobo explain contributes to technical efficiency, but it can also be associated with the problems just discussed. They describe models, including one operating in Bogotá (the TransMilenio Project), in which authorities seek tenders to the rights to operate particular routes. This is an example of restricting entry, but at the same time introducing competition *for* the market. In terms of services quality and the policy problems, the project led to faster trip times, fewer accidents involving buses, and lower pollution levels

An alternative would have been to establish a monopoly for the provision of the services. But that leads to either prices that are set too high by the monopolist or else an excessive regulatory burden, in which the regulator is at a disadvantage compared to the operator in terms of access to information about costs. The hybrid model of competition for the market is an attempt to establish a scheme that reduces the regulatory burden and solves the problems identified but does so in a way that is no more restrictive of competition than necessary.

Capacity Building

The target of capacity building is to reduce the costs of, and the time taken to reach, the higher level of participation in the world economy (Findlay, 2003). From this perspective, capacity building includes measures to reduce adjustment costs in the economy and to reduce the costs of the institution building required to replace the older and inefficient forms of policy with those that match the international commitments.

Examples of capacity building include sharing experiences of the design and management of the reform process, such as the design of the regulatory arrangements to support private-sector participation in the provision of transport services that were discussed above. Other examples are the design of competition-policy institutions and cooperation on the application of competition-policy instruments across national borders. The latter could also include support for the implementation of the principles of the Reference Paper on Basic Telecommunications and their application to other sectors.

The costs, and the time taken to reap the full benefits of reform, can also be reduced by services liberalization itself. Services producers are large users of other service inputs. The ability of one service sector to respond to international competition depends on its own access to inputs at world prices, the same prices that its competitors are facing. Competitiveness depends on the performance, for example, of the education, transport, energy, telecommunications and financial sectors. The services of these sectors help reduce costs of adjustment elsewhere in the economy, and their performance depends in turn on the degree to which they are open to international competition.

Capacity building is especially relevant to participation in the WTO negotiating processes, but the priorities are not the technical issues in the WTO agreements. Instead they are the design of a strategy for trade-policy reform.

Findlay (2003) notes that it is often observed that 'trade policy starts at home'. In other words, the first step is to specify a development plan, which includes the priorities for policy reform. The design of a strategy for international commitments then follows from that plan.

Experience elsewhere suggests that it will be difficult for developing countries to resist specific requests by trading partners. If they allow their own policy changes to be driven solely by those requests, then policy development will tend to be haphazard and partial. As a result, there is a risk that foreign participants may capture a large part of the gains. It is also more likely that serious issues in implementation will confront developing country policy makers.

There is value in compiling information on the nature and extent of impediments. Findlay and Warren (2000) explain that this information helps establish policy priorities (e.g. in a 'tops down approach', reduce the most significant impediments first). It also provides a benchmark against which to assess the progress of reform and helps measure the extent of gains from reform, all of which helps support political coalitions in favor of reform. However, the methodologies for measuring impediments remain at early stages of development, and it is valuable to supplement that research with a series of business consultations. Business can also be encouraged to establish coalitions and forums in which these consultations might be conducted (many countries host an active coalition of service industries, for example). McGuire and Findlay (2005) review a methodology for assessing the degree of restrictiveness in services policy.

Establishing the links with the domestic development agenda is the main challenge in building an international strategy. This challenge should be the focus of cooperation on capacity building, Findlay (2003) argues. While the specification and implementation of a strategy in the WTO ultimately required substantial knowledge and understanding of the provision of the GATS and of negotiating tactics, the first step is, as always, strategic rather than tactical. This point is illustrated in the design of request-offer strategies, as examined by the OECD (2002).

Impact on the Poor

Competition and openness to trade may contribute to efficiency, but do they also contribute to targets for equity in the distribution of income and wealth? The impact of improved access to transport services is illustrated by an example developed by Radelet and Sachs (1998). Suppose that a region of a developing economy faces a perfectly elastic demand for its output and a perfectly elastic supply of purchased intermediate inputs that come from outside region. Suppose that the share of purchased inputs in gross value is 30 per cent. Then if transport costs are 35 per cent of the value of output and inputs, value added is 24.5 per cent of the value of output. If transport costs fall to 23 per cent of the value of output, valued added rises by 64 per cent to reach 40 per cent of the value of output.

Changes in transport costs even in the range used in this example make a significant difference to the value added available for distribution to the factors of production. If the payment to capital is fixed, then the amount of value added available to labor changes by an even greater proportion. This example illustrates the significance of transport-system efficiency for inland areas of a developing economy.

A more efficient transport sector will benefit people living in poor areas in a number of ways. First, as implicit in the example above, their terms of trade will improve. The costs of items they buy from the rest of the country will be less. The prices they receive for the items they export to the rest of the country will be higher. The opening up of markets due to improvements in transport and logistics services can also have effects on competition in the local markets to the benefit of local consumers of its services. For example, suppliers who previously had monopoly power are constrained by the options of supply from outside the region. Thus regulatory reform not only lowers costs, but its competitive effects force the passing on of those cost reductions to consumers in business and in households. Firms that previously earned rents from their protected position are clearly worse off, but overall the region will realize a welfare gain from the introduction of competition. In terms of the welfare of the group of people living in the poor area, this effect is even larger when those who captured the rents were not local firms.

Some localities may still not receive services at a quality typical of more developed areas after markets become more competitive. Governments often respond to this situation by subsidizing the provision of services. Subsidies might be arranged within the sector (supported by a regulatory structure that facilitates these transfers between consumers), or through explicit payments from the budget. There are important efficiency considerations in the design of these policies, both on the funding side and in terms of the manner in which the subsidies are applied.

Where services to the poor rely on cross-subsidies from other markets, opening those markets to trade and foreign investment runs the risk of undermining the basis of the transfers. Profits are competed away in those markets now more open and incumbent suppliers in rural or isolated areas then lack the resources to maintain the subsidies. China's commitments to rail reform were mentioned earlier, but one important question in their implementation will be how China meets the policy obligations to maintain services to some relatively isolated areas.

Research on the effects of infrastructure reform in Latin America (summarized in World Bank, 2002b) highlights some of the key elements in an effective response to concerns about the impact of reform on poor communities. This work showed that where competition occurs and regulation is effective, the cost of services can fall, although there are also examples of situations in which tariffs have risen to cover costs of provision. The reforms reviewed in the work also increased the provision of infrastructure services by the private sector. With respect to impact on poor areas, the work identifies the following five main ways in regulatory policy that can promote distributional objectives:

- *Setting investment targets.* Including targets for investment in new services at the time of awarding contracts or concessions to private providers (e.g. the extension of bus services in isolated areas).
- *Being flexible with respect to price and quality combinations.* Adopting a regulatory structure where standards vary between geographic areas (different vehicle standards for bus services in isolated areas).

- *Allow liberal entry of infrastructure providers.* Removing barriers to entry by suppliers from the informal sector.
- *Involving communities in the regulatory process.* Adopting different forms of consultation to contact a wider range of types of people in the community, including delegation of responsibility to lower level governments.
- *Subsidies.* Attention to the design of subsidy policy, for example, checking that the subsidies are received by its target households, financing the subsidies at least cost, delivering the subsidy efficiently (perhaps including in the form of a cash payment) and employing competitive processes in identifying providers of subsidized services (these aspects are also discussed by Gruen (2001) and Petrazzini (1996)).

Role of International Negotiations

Three questions about the links between the sorts of policy reforms discussed so far and international negotiations are reviewed in this section. These questions are the extent to which international negotiations can help domestic reform, what we can learn from the negotiations completed so far, and to what extent it is worth holding back on commitments in international negotiations in order to preserve policy flexibility.

How Can International Negotiations Help to Support Domestic Reform?

Access to domestic markets by foreign providers adds to the scope for competition either in the market or for the market, as explained already. That access could be provided through unilateral action by the host economy of those projects. But one reason for making the contribution in the context of international negotiations is to add to the credibility of the policy change. Mattoo (2002) explains this point in more detail. Projects in this sector are relatively long-lived and involve substantial sunk costs, including losses that might be incurred in the early years. Investors will seek some commitment by government that the policy environment in which the project operates will not be reversed, and that future policy changes promised will be carried out.

The GATS provides a way to add to the credibility of policy statements. Those reforms that are reflected in the GATS commitments are binding, including those to be applied at a future date. If the policy change is not made, then trading partners can seek compensation (Mattoo, 2002: 283).

A second contribution of participation in the GATS is that it may provide an opportunity to secure access to export markets for domestic-service providers. Mattoo (2002) explains that for some countries the reciprocity that the GATS offers may be important, especially when the ability to reform is 'constrained by domestic opposition (p. 285). The market-access opportunities that trading partners might provide as part of a package of commitments may be sufficient to shift the balance in the domestic policy-making process to support reform at home. Mattoo also notes, however, that in many countries this reciprocity is not important since the liberalization can be undertaken unilaterally because of the nature of its benefits and the adjustment costs associated with its implementation.

A third contribution is the direction that the GATS may provide to domestic regulatory reform. Examples have already been noted. The principles established for telecommunications are relevant to other service sectors. This experience provides a direction for change in domestic regulation in which entry might be impeded by lack of access to an essential facility. The GATS negotiations to date have also developed principles that apply to other regulatory measures, to help make sure they are not more restrictive than necessary to achieve their regulatory purpose. An example would be the application of policy on universal service obligations: as noted already the subsidies required to support that policy could be collected in ways that impede trade, or they could be funded from a broader tax base. The principle of adopting methods that are no more restrictive than necessary directs policy reform to the latter models.

What Have International Negotiations Achieved?[5]

To what extent have trade agreements delivered any benefits along the three dimensions? It has already been noted that the commitment on transport and distribution services negotiated during the Uruguay Round did not imply any actual liberalization. In other words, the GATS has not proved useful, so far, as a vehicle to advance market opening in this sector. But have existing GATS commitments lent credibility to domestic policies and prevented backsliding?

No research has been conducted to answer this question with confidence. Most likely, the contribution of commitments is likely to differ from country to country depending on the quality of the overall investment climate and alternative assurance mechanisms for foreign investors. For example, many bilateral investment treaties already afford foreign investors compensation in case of expropriation and offer investor-state dispute settlement.

---

[5] This section is adapted from Findlay and Fink (2005).

The GATS has also had limited success in promoting regulatory cooperation. Some WTO members that made commitments on maritime transport during the Uruguay Round promised to make available port services to incoming ships on "reasonable and non-discriminatory terms." But the number of such commitments is limited, and existing commitments are limited in scope. For example, no standard set of regulatory principles exists in any of the transport sectors—in contrast to telecommunications, for which a more detailed Reference Paper was established.

Actual liberalization was negotiated in the context of WTO accession, notably China's accession commitment in transport and distribution. While this serves to illustrate that, in principle, the GATS can be a vehicle for trade liberalization; it also reflects the asymmetries inherent in non-reciprocal negotiations towards WTO accession. For China, the accession commitment pushed reform beyond the domestic deregulation that had been already undertaken in some transport sectors. It helped overcome opposition to foreign entry and from the perspective of foreign investors established a credible reform timetable that encouraged their entry in anticipation of further reform (Luo and Findlay, 2004).

Finally, have regional trade agreements been more successful than the GATS in opening up transport and distribution markets? Some commentators argue that regional agreements offer the possibility of a more focused exchange of commitments, as there are fewer possibilities on free-riding by members who do not actively participate in multilateral

---

Box 9.5. NAFTA and Mexico–U.S. Liberalization of Cross-border Road Transport[1]

While the U.S. allowed Canadian trucks to operate inside the U.S. even before NAFTA, it held up access to Mexican trucks (with a few exceptions). The grounds were that Canada had provided reciprocal access whereas Mexico had not. The North American Free Trade Agreement (NAFTA) had required the U.S. to allow Mexican trucks into the border states by 1995 and to the rest of the country by 2000. However, implementation of those commitments was delayed and explained on the grounds that Mexican trucks were unsafe. Despite this, Mexican trucks were allowed to operate in a 20 mile zone along the U.S. border where goods are transshipped to U.S. trucks. The delays and long lines involved contributed to the incentive to use lower quality trucks for performing these services, exaggerating the apparent problem of Mexican trucks meeting U.S. safety standards. Mexico challenged the moratorium in a NAFTA tribunal. In 2002 President Bush ordered that all U.S. roads be opened to Mexican trucks. However the claim was then made by labor and environmental organizations that this could not happen until an environmental assessment of the change had been completed. The U.S. Supreme Court rejected that argument in June 2004. However, U.S. standards continue to be costly to meet, including the cost of the insurance required. Oscar Moreno, a director of Mexico's national trucking chamber of commerce observed that 'our grandchildren will be dealing with these rules before there is a great flood of drivers going north'. Questions also remain about how the U.S. security agencies will screen Mexican drivers.

Note: [1] Adapted from "The Truck Stops Here," *Wall Street Journal*, June 9, 2004, Editorial; and "Access to U.S. Highways Comes at Cost for Mexican Truckers," *Knight Ridder Tribune Business News*, June 12, 2004; "U.S. Roadways Opened to Mexican Trucks," Law Center CNN, June 8, 2004: and "U.S. Opened to Mexican Trucks," June 8, 2004, available at: www.axcentral.com. The historical background is available from a panel report, "In the Matter of Cross-border Trucking Services," Secretariat file USA-MEX-98-2008-01, Final Report of the Panel, February 6, 2001, available at: http://www.nafta-sec-alena.org/app/DocRepository/1/Dispute/english/NAFTA_Chapter_20/USA/ub98010e.pdf This material is also reviewed by Condon and Sinha (2001).

Source: Adapted from Findlay and Fink (2005).

negotiations (Schwartz and Sykes, 1996). However, a regional and preferential approach to reform suffers from the costs of trade and investment diversion. Furthermore, despite the rapidly increasing number of regional agreements, they do not seem to have been more successful than the GATS.[6] Probably the most prominent attempt at liberalization—the opening of cross-border trucking between Mexico and the U.S. under NAFTA—has been unsuccessful. In 2004, ten years after the agreement was signed, not a single Mexican truck had crossed the American border, although recent court rulings seem to have finally cleared the way for cross-border competition to emerge (see Box 9.5).

What Can We Learn from the International Rules that have been Designed and Commitments that have been Undertaken?

Commitments in the GATS have reflected 'existing levels of unilaterally determined policy rather than liberalization achieved through a reciprocal exchange of "concessions"' (Mattoo, 2002: 285). An example of the sort of bargaining that might have been expected was an exchange of commitments under mode 3 to developed countries with those on mode 4 to developing countries. However, the benefits of that sort of exchange appeared to be insufficient to surmount the various domestic political hurdles in both sets of economies. Nor does there appear to have significant trading across sectors within the GATS.

As already discussed, this sort of trading may not be important in services negotiations. Reasons for its application in goods included the political economy effects already discussed as well as concerns about the terms of trade effects of liberalization (in which export prices fall relative to import prices), which might be ameliorated as a number of economies open their markets simultaneously. These sorts of gains, however, are less important in services, where most of the benefits of reform are captured by the home economy. The more important motivation for international commitments is therefore to add credibility to domestic policy.

One qualification of the GATS role in this respect is that it allows commitments to be presented in a form that undermines their value. Mattoo (2002: 283) provides examples of the expression of the commitments that are not clear or qualified and urges a 'purge of the schedules' of this sort of language in the next round.

The question also arises of whether the Reference Paper on Basic Telecommunications can meet the expectations created for it as a model to other infrastructure sectors,

---

[6] For a recent review of regional agreements in services, see Mattoo and Sauvé (2004) and Chapter 6 of this *Handbook*.

including transport. Fink responds (box 5.7 in Gamberale and Mattoo, 2002) to this question with some concerns about its "vague language" from which it would be difficult to derive "far-reaching obligations" and his concern that the Paper would only limit the "most egregious departures from pro-competitive regulation" (p. 294). However there is, as Fink points out, opportunity as experience accumulates to strengthen the application of the principles.

Is It Worth Not Making Commitments in order to Preserve Policy Flexibility?

Members may wish to retain flexibility for a variety of reasons, including the use of commitments in subsequent negotiations that provide their exporters with greater market-access opportunities, to stage the process of liberalization given the uncertainties that might be perceived in the adjustments required and the costs of those adjustments, and to maintain the opportunity to apply policies that meet the interests of particular communities, such as isolated areas or relatively poor districts. However, it is argued here that the GATS already offers WTO Members flexibility in the presentation and timing of the implementation of their reform programs and in managing both adjustment costs and social policy objectives.

On the first point, of the value of 'negotiating coin', the observation has already been offered that the value of the GATS in this respect may be limited, and that it is greater value as a source of evidence of a binding commitment to a policy change, which is important because of the nature of the investment in infrastructure services, like transport.

On the second point, of the value of spreading out the liberalization program and managing the adjustment costs, the GATS permits exactly this. Members can schedule commitments over time. The value of making that commitment in a formal way in the GATS is that it avoids the pressure that might develop to reverse policy, designed to achieve the sorts of gains from openness examined here, but which has not yet been implemented. However, the assessment of the effects of policy reform is often extremely difficult, especially in the service sector because of the nature of the impediments applied. This adds to the uncertainty among policy makers and leads to a case for increased policy research and advice in these areas (World Bank, 2004).

On the third point, of the operation of pro-poor policy, the GATS does not prevent the pursuit of social objectives, through subsidies or universal service obligations, even if the sector in which those policies apply has been scheduled. As discussed above, there are options for the pursuit of social objectives alongside the commitments to policy

---

Box 9.6. Trade in Transport Services: Competition and Reliability, Issues and Trade-Offs

---

Marc H. Juhel

It is commonplace today to state that a country's trade performance relies to a significant extent on the efficiency and reliability of transport services. Apart from a very limited subset of traded commodities—software, for instance—most traded products still need to be physically carried from point of production to market. And the cost and time it takes to carry them often is a decisive factor in opening up external markets.

Conventional wisdom will also say cost-efficiency in transport services usually results from competition between transport services providers; hence the importance of opening up markets for trade in transport and ancillary services. This holds true indeed in many instances, in particular in countries where transport has long been considered a strategic activity to be restricted to public, government-owned, monopolies: ports, railways, air transport, and even road freight transport or key services like freight forwarding activities, which have long been and sometimes still are administered by government corporations, with no allowed access to any private provider. However, the shortcomings and built-in inefficiencies of this monopoly-supply model have over the years become impossible to miss. Most parts of the transport sector in many developing countries today are operated by private companies or are in the process of being transferred to private operators through various means, from management contract to concessions and outright sale of assets.

Now, the question becomes, under which conditions does this transfer to private supply of transport services actually foster competition, and therefore cost-efficiency of delivered services, and eventually increased trade competitiveness? To answer this, we must turn from the supply to the demand side: what does international trade expect today from transport services? The main answer is: guaranteed delivery. Time and cost reliability and predictability are key for integration within the multinational supply chains that provide access to the most developed markets. And if the proposed economic growth strategy recommended to developing countries, including the least developed ones, hinges on promoting external trade and access to foreign markets, then cost and time reliability of transport services is paramount.

This statement leads to consideration of the conditions in which increased competition between transport-services providers, which typically helps bring costs down, also contributes to increase reliability in delivery times. In markets where sustained transport flows are large, the case is clear in so far as time reliability becomes a marketing element on its own. Transport providers compete on delivery time as well as on costs, and more often than not a higher standard in guaranteed delivery will offset a higher cost for many shippers serving time-sensitive markets, and as we know, basically all multinational supply chains are today time-sensitive.

However, the case may become less clear when considering markets with thin transport flows, as in many developing countries. For reasons of convenience, speed, safety, and inter-operability, international trade relies heavily on containerized traffic, so the ability for a country to be served by efficient container services is an important asset for its external trade competitiveness. But efficient container services demand significant investments in terminals, handling equipment, and yard management systems. To be financially viable without overcharging the traffic to be served—which would defeat the competitiveness purpose—those investments will require a minimum activity threshold in terms of tonnage, or number of containers. As a result, many ports with modest containerized traffic, when seeking to attract a private operator to modernize and develop their container terminal, often through a concession contract, are faced with the request to protect the facility from on-site competition for a period of time as a prerequisite for submitting a bid.

To an extent, this may look like the infant industry argument in the protectionism debate. But it has some merits considering that potential competitors in a given location may have very different economic rationales. That is, an independent terminal operator will consider the specific terminal as a stand-alone profit center, while a shipping line may want to set up its own dedicated facility in an integrated multimodal operational perspective, where the financial performance of this particular facility is just an element of a broader business strategy. Understandably, the former, when bidding for a concession under such circumstances, will want to get a measure of protection, usually temporary, against the latter. The issue for the concessioning authority, or the regulatory body, will then be to assess the merits of the case in view of the expected level of activity, and protect itself against any potential rent-seeking behavior by specifically defining the scope of the protection granted (in time, no more than a few years, or in tonnage handled) and simultaneously implementing an effective tariff regulation policy.

The case becomes more complicated still when considering international corridors serving landlocked developing countries (LLDCs). These countries typically generate relatively modest traffic flows, but those are nonetheless critical to their economic development. Moreover, bearing in mind the reliance on small and medium enterprises (SMEs) to spur growth, enabling these SMEs to plug into international trade channels is a compelling necessity, which brings us back to the efficiency and reliability of transport services.

The challenge in such a situation therefore is: which transport services organization will best be able to offer guaranteed delivery despite limited traffic and geographical remoteness? In operational terms, guaranteed delivery and reliability of services supply translate into scheduled services. But scheduled services in thin transport markets inevitably means running with pervasive overcapacity, at a cost. Most shippers will gladly accept to pay this additional cost to benefit from guaranteed scheduled services, which for many will mean increased market opportunities overseas, including fitting into just-in-time multinational supply chains. However, in a situation in which free riders can set out to cream-up the market by targeting only the biggest shippers—for instance through chartering arrangements, where in essence the risk in terms of capacity usage is shifted from the carrier to the shipper—the provider of scheduled transport services may find himself cornered in a situation where the price of maintaining its services, mainly for SMEs, will just become uncompetitive because of too narrow a market base. In such a case a degree of protection may well be warranted, provided it is governed by a clear regulatory framework protecting against supplier abuse.

A related case can be found in the vertical integration phenomenon, which will also raise questions of the ability to crowd out competition on individual segments of an international transport chain. Considering again a landlocked country served by a single import/export corridor, it is easy enough to understand that in order for an international transport operator to issue a door-to-door transport contract between this country and an overseas destination, with a guaranteed delivery clause, he will want to control every link in the chain. Which could mean, for instance, for a shipping line to operate the container terminal in the port of export, then the railway services to the border, and maybe have the trucking company reaching to the production area in the landlocked country (or if not operate directly, have longstanding agreements with rail and truck operators). Now this runs against the trend towards unbundling transport services to foster competition on different transport segments. But in the case discussed above, unbundling may sometimes result in the impossibility for the landlocked country's shippers to get access to door-to-door services, which may keep them out of markets critical for them. So the way to bring competition pressure to bear on such a scheme will usually not be through competition on individual segments, but through the promotion of another competitive corridor altogether, like Dakar/Bamako/Ouagadougou against Abidjan/Ouagadougou/Bamako, or Mombasa/Kampala against Dar-Es-Salaam/Kampala. This will have a lot to do with trade and transport-facilitation measures to make it actually possible for real competition on price and quality of services to unfold.

The previous examples highlight the need for extended market access in provision of transport services, allowing in particular access to foreign providers. In many situations, it will be a prerequisite for availability of multimodal door-to-door services, a necessity in today's world for competitive access to regional and international markets.

Finally, how can we ensure that poor constituencies can still be served when opening up transport services market to commercial forces? In situations where any financial profitability on standard commercial grounds is still far off because of affordability and market-base issues, it can often still be possible to enlist private-sector skills through negative concessions, whereby a contract is offered based on minimum service standards in terms of quality and coverage, with a maximum allowed fare, and awarded to the bidder asking for the lowest subsidy to run the operations. This scheme has been used numerous times for urban transport and suburban rail services, in Latin America and elsewhere.

> To summarize, opening up the market for trade in transport services is indeed a necessity. Competition policy must sometimes be adjusted to ensure that it does not run against guaranteed delivery services in thin transport flows. Vertical integration may be preferred to unbundling but competition opportunities should then be nurtured on a broader regional scale, and adequate regulation always enforced to prevent rent-seeking.

change that do yield benefits to poorer communities, but those options can also be demanding in terms of bureaucratic resources and capacity.

References

Adlung, R., A. Carzeniga, B. Hoekman, M. Kono, A. Mattoo, and L. Tuthill. 2002. "The GATS: Key Features and Sectors," in B. Hoekman, A. Mattoo, and P. English (eds.), *Development, Trade and the WTO: A Handbook*. Washington, D.C.: World Bank.

Atinc, T. M. 1997. "Sharing Rising Incomes: Disparities in China." Washington, D.C.: World Bank.

Bronckers, M. and P. Larouche. 1997., "Telecommunications Services and the World Trade Organization," *Journal of World Trade* 31(3): 5–48.

Brook Cowen, P. J. 1997. "The Private Sector in Water and Sanitation—How to Get Started," Public Policy for the Private Sector, Note No. 126. Washington, D.C.: World Bank.

Choi, D-H., J. Kim, and C. Findlay. 1997. "Transport Services Liberalization in APEC," *Asia Pacific Economic Review* 3(2).

Clark, X., D. Dollar, and A. Micco. 2001. "Maritime Transport Costs and Port Efficiency," Mimeo, Washington, D.C.: World Bank.

Condon, B. and T. Sinha. 2001. "An Analysis of an Alliance: NAFTA—Trucking and the US Insurance Industry," *The Estey Centre Journal of International Law and Trade Policy* 2(2): 235–45.

Deardorff, A. 2001. "International Provision of Trade Services, Trade, and Fragmentation," *Review of International Economics* (May) 9(2): 233–48.

Ergas, H. and C. Findlay. 2003. "New Directions in Australian Air Transport," *Agenda* 10(1).

Estache, A. and G. de Rus. 2000. "The Regulation of Transport Infrastructure and Services: A Conceptual Overview," in A. Estache and G. de Rus (eds.), *Privatization and Regulation of Transport Infrastructure: Guidelines for Policymakers and Regulators*. Washington, D.C.: World Bank.

Estache, A. and A. Gomez-Lobo. 2004. "The Limits to Competition in Urban Bus Services in Developing Countries." World Bank Policy Research Working Paper 3207 (February).

Findlay, C. 2003. "Services." Background paper for the U.N. Millennium Project Task Force Trade, (March).

Findlay, C. and T. Warren (eds.). 2000. *Impediments to Trade in Services: Measurement and Policy Implications*. London: Routledge.

—— and C. Fink. 2005. "Trade in Transport and Distribution Services," Mimeo (January).

Fink, C., A. Mattoo, and I. C. Neagu. 2002. "Trade in International Maritime Services: How Much Does Policy Matter?" *The World Bank Economic Review* 16(1): 81–108.

François, Joe and I. Wooton. 2001. "Trade in International Transport Services: The Role of Competition," *Review of International Economics* (May) 9(2).

Gamberale, C. and A. Mattoo. 2002. "Domestic Regulations and Liberalization of Trade in Services," in B. Hoekman, A. Mattoo, and P. English (eds.), *Development, Trade and the WTO: A Handbook.* Washington, D.C.: World Bank, pp. 290–303.

Goldstein, A. 1999. "Infrastructure Development and Regulatory Reform in Sub-Saharan Africa: the Case of Air Transport," Technical Papers, Development Centre, OECD (October).

—— and C. Findlay. 2003. "Liberalization and Foreign Direct Investment in Asian Transport Systems: The Case of Aviation," paper presented at the OECD–ADB Experts Meeting on FDI in Developing Asia, October.

Graham, E. M. and E. Wada. 2001. "Foreign Direct Investment in China: Effects on Growth and Economic Performance," Institute for International Economics Working Paper No. 01-03.

Gruen, N. 2001. "Beyond the Safety Net—A View from Outside," presentation to the APEC Telecommunications Working Group, Canberra, March.

Hummels, D. 2001. "Time as a Trade Barrier," available at: http://www.mgmt.purdue.edu/faculty/hummelsd/research/time3b.pdf

Limao, N. and T. Venables. 2001. "Infrastructure, Geographical Disadvantage and Transport Costs," *World Bank Economic Review* 15: 315–43.

Luo, W. and C. Findlay. 2004. "Logistics in China, Accession to the WTO and Its Implications," in D. Bhattasali, W. Martin, and S. Li (eds.), *China and the WTO: Accession, Policy Reform and Poverty Reduction Strategies.* Oxford: Oxford University Press.

McGuire, G. and C. Findlay. 2005. "Services Trade Liberalization Strategies for APEC Member Economies," *Asian-Pacific Economic Literature* 19(1): 18–41.

McGuire, G., M. Schuele, and T. Smith. 2000. "Restrictiveness of International Trade in Maritime Services," in C. Findlay and T. Warren (eds.), *Impediments to Trade in Services: Measurement and Policy Implications.* London and New York: Routledge.

Mattoo, A. 2002. "Negotiating Improved Market Access Commitments," in B. Hoekman, A. Mattoo, and P. English (eds.), *Development, Trade and the WTO: A Handbook.* Washington, D.C.: World Bank.

—— 2003. "China's Accession to the WTO: The Services Dimension," in D. Bhattasali, L. Shantong, and W. Martin (eds.), *China and the WTO Accession, Policy Reform, and Poverty Reduction Strategies.* Oxford: Oxford University Press.

—— and P. Sauvé. 2004 "Regionalism and Trade in Services in the Western Hemisphere: A Policy Agenda," in A. Estevadeordal, D. Rodrik, A. M. Taylor, and A. Velasco (eds.), *Integrating the Americas FTAA and Beyond.* Cambridge, MA: Harvard University Press.

Naughton, B. 2002. "Provincial Economic Growth in China: Causes and Consequences of Regional Differentiation," in M-F. Renard (ed.), *China and Its Regions: Economic Growth and Reform in Chinese Provinces.* Cheltenham, UK: Edward Elgar.

Nikomborirak, D. and C. Findlay. 2003. "Liberalization of Air Transport Services," in W. Martin and M. Pangestu (eds.), *Options for Global Trade Reform: A View from the Asia Pacific.* Cambridge: Cambridge University Press.

OECD. 2002. "Managing 'Request-Offer' Negotiations under the GATS," Working Party Paper of the Trade Committee, TD/TC/WP(2002)13. Paris: OECD.

Oum, T. H. and C. Yu. 1998. *Winning Airlines: Productivity and Cost Competitiveness of the World's Major Airlines.* Boston: Kluwer Academic Publishers.

Pedersen, P. O. 2000. "The Changing Structure of Transport Under Trade Liberalization and Globalization and Its Impact on African Development," Working Paper Subseries on Globalisation and Economic Restructuring in Africa, no. vii, Centre for Development Research, Copenhagen (January).

Petrazzini, B. A. 1996. "Competition in Telecoms—Implications for Universal Service and Employment," Public Policy for the Private Sector, World Bank Group (October).

Pollitt, M. G. and A. S. J. Smith. 2002. "The Restructuring and Privatization of British Rail: Was It Really that Bad?" *Fiscal Studies* 23(4): 463–502.

Radelet, S. and J. Sachs. 1998. "Shipping Costs, Manufactured Exports and Economic Growth," paper presented to the American Economic Association Meetings, Harvard University, Mimeo, available at: http://www2.cid.harvard.edu/hiidpapers/shipcost.pdf (accessed July 31, 2002).

Rose, E. 2004. "Reworking the Model," *Airline Business* (March) pp. 58–60.

Schwartz, W.F. and A. O. Sykes. 1996. "Toward a Positive Theory of the Most Favored Nation Obligation and Its Exceptions in the WTO/GATT System," *International Review of Law and Economics* 16: 27–51.

Trujillo, L. and T. Serebrisky. 2004. "An Assessment of Port Reform in Argentina: Outcomes and Challenges Ahead," World Bank Institute, available at: http://www.worldbank.org/wbi/regulation/pubs/portreform_argentina.html

U.K. Department for Transport. 2004. "The Future of Rail," White Paper, The Stationery Office, London, available at: http://www.dft.gov.uk/stellent/groups/dft_railways/documents/pdf/dft_railways_pdf_031105.pdf (accessed January 20, 2005)

World Bank. 1996. "Container Transport Services and Trade: Framework for an Efficient Container Transport System," Report No. 15303-CHA. Washington, D.C.: World Bank.

World Bank. 2002a. "Transport Services: Reducing Barriers to Trade," *Global Economic Prospects 2002.* Washington, D.C.: World Bank.

World Bank. 2002b. "Building Institutions for Markets," World Development Report 2002. New York: Oxford University Press.

World Bank. 2002c. "Global Economic Prospects and the Developing Countries: Making Trade Work for the World's Poor," Report No. 23590. Washington, D.C.: World Bank.

World Bank. 2004. "Making Services Work for Poor People," World Development Report 2004. New York: Oxford University Press.

World Trade Organization. 1999. "Structure of Commitments for Modes 1, 2 and 3," Background Note by the Secretariat, S/C/W/99, March 3.

10 Trade in Services Telecommunications

Peter F. Cowhey and Jonathan D. Aronson

This chapter focuses on trade arrangements for international telecommunications and information services. It is organized in four parts. After a brief preview of the key messages, the first part provides background on the major changes that have transformed and globalized communications and information technology during the past two decades. The second part reviews the agreements that have altered the governance mechanism that manage international telecommunications that came out of the Uruguay Round (1994), the Basic Telecommunications Agreement (BTA) (1997), and other international agreements. It also examines the regulatory choices tied to competition and trade in telecommunications services. Finally, the third part provides an overview of the international telecommunications/IT issues that are under consideration in the Doha Round negotiations. It seeks to explain what the industrial countries are seeking, why they argue that these additional reforms are desirable, and whether and under what circumstances these arguments might make sense to developing countries and their negotiators. Costa Rica's telecommunications services commitments in the U.S.–Central American–Dominican Republic Free Trade Agreement are described in Annex 1 of this chapter. In Annex 2 to the chapter, the experiences of Ghana and South Korea are considered as they adapted their national systems to the post-1997 telecommunications reality.

Introduction: A Preview of the Key Messages

There are ten key, interrelated messages that might be drawn from what follows.

1. Robust and inexpensive telecommunications and information technology is a key to growth: Global markets are important for long-term economic success. Even the most basic engagement with export markets requires increasingly sophisticated communications links. For example, Wal-Mart buys in large volume from China, but only from suppliers that they interact with by modern data communications. Similarly, the tourist, convention, and entertainment industries are a steadily growing share of the world economy, but they all require a sophisticated communications infrastructure.

2. Benefits of Competition: Countries need competition, not because it is perfect, but because everything else is even worse. Telecom monopolists always used to claim that their industry was special and that monopoly was the only possible approach to allocate scarce resources efficiently. The last 20 years have decisively demonstrated that telecommunications is in fact an ordinary industry and that, like other industries, efficiency benefits if effective competition is introduced.

3. The Path to Competition: Many countries believe that they can stage a gradual assent to competition. They begin by partially privatizing the traditional monopolist, with a strategic foreign investor. They next create a duopoly for cellular services. More competitors, if ever permitted, are phased in slowly over time, but still with an eye to limiting the number of entrants in order to make investment more attractive. Meanwhile, they permit competition in value added services, subject to various restrictions designed to force newcomers to use the infrastructure of the traditional carriers and restrict new applications such as Voice over the Internet (VoIP). This strategy has already proven less productive than a more rapid movement to competition. Just as importantly, it is probably not sustainable in a world of rapidly changing technology.

4. Benefits of Trade Negotiations: Trade negotiations are curious when it comes to winners and losers. You win on a point when the other country allows your products into their markets so their consumers and businesses get to pay less money for them. You lose (make a concession) by letting others sell into your market or invest in your market so that your consumers pay less money for goods and services than otherwise. When you make a concession you are redistributing benefits from a few, large concentrated interests to consumers. So, this is hardly "losing" in the traditional sense. You do need to allow for adjustment costs, however, to those who lose while creating a more efficient market.

5. Trade negotiations should reinforce a strategy for domestic market reform: A country should make commitments on telecommunications services in trade deals at the WTO (or any other bilateral or regional level) because they advance a plan for reform of the regulation of the telecommunications market. Some specific decisions required for a successful trade negotiation may be politically uncomfortable, but a good trade bargain will allow a developing country to strengthen its reform plan and gain added economic benefits from the reforms.

6. Need for Transparency and Predictability: Developing countries that are seen by foreign countries and investors as stable, predictable, transparent, and with low levels of corruption will be more likely to attract significant amounts of foreign investment. The regulatory principles advanced in trade agreements can anchor a strategy to enhance transparent predictable regulation.

7. Creation of regulatory authorities: Most countries now recognize that telephone companies (or PTT ministries) should not be in charge of their own oversight. But

they are slow to invest in creating competent, independent regulators who have necessary enforcement powers and the ability to collect and analyze market information.

8. Trade commitments as a way of reinforcing the credibility of anti-corruption plans: The perspective in many developed countries is that corruption is pervasive in developing countries and that the cost of doing business is therefore higher than in industrial countries. Investors will only invest if they adjust the risk/reward ratio so that they earn more profits quicker than they otherwise might be willing to accept. To the extent that a country is viewed as having laws and institutions that are reasonably honest and reliable, they are more likely to be able to attract outside funds. Botswana is an example of a country that is viewed as well run despite its small size and low levels of development. It has been quite successful in dealing with international financial markets. Trade commitments on telecommunications services can enhance the credibility of measures designed to combat corruption.

9. Restrictions on Foreign Investment: It is common in developing countries to limit foreign investment to minority ownership shares However, the most successful economies have steadily moved to remove these restrictions on telecommunications. Retaining investment limits means that foreign suppliers worry that they cannot exercise effective management control. This raises the risks of investment and requires a higher return on investment. Many countries increase this rate of return for foreign investors by limiting competition, a policy with its own negative impact on market efficiency.

10. Trade commitments cannot substitute for political will: Pro-competitive regulation to enforce trade commitments is essential because the transition to competition always faces significant political resistance. Unless political leadership believes that basic goals of economic and social development require a robust communications and information technology infrastructure supplied by competitive market forces, regulators will fail.

Trade negotiators are not telecom experts, nor should they have to be. But it is almost impossible to negotiate on this complex market without understanding a few fundamentals about the basic technology—which is changing dramatically—and the economics of the different segments of the market. This chapter is built on key trends that are transforming the telecom/information technology landscape. We begin with the baseline for the market—the design and economics of the traditional wired network—and then look at the changes.

In an annex to the chapter, Roberto Echandi discusses the specific commitments of Costa Rica with regard to telecommunication services in the context of the North American Free Trade Agreement (NAFTA) with the United States.

Traditional Network Architectures and Economics

The WTO's Basic Telecommunications Agreement (BTA) of 1997 primarily focused on wireline networks, and many of the regulatory concepts that were translated into the BTA flowed from these traditional networks. So, a brief understanding of these networks is desirable as a starting point.

The architecture of the traditional phone network was hierarchical and analog circuit-switched. Complex and extremely expensive large central-office switches oversaw traffic routed by smaller, more local switches over a carefully planned pattern designed to conserve scarce transmission bandwidth and switching capacity. The key role of central-office-switching systems meant that they performed numerous specialized functions that were vital for operation of traditional phone systems, including billing. It is often not practical for competitors to duplicate these capabilities in a timely, cost effective manner.

Box 10.1 reviews the economics of wired networks more closely. There are three points of importance. First, there are large economies of scale and scope (size and complementarity of functions) in networks. For a long time engineers and economists thought that these justified monopolies. Later, they realized that the inefficiencies of monopoly probably offset all of the theoretical gains from larger economies of scale and scope. More rapid technological innovation further reinforced this conclusion. Second, it is possible to share network capabilities efficiently among multiple operators, but this usually requires regulatory intervention for some period of time. Third, there are significant network externalities in communications—the network is more valuable to everyone as more people are connected. This justifies policies to subsidize universal service so long as they are designed efficiently.

Box 10.1. Economic Principles of Telecommunications

Economists note that telecommunications networks have special cost characteristics: A correct analysis of telecommunications networks has to begin by recognizing that, *in theory*, there is a potential for natural monopoly, especially for the local wired network. Network operators may incur large sunk costs that cannot be redeployed, suggesting that these firms may have declining long-run average cost schedules. These cost schedules can result in natural monopoly in those segments of the industries where the minimum optimal scale of production is large relative to the market demand. However, the case for natural monopoly is much weaker for long-distance (including data) and mobile-wireless networks.

For all forms of communications the regulation of monopoly is imperfect and costly: Even a high-minimum, efficient scale of operation for major network facilities does not necessarily justify monopoly on a national scale. Potential market failures in unregulated industries based on technologies exhibiting scale economies have to be compared with potential regulatory failure when the government tries to regulate natural monopoly. Although regulating imperfectly competitive industries is not entirely without costs, these costs are lower when regulators can deal with several competitors in an oligopolistic market rather than with a monopolist. For one thing, oligopolistic competition yields important economic information for regulators. For another, the presence of some competitive constraints means regulators have options other than the micromanagement of carrier costs and revenues. Moreover, competition between two local network operators with declining long-run average cost curves may result in a downward shift of these curves, generating efficiency gains that outweigh the loss of scale economies caused by the moves up along the cost curves. Frequently, competition will induce major reductions in transaction costs that more than offset any losses on scale economies. Finally, in markets characterized by pricing that is only vaguely associated with efficient costing, it may not matter whether new entrants can match the lowest theoretical costs of incumbents. There may still be substantial welfare gains from pricing and service innovations by new entrants.

Network externality effects are also extremely important: Networks are more valuable if there are more people utilizing them. (Shapiro and Varian, 1998) This externality is especially important to interconnection and universal service policies. In developing and transition economies where teledensities (communications lines per 100 people) are rather low, the network externality effect may be pronounced. In this case the marginal social welfare benefit of adding new subscribers to the relatively small network may be large, justifying subsidies that will allow additional users to access the network.

In developing countries the spatial distribution of potential subscribers also is an especially important factor in telecommunications infrastructure deployment. High spatial concentration of users is particularly favorable because it allows the utilization of the economies of density and scope, resulting in lower operating costs for telecommunications networks in concentrated urban areas. Telecommunications services in low-density areas have also traditionally been cross-subsidized by more profitable telecommunications services in concentrated urban areas. Therefore, a relatively uneven demographic landscape with large population concentration in a few select areas could also facilitate the penetration of telecommunications networks in sparsely populated rural areas. The challenge is to subsidize low concentration regions in a way that is efficient and not harmful to competition.

Three giant changes have transformed the structure of telecom services since 1980. The traditional services on the telephone network were local phone, long distance and international long distance services. Later, fax services became prominent as telegraphs and telex shrank to a tiny piece of the market. The telephone network technology also was relatively inflexible so there were separate specialized networks for broadcasting.

The changes in the size of market segments reflect these trends. When the BTA talks seriously recommenced in 1994, the world telecom services market of $517 billion was about 16 per cent data and 10 per cent mobile. In 2001 the world telecom services market was $968 billion even though competition had caused prices to plunge in many of the world's largest markets. Just as strikingly, data revenues were about 18.5 per cent even though data were, by volume, now equal in size to voice traffic. In the meantime, mobile had grown to about 33 per cent of world telecom revenues. International traffic had slipped from more than 8 per cent of the total revenue to less than 8 per cent. The equipment market declined in its size relative to services during this period as it grew from $158 to $264 billion. This meant it went from roughly 23 per cent of the services market to less than 21 per cent.[1]

These changes overlapped but there was a rough sequence. First, during the 1980s traditional fixed-wired services became segmented between consumer and business

---

[1] ITU-D, Key GlobalTelecom Indicators.

services. This was associated with the rise of private corporate networks. Second, computing networks evolved into the Internet architecture, which provided a totally new way for organizing all forms of communications networking. In parallel, the total data transmission capacity (measured by the amount of data that could be transmitted per second) exploded. Today, the internet architecture and broadband capacity are erasing traditional distinctions between services (e.g. broadcast versus voice telephone service). Third, wireless and especially mobile networks have supplanted wired networks as the predominant form of connectivity in developing countries and, to a lesser extent, developed countries.

The Rise of Corporate Networks Leads to Competition in Basic Services

As computer data networking grew in the 1970s and major companies became more communications intensive in their operations, two major adaptations took place in the regulation and business of phone networks. The policy of the United States, where most of these changes began, set a direction eventually mimicked by most major markets. The U.S. decision makers believed that computing offered a major new opportunity for creating revolutions in business models. They also recognized that then existing monopolies had inefficient pricing and supply structures. Their goal was to free the new computer companies from the inefficiencies of the old telephone system without breaking up the monopoly.

So, the Federal Communications Commission required the telephone companies to lease simple transmission capacity (without telephone switching) on a cost-oriented basis to companies wanting to run their own internal telephone and computer networks. This was the origin of the "private leased circuit" segment of the telecommunications market that appears in the BTA schedules. The United States also authorized independent service providers to lease transmission capacity from phone companies, install their own phone switches and computer equipment, and to provide private telephone and data transmission capacity to corporations. This spawned a new wholesale market comprised of new operators who leased capacity in bulk from phone companies and then engaged in "resale" to individual companies. It also greatly enhanced the ability of computer-systems designers to create architectures for data networks that were independent of the architecture of phone networks. Different software and transmission protocols could be devised. This eventually permitted the rise of the Internet.

As a business proposition, traditional phone companies focused on the market for private business networks featuring wholesalers who leased lines and resold them to private businesses for internal communications with special value added features such as customized billing systems and reliability guarantees. The data market, even in the mid-1990s, was still much smaller than voice or fax, but it was critical for selling a combined bundle of services to companies. Businesses were the largest single consumers of long-distance services in every country. As a rule of thumb, about five percent of the telephone customers, larger firms and government, accounted for close to fifty percent of the long-distance market in any industrial country. As a result, the ability of businesses to lower their costs of voice and improve the effectiveness of computer networking was a key driver of innovation in firms. To a significant extent the Value added telecom services and BTA negotiations were driven by firms seeking competition globally in the provision of these business service segments.

Creating a competitive market in business services soon lent itself to creating competition in long-distance services. It is important to recognize that the transmission capacity in a phone network has, to simplify greatly, two components—local transmission capacity (such as the connection to family residences or small businesses) and the larger scale transport circuits often called the backbone network (transmission capacity, typically fiber optic today, that links together the large office buildings in Tokyo or the long distance traffic between cities). For reasons of engineering and economics it is much easier for a new entrant to build its own backbone wired network than to duplicate local transmission capacity of a wired network (often called "the last mile") in a timely way. Thus, the operator who controls local wired transmission has significant strategic advantages that may allow the operator to restrict competition by other companies for some services. Since the introduction of competition in business services and (later) long-distance services, government regulators had to intervene extensively to make sure that transmission capacity, especially local capacity, was available to new entrants on cost effective and timely terms. Large users began to support competitive provision of the underlying telephone infrastructures, not just the ability to lease transmission from monopolies, in the hope that it would allow for more innovative and cheaper underlying network transmission systems.

Competition evolved still further to include the competitive provision of local telephone services, networks to support Internet Service Providers (ISPs) and provision of broadband connections to residences and small businesses through Asymmetric Digital Subscriber Line systems (ADSLs use special electronics to boost data capacity on the local transmission system). The problem for government regulators became even more complex. In addition to making transmission capacity available, they had to open up access to a number of other technological capabilities for "rental" by new entrants. These "network elements" ranged from billing systems to operations-support systems. Along with transmission and switching, regulators pledge to make them available on a cost effective and timely manner through "interconnection" regulations to new entrants. So long as the incumbent phone company has the ability and incentive to cut off competition by new entrants through denying effective access to these network elements, interconnection regulation is necessary. Over time, as in long distance transmission facilities in the United States, the incumbent can lose this power and regulation can be removed.

By the mid-1990s the business service and research users' computer networks evolved into the Internet. The difference between the architecture of the telephone and Internet systems explains some of the key stakes in the negotiations over communications services in the Doha Round.

THE RISE OF THE INTERNET

Data are replacing voice as the dominant use of major communication networks, thanks to the Internet, the Web, and the continuing sharp declines in computing costs. In addition, phones are becoming interchangeable with computers as witnessed by the latest cell phones (which have powerful micro-processors).[2] As a result every network of an effective economy will have to support data applications reliably. A modern economy requires a network that can carry vast amounts of information. This has two fundamental implications. First, the cost of data traffic needs to be inexpensive. Internet use, for instance, responds to pricing. Second, inexpensive and reliable data networking means an even more rapid acceleration of the collapse of much of the pricing structure for traditional phone services. Countries will need to depend on elasticities of demand to generate large amounts of flows of information at affordable prices instead of soaking a few well-healed users, many of them foreign, with exorbitant prices. Pricing policies that will attract flows therefore are necessary.

Altogether, Internet architectures are cheaper and more powerful than traditional phone networks.[3] It also means that, as transmission capacity expands and becomes cheaper (e.g. for leading edge users of broadband) the distinctions among broadcast,

---

[2] For example, the next generation of cell phones will have the capability of playing complete songs downloaded from the network. The trick will be to download songs and then store them in memory on the phone. High end phones will be like an I-Pod.

[3] A phone call, for example, took place because a central-office switch created a single dedicated circuit between the two telephones for the duration of the call. These circuits were analog (a technology not congenial to computing traffic) and wasted transmission bandwidth because most conversations only used a fraction of the dedicated circuit's capacity. The architecture of the Internet is the exact opposite of the phone network because it relies on digital computing logic. (All telecom traffic is organized into signals consisting of the binary 1s and 0s of computing systems.) It also uses a relatively flat architecture to transmit and receive packets. Put simply, phone calls, email, and movies are all organized into packets of binary digital information that include an address for where each packet should go, an error correction code, and some other basic features. Smart computers (routers) use a shared table of Internet addresses to figure out the most efficient way to route the packet traffic to its destination. There is no dedicated circuit; each packet could theoretically follow a different route, so bandwidth is used much more efficiently. There is no hierarchy of highly specialized phone switches; each router has software capable of making its own routing decisions. This decentralization of network intelligence on what are essentially powerful personal computers allows more flexibility in traffic management at lower costs, and it allows for much faster technology upgrades and innovation.

computing, and telephone networks start to dissolve. In networks serving large users, such as big banks, speed and bandwidth capacity already are high and constantly escalate. (A special concern for developing countries is that the level of high-end bandwidth available to their economies remains relatively low and expensive by global standards.) Generally, for households and small and medium sized enterprises, the distinction is made between narrow band (speeds roughly up to 64k) and broad-band (speeds of anywhere from 500 kb/s upwards). On wired networks these broadband capabilities for smaller customers usually arrive by means of either ADSL or cable-modem networks (delivering data over a cable television system with upgraded electronics and reliability). Both ADSL and cable-modem systems deliver Internet services.

The difference in architectures between the phone and Internet models of a network implies differences about risk-taking and innovation that will often show up in discussions about the risks and benefits of competition in trade negotiations. Traditional telephone-network engineering emphasizes careful conservative engineering to assure reliability and quality. Innovation is a process of elaborate international planning on standards. Questions are asked, and answered, exhaustively before heading off in a new direction. By contrast, the Internet approach emphasizes the application of the logic of Moore's law to networking. (Moore's law states that the power of computer chips doubles every eighteen months while cost remains constant.) The implications—rapid innovation to more powerful capabilities with plunging real prices for performance—fuel Internet architecture. Its designers have bet successfully that they can begin service innovations without complete solutions because they can ride the curve of the logic of Moore's law. Throwing ever increasing computing power at lower costs at a problem allows for flexible problem-solving. Moreover, it is not just computing. For example, the performance of both network-data storage and fiber-optic-network speed and capacity has grown more rapidly than the rates for computing in recent years.

The impact of the Internet is becoming ubiquitous. The Internet changes how a network is organized, the services it can provide, and its cost structure. These differences have significant implications for both telecom regulation and BTA commitments. The BTA was negotiated without full absorption of the implications of the Internet. Now, services specialists need to understand its impact. The Internet is a descendant of computer networking and, under many regulatory definitions, including perhaps the BTA definitions, it is therefore not a basic telecommunications service (e.g. a phone call) but a value added computing service. As just noted, regulators in most countries exempted computer networking from many of the rules for phone networks, including the funding of subsidies for universal service. (Broadcasting had a separate regulatory system for its specialized networks.) Thus, as the Internet becomes more ubiquitous and has greater bandwidth, it poses huge challenges because it is capable of incrementally upgrading to cover voice phone and video-style services. These are exempt from many regulations on traditional phone networks. Many phone companies already use Internet telephony (Voice over the Internet Protocol, or VoIP) to send some of their phone calls to other countries because, as computer messages under the regulations, they are exempt from more expensive interconnection charges for voice calls.[4]

Thus, when looking at the scheduling of commitments on market access, the following considerations are important:

1. At a minimum, countries with large corporate centers will be looking for ways to allow competition in the provision of private corporate networks for voice and data. They will also want competition in the wholesale/resale business that supports such corporate networking.

2. If a country schedules a commitment to competition in local or long-distance basic services, or competition in the provision of networking for ISPs or the provision of broadband networking for data, it also has to embrace a framework for interconnection regulation.

3. Countries have to make careful choices between commitments on competition in the provision of services and competition in the provision of network infrastructure that underlies these services. The overwhelming trend is to permitting competition in both. But many developing countries reserve the right to limit the total number of competitors providing infrastructure either temporarily or permanently.

4. The Internet and greater bandwidth mean that scheduling commitments for different market segments interact in new ways. For example, scheduling commitments for competition in value added computing networks and voice services may mean that a country has committed itself to permitting the provision of voice services as VoIP services exempt from local pricing and subsidy rules for traditional voice services. This can be avoided by special scheduling restrictions if a country so desires.

---

[4] The business model for communication carriers may change dramatically in the future. In the late 1990s, new competitors in the marketplace closely resembled traditional telecom companies except that they had leaner staffing and corporate cultures more attuned to marketing. This was much like the introduction of more competition in the main-frame computer industry in the 1950s when the rivals to IBM looked much like mini-IBMs. The impact of the new technologies may lead to completely new business models that reflect new cost structures and service opportunities. The goal of regulation should be to permit, not restrict, experiments with these business models. For example, the largest costs for a traditional telephone company include extensive marketing, billing, and general management systems. Wireless technology in low population markets, by contrast, could permit much smaller companies with much less expensive approaches to billing and marketing. Yet, policies restricting the number of entrants and requiring large networks by new entrants into a marketplace drive companies to replicate the old models of telephone companies. For example, Voice over Internet providers look much like Dell Computers in their staffing and production models. Like Dell, they use business models that are vastly different from those of traditional phone companies. The model for rural service in the future may be more like McDonalds than NTT. Technology may make local franchising systems more appropriate than large telephone companies. Vendors can supply the technology package and management practices on an expedited, low-cost basis. Entry regulations are the enemy of spontaneous experimentation.

THE RISE OF WIRELESS NETWORKING

If the rise of private business networks and the associated businesses of leased lines and resale define one great change and the emergence of the Internet is a second, then the third key change is the emergence of a genuine alternative to wired infrastructure for all but the highest bandwidth. Wireless networks now connect more users than do wired networks.

The divisions with wireless can be roughly represented as in Table 10.1.

Satellite was the first major fixed wireless system of the modern era. It was a substitute for conventional phone-transmission cables and made possible voice and data links for many poor countries with little or no connectivity to international phone cables. It also provided broadcast television on a global basis. Satellite services were originally provided almost exclusively through monopoly systems, mainly through the Intelsat system. The introduction of competition in satellite systems was a hotspot for the BTA negotiations, but this is not a major focus currently.

Terrestrial fixed-wireless systems can be broken down into licensed and unlicensed components. This classification depends on whether or not the system relies on spectrum that is licensed to one or a small number of suppliers (in theory, to control congestion and interference) or is on unlicensed spectrum open to all. Most licensed systems are descendants of microwave-relay systems that have been radically upgraded and serve as alternatives to wired cables. Experiments with broadband-data delivery over these systems in the booming marketplace of the late 1990s mostly failed. There is now a new generation of systems being examined for deployment. Many countries have set aside certain radio bands for unlicensed systems (i.e. wireless systems that require no license to provide services). Unlicensed systems—such as WiFi (or 802.11 b, for example)—use extremely low power so that they can deliver large bandwidth for short distances. They may have a large impact because they allow several users to cheaply and easily share a single broadband connection within an area. Rural applications of this technology may be especially attractive.

Wireless-mobile systems all use licensed spectrum. They pose major issues in controlling congestion and interference in highly complicated systems because they are designed to provide seamless connections to moving customers. First-generation services were primarily analog telephone services. Second-generation services were still predominantly voice oriented, but provided limited data capabilities and improved quality because they were digital. The two dominant technologies of the second generation

Table 10.1. Wireless Technology Systems

Fixed	Terrestrial (licensed and unlicensed)	Satellite (geosynchronous)
Mobile	Terrestrial (2nd and 3rd generation)	Satellite (low earth orbit systems)

were GSM and CDMA systems. The third-generation services, now being deployed after much financial speculation and subsequent delay in commercial application, are different versions of high-speed CDMA architectures. These are designed to provide voice and data up to 2.5 mb/s, although the actual speed is usually less than that. Thus, they are roughly equivalent to having a mobile wireless ADSL or cable modem link for data. As data speeds increase and prices decrease, new classes of applications, especially multimedia, are emerging.

The significance of wireless for society and regulation is huge. Wireless has opened the way to a vast increase in connectivity among countries. It is cheaper and faster to deploy than wired networks. However, communications regulators in many developing countries have so far treated it as if it were a luxury premium service for the better-off and business. As a result, they allowed mobile operators to price higher and flexibly and began competition in these services earlier than for wired networks. The result was better cash flow to build out the networks and more efficiency in their operation, plus greater attention to customer service through innovative marketing schemes. Pre-paid phone cards were particularly important for making the service practical for lower income customers.

Competition and trade challenges raised by wireless are discussed below. For now, note that 3G systems in particular (and their successor technologies) may force changes in the way that countries regulate competition of fixed wired networks.

Background on Previous Telecommunication Service Negotiations

While this chapter will focus on the WTO negotiations, bilateral and regional trade negotiations all will occur within the baseline of trade practices created in the Uruguay Round (1986–93). So, it is vital to think through the WTO picture to understand any negotiation.

TELECOM IN THE URUGUAY ROUND

The WTO agreement has a significance that goes beyond the specific commitments and the impressive number of signatories: 67 of 69 governments made significant liberalization commitments. One way to capture the extent of the agreement's impact is to look at its effect on markets. The U.S. government has calculated that approximately 85 per cent of the world market, measured by revenues, is covered by strong market-access commitments in the negotiations. With a few specific exceptions on particular issues or market segments,

Table 10.2. Participant Commitments

Participant commitments	Total governments, including other (77)
Voice telephone	63a 61b 64c 48d
Data transmission	70
Private leased circuit services	61
Terrestrial mobile telephone	67
Other terrestrial mobile services	67
Mobile satellite services / capacity	58
Fixed satellite services / capacity	57
Trunked radio services	21
Additional commitments Ref. Ppr.	–
Additional commitments (other)	64

Notes: a. Local telephone. b. Long distance telephone. c. International telephone. d. Resale.
Source: Adapted from WTO (some explanatory notes are excluded).

all the OECD nations essentially were bound to unconditional market access on January 1, 1998. And as noted in Table 10.2, a review of the major industrializing countries shows significant commitments on market access that increased rapidly over a period of a few years (typically after transition periods ranging from two to five years).

There remains a divide between the more advanced and less advanced developing countries. In the 1997 round of the telecom negotiation, most of the more advanced developing countries made offers on telecom services, and the chief concern of industrial countries in this round was to expand those offers to make them virtually identical to the industrial countries' offers. The market reforms and trade commitments in the larger developing economies make it more difficult for the less advanced economies to attract quality international investors. For the less advanced economies, the goal of industrial countries is to get them committed to the process. But there is no driving urgency for huge progress because the amounts of international traffic and payments are still quite small. U.S. bilateral trade agreements with Chile, Singapore, and Central America advance the BTA provisions incrementally by making implicit expectations of the BTA into explicit obligations, but they do not radically modify the BTA.[5]

The Annex on Telecommunications in the GATS

The General Agreement on Trade in Services (GATS) contains principles to situate the GATS within the WTO framework of principles and then deal with some of the special characteristics of services. The BTA is nested within these principles. The Annex on Telecommunications then applies these principles to telecommunications. Most of the

---

[5] See Sherman (2004) for an excellent overview of more recent agreements.

text addresses data networking and closed user groups. Given the importance of corporate and data services, a brief review of key characteristics is useful.

- The text on access and use of the Public Network (a network required by its license to be generally available to the public) spells out the rights of users to interconnect their private networks to the public network. While a country has a right to take measures to protect its network's technical integrity and achieve other reasonable goals (such as protecting data protection) the measures must be reasonably related to these carefully defined objectives. We discuss below the issues of setting standards and choice of telecommunications equipment by users.

- The Annex reaffirms the principles of national treatment and MFN for national offers and market conduct. National treatment (Article 17 of the GATS) and MFN (Article 2) provisions are at the heart of the WTO framework. The former means that foreign firms cannot be treated less favorably under domestic rules and regulations than local firms if a country has granted market access to foreign firms. Any plans to treat them less favorably must be taken as an exception in a country's schedule on market access. MFN means that a country cannot grant market access to one WTO country's firms without granting access on identical terms to all other WTO members' firms. MFN also means that countries cannot look at the national origins of a foreign firm to see if they will be regulated differently from other firms except on narrow grounds of WTO exemptions like national security. In the 1997 BTA, a major stumbling block to agreement on international services for two years in the negotiations was a disagreement over how to apply MFN obligations to national regulatory arrangements for services like international phone calls where countries had different rates for terminating calls from different WTO countries.

Schedule of Specific Commitments

Scheduling Market Access. One of the major challenges of trade in services is determining how to schedule market-access commitments. There are three principal modes for telecommunications. The two dominant are cross-border (mode 1 in scheduling parlance) and commercial presence (mode 3) that correspond roughly to delivering services through networks crossing national boundaries and the creation of a local business to provide the service, including scheduling of foreign investment liberalization commitments. Mode 3 is fairly meaningless without a right to foreign ownership and investment and, therefore, a central feature of the BTA is commitments on rights of foreign investment (in regard to which services and how much foreign ownership is permitted). (Trade pacts since the BTA have expanded on mode 1 entry by frequently stipulating that a company need not establish a commercial office in the country where a service is provided.) Consumption abroad is another mode of scheduling (mode 2), but this primarily relates to the rights of commercial users to have access to the local national network on terms and conditions conducive to the users being able to lease and reuse network facilities. Mode 4, presence and movement of natural persons, has clear theoretical salience because it allows suppliers and users to move necessary experts in and out of a country. But, given the larger controversy at the GATS over this mode, it is relatively little used in the BTA.

The negotiators of the Annex and BTA spent considerable effort on figuring out how to define the services. The Annex largely covers value added services for data and corporate use, including email. It does not cover the underlying network facilities that enable the services. The BTA covers both the underlying network infrastructure and the services provided on it, including leased transmission circuits and such end services as telephone and fax services. Box 10.2 contains the list of services.

Box 10.2. Basic and Value Added Telecommunications

Basic telecommunications include all telecommunication services, both public and private that involve end-to-end transmission of customer supplier information.

　Basic telecommunication services are provided:

- through cross-border supply
- and through the establishment of foreign firms or commercial presence, including the ability to own and operate independent telecom network infrastructure

Examples of basic telecommunication services:

　(a) Voice telephone services
　(b) Packet-switched data transmission services
　(c) Circuit-switched data transmission services
　(d) Telex services
　(e) Telegraph services
　(f) Facsimile services
　(g) Private leased circuit services
　(h) Other

- Analog/digital cellular/mobile telephone services
- Mobile data services
- Paging
- Personal communications services
- Satellite-based mobile services (incl. e.g. telephony, data, paging, and/or PCS)
- Fixed satellite services
- VSAT services

- Gateway earthstation services
- Teleconferencing
- Video transport
- Trunked radio system services

Categories covered by basic telecommunication commitments, unless otherwise specified:

- Local
- Long distance
- International
- Wire-based (including, e.g., all types of cables and, usually, radio portions of fixed infrastructure)
- Radio-based (all forms of wireless, including satellite)
- On a resale basis (non-facilities based supply)
- Facilities-based supply
- For public use (i.e. services that must be made available to the public generally)
- For non-public use (e.g. services provided for sale to closed user groups)

Value added telecommunication services:

Value added telecommunication services are telecommunications for which suppliers "add value" to the customer's information by enhancing its form or content or by providing for its storage and retrieval.

　Examples:

- On-line data processing
- On-line data base storage and retrieval
- Electronic data interchange
- Email
- Voice mail

Source: These materials are taken directly from the WTO website.

A key provision on scheduling is that it is "technology neutral." Unless a country takes an explicit exception, for example, a commitment to allow competitive provision of data services applies to both satellite and fiber-optic delivered data. Scheduling a basic telecom service, like packet-switched data transmission or fax services, implies coverage of local, long distance, and international service unless a country takes a specific exception.

RESTRICTIONS ON MARKET ACCESS

Many countries are willing to offer market access with some significant exceptions. They must state those exceptions in their schedule of market-access commitments. Box 10.3 provides an example for Korea. If a country wishes to restrict the total number of licenses for basic telecommunications carriers, it must note that. Many countries have a restriction based on availability of spectrum for commitments on wireless-mobile services. Some countries have restrictions on how international networks may connect to the national network in order to make it easier to monitor and control this traffic exchange. (We discuss the economic incentives for this choice in our discussion of settlement rates.)

Box 10.3. Korea's Final Schedule of Commitments on Telecom at the WTO

- As of 1998, liberalizes and permits foreign investment in wireline-based telephone services never before opened to full competition. Limits direct foreign equity ownership of facilities-based operators set to 33% (20% limit for Korea Telecom). Full competition permitted in non-facilities based provision (resale) of all telecom services as of 1998, except voice which will be permitted in 2001 (source: TIA online).
- Reference: Status of Liberalization and Deregulation of the Facilities-based Service Market (KISDI White Paper 2002).

Korea's final schedule of commitment in WTO agreement (source: KISDI, Dec. 2002)

	Before final request	WTO final request (February, 1997)
Limitation on foreign ownership	Wireline: prohibited / Wireless: 33% (Ownership of a person) Wireline: 10% / Wireless: 33%, KT: 1%)	From 1999, both Wireline and Wireless: 33% / KT: 20% From 2001, both Wireline and Wireless: 49% / KT: 33% *(Ownership of a person) Wireline: 10% / Wireless: 33% / KT: 3%
Largest foreign shareholder	Prohibited Representative: prohibited	Permitted from 1999 (except KT)
Foreign representative/board of directors	Board of directors: no more than 1/3	No limitation from 1998
Voice resale services interconnected to PTTN	Prohibited	Permitted from 1999 (foreign ownership restricted to 49%)
Resale Others	No limitation	Permitted to 100% from 1998
Number of service suppliers	RFP (Request for proposal)— a priori limitation	Restriction allowed only in case of frequency limitation
Cross-border service supply	Restriction possible	Permitted subject to the commercial arrangement with domestic licensed service suppliers Voice resale service interconnected to PTTN: until Dec. 31, 2000, permitted only by establishment of a company (legal person) within Korea
Regulatory principles	Application of domestic regulatory principles	Application of regulatory principles in Reference paper
One-way satellite transmission of DTH and DBS television services and of digital audio services	Restriction possible	No commitments

Source: WTO Agreement Korea, February 2004.

"PHASE IN" PERIODS

Countries may also decide that they are willing to make changes in the market, but refuse to do so all at once. They can schedule "phase-in" periods. As long as this takes place during a reasonable period, trade partners accept them. Moreover, by setting a binding future date for competition, a country encourages current local suppliers to begin improving their efficiency at once.

Some service commitments are ambiguous. Inevitably, technology and new business models challenge some of the categories in any scheduling system. For example, did the BTA commitment on voice services cover the Internet-based voice services? China, for example, specifically agreed upon accession to the WTO that voice-service commitments included Internet-based voice. But it phased in competition on all international voice services over a several-year period.

The WTO Reference Paper: A Major Achievement

A major achievement of the 1997 Agreement was the creation of the "Reference Paper" on pro-competitive regulatory principles, which was accepted by 67 countries making binding offers on market access (Arena, 1997). (The "Reference Paper" was scheduled as an "additional commitment" in national offers under Article 18 of the GATS.)[6] (See Box 10.4.)

Countries created the Reference Paper for two reasons. First, the negotiations were an opportunity to create a firm set of common understandings of how competition, or a transition to competition, must be governed. The principles are sufficiently broad to allow for diverse rules and practices but sufficiently specific to hold governments accountable for the fundamentals of market-oriented regulation. Second, countries distrusted any market-access commitment that was not backed up by enforceable rights in regard to the "invisible" barriers to competition and market access. In the telecommunications sector, a government's commitments to free trade may not be strong enough to guarantee real market access for foreign suppliers of services because of the high levels of market power. Monopolistic suppliers could frustrate competition from new foreign entrants despite trade liberalization commitments. The obligations of governments to create effective interconnection rules separate the regulator from the operator, and create a transparent decision process with rules that were least burdensome for competition are at the core of the principles.

---

[6] Arguably, countries bound themselves to competition principles in the general GATS framework. But what they meant for telecoms in practice could have become the basis for endless debate (as they already were in practice in industrial countries with competitive markets). The BTA negotiators agreed that there needed to be a specific translation of the GATS framework into more specific guidelines for telecoms.

Box 10.4. The WTO Reference Paper

The WTO Reference Paper has the following features. This summary reflects the major intent of the Reference Paper. It may also be noted that every country with market-access obligations also has further obligations under the GATS because the telecommunications agreement operates as an industry-specific code under this framework.

1. The regulatory body is separate from the operators and must employ procedures that assure impartiality in regard to all market participants. This obligation does not specify the form of the regulator—it can be an independent commission or a cabinet ministry—but it must be totally separate from the operators and must have transparent and objective procedures for creating and applying its licensing and regulatory policies. The criteria for licensing must be made available by the regulator. The regulator also must act on certain regulatory obligations, such as interconnection, in a reasonable period of time. Inadequate staffing and enforcement problems have frustrated some regulators in meeting these obligations.

2. It creates obligations for governments concerning their regulation of "major suppliers" of telecommunications services who have market power. A major supplier controls "essential facilities" for the public network that "cannot feasibly be economically or technically substituted in order to provide a service." Thus, the Paper is focusing on regulatory treatment of the dominant incumbent carrier. (As competition unfolds, most regulators define a threshold for defining when a dominant incumbent loses market power. One threshold is loss of 50 per cent of the defined market, such as domestic long distance service to households.) It does not demand, and implicitly discourages, symmetric treatment under regulation of the former monopolist and new entrants. In most cases new entrants do not have the power in the marketplace to restrict competition that would qualify a firm as a "major supplier."[1] However, at the insistence of the E.U., the regulatory principles recognize that suppliers may act collectively to exercise market power.

3. Governments must take measures to assure that major suppliers do not engage in anti-competitive practices, such as anti-competitive cross-subsidies, use of information obtained from competitors, or withholding timely technical information needed by competitors.

4. Governments will assure interconnection with a major supplier for competitors at any technically feasible point in the networks. The terms, conditions, and quality must be non-discriminatory (no less favorable to the competitor than the operating company of the major supplier). Interconnection must be timely and done at "cost-oriented rates that are transparent, reasonable, having regard to economic feasibility, and sufficiently unbundled so that the supplier need not pay for network components or facilities that it does not require for the service to be provided." The terms for interconnection must be publicly available and enforceable on a timely basis.

5. Governments may maintain policy measures designed to achieve universal service. However, they must be administered in ways that are transparent, non-discriminatory and competitively neutral. They should not be more burdensome than necessary to achieve the specific goal for universal service.

6. Governments will use procedures for the allocation and use of scare resources, including radio frequencies (plus telephone numbers and rights of way), that are timely, objective, transparent and non-discriminatory. This provision recognizes that spectrum allocation and assignment are difficult and controversial regulatory tasks. Therefore, the primary obligations are non-discrimination and transparency in a timely licensing system. Transparency includes making public how the spectrum is currently allocated and licensed.

Note: [1] There are cases when new entrants may have market power. The U.K. has ruled, for example, that all mobile-network operators have market power in regard to calls terminating into customers on their own networks. There are no substitutable sources of supply. In a calling-party pay system (used in most countries for mobile), the receiving party is indifferent to the cost charged for terminating a call. So, there is no countervailing market power to that exercised by the network operator. The United States has similarly ruled that competitors to incumbent local phone operators cannot abuse their control over termination of calls to their customers.
Source: Adapted from Cowhey and Klimenko (2002). Also see Sherman (1998).

The Interconnection Consensus in the Reference Paper

- Interconnection policy is the bedrock for regulating the transition to competition. The incumbent controlling the "essential" facility may try to deny access to customers to its rivals. The interconnection policy requires incumbents with essential facilities to share network economies with new entrants on economically efficient terms. (Noam, 2001; Laffont and Tirole, 1998) In addition to setting pricing rules, the policy ensures that non-price discrimination does not hamper entry. For example, new entrants need reasonable flexibility in choosing among the dominant carrier's network features. In addition, interconnection policies must address all the major barriers to entry. For example, customers do not want to change phone numbers in order to switch carrier services. A lack of local number portability will result in customer inertia.

- Interconnection policies are a transitional measure to deal with the market power of the traditional incumbent. As a complex form of regulatory micro-management of the market, this policy inevitably has costs. Some believe that it discourages investment by the dominant carrier (often called a "major supplier" in trade pacts), especially in new technologies (such as broadband service for residences). Others believe that it induces "too much" market entry (i.e. by setting the price of interconnection too low, it induces entry in the market that is not economically efficient). Yet it is equally clear that dominant carriers do have significant market power and often have an incentive to employ that power to discourage new entrants. Their position as a significant factor in the national stock market of transitional economies and as large national employers further bolsters their political influence.

- Disputes over interconnection. Requirements for interconnection go to the heart of competition, so vigorous disputes over its precise terms are to be expected. These regulatory and judicial disputes (especially in the United States) have created the impression in developing countries that there is no consensus on the correct principles and terms for the policy. But in fact a fundamental consensus exists in policies in industrial countries. Interconnection policy sets pricing for interconnection based on some version of long-run incremental costs. It requires the timely provision of leased-transmission circuit capacity, significant unbundling of the network elements available for interconnection, nondiscriminatory access to rights of way, and portability for telephone numbers when subscribers decide to switch carriers. And this policy uses a process featuring direct negotiations among commercial parties and a timely dispute-resolution mechanism that allows the regulator, relying on existing guidelines (such as the reference interconnection offer required in the E.U.) to settle matters that cannot be resolved during the commercial negotiations (Cowhey and Klimenko, 2002). Some trade agreements are including phrasing that gives support to this approach.

Disputes over interconnection pricing in industrial countries, for example, may focus on whether the basic form of interconnection between two local networks should cost $0.01 or $0.05 per call. However, the fury generated by these disputes has created the mistaken impression in many developing countries that estimates of costs in industrial countries vary wildly. Similarly, disputes arise over the precise range of elements of the network's functions that must be unbundled and available to new entrants, even though a consensus exists that several elements do in fact require unbundling.

- Setting costs for interconnection. Determining the costs of incumbents reliably is difficult, especially if we pay some attention to historic costs. The necessary data are simply missing in most countries. But there is no reason not to use some form of international benchmarking to help determine interconnection costs. A big enough pool of countries now exists to provide an appropriate reference group that can then be adjusted.

- Phasing out the obligation. As competition unfolds, specific market segments may no longer require interconnection rules. Local phone services still require interconnection but in some industrial countries broadband services to the home may no longer require interconnection rules.[7] This ability to phase out is clearly implicit in the BTA, but subsequent trade agreements have made the point explicit (Sherman, 2004).

- Interconnecting wired and wireless networks. The BTA negotiators focused their attention on wired to wired network connections when discussing obligations for interconnection. The growing magnitude of mobile and wireless networks has begun to concentrate attention on the interconnection of wired to wireless networks. Bilateral and regional trade agreements since the BTA more clearly state the interconnection obligations between the two types of networks (Sherman, 2004).

For a variety of reasons, most countries have treated these connections asymmetrically in favor of wireless operators. The wired network pays a high charge to terminate on the wireless network, but not vice versa. As the British regulator, Ofcom, has noted, the mobile wireless operators individually and collectively may be able to exercise market power to keep mobile termination charges high. And, as mobile becomes a significant share of all traffic, this means that wired networks have to terminate onto the mobile networks. Ofcom has now declared that this arrangement in Great Britain constitutes anti-competitive behavior. The U.S. is also examining the impact of high mobile termination charges in other countries on U.S. consumers, and the European Union is

---

[7] Regulators rightly pay attention to the costs of regulation. Interconnection rules are cumbersome and never perfect. At some point, there may be enough competition in network infrastructure to support broadband that, even if less than perfect, may justify reducing requirements for interconnection for broadband services. In this case the logic is that the costs of the regulation outweigh the remaining benefits of overcoming limited weaknesses in competition.

examining the problem within the E.U.[8] A variation on this problem is the use of high termination charges for roaming internationally over mobile networks. We discuss this in the context of international charging arrangements.

WIRELESS RESALE OPERATORS

Countries may be reluctant to encourage the build-out of more than three or four mobile-network infrastructures for various reasons (either based on estimates of the viability of large numbers of competitors with major infrastructure costs or concerns about the availability of adequate spectrum). In these countries there are still benefits for consumers from more suppliers. Thus, it may be desirable to allow the creation of operators who resell the services of infrastructure networks (often called mobile virtual network operators, or MVNOs). This should be seen as the mobile equivalent to resale and value added service networks. In the Doha Round, negotiators have to clarify if mobile services are understood to be subject to interconnection principles and if they are covered by market access commitments on resale.

Universal Service as a Key Challenge under the Reference Paper

The network build out challenge. Universal service is one of the most sensitive questions on telecoms for any trade negotiator. A brief review of fundamentals about universal service helps clarify the meaning of BTA commitments.

The demand for more network capacity is huge in transitional and developing economies. The traditional indicators of unfilled demand, such as waiting lists for phone service, vastly underestimate the actual pent-up demand. These indicators do not capture the large numbers of people who do not bother registering for telephone service and the even larger numbers who utilize capacity fully because of counter-productive pricing. When demand is unfilled, consumers lose.

---

[8] The European Commission has also declared that mobile-network operators have significant market power in regard to call termination on their networks. In the U.S. the "receiving party pays" system for charging means that consumers may exit if the networks charges a high fee for termination. Under the "calling party pays" system outside of the U.S., there is no incentive for the party receiving a call to care about high termination rates. A variation on this problem is the use of high termination charges for roaming internationally over mobile networks. Sherman (2004) points out that the U.S. FTAs in recent years have explicitly exempted mobile operators from regulation of termination charges. See Cowhey (2004), Ofcom (2003 decision), and E.U. decision (2003).

Inefficient subsidies and pricing. There are widespread concerns about the effect of trade liberalization on universal service. However, irrespective of the degree of competition, the usual mechanisms for providing universal service can become the enemy of greater economic efficiency and faster build-out. For example, the common practice of keeping local rates below costs to encourage universal service simply discourages investment in building out the local network.[9] This type of protection for consumers treats the wrong problem and also discourages investment in adequate network infrastructure. Low prices do no good if there is no network to provide the service.

Other rate distortions created in the name of equity significantly hinder the efficient provision of communications services and create political disincentives for competition. For example, relying on subsidies from urban to rural areas (a byproduct of geographic price averaging) can mean that poor urban workers subsidize phone services for the country estates of business leaders. Meanwhile, incumbent operators have a powerful political weapon to use against introducing competition: the argument that new entrants are likely to serve only urban areas (thus "skimming the cream" from the market).[10]

Keeping local rates artificially low also creates incentives to inflate the prices of domestic and international long-distance services (including data services). Inflated prices for these services constitute a significant tax on business. The extremely high cost of international calling is a barrier to small firms interested in export-oriented growth. All countries suffer from inflated rates for international services, including the United States. But the situation in virtually every developing country is far worse than it is in industrial countries. Rates for international services to and from most developing countries are so high that they are equivalent to a tariff of 100 to 500 percent on communications and data services. These escalated prices act as strong disincentives in the creation of an information-based economy.

The challenge is to move to cost-based rates for all services. Such rates will make investment in providing services economically viable. Coupled with competition among networks (wired and wireless) cost-oriented pricing will do much to extend the geographic coverage of networks. Changes in the global market for cross-border communications services will surely speed changes in the communications market domestically. Rate rebalancing will have to occur. Rebalancing often leads to short-term discomfort because of such effects as increases in the cost of local phone services. But rebalancing also makes it easier to manage the other economic fundamentals of this market transition, such as building out local networks that adopt new technologies more quickly (and thus enabling better and less expensive services). Rebalancing means that the cost of local service prices may rise (at least in some regions of a country), but many other prices will decline and tap significant

---

[9] Using revenues from long distance services to subsidize universal service (as is done in the United States) is also a bad idea because it distorts pricing and economic incentives for network development.

[10] A geographically averaged rate, which inflates prices for urban areas, makes entry into urban areas quite profitable. See Laffont and Tirole (1998).

demand elasticity.[11] One reason why mobile networks have been superseding wired ones in poor countries is because regulators treated them as premium services that did not require detailed price controls. For example, mobile pre-paid services are more cost effective for the poor and are a logical complement to rebalancing the rates for local wired services in order to make financing wired networks more feasible.[12] Vodacom of South Africa has discovered, for example, that demand for services outside of major cities in sub-Saharan Africa is much greater than predicted and capable of sustaining wider network build-out. (See Cowhey and Klimenko, 2002) for a longer discussion of rate rebalancing and universal service.)

HOW DO TRADE COMMITMENTS INFLUENCE THESE POLICY CHALLENGES?

Under the BTA regulatory principles, governments may maintain policy measures designed to achieve universal service. However, they must be administered in ways that are transparent, non-discriminatory and competitively neutral. They should not be more burdensome than necessary to achieve the specific goal for universal service.

The good news is that the BTA is consistent with a vigorous improvement in universal service policies that is sensitive to market-transition challenges in a particular country. Consider the implication of the Reference Paper principles for the challenge of reform of the subsidy system. Regulatory reform can advance universal service by making any system of subsidies more efficient, and therefore getting more output for the expenditure. For example, regulators have learned that making subsidies transparent, cost-oriented and less distorting of competition (as required in the Reference Paper) often forces financial reform. Some have gone further. Chile, for example, auctions subsidies off to the phone carrier offering the most build-out of the network in a rural region.

One frequently discussed challenge involves controversies over the pricing of new services made possible by technological innovation. Regulators can become mired in arguments about the cost of special services such as Internet video-conferencing. There is no perfect solution to such issues, but they are manageable under BTA commitments to competition. The Reference Paper does not forbid adapting universal service rules to new circumstances as long as the methods are competitively neutral, least burdensome, and transparent. All of these provisions induce the regulator to seek the most cost

---

[11] A corollary policy measure is greater flexibility for operators in setting prices. Price caps for broader baskets of services are one way of achieving this goal. As competition is introduced it is especially desirable to allow more flexibility in pricing plans for local services.

[12] This is a complex subject. Increasing prices for local wired line calls may cause subscribers to drop off the network but permit build-out because total revenues increase (Hodge, 2003). Mobile pre-paid services substitute for the wired ones for the poor. Such a subsidy, bundled into the calling party pay system, needs to be made transparent, cost-oriented, and competitively neutral.

efficient measures to promote universal service. In practice, voice over the Internet, VoIP, is the most prominent issue. Recall that it is arguably a value added computer service exempt from restrictions and pricing for traditional voice services (whose pricing is usually manipulated for universal service goals). Even if treated as a value added service, a country can still impose a requirement to finance universal service as long as it meets the criteria of the Reference Paper (e.g. transparent and least burdensome).[13] Whether or not a country should schedule a specific exemption on this matter in order to clarify its freedom to act is a matter of debate. In general, the wording of such restrictions is likely to be more of a source of misunderstanding than added protection.

Benefits of BTA for Dealing with World Capital Markets and Foreign Investors

A major problem for developing countries is that they often pay a premium for foreign capital investment due to "risk premiums" assessed by investors doubting the reliability of the national rules governing investment and market conduct (Levy and Spiller, 1996). When countries make major changes in regard to these rules, it often drives up the premium even if there may be merit to the specific choice.

The BTA Regulatory Principles can help establish flexible regulation that is credible. There are advantages of a phase-in road map, but it is not disastrous if initial decisions are wrong because, like privatizations with overly long monopoly periods, the disciplines of the WTO and the dispute system mean that changes in policy are transparent (including publicly available criteria for licensing), not random, usually tempered by some compensation, and explainable to the marketplace as not a signal that policy will be lightly reversed.

International Settlement Rates: A Particular Challenge to Interpreting Market Access and the Reference Paper

Why was this such a large issue? The traditional international regime for telecommunications services had created a system for international-switched telephone services that were fundamentally anti-competitive. For decades, rules backed by the International

---

[13] Many countries have created, at least temporarily, a "safe harbor" for the prices of new services over the Internet because of pricing inefficiencies in traditional communications services. Why visit the sins of the past on emerging technology? However, if regulators wish to impose universal service obligations on Internet telephony, for example, they may do so.

Telecommunications Union (ITU) sanctioned the "joint supply" of international phone services using accounting rates. An accounting rate is the negotiated transfer price for end-to-end international services jointly supplied by two national carriers. (Carriers conduct these negotiations and conclude a commercial contract to establish this accounting rate.)[14] Each carrier theoretically contributes half of the international switched (phone or fax) service (for example, taking the international call from a hypothetical mid-point in the ocean for out-bound traffic, and terminating the call to a local household in its country for in-bound traffic). For contributing this service, the national carrier is entitled to a fee usually equivalent to half of the accounting rate. This is the settlement rate. (We shall refer only to the settlement rate because it is the economically relevant concept.) Given that carriers negotiated the settlement rate on a bilateral basis, it is no surprise that these revenues created large economic profits.[15] A carrier more interested in making money from terminating international calls than originating them could use its monopoly control over termination to press carriers and press for large profits because networks are more valuable to all users if the network serves additional users.[16] In addition, the high profits gave countries an incentive to restrict competition, thus slowing innovation and build-out of global networks. This situation was particularly worrisome for U.S. carriers because the U.S. was at the hub of global multinational business networks and it had a population with strong immigrant roots. So, U.S. carriers had customers who especially prized global connectivity and the traditional system both increased prices and slowed innovation.[17]

---

[14] As an inter-carrier transfer price, the accounting rate is not the end price to consumers. Consumer prices traditionally had an additional large mark-up. On the traditional system, see Cowhey and Richards (1999) and Zacher and Sutton (1996).

[15] For example, global networking by AT&T required the use of a complementary asset in a foreign country that was controlled by a local monopolist. That created market power for foreign partners. Carriers controlling infrastructure essential to the provision of services have the incentive and variety of means to exercise market power. During the time of the development of the global-network infrastructure, some countries could threaten not to build out their network infrastructure (e.g. phone switches). Even after developing infrastructure, countries could threaten to disrupt service for a variety of reasons (ranging from poor maintenance to claims of protection of national sovereignty).

[16] On the value of the network to other users, see Shapiro and Varian (1998) and Noam (2001).

[17] Even though the settlement rate is not the end price to consumers, it influences consumer prices because of the net-settlement payment. For example, suppose the U.S. sent ten minutes of calls to Mexico at a settlement rate of fifty cents per minute and Mexico sent the U.S. a total of five minutes of calls at this rate. Then, the net-settlement payment from the U.S. to Mexico in this period was $2.50. The U.S. carrier had to recover this payment of $2.50 from its own customers, a significant cost element in its pricing decision (i.e. it significantly increased the cost for international services). In 1995, U.S. carriers made $5.4 billion in net-settlement payments to other countries, and this total was about $6 billion in 1997. Besides driving up rates for U.S. consumers, the FCC calculated that roughly 70% of the total net settlement payments represented a subsidy paid by U.S. consumers to foreign carriers. The average settlement rate paid by U.S. carriers in 1996 was 39 cents per minute; outside the OECD area and Mexico the average cost for U.S. carriers was well over 60 cents per minute in 1996 (Lande and Blake, 1997). To illustrate the problem with market performance from the viewpoint of consumer welfare, in August 1997 (after over a dozen years of competition) the FCC estimated that the average price of an international phone call from the U.S. was 88 cents per minute, compared to 13 cents for domestic long distance (Cowhey, 1999). These price differences existed despite

The BTA agreement opened the way to allowing competition in the provision of services across national borders, thus breaking the monopoly on termination of incoming foreign calls, and correcting this problem. However, during a transition to competition globally, it was possible that WTO members who retained monopolies on international services could manipulate the newly open markets in OECD nations' international services to increase the profits that they collected off international services. (This was called the "one way bypass problem in trade circles.) For this reason the United States took a unilateral regulatory measure after the BTA to impose price caps (called benchmarks) on what U.S. carriers could pay to foreign carriers for termination. (See Cowhey and Richards, 1999) This was intended to reduce profit levels on foreign termination very substantially, thereby reducing the incentives to manipulate international traffic flows in and out of the United States. This reduced the profitability of international traffic substantially, much to the displeasure of developing countries.

To the surprise of many analysts, the FCC price caps did not draw a WTO challenge. There were two reasons. Most countries had different settlement rates for different countries. The non-discrimination and MFN rules of the GATS might make different rates for the same termination service illegal. Therefore, the BTA negotiators agreed to a standstill where no country would make a WTO challenge on any settlement rate issue for two years. By this time the U.S. had already changed the market. In addition, the U.S. framed its regulation in such a manner that it likely would have withstood a WTO challenge because it was designed to stop anti-competitive behavior in a manner consistent with most favored nation and national treatment criteria.

New challenges on international services. Although trade negotiators might hear about the Benchmarks of the U.S., this has become largely a dispute at the margin of trade negotiations. Three new issues are of concern for current negotiations.

First, the interaction of market-access commitments and the Reference Paper for the delivery of international service is significant. Even if the FCC Benchmarks capped the level of settlement rates, these rates remained substantially profitable and many countries are reluctant to eliminate these profits immediately through full-scale competition. Thus, they seek some of the benefits of greater competition (more infrastructure build-out and consumer choices on quality and terms of service) while limiting erosion of settlement rates. To do so, Mexico, for example, allowed competition in both domestic and international long-distance services in its WTO offer both through leasing transmission capacity and building own network. But it put restrictions on its offer that it believed would give Telmex, the former monopolist, exclusive power to negotiate the settlement rates for Mexico. And it also restricted delivery of end-to-end international

---

negligible differences in the costs of transmission between the two types of calls. U.S. rates for international service were generally the lowest in the world, but they were still grossly inflated. The FCC believed that the efficient cost of termination for a minute of switched service (the function paid for by a settlement rate) was no higher than five to ten cents. In fact, it was probably closer to two to three cents.

services by international simple resale (which, by definition, was a service outside of the settlement-rate system) with a reservation on its market commitment. The United States, which paid nearly $700 million in settlement costs to Mexico, took Mexico to dispute resolution. Pending resolution of the Appeals process, the WTO has ruled against Mexico's efforts to restrict the bypass of settlement rates (by allowing U.S. carriers to lease circuits to carry their own traffic) and to give Telmex, the dominant carrier, sole authority to negotiate the settlement rates on behalf of all carriers, which violated Mexico's commitments on market access. The Reference Paper was read to require non-discrimination in the provision of interconnection to the domestic long-distance market and to forbid the handing of such power over settlement rates to the dominant supplier.

Second, carriers outside the United States have complained that U.S. carriers have exercised market power in regard to Internet traffic in and out of the United States. To simplify greatly, many users in Australia (for example) want access to U.S. websites. Far fewer users in the U.S. wanted access to websites in Australia. So, U.S. carriers through 2001 took the view that they would deliver traffic to and from U.S. websites for an Australian carrier at no charge if the Australian carrier agreed to transport the web traffic to and from the U.S. for both their users and for American users wanting to visit Australian websites. This is a rough description, but it gets to the heart of the two issues that have made Internet traffic exchange (ITE) at the global level both sensitive and hard to grasp. First, unlike settlement rates, the international exchange described above did not require the United States to share the cost of international transport. The foreign carrier provided all of the international transport capacity. The U.S. carrier only provided transport around the United States, a service that used to be bundled with provision of half of the international transport capacity under the settlement-rate system. This revision took place just as the United States was undermining the traditional settlement rate and jointly supplied service system that required carriers to share international transport costs. Many countries concluded that the United States intended to use its market power to force foreign carriers to shoulder a disproportionate share of international network costs. Protests over this commercial arrangement led to diplomatic disputes about what came to be called International Charging Arrangements for Internet Services (ICAIS). As explained in Annex 1 to this chapter, in terms of WTO diplomacy, these disputes would fall under the competition obligations of each country in regard to international transport. However, market changes since 2001 are causing this issue to ebb as commercial contracts change rapidly, the cost of transport continues to plummet, and less and less traffic requires transport to the United States (in part because services like Yahoo now put their web servers in each major geographic region).

Third, many industrial countries are now examining the merits of claims that mobile operators have significant market power in regard to terminating incoming calls. Under a "calling party pays" system the recipient of a call is indifferent to such charges. U.S.

international carriers estimate that around 22 per cent of their traffic to other countries now terminates on a mobile network. If the fees for termination are substantially above competitive levels, then some U.S. carriers are urging "benchmarks" for mobile termination fees in other countries.[18] There are complicated issues involved in assessing these claims and remedies. However, the initial positions of several major regulatory authorities indicate that this will be a major issue. Developing countries will have to assess their commitments on access for international services and interconnection in light of this growing controversy.

Standard Setting and Equipment Certification

Standard setting and equipment certification for compliance with codes on safety, reliability, and compatibility with the network remain critical for governments' retention of power over markets. These activities are largely covered by other WTO codes. But, two examples show how services intersect with these powers.

First, standard setting usually is undertaken by government or the private sector within a framework stipulated or recognized by government. A key turning point in the provision of communications services is the decision to liberalize competition in the equipment that enables the services, especially customer equipment such as mobile handsets or modems. Countries embracing competition rely on the approach called "no harm to the network" in certifying equipment for usage in their country. There are well established international practices to guide implementing this approach, which basically sets the onus on equipment makers to avoid harming the network rather than micromanaging the vendors. A somewhat more complicated, but again well established, set of practices guide certification of equipment using radio frequencies for compliance with non-interference guidelines. The satellite-service providers are extremely sensitive to the risk that they could hold a license to provide service in a country but not have the necessary approvals needed to certify, and thus sell, their equipment.

Second, a larger question is how to set standards for the network. The common phrase for emphasizing the private sector's role is that "standards should be voluntary, transparent, and industry led." However, sometimes governments will stipulate a mandatory standard for a service that implicitly or explicitly limits the range of service competition options. One prominent example in second generation mobile services is that the European Union made GSM into a mandatory standard for Europe while the United States allowed any technology meeting non-interference specifications, opening

---

[18] Typically the foreign wired operator imposes a surcharge on the U.S. carrier for passing the call on to the mobile network.

the way to CDMA systems. In general, the trend is away from mandatory standards in competitive service markets except in well defined exceptions.

Spectrum Allocation and Licensing

The WTO formula is to embrace a transparent, least burdensome and competitively neutral approach to spectrum licensing but let prior licensing decisions stand. Negotiators shied away from anything that would restrict national options from allocating spectrum as long as decisions were taken transparently. That said, there are at least four issues about spectrum licensing that need to be examined by developing countries and will be subject to inquiry in the bilateral negotiations that form the heart of WTO negotiations.

First, has the country established a national spectrum plan that is transparent? Are the processes that establish the plan transparent? Second, does the country embrace spectrum licenses that are service and technology neutral? Industrial countries are moving to the view that economic efficiency suggests, and technology now permits, that spectrum licenses should have fewer major conditions. For example, whether a spectrum band should be used for voice or data ought to be up to the licensee as long as it meets non-interference rules. The same applies to technology. While many countries still require a mandatory technology standard for a particular service, that approach is beginning to decline. Technology is too complex and fast moving to have governments try to micro-manage such matters if not absolutely necessary. Third, can spectrum licenses be transferred on a commercial basis among private actors? A resale market in spectrum is an additional commitment that a country could schedule in the BTA. Fourth, will more of the spectrum be set aside for unlicensed purposes, subject only to restrictions on power use or the design of receiving equipment or to avoid interference? There is no way to schedule such a policy in terms of a BTA commitment easily, but major trading partners will still want to know about the policy. They may also probe the policy concerning the interconnection of services provided on unlicensed bands and those on licensed bands.

Cross-country Evidence from Developing Country Case Studies

Today, there is a powerful need for countries to be plugged into cheap and powerful global data networking and communications. To be part of a global firm's global supply chain that supplies goods and services on demand, countries and companies must be connected and interconnected. From Benetton to Wal-Mart, firms that do not have instantaneous links to their production processes, warehouses, and distribution networks are out of the loop. For example, Wal-Mart, a giant buyer of Chinese goods, insists that all of their suppliers can interact with it via modern data communications.

Similarly, unless countries keep up with technological innovation, a niche advantage today can be gone tomorrow. One early innovator, Barbados, made important inroads by persuading American Airlines to locate their data entry operations there. America Airlines hired and trained entry-level workers, some of whom went on to establish their own enterprises. Further, to transport the daily receipts to Barbados, the airline flew on non-stop flight from New York, which boosted tourism. As technology proceeded, the data entry business vanished, but Barbados had a leg up for further progress. A more striking example is India that is currently benefiting from its investment in high technology education. Bangalore has emerged as a global software leader and the advent of affordable global communications and networks has boosted India as a global technology power, customer service center and as a prime destination for outsourcing.

The Internet has further propelled the importance of communications and information technology because it enables small businesses, rural villages, and residences to use information to improve their economic and social options. There is considerable case study evidence of the benefits of information kiosks for farmers trying to get better terms of trade through more accurate information on market prices and demand. More significantly, perhaps, there is evidence that web hosting is a powerful tool for boosting the export performance of less developed countries because information significantly shapes patterns of trade (Freund and Weinhold, 2000).

More generally, experience from around the world is quite clear that greater competition in the provision of telecommunications services results in better performance than monopoly provision of the same services. Competition generally leads to lower prices, improved service, more widespread access, and more rapid expansion of capacity, including Internet penetration (Petrazzini and Guerrero, 2000). The BTA accelerated, but did not guarantee the introduction of competition in various segments of the telecommunications market in developing countries. Ultimately countries embrace competition not because they are urged to do so by outsiders, but because it is perceived to be in their own best interest. The BTA and other treaties provide a justification for developing countries to act to limit the power of incumbent monopolists and an outside commitment to blame for doing what they want and need to do anyway, but without internal desire nothing will happen. Trade commitments also enhance the credibility of market reforms, and thus they earn higher rewards for countries in the global markets for investment capital and talented people. In Annex 2, two country cases from different regions—Ghana and South Korea—illustrate the opportunities and pitfalls of competition.

The Lay of the Land for the Doha Telecom Negotiations and Beyond

Much of the substance of telecommunications negotiation is technical and bilateral. These bilateral exchanges generally take the form of asking and answering detailed questions about the regulations of each others' market. Trade negotiators therefore need a keen understanding of what the rules in their own countries actually are. To be able to negotiate successfully, a delegation must have a detailed grasp of the key issues, be well-versed in the intricacies of their own rules, and a clear position. To be a player in multilateral negotiations, a nation and its negotiators must really understand the subtleties of what is taking place. Delegations that play it by ear will not be taken seriously and are likely to be written off as wasting everyone's time.

In most negotiations, the United States and E.U. take the role of the "demandeur." They ask for concessions and are usually quite open about what they might be willing to give in return. They are relatively transparent. In the realm of telecommunications in the Doha negotiating round, the United States and E.U. have emphasized their desire to achieve global, low cost connectivity. As in the past, the United States and E.U. also seek the removal of remaining national restrictions on foreign investment in the telecommunications and other sectors. The United States presumably would like to use details of regulatory policy to help achieve these goals. Conceivably, the United States also may consider using WTO negotiations to remove restrictions on wireless markets. The E.U. and the U.S. will presumably seek to use discussions of the Reference Paper and other trade agreements to advance an understanding of regulation close to their approach in order to make obligations of the Reference Paper more explicit and the mechanisms for assuring transparent effective regulation clearer.

A more intriguing question is whether or not the more prosperous of the non-OECD industrial nations will become leaders in seeking market opening through trade negotiations. Some developing countries wish to gain access to the markets of other developing countries in the process of the negotiation, mostly to extend their regional position. These factors are likely to be especially prominent in regional trade negotiations.

In the end, the most important task for the negotiator from a developing country is to work with those regulating the domestic market in order to have a coherent reform strategy. The goal is to use the trade negotiation to take on the politically hard choices of market change while getting higher return from international markets for these choices. This added return will occur by using a template of global reform to simplify some choices and using the binding nature of trade commitments to convince global markets that reforms are credible and domestic skeptics that future choices are now being formulated around new policy equilibrium.

Annex 1

THE ICAIS (INTERNATIONAL CHARGES FOR ACCESS TO INTERNET SERVICES) CONTROVERSY

The ICAIS controversy largely involves how U.S. carriers charge for international traffic to U.S. websites although it could apply to other countries. This Box briefly explains the issue and how the existing market-access commitments under the BTA would apply.

Internet web traffic between countries requires networks taking traffic from one country to the other. In mid-1996, for example, it was common that a user in one country would want something from a web-hosting server in another country and then (after getting information from the server) need the information to be sent back to its home computer. Given the early U.S. dominance of the web and its content, far more traffic seeking access to websites came into the United States than went out to the rest of the world. Reinforcing the balance of demand for U.S. content was the pricing and capacity structure for data transport internationally. Earlier competition and higher capacity demands led the United States to become the hub of international data networking. Internet traffic between two points within Europe or within Asia frequently transited through the United States in order to move at higher speed and lower costs.[19] The traffic flow of the Internet was the opposite of switched international services (that is, the United States received more traffic than it sent out), especially through the end of the 1990s.

A few major backbone data networks, called Tier I carriers, dominated long-haul Internet traffic in the mid-1990s. They agreed to "peer," or exchange traffic, with other Tier I carriers without charge. Typically, these networks charged smaller, regional and local networks for long-haul traffic transport. When U.S. carriers signed contracts with many foreign networks, they treated them as something more than a regional network but less than a true peer. For example, a U.S. backbone carrier might insist that an Asian carrier agree to be responsible for transporting all of the traffic of the U.S. carrier and the Asian carrier between the two countries. In return, the U.S. carrier would agree that once the Asian carrier's traffic arrived in Los Angeles, the U.S. carrier would transport it anywhere in the continental United States and bring the reply back to Los Angeles, where the Asian carrier would transport it back to its home country.

This is a rough description but it gets to the heart of the two issues that have made Internet traffic exchange (ITE) at the global level both sensitive and hard to grasp. First, unlike settlement rates, the international exchange described above did not require the United States to share the cost of international transport. The foreign carrier provided all of the international transport capacity. The U.S. carrier only provided transport around the

---

[19] TeleGeography, Hubs and Spokes: A Telegeography Internet Reader (Washington, D.C.: TeleGeography, 2000), 15–26.

United States, a service that used to be bundled with provision of half of the international transport capacity under the settlement rate system. This revision took place just as the United States was undermining the traditional settlement rate and jointly supplied service system that required carriers to share international transport costs. Many countries concluded that the United States intended to use its market power to force foreign carriers to shoulder a disproportionate share of international network costs.[20] Discontent was so strong that the ITU's 2000 World Telecommunications Standardization Assembly passed a resolution that endorsed governments making bilateral arrangements for Internet traffic exchange to ensure fair cost-sharing. The United States dissented from this resolution.[21]

Second, the primary alternative to the settlement rate system is to assemble networks through complex "make or buy" decisions. For example, a carrier can build its own dedicated network to all the major world websites and pay no one else for transport (assuming that all the markets are open to competition and foreign entry), or it can rent transport from another carrier (ISR is one example of renting capacity). If it rents, it can use a variety of methods. Backbone capacity is exploding internationally and domestically for long-haul traffic, and control of that capacity is finally diversifying significantly. This means that a more competitive market is emerging. It may require some time to reach an efficient equilibrium but the ingredients are there.[22] In some regions of the world, government policy may hinder this development but certainly not in the United States or the North Atlantic region. At least in major traffic markets, including the United States (where most of the complaints about ITE have focused), the long-haul transport market is becoming efficient.[23] Further reducing the magnitude of the problem

[20] The early peering agreements did not distinguish between incoming and outgoing traffic. That is, once a Japanese request for a reply from a U.S. web server in Chicago arrived in the United States, the U.S. backbone carrier agreed to take the Japanese traffic to the server in Chicago and take the server's response back to Los Angeles to be handed back to the Japanese carrier. Thus, in this model there was no true international traffic balancing, and even local termination (going to Chicago) and origination (returning from Chicago) services were co-mingled. Whether this worked in favor or against the interests of the Japanese carrier financially is arguable. But, in the late 1990s, it was a less transparent market where U.S. carriers had the trump card (transport access to U.S. web servers and their content).

[21] "U.S. Plays Role of Dissenter at ITU's World Standards Meeting," Telecommunications Reports International, October 13, 2000, 116–17. Compliance with such resolutions is voluntary under international law.

[22] Many other developments, such as the practice of mirroring for websites (whereby U.S. websites are set up in Asia to reduce service-time delays) and the decline of the dominance of U.S. content and the English language on the Web have also changed the original contracting problem. See Report on OECD Workshop "Internet Traffic Exchange," June 7–8, 2001 (Available at OECD website at <http://oecd.org/EN/home>). On this issue also see TeleGeography 2001, 58–9. As the Internet continues to grow and become more sophisticated, the peering/settlement system will also confront questions about how to manage pricing while dealing with quality of service issues. See Richard Cawley, "Policies to support the scaling and extensibility of the Internet: Principles to Guide Settlements Policy Consistent with Technical and Pricing Development of Internet," available at: http://www.ksg.harvard.edu/iip/cai/cawley.htm

[23] Another problem is the possibility of a backbone-carrier market where the major carrier(s) have the ability and incentive to maintain prices over efficient competitive levels. The U.S. Department of Justice and the European Commission competition authorities worried about this risk if they permitted a merger of WorldCom and Sprint (who, at the time of the proposed merger, controlled 53 per cent of the U.S.

is the growing diversification of web content and web servers globally. More web content and traffic is now created outside the United States than was created in the late 1990s. Major websites (such as Yahoo) now set up "mirror servers" around the world to deliver even U.S. content more efficiently and quickly. Traffic to mirror servers never enters the United States.

The favorable competitive trend on long haul does not fully clear up the issue. The control of the last mile (or kilometer) of transport for terminating or originating services to websites is very similar to two familiar issues concerning local interconnection arrangements. First, do the companies that control local networks have the ability and incentive to discriminate against other carriers in a way that harms consumers? Inter-exchange carriers (such as Internet backbone providers) constitute a significant share of the data traffic revenues of such U.S. Bell operating companies like Bell South. Arguably, discouraging this profitable wholesale market is not in the local carrier's interest. However, this is one area where regulation has been reasonably effective (as opposed to detailed unbundling of the local network), especially for well-entrenched data networks that have established long-term contracts for capacity supplemented by direct ownership of facilities to the largest customer sites. There have been complaints that newer entrants do less well in obtaining this access. Second, if there is any question of market power, have regulators taken measures to improve the transparency of the market? Some complaints have focused more on the need to improve information about peering arrangements for market participants than on demands for specific regulation of financial arrangements.[24] If there was a problem in regard to these issues a country could bring a complaint under the market access commitments of OECD countries in the BTA.

Annex 2

CASE STUDIES OF TELECOMMUNICATIONS COMPETITION

Ghana

Ghana made a significant market access commitment in the BTA, but the results have been disappointing. Weak government institutions have made it more difficult to introduce competition. In signing on to the BTA, Ghana placed two significant limitations on

---

backbone network). Eventually they required a divestiture of MCI's transmission capacity to Cable & Wireless. The risk was one well understood in competition policy. The explosive growth of the backbone network in the United States and Europe reduces the likelihood of risk, but the question is subject to empirical investigation using the tools of competition analysis.

[24] TeleGeography 2000, 28.

market access. First, across-the-board joint ventures with Ghanaian nationals were required. Second, except in underserved population centers, a duopoly was mandated and bypass of the duopoly providers was not permitted. These limitations applied to fixed-network infrastructure and for local, domestic-long distance, and international service. Terrestrial and satellite-based mobile services were required to make commercial arrangements with duopoly providers for voice services and were not allowed to bypass the network facilities of the duopoly providers for non-voice services.

In December 1996 Ghana created the National Communications Authority to serve as an independent regulator. Unfortunately, its independence was constrained politically because: (1) all of its members were appointed by and could be removed by the President, at any time; (2) many of its high officials were former Ghana Telecom professionals; and (3) the NCA remained in many ways subservient to the Minister of Communications. The NCA has never functioned as envisioned, in part because implementing legislation has never been passed by Parliament. Its independence has decreased to the point that the Minister of Communications was serving as chair of its Board in 2003.

Also in December 1996, Ghana partially privatized its inefficient incumbent telecommunications monopoly, Ghana Telecom, by selling a minority share and ceding management control to Telekom Malaysia for a period of five years. At the same time a license was sold to Westel to build and operate a competing telecom network. Westel never established a foothold. Although it invested about $26 million in its network between 1997 and 2002, by March 2002 it had only 2,621 subscribers. In the absence of pro-competitive regulation, Westel had few incentives to compete aggressively and Ghana Telecom had fewer incentives to reform.[25] As a result, Ghana Telecom also underperformed its promises, reaching only 241,000 lines by 2002. By 2001 Malaysia Telekom was disenchanted in its investment and was seeking a buyer for its share of Ghana Telecom. In February 2002 the new Kufuor government, distrustful of the agreements of its predecessors, abrogated Telekom Malaysia's management agreement, although it honored their 30 per cent ownership share. Ultimately, the Norwegian firm, Telenor, was hired to provide management services for Ghana Telecom.

Cellular entry into the market was first allowed in 1992. By 1996 three mobile cellular firms had entered the market. Mobitel began operations in 1992–3; Celltel began in 1995; Spacefon, the most aggressive of the three entered the market in 1996. All three providers interconnected through Ghana Telecom. But, Ghana Telecom was not content to be kept out of the mobile market and launched its own service, OneTouch, in 2000. Although OneTouch is supposed to operate as a separate business unit from the rest of Ghana Telecom, the extent to which this separation is real is not clear. Given the weakness of the regulator, Ghana Telecom has frequently been charged with manipulating

---

[25] The Westel case also illustrates another hard-earned lesson from competitive markets—not every competitor competes well. Markets routinely see most entrants fail. Freedom to enter allows experimentation until competitors with better strategies and mixes of assets emerge.

interconnection to the detriment of its competitors and providing unfair cross-subsidies and unequal treatment.

Still, mobile use is expanding rapidly, and has recently overtaken fixed-line telephony in terms of the number of subscribers. As of September 2003, there were approximately 702,000 subscribers, about 93 per cent of whom were digital subscribers. Scancom had 367,000 subscribers and Ghana Telecom had 210,500.

According to ITU Telecommunications indicators, relative to other African countries, between 1996 and 2002 Ghana has improved more rapidly on fixed line telephony penetration (0.44 in 1996 to 1.16 in 2001) than some others (Kenya: 1.02 in 1996 to 1.03 in 2002 or Cameroon: 0.52 in 1996 to 0.66 in 2001), but it has not done as well as Cote d'Ivoire (0.95 in 1996 to 2.04 in 2002) or Senegal (1.11 in 1996 to 2.29 in 2002). Although its mobile penetration has increased, Ghana (0.07 in 1996 to 0.93 in 2001) has significantly lagged other African nations like Kenya (0.01 in 1996 to 4.15 in 2002), Cameroon (0.03 in 1996 to 3.57 in 2002), Senegal (0.03 in 1996 to 5.65 in 2002), and Cote d'Ivoire (0.10 in 1996 to 6.23 in 2002). Further, competition and privatization as practiced in Ghana have so far had minimal impact on underserved rural areas. Most of the growth has occurred around Accra and other larger cities. A particularly striking scene in Accra is the growth of large sophisticated Internet cafes and entrepreneurial Internet Service Providers geared to small businesses. Providers of these services all complain of inadequate and over-priced communications infrastructure. They report that a vigorous "grey market" exists for network connectivity to overcome the weaknesses of the official prices and sources of supply.[26]

South Korea

By contrast, in the early 1990s South Korea became persuaded that it was in its own interest to embrace greater competition. In 1991 it licensed a second business operator for international services. Mobile competition was introduced in 1994 and long-distance competition a year later. In 1996 South Korea established a more competitive market structure by approving 27 new service providers in seven areas, including international telephone service, PCS, and wireless data communications. After the signing of the BTA, opportunities for domestic service providers and equipment manufacturers to compete outside of Korea improved significantly.[27]

The Ministry of Information and Communication succeeded the Ministry of Communications in December 1994 to unify IT functions under one ministry and to nurture information technology as an engine of economic growth for South Korea. The MIC's goals are to accelerate the deepening of the use of IT in government and the whole

---

[26] Based on author interviews in Ghana in 2003.
[27] Lee et al. (1997, 2001). Author interviews, 2002.

economy, promote the IT industry as a research and production driver for growth, and deregulate and liberalize markets. The MIC is supplemented by the Korea Communications Commission, established in 1992, to regulate the telecommunications and IT industry and to ensure fair competition. The KCC arbitrates disputes involving carriers, oversees interconnection arrangements between carriers, and investigates complaints of unfair competitive actions. KCC's independence was further ensured through amendments to the Telecommunications Act passed in November 2002.

During the Uruguay Round negotiations, South Korea agreed to open its value added telecommunications services markets and also recognized that liberalization and competition in basic telecommunications were not only inevitable, but desirable. South Korea explicitly tried to take advantage of the agreement to restructure it domestic telecommunications market. South Korean authorities emphasized "domestic competition first and global competition afterwards" to improve the competitiveness of domestic industries and "gradual market liberalization," which supposedly served the purpose of minimizing any negative impact of a sudden influx of foreign capital. However, a more likely reason for the delay was the desire to exercise greater control over technology decisions of market operators. This was easier in the absence of foreign management and investment control.

In response to the demands of the other industrial countries for more market opening as part of the BTA, in 1998 South Korea permitted for the first time foreign investment in wireline-based telephone services (up to 33 per cent ownership of facilities-based operators and up to 20 per cent in Korea Telecom). (See Box 10.3) for the Korean offer.) The aggregate ownerships limits were lifted to 49 per cent for both in 2001. Full competition in resale of all telecommunications services except voice was allowed in January 1998, and full voice competition followed in January 2001.[28] The limit on resale was designed to avoid the kinds of manipulation of international traffic under the settlement rate system that the United States had identified as a risk. The value added services market was entirely opened in 2001, and Korea gradually relaxed restrictions on foreign investments in facilities-based telecommunications. By 2003 most regulations were lifted except for ceilings on foreign investment in facilities-based services (49 per cent) and restrictions on foreign investors becoming the major shareholder in Korea Telecom.

As in many countries the reduction of government ownership of the traditional monopolist, Korea Telecom, was slow and complex. Korea's monopoly common carrier for all wireline services and later for Internet access was split off from the Ministry of Postal Service in 1982. Privatization proceeded gradually by selling off its stock from

---

[28] In the wake of the Asian financial crisis, Korea adopted an even more aggressive set of policies to prompt recovery. In the summer of 1998 the Korean government abruptly changed policy in favor of economic stimulation through monetary and fiscal expansion. The government also simultaneously promoted corporate sector restructuring, financial sector restructuring, public sector restructuring, and labor market reform. Stephan Haggard (2000) for the Institute of International Economics.

1987 to 2002. Turning this formerly government-owned company into an efficient private firm was a major advance. But concerns remain over privatization, given the huge proportion of the national economy that it represents and anti-competitive possibilities. This led the government to create an independent management cadre, to limit the shares of ownership that any one investor could hold, and to disperse its shares widely to individualism institutional investors and eventually to international investors. Both KT and SK Telecom, the wireless leader, has foreign ownership in the mid-40 per cent range and both now favor lifting the current 49 per cent ceiling on foreign ownership.

Competition was introduced for KT for international phone service in 1990 and for domestic long-distance service in 1995. (Dacom and Onse Telecom now compete in both areas.) The government established a wireline competitor, Hanaro Telecom, for local service that began service in 1999, but has so far made only small inroads into KT's market. In early 2004 KT's market share in local service remained at 96 per cent, its share of the domestic long-distance market had fallen to 79.7 per cent, and it retained 46 per cent of the international telephone service market.

Initially, Dacom received a nationwide monopoly for high-speed wireless internet provision. KT was allowed to provide Internet Access in 2000 and quickly took a strong position as competition in wireline-broadband access and the growing substitution of wireless for wired-spurred innovations in broadband service. Korea benefited from demography also. The strong concentration of population in urban areas with high-rise housing of recent origin facilitated residential broadband networks. Korea emerged as one of the leading countries for broadband Internet access.

An even greater success for Korea came in the wireless market, which now greatly exceeds wireline. Cell phone subscribers in Korea grew from under two million at the start of 1996 to reach 35 million by the third quarter of 2003. SK Telecom is the largest player but KTF (a subsidiary of KT) and LG Telecom both have healthy shares of the market. Vigorous competition has also spurred innovative services. Korea is one of the leaders in mobile-data markets. A striking characteristic of the market is the leadership in use by teenagers, thus making applications like downloads of ring tones into popular items. In addition, broadband data emerged first as a service in Korea. Korea was the first country to offer widespread 3G wireless service and continues to be a leader in wireless use and penetration. Koreans also are among the most active users of text messaging and wireless-data transfer anywhere.

KTF's second place position in the wireless market has created an unusual political opportunity for innovative regulation in wireless services. Most recently, it introduced mobile-phone-number portability in October 2003. And it also put price caps on the charges for terminating calls from wired onto wireless markets.

The producers of wireless equipment also have prospered as a result of providing equipment for its innovative service market. Samsung Electronics, which controls just over half of the domestic wireless equipment market and is a vigorous competitor worldwide, is now larger in terms of sales and market cap than Sony. LG Electronics is also a major global player.

This leadership in wireless technology represented a strategic gamble by a government that was willing to dictate technical standards in services in order to support innovation in the equipment market. Specifically, South Korea gambled on CDMA technology for second- and third-generation technologies. (This strategy worked in part because Korean suppliers were able to achieve a leading position in the U.S. market that also introduced CDMA technology in the same time frame.) This dictation of standards was typical of many governments in the 1980s and early 1990s, but it has become less common today because trade rules discourage such industrial policies, and experience has shown that governments often fail to guess right when picking standards. However, South Korea remains active in intervening in this area, and today is trying to impose a new mandatory standard for wireless technology that has been designed in Korea. This is becoming subject to a trade dispute.

In short, thoughtful regulation coupled with significant domestic competition and selected international partnerships and competition have propelled South Korea into a global leadership role. The goal of modernizing the economy by facilitating powerful and inexpensive communications and information technology services was reinforced by the general decision to rely more on market forces after the Asian financial crisis. This was complemented by a related growth in advanced technology equipment production. Together, these factors provided the political motivation for the difficult choices.

Annex 3

COMMITMENTS OF COSTA RICA ON TELECOMMUNICATION SERVICES IN THE CONTEXT OF THE U.S.–CENTRAL AMERICA–DOMINICAN REPUBLIC FREE TRADE AGREEMENT (DR-CAFTA)

Roberto Echandi

Introduction

This Annex explains the scope and content of the commitments undertaken by Costa Rica in telecommunication services in the context of the U.S.–Central America–Dominican Republic Free Trade Agreement (DR-CAFTA). Two fundamental issues are addressed: (1) the nature and practical implications of the structure of Chapter 13, "Telecommunications," of the DR-CAFTA and its respective Annex; and (2) the scope and content of each of the four parts of Annex 13, "Specific Commitments of Costa Rica on Telecommunications Services."

The Structure of Chapter 13 and its Annex

In the chapters on services in DR-CAFTA, the Parties involved assume a series of obligations, but also acquire a series of rights. These rights can benefit the States themselves or benefit their respective service providers. In many cases, the obligations assumed by a country are the same as those assumed by the rest of the Parties of the Free Trade Agreement, that is, they are symmetrical. However, that is not the case of the commitments assumed by the DR-CAFTA Parties on telecommunications. Note 1 to Chapter 13 expressly states the following: "In place of the obligations established in this Chapter, Costa Rica shall undertake the specific commitments set out in Annex 13."

Pursuant to note 1 cited above, in the territory of the other Parties of DR-CAFTA, Costa Rica and its service providers will benefit from all the rights granted by Chapter 13. However, the obligations undertaken by Costa Rica relative to the other DR-CAFTA Parties and their service suppliers, are exclusively limited to the obligations included in Annex 13.

Reach and Content of Annex 13

Annex 13 is divided into four sections, as follows:

1. *Preamble.* The preamble states the object and purpose of the Parties when negotiating the content of the Annex. The importance of the elements included in the preamble stems from the fact that they will serve as a supplementary source of interpretation of the rest of the text of Annex 13.

   The preamble acknowledges the unique nature of the Costa Rican social policy on telecommunications. Further, it reaffirms the decision to ensure that the process of opening of the telecommunications services sector must be based on the terms of the Constitution of Costa Rica. A key aspect of the preamble is that the process of opening of the telecommunications sector shall be to the benefit of the user and shall be based on the principles of graduality, selectivity, and regulation, and in strict conformity with the social objectives of universality and solidarity in the supply of telecommunications services in Costa Rica. Furthermore, it is explicitly recognized that the Costa Rican Institute of Electricity—"ICE" a public enterprise and main provider of telecommunications services in Costa Rica—will be a participant in the future competitive market. Thus, the preamble explicitly clarifies that there is not any commitment to privatize this institution.

2. *Modernization of ICE.* Section II of the Annex includes the obligation on the part of Costa Rica to promulgate a new legal framework in order to strengthen the ICE, through its appropriate modernization, by December 31, 2004. This is an obligation assumed by Costa Rica, which, as well as any other included in the Annex, in

principle would be effective once the Treaty has entered into force. If at that date, Costa Rica has not yet promulgated this legal framework, technically the country would be violating its treaty obligations under DR-CAFTA. However, due to the fact that the inclusion of the commitment of modernization of the ICE within Annex 13 was at the request of Costa Rica, and not of the U.S. or any other DR-CAFTA Party, it is unlikely that the mechanism of dispute settlement would be used in order to enforce this obligation.

3. *Commitments of Selective and Gradual Opening of the Market.* Section III of Annex 13 includes two main obligations for Costa Rica. First, there is a market-access stand-still, and second, there is the commitment for a gradual and selective opening of three telecommunication services. The market-access standstill obligation is an important feature of the Annex, as not all telecommunications services in Costa Rica are currently under public monopoly. A limited number of services are open to competition, for instance "radio messages" services and beepers. The market-access standstill entails that Costa Rica will not be able to extend the public monopoly regimen to services that already are open to competition in accordance with current Costa Rican legislation as of January 27, 2003.[29] In other words, Costa Rica will not be able to extend the public monopoly beyond the level existing level at the date the negotiation started.[30] It should be clarified that the market-access standstill obligation does not limit in any manner the prerogative of Costa Rica to enact modern legislation to regulate the telecommunications sector.[31] This provision neither implies that Costa Rica will have to grant retroactive benefits nor that it will have to "freeze" any frequency assigned or use of the "radio-frequency" spectrum.[32]

In addition to the market standstill commitment, in Section III.2 of the Annex, Costa Rica assumes the obligation of permitting, on a non-discriminatory basis, competition between telecommunications service providers so that they can provide directly to consumers three specific types of telecommunications services: private network services and Internet services by January 1, 2006 and mobile wireless services by January 1, 2007. The content of Section III.2. warrants several clarifications.

First, in accordance with this provision, Costa Rica does not grant the United States any right of exclusive access to the Costa Rican market. It should be noted that the obligation assumed consists in allowing competition on a non-discriminatory

---

[29] January 27, 2003 was the date the DR-CAFTA negotiations started.

[30] The determination of the scope of the monopoly of the telecommunications sector has been a subject of debate in Costa Rica. Nevertheless, paragraph III.1 does not prejudge which services are open to competition in accordance with Costa Rican legislation.

[31] On the contrary, Section IV of the Annex explicitly refers to the need for Costa Rica to issue a regulatory framework for telecommunications services. In this respect, Section IV of the Annex specifies a date to fulfill this objective, i.e. January 1, 2006 at the latest.

[32] This aspect is not regulated in Section III of the Annex, but very generally in its paragraph V.4.

basis, rather than granting an exclusive preference to telecommunications service providers of the U.S. or Central America.

Second, Section III.2 includes a paragraph (b), where it is stated that the commitment to allow competition in the supply of telecommunication services on a non-discriminatory basis shall also apply to any other telecommunications service that Costa Rica unilaterally decides—and not pursuant the terms of Annex 13—to permit in the future. Thus, any additional opening in the market that takes place in the future will be automatically bound for non-discriminatory competition under the terms explained.

4. *Regulatory Principles.* Section IV of the Annex establishes the obligation of Costa Rica to promulgate, at the latest on January 1, 2006, a regulatory framework for telecommunications services that should comply with the principles included in this Section. The formulation of these principles, which derive from the principal international instruments that govern trade in telecommunications services, was drafted in quite general terms. The rationale for this approach was to provide Costa Rica with enough room to maneuver to specify these principles when enacting the legislation at the national level.

The purpose of these regulatory principles is to serve as a guide for the regulation of the telecommunications sector and not to affect the commitments of market access that Costa Rica would assume according to Section III of the Annex. Thus, nothing is stipulated in Section IV can be interpreted in the sense of expanding the commitments of market access assumed under Section III of the Annex. The principles included in Section IV are the following:

1. *Universal Service.* Costa Rica will have the right to define the kind of universal service obligations it wishes to maintain, which will not be considered anti-competitive per se, provided they are administered in a transparent, non-discriminatory, and competitively neutral manner and are not more burdensome than necessary for the kind of universal service defined.

This is one of the most important principles for Costa Rica, since it implies clearly that the country will enjoy room to maneuver in order to design a system of universal coverage, in accordance with the principle of solidarity in the supply of telecommunication services, where not only the ICE, but all the other suppliers of telecommunications services—nationals or foreigners—would have an obligation to contribute.

2. *Independence of the Regulatory Authority.* In order to guarantee the adequate supply of telecommunications as a public service, Costa Rica should have a regulatory authority of telecommunications services, which should be separate and not accountable to any supplier of these services and impartial with respect to all market participants. The Annex does not prejudge whether the regulatory authority could be

built within the framework of an existing regulatory body. This point, as well as the other principles, would be specified through national legislation.

3. *Transparency.* Annex 13 guarantees access of the public to information on the procedures, agreements or offers related to interconnection. Further, this provision states the obligation to make available to the public all licensing or authorization criteria and procedures required for telecommunications service suppliers, and the terms and conditions of all licenses or authorizations issued.

4. *Allocation and Use of Scarce Resources.* Annex 13 also provides that Costa Rica shall ensure that procedures for the allocation and use of limited resources, including frequencies, numbers, and rights of way, are administered in an objective, timely, transparent, and non-discriminatory manner by a competent domestic authority.

5. *Regulated Interconnection.* This provision is directed to offer to the service providers of telecommunications the possibility to be able to be interconnected to the public network of telecommunications in a timely fashion, under non-discriminatory terms, conditions, and cost-oriented rates that are transparent, reasonable, and having regard to economic feasibility. This is not a provision of market access. Instead, this guarantee stems from the recognition that it is not possible to provide telecommunication services—at national or international levels—if there is not interconnection of networks among the different suppliers of telecommunication services.

6. *Access to and Use of the Network.* This guarantee is not exclusively directed to service providers of telecommunications, but to all sorts of companies that, in order to provide their services, need to have access to and to use—not to provide—public telecommunications services. This would apply, for example, to a bank that intends to have a network of automatic teller machines and branches in the entire national territory. In this case, the logic of the provision is that the telecommunication service providers do not deny to the bank access to the networks or the use of the public telecommunications services. This obligation is not absolute. The last phrase of paragraph IV.6 stipulates that Costa Rica can impose conditions to the access to and the use of networks or public telecommunications services in order to safeguard the public-service responsibilities of providers of public-telecommunications networks or services, in particular their ability to make their networks or services available to the public generally, or protect the technical integrity of public-telecommunications networks or services. Furthermore, it is important to clarify that this provision grants no right to a service provider of telecommunications not authorized to offer telecommunications services in the country.

7. *Supply of Information Services.* With this provision, Annex 13 purports to make the distinction between two different types of services: on the one hand, public-telecommunications services - any telecommunications service that a Party requires, explicitly or in effect, to be offered to the public generally—and on the other hand, information services—services that generate, store, transform, or process data that

use telecommunications as a transport means. While part of the first services are subject to the public monopoly in Costa Rica, information services are not, and therefore can be offered by any public or private corporation. Furthermore, while public-telecommunications services are a public service and as such should be clearly regulated and subject to State supervision, information services are not public services, but private, and as such should not be subject to the same regimen as public-telecommunication services.

Recognizing that information services are not public utilities, paragraph IV.7 establishes for this type of services that Costa Rica cannot require a company to provide information services to the general public or justify its rates in accordance with its costs and register its rates for such services. It is noteworthy that it corresponds to what Costa Rica defines is an information service for the purpose of this paragraph.

8. *Competition.* In view of this principle, Costa Rica will maintain adequate measures to prevent important providers from using anticompetitive practices. The rationale of this provision is to ensure for the country a legal framework capable of promoting fair and transparent competition in the market. These regulations could also be applied to all other operators who enter the national market, and not just the important suppliers.

9. *Submarine Cable Systems.* Paragraph VI.9 is a guarantee that is applied only when a telecommunication provider is authorized to operate submarine cable systems as a public telecommunication service. In this situation, Costa Rica shall grant to this provider reasonable and non-discriminatory treatment for access to submarine cable systems—including landing facilities—in its territory. Again, in view of note 6 of the Annex, this obligation per se does not imply granting any right or duty of access to the telecommunications market in Costa Rica.

10. *Flexibility in the Choice of Technologies.* Pursuant to this principle, Costa Rica may not prevent suppliers of public-telecommunications services from having the flexibility to choose the technologies that they use to supply their services, subject to requirements necessary to satisfy legitimate public-policy interests.

Conclusion

Annex 13 of the DR-CAFTA illustrates two fundamental aspects of international trade negotiations with small developing countries. First, the structure and contents of the Annex represent an example of how international trade agreements can be crafted in order to achieve a balance between two often contradictory objectives when negotiating highly sensitive political issues: on the one hand, to foster certainty and predictability for business transactions through sound and clear rules and disciplines, and on the other, to allow the countries concerned—especially those undertaking commitments that entail reforms to domestic regimes the right margin of policy space to be able to specify those rules and disciplines according to national idiosyncrasy. Annex 13 of the DR–CAFTA illustrates how such a delicate balance can be achieved.

The Annex provides for very specific and clear commitments for Costa Rica, not only with respect to the opening of the telecommunication sector to competition, but also regarding the enactment of a new legal framework to regulate the sector. By providing clear, but general principles, the Costa Rican authorities will have enough policy space to specify those rules and disciplines according to their national needs and policy objectives.

For instance, Annex 13 safeguards the right of Costa Rica to preserve the universal coverage of telecommunications services. This Annex delegates to the Costa Rican lawmaker not only the definition of the specific features and policy objectives that such universal system may have, but also the identification of the means to make such universal system effectively work. Since the obligations imposed on the service providers are transparent, non-discriminatory, and competitively neutral and not more burdensome than necessary for the kind of universal service defined, the Costa Rican authorities have significant policy space to craft the kind of universal service desired. This approach is also applicable for the other regulatory principles included in Annex 13.

The second key aspect that Annex 13 of the DR–CAFTA illustrates with respect to international trade negotiations with small developing countries is even more important. Annex 13 illustrates how the rationale of the DR–CAFTA negotiations—as with most other international trade negotiations in the context of developing countries—is not limited to improve conditions of access into key export markets for developing countries, or to enable the former to increase their exports, or attract increased investment inflows and diversify their export supply. Without doubt, all these objectives, aimed at improving the conditions through which developing economies integrate themselves to international markets are extremely important. However, these goals are only part of the story of the importance of free trade agreements for smaller developing economies.

The other main impact that a free trade agreement like the DR–CAFTA can have, and that is clearly illustrated by Annex 13, consists in the trade agreement becoming instrumental to foster key domestic reforms that Costa Rica should have undertaken a long time ago in order to foster the process of modernization of their institutions and promote sound, fair and sustainable economic development. In this sense, Annex 13 is an example of how the DR–CAFTA is then about domestic reform, a catalyst for internal change aimed at modernizing the economies of the region. Any process of reform always faces resistance by vested interests. In the case of small developing countries, institutions often are very vulnerable and permeable to pressures of particularly politically strong pressure groups. In such contexts, the negotiation of international trade agreements can represent a mechanism to exert external pressure to make domestic reform feasible.

The process of opening the telecommunications sector in Costa Rica is a case on point. For more than a decade, Costa Rica has attempted to open the State monopoly in the telecommunications sector. However, the political pressure exerted mostly by public-sector unions has impeded a national consensus, making governments doubtful as to whether to use their political capital to foster the reform of the sector which is so badly needed by the Costa Rican economy. Within this context, had the DR–CAFTA Parties failed to ask Costa Rica to undertake any commitment in the telecommunications sector, it is very likely that the opening of the State monopoly in telecommunications would not be at the top of the Costa Rican domestic political agenda as it is today.

References

Arena, A 1997. "The WTO Telecommunications Agreement: Some Personal Reflections," *Tele-Geography.* Washington, D.C.: TeleGeography.

Baier, S. L. and J. H. Bergstrand. 2001. "International Trade in Services, Free Trade Agreements, and the WTO," in R. M. Stern (ed.), *Services in the International Economy.* Ann Arbor: University of Michigan Press, pp. 157–83.

Cowhey, P. 1999. "FCC Benchmarks and the Reform of the International Telecommunications Market," *Telecommunications Policy* 22: 899–911.

—— 2004. "Cross-Border Telecommunications Services: Competition and Trade Policy in the Next WTO Round," in D. Geradin and D. Luff (eds.), *Trade in Telecommunications and Audio-Visual Services in the Context of the WTO: Towards Convergence?* Cambridge: Cambridge University Press.

Cowhey, P. and J. E. Richards. 1999. "Dialing for Dollars: Institutional Designs for the Globalization of the Market for Basic Telecommunications Services," in A. Prakash and J. Hart (eds.), *Coping With Globalization.* New York: Routledge, pp. 148–69.

—— and M. Klimenko. 2002. "Implementing Telecommunications Liberalization in the Developing Countries after the WTO Agreement on Basic Telecommunications Services," *Journal of International Development* 12: 265–81.

Federal Communications Commission. 1997. "In the Matter of International Settlement Rates," Report and Order, IB Docket No. 96–261.

Freund, C. and D. Weinhold. 2000. "On the Effect of the Internet on International Trade," International Finance Discussion Papers, No. 693, Board of Governors of the Federal Reserve System.

Haggard, S. 2000. *The Political Economy of the Asian Financial Crisis.* Washington, D.C.: Institute of International Economics.

Hodge, J. 2003. "WTO Negotiations in Telecommunications: How Should SADC Countries Respond?" SATRN Report No. 2 (January). Available at: http://www.tips.afrihost.com/research/papers/pdfs/660.pdf

Hufbauer, G. C. and E. Wada. 1997. *Unfinished Business: Telecommunications After the Uruguay Round.* Washington, D.C.: Institute for International Economics.

Laffont, J-J., P. Rey, and J. Tirole. 1998. Network Competition: I. Overview and Non-discriminatory Pricing, *The Rand Journal of Economics* 29(1): 1–37.

Lande, J. and L. Blake. 1997. "Trends in the U.S. International Telecommunications Industry," Industry Analysis Division, Common Carrier Bureau, Federal Communications Commission.

Lee, M-H. and H-Y. Lie. 1997. "WTO Negotiations on Basic Telecommunications and Future Course of Korea's Information and Telecommunications Industry," *KISDI*, pp. 65–104 (Spring).

Lee, N. C. and A-Y. Lie. 2001. "Korea's Telecom Services Reform through Trade Negotiations," *KISDI*, pp. 77–114 (Spring).

Levy, B. and P. Spiller (eds.). 1996. *Regulations, Institutions, and Commitment: Comparative Studies of Telecommunications*. Cambridge, M.A.: Cambridge University Press.

Noam, E. 2001. *Interconnecting the Network of Networks*. Boston, M.A.: MIT Press.

Noll, R. 2000. "Telecommunications Reform in Developing Countries," in A. O. Krueger (ed.), *Economic Policy Reform: The Second Stage*. Chicago: University of Chicago Press.

Petrazzini, B. A. and A. Guerrero. 2000. "Promoting Internet Development: The Case of Argentina," *Telecommunications Policy* 24: 89–112.

Shapiro, C. and H. Varian. 1998. *Information Rules: A Strategic Guide to the Network Economy*. Cambridge, M.A.: Harvard Business School Press.

Sherman, L. B., 1998. " 'Wildly Enthusiastic' About the First Multilateral Agreement on Trade in Telecommunications Services," *Federal Communications Law Journal* 51: 62–110.

Sherman, L. 2004. Telecommunications Trade Agreements (Argus Consulting).

TeleGeography, Inc. 2000. *TeleGeography, 2001*. Washington, D.C.: TeleGeography.

TeleGeography, Inc. 2001. *TeleGeography, 2001*. Washington, D.C.: TeleGeography.

Zacher, M. with B. Sutton. 1996. *Governing Global Networks: International Regimes for Transportation and Communications*. Cambridge, M.A.: Cambridge University Press.

11 Trade in Health Services and the GATS

Richard Smith, Chantal Blouin, Nick Drager, and David P. Fidler

Introduction[1]

Globalization is one of the key challenges facing health policy makers in the twenty-first century. While effects on health from, for example, cross-border flows of infectious disease and the advertising of unhealthy lifestyles are important aspects of globalization, a significant challenge concerns the globalization of the health sector itself: direct trade in health-related goods, services and people (patients and professionals). Trade in health services will be affected by changes in general trade liberalization, international legislation, and international institutions; in return, it will itself impact on national economies. (See WHO/WTO, 2002.)

However, to date the health sector has been relatively unaffected by trade, as it remains a predominantly domestic service-oriented sector. Throughout history, most trade liberalization has concerned the movement of goods, and, to a lesser degree, people. However, while services (such as banking, education, and telecommunications, as well as health) account for only about 20 per cent of global trade (on a balance-of-payments basis), the health sector is the fastest growing. Much of this increase in service-related trade has resulted from changes in technology, which make e-commerce and telemedicine technical possibilities; from easier travel and border restrictions, which make temporary movement of patients and professionals feasible; and from the rise of transnational corporations, which makes the ownership and management of health-care facilities more feasible.

A recent, and critical, development in international legislation concerning trade and health services has been the WTO GATS negotiations aimed at the further liberalization of trade in services.

---

[1] This chapter has been adapted from Drager and Fidler (2004) and Smith et al. (2006). Other useful references include: Adlung (2002), Adlung and Carzaniga (2001), Chandra (2002), Fidler et al. (2004), Hilary (2001), Krajewski (2003), Pan American Health Organization/World Health Organization (2002), Sinclair and Grieshaber-Otto (2002), Woodruffe and Joy (2002), World Trade Organization (2001), and Yach and Bettcher (1998a, b).

The pace of development of GATS commitments, and especially their binding nature, has created a fresh imperative to establish how health services will be affected. More specifically, it has raised concerns that the spread of globalization threatens to outpace the ability of governments and nations to adjust to the new commitments, let alone guide them (Adlung, 2002; Price and Pollock, 1999). In this respect, the potential risk associated with trade in health services is further increased with the added complication of conflicts, or misunderstandings, between the trade and health sectors. This causes further confusion in estimating the potential benefits and risks of trade liberalization in health services. National ministries of trade (and perhaps finance and foreign affairs) often make GATS commitments in isolation from health ministries, yet their decisions have an impact on health, of which they have limited knowledge. Conversely, ministries of health typically have very limited knowledge of trade issues. A critical factor in globalization and trade in health services is therefore to address this asymmetry of information by enabling ministries of health to make informed and comprehensive presentations to ministries of trade concerning decisions to be taken under the GATS.

The main purpose of this chapter is to elucidate from both the trade and health perspectives the nature and implications of international trade in the health sector, and thus to assist in the formulation of trade policy and in international negotiations in the health sector. Health policy makers require tools to assist them in evaluating the liberalization of national health systems utilizing currently available data, in formulating the development of systems to improve the collection of data relevant to these decisions, and in participating in the negotiation process.

Countries are encouraged to embed the health-policy principles summarized in Box 11.1 in the process of managing the GATS.

Box 11.1. Health Policy Principles to Guide Liberalization of Health-Related Services

---

- Liberalized trade in health-related services should lead to an optimal balance between preventive and curative services.
- Involvement of both private industry and civil society is important to ensure that liberalization of health-related services promotes participatory health policy towards achieving national goals.
- Improving access and affordability of health-related services should be a goal of liberalization of trade in health-related services.
- Developing countries, and least-developed countries in particular, deserve special consideration in the process of liberalizing trade in health-related services.
- The status of health as a human right should inform and guide proposals to liberalize trade in health-related services.

Source: Adapted from Smith et al. (2006).

Choices Under the GATS

In key areas of the GATS, governments face choices about the breadth and depth of liberalization of trade in health-related services and the impact of such liberalization on health policy. In fact, countries are free to decide whether liberalization in the health sector should be pursued or not and to what extent. Countries are not obliged to liberalize health services if they do not wish to do so. These choices make it imperative that health officials understand the structure and substance of the GATS, collaborate with other government agencies on GATS implementation and liberalization, and act to ensure that the GATS process does not adversely affect national health policy (see Box 11.2).

Key Provisions of the GATS

The GATS creates the multilateral legal framework for international trade in nearly every type of service. The Agreement's 29 articles establish the scope of its rules coverage, impose general obligations, structure the making of specific commitments, construct a process for progressive liberalization of trade in services, and link the treaty to the WTO's dispute settlement mechanism. The key provisions for health policy are described below and summarized in Table 11.1.

Box 11.2. Points for Policy Makers

- GATS establishes the multilateral legal framework for international trade in services among WTO members.
- The scope of GATS is very broad, which means it applies to a wide range of health-related services.
- GATS covers policies, practices and laws that affect trade in services among WTO members.
- GATS contains general obligations and disciplines, such as MFN treatment, which apply to all measures affecting services within the scope of the Agreement.
- GATS allows WTO members to make specific commitments on market access and national treatment and to tailor those commitments to national policy ends.
- GATS sets the objective of progressive liberalization of trade in services, meaning that WTO members will negotiate over new specific commitments in service sectors subject to the Agreement.
- The process of progressive liberalization under the GATS requires the active involvement of health policy makers.
- Before making any specific commitment under GATS, governments should ensure that they have thoroughly assessed the implications of opening health systems to foreign providers and the potential costs and benefits of making legally binding commitments. Countries may wish to experiment through autonomous liberalization of certain health related services, and only make commitments under GATS after a careful assessment of its effects.

Source: Adapted from Smith et al. (2006).

Table 11.1. Articles of GATS of Greatest Relevance to Health Policy

Topic (GATS Articles)	Substance of the GATS Provision (Note that a number of articles contain further detail that are spelled out in GATS)
	SCOPE OF GATS (PART I)
Scope and definitions (Article I)	GATS applies to measures by WTO members affecting trade in services. Trade in services is defined as the supply of a service (1) from the territory of one WTO member into the territory of any other WTO member; (2) in the territory of one WTO member to the service consumer of any other WTO member; (3) by a service supplier of one WTO member through commercial presence in the territory of any other WTO member; and (4) by a service supplier of one WTO member through presence of natural persons of a WTO member in the territory of any other WTO member.
	"Services" includes any service in any sector except services supplied in the exercise of governmental authority.
	A "service supplied in the exercise of governmental authority" means any service that is supplied neither on a commercial basis nor in competition with one or more service suppliers.
	GENERAL OBLIGATIONS AND DISCIPLINES (PART II)
Most-favored-nation treatment (Article II)	With respect to any measure covered by GATS, each WTO member shall accord immediately and unconditionally to services and service suppliers of any other WTO member treatment no less favorable than that it accords to like services and service suppliers of any other country.
Domestic regulation (Article VI)	The Council for Trade in Services shall develop any necessary disciplines on measures relating to qualification requirements, technical standards, and licensing requirements to ensure that such measures do not constitute unnecessary barriers to trade in services. Such disciplines shall aim to ensure that such requirements are, inter alia, not more burdensome than necessary to ensure the quality of the service.
Monopolies and exclusive service suppliers (Article VIII)	If a WTO member grants monopoly or exclusive service rights regarding the supply of a service covered by specific commitments, then that WTO member must make compensatory arrangements with any WTO member adversely affected by such granting of monopoly or exclusive service rights.
General exceptions (Article XIV)	WTO members may restrict trade in health-related services in violation of general obligations or specific commitments when such restrictive measures are necessary to protect human, animal, or plant life or health, and the application of which does not constitute a means of arbitrary or unjustifiable discrimination or a disguised restriction on trade in services.
	SPECIFIC COMMITMENTS (PART III)
Market access (Article XVI)	With respect to market access through the modes of supply identified in Article I, each WTO member shall accord services and service suppliers of any other WTO member treatment no less favorable than that provided for under the terms, limitations, and conditions agreed and specified in its Schedule of Specific Commitments. WTO members must list measures restricting market access they wish to maintain in sectors subject to market access commitments.
National treatment (Article XVII)	In the sectors inscribed in its Schedule of Specific Commitments, and subject to any conditions and qualifications set out therein, each WTO

(Continued)

Table 11.1. (*Continued*)

Topic (GATS Articles)	Substance of the GATS Provision (Note that a number of articles contain further detail that are spelled out in GATS)
	member shall accord to services and service suppliers of any other WTO member, in respect of all measures affecting the supply of services, treatment no less favorable than that it accords to its own like services and service suppliers.
	PROGRESSIVE LIBERALIZATION (PART IV)
Negotiation of specific commitments (Article XIX)	WTO members shall enter into successive rounds of negotiations with a view to achieving a progressively higher level of liberalization in trade in services.
Modification of schedules (Article XXI)	To withdraw or modify a Schedule of Specific Commitments, a WTO member must make compensatory arrangements for WTO members adversely affected by such withdrawal or modification; and such compensatory arrangements are then available to all WTO members on a most-favored-nation basis.
	INSTITUTIONAL PROVISIONS (PART V)
Dispute settlement and enforcement (Article XXIII)	Disputes that arise under GATS are subject to the WTO Dispute Settlement Understanding.
Council for Trade in Services (Article XXIV)	The Council for Trade in Services shall facilitate the operation of GATS and advance its objectives.

Source: Adapted from WTO (www.wto.org).

Scope of the GATS

The GATS applies to all measures by WTO members affecting trade in services (Article I:1). The GATS defines all elements of this rule—"measures," "affecting," and "trade in services"—broadly. For example, the GATS covers all possible ways in which services are provided

---

Box 11.3. Modes of Service Supply under GATS and Health Opportunities and Risks

Supply modes	Opportunity	Risk
Mode 1: Cross-border supply of services (telemedicine, e-health)	Increased care to remote and under-served areas	Diversion of resources from other health services
Mode 2: Consumption of services abroad (patients traveling abroad for hospital treatment)	Generates foreign exchange earnings for health services of importing country	Crowding out of local population and diversion of resources to service foreign nationals
Mode 3: Commercial presence (establishment of health facilities in other countries)	Creates opportunities for new employment and access to new technologies	Development of two-tiered health system, with an internal brain drain
Mode 4: Presence of natural persons (doctors or nurses practicing in other countries)	Economic gains from remittances of health-care personnel working overseas	Permanent outflow of health-care personnel, with loss of investment in educating and training such personnel

Source: Adapted from Smith et al. (2006).

(see Box 11.3). The GATS scope is expansive and overlaps significantly with the wide range of activities that governments undertake in regulating health-related services.

The Agreement excludes from its coverage services supplied in the exercise of governmental authority (Article I:3(b)). Services supplied pursuant to governmental authority only fall within this exclusion if the services are provided neither on a commercial basis nor in competition with one or more service suppliers (Article I:3(c)). The scope of this exclusion remains ambiguous and controversial, meaning that this provision deserves close attention from health ministries. Various members have used different techniques to avoid the ambiguities associated with Article 1:3. Some have decided not to undertake commitments at all, others have sought to narrow the scope of commitments to the commercial segment only.

General Obligations and Disciplines

For all measures affecting services within the GATS scope, the Agreement imposes general obligations and disciplines. From a health-policy perspective, the most important general obligations involve rules on domestic regulation of services, specifically disciplines on granting or extending monopoly or exclusive service rights and the duty to engage in negotiations to develop rules on domestic regulation, subsidies, government procurement, and emergency safeguards. While some general obligations, such as the rules on extending monopoly or exclusive service rights, present health policy with challenges, the development of rules on domestic regulation, subsidies, government procurement, and emergency safeguards remains an on-going process that health ministries should monitor.

Specific Commitments

GATS creates a structure for countries to make specific market-access and national-treatment commitments in service sectors in which they wish to liberalize trade. Market-access commitments remove barriers to foreign services, and national-treatment commitments require that foreign and domestic services be treated the same. Under GATS, each WTO member decides for itself whether to make binding market access and national-treatment commitments.

At the same time, GATS imposes a "list it or lose it" process on countries making specific commitments. When making market-access or national-treatment commitments, countries have to list all measures they wish to retain that would otherwise violate the specific commitment being made. Some measures that restrict market access may be important for health policy reasons, such as limitations on the number of service suppliers through an economic needs test, which illustrates the importance of thoroughly analyzing proposals to liberalize trade in health-related services.

Progressive Liberalization

Countries will face decisions whether to liberalize trade in services through market-access and national-treatment commitments in periodic negotiations designed to produce the progressive liberalization of trade in services.

Managing the GATS Process from a Health Policy Perspective

The structure and substance of the GATS create a challenge for ministries of health to develop capabilities to manage the GATS process effectively from a health-policy perspective in two key areas: (1) evaluating requests for, and offers of, specific commitments; and (2) negotiations on GATS rules.

With respect to the request/offer process and specific commitments, at the heart of this challenge will be the assessment of other countries' requests for, and a country's own offers of, liberalization in health-related services. Requests will seek, and offers will make, new

---

Box 11.4. Key Questions for Monitoring the Impact of GATS on Health Policy

In connection with a request for, or offer of, market access and/or national treatment commitments in a health-related service sector:

- To what extent is the sector already open to foreign service providers, and what have been the regulatory concerns posed by existing foreign competition?
- Do the commitments fit the strategies and directions identified by national health policy?
- What effect would the commitments have on government-provided health-related services?
- What regulatory burdens would the commitments create for the government in health-related sectors?
- Would the commitments eliminate or weaken regulatory approaches necessary for the protection and promotion of health?
- What scientific and public-health evidence and principles can be brought to bear to analyze the possible effect of the commitments?
- Can the commitments be crafted both to protect health policy and to liberalize trade progressively?

Source: Adapted from Smith et al. (2006).

specific commitments on market access and national treatment. Health-policy analysis of GATS indicates that requests for new market-access commitments will pose the most difficulties for health policy makers because measures that restrict market access may be used by health ministries to pursue domestic health-service objectives.

The tabling of requests for, and making offers of, specific market access and national treatment commitments will raise questions that health-policy makers will have to address (see Box 11.4).

Negotiations on GATS Rules

The GATS process also involves negotiations on GATS rules on domestic regulation, subsidies, emergency safeguards, and government procurement. These negotiations also deserve the attention and analysis of health ministries because of the potential to adopt rules that would affect health policy, especially with regard to rules on domestic regulation.

Building Capacity at the National Level to Inform the GATS Negotiations and Monitor Health Implications of GATS

Although experts acknowledge that the GATS has yet to significantly affect trade in health-related services, the potential for the GATS to do so through the progressive liberalization process is substantial. In the GATS negotiations, countries may be receiving requests from and may consider submitting offers to other WTO members for market-access and national-treatment commitments in many different health-related service sectors. Such requests/offers will place a premium on a government's ability to develop inter-agency cooperation and collaboration in order to ensure that decisions made on new specific commitments do not adversely affect national health policy and regulatory capabilities. Health ministries were not actively involved in the Uruguay Round negotiations on GATS, but should be encouraged to be pro-active about their responsibilities with respect to the current GATS process (see Box 11.5).

Building GATS capacity at the national level will require countries, among other things, to analyze their current level and types of trade in health services, the benefits and costs that existing trade has produced, the barriers to expanding such trade and the policy objectives behind those barriers, those who stand to gain and lose from liberalization proposals, and the regulatory and policy changes needed to harness liberalization for the maximum benefit to health (See Box 11.6).

Box 11.5. Checklist for Policy Makers on Trade in Health-Related Services

---

- Identify a focal point for trade in health-related services within the Ministry of Health.
- Establish contacts and systematic interactions (e.g. a GATS working group) with trade and other key ministries and with representatives from private industry and civil society.
- Collect and evaluate relevant information on the effect of existing trade in health-related services within the country.
- Obtain reliable legal advice not only on the GATS but also on other international trade and investment agreements (e.g., bilateral investment agreements) that may affect trade in health-related services.
- Develop a sustainable mechanism for monitoring the impact of trade in health-related services generally and the GATS process specifically.
- Utilize the information and technical assistance provided by WHO on matters concerning trade in health-related services.
- Subject all requests for, and offers of, liberalization of trade in health-related services to a thorough assessment of their health policy implications.

Source: Adapted from Smith et al. (2006).

Box 11.6. Elements of a General Framework for Country Analysis of GATS

- General macro-economic and trade environment in the country.
- State of the domestic public health and health care systems.
- State of trade and investment in health-related service sectors.
- The quality of information on the health sector.
- Institutional capacity and capabilities for handling liberalized trade in health-related services.

Source: Adapted from Smith et al. (2006).

The World Health Organization (WHO) Work on the GATS and Policy Recommendations to Date

The WHO work on the GATS has, to date, focused on collecting evidence on the potential and actual impact of the GATS on the functioning of health systems. These efforts involve:

- collecting data on trade in health-related services;
- undertaking a wide range of country-based studies;
- conducting regional and national training programs;
- supporting a legal review of GATS from the perspective of health policy;
- developing a Handbook on Trade in Health-Related Services and GATS; and
- tracking and disseminating information on GATS negotiations.

The following general policy recommendations noted in Smith et al. (2006) are based on this work to date:

- Get Your House in Order: National stewardship of the health system in the context of the GATS requires a sophisticated understanding of how trade in health-related services already affects and may affect a country's health systems and policy.
- Know the Whole House, Not Just Select Rooms: The GATS process can affect many sectors related to health, and this places a premium on health ministries understanding the importance of a comprehensive outlook on trade in health-related services.
- Remember Who Owns the House: The GATS provides countries with choices and does not force them to make liberalization commitments that are not in their best interests. If a country is unsure about the effects of making specific commitments, it is fully within its rights to decline to make legally binding commitments to liberalize.
- Home Improvement Means Health Improvement: Health principles and criteria, as outlined in Box 11.1, should drive policy decisions on trade in health-related services in the GATS negotiations.

Conclusion

The GATS constitutes a very important agreement from the perspective of health. Unlike the relationship between health and other WTO agreements, the GATS and health interface will be most significantly shaped by the ongoing and subsequent efforts to progressively liberalize trade in services. In this light, countries must develop informed and sophisticated approaches to managing the GATS process, its results, and future liberalization efforts. The WHO is developing capabilities to assist countries in this endeavor but, without commitment by national governments, the protection and promotion of health in the GATS process may be compromised.

"Top Ten" Key Questions Concerning Trade in Health Services and the GATS: Why are Current Levels of Trade in Health Services Low?

There is considerable evidence that the overall level of GATS commitments in health is extremely low, which itself is seen as a reflection of an overall low (although increasing) level of trade within health services. Indeed, apart from education, no service sector has fewer GATS commitments than health. Further, of the countries that have made commitments, the number of sectors committed is positively related to levels of economic development. That is, developed countries appear to find it either easier or more economically beneficial to submit relatively extensive schedules than do developing countries.[2] Overall, of the four relevant subsectors, medical and dental services are the most heavily committed (62 members), followed by hospital services (52 members), and services provided by midwives, nurses, etc. (34 members). This general pattern suggests that it is politically easier or more economically attractive for administrations to liberalize capital-intensive and skill-intensive sectors than labor-intensive activities.

Given that commitments and negotiation activity are so low in health compared with other service sectors, the key question is therefore why they are so low, and whether this indicates that countries should be unconcerned about trade in health services or GATS-related commitments. In this respect, there may be two reasons for such low levels of current activity. The first is the presence of government monopolies offering services free or below cost. This would especially affect commitments under mode 3 (commercial presence), but also other modes as well. However, although this may be a part of the reason, total monopoly situations are rare, and most countries have both a public and a private health sector. Second, there do not appear to be any "pace setters" in the health sector, compared, for example, to the role played by the United States, the European Community and other OECD countries in areas such as telecommunications and financial services.

Nonetheless, this does not imply that trade in health services will not assume greater significance in future GATS negotiations. For example, it may be argued that the GATS process is so new that other sectors, which were already more liberalized, were easier to commit to first, and once these are underway attention will turn to other areas. It may also be argued that new technologies are making health more amenable to trade. Similarly, saturation in other markets may lead to health being seen as a growth area, especially as more countries increase the role of the private sector in health services. Overall, however, the lesson may be that, once developed countries have "saturated" their own markets, they will be likely to move on to see how to exploit other markets. At the same time, it might be suggested that while developed countries have their trade focus on other sectors,

---

[2] This generally applies, although there are some interesting anomalies, such as Canada not undertaking commitments in any of the four relevant subsectors (medical and dental services; services provided by midwives, nurses, physiotherapists, and paramedical personnel; hospital services; and other human health services such as ambulance services and residential health facility services), and the United States and Japan scheduling only one, while Burundi, The Gambia, Lesotho, Malawi, Sierra Leone, and Zambia have all included at least three subsectors.

developing countries might take advantage of this vacuum in trade to pursue their own agendas, either in health or in other sectors linked with health.[3]

How Will the GATS Legally Affect a Country's Health Policy?

Two core issues determine the answer to this question. First, does the specific health-related service in question fall within the remit of the GATS? The GATS applies to health-related services provided for profit, but controversy exists about the application of the GATS to government-provided services. The GATS excludes services provided pursuant to the exercise of governmental authority as long as such services are not provided on a "commercial basis" or "in competition" with other services. How WTO members define these terms will determine whether government-provided health-related services fall within, or are excluded from, the GATS.

Although many legal experts expect the exclusion to be interpreted and applied narrowly, the ambiguity provides an opportunity for the health-policy community to influence the interpretation of this exclusion in a way that is sensitive to health-policy concerns. For example, WTO members can clarify what "commercial basis" and "in competition" mean in a way that excludes the provision of most government-provided health-related services.

Important here is also influencing the WTO to insist that the "burden of proof" concerning whether a government-supplied service benefits from the exclusion should fall on the WTO member claiming that the exclusion does not cover a government-supplied service (i.e. a WTO member complaining about a possible GATS violation).

Second, when a health-related service falls within the GATS, what GATS "rules" are most significant in affecting health policy? These are fourfold:

- The general obligations and disciplines of the GATS affect health policy. Essentially, these are obligations that apply to trade in all service sectors covered by GATS, and comprise the MFN obligation and various obligations that relate to domestic regulatory powers. The MFN obligation probably does not significantly affect health policy. However, the general obligations affecting domestic regulatory powers may be significant, as they may interfere with the ability of a member to regulate services domestically, such as in regard to licensing and qualification requirements, or technical standards. At present, however, WTO members have negotiated no disciplines

---

[3] See Box 11.7 at the end of the chapter for a discussion of the GATS and the health of poor people especially in less-developed countries.

on domestic regulatory powers in the area of health-related services. Overall, in terms of the general obligations and disciplines of the GATS, their present impact on health policy is not particularly troubling. The general obligations that are universally binding are not large in number or worrying for health policy. The low level of specific commitments made to date in health-related sectors mitigates the effect of the general obligations linked to specific commitments. More concerns may arise in the future, however, if the level and nature of specific commitments in health-related sectors increase and as WTO members negotiate additional multilateral disciplines on trade in services.

- Rules governing the making of specific commitments and progressive liberalization will also affect health policy. Many suggest that rules on specific commitments allow WTO members to retain flexibility and discretion in calibrating where and how much to liberalize trade in services. What this perspective obscures, however, is that the policy freedom and flexibility that WTO members have to make specific commitments disappears once specific commitments are made, perhaps locking WTO members into liberalization commitments that may turn out to be bad policy moves. Further, the flexibility of the specific commitment provisions cannot be isolated from the duty to participate in successive negotiating rounds to progressively liberalize trade in services. The political dynamic created by the duty to negotiate progressive liberalization may, over time, be detrimental to a government's ability to provide and regulate public-interest services such as health. The GATS rules on making specific commitments require that members exercise great care and foresight in listing the types of market-access restrictions or national-treatment restrictions that they want to maintain or adopt in the future. The broad scope of the GATS therefore creates an enormous challenge for members, with pressure to undertake the complex and difficult process of scheduling specific commitments with little margin for error.

- In the event a health-related measure affecting trade in services violates the GATS, the treaty contains exceptions to its obligations, including an exception specifically on health. The health exception justifies violations of GATS rules when the measures in question are "necessary to protect human, animal, or plant life or health." WTO members attempting to use this exception must demonstrate that their measures are the least trade restrictive measures reasonably available to them to achieve the level of health protection sought.

- The GATS "institutional framework," and particularly the dispute settlement mechanism, are also important parts of the GATS for health policy. Other contexts demonstrate that the WTO dispute settlement mechanism will not adopt a deferential attitude toward members, arguing that their behavior protects human health. At the same time, these rulings suggest that the WTO dispute settlement process is capable of producing rulings that recognize the importance of protecting human health within a system designed to liberalize international trade.

The relationship between the GATS and health policy may be most significantly shaped by the ongoing and subsequent efforts to progressively liberalize trade in health-related services and the negotiation of further multilateral disciplines on domestic regulatory powers. The challenge for health policy is to manage this international legal process in an informed and sophisticated manner in order to ensure that the evolving law of the GATS recognizes and respects WTO member rights to promote and protect health. It is vital therefore that countries have a clear idea of the effect that liberalization will have on their respective health systems.

What Effect Might Liberalization have on National Health Systems?

The effect of liberalization on a country's health system will crucially depend upon the extent to which the private sector does, or is able to, participate in the provision of health services. A potential concern with the GATS is that it may cause countries to overlook the issue of commercial-health-service provision and finance in the move to discuss the level to which foreign participation in the market may occur. However, the core issue remains whether a country wishes to have, or expand, private-sector involvement in the provision and/or finance of health services. This will be an issue related to, for example, national budget priorities, the desire to increase available resources, questions about the efficiency of resource use, ensuring that public policy objectives (such as universal provision of high-quality care) are met, and so forth.

If commercialization of health care is desired, the question becomes whether to allow participation by foreign suppliers. It is only at this stage that the GATS comes into play. The GATS only deals with the treatment of foreigners, not nationals, and the GATS has nothing to say on the debate over whether to allow private provision per se. This may involve some of the following considerations: the desire to increase the efficiency of national private providers by exposing them to competition; the use of foreign suppliers to meet key shortages in the short- to medium-term; the desire to have access to new technologies or skills that may not be available from national suppliers; and the desire to increase the facilities and services available to health-care consumers beyond what the domestic suppliers can provide. Equally, consideration must be given to how to ensure the quality of foreign providers and the impact of foreign suppliers on local suppliers and on the system for health care as a whole.

What are the Likely Benefits from Greater Trade in Health Services?

Foreign investment in health facilities represents a transfer of resources whose ramifications reach beyond the health sector, including indirect effects on growth, income, and employment, and in other sectors, such as construction, transport, and communication. Health tourism can become an area in which developing countries are competitive exporters. Some countries with health personnel surpluses can also make important economic gains from remittances from the temporary movement of health professionals. From the standpoint of public health, it might prove too narrow a view to consider only the direct effects on a population's health status of increased foreign presence in, for example, a country's hospital sector. Broader routes of causation, leading from the liberalization of trade and investment to development and from development to better population health, may be equally significant in this connection.

In addition to the economy-wide benefits, trade in health services can have positive impacts on the national health system in a variety of ways. Foreign investors can bring in additional resources, new technologies, and new management techniques that can improve the provision of services and financing of the system. These can improve working conditions and therefore reduce the likelihood that health professionals leave the country. Foreign insurers may contribute to reduce the heavy reliance on out-of-pocket payments for health services found in many developing countries. The potential of trade in health services can be harnessed to benefit the whole health system, not merely a small group of patients. However, this will require a strengthening of the stewardship and regulatory functions of national governments.

What can be Done to Limit the Possible Risks of Trade?

A key concern with respect to liberalizing trade in health services is the effect on equity of access and quality of care. There are limits to the extent to which governments can influence the level and structure of trade in health services. However, it is important to bear in mind that:

- The GATS does not impose any constraints on the terms and conditions under which a potential host country treats foreign patients, so, for example, foreigners may be charged extra for treatment and these proceeds used to enhance the quantity and quality of basic domestic supplies.

- There are no legal impediments in the GATS that would affect the ability of governments to discourage qualified staff from seeking employment in the private sector, whether at home or abroad, such as through deposit requirements or guarantees that would make it financially unattractive for young professionals to capitalize immediately on taxpayer investment in their education by seeking higher incomes.

- It is difficult to see any crowding-out effects, to the disadvantage of resident patients, that could not be addressed through adequate regulation that would not normally violate GATS provisions. For example, a country might require all private hospitals to reserve a minimum per centage of beds for free treatment for the needy, to offer some basic medical services in remote rural areas, or to train beyond the number required for the purposes of these institutions.

In addition to the foregoing, there are a number of key limitations that may be made by members in their GATS commitments. Horizontal limitations apply across all committed sectors and typically reflect economy-wide policy concerns and objectives. These include, for example, restrictions on the physical presence of foreign suppliers, foreign equity ceilings, or restrictions on the legal form of establishment (e.g. joint ventures only). In contrast, vertical limitations refer to specific limitations under each GATS mode. For modes 1 and 2, these mainly concern the nonportability of insurance entitlements. Mode 3 and 4 limitations tend to be covered under horizontal limitations. For example, in mode 3, some countries have reserved the right to restrict the commercial incorporation of foreign health-care providers, and in mode 4, quota-type restrictions, mainly setting a ceiling on numbers of foreign employees or denying access to all persons not considered to be specialist doctors, have been frequent. Furthermore, economic needs tests (ENTs) have also been frequently referred to in limitations under modes 3 and 4, mostly for hospital services but also for medical and dental services.

When, and How Best, Might Negotiations be Undertaken?

In undertaking liberalization, the consequences should be carefully considered, and in particular the timing and pace of liberalization must be well thought out. In a public-monopoly environment, the production, financing, regulation, and control of a service tend to go hand in hand, whereas the move toward competitive systems necessarily implies a separation of tasks and functions. Liberalization may therefore presuppose regulation to meet the multiplicity of legitimate objectives involved. This is a challenging task, not least for developing countries lacking regulatory experience. However, there is nothing to prevent administrations from joining forces to exploit possible synergies and/or mandating competent international organizations to propose model solutions. Regulatory approaches developed for telecommunications in recent years, under the auspices of the International Telecommunication Union, could inspire work in WHO and comparable bodies in other areas as well. The technological and economic forces working toward global market integration are unlikely to leave the health sector unaffected, and timely action by governments would seem to be desirable.

What is the Relationship between Trade in Health Services and Other Sectors?

Trade policy becomes a health-policy issue not only for how it affects health systems, but also for how it influences the many social, environmental, and economic determinants of health. Health services, although an important determinant of health, are not the primary determinant of health, especially in developing countries. Rather, the greatest influences on population health are education, income (and thus employment), gender, nutrition, and access to clean water and sanitation. Thus, any assessment of the impact of trade liberalization should include the impact of trade-policy commitments on the foregoing influences and equitable access that is strongly associated with population health.

Clearly, each population health determinant is influenced by domestic public policies, but crucially these domestic public policies are influenced by numerous bilateral, regional, and global trade agreements, of which GATS is just one. It is therefore important for developing countries to consider important nonmedical (social, environmental, economic) health determinants, how they are presently considered in policy discussions of nonhealth sectors (e.g. environment, education, transportation, energy, finance, social services, housing) and what analytical and human resource capacity is available in the health ministry, or in collaboration with university researchers and nongovernmental organizations, to engage in assessments of nonhealth policies on health determinants.

Should Trade Liberalization be Under GATS or Other Trade Agreements?

Thus far, discussion has focused mostly on the GATS. However, the core question concerning trade liberalization in health services is whether these reforms should be undertaken under the GATS or under other trade agreements? There are many, issues relating to this question, the two most important being:

- Can GATS commitments in one area be used effectively as a bargaining chip to negotiate better market access or to achieve other goals with trading partners in another area? For example, a commitment in health services may be offered in exchange for a reduction in agricultural subsidies from other members of the WTO.

- Will foreign investors see binding trade reforms under GATS as an insurance policy that their entry into a market, and their nondiscriminatory treatment, is guaranteed? If so, will this encourage investor confidence and lead to greater foreign investment in the sector in which the commitments were made?

Whether a country should consider liberalizing trade in health services in the context of a regional trade agreement, but not under the GATS, will depend upon the country's assessment of, among other things, whether its trade interests are regional or global (e.g. while some countries may feel more comfortable opening up to foreign investment from their neighbors, their export interests—such as in temporary movement of personnel—may be more global in character).

Other factors to consider include the extent to which the key shortages expected to be met by trade can be met from the parties to the regional agreement, rather than on a global basis; the relative costs and benefits of negotiating effort, relative negotiating power, and the scope for leveraging the outcome of one process in the context of another.

Of course, even if countries do not make commitments under the GATS or health services, trade itself will continue as it has for some time, independent of the GATS. Thus, whether or not a country decides to make GATS commitments on trade in health services, it will still need to deal with many of the issues and challenges that arise from that trade. So, should a country commit under GATS or not? This hinges almost entirely on the following crucial issue.

What is the Single Most Important Issue in Determining Whether to Commit under the GATS?

The issue of policy reversal is perhaps the most important element of doubt over whether liberalization should take place within the GATS or without.

Making commitments under the GATS is very different from undertaking liberalization unilaterally within a country's own policy framework. By committing a sector to the GATS, the country must abide by specific GATS rules on market access and national treatment in relation to that sector, as well as the general GATS rules governing all services. Unlike a country's own unilateral decisions, which can be reversed if they are found to be damaging, the GATS commitment is binding and effectively irreversible. This requires a far higher threshold of certainty before countries decide to make any commitments, particularly in crucial service sectors such as health, under the GATS. In assessing the likely impact of the GATS on health, the central questions facing policy makers are therefore actually very simple, and very stark:

- Will increased trade in these services lead to better health outcomes?
- Will increased liberalization of trade (more competition from foreign private health care companies) lead to better health outcomes?
- Will making a GATS commitment in these sectors offer any additional advantage that will lead to better health outcomes?

Of course, the implication here is clear: "if the answer to any of these is negative, or in doubt, then a country should not make GATS commitments."

Overall, we conclude that members who would like to open their health sector to foreign providers should consider "experimenting" with liberalization outside of GATS before making GATS commitments. Members can liberalize trade in health-related services unilaterally, if they wish, without accepting binding commitments in their national GATS schedules of specific commitments. Such unilateral liberalization would allow WTO members to experiment with such policies in a way that permits them to reverse course on market access or national treatment if the experiment produces unsatisfactory results. Although this seems straightforward, answering these questions will require a considerable level of information and analysis.

How Might a Country Best Obtain the Information Necessary to Inform Policy?

Data on the impact of trade liberalization on health, health services, or the economy are scarce. That data are scarce really reflects three interrelated issues: that there has been no imperative to assess the data before (for instance, routine data tend not to be broken down into health sector categories that would be required); there is no existing "tool" that may be used to determine what, and how, such data may be collected; and countries often lack human and physical capital to collect the required data.

A framework can be designed—see boxes 11.4 and 11.6—to assist countries in gathering information that would help policy makers understand the nature and implications of international trade in the health sector, and thus assist them in formulating trade policy as well as in participating in international negotiations concerning the health sector. In doing so, the framework will also assist in the identification of information and data gaps, and thus help prioritize, streamline, and coordinate data collection in this area. It should also help to avoid duplication of information and effort in assessing the opportunities and risks involved in engaging in wider trade liberalization in health services. Furthermore, by proposing a common format and standard questionnaire, the framework will hopefully facilitate the establishment of a common database and data-collection techniques and greater sharing of experiences and data across countries, thus enabling cross-country learning and comparative assessment of the effects of autonomous or GATS-related liberalization.

The framework is designed to gather information from a variety of sources, and in a variety of formats (quantitative and qualitative). It is therefore not possible, or necessarily desirable, to produce a "mathematical" algorithm for determining a country's approach to trade liberalization in health services (within or without the context of GATS). Rather, the framework pulls together, in a systematic manner, the most relevant items of information that policy makers will need to assist them in this respect and to work through the complex economic, sectoral, social, and international issues that surround trade liberalization and health services. In this way, the framework achieves three goals. First, it creates awareness of and sensitization to issues with respect to trade liberalization and health services. Second, the framework helps users to identify and formulate policy at the national, bilateral, regional, and multilateral levels. It is expected that the framework exercise will help countries to identify areas and issues on which to focus and prioritize in terms of policy measures and initiatives at various levels, with a view to facilitating trade in health services while ensuring the associated gains and mitigating the associated adverse effects. Third, the framework should help to identify gaps in data and information, and in existing data collection systems and procedures. It is expected that identification of such limitations will provide the basis for establishing appropriate procedural, organizational, and institutional structures and systems to improve the state of data and information relevant to understanding and assessing trade in health services.

Box 11.7. The GATS and the Health of Poor People

Shantayanan Devarajan*

The prospect that the General Agreement on Trade in Services (GATS) will include health services is causing considerable concern in the health community. Acknowledging that the GATS provides an opportunity for improving health outcomes, the authors of this chapter advocate a cautious approach. They argue that liberalization in health services should "ensure the necessary policy and regulatory space governments require to promote and protect the health of their populations, particularly those in greatest need." They point out that countries are not obliged to liberalize health services if they do not wish to do so.

Since when have governments been promoting and protecting the health of those in need? Many, if not most, governments today are failing to meet the health needs of poor people. The child mortality rate for the poorest 20 per cent of the population of Bolivia is almost five times that for the richest 20 per cent. These rates can be reduced by spending on those things that affect child deaths, such as safe water, sanitation, immunization, and information about well-child care. Yet the lion's share of government health spending goes towards clinical services—and that too mainly to the non-poor. In Guinea, 48 per cent of public spending on health accrues to the richest quintile of the population, while less than 8 per cent goes to the poorest 20 per cent. Worse still, the quality of the services that poor people receive is often appalling. One symptom is the high degree of absenteeism of doctors in primary health centers. In Bangladesh, the rate is 74 per cent.

In such settings, the introduction of trade in health services is unlikely to affect the services that poor people receive. The trade will be in the high-end clinical services typically enjoyed by the non-poor. But the situation is worse than that. The resistance to GATS may be a reflection of the special interests that have captured public-health expenditures for themselves. The reason why so much of public spending on health benefits the rich has to do with the absence of insurance markets. The rich do not suffer from child mortality, but they do suffer from catastrophic illnesses just as the poor do. Without well-functioning insurance systems, the rich need a way to protect themselves from these catastrophic illnesses (or more precisely, from the income losses associated with them). So they capture the government health budget, and use it to spend on tertiary hospitals in urban areas, as a substitute for a comprehensive insurance scheme. Furthermore, there is a coalition between the people who capture the public health budget, and the government service providers (doctors, nurses) who are chronically absent from their posts in primary health clinics. The doctors would rather not serve in remote, rural areas—so they have an incentive to keep the tertiary urban hospitals funded as well.

The liberalization of trade in health services can upset this system by introducing competition. It is not surprising, therefore, that the resistance to the GATS comes from some health ministries. But should we allow the health ministries—the same ministries that have failed to deliver quality health services to poor people—to lead the discussion on whether trade in health services should be liberalized?

In sum, the GATS is unlikely to have a direct effect on the health of poor people because the health services they receive are not the ones being liberalized. But it could have an indirect, beneficial effect if it helps countries break out of the trap of capture of the health budget by the rich and the health-service providers, releasing resources for improving the health of the poor.

Notes: * Many of these ideas stem from my work on the World Development Report 2004, *Making Services Work for Poor People.* I am grateful to my fellow team members, especially Jeffrey Hammer and Agnes Soucat for their collaboration. The views expressed are my own and not necessarily those of the World Bank.

References

Adlung, R. 2002. "Health Services in a Globalizing World," *EuroHealth* 8: 18–21.

——and A. Carzaniga. 2001. "Health Services under the General Agreement on Trade in Services," *Bulletin of the World Health Organization* 79(4): 352–64.

Chandra, R. 2002. "Trade in Health Services," *Bulletin of the World Health Organization* 80(2): 158–361.

Drager, N. and D. P. Fidler. 2004. "Managing Liberalization of Trade in Services from a Health-Policy Perspective." *Trade and Health Notes* 1 (February). Available at: www.who.int/trade/resource/en/GATSfoldout_e.pdf

Fidler, D. P, C. Correa, and O. Aginam. 2004. *Legal Review of the General Agreement on Trade in Services (GATS) from a Health Policy Perspective.* Geneva: World Health Organization.

Hilary, J. 2001. *The Wrong Model: GATS, Liberalization and Children's Right to Health."* London: Save the Children.

Krajewski, M. 2003. "Public Services and Trade Liberalization: Mapping the Legal Framework," *Journal of International Economic Law* 6(2): 341–67.

Pan American Health Organization/World Health Organization. 2002. "Trade in Health Services: Global, Regional, and Country Perspectives." Washington, D.C.: Pan American Health Organization.

Price, D. and A. M. Pollock. 1999. "How the World Trade Organization is Shaping Domestic Policies in Health Care," *The Lancet* 354: 1889–92.

Sinclair, S. and J. Grieshaber-Otto. 2002. *Facing the Facts: A Guide to the GATS Debate.* Ottawa: Canadian Centre for Policy Alternatives.

Smith, R., C. Blouin, and N. Drager. 2006. "Trade in Health Services and the GATS: Introduction and Summary," in C. Blouin, N. Drager, and R. Smith (eds.), *International Trade in Health Services and the GATS: Current Issues and Debates.* Washington, D.C.: World Bank.

Woodruffe, J. and C. Joy. 2002. *Out of Service: The Development Dangers of the General Agreement on Trade in Services.* London: World Development Movement.

WHO/WTO (World Health Organization/World Trade Organization). 2002. *WTO Agreements and Public Health—A Joint Study by the WHO and the WTO Secretariat.* Geneva: World Health Organization.

World Trade Organization. 2001. *GATS Fact and Fiction.* Geneva: World Trade Organization.

Yach, D., and D. Bettcher. 1998a. "The Globalization of Public Health: Threats and Opportunities," *American Journal of Public Health* 88: 735–8.

——1998b. The Globalization of Public Health: The Convergence of Self-interest and Altruism," *American Journal of Public Health* 88: 738–41.

12 E-Commerce Regulation: New Game, New Rules?

Carlos A. Primo Braga*

Introduction

The rapid expansion of electronic commerce (e-commerce) is impacting economic activities both at the national and international levels. E-commerce is still in its infancy, but it is often identified as one of the main drivers of the economic and social changes associated with the "networking revolution."[1]

There is broad consensus that the establishment of the regulatory environment under which economic agents practice e-commerce plays an important role in shaping the impact and depth of these transformations. Most countries have by now introduced domestic legislation devoted to foster an adequate "digital" environment with special emphasis on the rules and regulations relevant for e-commerce. At the international level, debate is also ongoing not only under the auspices of the World Trade Organization (WTO), but also in many other forums (e.g. OECD, WIPO, ICANN, ITU). This chapter reviews the case for multilateral rules and the challenges faced by regulators around the world to cope with the extra-territorial implications of e-commerce.

The chapter is organized as follows. I first discuss the economic dimensions of e-commerce and the most relevant regulatory issues for its expansion. I then analyze the case for multilateral rules concerning e-commerce, focusing on ongoing discussions on trade-related issues in the WTO. A final section concludes.

E-Commerce and the Regulatory Environment

As reviewed in Primo Braga et al. (2003), a major technological driver of the "networking revolution" has been the exponential growth of computer processing power. Since the 1970s, the number of transistors on a chip has been doubling roughly every

---

[1] The dramatic growth of the Internet and the rapid roll-out of wireless networks are the hallmarks of the "networking revolution." See, for example, InfoDev. (2000). For a discussion of the role of e-commerce in the emerging "networked society," see Drucker (2002).

18 months.[2] Transistor density per chip, in turn, drives performance and as the costs per chip have remained stable, the performance/cost ratio of computing devices has increased dramatically. By 2000, one could buy computer devices with 66,000 times the processing power per dollar of what was available 25 years ago. Moreover, this trend is expected to continue at least until 2010 when computing devices are expected to have 10 million times the processing power per dollar as compared to the computers available in 1975.[3]

Another major technological trend of the last three decades has been the expansion of communication networks. The growing convergence of telecommunications and information technology that started with the introduction of digitally enabled automated exchanges is expected to continue as improvements in the technology of feeding and extracting signals into optical fibers and the wireless explosion reshape the "physical" layer of networks. In the same vein, the emergence of packet-switching networks relying on the Internet protocol at its code layer and software developments affecting the structure and usability of the content layer are expanding further the reach and the attractiveness of networks both for consumers and firms. Table 12.1 illustrates the concept of "layers" in the context of modern communication systems.[4]

There are many working definitions of e-commerce.[5] In the WTO Work Program on Electronic Commerce, for example, e-commerce "is understood to mean the production, distribution, marketing, sale or delivery of goods and services by electronic means."[6] Such a broad definition encompasses not only electronic transactions over open-access networks (the Internet), but also electronic data interchange (EDI) over proprietary networks. As pointed out in Costa (2001), purchasing "is a four-step process of search, order, payment and delivery," and electronic networks can play a role in one or more of these steps. For our purposes, we will consider e-commerce to take place whenever a commercial transaction is conducted online, even if its realization requires physical delivery of the product.

Table 12.1. The Layers of Communication Systems

Content layer (services, images, and applications transmitted by the network)

Code layer (protocols and software that make the network run)

Physical infrastructure layer (wires, cables, computers, satellites across which bits of information travel)

---

[2] This is often referred to as "Moore's Law" after Gordon Moore, the Intel Corporation founder who first observed this trend.

[3] For more details about the drivers of the "information revolution," including Metcalf's Law on network externalities effects, see Shapiro and Varian (1999) and Brad De Long's Home Page section on "Information Economy," available at: http://econ161.berkeley.edu/E_Sidebars/E-conomy_figures2.html

[4] For a discussion of this concept see, for example, Benkley (2000). Note that throughout this chapter, the terms "modern communication networks" and the Internet are used interchangeably.

[5] For details see Primo Braga and Eskinazi (2002).

[6] See WTO (1998).

Table 12.2. Regulatory Environments and Networks: Areas of Relevance for E-Commerce

	Telecom regulation	Competition policy	Intellectual property rights	Taxation	Trade policies	Internet governance	Consumer protection	Privacy and data protection	Content regulation	Security and cyberlaws
Content layer		A	A	A	A		A	A	A	A
Code layer	B	B	B	B	B	B		B	B	B
Physical infrastructure	B	B	B	B	B			B	B	B

Notes: A—denotes areas of direct impact of the identified regulation/policy on e-commerce. B—denotes areas of indirect impact of the identified regulation/policy on e-commerce.

Electronic marketplaces can make trading easier and more efficient than ever. By 1991, the Internet had around three million users worldwide. By the end of year 2004, it is estimated that the global online population will have surpassed 900 million.[7] E-commerce has also expanded dramatically in recent years. From almost zero in 1995, e-commerce transactions passed the $100 billion mark by 1999, and most estimates indicate that they have surpassed $1 trillion in 2003.[8]

E-commerce has the potential of transforming existing trade networks and reducing the handicap of geographical isolation. Firms around the world can now experiment with new ways to contest international markets and countries can further benefit from international specialization. Moreover, in the case of services and digitized goods, e-commerce allows bypassing conventional distribution channels, fostering international market integration. Needless to say, these opportunities can only be realized if certain minimum requirements with respect to access to infrastructure (connectivity) and basic skills (digital literacy) are met.

E-commerce opportunities are influenced by the operations of the three layers of modern networks. The more efficient the physical infrastructure, the greater is the potential for expansion of e-commerce. The quality of the coordination for the allocation of unique IP-addresses and for the development of compatible protocols, in turn, affects the efficiency of the network and its capacity to support e-commerce. And the relevance of the services available in the content layer is the main determinant of the scope of e-commerce.

Many governmental policies affect each one of these distinct layers, as noted in Table 12.2. In what follows, the relevance of these policies for e-commerce activities is briefly reviewed in a qualitative fashion.

Competition Policy and Telecom Regulation

Competition is the key to driving prices down and encouraging innovation in the networked economy. For the sake of simplicity, the regulatory "taxonomy" adopted here assumes that telecom regulation deals with issues of entry/ownership, pricing and fairness (universal service obligations), while competition policy deals meanly with anti-competitive practices and the implications of merger and acquisitions for competition in the industries operating in the distinct layers of the network.

---

[7] For a summary of Internet statistics see, for example: http://www.clickz.com/stats/

[8] The economic importance of e-commerce rests less in its current size than in the likely speed of its expansion. Estimates for e-commerce transactions vary widely, but most analyses suggest that global e-commerce was in the $1.4 to 3.8 trillion range in 2003 (UNCTAD 2003).

There are three areas of particular concern regarding competition at the level of modern communication networks: (1) the promotion of the contestability of incumbent networks; (2) the control of anti-competitive practices; and (3) the implementation of appropriate interconnection policies, so that large as well as small actors can access the infrastructure.[9]

There is a large literature on the impact of the wave of reforms that swept through the basic telecommunications sector (the key sector at the level of the infrastructure layer) in the last two decades.[10] Some of the stylized facts of this literature can be summarized as follows:

- Sector reform involving both liberalization and privatization tends to increase teledensity and telecom productivity (e.g. mainlines per employee).
- The sequence of reforms matters. Delays in introducing competition (e.g. the award of a period of market exclusivity) in the context of privatization efforts tends to adversely affect performance, although mobile services competition can mitigate the adverse impact of such a strategy for fixed-line operators.
- Countries that have given priority to raising proceeds for the government (e.g. by delaying competition) tend to experience higher prices at the consumer level and/or smaller declines over time vis-à-vis those that emphasize competition, particularly, in view of rebalancing efforts to adjust local call prices.
- The quality and independence of the regulatory authority also impact positively on teledensity and productivity.
- Universal service obligations have to be managed carefully since unrealistic rollout targets can be socially wasteful.
- Sector reform is positively correlated with Internet penetration and the potential for e-commerce expansion.

In short, competition in areas of relevance for e-commerce has been typically fostered by market-oriented telecom reform. As discussed below, multilateral rules in this area have played a complementary role, but most of the action is occurring at the country and/or regional (in the case of the E.U.) levels.

---

[9] See OECD (2000) for a more detailed discussion of this theme.

[10] The history of the telecommunications industry is characterized by a "pendulum" movement in terms of its ownership. Many telecom companies started their operations around the world as private enterprises. By the 1970s, however, there were few cases (e.g. the Philippines, Spain, the United States) in which these operators had remained as private entities. In most countries, telecommunication services were provided by monopolistic state-owned enterprises, often rationalized as the proper response to natural monopoly conditions and strategic considerations. The poor record of most state-owned telecom operators in delivering quality services and expanding the coverage of their networks, as well as rapid technological progress in the sector (eroding the natural monopoly argument), contributed to changing the terms of the debate. The push towards competition and privatization was also fostered by the fiscal needs of governments. For further details see, for example, Primo Braga and Ziegler (1998), Beardsley et al. (2002), and Fink et al. (2003).

Competition, however, is not an issue only at the level of the infrastructure layer (which has been dealt with mainly via telecom policy). As illustrated by the Microsoft case in the U.S. and in the E.U., Microsoft's dominance in PC operating systems and consumer applications has led to concerns about its capacity to exercise market power into complementary parts of the network (e.g. workgroup servers) in view of the importance of interoperability of software systems in a networked environment. As a consequence, competition authorities in both cases have intervened (even though with different remedies) to address this type of concern.

It is also worth noting that some countries have been relying on government procurement policies to address perceived anti-competitive practices in the market for software. Peru, for example, began discussing legislation requiring the use of open-source software in publicly funded IT projects in 2002. In the same vein, Brazil (mainly at the level of municipalities) and some European countries have been considering legislation that favors open-source solutions.

Intellectual Property Rights

Intellectual property rights (IPRs) play a critical role in the process of innovation (generation of new knowledge) in market economies. Over the last 15 years there has been a clear trend toward the strengthening of IPRs around the world, a process closely associated with multilateral negotiations.[11] Although such developments as the outcome of the WTO Ministerial Conference in Doha in 2001 and the subsequent waiver (August 2003) for trade in drugs produced under compulsory licensing suggest that this trend may be reversed, IP owners will continue to press for higher standards of protection at national and international levels. These interests are not necessarily aligned with those of consumers and content-access providers (e.g. Internet service providers).

Copyright and trademarks play an important role in influencing the dissemination of content in cyberspace. Their protection goes beyond the content layer, also affecting the code layer given the potential implications of trademarks for domain names. The Internet not only opened new possibilities for dissemination of information, but also expanded the scope for activities that may infringe on someone's IPRs. With a few computer strokes, one can download copyrighted material in bulletin boards around the world in an anonymous fashion. It can be argued that this is simply another chapter in the history of technological progress and that, as in the case of photocopying, audio, and videotape capabilities, the law will adapt—as time goes by—to face these new challenges. The expansion of legitimate videotape rental facilities around the world illustrates how the legal system can cope with decreasing costs of copying, while enforcing the protection of IPRs.

---

[11] For details see, for example, Primo Braga (1996).

The costs of enforcing IPRs in a network environment, however, can be substantial. Digital technologies are not only reducing reproduction costs, but are also dramatically changing distribution costs. Nowhere is this better illustrated than in the market for music. Illegal downloading of music on the Internet has significantly affected the music industry, with sales lost to Internet "piracy" estimated at roughly $2.4 billion per year, and the industry has experienced a related decline in global music sales of roughly 7 per cent per year over the last two years.[12] The industry has been following a two-track strategy in fighting this phenomenon: (1) initiating legal action against websites that allow file-sharing; and (2) experimenting with new business models (e.g. Apple's iTunes) that allow for legal download of music for a fee. The costs of legal enforcement, not to mention the public-relations implications, limit the overall impact of the two-track strategy. The adoption of new business models, in turn, is a positive development that illustrates the scope to explore e-commerce as an opportunity opened by digital technologies.

Another important dimension of the impact of IPRs in networks concerns its role in fostering innovation. As pointed out by Lessig (2001), the explosion of creativity and innovation associated with the Internet has occurred, ironically, in a setting that had at its core a non-proprietary approach to the protocols and, in part, to the content on the network. According to this view, attempts to strengthen protection—as illustrated by the drive toward the application of patents to software and business processes in the United States, and the sui-generis approach to database protection in the European Union—may chill innovation by fostering rent-seeking and confining the "commons" under which cyberspace has prospered. Moreover, as just discussed, stronger IPRs may also conspire against the interoperability of software, affecting the growth (and the value) of networks.

Taxation

The taxation of e-commerce poses several challenges to tax authorities. First, there is the question of definition of digital products, since so-called "soft goods" (e.g. software, books, music) can be treated either as goods or services. The treatment in each case will vary, depending, for example, on whether or not services are taxed in the relevant tax jurisdiction. Second, the treatment of indirect taxes (e.g. value added taxes) raises not only questions of enforcement, but also requires clarification of concepts such as the "place of permanent establishment" for e-commerce firms. A firm may not be physically present in a tax jurisdiction, but have a website hosted in a local ISP in order to provide an efficient interface to local consumers. If the website hosting is considered as evidence of permanent

---

[12] See Burt (2004). For a detailed discussion of music piracy and copyright in the "digital age," see Bach (2004).

establishment, then local authorities could in principle tax sales associated with that website. If not, then the firm would not be required to collect sales tax. Third, the issues of permanent establishment and the characterization of income generated by e-commerce (business profits or royalty income) are also critical for direct tax purposes (e.g. income tax).[13]

International Trade

Trade policies can also significantly influence the prospects for e-commerce expansion. In theory, e-commerce operates in an electronic space that is not bound by geography or national borders. And, in practice, most e-commerce is currently free from customs duties (in large part because of the technical difficulties of applying duties to these flows). But trade policies—in particular, quantitative restrictions to service suppliers—can be used to impair international transactions.

E-commerce typically occurs under the guise of cross-border trade in services as discussed above. In this context, most of the concerns associated with market access for e-commerce are related to the content layer of networks. Market access barriers affecting other layers (e.g. tariffs and QRs on information and communication technology equipment which are the building blocks of the physical layer), however, are also relevant.

Moreover, trade policies are intimately associated with domestic regulation in areas of relevance for e-commerce activities. Market access commitments can be affected (or even nullified) by decisions on foreign direct investment or taxation, for example. Constraints on the establishment of service suppliers can hinder the scope of cross-border transactions in the content layer. In the same vein, value added tax (VAT) rebates that favor domestic products (as illustrated by China's treatment of semiconductor chips) can be construed to discriminate against foreign producers.

Internet Governance

The architecture of the Internet is based on an end-to-end design (i.e. a design that is neutral across applications and controlled from the "edge" by users that operate "intelligent" terminals across a "dumb" network that is focused on transmitting packets of information as efficiently and flexibly as possible). This differentiates Internet-based networks from conventional telecommunications networks and puts a special value on

---

[13] For a detailed discussion of taxation issues, see Mann et al. (2000).

the rules-of-the-game adopted for guaranteeing a smooth operation of the many networks linked by Internet protocols.[14]

These rules (covering the code layer) deal mainly with issues such as: the coordination and administration of the Domain Name System (that translates domain names into machine-readable numerical addresses) and its root servers; the administration/allocation of IP-addresses; and the development of protocols and standards. Some of these functions are quite technical, but essential for the stability of the network (e.g. IP addresses need to be globally unique and domain names should allow proper global identification). Most of these functions are currently implemented by the Internet Corporation for Assigned Names and Numbers (ICANN)—a private international organization, incorporated under California law—and its associated Regional Internet Registries. As pointed out by Holitscher (2004), these coordinating activities have the potential of generating/redistributing wealth (e.g. via the creation of new Top Level Domain names) and the control of ICANN has generated a great deal of debate in view of perceptions about the U.S. government influence on its operations.

Consumer Protection

This is another area in which e-commerce has opened new challenges to governments. On-line transactions are often characterized by lack of transparency (in terms of responsibilities of the seller, warranties, refund arrangements, etc.) and legal uncertainty with respect to the relevant jurisdiction for consumer complaints, not to mention difficulties with enforcement. Cyberspace allows fraud and deception to be explored in a networked fashion, compounding the potential reach and impact of illegal activities. Unless consumer protection can be enforced under reasonable terms, trust (a critical variable for the expansion of e-commerce) in the new medium is unlikely to evolve in a positive fashion. At the same time, excessive regulatory burden can inhibit entry by small enterprises into this market. For example, the adoption of "country-of-destination" principle, according to which the law and jurisdiction to be applied in c-commerce disputes are the ones of the country of residence of the consumer, illustrates a counter-productive approach in a world characterized by different consumer protection standards.[15]

---

[14] For a discussion of Internet architecture, see, for example, Denton (1999) and Lessig (2001).
[15] For further details, see ICC (2003).

Privacy and Data Protection

Appropriate privacy- and data-protection policies are also fundamental aspects of a sound regulatory environment. These policies are particularly relevant for business-to-consumer transactions, as consumers are reluctant to engage in online transactions if these issues are not properly addressed.[16]

Technology-based solutions can play an important role in this context. The growing reliance on cryptography and protocols such as Secured Electronic Transactions (SET) that enable consumers to use credit cards, without directly revealing information online (a third party verifies and transfers funds between the buyer and seller) illustrate this. Still, unless the local regulatory authorities have the capacity to engage the private sector in a meaningful dialogue on how to adopt such solutions, concerns about unfair market advantages can hinder their introduction and effectiveness.

It is also important to recognize that expansive jurisdictional interpretations—as illustrated by the EU Data Protection Directive that requires foreign website operators to comply with EU privacy laws even though they are not established for business in the EU—may generate international friction.

Content Regulation

There are legitimate regulatory objectives associated with efforts to protect the public, and children in particular, from objectionable content (e.g. pornography) and to combat unlawful and/or harmful content (e.g. gambling, material promoting hate speech, racism, or violence). Government authorities often attempt to censor information and/or control access to Internet sites based on subject matter. Needless to say, regulation in this area can easily disguise repressive actions and protectionist motivations. This is an area in which the scope for international harmonization is limited, given wide differences in societal values. Emphasis on self-regulation and technological solutions (e.g. content filters) has been the route supported by e-commerce firms with a view to minimize regulatory burden.

Security and Cyberlaws

As pointed out in Mann et al. (2000: 206), security is often listed as the top concern of commercial enterprises as far as barriers to e-commerce expansion are concerned. Over

---

[16] OECD (2001).

the last few years, the number of security incidents in the Internet has grown at a fast pace. The explosion of viruses (often in connection with spam email) and "worms" (malicious code that can identify vulnerable targets on the Internet without direct human involvement) has generated significant economic damage, which is currently estimated to run into hundreds of billions of dollars per year. In the same vein, cybercrime (e.g. identity theft, "phishing" scams) is on the rise, further contributing to demands for international collaboration.

Many countries have implemented cyberlaws addressing issues like authentication (e.g. the role of digital signatures) and certification (e.g. the liability of certification authorities), as well as the acceptability of paperless records in courts. Conflicting approaches in this area and in the treatment of technologies adopted to secure electronic transactions (e.g. encryption) continue to hamper e-commerce activities and harm user confidence in the medium.

Summing up, e-commerce activities are potentially affected by a myriad of regulatory environments and policies as described above.[17] In theory, the regulatory framework supporting e-commerce should be governed by consistent principles, leading to predictable results regardless of the legal framework in which a particular buyer or seller resides. In practice, regulatory policies do reflect societal values and in this context friction across national jurisdictions is inevitable. Against this background, there is a natural tendency to look for multilateral forums as a mechanism to advance the debate on the regulation of e-commerce.

The Case for Multilateral Rules[18]

To what extent can multilateral rules for e-commerce minimize the potential for regulatory conflict identified above? The desirability of multilateral responses is influenced by the perspective adopted in evaluating the issues raised by e-commerce. At one extreme, there are those who would argue that nothing new is required to deal with these issues. From this perspective, existing regulatory regimes in the fields of telecom, competition, intellectual property rights, etc., can cope with most e-commerce issues. At the other extreme, there are those who argue that "cyberspace" cannot be ruled by existing legal and regulatory environments.[19] In this perspective, "cyberspace"

---

[17] The summary mapping provided in this section is by no means comprehensive. The regulation of financial services, for example, can also have significant implications for e-commerce, affecting entry in Internet banking and the use of electronic transfers as a form of payment.

[18] This section relies extensively upon Primo Braga and Eskinazi (2002).

[19] For an example of this extreme perspective with respect to IPRs, see Barlow (1994).

constitutes a mythical "seventh continent," with no political borders, operating in a 24 × 7 × 365 environment.[20] In such a "space," national regulations are bound to conflict and unless supranational solutions or effective forms of international cooperation are fashioned, e-commerce will not be able to live up to its full potential.

It should come as no surprise that the truth is somewhere in between these extreme views. Some issues are to a certain extent unique to e-commerce—e.g. the need for international cooperation concerning the code layer of networks (i.e. Internet governance). Even in such areas, however, one could argue that the problems are not necessarily new, simply reflecting the need for coordination in a networked environment. International interconnection norms, agreed under auspices of the International Telecommunications Union (ITU) many decades ago, eliminated the need for telegrams to be printed at each border post, walked across, and retyped.[21] In short, the potential for cooperative solutions under international treaties, which are fully compatible with the principle of national sovereignty and independent jurisdictions, has a long tradition in the communications field.

Table 12.3 identifies some of the most prominent "deeper integration" issues (i.e. those associated with differences in national regulatory regimes) and existing international agreements and/or cooperative arrangements that have emerged over the past few years, as well as forums where clarification discussions are ongoing. Most of these arrangements have taken the form of non-binding guidelines. A notable exception is the Basic Telecommunications Agreement (and the related Reference Paper) under the General Agreement on Trade in Services (GATS) of the WTO.

As pointed out in Primo Braga and Eskinazi (2002), the pursuit of deeper integration arrangements by governments and industries in trade-related areas is nothing new. The networked environment, however, offers new opportunities for public-private partnerships in this area (e.g. ICANN), as well as new forms of dispute resolution illustrated by the creation of the WIPO domain name dispute resolution body, which provides holders of trademark rights with an administrative mechanism to challenge bad-faith registration of Internet domain names that correspond to those trademarks.

Forming consensus and international cooperation on issues where national systems are more entrenched (e.g. taxation, commercial law, privacy legislation) is far more complicated, however. The WTO framework is often referred to as the most obvious institutional umbrella for multilateral commitments associated with e-commerce issues. In what follows, a brief review of the status of the debate on trade-related e-commerce issues in the WTO is provided to illustrate the challenges faced for the implementation of binding multilateral rules.

---

[20] See, for example, Rischard (2002).   [21] See Murphy (1994).

Table 12.3. Deeper Integration Issues Related to E-Commerce

Topic	Scope for international conflicts	Existing international agreements, cooperative arrangements, and forums for debate
Taxation	Jurisdictional arbitrage, enforcement problems	OECD Tax Framework Conditions
Privacy, consumer protection, content rules (pornography, gambling, hate propaganda)	Different national approaches; some countries prefer strict rules, others self-regulation.	OECD Guidelines for Consumer Protection and the Protection of Privacy.
Protection of intellectual property	Foreign infringement of national copyright laws, trademark-infringing domain name disputes	WIPO Copyright Treaty, WIPO Performance and Phonograms Treaty, WIPO domain name dispute resolution body
Legal liability, cybercrime (hacking, Internet fraud)	Extra-territorial application of national laws	Council of Europe Cybercrime Treaty, Hague Convention (to be adopted)
Internet governance	Interconnectivity and interoperability of IP-based networks, allocation/creation of gTLDs	ICANN
Telecommunications regulation Competition laws	Pursuit of discriminatory rules against foreign providers Procedural fairness and different interpretations on anti-competitive behavior	Basic Telecommunications Agreement (GATS/WTO) One of the original Singapore Issues considered for negotiations in the WTO's Doha Round; increasingly being addressed in Regional Trade Agreements
Trade-related issues associated with e-commerce	Market access, national treatment, jurisdiction and applicable law, customs duties on electronic transmissions	Clarification efforts under the "Work Program on Electronic Commerce" of the WTO

Source: Adapted by the author from Primo Braga et al. (2001).

E-Commerce in the WTO

The pursuit of negotiations on e-commerce in the WTO is rationalized as a way to ensure "fair trade" or an equality of competitive opportunities for foreign and domestic firms in this new area of economic activity. Negotiations could, in principle, cover both "deep" integration issues (i.e. those dealing with differences in national regulatory regimes) and the "shallow integration" agenda (i.e. the elimination of discrimination at the border).

From a WTO point of view, e-commerce is a vehicle for international trade in both goods and services. It involves a mix of telecommunications, information, financial, and transportation (e.g. express delivery) services. However, the products that are bought and sold may be digitized or tangible goods, or they may be services (access to databases, consulting, advice, and so forth). These products will often be protected through IPRs. Thus, international e-commerce is affected by rules under the GATT (the General Agreement on Tariffs and Trade), GATS (the General Agreement on Trade in Services), and TRIPS (the Agreement on Trade-Related Aspects of Intellectual Property Rights), the three pillars of the WTO.[22]

Starting in 1997, WTO members began to wrestle with the questions of if and how e-commerce should be dealt with in the WTO. What areas of the existing agreements needed clarification and/or could benefit e-commerce expansion via additional commitments? How to deal with deep integration issues (e.g. taxation, privacy, consumer protection) to ensure that they do not become a barrier to trade? Last but not least, should e-commerce-specific disciplines be negotiated?

Clarification Issues

An important area for clarification of WTO rules with respect to e-commerce refers to the classification of products bought and sold. Should e-commerce be treated as a service and be subjected to the GATS rules? If so, should e-commerce be regarded as a mode 1 (cross-border trade) or mode 2 (movement of consumer) type of transaction? The United States, for example, has argued that treating all e-commerce transactions as services raises the danger that policy regimes may become more restrictive than the status quo, because many WTO members have not made specific commitments on products that are traded electronically (such as software or database access). Conceptually, however, it is extremely difficult to define what distinguishes goods from services. From a practical point of view, the treatment of e-commerce as services—a position supported by the European Union (E.U.)—may therefore prevail.

Even if such a choice is made, however, the question of clarifying the applicability of different modes of delivery under the GATS to e-commerce transactions remains open to debate. In the GATS schedule of commitments, many WTO members made more liberal commitments under mode 2 than under mode 1, in large part because many did

---

[22] Moreover, the Information Technology Agreement (ITA)—a self-contained sectorial negotiation—has reduced to a zero tariff level all products covered under its declaration. The 61 signatories of the ITA (as of 2004) have submitted these commitments, covering more than 90 per cent of the world trade in information technology products under the GATT. This illustrates the impact of the WTO on the infrastructure layer of the global information system.

not have any interest in being restrictive on mode 2—movement of the consumer—and did not associate this mode with e-commerce. However, it has been argued that if a person buys a product from a firm located in a foreign country through e-commerce, this is akin to the consumer physically moving to the location of the provider.[23] The only difference is that the "movement" takes place by interacting with the server of the enterprise. The distinction between modes also has potential implications for enforcement of contracts. Under mode 2, presumably the legal regime of the provider applies in case of a dispute, whereas under mode 1, it may by the buyer's legal system that applies. Determining which jurisdiction applies is something that has not been addressed under the GATS and illustrates the inevitable "deep integration" nuances that e-commerce discussions will bring to bear.

Classification issues can also play a role in determining the reach of multilateral disciplines. In an ongoing dispute in the WTO, Antigua and Barbuda have argued that U.S. laws that prohibit gambling over wires across state lines and that have been used to constrain international online betting are in breach of U.S. commitments under the GATS.[24] The issue here is to what extent the services category of "other recreational services"—a category that is part of U.S. commitments under the GATS—encompasses online betting. Also being discussed in this context is the "public morals clause" that gives flexibility under the GATS for a Member country to use trade instruments to "protect public morals." The final outcome of this dispute will further illustrate the extent to which nations are willing to uphold the primacy of national law vis-à-vis multilateral disciplines as they apply to "cyberspace."

New Commitments

The most visible outcome of the debate on e-commerce in the WTO so far was the decision at the 1998 WTO Ministerial that electronic delivery of digitized goods and services would be free from customs duties. This commitment was temporary, and one of the questions confronting members is whether to make this exemption permanent. No agreement on this could be reached at the 1999 Seattle Ministerial. Members could only come up with a draft agreement that the 1998 moratorium would be extended. At the 2001 WTO Ministerial Conference in Doha, once again, members committed to extend the moratorium on a temporary basis. This commitment was expected to be reaffirmed at the Cancun Ministerial in 2003, but in view of the collapse of the negotiations, no formal decision was taken at that time.

The net effect of the ban on duties is to act as a subsidy to products that can be digitized, and therefore as a tax on transport services and producers who do not

---

[23] See Mattoo and Schuknecht (2000).   [24] See WTO (2004).

(cannot) use the Internet as a mode of supply. At the margin, both customs and sales tax revenues will also fall (as sales taxes, even if formally applicable, are difficult to collect). There has been a vigorous debate on the merits of making this ban permanent (note that the ban does not extend to goods ordered over the net—these remain subject to tariffs).

Mattoo and Schuknecht (2000) argue that much of this debate misses the point. If a WTO member has made a commitment in a particular sector to provide national treatment, then all discriminatory taxes are already prohibited and so the ban adds nothing. Conversely, if a member has not made a national treatment commitment, it remains free to impose discriminatory internal taxes other than customs duties, so again the ban has little value. Based on this analysis, it seems reasonable to argue that the most effective route to ensure liberalization of electronic commerce is to expand the GATS specific commitments.

"Deep Integration" Concerns

Such a minimalist "shallow integration" approach, however, does not address the many "deep integration" issues associated with e-commerce debates.[25] Accordingly, a case can be made that unless specific disciplines for e-commerce are negotiated under the WTO, the potential for inadequate national regulations to constrain the expansion of global e-commerce remains a relevant issue.

Deeper integration is inherently more difficult to achieve than shallow integration. In contrast to trade policy—where there are clear-cut policy recommendations that unambiguously increase global welfare—when it comes to regulation and market structure there are few hard and fast "rules of thumb" that governments can rely on to ensure that trade agreements will enhance welfare. Preferences across societies differ depending on local circumstances, tastes, and conditions, resulting in differing demands for regulation. The type of intervention may also differ across jurisdictions depending on economic systems, the strength of administrative capacity and required institutions, not to mention the level of development. It is also important to recognize that there are many different ways to pursue "deep integration." They can range from the pursuit of minimum standards of regulation within a specific agreement (such as the Reference Paper on Telecommunications under the GATS) to more ambitious efforts to harmonize regulatory regimes, as in the case of the EU.[26]

The push for incorporating cooperative arrangements into formal trade agreements is that trade sanctions are often regarded as an effective enforcement device. However, unless there is clear link between the particular regulatory issue at hand and the

---

[25] For a review of these broader issues, see Mann et al. (2000).
[26] For a discussion of different formats of services liberalization, see Hoekman and Primo Braga (1997).

contestability of (access to) markets, embedding regulatory disciplines into trade agreements is not necessarily an optimal solution.

The debate around e-commerce illustrates the difficulties that arise in view of different social preferences concerning regulation. Some governments favor strong control and regulation; others opt for a more liberal, hands-off approach. Those in favor of government intervention argue that the Internet can bring their citizens face to face with pornography, gambling, or fraud and note there is no reason why e-commerce should be exempt from taxation or the type of trade controls that apply to mail-order within and across national borders. Those in favor of a more liberal approach argue that the Internet has the potential of transforming the functioning of economies, and that government intervention could have detrimental consequences by slowing down the growth of networks and the pace of innovation. They also argue that new technologies increasingly offer solutions for Internet users to protect themselves against undesired messages or fraud, and that market forces will be more effective than government intervention in ensuring contract enforcement.

As pointed out in Bach and Erber (2001), these two different approaches to regulation are often associated with different perspectives about the role/impact of e-commerce. Those in favor of government regulation and early multilateral harmonization efforts tend to see e-commerce as simply entailing new technical alternatives for trade transactions. Under this perspective, the adoption of ex-ante multilateral regulation can diminish transaction costs for economic actors, as national regulatory regimes become more homogeneous and the search costs associated with learning about different regulatory environments are minimized. This is, in essence, the approach followed by the EU. Those resisting negotiations on comprehensive new multilateral regulatory rules for e-commerce, tend to perceive e-commerce as a new "economic frontier" that significantly affects the way trade is performed. As a consequence, early harmonization can hinder social learning and self-regulation should be favored. This, in turn, is the approach championed by the United States.

It is important to note that in many cases harmonization is not required in order to ensure access to markets; all that is necessary is to accept regulatory competition. For example, jurisdictions may have different approaches to taxation and privacy regulations. One country may restrict the exchange of personal data and seek to tax internet transactions, while another may have a more lax approach to privacy—leaving it to consumers to decide whether to allow their data to be used by third parties, and only requiring that consumers be told that data may be sold and relying on other sources for tax revenue. Such differences will have implications for the incentives of firms to choose across jurisdictions, illustrating the potential for regulatory competition.

The problem is that many governments are unwilling to accept such competition and seek to defend their norms. A way to do this is through harmonization—seeking to impose national (or regional) standards. One observes such attempts in the area of both taxation and privacy rules. Thus, the E.U. has been resistant to any relaxation of European privacy regulation, forcing the U.S. to negotiate a special arrangement under which U.S.-based firms guarantee not to violate such norms when engaging in transactions with E.U. consumers. The problem is that such deals are unlikely to be available to developing countries, creating potential for de facto discrimination. Developing countries may be forced to harmonize to allow trade to occur. However, attaining stringent standards may be costly for them, requiring major investments in infrastructure and institutions. Special efforts will be required to ensure that policy integration does not entail "implicit" discrimination.

Concluding Remarks

This chapter has reviewed the evolving international regulatory environment under which e-commerce is transacted. The variety of policies that can influence e-commerce and the emergence of new governance issues that require global coordination illustrate the problems faced by policy makers in this area. Moreover, the rapid expansion of networks has increased the potential for cross-border disputes.

It is unlikely that competition among national regulatory regimes will promote regulatory harmonization in the near future. In the same vein, the negotiation of new sets of rules at the multilateral level is bound to proceed at a much slower pace than what would be desirable from the perspective of e-commerce firms.

Policy makers in developing countries face major challenges to lay the foundations for a sound regulatory environment for e-commerce. The usual problems of institution building and scarcity of trained personnel for regulatory functions are in this case compounded by the novelty of some of the issues being discussed. Against this background, there is a natural tendency to look for multilateral forums as a way to advance the debate on global regulations for e-commerce that could then serve as parameters for shaping national regulatory regimes. For developing countries, this could reduce transaction costs in the process of searching for appropriate regulatory solutions. And for the global economy, the network externalities associated with the reduction of international frictions generated by distinct regulatory solutions can also be substantial. Needless to say, these benefits have to be weighed against the potential negative effects of inadequate regulatory solutions that may emerge from this process.

An analysis of the capacity of the WTO—as an obvious organization to advance this agenda—does not provide much hope for rapid regulatory convergence with respect to e-commerce. In reality, the main contribution that the WTO can offer at this stage concerns the expansion of the coverage of specific commitments under the GATS. These entail mainly shallow integration issues—the elimination of discrimination (committing to the national treatment rule) and allowing foreign providers to contest (market access) local markets. Such commitments must cover not only Internet and telecommunications "backbone" services, but also financial services, information technology services, business process outsourcing, and the distribution services that are vital elements for the delivery of goods that cannot be digitized.[27] In the same vein, the expansion of the commitments associated with the ITA under the GATT would foster the expansion of the infrastructure layer in support of e-commerce activities.

As far as deep integration is concerned, most of the action will continue to occur outside the WTO. Regulatory convergence, when appropriate, should be explored in specialized forums that have the required technical expertise. The main role of the WTO should be to encourage such efforts and allow for competition between regulatory regimes while disciplining discriminatory behavior. This should also include the monitoring of preferential "deep-integration" agreements between members with a view of constraining discrimination against third parties.

References

Bach, D. 2004. "The Double Punch of Law and Technology: Fighting Music Piracy or Remaking Copyright in a Digital Age?" *Business and Politics* 6(2).

Bach, S. and G. Erber. 2001. "Electronic Commerce: A Need for Regulation?" in K. G. Deutsch and B. Speyer (eds.), *The World Trade Organization Millennium Round*. London and New York: Routledge.

Barlow, J. P. 1994. "The Economy of Ideas: A Framework for Rethinking Patents and Copyrights in the Digital Age (Everything You Know About Intellectual Property is Wrong)," *Wired* (March): 84–129.

Benkley, Y. 2000. " From Consumers to Users: Shifting the Deeper Structures of Regulation," *Federal Communications Law Journal* 52: 561–3.

Beardsley, S. et al. 2002. "Telecommunications Sector Reform—A Prerequisite for Networked Readiness," in *Global Information Technology Report, 2001–2002—Readiness for the Networked World*. Oxford: Oxford University Press.

Burt, T. 2004. "Music Industry Widens Internet Lawsuits," *Financial Times* (March 31): 7.

Costa, E. 2001. *Global E-Commerce Strategies for Small Businesses*. Cambridge, MA: MIT Press.

Denton, T. 1999. *Netheads vs. Bellheads*. Available at: http://www.tmdenton.com/pub/index.htm

Drucker, P.F. 2002. *Managing in the Next Society*. New York: St. Martin's Press, pp. 3–24.

---

[27] See Mattoo and Wunsch (2004) for an analysis of critical services relevant for e-commerce and how best to promote lock-in of liberal trade regimes in this area.

Fink, C., A. Mattoo, and R. Rathindran. 2003. "An Assessment of Telecommunications Reform in Developing Countries," *Information Economics and Policy* 14: 443–66.

Hoekman, B. and C.A. Primo Braga. 1997. "Protection and Trade in Services: A Survey," *Open Economies Review* 8 (3): 285–308.

Holitscher, M. 2004. "Internet Governance Revisited: Think Decentralization!," paper submitted to the ITU workshop on Internet governance. Geneva: ITU, mimeo.

ICC. 2003. *ICC Compendium on ICT and E-Business Policy and Practice.* Paris: International Chamber of Commerce.

InfoDev. 2000. "The Networking Revolution: Opportunities and Challenges for Developing Countries," InfoDev Working Paper. Washington, D.C.: World Bank.

Lessig, L. 2001. *The Future of Ideas._*New York: Random House.

Mann, C. L., S. E. Eckert, and S. C. Knight. 2000. *Global Electronic Commerce: A Policy Primer.* Washington, D.C.: Institute for International Economics.

Mattoo, A. and L. Schuknecht. 2000. "Trade Policies for Electronic Commerce," Policy Research Working Paper 2380. Washington, D.C.: World Bank.

Mattoo, A. and S. Wunsch, 2004, "Pre-empting Protectionism in Services: The GATS and Outsourcing," Policy Research Working Paper 3237. Washington, D.C.: World Bank.

Murphy, C. 1994. *International Organization and Industrial Change: Global Governance Since 1850.* New York: Oxford University Press.

OECD. 2000. "Information Technology Outlook 2000." Paris: OECD.

OECD. 2001. "Electronic Commerce," *Policy Brief.* Paris: OECD.

Primo Braga, C. A. 1996. "Trade-Related Intellectual Property Issues," in W. Martin and L. A. Winters (eds.), *The Uruguay Round and Developing Economies.* Cambridge: Cambridge University Press.

—— 2005. "E-Commerce Regulation: New Game, New Rules?" *The Quarterly Review of Economics and Finance*, 45: 541–58.

—— and V. Ziegler. 1998. "Telecommunications in Latin America and the Caribbean: The Role of Foreign Capital," *The Quarterly Review of Economics and Finance* (Fall) 38: 409–19.

Primo Braga, C. A. and R. Eskinazi. 2002. "WTO Rules on Electronic Commerce: Opportunities and Challenges for Developing Economies," PSIO Occasional Paper: WTO Series Number 04. Geneva: Geneva: Institute Universitaire de Hautes Etudes Internationales.

Primo Braga, C. A., C. Fink, and B. Hoekman. 2001 "Telecommunications, E-Commerce and Developing Countries: What Can the WTO Do?" in P. Guerrieri and H-E. Scharrer (eds.), *Trade, Investment and Competition Policies in the Global Economy.* Hamburg: Istituto Affari Internazionali and Hamburg Institute of International Economics.

Primo Braga, C. A., J. A. Daly, and B. Sareen. 2003. "The Future of Information and Communication Technologies for Development," Working Paper Development Gateway. Washington, D.C.: Development Gateway Foundation.

Rischard, J. F. 2002. *High Noon: Twenty Global Problems, Twenty Years to Solve Them.* New York: Basic Books.

Shapiro, C. and H. R. Varian. 1999. *Information Rules: A Strategic Guide to the Network Economy.* Boston: Harvard Business School Press.

UNCTAD. 2003. *E-Commerce and Development Report 2003.* New York and Geneva: United Nations.

WTO. 1998. "Work Programme on Electronic Commerce," Document WT/MIN(98)/DEC/2. Geneva: World Trade Organization.

WTO. 2004. "United States—Measures Affecting the Cross-Border Supply of Gambling and Betting Services," Document WT/DS285/5/Add.3. Geneva: World Trade Organization.

13 The Temporary Movement of Workers to Provide Services (GATS Mode 4)*

L. Alan Winters

This chapter considers the case and the means for liberalizing the temporary flow of labor between countries for the purpose of providing services: mode 4 of the GATS. Despite being until now a mere bit-player in the GATS drama, mode 4 is at last starting to command some attention from negotiators and policy makers. This chapter, and the papers it draws on,[1] argue that this is long overdue and that serious efforts to liberalize the temporary movement of natural persons (TM) from developing to developed member countries could generate very large mutual benefits.

The very heart of international trade, be it in goods or in factors, lies in exploiting differences. The larger the differences, the larger the potential gains from opening up international trade. In the case of TM, potentially large returns would be feasible if medium and less skilled workers, who are relatively abundant in developing countries, were allowed to move and provide their services in developed countries. The review of existing empirical studies of factor mobility and the new estimates described in this chapter agree that there are huge returns to even relatively small movements of labor. An increase in developed countries' quotas on the inward movements of both skilled and unskilled temporary workers equivalent to 3 per cent of their workforces would generate an estimated increase in world welfare of over US$150 billion per annum.

The mass permanent migration of less skilled workers raises fears in developed countries over the erosion of their cultural identity, problems of assimilation and the drain on the public purse. These need be much less pressing with TM, providing that governments correctly inform their citizens and take steps to make "temporary" credible. Objectively speaking, the biggest concern about TM is its competitive challenge

* This chapter was prepared while the author was Professor of Economics in the University of Sussex, U.K. He has subsequently become Director of the Development Research Group of the World Bank. Neither of these institutions bears any responsibility for the views expressed herein. The author is grateful to Carsten Fink, Roman Grynberg, Aaditya Mattoo, Maurice Schiff, Terrie Walmsley, Zhen Kun Wang, and Gianni Zanini for discussion on various aspects of the material in this chapter and to Pedro Martins, Audrey Kitson Walters, and Natasha Ward for logistical and research support.

[1] Winters et al. (2003a, b); Walmsley and Winters (2002); and Winters (2003).

to local less skilled workers. This is neither more nor less than the challenge posed to such workers by imports of labor-intensive goods from developing countries, which has been overcome by the weight of economic gain that trade could deliver and by policies to ease adjustment among local less skilled workers in developed countries. Applied with the same sensitivity and the same sorts of policies as trade policy reform in goods has received in the past, the temporary movement of less skilled workers between countries would offer the chance to reap some very large gains from trade.

For the sake of concreteness, the chapter focuses on the multilateral liberalization of TM via the GATS. Many of the arguments, however, generalize to unilateral, bilateral or regional liberalizations and some of the lessons are drawn from such arrangements. Similarly, the chapter also focuses on developing to developed country flows although nearly all of the analysis would equally apply to developing-country TM.

The chapter comprises seven parts. First discussed is the extent and nature of TM and the barriers to it. Then there is a discussion of ways in which we might think of and model the liberalization of mode 4. This is based on two polar alternatives—treating it as perfectly akin to goods trade and treating it as perfectly akin to labor migration. The second section summarizes an estimate of the benefits of mode 4 liberalization treating it as akin to migration. This is argued to be a reasonable assumption in the context of the sort of models that economists have to use for this sort of exercise, and it suggests the very large economic benefits already alluded to. The third section examines the simple gains from temporary movement of persons as part of mode 4 liberalization. To examine these gains this section presents the logic of computable models to understand the gains of TM of persons as well as its effects on different economic sectors. The fourth section discusses ways in which the polar forms of thinking about TM may be relaxed in future empirical exercises to try to refine the estimates of the effects of liberalization. The fifth section discusses practical issues that may be negotiated in the GATS to make TM a reality. It cautions not to stake everything on achieving a clean, elegant, and comprehensive agreement on mode 4. Many issues are still very complex and sensitive and the overriding requirement an increase in actual mobility rather than an elegant solution. The sixth section asks what benefits does GATS mode 4 bring to countries wanting to liberalize TM. The final section considers briefly the arguments for and technicalities of compensating domestic workers who are disadvantaged by inflows of workers from abroad. Box 13.5 at the end of the chapter has a discussion of the U.S. experience with TM.

In the first addendum to the chapter, Demetrios G. Papademetriou discusses the U.S. experience with the temporary movement of service providers. In the second addendum, Sherry Stephenson discusses mode 4 issues in the Latin American context.

The Nature and Extent of Temporary Mobility: Analytical Objectives

The objectives of the discussion that follow include:

- Observe the magnitude of flows of temporary workers in the world economy, distinguishing skilled from unskilled labor, and between net suppliers and net demanders of labor.
- Understand the limitations of data and proxies that are used to measure the size of TM (why data on bilateral flows are important).
- Note the current low level of scheduled concessions in GATS mode 4.
- Identify the main barriers to TM.

Temporary vs. Permanent Migration

The official statistical distinction between temporary and permanent migration is usually between stays of less than or more than one year. This is the threshold at which for many purposes residence is held to have changed. For economic and policy purposes, however, one would wish to be more subtle. Many permanent, or at least very long-lived, migrations start as ostensibly short-term temporary movements and some comprise solely a sequence of such contracts. On the other hand some migrations of over one year are nonetheless explicitly intended to be temporary, as, for example, when managers move to one of their firm's off-shore branches, with diplomatic postings and the U.S. H1-B visa for highly skilled workers. Hence inevitably there is only a relatively weak association between what is reported (if temporary mobility is reported at all) and what one would really like to know.

The distinction between temporary and permanent migration is potentially important economically in several ways. Temporary workers are less frequently accompanied by their families, and so usually make less call on public services per unit of their output than do permanent migrants. Temporary workers typically invest less in integrating themselves into local society, which may either increase tension, if they are more readily perceived as outsiders, or reduce it, if they are seen as less demanding or threatening to local cultures as a result. They also invest less in acquiring host-country-specific skills. Thus a stream of, say, ten one-year migrants is likely to be less productive in the host country than a single ten-year migrant. It is not, of course, as likely back in the home country, because there will be ten "somewhat skilled" rather than one "very skilled" worker (if the long-term migrant returns at all). (We assume in this—quite reasonably—that skills learned abroad will normally enhance home productivity as well.) Relatedly, temporary migrants tend to remit a higher percentage of their incomes to their home countries than do permanent ones.

Local attitudes towards temporary and permanent migrants may differ, although not necessarily in the same way in all countries. The two principal fears of migration are the displacement of local workers from (premium) employment and the threat of cultural dilution. One interesting reflection due to Aaditya Mattoo is that the relative importance of cultural and displacement fears can influence host countries' preferences between temporary and permanent migration. In Europe, intense cultural xenophobia coupled with relatively benign policies for displaced workers favor TM. In the U.S., on the other hand, with a disposition towards migration and a relatively harsh labor market, the labor unions (and hence, to some extent, policy in general) favor permanent immigrants who can be unionized and incorporated into "the system" to potential "hit-and-run" competition from temporary migrants, especially if they are delivered by overseas firms which have the right to bring in their own workers.

The Extent of Temporary Mobility

This section starts by defining temporary labor mobility or migration (TM) and asking how it differs economically from permanent migration. It then attempts to quantify the extent of TM. The main points follow.

GATT traditions, as well as policy-makers and some economists, relate the importance of a liberalization to the size of the existing trade flow that it affects. If you believe this, skip this session and get a coffee because current mobility is very low. Karsenty (2000) estimates that "compensation of employees," the closest official measure that we can get to mode 4, accounts for just 1.4 per cent of total service earnings. Walmsley and Winters (2002) estimate that, very roughly, there were 7.2 million skilled and 34.2 million less-skilled temporary migrants in the world economy in 1997. These are pretty small numbers, but, as is argued below, they reflect the importance of the restrictions on the movement of labor rather than the lack of it.

Table 13.1 reports Walmsley and Winters' figures in more detail. Even in the kindest light, they are very approximate and in some cases clearly wrong—e.g. the absence of temporary migrants (i.e. residents temporarily working abroad) from the U.S., Canada, the U.K. and Germany. Nonetheless they are probably the best estimates available. There is very little information on bilateral flows—which workers end up where (although scholars are starting to work on it). Such data will be very important, especially so, given that migratory flows tend to follow established routes because immigrants prefer to move to places where there are already compatriot communities and because existing communities are major providers of information about opportunities for people back home.

Table 13.1. The Temporary Movement of Unskilled and Skilled Workers: Estimated Stocks in 1997 (000s of people)

Region	Unskilled temporary workers[a] 1997	Unskilled temporary migrants 1997	Skilled temporary workers 1997	Skilled temporary migrants 1997
U.S.	4,140	0	767	0
Canada	222	0	41	0
Mexico	0	2,529	0	204
U.K.	989	0	183	0
Germany	4,339	0	804	0
Rest of E.U.	3,526	4,060	747	3,945
Rest of Europe	1,919	238	355	232
Eastern Europe	27	474	5	53
Former Soviet Union	65	670	12	74
Australia and New Zealand	176	0	33	0
China	128	593	61	38
Japan	366	324	68	324
Rest of East Asia	299	139	55	30
South East Asia	1,696	7,100	647	972
India	16	1,198	3	49
Rest of South Asia	174	2,907	12	60
Brazil	584	1,789	108	127
Rest of Latin America	1,055	3,087	465	273
Middle East and Northern Africa	13,542	7,130	2,603	600
Southern Africa	866	1,266	160	95
Rest of World	78	703	21	73
Total	**34,207**	**34,207**	**7,150**	**7,150**

Note: [a] The temporary workers of a country are workers from elsewhere temporarily working in that country. Temporary migrants are residents of the country temporarily working elsewhere.
Source: Adapted from Walmsley and Winters (2002).

Table 13.2 (adapted from Nielson and Cattaneo, 2003) presents one of the few bilateral analyses available—and one of the most important—the U.S. Two of the largest flows—for "specialty occupations" and inter-corporate transferees—are firmly at the skilled end of the range. Workers in both classes are substantially provided by other developed countries, although India and China are the largest providers of the specialty occupations (see Table 13.3). "Exchange visitors" include many cultural and educational exchanges but may also include workers. Europe is the predominant supplier here. The only potentially unskilled flow—non-agricultural workers—is small, dominated by North America and officially capped at 66,000 per annum.

Table 13.3 (also adapted from Nielson and Cattaneo, 2003) gives a breakdown of H1-B visa beneficiaries by occupation, age, qualification and wage. It makes clear the relatively high levels of skills involved, although the immense dominance of the information and computer technology (ICT) industries is somewhat idiosyncratic and has since eased somewhat. H1-B visas cover much more than potential mode 4 applications, however.

Table 13.2. Geographic Origin of Non-immigrants to the United States: Selected Visa Categories of Most Relevance for Mode 4, 2001

	All countries	Europe	Asia	Africa	Oceania	North America	Carib-bean	Central America	South America
Registered nurses (H1A)	627	146	272	13	14	127	12	2	55
(H1C)	29	16	3	—	—	4	2	—	6
Specialty occupations (H1B)	384,191	111,382	178,411	8,573	9,499	37,554	3,693	2,982	38,251
Nonagricultural workers performing services unavailable in the United States (H2B)	72,387	3,411	1,893	809	1,916	62,673	10,503	4,723	1,483
Industrial trainees (H3)	3,245	1,218	1,076	95	56	294	50	45	502
Workers with extraordinary ability/achievement (O1)	25,685	14,981	3,504	422	1,579	2,464	311	163	2,686
Workers accompanying and assisting in performance of O1 workers (O2)	3,834	1,356	744	72	175	1,172	642	18	296
Internationally recognized athletes or entertainers (P1)	42,430	15,387	2,112	948	999	18,926	4,941	1,163	3,880
Artists or entertainers in reciprocal exchange programs (P2)	3,877	201	148	22	18	3,406	90	23	73
Artists or entertainers in culturally unique programs (P3)	9,484	3,095	2,682	548	63	1,971	1,618	47	1,053
Workers in international cultural exchange programs (Q1)	2,388	1,389	394	333	3	239	7	2	26
Exchange visitors (J1)	339,848	210,123	59,007	12,292	11,788	20,993	3,582	3,639	24,441
Intracorporate transferees (L1)	328,480	162,672	72,837	4,108	12,334	42,519	1,675	2,282	33,547

Source: Adapted from Nielson and Cattaneo (2003).

Table 13.3. Profile of H1B Beneficiaries by Top Ten Industries, United States, Fiscal 2001

Industry (NAICS code)	Number of beneficiaries	Median age (years)	Master's degree or higher (percent)	Median income	Leading country of birth (percent)
All industries	331,206	29	42	$55,000	India (49)
Computer systems design and related services (5415)	141,267	28	33	56,500	India (75)
Colleges, universities, and professional schools (6113)	15,372	34	93	36,999	China (24)
Management, scientific, and technical consulting services (5413)	12,721	28	41	55,000	India (54)
Architectural, engineering, and related services (5417)	12,148	30	42	50,000	India (26)
Telecommunications (5133)	9,638	29	48	69,000	India (39)
Scientific research and development services (5417)	6,929	32	81	55,291	China (24)
Semiconductor and other electronic component manufacturing (3344)	6,171	29	65	71,000	India (36)
Communications equipment manufacturing (3342)	4,383	29	58	68,000	India (36)
Accounting, tax preparation, bookkeeping, and payroll services (5412)	4,213	29	36	43,000	India (17)
Securities and commodity contracts intermediation and brokerage (5231)	3,676	28	45	75,000	India (21)

Notes: Based on all beneficiaries with known level of income, education, or occupation. NAICS = North American Industry Classification System.

Source: Adapted from Nielson and Cattaneo (2003).

Some are for manufacturing industry and many of them generate applications for "green cards" i.e. permanent migration. Indeed, the H1-B visa is probably equally much a screening device for potential permanent migrants as a way of temporarily meeting skills shortages.

A major and conscious supplier of temporary labor—perhaps the world's largest relative to its population—is the Philippines. Figure 13.1 shows the great importance of overseas employment to GDP, while Table 13.4 reports the number of service providers deployed abroad for some skills and some markets. Note the prominence of the Gulf states, the main one of which, Saudi Arabia, is only a recent WTO member. The data are partial and Francisco (2003) estimates that over 1995–2000

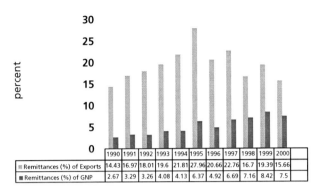

Figure 13.1. Remittances from overseas workers as percent of GDP and exports (1990–2000)
Source: Adapted from Francisco (2003).

between 127 and 198 thousand workers were deployed abroad each year. In addition, the Philippines provided 230,000 seafarers in 2000, way beyond the 83,000 from Indonesia which is ranked second. The Philippines is interesting in that it encourages overseas work and helps to organize it through the Philippines Overseas Employment Administration. It believes itself to be a major victim of mobility restrictions in other countries.

The contribution of the GATS mode 4 to temporary mobility is very small so far. WTO (1998) reports the relatively small number of scheduled concessions in mode 4 compared with other modes, while Carzaniga (2003) describes how mode 4 commitments are far shallower than elsewhere in the GATS. No individual country has scheduled "none" (i.e. no restrictions) and "horizontal restrictions" are relatively more important for mode 4 than other modes of providing services. Of the 400 scheduled concessions recorded, 287 pertain to managers, executives, and specialists and only 69 refer to lower-skilled occupations "business seller" or "other."

This brief sketch of the figures suggests that there is a great deal to "play for" in the GATS mode 4 negotiations, but they also raise a question as to whether mode 4 brings anything significant to the temporary mobility table (Table 13.1). We return to the latter question below.

Barriers to Labor Mobility

There are strong natural barriers to labor mobility. Most of us have strong attachments to our home regions as one can see within countries where large real income differences persist between regions even in the absence of legal, linguistic or cultural barriers. On top of this, international migrants face problems of language and culture as well as the

Table 13.4. Overseas Service Workers from the Philippines, by Occupation and Country (1995–2000)

Profession / Skill	Destination	Number
Nurses	Saudi Arabia	19,885
	U.K.	4,118
	Libya	1,488
	Singapore	1,241
IT (Computer programmers and related workers, systems analysts)	U.S.	2,730
	Saudi Arabia	1,358
	Singapore	125
	Australia	102
	UAE	57
Accountants	Saudi Arabia	988
	Northern Marinas Island	211
	U.S.	180
	Papua New Guinea	129
	UAE	129
Engineers	Saudi Arabia	7,945
Domestic helpers and related household workers	Hong Kong	136,339
	Saudi Arabia	54,522
	UAE	27,692
	Taiwan	23,618
	Kuwait	20,454
	Malaysia	15,331
	Singapore	7,919
	Canada	6,133
	Italy	6,093
	Brunei	4,781
Choreographers and dancers	Japan	153,181
	Malaysia	145
	Taiwan	16
Composers, musicians and singers	Japan	53,989
	Malaysia	257
	Singapore	256
Electricians	Saudi Arabia	14,630
	Hong Kong	1,085
	Qatar	1,022
Waiters, bartenders and related workers	UAE	7,368
	Saudi Arabia	6,111
	Bahrain	1,1179
	Kuwait	1,079

Source: Adapted from Francisco (2003).

loss of the functional social networks they have at home. Thus, within the E.U., migration has remained low even in the face of huge income disparities between countries and in the absence of formal barriers.

Beyond these "natural" barriers, migrants, both permanent and temporary, face a host of official and regulatory restrictions. Most obvious are the migration

Table 13.5. Commitments on Mode 4 by Type of Person (Horizontal Commitments), April 2002

		No. of entries	No. of aggregate entries	% of aggregate entries
Intra-corporate transferees	Executives	56	168	42%
	Managers	55		
	Specialists	56		
	Others	1		
	Executives	24	110	28%
	Managers	42		
	Specialists	44		
Business visitors	Commercial presence	41	93	23%
	Sale negotiations	52		
	Contract suppliers	12	12	3%
	Other	17	17	4%
	Total[a]	400	400	100%

Note: [a] Total number of entries by those WTO Members that have included commitments on mode 4 in the horizontal section of their schedules.
Source: Adapted from Carziniga (2003) based on WTO Secretariat.

regulations embodied in visa policies. Virtually all countries restrict the potential flow of immigrants very severely via this route by merely excluding migrants or, more likely, permitting only the most special of migrants access—e.g. via scoring systems such as Canada's designed to pick up the most able migrants, or in terms of political asylum whereby only the most vulnerable of people are offered sanctuary. Temporary migrants are typically processed in exactly the same way as potential permanent migrants with very high levels of screening and delay. This is a strong discouragement to TM.

In many countries visa regulations permit entry to foreign workers provided that their services are held to be necessary to the local economy via so-called "economic-needs" tests. In some cases these are operationalized by essentially arbitrary decisions by the immigration service. In most they entail the potential employers undertaking extensive bureaucratic processes to prove their needs. This makes TM unattractive except in case of the greatest need.

Even when visa regulations do not prevent mobility, other regulations can. For example, many professions are licensed, and licenses are hard to acquire for people with foreign qualifications or foreign experience. In some cases nationality is a qualification, e.g. for the CEOs of financial institutions in some countries. Practical issues such as the transfer of pension rights or access to health facilities can make mobility expensive and unattractive.

The Basic Economics of Temporary Labor Mobility: Analytical Objectives

The objectives of the discussion to follow are:

- Appreciate the two polar approaches to modeling the liberalization of mode 4—as akin to trade in goods and as akin to permanent migration, and understand the rationale of the models and their assumptions.
- Recognize the potential gains from liberalizing TM and also that some short and long-run adverse effects may emerge.
- Be able to distinguish TM from international migration (in terms of social-economic challenges).
- Clear understanding of the limitations of both models.

The Temporary Movement of Natural Persons, as the GATS calls temporary mobility (TM), can be thought about under two existing analytical paradigms and in truth lies somewhere between them. At one extreme it can be viewed as no different from cross-border services trade (mode 1), which, in turn, is often argued to be analytically no different from ordinary goods trade. For example, a consultant traveling to Washington to deliver a course module in person is analytically close to a paper being sent in hard-copy form, electronic form or even delivered by video-link. Hence one part of the "mode 4 story" is the trade story with which we are perfectly familiar.

At the other extreme, TM has much in common with 'traditional' long-term migration, whereby workers actually relocate from one country to another. This is particularly true where periods of stay are long or where a particular job in country B is filled by a circulating flow of temporary workers from country A, each being replaced by another as her contract expires. While such a "revolving door" provision differs from permanent migration in terms of its implications for social integration, network formation and the inter-generational spill-overs from education, the basic fact that country B gains a worker while country A loses one is common to both. The "revolving door" model could be particularly relevant to agency-provided flows of middle-level professional workers such as nurses and teachers. Hence a second strand of thought about TM is based on the economics of factor mobility, and since this is less familiar to trade negotiators than the trade literature, we devote some time to it here.

Neither of the polar models—trade or migration—captures the full character of TM, however, so we also need to devote some time to refining those models which represent its peculiarities more satisfyingly.

Temporary Mobility as International Trade

At its simplest, trade in services is no different from trade in goods, for which there is now widespread acceptance of the benefits of a relatively liberal trading regime. For example, exchanging goods or services across international borders facilitates:

- reaping economies of scale;
- the benefits of specialization according to comparative advantage;
- learning by doing and developing expertise by concentrating on particular sectors;
- importing better technologies; and
- stronger competition.

All of these benefits potentially apply equally or even more strongly to services as to goods because:

- services as a whole account for a greater share of income (and, usually, employment) than industry and agriculture together; and
- trade barriers are generally higher in services than in goods—especially where TM is involved;
- many barriers explicitly and dramatically reduce competition in the service sector, which can be very costly in efficiency terms; and
- many services are necessary inputs to other sectors, so that their provision influences the efficiency and competition in other parts of the economy—e.g. communications and transportation, or banking. Thus liberalization in these sectors can have broad and deep indirect effects. For example, improved services can create completely new markets for other goods, which, as Romer (1994) shows, can induce dramatic welfare improvements: improved transport and communications can allow peripheral farmers to sell in the cities or to obtain previously unavailable credit that could dramatically increase their output.

Thus, for example, using a simple static computable general equilibrium model, Hertel et al. (1999) suggest that, while reductions in the tariff equivalents of trade barriers of 40 per cent in agriculture and manufacturing will each raise global welfare by about $70 billion per annum, a similar liberalization in services could contribute over $300 billion. One should not take these modeling estimates too literally and TM is only part of service delivery, but the orders of magnitude are striking and even a small share of so large a benefit renders mode 4 significant.

The broad principles of international trade theory apply to both goods and services, but we should not take the equivalence too literally. Services are non-storable and often non-transportable; they are subject to greater problems of moral hazard and asymmetric information and, as a consequence, are much more frequently managed via regulation rather than, say, simple taxes; services frequently cannot be produced in stages, frustrating intra-service intermediate trade. None of this argues for wholly unregulated international trade in services. Governments will always have a fiduciary role in regulating many services, to counter the problems that arise from market failures such as moral hazard or asymmetric information. Rather, as Mattoo (2000) notes, services trade liberalization—including that of TM—calls for ensuring:

- that such regulations are geared to solving market failures rather than to protection;
- that they do so in "trade efficient" ways; and
- that, above all, they enhance rather than curtail competition.

TM differs even further from goods trade than other service trade because it is impossible to separate the delivery of the service from the welfare of the provider, about whom we care.[2] This can make policy decisions more complex. For example, developed country labor may object to the importation of cheap labor-intensive goods (e.g. shirts) from the developing world, but once the goods are in the country, there is little that labor can do to prevent their sale and circulation within the economy. If they object to developing-country service workers from entering the country, on the other hand, even if the government allows inflows, labor can, by discrimination and direct action, impose continuing costs on those workers. This example also illustrates the further difference that inflows of workers are potentially much more challenging to host societies than are inflows of goods or even of cross-border service flows or foreign-owned firms. They may appear to threaten cultural and social identities directly rather than just indirectly via the generation of income through economic activity. These contrasts do not invalidate the insights gained from the equivalence of services and goods trade, but they do add to them.

The parallel with goods-trade liberalization also serves as a challenge to populist arguments that services require generalized "infant industry" protection or that they have national security dimensions. The analysis of these arguments for goods trade— e.g. Baldwin (1969) and Winters (1991) respectively—shows that they apply only in the presence of very specific market failures and thus that they will require detailed justification if they are to be applied to services.

Before proceeding, we should recall that although goods trade liberalization is now widely accepted as one of the key components of the policy cocktail required for growth and efficiency, it is not without its challenges. Neither will services liberalization be. In particular, trade reform is strongly redistributional, both between producers, governments, and consumers, and within those groups. While widespread reform seems likely to benefit nearly everyone eventually (what Max Corden (1984) called the "Hicksian

---

[2] The same is true of mode 2 (movement of consumers), but not of mode 3 (establishment— i.e. movement of capital because capital does not experience welfare per se.

optimism"), there are likely to be short-term hardships, and we cannot rule out there being long-term casualties. There is a substantial political economy literature on the way in which these redistributions affect the prospects of reform—e.g. Rodrik (1995)—and a further literature discussing the need for, and design of, complementary and compensatory policies to counteract their adverse effects—see, for example, DfID (2000) and Sapir (2001). McCulloch et al. (2001), Winters (2002) and Winters et al. (2004) offer detailed discussions of the way in which trade liberalization might affect poverty, while Winters (2003) considers explicitly the possible impacts of the Doha Development Agenda on poverty. All of these issues are likely to be as relevant to mode 4 as to goods-market liberalization, and we should consider the lessons learned from the latter.

Temporary Mobility as Factor Mobility

The second analytical approach to TM is to treat it like migration. It is important to stress that TM is *NOT* international migration as usually understood—although in administrative practice the two have tended to merge. As we shall see later, TM has fewer of the cultural, social or political challenges that are associated with international migration because it explicitly does not entail shifts in residence. However, its direct economic consequences can be thought of as those of migration: workers enter a country temporarily to carry out particular jobs and thus labor inputs in one economy are reduced while those in another are increased.

At its simplest, the motive for a worker to work abroad is that real wages are higher there. Corresponding to these different wages are different productivities. In reasonably competitive labor markets, workers are paid the value of their marginal products—firms pay workers the value that they generate—and even where this is not true, the differences are not usually very large.[3] Thus provided that productivity is at least partly a function of where the work is carried out and not just a characteristic of the individual workers, we can be confident that when a worker moves from a low wage to a high wage country, productivity increases and world aggregate output rises, offering scope for economic gains.

In the extreme case in which workers from different countries are identical and productivity is purely a function of location, the increment in output when a worker moves is equal to the difference in wages between the two countries involved. In an early

---

[3] The main reason for differences between wages and (long-run) productivity is market power: if workers can restrict their supply to a firm and if that firm reaps excess profits from market power in the goods market, then workers can share the rents. Alternatively, if firms can control the number of jobs in a labor market, they can drive wages below marginal products. Regulation could have either of these effects, depending on its form.

computable general equilibrium (CGE) model of this case, Hamilton and Whalley (1984) suggest that if labor were able to move between regions sufficiently to equalize wages globally, world income could increase by 150 per cent or more! Varying the assumptions—e.g. to reflect higher dependency ratios in developing than developed countries, different costs of living in different countries, or incomplete wage equalization—moderates these results a bit but still allows gains far in excess of anything observed in the trade liberalization literature.

Figure 13.2 illustrates the economics of this case in a simple partial economic framework. Suppose the horizontal axis $O_B O_A$ represents the world stock of labor and the vertical axis the wage and the value of the marginal product of labor. In country B labor is demanded until the wage (W_B) equals the marginal product (MPL_B), so plotting MPL_B against employment in B relative to origin O_B we have a demand curve for labor in B. (As employment increases, moving right from O_B towards O_A, the marginal product of labor falls, so that higher employment is only possible with lower wages.) Labor not employed in B is assumed to be employed in A and MPL_A is measured relative to the right-hand origin O_A and generates wages W_A.

Suppose that initially labor allocation is at L_O: $O_B L_O$ workers in B and $L_O O_A$ in A. From MPL_B, the wage in B has to be W_B, while that in labor-abundant A is W_A. Now suppose that labor can move until the wage is equal in A and B. This implies that the marginal products must be equal, so that the equilibrium allocation is at L_I. What are the gains? Consider allocation L_O again: at L_O workers in B produce output worth W_B and those in A output worth $MPL_A = W_A$. Thus if we shift one worker from A to B (i.e. made a tiny move to the right of L_O) we lose W_A but gain W_B — a gain of (W_B-W_A). Now move another worker, MPL_B has fallen ever so slightly and MPL_A has risen ever so slightly, but we still gain very nearly (W_B−W_A). If we carry on doing this until we get to

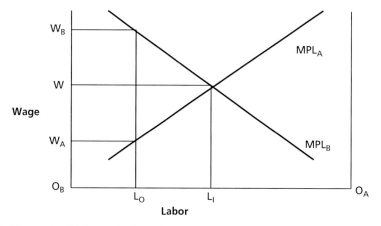

Figure 13.2. The costs of labor misallocation

L_I we will always gain the difference between MPL_B and MPL_A appropriate to the labor allocation that we have reached on the way between L_O and L_I. That is, the whole shift from L_O to L_I will increase world output by the area of triangle bounded by L_0, L_1 and the two MPL curves. This is, in principle, the number that Hamilton and Whalley (1984) calculate. Note that to make the calculation we need to know the shape of the MPL functions in each country and the final allocation L_I. In a multi-country world, given all the frictions involved in migration and the absence of any observations remotely close to the free migration point L_I, this is very difficult.

Such extreme mobility is not conceivable practically, but the same model underlies a much simpler back-of-the-envelope calculation. Winters (2001) suggests the possibility of global gains of over $300 billion per annum from modest increases in labor mobility. Suppose, very conservatively, that in moving from a low to a high-income country, a worker could make up only one-quarter of the productivity or wage gap between the two countries. (That is, assume that three-quarters of observed wage gaps are due to differences in individual characteristics such as health, education or culture, and hence that they would persist even after developing country workers started to work in the rich countries.) Suppose also that 50 million additional developing country workers worked abroad in any year, equivalent to an increase of about 5 per cent in industrial countries' populations. With a wage gap of, say $24,000 per annum, the gains would be $300 billion per annum![4]

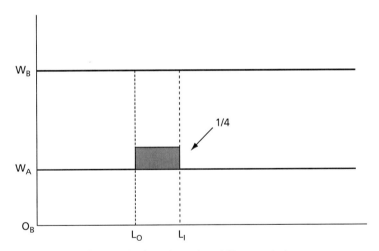

Figure 13.3. The benefits of a small relaxation of mobility restrictions

[4] Labor costs per manufacturing worker, which are an indicator of productivity, were about $32,000 in the U.S. in 1990–4, compared with $1,192 in India, $1,442 in Lesotho, $5,822 in China, and $6,138 in Mexico; high-income countries' population was 927 million in 1997 (World Bank, 1999).

Figure 13.3 illustrates this case. It is basically the area of Figure 13.2 around L_O greatly magnified. For very small movements of labor along the labor axis, we can ignore the slopes of MPL_A and MPL_B—all that matters effectively is the distance between them.

Temporary Mobility and Poverty

Temporary mobility, or indeed any migration, has potentially mixed implications for poverty in developing countries. The mobile workers themselves are unlikely to be from the poorest segments of society, who are generally too disconnected from the world economy to know about opportunities and too unskilled to be able to take advantage of them. The poorest may gain by moving into the jobs vacated by the mobile workers or because, attracted by the possibility of migration, they choose to become more educated. On the other hand, if migration removes the more skilled and/or entrepreneurial of workers from the sectors employing the poor, their opportunities for economically advantageous work may decline.

A second link between TM and poverty is via remittances. If these boost overall economic activity, the poor are likely to gain in the long run. More directly, they may be recipients of remittances if they have relatives who have moved. The Inter-American Dialogue (2004) writes:

There is no question that remittances reach low-income families and significantly increase their purchasing power and standard of living. In Honduras, Nicaragua, El Salvador, and a few others of Latin America's poorest nations, remittances may be more than doubling the incomes of the poorest 20 percent of the population. A large fraction of remittances is sent to rural areas, where incomes are far below national averages. In Mexico, for instance, communities with populations under 30,000 receive around 40 percent of remittances. Without them, many of these communities could not survive.

They also note that:

Remittances, however, are not a free good. Their cost is mostly borne by low-income migrants and their families in the United States. The average Salvadoran immigrant, for example, transfers upwards of 10 percent of his or her income to relatives back home. These payments often require that migrants reduce already meager expenditures on themselves, their families, and their children. They buy less housing, education, and health; save very little; and often work exceedingly long hours. These are mostly people who earn very little to begin with. According to the 2000 U.S. Census, more than 40 percent of Latinos earn less than $20,000 a year, and over 70 percent take home less than $35,000 a year.

Central America is arguably special with respect to remittances. Most of its poor have at least some education and connection with the world economy and have, formally or informally, good access to the U.S. with its huge demand for unskilled labor. This view is supported by the conclusions in World Bank (2003) about remittances in Lesotho. This report documents the heavy reliance of the Lesothan economy on remittances from miners working in South Africa, the recent strong declines in this flow of income and the fact that the burden of the decline falls primarily on relatively better off and urban households.

A third possible link is via aggregate income. Labor movements affect countries' relative outputs and hence their terms of trade, with the country of emigration typically experiencing an improvement. The country of immigration may show a growth in productivity either because it receives "better than average" labor from migration (migrants are typically above average in ability, dynamism, etc.) or because the inflows increase the returns to capital and the new investment that that induces is more productive than average.

Temporary Mobility and International Investment

In the original negotiation of the GATS the intention was that there would be a rough reciprocity between liberalization in mode 3—the establishment of service outlets (FDI), which, in the mercantilist calculus of the GATT and GATS, was of most interest to developed countries—and that of mode 4 which was expected to be of more interest to developing countries. In the event, this reciprocity was never achieved despite (or perhaps because of) the decision to allow mode 4 negotiations to extend beyond the completion date for most elements of the Uruguay Round. Few concessions were scheduled in mode 4, and those that were mostly referred to skilled labor and intra-corporate employees, i.e. to mainly developed rather than developing country interests.

There is a related question of positive economics: are modes 3 and 4 complements or substitutes? There are certainly complementary aspects, such as intra-corporate transferees, and there is plenty of economic theory that suggests that migration and international trade are complements—see, for example, Markusen (1983). Moreover both modes 3 and 4 refer to services for which producers (or factors of production) move to where the service is delivered and consumed. Thus in most cases it will be important whether capital moves from A to B or labor from B to A, because, unlike with goods or cross-border services where the final product can be traded through space, it matters here whether output of these services is produced in A or B. Overall, therefore, there is probably not much case for expecting modes 3 and 4 to be substitutable, and some case for expecting complementarity.

The Simple Gains from Temporary Movement—
New Estimates:[5] Analytical Objectives

The objectives of the discussion to follow are:

- Understand the logic of the computable model of the gains form TM and its assumptions (modifications to the GTAP model).

- Realize the likely gains from mode 4 liberalization. Identify potential winners and losers and the reasons for their different experiences. Note the differences between skilled and less skilled TM flows.

- Explore the importance of the assumptions of the model and their likely impact on the results.

- Derive implications for the mode 4 liberalization process.

Which countries would benefit from liberalizing the restrictions on the temporary movement of natural persons (TM) and by how much? This section summarizes some recent modeling results derived from a global applied general equilibrium model of south–north temporary movement of labor. The method is to fit a computable model to data from a base year (1997) and then ask how the outcome would have differed if there had been freer labor mobility in that year. Thus the results are not predictions of the actual future effects of a policy change, but rather quantitative thought experiments to suggest possible orders of magnitude in a realistic but hypothetical world.

In the absence of quantifiable data on restrictions to services trade per se, Walmsley and Winters (2002)—WW—model TM as the movement of workers from one country to another. This clearly overlooks a huge array of institutional details in actual and potential schemes for the temporary mobility of labor—some of which we turn to below. However, as argued above, in terms of the effects on narrowly economic variables, the approach is not seriously misleading, especially in the sort of model that is used. That is, ultimately, TM means that fewer workers produce at home and more do so in the host country.

The bottom line of the modeling exercise is that increased mobility equivalent to 3 per cent of the receiving countries' work forces would generate $156 billion per year in extra economic welfare in 1997 prices. These gains are shared between developing and developed countries and owe more to less-skilled than to skilled-labor mobility. The results from numerical models such as we are about to explore are informative, but one cannot possibly rely on the specific numbers that they generate.

---

[5] This section is based on Winters et al. (2002) and Walmsley and Winters (2002), from which more details of the modeling and results may be obtained.

The Model

The model and data used in Walmsley and Winters (2002) (WW) are described in more details in the Annex below. They are based on the GTAP model and database developed by Hertel (1997). The version of GTAP that is used is a standard applied general equilibrium model that assumes perfect competition; consequentially the exercise contains none of the scale or clustering effects which often figure in the skilled migration literature—see below. In each of several regions, a single household is assumed to allocate income across private and government consumption, and saving in fixed proportions. Demand for domestic and imported goods then depends on income and relative prices. Firms minimize the costs of production. They combine intermediate inputs, from domestic and imported sources, with primary factors to produce commodities for the domestic and export markets. Demand for factors of production (land, skilled and unskilled labor, capital and natural resources) depends on output and relative prices. Prices adjust to ensure that demand equals supply in every market.

WW modify the standard GTAP model to incorporate the movement of natural persons.. We start by distinguishing the terms "temporary migrant" and "temporary worker": A temporary migrant leaves his or her home region to become a temporary worker in a host region.

Changes in the economic welfare of permanent and temporary workers are related to their income flows deflated by prices in their place of work. The welfare of temporary migrants is found by summing the welfare changes of temporary workers across host countries and sharing it out over the various home countries, according to their shares in total TM. Once the welfare changes of temporary migrants are determined, welfare by home region, regardless of temporary residence, can also be calculated by simply summing the relevant changes.

The Experiments

The experiments assume that "skilled" and "unskilled" quotas on the movement of natural persons increase in traditionally labor-importing regions, supplied by temporary migrants from a number of traditionally labor-exporting countries according to their labor-force shares. The quotas are increased by an amount that would allow the quantity of labor in the host (or labor importing) countries to increase by 3 per cent equivalent to 8 million skilled workers and 8.5 million unskilled.[6] For example, in the

---

[6] By this we mean the number of workers (actual bodies) increases by 3 per cent of the labor force. Because relative productivities differ, this does not mean that the effective labor force increases by 3 per cent, since the labor force is increased by the number of equivalent workers.

case of the U.S., the increase in the quota would amount to 2.7 million unskilled temporary workers and 2.4 million skilled temporary workers. China as a supplier of temporary workers, would then supply 2.4 million of the total 8.5 million unskilled workers required and 0.49 million of the total 8 million skilled workers required worldwide.

Increasing developed countries' quotas on both skilled and unskilled temporary workers increases world welfare by an estimated US$156 billion in 1997 prices—about 0.6 per cent of initial world income. Tables 13.6 and 13.7 give some geographical details, but, for these, care must be taken to distinguish "home" country residents—those who start off in a country but some of whom move temporarily—from "host" country residents—the set of people who end up there after movement has occurred. Treating a country as a "home country" refers to its permanent workers who never leave plus its temporary migrants who work abroad—loosely speaking a nationality-based concept. Treating it as a "host country" refers to the permanent workers plus the temporary workers from elsewhere who work there—a residence-based concept.[7]

In aggregate terms the main gainers for liberalizing TM are the initial residents of the developing (labor-exporting) economies, as we can see from Column V in Table 13.6—developing countries as "home" countries. Most of this increase is the result of the higher incomes earned by the people who actually move (Column III). They are now able to earn higher wages in the developed countries, as shown in Column II of Table 13.6 under "welfare of temporary workers." (Recall that each mobile worker is both a "temporary worker" and a "temporary migrant," so columns II and III report the welfare of the same set of people allocated once by residence and once by nationality.) Despite the remittances they receive, permanent residents in the developing countries generally lose from the outflow of temporary migrants (Column IV in Table 13.6). The decrease in labor supply reduces the returns to capital and other factors of production (Column IV in Table 13.7) because those factors have less labor to work with.[8]

Combining the results for permanent residents and (the few) temporary workers already located there gives the outcomes for developing countries as host countries (Column VI of Table 13.6); in general these economies record losses, but recall that this excludes the benefits experienced by the temporary migrants who are working abroad.

---

[7] Note, however, that in Table 13.6 even 'labor exporters' record effects on temporary workers. The reason is that, although WW do not vary their number in the experiments, most labor exporters have a number of temporary workers in their base data, and as wages change, so does the economic welfare of these workers. The changes parallel those of permanent residents in these countries. A similar explanation applies for labor importers and temporary workers.

[8] In South Asia the welfare of permanent residents increases because the increase in remittances outweighs the decline in labor and capital income. This increase in income increases the demand for domestic goods and attenuates the decline in production in the economy. It allows the real wages of both skilled and unskilled workers to rise.

Table 13.6. Economic Welfare by Region and Class of Worker [a]

I Regions	II Welfare of temporary workers	III Welfare of temporary migrants	IV Welfare of permanent residents [b]	V Welfare by home region III + IV	VI Welfare by host region II + IV
Developed countries	175960	68577	6982	75559	182942
Developing countries of which	−5002	98984	−20685	78301	−25688
FSU and CEECs	−25	12511	−4991	7521	−5017
East and SE Asia	−762	29647	−12192	17456	−12955
South Asia	−53	4158	16377	20535	16325
Latin America	−718	30980	−12457	18523	−13175
Africa	−3444	21688	−7422	14266	−10866
TOTAL[e]	170932	170704	−14626	156078	156306

Notes: [a] US$ millions. [b] Permanent residents who do not move temporarily. [c] "Home" refers to people originating in the specified country regardless of where they work or live. [d] "Host" refers to people living in the specified country regardless of where they originated from. [e] Includes a small "rest of the world" region.
Source: Adapted from Walmsley and Winters (2002).

Table 13.7. Percentage Changes[a] in the Real Wages of Skilled and Unskilled Workers

I Regions [b]	II % Change in real wage of skilled labor	III % Change in real wage of unskilled labor	IV % Change in rental price of capital	V % Change in real GDP [c]	VI % Change in terms of trade
Developed countries	−1.02	−0.61	0.78	1.05	−0.24
Developing countries of which	5.13	0.12	−0.52	−0.91	0.53
FSU and CEECs	4.40	−0.48	−0.70	−1.03	0.18
East and SE Asia	4.94	0.02	−0.49	−0.88	0.28
South Asia	5.92	0.60	0.59	−0.48	4.55
Latin America	4.67	−0.21	−0.63	−0.88	0.06
Africa	5.75	0.20	−1.02	−1.39	0.37

Notes: [a] Percentage changes in variable from base case. [b] Weighted averages of results for the regions distinguished in the model—weights are skilled workers, unskilled workers, GDP, GDP and GDP respectively for columns II–VI. [c] Readers are reminded that Real GDP is not a measure of welfare. Real GDP is a measure of production, while welfare is a measure of the utility achieved from consumption, which depends among other things, on remittances received.
Source: Adapted from Walmsley and Winters (2002).

The loss of these factor inputs reduces aggregate output in the developing countries, real GDP, in the labor-exporting countries (Column V in Table 13.7), and because the outflow of labor is biased towards skilled labor, skilled workers' real wages rise in developing countries (Column II in Table 13.7).[9] Developing economies generally experience improvements in their terms of trade as the fall in their GDP reduces the

---

[9] By assumption, the relaxation of quotas reflects the skill mix of developing countries and so is substantially more skill-intensive than the typical developing country's labor-force endowment.

supply of the varieties of goods that they produce and so drives up their prices. Developed countries experience a corresponding decline.[10]

While the developing countries are the main beneficiaries of the increase in quotas, the initial residents of most of the developed countries also experience increases in welfare from the higher returns to capital and the increase in taxes collected. (In fact, for technical reasons spelt out in WW, the estimates in Table 13.6 for developed countries' permanent residents welfare is understated.) Real GDP increases substantially in the developed economies, but in most cases the terms of trade decline as higher output drives down the prices of exports relative to imports. Also note the strong positive effects on developed countries' temporary migrants in Table 13.6—i.e. those who have left a developed country to work abroad. This reflects the fact that over half of the stock of skilled temporary migrants identified in WW's database comes from the "Rest of the EU" region (E.U. less than U.K. and Germany). With their unavoidably crude pro-rata way of allocating these over destinations, many of them are allocated to developing countries (mostly in the Middle East), where they benefit from the strong increase in skilled wages.

Table 13.8 considers the effects of relaxing the skilled and unskilled quotas separately. Notably, both the developed and developing countries would benefit more from the liberalization of restrictions on unskilled labor than on skilled labor. For developing (labor-exporting) countries, the reason is that, while skilled temporary migrants can greatly increase their earnings by moving, the negative effect of their loss on their home economies is considerable. Thus, for example, while the skilled temporary workers improve their welfare by $61 billion, permanent residents in the developing world lose $34 billion while those in the developed world break even.

Turning to unskilled mobility, the temporary migrants from developing countries gain $38 billion in all, and their remittances more than offset their original (low) contribution to home output, so that the welfare of those who remain behind also rises. For the developed (labor-importing) regions, higher quotas on unskilled labor are also more beneficial in terms of welfare than are those on skilled workers, although most of the effect comes from the welfare of developed countries' temporary migrants, an effect which is not currently completely convincingly modeled by WW.

The distinction between the net benefits of skilled and unskilled mobility should not be over-emphasized, however. The WW model is very simple and ignores all the potential subtleties associated with the brain drain. These may either increase the home country benefits of emigration, via things like increased output of skilled workers, or reduce it (possibly below zero), by removing the best individuals or undermining the

---

[10] These two effects do not perfectly balance in Table 13.8 because the figures given are averages of many regional/country effects rather than reflecting only net trade between the developed and developing country blocs.

Table 13.8. Welfare Decomposed According to Effects of Increasing Skilled and Unskilled Quotas[a]

I Region	II Welfare of permanent workers (unskilled[b])	III Welfare of permanent workers (skilled[c])	IV Welfare of temporary migrants (unskilled[b])	V Welfare of temporary migrants (skilled[c])	VI Welfare of home region (unskilled[b]) II + IV	VII Welfare of home region i
Developed countries	6,860	121	50,587	17,989	57,447	18,111
Developing countries of which	13,097	−33,781	37,676	61,309	50,773	27,528
FSU and CEECs	205	−5,196	3,418	9,094	3,622	3,898
East and SE Asia	2,331	−14,523	9,558	20,089	11,889	5,566
South Asia	9,295	7,083	1,789	2,369	11,084	9,452
Latin America	−158	−12,298	13,216	17,763	13,059	5,465
Africa	1,424	−8,846	9,695	11,993	11,119	3,147
TOTAL[d]	20,181	−34,807	89,346	81,358	109,527	46,551

Notes: [a] US$ millions. [b] This is the welfare of the whole population when only quotas on unskilled workers are relaxed. [c] This is the welfare of the whole population when only quotas on skilled workers are relaxed. [d] Includes a small "rest of the world" region.
Source: Adapted from Walmsley and Winters (2002).

creation of a critical mass of skilled workers. Similarly the model misses any costs related directly to the number of people who move—transportation, subsistence, racial discrimination. Thus while the results are stark and certainly remind us of the potential benefits of unskilled worker mobility, one should not take the results too literally.

Table 13.9 summarizes some alternative estimations. These show that the precise details of the experiment do not undermine the basic results, and that the model is essentially "linear" for this kind of experiment. The basic reason for both features is that by far the most important component of the results is the shaded rectangular in Figure 13.3 replicated for each country and labor market. Each TM-individual creates extra value according to the assumed catch-up productivity, and thus the aggregate effect depends almost wholly on the assumed catch-up parameter and how many people move.

Alternative II separates the economy into two labor markets for each kind of labor—services and the rest. It then confines the inflow of labor to the developed countries' service sectors. The inflows result in a large expansion in services at the expense of the other sectors. Services sector wages decline (by between 1per cent to 2 per cent), while those in the other sectors increase substantially (by between 1 per cent to 3 per cent). Capital is replaced with the cheaper skilled labor in the services sector, allowing it to move to other sectors - agriculture and manufacturing. Developing countries see the opposite result. Their services sectors decline by more and their non-services sectors by less than in the unrestricted increases case (or even expand).

Restricting temporary labor to services reduces the benefits of TM because it prevents workers from taking advantage of increasing wages in other sectors. However, the loss

Table 13.9. Welfare[a] Results for Sensitivity Analysis

	Labor importing developed countries	Labor exporting developing countries	Total	% of Standard simulation (Row I)
Standard[b]	75558	80521	156078	100
Services only	73,790	78,683	152,470	98
% of current temporaries	85407	72330	157738	101
Endogenous labor			152,038	97
75% of productivity gained	120931	114614	235545	151
25% of productivity gained	30128	46237	76365	49
6% shock	138921	168356	307278	197
Trade liberalization	45052	59241	104293	67

Notes: [a] US$ millions. [b] Shock is equal to 3% of labor and assumes temporary workers gain 50% of host regions productivity.
Source: Adapted from Walmsley and Winters (2002).

from the restriction is not very large—benefits of $152 billion compared with $156 billion because the changes in wages are very small compared with the differences in wages between developed and developing economies. Thus, at least for the initial stages of a liberalization, restricting new temporary labor to only the services sectors (as mode 4 will do) will not seriously reduce the gains relative to those available under unrestricted mobility. Moreover, the assumption of completely separate labor markets is too extreme.

The standard results are also basically unaffected if one assumes that developing countries have perfectly elastic supplies of unskilled labor.[11] Similarly, if temporary workers are provided according to current shares of temporary workers rather than of labor forces, it hardly matters. If we assume that incoming workers catch up only one-quarter of the gap between their home and host country productivities (rather than one-half), the benefits are roughly halved, while, if we assume a three-quarter catch-up (i.e. increase the catch-up parameter by 50 per cent), the benefits are increased by 51 per cent. Gains are similarly proportional to the size of the liberalization, very nearly doubling if quotas expand by 6 per cent rather than 3 per cent of the work force. Finally, by way of comparison, we find that the complete abolition of all goods trade restrictions in the WW model generates only $104 billion of welfare gains compared with $156 billion from a limited relaxation of restrictions on labor movement.

It bears re-iterating: do not take these numbers literally. They are just orders of magnitude. They are not subject to much uncertainty in terms of the experiments that we run, but they are very uncertain once we recognize the inadequacies of the original

---

[11] If labor is perfectly elastic in supply in the developing countries, wages do not rise as emigration occurs. Rather as workers leave for abroad, replacements are sucked out of essentially unproductive tasks such as very low quality agriculture. Hence the developing country fails to see wages rise but equally does not see employment fall. These factors have approximately off-setting effects on aggregate income.

data, the crudity of the modeling of TM, and the extremity of the modeling assumptions. Nonetheless, backed up by the simple back-of-the-envelope exercise in Winters (2001), the results suggest startlingly large benefits to freeing up the temporary movement of labor. Even for a limited liberalization, they are far larger than the benefits available to a complete goods-market liberalization, and they are also larger for unskilled than for skilled labor mobility. If they do nothing else, these results should challenge negotiators to think hard about the priorities they bring to a negotiating round.

Mobility Between Sectors

A major issue in the foregoing exercise modeling TM as migration is the implicit assumption that the work force of permanent and temporary workers is costlessly distributed across sectors within the economy according to labor demand. This is clearly not literally true and, if it were seriously violated, it would pose serious challenges as we contemplate larger and larger TM flows, for they would be likely to disturb inter-industry relativities very strongly.

Virtually all trade liberalizations modeling exercises involve the assumption of perfect long-run mobility of each kind of labor between sectors and the consequent equalization of real wages for each kind across sectors. Some models allow for real wage differences between sectors that reflect the sectors' non-pecuniary advantages or disadvantages (i.e. non-monetary factors such as safety or anti-social hours). These are assumed to be unvarying and proportional to the wage so that, in fact, all wages move up and down by the same proportion together. Other models allow for upward-sloping aggregate supply curves of labor to reflect the way in which higher real wages will be needed to attract more people into the work force. None of these, however, addresses the issue that seems most pertinent to TM under the GATS, namely the frictions on moving between sectors.

Suppose that all of the temporary workers permitted to enter a country initially enter a particular sector, j. If the labor in sector j were wholly specific to that sector, wages would fall and employment and output would rise. There would be spill-overs to other sectors via demand (because the price of j and incomes would have changed), but no direct labor-market effects on other sectors. The effects of TM would be highly con-centrated on sector j. If on the other hand, labor were perfectly mobile between sectors, the incipient wage decline induced by the extra workers in sector j would immediately drive some of the existing workers out of j into other sectors, reducing wages in other sectors. Ultimately, wages would change by the same small amount in all sectors, and the shock to the sector j would be much smaller than in the sector-specific case.

Which of these stories is more plausible? In the very short-run, labor is fairly sector-specific, especially if workers have sector-specific skills, so that impacts are deep and narrow. Kletzer (2001), for example, finds quite long-lived unemployment and wage cuts for some of the workers losing their jobs in import-competing sectors. In the longer run, however, most economies show a good deal of flexibility and so impacts are broader and shallower. Borjas and Freeman (1992) show that U.S. regions that attract large immigrant inflows experience corresponding declines in internal inflows or increases in worker outflows, for, in the long run, their work forces seem to be no different from what would be expected in the absence of immigration. Given that it is probably less costly to switch sectors than locations (especially for the less skilled), we might take this as evidence to support the single labor-market assumption. The fact that workers' attitudes towards globalization owe more to their skills levels than to their sectors of employment (Scheve and Slaughter, 2001) also suggests fair degrees of mobility.

Refining the Estimates: Analytical Objectives

The objectives of the following discussion are:

- Distinguish between flows of skilled and business professional workers from more developed to less developed countries and the flows (both skilled and unskilled workers) from less developed to more developed countries.

- Appreciate both the potentials for "brain gain" and the dangers of "brain drain."

- Note the importance of information about the size of the barriers to services for future empirical exercises.

Before going onto the details of negotiating TM, it is useful to consider some general issues surrounding migration and how they may vary between permanent migration and temporary mobility (TM). Within the general heading of labor mobility, it is useful to distinguish three particular dimensions: the flow of unskilled workers from less developed to more developed countries;[12] the flow of skilled and business professional workers from more developed to less developed countries; and the flow of skilled and professional workers from less developed to more developed countries. Of course there are flows between pairs of countries at roughly equal levels of development, but they raise fewer economic issues. Implicit in this classification by level of development is that countries have general advantages that affect their productivity in all sectors (and usually of all factors of production). This means that, at first, we can think of the general issues entailed in mobility free from sectoral complications.

---

[12] We deliberately use the terms 'more' and 'less' developed here to convey that what matters is their relative level of income, not their absolute levels as in the normal developed/developing divide.

Flows from More to Less Developed Countries

The main issue here is the right of developed country firms to send specialists to their plants in developing countries, so-called intra-corporate transfers. In some cases it is highly skilled technical workers who are required, often at short notice and for short periods. Such workers are necessary for commissioning new plants and equipment, repairing and maintaining such equipment, and for providing intra-firm services such as accounting, designs or legal advice. In other cases, the interest is in the mobility of managers—either senior managers to oversee major functions or the regular rotation of middle management. Firms already see these various flows as a means of increasing local efficiency and of integrating their operations on a global scale, and one presumes that they increase global output (as well as the multinationals' profits). Indeed, they are central to the dissemination of both hard and soft technologies to the developing world, and so apart from very long-run concerns about the incentives they create or destroy for human capital formation, they are potentially an important contributor to development.

Tang and Wood (1999) have shown in a simple model that, as with most migration driven by wage differences, such business mobility increases world output. Not surprisingly they find that it narrows the skills gap (the difference between skilled and unskilled wages) in the developing host countries (unskilled wages rise because there is more skilled labor to work with) while widening it in developed countries. In the latter country unskilled workers suffer from having fewer skilled workers to cooperate with and from the competition from cheaper unskilled labor abroad. In the developing country, output (GDP) increases, and although part of it accrues to the mobile skilled workers who are from the developed country, part accrues at home in terms of higher unskilled wages and tax revenues. Such mobility will, in this model, reduce the developing country's skilled-wage and so, in the absence of any off-setting factors, reduce the incentive for education; and this is re-enforced by the fact that, once mobility is permitted, the multinational corporation (MNC) might be able to do less local training. Hence there is a possibility—although at present we can say no more—of longer-term costs to the developing country. Analytically it has parallels with the arguments surrounding the so-called "beneficial brain drain" that the next subsection considers.

Skilled Labor from Less to More Developed Countries

The second element of labor mobility is the flow of skilled workers from developing countries—the so-called brain drain. The value of skilled labor to a well-functioning economy has never been plainer and in certain sectors—e.g. IT, education and health— developed countries are now actively seeking to recruit from abroad.

One's immediate reaction is that if the advanced economies gain from skilled immigration, the developing countries from which skilled workers emigrate must necessarily lose. Indeed, this is not an implausible scenario: the loss of the services of skilled people, even temporarily, reduces total output, and hence the tax base and scale economies. Depending on the extent of the skilled workers' absences, it could also reduce an economy's entrepreneurship, its ability to absorb new technologies, and various positive spill-overs from skilled to other workers and society in general.

But, in fact, straight loss is far from inevitable, and is less likely with TM than permanent migration. For example, skilled workers from developing countries are likely to be more productive and have higher earnings in advanced economies, and the share of their higher earnings that they send or bring home with them may more than fully offset the loss of their services locally. This is particularly true if the developing country had not been making optimal use of the skilled labor initially, say for bureaucratic reasons or because the necessary complementary inputs were not available. These arguments have been made previously about remittances from permanent or quasi-permanent migrants, but they apply with even more force to TM. Such evidence as we do have suggests that remittances are higher for shorter-term migrants.[13]

Workers abroad are potential sources of ideas, technology, markets or networks for those who remain behind, increasing the latter's productivity and market opportunities. Again this applies to permanent migrants, but the spill-overs are likely to be stronger if the workers with foreign experience spend more time living and working in their home economies. Under these circumstances TM will boost local productivity as returning skilled workers instruct or inspire local colleagues. It is true, however, that TM may be less effective at building up foreign networks than permanent migration or in encouraging workers to learn the practices of their host nations. Thus, ultimately the extent of spill-overs is an empirical matter.

There is also likely to be far higher turnover among temporary than among permanent migrants—i.e. if a country could send N of its residents abroad at any one time, the stock of residents with experience of working abroad will far exceed N under TM. Thus the increased skills and incomes associated with mobility are likely to be more widely spread under TM than permanent migration, albeit that the increments for any individual are likely to be lower. Thus the spillovers are likely to be broader, and to the extent that breadth determines their effect, stronger. Breadth is a key factor for network externalities—your own benefit depends on how many other people also have access to the facilities or knowledge required—and also where a critical mass of support must be accumulated before a change can occur. The last seems very plausible for cases where

---

[13] In fact, the repatriated earnings of TM workers are unlikely to be recorded as remittances in the Balance of Payments accounts. If workers carry their earnings home, they probably will not be recorded at all, whereas if they are repatriated by their employers or the purchases of the contracts they work on, the earnings will be recorded as service exports or profits earned abroad.

overseas experience encourages local workers to adopt different practices or institutions. If lots of people have experienced the benefits of the alternative ways, they are more likely to be introduced than if only a few have.

A further possibility is that TM increases the returns to education and that the resulting increase in the supply of skills exceeds the actual loss of skilled inputs through TM, leaving the domestic economy in the developing country a net gainer of skills. The small amount of evidence on these arguments is mixed—see the survey by Commander et al. (CKM) (2004), which analyses the arguments in some detail—but there are certainly cases where supply has increased strongly as migratory opportunities have increased—e.g. nurses in the Philippines, IT workers in India. One can think of several reasons why, again, TM may offer greater scope for gains than does permanent migration. For example, under the latter the rewards to education are high but arrive with relatively small probability (i.e. that of getting one of the favored jobs abroad), whereas with TM the rewards are smaller but more likely since more people will be affected by them. If the resulting increase in the supply of skilled workers exceeds the actual loss through TM or migration (something that is more likely under TM), the domestic economy in the developing country is a net gainer of skills and hence, possibly, of net income and welfare.

Finally, workers who are abroad only temporarily are also more likely to pay their income taxes in their home rather than their host countries. Under current law, this depends on how temporary they are, and it is potentially a major—and negotiable—consideration in the allocation of the benefits of TM between host and home countries.

Clearly developing countries' policies towards skilled TM should depend heavily on the net balance of these effects, and this is currently very uncertain. Moreover, the balance is likely to vary by sector and by country as Beine et al. (2001) suggest. For example, highly skilled workers seem to benefit from clustering together and also from operating in larger markets. The more people there are to benefit from their good ideas the greater their worth)—see CKM section 7. Thus one can imagine the following taxonomy of countries:

- Very small economies, which could never generate the market or society size to make acquiring skills very profitable; these are more likely to gain from migration, via remittances, network effects, etc.

- Very large economies, which can reliably create the mass of skilled workers necessary for efficiency; these will lose the output of skilled migrants but only on the margin: the fundamental existence of skill-intensive sectors and spillovers will not be undermined and the effects of migration may well be offset by remittances, etc.

- Medium-sized economies which, on the other hand, may be prevented by migration from reaching the critical mass of skills necessary to achieve local "take-off" in high skill activities; these could suffer a quantum decline in local value added that no remittance or networking could ever overcome.

This is all speculation at present and we have little idea of what small, medium, and large means in this context, but it does at least warn us that attitudes to TM and to migration should probably differ between developing countries.

Unskilled Mobility from Less to More Developed Countries

While not entirely frictionless, flows of skilled workers are much easier for developed countries to handle politically than is general migration: skilled workers appear to meet obvious shortages and are generally much easier to assimilate. But the real gains from trade, be it in goods or in factors, come from exploiting differences. Hence it is the flow of unskilled (or, strictly, less skilled) workers from less developed to more developed countries that promises the larger returns. Not only is the proportionate gap in productivity between host and home countries likely to be largest here, but so too are the numbers of people available to move.

But there are formidable political problems associated with large-scale permanent unskilled migration. Host countries fear cultural and integration problems because the unskilled are less likely to adapt to Western culture; they fear drains on the public purse; the jobs that unskilled immigrants take do not command immediate respect and appear to be at the expense of the employment of local unskilled workers—who currently appear still to be in excess supply. Given the ability of various lobbies to ensure that protection in OECD and middle-income countries is skewed towards supporting unskilled wages and employment, it is no surprise that the same forces have been able to resist immigration so effectively.

TM can offer a way out of this dilemma. Although it will clearly deliver only some of the economic benefits available from straight migration in terms of output and income, it avoids most of the latter's political costs. The incentives and ability of migrants to learn about their new environment and for local firms to use them will be lower for temporary than for permanent migrants, but temporary movers pose fewer cultural or integration threats and make virtually no call on public services. Thus, the main challenge posed by a well-run TM scheme is the increase in competition that it poses for indigenous low-skill workers. This is qualitatively the same challenge as is posed by imports of labor-intensive goods from the developing world, and it has the same aggregate gains and distributional consequences (losses for the low-skilled, gains for everyone else). Formidable though it has been, the resistance to the liberalization of imports of labor-intensive goods has been at least partly overcome in the past by the weight of the economic gain that trade can deliver and by policies designed to ease adjustment among the local unskilled. Applied with the same policies and sensitivities as trade policy reform in goods has received in the past, TM among less skilled workers offers the chance to reap some of the large gains described above.

One cannot argue, regrettably, that TM faces no cultural, social or political objections—xenophobia is not so selective—and it is true that permanent migration may eventually become less threatening because permanent migrants assimilate into the local culture where temporary ones do not. On the whole, however, it seems reasonable to expect that a scheme in which temporary migrants were known to be temporary would be less threatening in these dimensions. One interesting thought is that the relative importance of cultural and job displacement fears may influence host-countries' preferences over temporary or permanent migration. In Europe, intense cultural xenophobia coupled with relatively benign policies for displaced workers favor TM. In the US, on the other hand, with an historical disposition towards migration and a relatively harsh labor market, the labor unions (and hence, to some extent, policy in general) favor permanent immigrants. They can be unionized and incorporated into "the system" in contrast to "hit-and-run" competition from temporary migrants, especially if the latter are delivered by overseas firms that have the right to bring in their own workers.

As their populations age and as average levels of training and education rise, the scarcity of less skilled labor in developed countries will increase. Given that at least in some occupations there is really no substitute for human labor—e.g. in the caring occupations, personal services, and delivery of goods—the benefits of TM will increase through time. Thus while recognizing the formidable political challenges it poses, TM actually offers a strong long-run identity of interest between developing and developed countries.

Refining the Estimates of the Benefits of TM

The major challenge to modeling the effects of mode 4 liberalization as a simple trade liberalization is the complete absence of information about the size of the barriers to services trade. (This is true of virtually all services trade, not just that delivered by TM.) Using TM to deliver services faces both para-tariffs, such as the costs of visas, social security taxes, additional health insurance, registering qualifications, etc., and quantitative restrictions, in both specific form, such as the failure to recognize foreign qualifications, and in the general form of immigration restrictions. Often several restrictions will have to be relaxed before an increase in trade can occur.

One way of refining the empirical estimation of the costs of mode 4 restrictions is to quantify these barriers for specific sectors. This approach amounts more or less to preparing a 'business plan' for the provision of service X in market A by residents of country B. Taking the wage in B for the workers concerned as given, one would need to quantify the additional costs of providing the service in A. Some would be obvious—e.g. subsistence, insurance,[14] travel—while others could be less so—e.g. the need for advertising, or discounts for customers' uncertainty about quality or reliability. Yet more would be policy-related: current regulations may require electricians to complete a full training course in country A, but if objective criteria were applied with goodwill, one might conclude that merely re-examining foreign-trained electricians was sufficient.

Given the cost of B-residents supplying a service in A (which will clearly depend on the scale of operations assumed), one could compare this with the existing price in A.[15] A small relaxation in the quota of TM would then generate rent equivalent to the difference between the two costs—which would presumably be shared between the consumers, the mobile workers and the firms/institutions facilitating their mobility. If the relaxation in quota were non-marginal, one would strictly need estimates of the elasticities of supply of temporary workers and demand for the service in order to calculate the new equilibrium (as in Figure 13.2). One might guess at these values, but they are highly uncertain. However, for the sort of small relaxations of TM that we can contemplate in the near future, allowing the rent margins to change as trade increases is a second-order issue.

Clearly any exercise such as this will be highly sector-specific and subject to wide margins of error. Moreover, while the calculations suggested might indicate the private returns to TM, they would not necessarily immediately generate estimates of the overall welfare benefits of liberalization. This is because many of the necessary monetary costs of TM—e.g. those related to training and testing workers—contain elements of rent and/or subsidy themselves. These per-unit rents and subsidies need to be quantified and the new volumes of activity to which they apply predicted in order to calculate the gross losses or gains that they imply. The location in which the rents accrue also needs to be identified if one wishes to apportion net benefits between countries. In addition, one must recognize that if the liberalization of TM boosted demand for these "mobility services" the rents entailed could increase to absorb much of the net gain.

Issues for Negotiation: Analytical Objectives

The objectives of the following discussion are:

- Understand the relative attractions of bringing WTO rules into domestic employment law compared with introducing sub-contracting schemes for TM labor.

---

[14] Winters et al. (2002) argue that temporary workers should cover accident and medical insurance privately.

[15] If productivity necessarily varied between home and overseas workers, one would need to allow for this in the wage comparisons, but not if one is comparing the cost of a delivered service.

- Understand how existing temporary labor schemes can contribute to the TM discussions/negotiations.
- Understand the strengths and weaknesses of possible proposals on GATS mode 4.
- Note the practical importance of technical implementation issues in the TM liberalization process such as the recognition of qualifications and the wage parity rules.

Templates for Agreement—Existing Schemes

Temporary mobility is a well established phenomenon outside the WTO, with many countries operating temporary labor schemes for specific sectors and with specific partners. For example, Britain allows working-holidays for young people from Commonwealth countries, who are allowed to work in non-professional jobs for up to two years. Its seasonal agricultural workers scheme, originally intended primarily to promote cultural interchange for young people from Eastern Europe, allows a small number of workers to enter for up to ten months and is now largely driven by agricultural demand for labor. There is no work permit requirement for au pair workers who must be single, aged 17 to 27, from a limited set of countries, and stay is no longer than two years. There are also a number of business-related visitors who do not require work permits: those investing significant amounts in U.K.; and entrepreneurs and skilled workers with innovative ideas to enter the U.K. to establish a new company and work in the areas of science and technology and e-commerce.

Better known perhaps are the German foreign-guest-worker schemes that were used to fill gaps in the domestic labor market after 1955. These programs, based upon bilateral government agreements, were intended to provide a rotation of workers for the German economy. The early guest-workers program, however, not only filled the gap in the labor market, but also led to a good deal of permanent immigration. After the first oil crisis in 1973/4, Germany stopped recruiting foreign guest-workers and started to develop a series of migrant worker programs. These programs were more carefully designed to prevent workers from settling down in Germany.

One such design feature was subcontracting agreements. These agreements, between German and foreign firms, were initiated in the early 1980s but were most important in the 1990s. For example, a Czech or Polish firm would agree to do the brickwork on a German building, and would supply both the construction workers and the supervisory engineers to direct their work. The foreign company providing services retained the rights to give instructions to its employees working on the customer's premises. Draft subcontracting agreements had to be submitted for approval to the German Employment Service, which verified that the agreement provided for the payment of prevailing wages and acceptable working conditions, and that the foreign firm actually paid its workforce the agreed amounts. Social security contributions for the project workers were paid through the foreign company according to the provisions in its home country. In case of non-compliance, including workers who over-stayed their contract, fines were imposed on the German domestic (hiring) company, hence internalizing much of the enforcement burden. Foreign firms could be excluded from the bilateral agreements if they exceeded the job quotas allocated to them, employed workers without a proper work permit or paid wages below agreed level. In order to prevent illegal employment, employment officers carried out strict check-ups without notice on the construction sites. Foreign workers, were required to come to Germany without their families, and could stay only for a maximum of two years. They were paid partly in German marks and partly in their home currencies, and some of their wages remained with their employing firms (i.e., the subcontractors) until they returned home. There were no firm-specific quotas allocated to German companies on the number of subcontracted foreign workers, but there were industry-by-industry quotas and a countrywide quota, of 100,000 in 1992.

These existing bilateral or plurilateral temporary mobility schemes are interesting because they offer models for achieving a broader range of less-skilled TM within the context of the GATS. Even if the results of the Doha Development Agenda negotiations are limited, TM will remain on the agenda in future and so it is worth thinking about what might usefully be achieved in this context. Thus in the rest of this section we explore some practical proposals for advancing TM within the GATS.

First, however, a word of caution. A notable characteristic of the GATS, especially in the area of mode 4, is imprecision. This starts with the definition of the phenomenon itself and continues through to the details of any negotiating concessions that are made. Tidying up some of these loose ends may be a good use of negotiation effort, but not inevitably so. Most of the ends are loose, not because they were not thought of, but because they could not be tied up in the Uruguay Round. Unless circumstances have changed, tidying up could become divisive and actually prevent substantive progress. Thus, developing country negotiators need to exercise fine judgment about what to pursue in the mode 4 talks. We consider various concrete proposals in these terms below.

Domestic Employment

First consider the status of domestic employment under GATS. It is unclear whether the GATS must, can, or cannot govern the employment of foreign nationals by domestic service firms—see WTO (1998) or Winters et al. (2003a).

The GATS defines mode 4 as "the supply of a service ... by a service supplier of one Member, through the presence of natural persons of a Member in the territory of any other Members" (Article I 2(d)).[16] This definition focuses on the ability of a service provider to cross the border in order to provide a service rather than the conditions under which that movement takes place. The latter is the business of negotiation and of the specific commitments that member countries schedule under the GATS. However, the Annex on Movement of Natural Persons Supplying Services under the Agreement, which is an integral part of the GATS, states clearly that the GATS does not apply to measures affecting access to the employment market of a Member or to measures regarding citizenship, residence or employment on a permanent basis.[17] This seems pretty unambiguous, but unfortunately the Annex has previously stated that it applies to two categories of measures: (a) those affecting natural persons who are "service suppliers of a Member, and (b) natural persons of a Member who are employed by a service supplier of a Member in respect of the supply of a service." Both of these latter categories raise ambiguity when combined with Article I 2(d).

To treat jobs in a domestic firm differently from identical jobs in a foreign firm seems perverse, for it can result in exactly the same service provided by the same person being treated differently according to arcane details of firm ownership or history. However, whatever the legal situation, the costs and political risks of bringing the WTO into domestic employment law are likely to be high.

Within the WTO, revising the structure of the GATS agreement to clarify the situation would involve amending the charter, which de jure requires the assent of a substantial majority of WTO members and de facto the assent of all of them. Scheduling concessions within the current structure, on the other hand, is a matter merely for those countries who wish to take part in a round or act unilaterally.

Trade specialists see TM as a technical issue of economic efficiency and distribution that should be debated in terms of outcomes rather than structures and legalities. Immigration and labor-market officials, on the other hand, see it in terms of labor standards, culture, internal security, and citizenship, and fear that migration could unleash potentially overwhelming forces on societies unless it is carefully managed. It is very far from clear that electorates and governments will back the trade community's functional view over these sensitivities, and so seeking to clarify the GATS in this dimension could just lead to deadlock.

A second danger concerns the existing temporary foreign worker programs that typically view domestic firms as the employing entity. These show that TM is feasible and offer illustrations of and, sometimes, solutions to the fundamental question of how

---

[16] Supply of a service is qualified in Article XXVIII(b) to include 'the production, distribution, marketing, sales, and delivery of a service'.

[17] It also states that Members are free to regulate the entry and stay of individuals in their territory provided that regulations do not "nullify or impair the benefits accruing to any Member under the terms of a specific commitment."

to manage it. Incorporating these into the GATS is superficially attractive but poses several technical challenges and one major political threat.

If current foreign-worker schemes were scheduled in the GATS, they would have to be bound, making them much less flexible for host governments. Given the absence of a safeguards mechanism in the GATS (and the likelihood that any safeguard would be essentially commercial in nature), and given that the general exceptions in the GATS do not mention internal security or social policy, this could be viewed as a profound political disadvantage by developed country governments. At present they tend to view these agreements as taps that can be turned on and off as (political and economic) circumstances dictate. Indeed, as we saw in Germany in the early 1970s, the ability to shift the burden of adjustment to foreign workers is very attractive politically—surrendering that right would be quite a sacrifice.

With one exception, subjecting foreign workers to national treatment would not be particularly demanding.[18] The exception is that governments would probably wish to place additional regulations on foreign workers to guarantee their temporariness. Thus, for example, rules requiring some of their pay to be deferred until they leave, or even excluding them from social security/insurance systems may have to be registered with the WTO as exceptions to national treatment.

A much greater challenge is the most favored nation MFN rule.[19] The bilateral nature of most existing agreements reflects broad political or cultural objectives. Extending them would probably encounter resistance not only from the currently preferred sending countries, but also within the host countries. Of course the same arguments were made over pre-GATT preferential trading arrangements in goods, and gave rise to the exceptions for customs unions permitted by the GATT's Article XXIV. However, the cultural argument was less powerful among host-country residents in that case because goods are one thing, but inflows of real people quite another. Given the large pools of population outside the traditionally preferred regions, one could certainly anticipate strong changes in the sourcing of temporary workers if they were switched to a MFN basis. Indeed, the wish to manage who, as well as what number, has access to its country is usually a major consideration for governments, and the desire to maintain flexibility in this regard may indicate that at least in the foreseeable future country-specific agreements are required. One approach would be to make these bilateral or regional. However, this could reinforce current tendencies to carve the world economy into exclusive trading blocs, which is a serious political danger to the current liberal order. The pragmatic alternative is to recognize the force of these nationally based considerations and seek to accommodate them into the WTO. The dangers of such accommodation are

---

[18] National treatment requires that foreign goods, firms, workers, etc. be treated no worse than equivalent domestic ones. It is a fundamental pillar of the WTO.

[19] The MFN rule requires that all foreign entities receive the same treatment as the most favored one—i.e. no discrimination. It too is fundamental to the WTO, although exceptions are permitted.

not small—it could merely validate fragmentation—but it may be worth considering in this area alone.[20]

Box 13.1. The Indian Proposal on Mode 4

The most comprehensive developing country proposal on mode 4 is from India. It provides not only concrete suggestions for areas of further liberalization in mode 4, but also detailed administrative procedures relating to mode 4 visas and work permits and the recognition of qualifications. It reflects the view and addresses the issue that there is a significant imbalance between current commitments on mode 3, commercial presence, and those on mode 4, natural persons.

The Indian proposal first points out that existing mode 4 commitments are largely linked to commercial presence, which is of very limited use to developing countries who are interested primarily in movement of independent professionals and other persons. It then goes on to make the following points:

1. De-linking commitments of mode 4 and mode 3 by adding another category "Individual Professionals" to the existing categories. This reflects India's focus on the competitive end of the professional market where the competition from large transnational suppliers is at minimum.

2. Further expansion in the scope of categories to include middle and lower level of professionals into the existing coverage of "other persons" and "specialists." This clearly addresses the concern of many developing countries. They feel that their comparative advantage lies, not in highly skilled professionals, but in middle and lower level professionals. Allowing middle and lower levels of skilled workers to provide their services across borders starts to address the fact that trade is most beneficial when it starts to address differences between countries. Such mobility would benefit both developing country service providers and receiving countries' users/consumers.

3. Uniform definitions and coverage of broader service personnel categories. India calls for using the ILO's International Standard Classification of Occupations for the WTO services Sectoral Classification.

4. Like the other countries, India identifies the need for clarity in the definition of and multilateral disciplines on the application of Economic Needs Tests, if calls are to be made subject to such tests and for consensus to be achieved on what such categories should be.

5. The recognition of qualifications is a concern in both developed and developing countries, although it is more an issue for the latter. India proposes the establishment of multilateral norms to facilitate the recognition of academic as well as the recognition of work-related qualification.

6. India proposes the exemption of developing country professionals from social security contributions in their host countries.

7. It is important that temporary service providers under the GATS should be separated from permanent labor flows, so that normal immigration procedures would not hinder the commitments made on TM. In this spirit, India suggests introducing a special GATS visa for mode 4 temporaries, or at least a special sub-set of administrative rules and procedures within the overall immigration policy framework. Its intention is to ensure that mode 4 mobility lies outside the normal immigration procedures and would be flexible and renewable. The most sensitive and well known issue of how to prevent individual service providers from entering the host country's permanent labor market is recognized by admitting the need to establish "adequate in-built safeguard mechanisms," but no suggestion is made as to what these might be for the establishment of Multilateral Norms to reduce the scope of discriminatory practices in the use of Economic Needs Tests.

Source: "Proposed liberalization of movement of professionals under the General Agreement on Trade in Services (GATS)," Council for Trade in Services, S/CSS/W/12, November 24, 2000, Geneva. Summary as elaborated by Winters et al. (2003a).

---

[20] Pragmatism characterized the early years of the GATT, and perhaps accounted for its survival—e.g. the GATT permitted the creation of the European Economic Community (EEC) and restrictions on textile trade despite their being obviously contrary to its rules.

Box 13.2. The United Kingdom's: GATS Visa Scheme

This concession is intended to facilitate access to U.K. service contracts by non-E.U. based companies or organizations who employ persons having high level professional skills whose entry to this country would otherwise be subject to visa and work permit restrictions.

The service sectors for which the GATS work permits can be issued are: (1) legal services; (2) accountancy services; (3) bookkeeping services; (4) taxation advisory services; (5) architectural services, urban planning, and landscape architectural services; (6) engineering services; (7) integrated engineering services; (8) advertising; (9) management consulting services; (10) services relating to management consulting; (11) technical testing and analysis services; (12) translation services; and (13) site investigation services.

For the services listed from 6–13 the service contract needs to meet the requirements of an "economic needs test."

In order to qualify for a GATS work permit, the person(s) required to work on the contract in the U.K. is(are) expected to have: (i) a recognized degree level qualification; (ii) professional (with minor exceptions in three sectors) qualifications; and (iii) 3 years professional experience in the sector, the last 12 months of which should have been as a formal salaried employee of the organization who have been awarded the service contract.

The GATS agreement only extends to organizations of those countries who are members of the World Trade Organization (WTO) and who have signed up to the agreement. Decisions on GATS applications are made against the following criteria:

- The service contract must not exceed a period of three calendar months.
- The person will not be permitted to stay in the U.K. under this agreement beyond three calendar months in any 12 month period.
- The service provided must fall within one of the service sectors listed above.
- The person must have the qualifications and experience listed above.
- The person should have spent 12 months in the organization, as a formal salaried employee.
- The agreement does not extend to self-employed individuals, or to employment agencies or similar organizations who do not formally employ workers but simply supply or hire them out.
- The contract must have been awarded through an open tendering procedure or any other procedure that guarantees the bona fide nature of the contract (e.g. economic needs test).

The permission for employment in the U.K. is granted on the condition that there is an intention to leave the U.K. once the work on the service contract has been completed or the maximum period of three calendar months in 12 has been reached.

Source: Winters et al. (2003a).

The major political threat inherent in bringing current schemes into the GATS is the need to ensure that any GATS-based liberalization of TM generates genuinely additional labor movement. The many extant formal and informal routes to labor mobility from developing to developed countries generate a good deal of income for both parties. When mode 4 is negotiated, extreme care must be taken to ensure that any resulting codification of the rules does not restrict existing flows. Despite their obvious short-term political attractions, suggestions that the GATS should be used to turn illegal immigrants into legal ones are dangerous for precisely this reason. Unless that were accompanied by a huge liberalization in official numbers (because almost certainly the allocation of quotas would lead to under-filling by many potential supplying countries), it would restrict rather than enhance actual movement. No deal at all would be better than this. Rather we should be exploring the Indian suggestion for creating a GATS visa, which would create a new route for mobility of an explicitly temporary kind (WTO document S/CSS/W/12, November 24, 2000).

The main details of the Indian proposal are given in Box 13.1. Details of the U.K.'s actual practice for GATS visas are given in Box 13.2. It is plain that they are still far apart.

Sub-contracting

Sub-contracting schemes are the second way in which mode 4 negotiations can include lower-skilled workers, and Winters et al. (2003a, b) suggest initially focusing negotiating effort in this area. First, there is no dispute about its inclusion in the GATS and its appropriateness for negotiation. Second, with well-defined parties on both sides of the transaction—incorporated firms—the enforcement of the conditions imposed for mobility is much easier than it is for individual workers.[21] The principal disadvantage of sub-contracting is that it is inflexible and for some services infeasible. The sub-contracting firm has to be approved by the host authorities, and if approval is conditional, any change in its operations will need approval. This is a bureaucratic burden, but more importantly, it reduces the contestability of markets.

One common condition for sub-contracting is that mobile workers have prior employment with the sub-contracting firm. This requirement is intended to ensure that the individuals concerned are genuinely attached to a well-defined undertaking to which they can return and which, if necessary, can guarantee their return after the completion of the project. Pre-employment requirements also apply to intra-corporate transferees and so there is some existing well-defined practice in this area. However, pre-employment would be a major burden for firms set up largely for the purpose of exporting services with less-skilled labor, for it would involve periods of low or zero productivity at home during the qualification phase. Notice in Box 13.2 how employment with an agency does not qualify as employment for a U.K. GATS visa.

Despite its flaws, concentrating on sub-contracting as a means of effecting mode 4 concessions could offer substantial economic benefits to developing country exporters. It offers the greatest chance of extending mode 4 to lower-skilled workers, and it

---

[21] Care is necessary over the definition of sub-contracting: it is important that sub-contracted labor can be managed and directed by host country managers as well as via sub-contracted managers. If this were not the case, sub-contracting would be feasible only for major importers of services.

responds to most of the developed countries' concerns about ensuring the exit of temporary workers at the end of their terms of service provision. Tactically, it seems best to follow this line of least resistance in order to reap some early gains and achieve some dynamic in mode 4 negotiations. If successful, attention could then be switched to employment schemes and domestic employment.

Implementing a TM Agreement

There are a number of knotty technical implementation issues to solve if TM is to work. At least at first, it will involve quotas. This is not a problem per se—indeed, quotas offer a natural specie with which to negotiate. But quotas need to be allocated not only over sending countries—see above—but between workers. The easiest way is first-come first-served, with mobility ceasing once the quota has been exhausted. Logically one would apply the quota to the stock of workers since that is what governments wish to control. Hence, once the quota was full, governments would issue new licenses only to the extent that old ones had been turned in. An alternative would be to ration admittances and rely on exit-enforcement to ensure that the stock of foreign workers did not become "too large."

A second practical issue is security clearance for potential entrants. This would have to be the same process as applied to permanent migrants and be wholly separate from obtaining a GATS entry license—both security clearance and a GATS license would be required for entry to provide services. The need to obtain clearance obviously generates uncertainties for service providers, but these are not much different from those currently facing many travelers who have to obtain airline tickets before applying for their visas. If GATS TM is to work, however, it is necessary that security clearance be reasonably reliable and speedy, and that it not be captured for protectionist purposes. National authorities should be explicit about what is required for security clearance and ensure that it is applied even-handedly across professions and skill-levels. After all, to the extent that we know who poses the threats to security, professionals and students are as well represented in the high-risk group as are less-skilled workers.

Perhaps the most sensitive TM issue is ensuring that it is temporary. Without such assurances, it will be hard to convince immigration officials that mode 4 does not undermine border integrity or labor officials that it does not undermine labor law or local job markets. The German sub-contracting schemes are instructive in several ways. They involve fairly rigorous investigation of sites where temporary workers are likely to be employed to locate transgressors. They place an enforcement responsibility on local companies—the beneficiaries of cheaper services provided from abroad. They require the overseas (sub-contracting) firm to ensure the exit of their workers. And, at least in their early form, part of the payment was withheld until the workers returned home.

The "wage parity" regulations in many foreign worker programs require that foreign workers be paid the prevailing local wage rate when they temporarily work in a developed country.[22] Paying prevailing local wages on temporary foreign workers is a one-stone-two-birds measure. It is intended to protect local workers from wage erosion and, presumably, to sweeten the pill of foreign competition, while, at the same time, serving to protect foreign workers from being "exploited."

The problem of imposing a minimum wage/price is that it clearly reduces the potential volume of, and benefits from, trade. The principal losers are host-country consumers, but such regulations may also prevent developing countries from exploiting their comparative advantage. In particular, given the difficulties of finely classifying occupations and subtle differences in skills, wage parity could become a total block on TM. Within any recognized skills category, developing country nationals may be less skilled or experienced than local workers and hence unable, initially, to maintain marginal productivities equal to local wages. (And this problem could get worse as labor shortages drive up local wages.) Thus efficiency and a genuine commitment to mobility require that means be found whereby foreign temporary workers can offer themselves at wages appropriate to their skills.

It is also important to note that wage parity does not necessarily prevent wages in developed countries from falling. The prospect of being able to recruit more cheaply abroad can encourage employers to constrain or even reduce domestic wages precisely because domestic and foreign workers must be paid the same wage. That is, the regulation prevents paying a premium to domestic workers, which in some circumstances employers might be willing to do.

These arguments are long-run ones, however; under current circumstances wage parity could serve developing country interests. Given the excess demand for temporary workers, there are scarcity rents to be made by employing them. Wage parity helps to ensure that these go to the workers rather than the employers. In the absence of wage parity, strong competition to supply temporary labor would drive down its price towards a level defined by the wage in developing countries plus the costs of mobility. Employers in the developed country would still gain marginal value equal to the developed country local wage (because wages equal the value of marginal products in the initial equilibrium) and so they would obtain the surplus. With wage parity, on the other hand, employers have to pay the developed country wage and so the worker receives the rent. On this analysis, wage parity is beneficial to developing countries in the medium term (while quotas persist), provided that the "skills-definition" problems alluded to above is not too severe. Thus, while wage parity is not a policy that

---

[22] Wage parity is not a requirement that foreign workers be paid the local minimum wage—a much less intrusive policy. It is that they be paid the wage prevailing in their sector.

commends itself in long-run economic terms—almost no price-fixing measure does—it has a robust and pragmatic political, and short-run social appeal. Thus, as we enter the nearly uncharted waters of mode 4 liberalization, developing countries should not spend effort trying to counter it, although eventually it should be revisited.

All developed countries collect social security contributions from (legal) foreign temporary workers.[23] The workers, however, do not, establish entitlements to social security benefits in return. For example, in the U.S. for a person to receive social security he/she must work for ten or more years, which obviously precludes temporary workers. Such "excessive" social security taxes are effectively tariffs on the provision of services via mode 4, and, as such, candidates for liberalization. However, tariffs are more transparent and porous than non-tariff barriers (NTBs) such as numerical quotas and worker licensing procedures. Experience in the goods market suggests that NTBs are more costly than tariff barriers and hence should be higher priorities for liberalization. Thus, we would not suggest investing heavily in negotiations on this issue, although it may be that promising to return contributions on departure could be a useful means to encourage return. In this case developed countries might offer it very "cheaply."

Social (health) insurance has to be available the instant a worker arrives in a country and, of course, provided in that country. Thus to avoid concerns about the exploitation of host-country facilities, short-run social insurance (health) and long-run social protection need eventually to be separated for temporary foreign workers. Host governments could then legitimately insist that service providers be fully insured for work-related accidents and health before they can enter the country, while long-run social protection could be handled by refunds or perhaps by requiring employers or users of overseas contractors to fund the workers' social security contributions at their home rates.

One of the areas of great confusion in the current GATS is uncertainty about the definition of skills and occupations. Without clear definitions, regulatory authorities have huge discretion in deciding what constitutes a specialist (and, presumably, in changing the definition according to political/labor market pressures). These problems reduce the transparency and credibility of commitments and ultimately discourage countries from negotiating in this area. Two steps are required: (a) uniform definitions and coverage of service personnel categories; (b) the agreed list should include middle and lower level of professionals. There is much to be said for merely adopting the ILO's existing list. This would save time and effort and would also avoid the temptation to design the classification in a fashion that permits powerful players to make carve-outs in the very places where liberalization would be most effective.[24]

---

[23] Some of them also collect income tax from visitors, and many of the same considerations apply in this case too.

[24] Trade scholars are well aware of the way in which tariff schedules tend to become excessively detailed in the most sensitive sectors.

Practices and policies regarding professional and technical qualifications can severely restrict the ability of natural persons to move across borders. It would clearly advance the cause of TM if these frictions could be overcome. Given governments' fiduciary responsibilities for ensuring the quality and safety of many services, merely ignoring qualification issues is not an option. Rather, it will require careful case by case work to define levels and match the current ranges of formal qualifications, skills and experience to them. It is essential to find a way to recognize that countries vary substantially in the degree to which they rely on formal academic qualifications as opposed to on-the-job training and experience in defining suitable qualifications. Mattoo (2000) has suggested a "necessity test"—that certification be no more burdensome than is consistent with declared objectives—e.g. using exams to test competence rather than long pseudo-apprentices for foreign workers.

Economic needs tests (ENTs) permit entry to temporary workers only if there is an "identified need" for them: loosely speaking, if there is no domestic worker who could do the job—see Box 13.3. In essence, ENTs are like the import quotas used in the import-substitution regimes of old. These were designed to support domestic suppliers by excluding imports from any sector in which there was domestic supply, and they resulted in huge inefficiency via the high costs and low quality of the domestic goods so protected. Moreover, at present, the wording of ENTs is vague, and each country tends to have its own interpretation. The effective liberalization of TM requires that members agree to develop a common code of practice for ENTs (as suggested under the E.U. proposal) with the objective of rendering them specific, transparent and non-discriminatory, and defining their application criteria.[25] For the long run most economists would advocate the abolition of all ENTs: not so much because that will help developing countries as providers of temporary labor but because doing so will help them as

---

Box 13.3. The Recruitment of Nurses in the U.S.

The U.S. H-1A visa scheme is designed for registered nurses from overseas to work in the U.S. To be permitted to recruit abroad, however, the employing clinic must prove that it will suffer substantial disruption if it does not hire foreign nurses; that it had taken timely and significant steps to recruit sufficient nurses on the domestic market; that the employment of foreign nurses would not adversely affect the wages and working conditions of other nurses; and that it will pay the prevailing wage. The first three of these conditions constitute a rigorous economic needs test that seems likely to curtail recruitment significantly.

Source: Winters et al. (2003a).

---

[25] The E.U.'s submission to the WTO argued that regimes subject to ENTs not meeting these criteria were essentially unbound regardless of their other conditions.

recipients. Given the sensitivities and difficulties of liberalizing mode 4, however, it may not be an immediate priority.

What Can Mode 4 Offer? Analytical Objectives

The objectives in the discussion that follows are:

- Note the benefits that GATS mode 4 brings to countries wanting to liberalize TM.
- Explore the different options for developing countries seeking to gain more liberal access to labor markets.
- Explore possible explanations of why GATS mode 4 is hardly used.

Why use the GATS?

As noted above, TM occurs and is attracting considerable policy attention at present, but GATS mode 4 is hardly used at all. This calls for some thought.

Breining et al. (2003) speculate about what the GATS might bring to temporary mobility in the health sector, specifically, the flow of doctors from India to the U.K. They observe that medical mobility already satisfies many of the conditions that informed scholars of mode 4 such as Mattoo (2000) urge on negotiators. For example, to qualify to practice in the U.K., doctors need to prove their competence via a test of competence and language (the PLAB), not undergo duplicative training or meet extensive residence requirements as are found with some other professions. That is, in Mattoo's terms, the qualifications test focuses on the necessary fiduciary issues rather than irrelevant formalities. Moreover, the World Health Organization (WHO) accreditation of medical training facilities internationally goes a long way towards achieving mutual recognition in qualifications, for the U.K. recognizes medical training given in any WHO accredited institution.

Moreover, if the GATS is viewed by either party as an appropriate mechanism, India and the U.K. are almost as good a pair of negotiating partners as one is likely to find.[26] India is the U.K.'s principal supplier of non-European Economic Area (EEA) doctors and the U.K. (one of) India's principal markets.[27] This maximizes the internalization of

---

[26] Even though health and education are national competences in the E.U., the formal negotiation would be between the E.U. and India, because the Commission has responsibility for all negotiations in the WTO, even where, as here, the issues at stake are national competences.

[27] The U.K. is obliged to recognize qualifications from the EEA and to impose no restrictions on the employment of EEA nationals.

the negotiation and in so doing will encourage agreement. Internalization is the extent to which the two parties to the talks can keep the benefits of improved market access to themselves even though they are obliged to throw any agreement they reach open to all WTO members through the MFN clause.[28] In the GATT—and hence implicitly by extension in the GATS—the "benefits" of a deal are held to be proportional to the level of current trade in the good or service concerned.

Despite these apparent advantages, doctors never figure explicitly in GATS mode 4 commitments and medicine is not included in the sectors for which the U.K. will now issue "GATS visas" (see www.workpermits.gov.uk) or in favored sectors in the E.U.'s GATS offer to talk to the Doha Round—see Box 13.4.[29]

How can this be explained? Partly it may just be that the mobility of health workers is well established and is seen by government as part of the employment nexus rather than the trade nexus—i.e., no one thought of using the GATS in this context. In addition, however, it seems that a desire for flexibility plays an important role, especially in the European context. European countries appear to want to be able to target specific countries for specific services, especially where language, culture, or qualifications are concerned—for example the green card introduced in Germany for Indian IT specialists or the preference for nurses from the Philippines in the U.K.[30]—or where they seek to offer preferences such as the training worker schemes available to workers from the former CMEA countries. The GATS limits both these features by requiring binding (i.e., non-reversible) commitments and the application of the MFN clause (i.e., no discrimination among sources) except, perhaps, for a temporary period.

On the Indian (developing country) side, there may be legitimate worries about the brain drain of doctors from India to the U.K. Hence they may wish that labor mobility be accompanied by safeguards to protect skills in the countries of emigration. One of the issues that needs to be explored here is how far such concerns should apply to mobility under the GATS. The fact that so much U.K. medical immigration is already ostensibly temporary but actually permanent suggests that they may apply here as well. However, since the general application of the GATS mode 4 seems likely to be accompanied by greater efforts to ensure that temporary labor does not turn into permanent residence— see, for example, Winters et al. (2003a)—it could be that bringing doctors in under the GATS would increase return rates rather than the reverse. On the other hand, in the absence of fierce self-denying regulations about the re-recruitment of GATS personnel after a short return to their home countries, a GATS window for doctors could just improve the efficiency with which the U.K. authorities are able to screen applicants. Such regulations seem almost unimaginable except on a voluntary basis such as that on

---

[28] See Finger (1979) or Winters (1987) on internalization.

[29] Box 13.4 also makes clear the E.U.'s exclusive focus on skilled TM. See Box 13.5 for a discussion of U.S. experience and policies with regard to TM.

[30] Collantes (2002).

Box 13.4. The European Communities' Offer on Mode 4, 2003

The European Communities' Offer on mode 4 covers people traveling to the E.U. to provide services for a limited period of time. It offers the following improvements over the status quo.

- Overseas companies, who have a contract to provide certain services with a client in the E.U., will be able to send skilled personnel to the E.U. to provide these services for up to six months at a time (within a period of 12 months). The maximum contract period is 12 months. The E.U. already has commitments in this area, but the proposal extends the number of sectors covered to 22 (e.g. legal, architectural, engineering, and computer services), as well as the permitted length of stay and length of the underlying contract (previously three months for stay and contract). The offer does not, however, apply to important services such as research and development, construction, higher education, and entertainment.

- The creation of a new sub-category of contractual service suppliers is offered: self-employed highly skilled people will be able to enter the E.U. for up to six months to provide services in the following sectors: (i) architectural; (ii) urban planning and landscape architectural services; (iii) engineering; (iv) integrated engineering services; (v) computer and related services; (vi) management consulting; (vii) services related to management consulting; and (viii) translation services.

- Corporate managers and specialists will be allowed to stay for an extended period of three years.

- A service company with a graduate training program will be able to transfer its "managers of the future" for up to one year's work experience with an affiliated company in the E.U.

In all cases, existing rules governing working conditions, minimum wage requirements, and any collective wage agreements in the E.U. will continue to apply.

Source: Winters et al. (2003a).

---

which DfID (2000) has persuaded the U.K. government not to recruit in doctor-deficit countries already.

If, despite the misgivings above, the Indian government wished to encourage the mobility of doctors abroad, one should enquire whether the current form of mode 4 of the GATS provides a useful means of doing so. On the one hand, the MFN clause of the GATS could be viewed as increasing the competition for places experienced by Indian doctors, for strictly it obliges the U.K. to consider all qualified doctors. It might also increase the bureaucratic cost of mobility; since the U.K.'s current "permit-free" schemes for doctors are fairly light-handed relative to other arrangements for international mobility.[31] On the other hand, GATS bindings would increase long-run predictability, removing the possibility of sudden changes as U.K. conditions changed. This last benefit could be important if the flow of doctors ultimately depends on investing in new training facilities in India.

---

[31] Once an overseas doctor has a training job in a U.K. hospital, he/she has no need to apply for a work permit. By "training jobs," Breining et al. and Kangesniemi et al. (2004) mean jobs for junior doctors who undertake a great deal of clinical work, but who also received advanced training in their specialties. They are typically time-limited and expire when training is completed.

From the U.K. perspective, the most important reason for binding TM under the GATS would be the need to assure future market access in order to encourage others (i.e. India, at present) to invest in the training of doctors and U.K. health providers to place more reliance on the steady inflow of doctors from abroad. This, of course, is the traditional argument for binding market-access barriers on goods in the GATT. It amounts to saying that the U.K. does not have a comparative advantage in the early stages of training doctors—school and undergraduate study—perhaps because they are rather labor intensive or because U.K. education technology (schools policy) is not very strong. The U.K. could still have comparative advantage in the later stages of medical training via its endowments of capital and rich patients on whom to practice, or via its strong public-sector orientation that stresses training. On this view, the GATS would help in "slicing up the value-chain" of medical education, exactly the circumstance in which, in goods markets, stable low trade barriers are held to matter most.[32] The UK may also wish to diversify away from India as a source of supply of doctors as competition for Indian doctors increases or supply decreases, and making an explicit commitment in the GATS may help here too. Finally, of course, offering medical services may be a relatively "cheap" concession to make under the GATS in constructing a package deal.

What Can Developing Countries Offer in Negotiation?

Assuming that the developed countries are willing to enter mode 4 agreements, it is useful to ask what developing countries can do to re-enforce that willingness. The first and most obvious quid-pro-quo is binding the access to their own TM markets. Industrial countries are very anxious to secure assured mobility for intra-corporate transferees—both managerial and technical. In order for their firms to be able to plan managerial careers, integrate their global operations, and install sophisticated equipment that requires overseas technicians, this access needs to be assured, i.e. it needs to be bound. Thus even if transfers are currently feasible, it is valuable to see them bound under the GATS. Similarly, developed country governments wish their nationals to have access to developing country services markets as independent service providers. This is politically a less pressing need than intra-corporate transferees, however, because independent traders are a less well-organized lobby than the large firms.

Such requests by developed countries suggest room for a negotiation within mode 4, but developing countries should not become more restrictive in these dimensions as a negotiating ploy. Both intra-corporate transferees and overseas professionals offer

---

[32] Hummels et al. (2001).

developing countries potential gains as importers—efficiency, knowledge, networks, etc. This is exactly the same as the case in goods trade, and the advice is the same. Generally, and subject to a suitable regulatory environment being in place, trade regimes should be liberal. Moreover, individual developing countries have very little negotiating power with which to force developed country hands. Hence they should be very selective in what they seek to hold back as negotiating specie and see negotiations at least as much as an opportunity to introduce good policy on imports at home as to open up export markets.

Going further, it is worth asking what developing countries can offer on their side of a TM agreement to encourage developed countries to sign one rather than act purely unilaterally. There is no prospect these days of controlling the outflow of people, so the aim should be to increase the value of such schemes to the developed partner as well as to themselves. This suggests that developing country governments seek means: (a) to make the administration of TM agreements more effective; (b) to ensure that workers are available; and (c) to minimize the problems of brain drain. The most attractive intermediate goal that developing countries can offer here seems to be to assist developed countries to make mobility actually temporary.

For less-skilled workers, developing countries might offer things such as:

- assistance in certifying (maybe licensing) employment agencies, including information transfer;
- convenient means of repatriating social security payments made during temporary work abroad;
- clear and reliable certification of qualifications; and
- policies at home to ease the repatriation of TM workers.

On the skilled front, the same sorts of offers might be appropriate, plus:

- Assistance in selecting workers to work temporarily abroad (as for example, happens with training placements for junior doctors coming to the U.K. under the Overseas Doctors Training Scheme (see Kangasniemi, Winters and Commander, 2004).

- Ensuring jobs are available for returnees returning at the end of their contracts (i.e., at a known future time).

- For education services that are not universal (upper secondary level and above), governments might insist on students signing contracts to repay (part of) their education costs if they leave the country permanently. The optimal contract would probably allow a certain period abroad for training and earnings-enhancement purposes followed by a requirement to deliver so much service at home.

These examples obviously need refining and details may well vary by profession or skill. On the other hand, some uniformity is probably desirable in order to discourage developed countries from cherry-picking favored high skill workers for permanent migration.

Reflection suggests that these contributions towards TM schemes are easier to offer and manage bilaterally (maybe regionally) than globally. This further raises the issue of whether the GATS with its MFN clause is the right way to go. Oye (1992) suggests that regionalism does have a role in liberalizing markets that are too restricted or too complex for non-discrimination to work. TM might fall into that class, but recall that in bilateral or regional negotiations developing countries generally have even less influence than in WTO negotiations.

Compensatory Policies: Analytical Objectives

The objectives of the following discussion are:

- Note the potential negative effects of a mode 4 liberalization (in the short and long-run).
- Explore which compensation/adjustment measures can be used to counteract these effects based on theory and experience of previous schemes.
- Assess arguments for compensating domestic workers who are disadvantaged by inflows of workers from abroad.
- Appreciate the need to treat mode 4 liberalization with sensitivity, especially over timing and sequencing.

We argued above that admitting less-skilled workers under a mode 4 liberalization is fundamentally no different from admitting imports of labor-intensive goods under a GATT liberalization. Both raise general welfare, but threaten indigenous less-skilled workers. This sub-section briefly considers how strong that parallel is and what lessons goods market liberalization has for mode 4.

The postulated equivalence seems a good one so far as the nature of the shock is concerned. However, there are questions about whether the scale is equivalent. In developed countries, services are substantially larger employers than manufacturing and primary sectors and while they employ large numbers of highly skilled workers, they also employ a high proportion of societies' less able members. Sectors such as personal care, janitorial services and much hotel work offer havens for the unskilled, and given that any society will have some people in such categories, they play a role both in terms of providing these people with income and allowing them the self respect of contributing. Indeed, these sectors have often been characterized as providing the jobs to which displaced unskilled manufacturing employees can be moved when their sectors have been liberalized, although Kletzer (2001) suggests this is much less true in reality than in perception. However, their existence has helped to ease adjustment in goods sectors in a way that will not be feasible when they themselves come under pressure.

If all low-grade service jobs in the developed countries were costlessly contestable by residents of the poorest developing countries at those countries' wage rates, the indigenous unskilled would indeed be squeezed very hard. However, that is clearly too extreme a view, for the natural protection of distance, culture and experience will all maintain wage premia in the developed countries relative to the developing world. And at least in the foreseeable future one is talking only about partial liberalization. Nonetheless, it does seem reasonable to expect that a vigorous mode 4 liberalization will pose significant adjustment strains.

What could be done? Consider, first, the long run. It is important to realize that the displaced unskilled workers could be compensated out of the general gains from liberalization. But that would require a willingness to be taxed and make transfers on the part of the more able majority, and the construction of a tax system that did not seriously discourage effort. If there are significant numbers of natives who could not make 'a decent living' in the sheltered sectors, one would have to rely on more or less permanent transfers on a large scale and it is not clear that societies have yet really mastered this technically. (Think of the social dysfunction and distress among many indigenous peoples at present.) The sort of subsidies that might be necessary would be housing subsidies for nationals or income top-ups that brought a national's wage up to acceptable levels even if his employer paid only the developing country wage.

This discussion suggests that there is a huge return to trying to ensure that there are fewer nationals on the bottom rungs of the skills ladder. This, in turn, suggests an ever-increasing use of the education sector to increase individuals' endowments of human capital, and might also entail finding ways of allowing all nationals to hold a reasonable stock of other capital. Capital owners are major beneficiaries of the inflow of workers from abroad, so if profit streams were equitably distributed, nationals would have reasonable living conditions even if they had low earning power. Exactly how such capital transfers were handled would need careful thought in order to balance freedom and personal responsibility with the assurance that the income flow would remain intact. This is exactly the debate that developed countries are having over pension plans, and one could indeed think of this problem as being akin to a lifetime pension.

Turning to the shorter term and recognizing that even the most aggressive liberalization will proceed relatively slowly compared to the size of the overall economy, one can draw better parallels with goods-trade liberalizations. There are broadly four approaches that deserve comment. First, sensitive sectors are just left out of the process of liberalization. We all know that this is what happens, but it does not make it good economics. If we are serious about mode 4—and we should be for the sake of both developed and developing countries—we should tackle some of the major sectors early on.

Second, liberalization can proceed slowly. This does not mean so much taking a small step and then waiting before deciding to take another, but rather planning a long transitional period for a known adjustment. The key here is credibility. If the liberalization is not credible, long adjustment periods are an invitation to lobby for their reversal, but if the end point is firmly expected at a date certain in the future, the gradual introduction of change can give individuals a chance to adjust more gently. One should not believe that slow adjustment is always better, but just that unless there are obvious externalities, it is better to give private actors the information and let them decide the best speed of adjustment. Also tied up with the timing is the question of the macroeconomic cycle. It is manifestly more difficult to get acceptance of liberalization if the economy is weak, and the costs of shifting employment between sectors are greater because transitional unemployment spells are longer in depressed economies. Thus there is something to be said for planning mode 4 liberalization to occur during the boom rather than the recession. This raises the question of whether a safeguards clause is necessary for mode 4 (or other services as well). Such clauses are likely to be subject to a good deal of abuse, but in terms of political reality, they may be desirable.

The third approach to compensation is specific trade-related compensation schemes. Among these the best known is the U.S. Trade Adjustment Assistance Act. This offers a composite of measures to support an industry damaged by liberalization with loans and assistance plus measures to compensate the displaced workers, including benefits to support income and training services.

The TAA was established by the Kennedy administration in 1962 as a quid pro quo for the wave of liberalization led by the Trade Expansion Act (TEA) in the United States and the Kennedy Round in the GATT. It provides trade-displaced workers with extended unemployment benefits, relocation expenses and (compulsory) training as a bridge to a new job with similar levels of income and benefits.[33] Several evaluations of the TAA program have shown that it provides additional income for temporarily displaced workers, many of whom obtain alternative employment relatively quickly anyway. But it fails to assist significantly those permanently displaced by trade-related closures. In addition, Decker and Corson (1995) suggest that training does not increase the future earnings of displaced workers.

Nonetheless, the TAA forms the basis of the North American Free Trade Agreement Transitional Adjustment Assistance (NAFTA-TAA) program, established in 1993. This assists workers who lose their jobs or whose hours of work and wages are reduced as a result of trade with Canada or Mexico by providing them with the opportunity to engage in long-term training while receiving income support.

Canada and Australia have operated similar schemes at various times in the past—the General Adjustment Assistance Program (GAAP) in Canada, and the Special Adjustment Assistance (SAA) in Australia—and with similarly unconvincing effects. Overall, experience with trade adjustment assistance has not been particularly happy. Schemes are often bureaucratic, providing limited benefits to a small category of workers who

---

[33] See Kapstein (1998) for a history of the TAA.

might well have found alternative jobs anyway, while providing little long-term assistance to the permanently displaced. Decisions on whether a worker is displaced due to government trade policy or some other shock have inevitably been rather arbitrary, leading to resentment among workers who fail to qualify for the benefit. In some cases, such schemes have assisted firms in moving to activities better reflecting comparative advantage, while in others they have inhibited such a move.

It is notable that the Europeans and Japanese have no such specific compensation schemes. This is argued by Sapir (2001) to be partly because their less effective markets have given them a degree of insulation against trade shocks, and partly because of their much deeper general social protection systems. The latter are the fourth approach to adjustment to consider They avoid the problem of attributing an individual's problems to trade and of prioritizing trade-related losses above those with other causes, but they are expensive and arguably bad for incentives. The preservation of the social security system is often quoted as one of the aims behind Europeans' resistance to immigration, but in fact, TM, which offers the foreign workers no rights under the system, helps to get around these fears. Nonetheless, the European models are under budgetary pressure and their future is not entirely secure. A major shock from a mode 4 liberalization, even if temporary, could pose serious problems if not appropriately anticipated.

This section has argued that the adjustment stresses that mode 4 liberalization could engender are real. They cannot be wished away because they will be both large and concentrated on a vulnerable section of society. In the short run, sensitivity about the timing and extent of liberalization may contain the pressures, and existing compensatory schemes can cope with those that actually arise. In the longer run, when deeper liberalization has been achieved, more active redistribution will be required to try to ensure that fewer nationals of developed countries are actually in the sectors competing with foreign workers. This requires education and training as well as thought being given to asset distribution.

Annex: Modeling Temporary Mobility

The model and data used in Walmsley and Winters (2002) (WW) are based on the GTAP model and database developed by Hertel (1997). The version of GTAP that is used is a standard applied general equilibrium model which assumes perfect competition,[34]

---

[34] "General Equilibrium" refers to the fact that shock effect, in principle, affects all sectors and all markets—goods, services, and factors. All are required to return to equilibrium after a shock or policy change. "Perfect Competition" assumes very many forms in a sector producing a homogenous output under constant returns to scale.

Box 13.5. The Temporary Movement of Service Providers: The U.S. Experience

Demetrios G. Papademetriou

United States immigration policy is inextricably interwoven with the economic, political, social, and cultural life of the country. The U.S. immigration system thus accommodates both permanent and temporary ("non-immigrant") admissions, although under an elaborate and complicated legal regime. The system includes many forms of temporary movement, including the movement of service providers.

Such movement has been the subject of very active negotiations in the General Agreement on Trade in Services (GATS), and particularly in the mode 4 mechanism for the Temporary Movement of Natural Persons (TMNP). In recent years, however, the U.S. Congress and, increasingly, the White House, have been taking a more politically "pragmatic"—"timid" would be a better term—approach to trade in services negotiations, and one notices an increasing tendency to make decisions about trade openings on domestic political considerations.

The U.S. admits large numbers of high, middle, and low skilled workers to work temporarily in the United States. Since the most recent national "comprehensive" immigration reform, the Immigration Act of 1990 (P.L. 101-649), and subsequent, more targeted amendments to the U.S. Immigration and Nationality Act, there are now more than 70 categories and sub-categories of non-immigrant visas. The "H" class of visas is among the most important for the mobility of service providers, but other visas also facilitate trade in services (most notably, the "B," "E," and "L" visas).

The "H" visa has been in existence since the early 1950s, but has been split into a number of sub-categories since the late 1980s, creating special categories for nurses (H-1A), seasonal agricultural workers (H-2A), temporary workers for employment in fields other than agriculture (H-2B), trainees (H-3), and family members of these temporary workers (H-4). But the most relevant nonimmigrant category in the United States for the purposes of this discussion may be the H-1B visa, a classification designed to allow the entry of persons in "specialty" occupations who are professionals of one type or another. These occupations run the gamut from nuclear scientists to runway models. Not all of the persons included in the H-1B category qualify as temporary service providers as defined by the GATS Mode 4 criteria. Nonetheless, a large proportion of temporary worker mobility in the United States falls under the H-1B category.

Temporary worker programs in the United States, and particularly those related to the provision of services, have evolved primarily as a result of politically motivated decisions in support of certain economic sectors or activities. To most in the U.S. Congress, it has been the economics of a sector and its influence with legislators, rather than a sense of greater trade opportunities or a commitment to the concept of a more open trading regime, that has been the motivating force for inventing and supporting such visas. This is an important point to bear in mind.

The role of the U.S. Congress on immigration matters is critical to understanding what may or may not be possible in mode 4 negotiations. Perhaps paradoxically, the world community, in trying to achieve greater GATS mode 4 liberalization, is in many ways negotiating with the least influential branch of American government on any immigration issue, the Executive branch. While the American system of government divides responsibility among its three main branches on most issues, the U.S. Congress controls and (micro)manages the immigration system with extreme zeal. Hence, the WTO, other international organizations, and foreign governments discussing issues with the United States Administration that relate to immigration are not dealing directly with the true decision makers. To make the point as starkly as possible, the political management of the temporary mobility of service providers is seen by the Congressional committees that have jurisdiction over immigration as an immigration issue, not a trade one, and treat it as such most of the time—the best efforts of trade negotiators and trade-friendly legislators to shift the intellectual and jurisdictional terrain notwithstanding.

United States policy on the temporary movement of service providers is thus shaped to an extraordinary degree through very painful political negotiations, and reflects first and foremost the ability of key legislators to agree on the set of compromises that will deliver a winning vote tally. In setting policy in this area, there are four key principles that the United States in particular struggles with at all times. These principles are deeply relevant to mode 4 negotiations and must be understood better by the international community if progress is to be made.

- *Smaller is better.* The United States seems to have found it easier to reach agreement on mobility in smaller negotiation settings than in larger discussions, such as the FTAA or GATS. As a result, the most detailed and in some ways far-reaching agreements on the movement of professionals (temporary or otherwise) have taken place in bilateral arrangements, such as the U.S.–Canada Free Trade Agreement in 1988, or regional trade agreements, such as the North American Free Trade Agreement (NAFTA). In all fairness, these agreements also took place during an era when the U.S. Congress was much more willing to defer to the Executive branch on trade, and before the immigration subcommittees and immigration skeptics more generally became aware of what trade negotiators were doing on mobility. Since then, much has changed politically. As a result, the following rule of thumb now seems to obtain: because the stakes involved and the intensity of the contentiousness of negotiations increase exponentially in multilateral negotiations, agreements on politically ultrasensitive issues such as immigration are easier to develop at the bilateral level, slightly more difficult at the regional level, and much harder at a global level.

- *Protecting U.S. workers.* When many of the temporary movement of persons categories were created, the discussion made two antecedent assumptions about its effects on U.S. workers and society that are now deeply controversial, at least politically so. First, that "temporary movement" is indeed temporary. Second, that such movement has no adverse effects on U.S. workers. Neither of these assumptions has been shown to be analytically robust enough to be able to sway Congressional leaders responsible for immigration policy. In fact, U.S. policy makers are increasingly sensitive to arguments that temporary migration "bleeds" into permanence and may in fact be causing adverse wage and job opportunity effects on native and other legal workers. Despite this emerging consciousness, however, the United States has not moved to address the resulting distributional strains, nor has it considered at all the idea of "compensatory" policies toward its own workers.

- *Deference to the employer.* In the constant tension between employer and employee interests in U.S. immigration policy (and especially the regulation of temporary migration), the government traditionally leaned toward the interests of the employer. As a result, U.S. policy generally deferred to employer needs in making admissions decisions, and focused most of its regulatory and investigative energy instead on enforcing the terms and conditions of employment. Thus, and with the exception of the security considerations of the post-September 11 environment, the United States has developed an enforcement regime on temporary entries that targets what might be called 'post-entry controls'. Specifically, the government notes the employer's promises ("attestations") prior to the admission of temporary workers, and tries to control the discrepancies between those promises and the reality of the terms of the foreign worker's employment. The reality on the ground, however, is that even the enforcement of the terms and conditions of employment is sporadic and awkward at best.

- *The question of duration of stay.* Trade negotiations and U.S. immigration legislation alike assume that the form of mobility they are discussing is exclusively temporary. However, the reality of the matter is that such movements have never been, are not now, and will never be purely temporary. The United States has begun to acknowledge this fact by making the H-1B visa into the first truly and openly 'transitional' visa in its history. H-1B visa holders are thus no longer true temporary migrants but transitional arrivals, many of whom will adjust their status into that of permanent immigrants by passing certain regulatory screens. Recent legislation further facilitates this process by allowing H-1B applicants for permanent residence to remain in the U.S. legally until a permanent visa becomes available. This development, together with the emerging agreement that H-1B visa holders should be able to change employers—what is known as "visa portability"—have made key segments of U.S. civil society and especially the U.S. organized labor movement more amenable to such visas. The reason is self-evident. Both sectors are more keen to work with people who have full rights and access to unionization as opposed to people with truncated rights.

United States policies on the temporary movement of service providers reveal a strong, continuing, but also schizophrenic interest in the use of temporary immigration to enhance U.S. international competitiveness. The challenge remains for the international community to be mindful of the overall tendency toward openness, yet be aware of the political considerations that make such openness an uncertain proposition.

Box 13.6. Mobility of Service Providers in the Caribbean Region

Sherry Stephenson

One of the most remarkable and successful experiences with the liberalization of services under Mode Four has taken place in the Caribbean; in particular inside the Caribbean Community and Common Market (CARICOM), comprised by fifteen member states: Antigua and Barbuda, The Bahamas, Barbados, Belize, Dominica, Grenada, Guyana, Haiti, Jamaica, Montserrat, Saint Lucia, St. Kitts and Nevis, St. Vincent and the Grenadines, Suriname and Trinidad and Tobago (of note: The Bahamas does not participate in the Common Market, and Haiti is not yet a full member, so does not apply all of the various CARICOM protocols).

CARICOM members, recognizing the critical importance of services trade, which plays a dominant role in the economies of the region, have undertaken a comprehensive liberalization of intra-CARICOM trade in services through the signing of Protocol II in 1998 on "Establishment, Services, and Capital". The protocol is at the heart of the creation of the CARICOM Single Market and Economy (CSME) because it is the instrument through which the Single Market is to be brought into effect. Protocol II grants the right of establishment or of unrestricted foreign direct investment by community nationals, the right to provide services, and the right to transfer capital to any CARICOM national within the community. Protocol II prohibits the introduction of new restrictions on the provision of services. It also significantly expands the commitments of CARICOM member states to allow the free movement of labour. The exercise of these rights should result in the creation of a single economic space, to be brought fully into effect in January 2008.

The most relevant elements of Protocol II are: the provision guaranteeing unconditional national treatment to all members of CARICOM for the free movement of services, labour and capital along with the obligation not to impose any new restrictions once the protocol enters into force. The process of actually liberalizing existing restrictions on services trade in CARICOM to make Protocol II a reality has followed a two-step approach: first, the elaboration of inventories of restrictions; and, second, the removal of restrictions.

Labour mobility constitutes a cornerstone of CARICOM's Single Market and Economy (CSME). Besides Protocol II of 1998, CARICOM has also adopted specific legislation to foster the free movement of persons in the form of The Skilled National Act of 1995. Both together have meant that CARICOM has gone further that any other regional agreement except the European Union in fostering labor mobility, both temporary and permanent, certainly surpassing all other trade agreements in the Western Hemisphere.

The primary elements of the policy covering the free movement of CARICOM nationals include:

- Free movement of university graduates, other professionals, and skilled persons and occupations as follows: Graduates from University of West Indies, University of Guyana, and University of Suriname; graduates of other recognized institutions in the region; graduates of institutions outside the region; duly accredited media workers; sport persons, musicians and artists; workers in the Tourism and Entertainment industries; any other skilled person eligible under Articles 35d and 36a of Protocol II.

- Freedom of travel and exercise of a profession: includes the elimination of a need for passports for travel within the region; facilitation at immigration points; elimination of requirements for work permits for CARICOM nationals.

- Other supporting measures including the harmonization and transferability of social security benefits; mechanisms for certifying and establishing equivalency of degrees and accrediting institutions; completion of a skilled register; coordination of social policies; development and promotion of a public education program on the policy of free movement.

Mobility of Service Providers in the Caribbean Region

Unlike the European Union, CARICOM does not provide for supranationality as regards the implementation of the Skilled National Act; therefore, each state needs to enact specific legislation to bring the requirements of Protocol II into effect at the national level. By 2005, twelve of the fifteen CARICOM Member States had enacted legislation to implement the Skilled National Act, as is seen from the list below elaborated by the CARICOM Secretariat (keeping in mind that The Bahamas has opted out of the labour mobility requirements of the CSME, while Haiti is not yet a full CARICOM member, and Monserrat is still rebuilding after the devastation of the recent volcanic explosion).

Member State	Legislation Enacted	Additional Steps Required
Antigua & Barbuda	Yes	Fully Operationalized
Belize	Yes	Regulations and administrative arrangements are still to be completed
Barbados	Yes	Fully Operationalized
Dominica	Yes	Fully Operationalized
Grenada	Yes	Fully Operationalized
Guyana	Yes	Fully Operationalized
Jamaica	Yes	Fully Operationalized
Saint Lucia	Yes	Fully Operationalized
St. Kitts & Nevis	Yes	Regulations and administrative arrangements are still to be completed
St. Vincent & The Grenadines	Yes	Fully Operationalized
Suriname	Yes	Fully Operationalized
Trinidad & Tobago	Yes	Fully Operationalized

—The success of CARICOM in effectively developing a process for the liberalization of the movement of natural persons—both on a temporary and more permanent basis—has undoubtedly has been facilitated by the relative homogeneity of CARICOM Member States (as compared with other regions) that share similar historical backgrounds, a similar language and common law legal tradition, and who all consider themselves small and vulnerable economies with similar income levels and sizes. Labour mobility for professionals has also been facilitated by the fact that the region has a common university-level system, constituted by the University of the West Indies with three main locations (Barbados, Jamaica and Trinidad and Tobago), as well as universities in Guyana and Suriname, the qualifications of whose graduates are recognized throughout the entire Caribbean community. Even though the program to date under the Skilled Nationals Act has only covered university graduates and skilled professionals, along with artists, musicians, media workers and sports and tourism persons, the implementation record of the member states has nonetheless been impressive. The intention of CARICOM is to expand this program further to additional categories of labour in the near future and include self-employed services providers, entrepreneurs, technical staff, managerial staff, supervisory staff, and spouses and immediate families of persons consuming services abroad.

Mobility of Service Providers in the Caribbean Region

In a 2005 regional economic study, the World Bank noted that, despite the lack of comprehensive data, intra-regional migration in the Caribbean was very significant. It also expected such labor flows to increase for two main reasons. First, the countries of the region had harmonized their social security systems, a key pre-condition for facilitating greater intra-regional labor mobility. And secondly, remaining restrictions on mobility were being further liberalized.

Labor mobility has supported the rapid development of the tourism, financial and construction sectors, by mitigating critical constraints, namely skill mismatches, high wages in some countries, and low productivity. The small size of most Caribbean islands exacerbates local skill deficiencies, especially in professional, technical, administrative and managerial positions in tourism, engineering, nursing, and teaching. Intraregional migration has also helped fill unmet labor demand in different countries at both the low and high ends of the skill spectrum. Today a large number of Haitians work in the Dominican agriculture sector and Guyanese in the Barbados construction industry. The result has been more uniform wages and greater efficiency of labor allocation within the region.[1]

[1] *Source*: "A Time to Choose: Caribbean Development in the 21st Century", World Bank, April 2005, Report No. 31725-LAC

consequentially this exercise contains none of the scale or clustering effects which often figure in the skilled migration literature—see below. In each of several regions, a single household is assumed to allocate income across private and government consumption, and saving in fixed proportions. Demand for domestic and imported goods then depends on income and relative prices. Firms minimize the costs of production. They combine intermediate inputs, from domestic and imported sources, with primary factors to produce commodities for the domestic and export markets. Demand for factors of production (land, skilled and unskilled labor, capital and natural resources) depends on output and relative prices. Prices adjust to ensure that demand equals supply in every market.

WW modify the standard GTAP model to incorporate the movement of natural persons as follows. They start by distinguishing the terms "temporary migrant" and "temporary worker": a temporary migrant leaves his or her home region to become a temporary worker in a host region.

Given that there is no information on bilateral flows of temporary labor, WW can say nothing about where temporary migrants from a given home region become a temporary workers, so WW postulate a global labor pool, which collects up the temporary migrants from all home regions and then allocates them across host regions. The temporary workers add to the supply of labor in the host region and are allocated across sectors within the region according to labor demand. In the host country temporary workers earn a wage for their labor, related to their productivity. Part of this wage is then sent back to the home region (via the global pool) as remittances. Within a country, the income of permanent and temporary residents plus net remittances received (inflows minus outflows) is then allocated across consumption, saving and government spending to maximize utility.

WW characterize changes in policies towards TM as increases in developed countries' quotas on inflows of temporary workers. Assuming that the quotas are always binding, i.e., that there is excess demand for places in the host countries, they can do this exogenously without having to model the incentives to move. They then assume that the new temporary workers are drawn from various home countries (mostly developing) according to the latter's labor force shares.

Having determined the number of temporary migrants leaving the home region and the number of temporary workers entering the host regions, WW estimate how these changes affect the effective supply of skilled and unskilled labor in terms of productivity units (i.e. after recognizing that temporary workers will make up only part of the difference in productivity between their home and host countries). Because there are no data on bilateral flows of workers, WW assume that a temporary worker initially has the same productivity as the average temporary migrant in the pool of mobile labor, which in turn, merely reflects the productivities of these workers in their home countries and the shares of each home country in the overall total of temporary migrants. Once working in the host region, however, the temporary worker acquires some of the productivity of the host region, and her productivity is assumed to equal the average productivity of a temporary migrant plus half the difference between that and the host region's productivity. That is, the productivity catch-up factor is one-half.

Once the temporary workers have left their home regions and entered the work force of the host region, they have to be allocated across sectors—in both countries. In the standard model, labor moves freely between sectors until wages are equalized across sectors for each type of worker. In the host regions, where the supply of labor has increased, wages are expected to decline, whereas in the home (sending) regions, they will rise. The extent of the change in wages will depend on the demand for labor—which in turn depends on the demand for production, which is driven by prices and income (both of which depend on wages).

Changes in the supply of labor and wage rates will ultimately affect the demand for other factors of production, notably capital. In the standard GTAP model, income includes all factor incomes (skilled and unskilled labor, land, capital and natural resources) net of depreciation and taxes. In the WW model also factor incomes have to reflect the distinction between the incomes of temporary and permanent labor, and be adjusted for the former's remittances to their home countries. The income of temporary workers in an economy is assumed to comprise their earnings less the remittances they send home (which, in turn, are assumed to be a given share of the wage). All other income, including that on land, capital etc., taxes and remittances received is assumed to be earned by permanent labor alone. Since there are no data on bilateral labor movement or remittances, remittances received have to be derived from average remittances from all temporary workers. Given that temporary workers in different host countries remit at different rates, changes in the geographical dispersion of temporary workers may therefore lead to changes in the average remittance rate. In order to calculate the overall effects of TM on the migrants from a particular home country, the income of the temporary labor by host region and labor type are aggregated across all host regions, and then distributed across home regions according to their numbers of temporary migrants in productivity equivalents.

Changes in the economic welfare of permanent and temporary workers are related to their income flows deflated by prices in their place of work.[35] The welfare of temporary migrants is found by summing the welfare changes of temporary workers across host countries and sharing it out over the various home countries, according to their shares in total TM. Once the welfare changes of temporary migrants are determined, welfare by home region, regardless of temporary residence, can also be calculated by simply summing the relevant changes. Table 13.A.1 summarizes the way in which income and welfare changes are summed to obtain national totals. We need to distinguish home- and host-country concepts. The former refers to all people starting off in a particular

---

[35] Technically, WW use Hicksian Equivalent Variation to measure changes in economic welfare. This expresses changes in money terms which can be summed across classes of workers to derive national aggregates.

Table 13.A.1. Accounting Concepts for the Temporary Flow of Labor from Country A to Country B

Income flow	Host concept	Home concept
PL_B	B	B
K_B	B	B
TL_B retained	B_T	A_T
TL_B remitted	A	A
K_A	A	A
PL_A	A	A

Notes: $PL_{j=}$ permanent labor in country j; $K_{j=}$ other factors in country j; $TL_{B=}$ temporary workers in B = temporary migrants from A. Retained—earnings retained in B by temporary workers. Remitted—earnings of temporary workers remitted to country A. A included in country A's total for permanent residents. B included in country B's total for permanent residents. A_T included in A's accounts under temporary migrants. B_T included in B's accounts under temporary workers.

country—essentially a nationality concept. The latter refers to all people actually located in a country after mobility has occurred—essentially a residence concept. At a practical level the only difference is the treatment of the income retained by temporary workers (A_T), which is attributed to the host country when we use the "host country" concept and the home country when one uses the "home country" concept.

References

Baldwin, R. E. 1969. "The Case against Infant-Industry Tariff Protection," *Journal of Political Economy* 77(3): 295–305.

Beine, M., F. Docquier, and H. Rapoport. 2001. "Brain Drain and Economic Growth: Theory and Evidence," *Journal of Development Economics* 64(1):275–89.

Borjas, G. J. and R. B. Freeman (eds.). 1992. *Immigration and the Workforce: Economic Consequences for the US and Source Areas*. Chicago: University of Chicago Press.

Breining, C., R. Chadha, and L. A. Winters. 2003. "The Temporary Movement of Workers: GATS Mode 4," *Bridging the Differences: Analyses of Five Issues of the WTO Agenda*. Jaipur, India: Consumer Unity Trust Society, pp. 111–46.

Carzaniga, A. 2003. "The GATS, Mode 4, and Pattern of Commitments," in A. Mattoo and A. Carzaniga (eds.), *Moving People to Deliver Services*. Washington, D.C.: World Bank, 21–6.

Collantes, V.A. 2002. "The General Agreement on Trade in Services (GATS): Liberalizing the Movement of Natural Persons (Mode 4): The Case of Filipino Nurses Moving to the UK and the US," Master thesis. Bern: World Trade Institute.

Commander S., M. Kangesniemi, and L. A. Winters. 2004. "The Brain Drain: Curse or Boon? A Survey of the Literature," in R. Baldwin and L. A. Winters (eds.), *Challenges to Globalization: The Economic Analysis*. Chicago: Chicago University Press.

Corden W. M. 1984. "The Normative Theory of International Trade," in R. W. Jones and P. Kenen (eds.), *Handbook of International Economics*. Amsterdam: North Holland, pp. 63–130.

Decker, P. T. and W. Corson. 1995. "International Trade and Worker Displacement: Evaluation of the Trade Adjustment Assistance Program," *Industrial and Labor Relations Review* 48: 758–74.

Department of Development. 2000. *Eliminating World Poverty: Making Globalization Work for the Poor*. Cm 5006. London: The Stationery Office.

Finger, J. M. 1979. "Trade Liberalization: A Public Choice Perspective," in R. C. Amarcher, G. Haberler, and T. D. Willet (eds.), *Challenges to a Liberal Economic Order*. Washington, D.C.: American Enterprise Institute.

Francisco, J. 2003. "Barriers to the Temporary Migration of Filipino Service Providers," in A. Mattoo and A. Carzaniga (eds.), *Moving People to Deliver Services*. Washington, D.C.: World Bank, pp. 179–90.

Hamilton, C., and J. Whalley. 1984. "Efficiency and Distributional Implications of Global Restrictions on Labor Mobility: Calculations and Policy Implications," *Journal of Development Economics* 14(1–2): 61–75.

Hertel, T. W. (ed.). 1997. *Global Trade Analysis: Modeling and Applications*. Cambridge: Cambridge University Press.

Hertel, T. W. et al. 1999. "Agricultural and Non-agricultural Liberalization in the Millennium Round." Available at: http://www.worldbank.org/reaserch/trade/archive.html/

Hummels, D., J. Ishii, and K. Yi. 2001. "The Nature and Growth of Vertical Specialization in World Trade," *Journal of International Economics* 54: 75–96.

Immigration and Naturalization Service. 2003. *2001 Statistical Yearbook of the Immigration and Naturalization Service*. Washington D.C.: Immigration and Naturalization Service.

Inter-American Dialogue. 2004. *All in the Family: Latin America's Most Important Financial Flow*. Washington, D.C.: Inter-American Dialogue.

Kangesniemi M., L. A. Winters, and S. Commander. 2004. "Is the Medical Brain Drain Beneficial? Evidence from Overseas Doctors in the UK." Mimeo, University of Sussex (April).

Kapstein, E. 1998. "Trade Liberalization and the Politics of Trade Adjustment Assistance," *International Labor Review* 137: 501–16.

Karsenty, G. 2000. "Assessing Trade in Services by Mode of Supply," in P. Sauvé and R. M. Stern (eds.), *GATS 2000: New Directions in Services Trade Liberalization*. Washington D.C.: Brookings Institution Press.

Kletzer, L. 2001. *Job Loss from Imports: Measuring the Costs*. Washington, D.C.: Institute for International Economics.

McCulloch, N., L. A. Winters, and X. Cirera. 2001. *Trade Liberalization and Poverty: A Handbook*. London: CEPR.

Markusen, J. R. 1983. "Factor Movements and Commodity Trade as Compliments," *Journal of International Economics* 14: 341–57.

Mattoo, A. 2000. "Developing Countries in the New Round of GATS Negotiations: Towards a Pro-Active Role," *World Economy* 23: 471–90.

Nielson, J., and O. Cattaneo. 2003. "Current Regimes for the Temporary Movement of Service Providers: Case Studies of Australia and United States," in A. Mattoo and A. Carzaniga (eds.), *Moving People to Deliver Services*. Washington, D.C.: World Bank, pp. 113–56.

Oye, K. 1992. *Economic Discrimination and Political Exchange: World Political Economy in the 1930s and 1980s.* Princeton, N.J.: University Press.

Rodrik, D. 1995. "Political Economy of Trade Policy," in G. M. Grossman and K. Rogoff (eds.), *Handbook of International Economics.* Amsterdam: Elsevier.

Romer, P. 1994. "New Goods, Old Theory, and the Welfare Costs of Trade Restrictions," *Journal of Development Economics* 43(1): 5–38.

Sapir, A. 2001. "Who's Afraid of Globalization?" in P. Sauvé and A. Subramanian (eds.), *Efficiency, Equity and Legitimacy: The Multilateral Trading System and the Millennium.* Chicago: Chicago University Press.

Shreve, K. E. and M. J. Slaughter. 2001. "What Determines Individual Trade Policy Preferences?" *Journal of International Economics* 54: 235–66.

Tang, P. J. G. and A. Wood. 1999. *Globalization, Co-operation Costs and Wage Inequalities* (January) Mimeo. Brighton: Institute of Development Studies, University of Sussex.

Walmsley, T. L. and L. A. Winters. 2002. *An Analysis of the Removal of Restrictions on the Temporary Movement of Natural Persons.* Discussion Paper No 3719. London: CEPR.

Winters, L. A. 1987. "Reciprocity," in J. M. Finger and A. Olechowski (eds.), *A Handbook on the Multilateral Trade Negotiations.* Washington, D.C.: World Bank.

—— 1991. *International Economics.* London: Routledge.

—— 2001. "Assessing the Efficiency Gain from Further Liberalization: A Comment," in P. Sauvé and A. Subramanian (eds.), *Efficiency, Equity and Legitimacy: The Multilateral Trading System and the Millennium.* Chicago: Chicago University Press.

—— 2002. "Trade, Trade Policy and Poverty: What Are the Links?" *The World Economy* 25(9): 1339–67.

—— 2003. "Doha and World Poverty Targets," in B. Pleskovic and N. Stern (eds.), *The New Reform Agenda*, Proceedings of the Annual Bank Conference on Development Economics. Washington, D.C.: World Bank, pp. 91–121.

Winters, L. A., T. L. Walmsley, Z. K. Wang, and R. Grynberg. 2003a. *Negotiating the Liberalization of the Temporary Movement of Natural Persons.* London: Commonwealth Secretariat, Economic Paper No. 53.

Winters, L. A., T. L. Walmsley, Z. K. Wang, and R. Grynberg. 2003b. "Liberalizing Temporary Movement of Natural Persons: An Agenda for the Development Round," *The World Economy* 26(8): 1137–61.

Winters, L. A., N. McCulloch, and A. McKay. 2004. "Trade Liberalization and Poverty: the Evidence So Far," *Journal of Economic Literature* 42(1): 72–115.

World Bank. 2003. "Integration into the World Trading Environment—Lesotho, Diagnostic Trade Integration Study" (June 11). Washington D.C:. World Bank.

WTO. 1998. "Presence of Natural Persons (Mode 4), Background Note by the Secretariat." S/C/W/75 (December 8). World Trade Organization, Geneva: Council for Trade in Services.

WTO. 2000. Document S/CSS/W/12 (November 24).

APPENDIX: A GUIDE TO SERVICES NEGOTIATIONS

Geza Feketekuty

Introduction

In the spring of 1979, two American trade officials with responsibility for the U.S. participation in the Tokyo Round of Multilateral Trade Negotiations under the aegis of the GATT were discussing a problem. The negotiations were heading into the final phase, and the United States had still not found a way of satisfying an important negotiating objective established by the U.S. Congress in the legislation authorizing U.S. participation in the negotiations. The legislation directed the President to negotiate a reduction in the barriers to trade in services, and American officials had pushed for action on this issue for several years without success. Since the two officials were on their way to a meeting of the Trade Committee of the Organization for Economic Co-operation and Development (OECD), a forum for cooperation on trade matters by developed countries, they hit upon the idea of asking the Committee to agree to a study of trade in services. The OECD was not the GATT, and a study was not the same as reducing barriers, but it would be a step forward.

When they reached Paris, they first broached the issue with the Chairman of the Committee, who agreed to give them a chance to sell the idea to a core group of the Committee that was to meet at a private dinner that evening to discuss the agenda of the meeting. The dinner guests, and later the Committee as a whole, had heard a great deal from the Americans about negotiating on trade in services and had universally agreed it was an outlandish idea. Nevertheless, they were all eager to conclude the negotiations, and a study seemed a cheap price to pay if it would take that issue off the table for the remainder of the negotiations. They therefore agreed in principle to the idea of a study, but deferred its content until after the negotiations were concluded.

When the American negotiators went home, they sold it to the services industry as a great breakthrough, which it eventually turned out to be, although that did not become apparent until after a number of years of discussion and struggle over the issue. Members of the GATT reached agreement at Punta Del Este, Uruguay, in 1986 to establish a Negotiating Committee on Trade in Services as part of the Uruguay Round of Multilateral Trade Negotiations, and reached agreement on the General Agreement on Trade in Services (GATS) in 1994.[1]

Agreement on the study did not magically convince other countries to do something they did not think made sense, but it provided a platform for an organized examination of the issue. Often that is all it takes in a negotiation. There are many issues that are not resolved simply because the people who would have to agree do not have the time to acquire all the information needed to make an informed decision. The other lesson of this story is that an idea raised at the right time may have a chance to be agreed, while at any other time it would have been rejected.

---

[1] The author of this chapter was the U.S. delegate to the OECD Trade Committee at the time, and one of the two officials involved. He subsequently assumed responsibility for building global consensus on the initiation of negotiations on trade in services. His subsequent efforts in building global consensus on the launching of negotiations are covered in two case studies, Aronson (1986) and Drake and Nicolaïdis (1992).

The OECD study initiated in 1980 ultimately demonstrated that information technology and globalization had changed the world, that, in this new world, trade in services had not only become a reality, but that it had also become crucial for productivity in manufacturing and for participation in the global economy. It also showed that trade in services faced barriers to trade just as trade in goods, that such barriers could be reduced through negotiations, and that their reduction would increase the productivity of the economy and create new opportunities for trade and growth.

Trade in services has become a key topic for trade negotiations, and will become even more important in the future. Globalization is knitting together the services component of national economies, and technological change is rapidly increasing the proportion of value added and employment that is generated through the services component of the economy.

This chapter will examine the negotiating processes that have evolved for negotiating issues on trade in services, how negotiations should be organized and prepared, and good negotiating habits used by successful negotiators.

Where, Why, What, and How Issues are Negotiated

We will focus first on where negotiations on trade in services take place, why governments negotiate in different venues and how the venues affect the outcome of negotiations, what is negotiated under the rubric of trade in services, how the negotiation on a particular issue moves from one venue to another, and how issues related to trade in services are negotiated.

Negotiating Venues—Where Negotiations on Trade in Services Take Place

The most visible, global negotiating forum for trade in services is the World Trade Organization (WTO). The GATS administered by the WTO provides both a global set of rules and a forum for the negotiation of national commitments. The negotiations in the GATS, however, are only the tip of the proverbial iceberg. Most negotiations over government measures that affect international trade and investment in services are under the surface of visibility. They take place through bilateral consultations and negotiations between the enterprises and governments most directly involved. Only systemic issues that cannot be resolved through bilateral consultations and negotiations are added to the agenda of global trade negotiations such as the current Doha Round of Multilateral Trade Negotiations in the WTO or regional/bilateral free trade negotiations such as the negotiations on the Free Trade Area of the Americas, the South Asian Free Trade Area Negotiations, or the bilateral free trade agreement between Korea and Chile.

Typically trade officials do not have direct policy responsibility for measures that affect international trade or investment in services. Trade officials therefore are usually cast in the role of intermediaries with the regulatory officials responsible for the formulation and administration of the regulations involved. This means that trade officials typically have to involve themselves in two sets of negotiations—internal and external negotiations. While the home government typically faces internal negotiations with the affected enterprises, the host government faces internal negotiations with regulatory officials.

The negotiation of issues affecting trade and investment in services is not the exclusive province of trade officials. National regulatory officials negotiate their own agreements with their counterparts, both bilaterally and multilaterally in specialized international organizations responsible for cooperation on regulatory issues in particular sectors. One such organization is the International Telecommunications Union, which is responsible for the development of international technical regulations for telecommunications.

Negotiating Objectives—Why Governments Negotiate on Services in a Trade Context

International negotiation on services within a regulatory context has a long history. Its objective has been to establish a mutually compatible regulatory framework for the delivery of infrastructure services such as shipping, rail transport, air transport, telecommunications and postal services between countries. The delivery of such services requires a mutually compatible regulatory framework because they fall under the jurisdiction of at least two countries, the country of origin and the country of destination. Regulatory officials responsible for the regulation of specific sectors such as air transportation have therefore negotiated both bilateral and multilateral agreements designed to establish some common ground rules for the enterprises delivering international services in that sector. In air transportation, officials negotiate bilateral landing right agreements, and they have also negotiated a multilateral framework agreement.

As is to be expected, national regulatory officials negotiating with each other to develop international ground rules for the delivery of international infrastructure services are largely concerned with how the agreement will allow them to achieve their regulatory objectives. Negotiations within a regulatory framework thus have a dynamic where each side in the negotiation is interested in giving up the least amount of regulatory sovereignty necessary to establish a basis for the provision of infrastructure services between the countries involved in the negotiations. Regulatory officials usually have neither the mandate nor the orientation to reduce regulatory or other trade barriers faced by service providers.

The negotiation of policy measures on services within a trade context is a relatively recent development that arose in the first instance from a desire by enterprises engaged in international trade and investment in services to obtain support from officials for the elimination of barriers to trade and investment in services. This is a function that trade officials have long provided for exporters of goods. In policy terms, a trade framework has made it possible to put an increased focus on the potential for stimulating economic growth through the expansion of international trade, competition, specialization and innovation in services.

Many barriers to trade in services are the result of misunderstandings between host government officials and foreign service providers, or inadequate information about regulatory objectives or commercial consequences. These kinds of trade barriers are best addressed through problem-solving negotiations, in the first instance between the foreign service provider and the host (i.e., importing country) government, and if necessary, between the home government of the foreign service provider and the host government (i.e. between the exporting country and the importing country. The objective of such problem-solving negotiations is to identify the least burdensome method (from a trade point of view) of achieving the regulatory objectives of the relevant laws and regulations. Bilateral problem-solving negotiations are usually the most efficient means of dealing with issues that can be resolved through the use of administrative discretion in the application of regulations. The resolution of issues that require changes in national laws and regulations, or even constitutional changes, in most cases requires more formal bilateral or multilateral negotiations or the invocation of a dispute-settlement process, as provided by the GATS in the WTO or in regional free trade agreements.

Ultimately no one venue provides the means for achieving all negotiating objectives. Negotiations on technical regulatory issues are best carried out directly between regulatory officials. Negotiations aimed at the reduction of trade barriers are best carried out by trade officials. Negotiations that are aimed at facilitating specific international transactions through adjustments in the administration of specific regulatory measures or requirements are best pursued through bilateral-problem-solving consultations or negotiations, while issues that require changes in national legislation are best carried out through formal, bilateral or multilateral negotiations within a trade framework. Over time we have seen the emergence of a degree of specialization among negotiating venues, and we can expect further innovation as governments seek out the most effective way of addressing increasingly complex regulatory and trade issues.

Scope of Negotiations—What are the Barriers to Trade in Services?

Barriers to trade negotiations in services are generally embedded in domestic regulations. Since services are invisible, governments cannot directly control trade in services at the point they cross the border. Officials may be able to observe transmissions of electronic signals or movements of natural persons, but they will have no real way of knowing what services are being exported or imported. For that reason governments seek to control trade in services through the regulation of the consumption of services by domestic residents or the production of services by locally established foreign suppliers. In addition, governments can seek to regulate the entry of foreigners who have the intention of producing a service, the exit of nationals who have the intention of consuming services abroad, or international payments associated with trade in services.

The focus of trade negotiations with respect to services is thus not on tariffs and quotas, as is the case for trade negotiations in goods, but on domestic regulations that limit the consumption of services produced abroad, the movement of services providers or consumers across the border, the ability of foreign service providers to establish themselves and to supply services in the host country, or the international transfer of money by consumers or producers of services.

The Negotiating Life Cycle of an Issue—How an Issue
Evolves from Informal Consultations to Formal Global Negotiations

An enterprise that faces a particular regulatory barrier that impedes its export of services should ideally first seek to deal with the issue directly through consultations with the responsible officials in the host government. Such contacts will enable the enterprise managers and officials most directly involved in the issue to sort out the specific facts in the case. It will also enable host-country regulators to take into account any special factors that may need to be considered in applying a regulation to a specific set of transactions. In many cases a trade or foreign investment issue identified by an enterprise as a trade problem is the result of a misunderstanding of the regulations by the exporter or investor, or a misunderstanding of the specific facts related to the proposed export or investment by the regulator. In other cases, the regulator may be able to reduce the regulatory burden without sacrificing the regulatory objective or violating the relevant laws and regulations.

A clear understanding of the regulatory issues will also better equip the prospective exporter or investor to communicate the nature of the issue clearly to the officials of the home government, if their intervention proves necessary. The willingness of an enterprise to expend the resources necessary to conduct such direct consultations is also usually a good test to the officials from whom they may seek help of how important the issue is to the enterprise. Small exporters, particularly in developing countries, may not have the resources to consult with the responsible officials in the importing country on a face-to-face basis. However, they could contact the officials involved through the mail or the Internet, or visit the economic/commercial section of the nearest embassy or consulate of the importing country.

The second step in the process of addressing a trade problem, if direct consultations with the host government fail to resolve the issue, is to consult with the commercial/economic officers in the home country's embassy in the host country, i.e. the exporting country's embassy in the importing country. The embassy may well be able to shed additional light on the issue, or to intervene on behalf of the enterprise with host-country officials. The embassy can also bring the issue to the attention of officials in the home government. Officials responsible for trade issues in the home government regularly read embassy reports on the problems faced by the country's exporters and investors in the host country. While embassy reporting cannot be a substitute for direct consultations with trade officials in the home country, it will facilitate the exporter's or investor's task of briefing home government officials and of persuading them to raise the issue with their counterparts in the importing country.

At the third stage of an orderly process for addressing a trade issue, the affected enterprise seeks to enlist officials in its home government in an advocacy effort. Trade and other officials at various levels of the hierarchy meet regularly with their counterparts in other countries to discuss issues of common concern and mutual trade and investment problems. In this third phase of the process, bilateral discussions and negotiations on a particular issue can move step by step to more senior levels, from discussions at a working level by desk officers responsible for trade and investment issues with a particular country to negotiations between senior trade officials, ending (for the most important issues) with negotiations between the trade ministers or even the heads of government. At some point during this process, the nature of the discussions are likely to move from an informal consultation process to a formal country-to-country negotiating process. Efforts to resolve issues during this phase of bilateral consultations and negotiations are motivated by an implicit reciprocity—you help me solve one of my problems and I help you solve one of your problems.

During the bilateral consultations and negotiations, officials from the two countries are likely to examine the trade effects of the measure, the regulatory objectives served by the measure and the potential for achieving the same regulatory objective through alternative, less trade-distorting regulatory measures. It also enables the two governments to test each other's perceptions regarding the applicability of various provisions and national commitments in international trade and investment agreements, and who is likely to obtain a favorable judgment if the case went to dispute settlement. While even the best arguments put forward during such discussions may not be able to overcome strong political resistance to policy changes that are likely to create adverse consequences for some domestic stakeholders, in a large number of cases bilateral discussions lead to mutually acceptable outcomes.

Trade problems that cannot be resolved through bilateral discussions are often incorporated in broader, formal negotiations such as multilateral trade negotiating rounds in the WTO, or regional/bilateral free trade area (FTA) negotiations. Such broader negotiating venues not only widen the potential for trade-offs among issues of interest to host countries, but may also make it possible to negotiate rules for repetitive problems or to bring other countries into the negotiations. An orderly, sequential process for addressing specific trade issues, from direct contacts between the enterprises and the host government, to bilateral consultations and negotiations, and ultimately multilateral negotiations or dispute settlement, provides for the most efficient means for addressing trade-negotiating issues. The sequential process serves as a filtering device. Issues that are less difficult and less important are dealt with directly by the affected officials and enterprises, or among working level officials, while more senior officials or political leaders address the more intractable issues that raise difficult political or legal problems. Naturally, only the most important issues, those that are of major commercial or policy significance, make it to the higher levels of government.

One obvious point is worth making. Countries become engaged in negotiations on trade in services either because they would like to address a barrier to their exports of services in another country, or because they want a quid pro quo from another country that has raised a services trade issue. As noted earlier, countries engaged in a two-way trade relationship, inevitably have trade or investment-policy related issues they would like to address with each other.

Where an importing country has little it wants from an exporting country and the issue raised by the exporting country is not covered by a national commitment in a trade agreement, the importing country can simply refuse to negotiate. Current practice gives sovereign countries considerable leeway to agree or not to agree on a trade matter on which they have not made a commitment. It is equally true that some importing countries in this kind of a situation may have non-trade reasons for negotiating on trade issues with another country.

How the WTO Structures Negotiations on Trade in Services

Negotiations on trade in services in the WTO focus on specific commitments by individual national governments and on rules that apply to all member countries. Countries negotiate specific national commitments bilaterally, with each country negotiating with every other member of the WTO. Since countries that have joined the GATS have committed themselves to apply most favored nation treatment (MFN) to most services sectors, countries have to extend the least trade restrictive treatment offered to any one country to all other countries that belong to the WTO. However, each country will seek to "sell" the same commitment to as many other member countries as possible.

Domestic regulations can restrain foreign imports either by discriminating against foreign suppliers or by restricting both foreign and domestic suppliers more than is necessary to accomplish the desired domestic regulatory objective. Under the provisions of the GATS, trade negotiations on services in the WTO cover both types of issues.

Negotiations aimed at the elimination of discriminatory provisions are called negotiations on national treatment, since national treatment requires the nondiscriminatory application of rules and regulations to both foreign and domestic suppliers. Negotiations aimed at the reduction or elimination of regulations that place quantitative constraints on both domestic and foreign producers on a nondiscriminatory basis are called market-access negotiations.

The national schedules of commitments are organized by sector, and within each sector, by mode of supply. Commitments fall into three categories: market access, national treatment, and other. Countries may also enter horizontal commitments on broad regulations that apply to all services.

In contrast to the negotiation of national market access and national treatment commitments, countries negotiate rules multilaterally, i.e. collectively. The negotiation of rules under the GATS focuses on the elaboration of existing Articles of the GATS agreement, or potentially the addition of new articles. Some rules apply to all regulations that affect trade in services, regardless of whether a country has made a specific commitment on that service. Other rules apply to all regulations that affect trade within sectors in which a country has made commitments. Still other rules apply only to regulations that affect trade in specific services covered by national commitments.

The negotiating procedures and the negotiating dynamics in rules negotiations are quite different from the procedures and dynamics of the negotiation of national commitments on market access and national treatment. The bilateral negotiation of specific national commitments takes the form of a bilateral bargaining process based on requests and offers, while the negotiation of rules involves an effort to build consensus among member countries on broad principles. We will explore the practical implications of these differences below.

Sectoral negotiations constitute a third category of negotiations that encompass both the negotiation of rules and national commitments that apply to a particular sector. As noted in the telecommunications chapter below, the General Agreement on Basic Telecommunications, for example, includes both a template for national commitments on the liberalization of particular segments of the public telecommunications market, and a Reference Paper that sets out guidelines for the regulation of competition in the provision of competitive telecommunication services.

Preparing the Negotiations—Laying the Analytical Foundations[2]

We now turn to the preparation of negotiations. Face-to-face negotiations are the culmination of a long and extended process of preparation. While many may think that the outcome of negotiations depends largely on the negotiating skills of individual negotiators at the bargaining table, good research and analysis and skillful shaping of a negotiating issue are often just as important, if not more important. A good negotiating outcome requires extensive analysis of the:

---

[2] An in depth treatment of the analysis of trade issues in preparation for negotiations can be found in a series of instructional manuals developed by the Institute for Trade and Commercial Diplomacy, and available on their website (www.commercialdiplomacy.org). They include a manual on the overall analytical framework (Feketekuty, 2001) and individual manuals on economic and commercial analysis, political analysis, policy analysis, and legal analysis.

- commercial issues at stake for all sides;
- macro-economic impact on the respective countries;
- trade-related domestic policy issues;
- laws and international rules that apply; and
- views and political influence of the stakeholders

Identifying and Consulting Stakeholders

The first step in preparing for international negotiations is to identify the domestic stakeholders. Stakeholders are groups in society, both inside and outside the government, who will be affected by the negotiations and therefore have a stake in the negotiating outcome. A stakeholder will be impacted positively, negatively, or not at all, depending on how the issues discussed at the negotiating table relate to their interests.

By their very nature, international negotiations involve people who represent governments, businesses, NGOs, and other entities that have a stake or interest in the outcome of the negotiations. While the individuals involved in the negotiation process bring their own ambitions and self-interests to the table, their mission is to serve as representatives of the organizations, bureaucracies, or enterprises to whom they are accountable.

Involving domestic stakeholders in the preparation of international trade negotiations among governments is consistent with principles of good governance, since those most directly affected by the negotiations will have the best information on how various negotiating outcomes will affect trade or the achievement of regulatory objectives. Involving stakeholders is also required for practical political considerations. Those most affected by a trade agreement will have a strong motivation to use the political process to ensure that the country's negotiating position reflects their interests, and by consulting them, trade officials can better influence and help shape their participation in the political process.

Starting the preparation of negotiations with the identification of stakeholders and consultation with stakeholders also makes sense because stakeholders are likely to be in a position to contribute, and in some cases help collect, basic information about the competitive strengths and weaknesses of national service industries, the problems exporters face in penetrating foreign markets, and the regulatory issues that are likely to arise in the course of the negotiations.

Asking domestic stakeholders to participate in the preparation of the negotiations also makes them feel as full participants in the process, making them loyal supporters of the negotiations as long as they are part of the process and their interests are addressed. At the very least, stakeholders included in the process will achieve a full understanding of the issues and the rationale for the negotiations, and they are likely to give the negotiators credit for including them in the process and for factoring their interests into the development of national positions, even if their interests are not fully satisfied. In summary, stakeholders are much more likely to support the final agreement negotiated by trade officials if they are consulted.

During the Tokyo Round of Multilateral Trade Negotiations, the U.S. Trade Representative (USTR) developed an elaborate system of private sector advisory committees that were consulted before, during and at the end of the negotiations. There were 45 committees, with a total membership of

600 private-sector representatives. In addition to the formal consultations with these committees, Ambassador Robert Strauss consulted extensively with top business executives, labor leaders, Members of Congress and politicians. As result of these efforts, he was able to obtain overwhelming approval of the Tokyo Round Agreements in the Congress. The Senate approved the Agreement by a vote of 96 to 3, and the House approved it with an equivalent majority. What was equally interesting is that the vast majority of Advisors, including representatives of industries facing increased competition from imports as a result of the agreements, fervently spoke in favor of the Agreement at industry gatherings and public meetings after the conclusion of the negotiations. The advisory process played an important role in all subsequent trade negotiations in which the United States participated, though not always with the same results in terms of Congressional votes.

Not every country has the resources to establish the same kind of elaborate system as the United States, but then most smaller and less resource-rich countries do not have as many key stakeholder groups who are likely to have a substantive interest in negotiations. Every government has the ability to develop a consultative process appropriate to its economic and institutional circumstances.

We identified two categories of domestic stakeholders: the various government ministries and departments responsible for administering the regulations likely to be covered by the negotiations, and the enterprises producing the services likely to be covered by the prospective negotiations. The stakeholders in the government can include not only officials in the central government, but also officials at a sub-central level, e.g. states, provinces, etc., where responsibility for the regulation of services is exercised at a sub-central level. Stakeholders from the services industries include both the various industry associations in services and the major enterprises producing services. Other stakeholders can include labor unions representing services workers, NGOs with a focus on services, and consumer groups.

Having identified the major stakeholder groups, the negotiator has to decide who should be consulted either individually or as a group, who should be invited to participate in meetings organized to discuss the negotiations, and who should be invited to join various consultative bodies established to support the negotiations. The consultation process should be built around three concentric circles. The innermost circle should consist of the stakeholders within the central government, i.e. the key ministries and departments responsible for trade issues and for the regulations covered by the negotiations. Each such ministry, department or agency should be asked to designate an individual who will participate in an inter-ministerial or inter-agency group responsible for the negotiations. In many countries such a group is given decision-making power. In other countries the group can give formal advice to the trade negotiator, but does not have the power to make decisions.

Where sub-central governments have a key role in regulating services, the trade negotiators may also have to establish a separate forum for consulting officials from sub-central governments. Consultations with sub-central government officials will inevitably be less frequent than the consultations among central government departments, since the representatives involved may have to travel some distance to participate in meetings.

The second concentric circle is made up of representatives of key private-stakeholder groups who are invited to participate in various advisory bodies. These advisory bodies can give negotiators direct feedback on proposed negotiating positions and serve as a vehicle for building consensus with the most influential private stakeholders. Such advisory bodies can also serve as sources of information on trade opportunities and problems, industry practices, and the most vexing barriers to an expansion of trade.

It is neither practical nor necessary to include representatives of every enterprise, industry association, union, NGO or sub-central government in the consultation process. Optimally, negotiators should involve the most influential and interested individuals from these groups, individuals who are respected by their peers by virtue of their reputation, who can influence the domestic political debate by virtue of their political clout, and who will spend the time to become informed by virtue of their interest in the negotiating outcome. Such individuals will often be found in the largest enterprises or most widely representative organizations, but not always.

Since the objective of the negotiations is to expand trade, special care should be taken to include representatives of the most competitive industries that have a keen interest in expanding their exports. Ultimately, negotiators will have to count on their vocal support in building domestic political support in favor of the negotiations. It is also wise to include some vocal opponents to take some of the edge off their opposition.

The identification of the most relevant domestic stakeholder groups and the most influential individuals in such groups is best accomplished by talking to academic and industry experts in the field and to journalists who cover services industries. By getting in touch with recommended individuals, trade officials can get a fair idea of the organization's potential interest in participating in an advisory process and the contribution that individuals at various levels in the organization could make to the consultative process. Ideally, an organization included in the consultative process will have interested individuals at both the top and middle levels of the organization, and staff experts who can brief them and support their effective participation in meetings.

Consultations with key private-sector stakeholders can take place either through private consultations with representatives of general business organizations such as chambers of commerce, key industry associations such as the Banker's Association, key companies, labor unions and interested NGOs, and firms. Most countries conduct such consultations to a lesser or greater extent. In addition to the consultations with individual stakeholders, the government may choose to establish an advisory body or committee to provide organized advice to the government negotiators. Private-advisory groups should be large enough to include representatives of the most important nongovernmental stakeholder groups.

Formal or informal advisory bodies can serve as a useful venues for building national consensus on the country's approach to the negotiations, for exchanging information on the progress of the negotiations, and for validating political support for any bargains struck during the negotiations. Formal advisory groups have proven to be useful and practical in both very large developed countries and small developing countries.

The third concentric tier is made up of all interested stakeholders, who may be invited to participate in briefings or conferences covering the negotiations. Individuals participating in briefings and conferences will have an opportunity to become educated on the issues covered by the negotiations, but will have only limited opportunity to provide direct, in-depth feedback on negotiating positions. Public briefings by government negotiators can be held in hotels, chambers of commerce, or research institutes. The resource requirement for conducting such briefings is modest, particularly when the briefings are held in facilities that can be provided by a stakeholder group.

Beyond the three concentric circles, negotiators will have to devise the means for informing the public at large on the evolution of negotiations. Since the press has the widest reach, the preparation of press releases and the organization of press briefings and press conferences has to be a core element of any communication strategy. Negotiators can also publish reports or white papers on negotiating issues, and establish a website with up-to-date information on the progress of the negotiations.

In practice, negotiators ideally will follow the following sequence of steps in identifying and organizing stakeholders:

- Draft a letter from the Trade Minister or other senior trade official to other government departments, ministries or agencies responsible for regulations that will be covered by the negotiations, asking them to appoint a senior official to an interagency committee that will review negotiating proposals. Organize an introductory meeting, in which members of the Committee are brought up to date on the schedule for the negotiations and the state of preparations for the negotiations.

- Identify appropriate sub-central officials and invite them to join an advisory committee of sub-central officials who will advise trade negotiators on regulatory issues within their jurisdiction. Invite them to an initial briefing on the negotiations.

- Identify private-sector stakeholders, contact them through a phone call or personal visit, explain to them the nature of the upcoming negotiations and invite their participation in a briefing session or conference on the negotiations, and at that meeting invite their inputs into the negotiating process.

- Issue a press release on the briefing session or conference, and ask the press to publicize the conference, indicating that any interested organizations are invited to send a representative.

- Based on initial contacts and consultations with relevant experts, identify prospective members of a private sector advisory body, and extend invitations to become a member of the advisory body.

Assembling Information on National Interests and Issues

The next task of the services negotiators is to assemble and compile background information on the country's exports and imports of services, competitive strengths and weaknesses of domestic services industries, foreign regulatory barriers that inhibit national exports of services to other markets, and regulatory issues that might arise in the context of negotiations. Crucial help in the collection of such information can come from the country's export industries, particularly the most successful exporting enterprises. Such companies are found even in the smallest developing countries.

Help in assembling this information can also come from a number of international institutions such as the International Trade Center in Geneva and the multilateral development banks, and from bilateral economic development assistance agencies such as the U.S. Agency for International Development and the Canadian Economic Development Agency.

Collecting detailed official statistics on trade in services is a challenge in every country, because unlike data on industrial trade, data on trade in services usually lacks sufficient detail to provide information on trade in specific services, much less a consistent time series. Available data are likely to be aggregated on a sectoral level, e.g. fee-based banking services, professional services, maritime transport services, etc. The problem is, of course, even more difficult in small developing countries that lack the means for the organized collection of statistics on services.

To supplement the official statistics, negotiators should ask major exporters and industry associations in the individual services sectors to provide additional data that can provide insights at a product level. Asking stakeholders to supplement official data is particularly important for the newer information-based services and various professional services, services that are often too new or too dispersed to be adequately covered in official statistics. This is particularly important because in most countries, both developed and developing, the newer information based services are often the ones that have the greatest potential for export growth, though the export potential in these services often hinges on domestic regulatory reforms in areas as such as telecommunications, air transportation, and financial services. Accordingly, there is often a close link between what a country should ideally request from other countries, and the domestic regulatory reforms that it offers to other countries. Consulting businesses in these sectors is a challenge in some countries, where the principal export industries are located in cities at some distance from the capital, but it is important that the effort be made.

Initial information on the country's competitive strengths and weaknesses is provided by the trade data. Sectors that export are likely to be relatively competitive, while sectors with large imports are likely to be competitively weak. Trade data, however, do not tell the full story. A sector in which a country has a potential competitive strength may not show many exports because foreign trade barriers or domestic regulatory constraints inhibit such trade, or simply because the industry has not explored export opportunities. Additional insights into competitive strengths can come from economic studies carried out by academic experts, assessments provided by industry experts, and a review of the export performance of other countries at a similar stage of economic development and similar economic circumstances. Such studies are often available from academic sources and from intergovernmental organizations such as the World Bank and the International Trade Center.

Trade negotiators are unlikely to find the same kind of detailed quantitative data on trade, production and prices of services that are available for goods. Since governments cannot observe services crossing the border, they are not able to measure the flow of services across the border in the same way that they can measure the flow of individual goods across the border. Instead, governments have to compile data on trade in services by periodically asking exporters and importers of services to fill out questionnaires. Since filling out the forms is relatively costly for market participants, only a limited number of exporters and importers are surveyed, and the published data are based on projections based on these sample surveys. Data on trade in services consequently lack the kind of accuracy and detail available for trade in goods. Data are generally available only for broad industry categories and for relatively long time intervals.

The shortcomings of the trade data are compounded by the difficulty of making a quantitative assessment of the degree of protection provided by regulatory measures. It is much easier to calculate the protection provided by a tariff or a quota than the protection provided by a regulatory measure. Negotiators in services thus lack the kind of detailed data that would enable them to estimate the impact of negotiated reductions in particular barriers on exports and imports of specific services. In order to make up for the lack of detailed official data, trade negotiators in services have to rely more heavily on information that can be provided by enterprises. Extensive consultations with industry are therefore particularly important in preparing for negotiations on trade in services.

In assessing the country's competitive strengths and weaknesses, a country must openly confront any competitive weaknesses that result from the country's own regulations. Onerous regulatory requirements may prevent the country's enterprises in a particular sector from increasing the economic efficiency of its operations or from introducing new and more competitive services and marketing techniques. In fact, most countries involved in negotiations on services have found that domestic regulatory reforms are a prerequisite for the country's effective participation in the negotiations. In most cases this entails removing outdated regulations that made sense in the past in the context of different technologies and market structures but have now outlived their usefulness. In many cases it also entails the introduction of new regulations appropriate to a more market-oriented regulatory regime. In fact, as we have seen, many countries that liberalized capital controls and international financial transactions went through a subsequent financial crisis because they did not accompany liberalization with adequate prudential regulations.

Information about foreign trade barriers is best provided by industry. The necessary canvassing of the industry can be done either by the trade negotiators themselves, by consultants hired for the task, or by a general industry association. Insights into trade barriers can also be found in the surveys done by third countries, particularly third countries with large staffs. Fortunately, surveys and inventories of trade barriers compiled by countries with adequate resources are now often available on the Internet. In a services sector where a country is potentially export competitive, but the private sector is underdeveloped, studies of the experience of other countries at the same or slightly more advanced stage of economic development can prove useful. Such studies could analyze the factors that may have contributed to the other country's success in exporting. Officials and business managers in such countries may well be willing to share their insights and serve as allies in the negotiating process.

The best sources of information about regulatory issues are the regulatory officials in the home government, research institutes that specialize in regulatory issues, international professional bodies, international organizations such as the International Telecommunications Union (ITU) that are responsible for the development of technical regulations at a global level for particular services (such as telecommunications in the case of the ITU), and international organizations with a wide economic mandate that regularly carry out regulatory studies for their members, including the WTO, UNCTAD, the World Bank, the OAS, and the OECD.

Assembling Information on Foreign Interests and Issues

Once we understand a country's competitive strengths and weaknesses in services, domestic stakeholders and their interests, and the foreign trade barriers that hamper exports, we have to collect information about the countries with whom we will be negotiating. We need to understand the strengths and weaknesses of their services industries, their stakeholders and their interests, what difficulties the foreign government is likely to face in meeting requests for the reform or liberalization of regulations in services, and what they are likely to request in return.

Understanding the foreign stakeholders and their interests is important because it will tell us something about the likely foreign reaction to our requests and the requests they are likely to make of us. While it may not be possible to know precisely how the stakeholder interests will be reflected in the country's final negotiating position, it can give us some general ideas. Moreover, down the road, understanding the interests of the stakeholders who stand behind the government's position will enable us to enlist the support of the stakeholders with similar or converging interests, give us an idea where the other government can be pushed, and ultimately provide insights into possible win-win solutions to the negotiations.

In order to negotiate successfully, it is important to understand the interests and problems of both parties to the negotiations. The reason for this is simply that a successful conclusion of a negotiation requires the consent of at least two parties, which means that both sides to an agreement have to be satisfied that it meets their economic interests. Becoming familiar with the interests of negotiating partners allows for the development of more effective arguments in support of negotiating proposals, by enabling the negotiator to demonstrate how a negotiating proposal will advance the other side's economic interests. In many cases a government that has not taken the time to do a comprehensive analysis of its interests may not be even aware how particular proposals could advance their interests. Ultimately, understanding the interests of negotiating partners will help to shape proposals that will serve both countries' interests.

Collecting information about foreign stakeholders around the world sounds like a resource-intensive exercise that only large, rich countries could undertake, and it is certainly true that such countries can mobilize more resources to collect such information. However, most countries have commercial officers posted in embassies around the world who could collect this kind of information. The most successful exporting companies in the home country are another good source for this kind of information. Even small developing countries often have companies that have been successful exporters in particular sectors, and these companies are generally very knowledgeable about the views and interests of their counterparts abroad.

Another key source of information accessible to anyone, even in developing countries, is the Internet. Most large countries, particularly democratic countries, have established a considerable degree of transparency with respect to the views and interests of their key stakeholders. They do this because the Internet has become an important tool for influencing internal domestic debate, as well as building support among foreign stakeholders. The United States, in particular, has a great deal of transparency as a result of its culture, legal environment, and a vigorous press. Most key industry associations, large corporations, unions and NGOs in the United States maintain websites with information about their organization's activities and position on negotiating issues. Both companies and industry associations frequently prepare position papers to set out their views. The same is increasingly the case for principal stakeholder groups in other developed countries and the more advanced developing countries.

Analyzing the Data

In order to be useful, the information that is collected has to be organized and analyzed in a coherent manner. Collecting all the information needed to understand an issue can be time consuming, but it is relatively easy compared to analyzing the data. Some trade analysts think they have completed their work when they have compiled voluminous information. But developing an in-depth understanding of the relevance of the information for the issue at stake is far more challenging. Analysis consists of developing an understanding of how the information can shed light on the economic interests of stakeholders affected by a measure, the potential interpretations that can be given to relevant laws and regulations, the policy issues that may have to be addressed and ultimately how the issue can be shaped to maximize the chances for a successful negotiation.

The following describes how information can be used to prepare negotiating requests and offers in the context of WTO negotiations in services:

- Information drawn from export data, economic studies, industry surveys and studies of other economies can lead to the identification of services in which the country has or could develop competitive exports.

- Information about foreign regulatory barriers and industry assessments of their relative importance can lead to the identification of foreign regulatory barriers that should be targeted in the requests submitted to other countries in the first stage of the negotiations.

- Import data, economic studies, industry surveys, studies of other economies and inputs provided by domestic ministries or departments can lead to the identification of services in which the country has weaknesses, and in which liberalization commitments should only be made on the basis of long phase-in periods, or precluded altogether.

- Information on regulatory issues can help negotiators to frame a request or offer in such a way that it does not undermine the achievement of desired social objectives embedded in current regulations.

- Information on the positions and interests of both domestic and foreign stakeholders is crucial for the development of negotiating proposals that can win the support of domestic constituencies and are negotiable abroad.[3] Such information can also inform the development of negotiating strategies and tactics.

Preparing the Negotiations—Developing Domestic Consensus on Negotiating Objectives, Negotiating Strategy, and Negotiating Proposals

Analysis of the issues and of the stakeholders in a negotiation builds the foundation for the formulation of negotiating objectives, the development of a negotiating strategy, and the drafting of negotiating proposals. Negotiating objectives provide a sense of direction for the negotiations. A negotiating strategy provides a road map for getting to the desired negotiating goal.

---

[3] We will later explore the implication of the differences between positions and interests. Interests are the commercial interests, policy objectives, bureaucratic imperatives, or legal requirements that a negotiator must satisfy in a negotiation in order to obtain the approval of the home constituencies. Interests need to be distinguished from the negotiating position, which is what a negotiator is instructed to ask for at any particular phase of the negotiation. The negotiating position is dictated not only by the organization's interests, but also by the negotiating strategies and tactics of the parties.

A negotiating proposal is designed as the first step in engaging foreign negotiators in a dialogue and conveying an optimal negotiating outcome to domestic stakeholders. The documents that set out a country's negotiating objectives, negotiating strategy and negotiating proposals provide a common frame of reference for the country's negotiating team and their stakeholders.

This section will examine in greater detail the purpose and content of documents that set out a country's negotiating objectives, negotiating strategy and negotiating proposals.

Establishing Negotiating Objectives

Once the information described above has been collected and analyzed, we are ready to develop a set of negotiating objectives. It is important to establish a clear set of negotiating objectives in order to provide a focus for the preparatory work leading to a negotiation and for the management of the negotiation. The development of negotiating objectives is also the ideal way of building support among domestic stakeholders, particularly stakeholders who will have a crucial influence on the acceptance or rejection of the negotiating outcome by the ultimate decision makers and by officials who will have to implement the results. At the same time, the statement of negotiating objectives will need to be adjusted or fine-tuned as negotiators and their stakeholders learn more about the issues being negotiated and the constraints and interests of their negotiating partners.

In order to develop negotiating objectives, we have to compile and analyze information and consult with stakeholders. We have to actively build consensus among the key domestic stakeholders who can influence a political decision on the issues covered by the negotiations. Coalition partners at home can include key officials from other government departments or agencies, key executives from corporations or trade associations, experts from academia or think tanks, and key legislators and their staffs.

The country's negotiating objectives should be set out in a statement that is approved by the political leadership. Who has to approve a statement of negotiating objectives varies according to the importance of the issues and the political structure of the country. Comprehensive multi-lateral negotiations in the WTO that may have far-reaching consequences for the country may require not only the approval of the country's trade minister, but also approval by the country's other top economic leadership and the head of government.

A statement of negotiating objectives need not cover technical details, but rather should set out some broad strategic objectives and a set of negotiating priorities. It may also set out an accompanying domestic policy agenda. As noted earlier, the ability of a country's enterprises to take advantage of the liberalization of trade barriers by other countries may well hinge on domestic regulatory reforms designed to remove unnecessary regulatory burdens, while achieving important social objectives such as the protection of consumers, the stability of the financial system, or regulatory transparency. Moreover, the government may well find it desirable to ease the economic adjustment of import-sensitive sectors and firms to increased competition from foreign firms. Such assistance could help domestic firms adopt competitive technologies or business practices, or help workers in these industries to develop the skills needed in the export-oriented industries that are expected to benefit from trade liberalization.

Ideally, a country's negotiating objectives are formulated as part of a broader domestic-economic-development strategy. While most countries sooner or later need to face up to the connection between the domestic policy agenda and international trade negotiations, institutional issues often make it difficult to synchronize the domestic-economic-policy-making process and the trade-policy-making process in a seamless way. Linking negotiating objectives to broader domestic economic growth strategies is generally beyond the scope of responsibilities of trade officials and therefore requires leadership by the country's top political leaders.

Developing a Negotiating Strategy

In negotiations, like in war, good strategy is a critical factor in success, as has been demonstrated by numerous examples where the less powerful beat the more powerful through good strategy. Good strategy can also help the powerful to obtain their objectives without much conflict. The best generals are those who win a war with a minimum of bloodshed, or even without fighting a battle at all.

Negotiations are a process rather than a discrete event that begins and ends with a formal negotiating session. The more successful a negotiator is in building support outside the negotiating room for the preferred negotiating outcome and in developing a broad consensus on the basic legitimacy and fairness of a negotiating proposal, the easier it will be for the negotiator to achieve the desired results at the negotiating table.

A negotiator's bargaining strength inside the negotiating room is determined as much by the number of stakeholders at home and abroad who support the negotiator's preferred negotiating outcome and by the degree to which the wider stakeholder community considers the proposals to be legitimate and fair, as it is by the economic power of the country represented in international negotiations, or by the power of an individual domestic stakeholder at home. Support is built through the formation of coalitions of stakeholders dedicated to the achievement of common, or at least compatible, objectives. Legitimacy and fairness are built through public dialogue with policy experts, the press and the public at large, provided of course that the proposal is not arbitrary and can be defended on the basis of widely held principles of what is fair and legitimate.

A negotiating strategy is a plan for building support for a desired negotiating outcome. It needs to identify the means for obtaining the support of potential allies and for minimizing and overcoming the opposition of potential opponents. Building support is a process of aligning interests, aligning negotiating proposals and arguments in support of such proposals, and aligning supportive actions. A good strategy spells out in fairly specific terms how the desired negotiating outcome has to be shaped to meet the interests of the targeted coalition of supporters. It needs to describe the arguments that should be made to potential supporters to win their support, and the arguments that should be made to opponents to minimize their opposition or to win them over. It should lay out a menu of written and oral communications such as position papers, advocacy letters, testimony, press releases, speeches, conferences, and other communication tools that will be used to reach the targeted-stakeholder communities. It should include steps that can be taken to establish and communicate the legitimacy and fairness of the proposed outcome. Finally, a strategy should set out the parameters of a successful negotiating outcome by describing the possible elements of an outcome that could satisfy the interests of the parties to the negotiations.

A good strategy builds on the information that has been collected about the issues and the stakeholders in the information-collection and research phase of the preparations, and the subsequent analysis of that information. The better the information and the higher the quality of analysis, the better will be the negotiating strategy.

The development of a strategy for coalition building and for legitimizing negotiating objectives is particularly important for smaller countries participating in international negotiations, and to smaller companies or industries seeking to influence governments at home or abroad on negotiating issues. Large and powerful countries can more easily afford to pay less attention to alliances and considerations of legitimacy. But as history has shown, even powerful countries or powerful stakeholders within countries are unlikely to remain successful if they do not seek the support of allies and fail to establish the legitimacy of their desired negotiating outcomes. Building consensus is a labor-intensive effort, but once a consensus is built around a proposal, and the core ideas are firmly rooted as a new paradigm, negotiations tend to take on a life of their own, independent of the country or stakeholder group that may have made the proposal in the first place. A good negotiating strategy that maps out the formation of coalitions and the establishment of the legitimacy of desired negotiating outcomes is particularly important for the negotiation of rules. After all, ultimately every country that will be bound by the rule will have to agree to it. This can only be achieved through a good strategy. Issue and country-specific negotiations provide fewer opportunities for coalition building and issues of legitimacy and fairness are often difficult to judge in such negotiations. However, the problems inherent in communicating the relevance of a complicated technical issue, or worse, a whole catalog of technical issues, can be overcome through the skillful packaging of the issues and the desired results in easily understood language that is seen as inherently fair and legitimate. If the relevance of the issues involved and the desired negotiating outcomes are successfully communicated in ways that can be understood by the broader stakeholder communities, it is possible to apply the benefits of good strategy, to even the most technical and detailed negotiations.

Building global consensus in support of the negotiation of an agreement on trade in services, for example, was a multidimensional effort that required building support by a large number of stakeholder groups throughout the world, and establishing the legitimacy of the objective. While the United States led the early effort, changes in political leadership at the top resulted in a sharp decline of U.S. leadership during some years. During those periods, the momentum generated by the international consensus that had been built during the earlier years carried the effort forward on its own momentum, and overrode new U.S. positions that might have reversed aspects of the consensus that had been built. International negotiations can be best visualized as an aircraft carrier—it takes a considerable amount of energy to get it moving, but once it is moving in a particular direction, it is difficult to change its course.

In Annex 1 below, the use of strategy in negotiations is provided by the experience of the U.S. negotiating team to use the OECD Study on services discussed in the introduction as a stepping stone towards global consensus on the launching of negotiations on trade in services.

Developing Negotiating Proposals

The next step in the preparation of negotiations is the development of negotiating proposals. A negotiating proposal represents the opening position in a negotiation, and should be designed to evoke responses from negotiating partners that will help frame the negotiations. In framing a negotiating proposal, a country needs to consider not only its negotiating objective, but also the views and interests of its negotiating partners. Like a game of chess, a negotiation is an interactive process of moves and countermoves, and the wise negotiator will think ahead to map out how the sequence of moves will eventually lead to the desired negotiating outcome. This is, of course, the essence of negotiating strategy.

How a proposal is structured depends on the nature of the negotiations. A negotiating proposal in a bilateral negotiation aimed at the modification of a foreign regulatory measure can take the form of a discussion paper that describes desired changes in the regulation at issue. In the request/offer process that is used in the GATS to frame the negotiation of national commitments, the negotiating proposal takes the form of requests for liberalizing actions by trading partners. In the negotiation of GATS rules, the negotiating proposal takes the form of a white paper outlining the proposed rule and the rationale for such a rule. The process for initiating negotiations in the WTO under these procedures is described below.

DEVELOPING REQUESTS UNDER THE REQUEST/OFFER PROCEDURE IN THE WTO

Under the procedures currently in effect for the services negotiations under the Doha Round of Multilateral Trade Negotiations in the WTO, the negotiation of specific national commitments proceeds on the basis of a request/offer procedure. Under this procedure, the negotiations are initiated through the bilateral submission of requests by each WTO member country to every other WTO member country that constitutes a potential export market for its services. Once the initial set of requests is made, countries schedule bilateral consultations, during which the country that has received requests is given the opportunity to ask clarifying questions. Subsequently, all countries that have received requests are given the opportunity to make bilateral offers. The initial exchange of requests and offers is often followed by subsequent rounds of requests and offers, and ultimately bilateral negotiations.

Requests can take the form of a request for national treatment, for the elimination of all market-access barriers in particular services or sectors, by mode of supply, or for the modification of specific regulatory provisions considered particularly restrictive by the country's exporters. For example, a country could ask for national treatment of foreign banks that have established themselves in the importing country (banking services provided by locally established banks under mode 3, which covers establishment). This means that any foreign bank would be treated in the same way as domestic banks with respect to the application of domestic laws and regulations. Alternatively, the request could focus on the removal of an onerous regulation, such as the requirement that foreign banks must make a large deposit at the Central Bank before they can establish themselves.

By keeping its initial request general, the requesting country might obtain more information about what the responding country considers a reasonable request. Based on the feedback provided by the importing country through bilateral consultations on the requests and the subsequent offer, the requesting country can more precisely target the requested regulatory changes in the second or subsequent round of requests. Ideally requests should follow the format set out in a country's national schedule.

While the exchange of requests and offers, and subsequent negotiations, under the normal request and offer procedure takes place on a bilateral basis, WTO members are required to give the best treatment they give to any one country to all other members of the WTO in accordance with the MFN principle that is embedded in the GATS Agreement. The only general exception to this rule applies to trade among members of a free trade agreement. Also, WTO members had a one time opportunity to exclude particular services from the application of the MFN provision at the time they joined the GATS.

An interesting tactical question is whether the requests submitted to other countries should cover all sectors, modes of supply and horizontal measures in which the country has an export interest. Negotiators may wish to leave some areas of interest out of their request if they are confident that other countries with more leverage will be pressing the country involved to liberalize that particular service, mode of supply or horizontal measure. By focusing its request on services, modes of supply or horizontal measures that are unlikely to be covered by other countries with negotiating clout, smaller or less developed countries may be able to focus their limited negotiating leverage more effectively on what is likely to make a difference for them.

Of course, there is a risk in leaving out areas of high priority for the country submitting the request in anticipation of what other countries are likely to request, because other countries with a stake in that issue may end up assigning a low priority to that service or mode of supply for reasons of their own. It is therefore best to make requests for services, modes of supply, or horizontal measures in which the country has a high interest, even if other countries can be expected to make similar requests.

A favored defensive tactic employed by countries that are reluctant to undertake major regulatory reforms in the course of the negotiations is to request regulatory changes that its trading partners will find impossible to meet, even if the requesting country does not have a real interest in the requested change. They do this in the expectation that it will deter the other country from pressing difficult requests. A country that does not have any real export interest may find this a useful tactic, but countries that have real export interests are better served by concentrating on those interests. If a request for the liberalization of measures that impede the export of a service of real interest causes political difficulty to another country, it still makes sense to include it in the request list. Even if the importing country is not in a position politically to make a full offer, it may be willing to make a partial offer that provides concrete commercial benefits.

Many developing countries with a limited ability to liberalize their services industry have been reluctant to make too many requests of other countries, for fear that it will come under excessive pressure to liberalize in import sensitive sectors. More often than not, countries are overly concerned about the potential negotiating pressure generated by an extensive request list. By not listing requests that reflect true interests, a country forgoes the possibility of offers that might advance its commercial interests. If the price the other country asks for making an offer is too high, the country making the request can always pull back on its requests in subsequent rounds.

Moreover, the process of submitting requests in areas of real interest to exporting industries may generate enthusiastic political support from these industries, thus expanding the limits of what may be politically feasible in liberalizing domestic measures. If, as is likely, other countries press for the liberalization of these same measures, the lack of negotiating leverage will not be the real issue anyway. Countries should construct a request list that reflects their true export interests, since this will signal the country's economic interests to the other negotiators, and increase the possibility that other countries will make favorable offers. As mentioned previously, a country needs to consider the adverse impact of its own regulations on the competitiveness of its enterprises when formulating requests and offers in international negotiations. Ideally, the formulation of requests and offers is accompanied by the development of a broader strategy for strengthening the competitiveness of the country's services industries.

At the Ministerial Meeting convened by the WTO in Hong Kong in the fall of 2005, ministers agreed to expand the bilateral request/offer process in services to include collective requests on a voluntary basis. Under this new procedure, groups of member countries can make requests for the liberalization or reform of measures in particular sectors or modes of supply to an identified list of other countries. This new procedure introduces a new dynamic in the negotiating process by establishing a common point of reference for negotiations on the particular sectors or modes of supply covered by the collective requests. In some ways, the subsequent negotiations can take on many of the characteristics of negotiations focused on rule making., in the sense that the challenge is to achieve a broad consensus among a group of countries on negotiating proposals and on negotiating outcomes.

FORMULATING NEGOTIATING PROPOSALS ON RULES IN THE GATS NEGOTIATIONS

In addition to the negotiation of specific national commitments, the negotiations on trade in services in the Doha Round of Multilateral Trade Negotiations in the WTO focuses on the development of rules that might be added to the GATS Agreement and on provisions of possible sectoral agreements. The negotiation of rules or sectoral agreements is generally preceded by a review of the issues by participating countries, and decisions on analytical studies that the WTO Secretariat may be asked to undertake. Upon completion of the analytical phase of the Negotiating Committee's work, member countries are likely to be asked to submit negotiating proposals, which are then reviewed in subsequent meetings of the Committee. At some point the Secretariat may be asked to compile all negotiating proposals that were submitted into an integrated analytical paper that describes and compares all the proposals on the basis of a common analytical framework.

Any country can submit a negotiating proposal at any time during the negotiating process. The timing of negotiating proposals needs to be based on various tactical considerations. The optimal time to submit a proposal depends on what a country hopes to accomplish with its proposal. For example, a country may choose to submit a proposal early during the negotiating process, even before countries are ready to consider proposals, in order to make a point concerning the feasibility of developing a rule that meets certain requirements under discussion. Such a proposal may help to derail skeptics who are trying to block the negotiations from developing in a certain direction. In tabling such a proposal, however, a country would need to consider that too much detail might scare off countries that have not yet reached a point where they are willing to contemplate certain types of rules or sectoral agreements. At a later stage in the process a country may choose to make a proposal that narrowly focuses on one aspect of the rule that best captures its particular interest or regulatory perspective, or the country may choose to submit a proposal that reflects a broad group interest, including its own. Once a large number of proposals have been tabled, a country may choose to submit a proposal that consolidates or bridges previous proposals in the hope that the new proposal could serve as a viable compromise solution.

Negotiating proposals can be submitted by individual countries, or by a coalition of countries acting together. If the coalition is wide enough and representative of a cross-section of countries, it can have considerable influence on the negotiating process. On the other hand, strategically crafted proposals by individual countries can turn out to be just as influential. Countries that are proactive in submitting negotiating proposals and in crafting group proposals can achieve considerable influence in the negotiating process, even if they are relatively small countries. The key to exercising influence is to master the technical details of the issue, to develop an in-depth understanding of the needs and views of member countries, and to surface proposals that can serve as the basis for building consensus.

A negotiating proposal should contain not only proposed language, but also the rationale underlying the proposal. The proposal should start out by placing the proposal in the context of the negotiations. This should be followed by an analytical section that lays out the issues that need to be addressed, by a description of the proposed text, and a final section laying out the rationale and why the proposal is the right solution for the problems posed.

Outward Looking and Defensive Strategies

Negotiators can follow a number of different strategies in pursuing their objectives in trade negotiations, or a combination of such strategies. A country might choose to pursue an outward looking strategy aimed at the global liberalization of barriers to international trade and competition. Alternatively, a country may choose to pursue a defensive strategy, if its primary consideration is making as few commitments as possible and the country does not attach much priority to obtaining liberalization commitments from other countries. Such a strategy makes sense in a multilateral negotiation, where a country may be willing to go along with a multilateral agreement that does not address any of its own problems as long as such an agreement does not require the country involved to make substantive commitments of its own.

OUTWARD LOOKING STRATEGIES

The most traditional, and perhaps the most common strategy pursued by trade negotiators is the mercantilist strategy. Negotiators pursuing this strategy seek to maximize the exports resulting from the reduction of foreign trade barriers and to minimize the increase in imports that might result from a reduction in the country's own trade barriers. The negotiators may well realize from their economic training that the country gains from obtaining foreign goods or services at cheaper prices if the country's own barriers are reduced, but domestic politics usually drives trade negotiators to a mercantilist policy, since import-sensitive industries are often better organized than export oriented industries. Moreover, in the final analysis, the liberalization of the country's own import barriers that are offered as "concessions" to foreign negotiators can simultaneously be presented to domestic consumers as gains for the country.

An alternative strategy that a country can pursue is a domestic reform strategy, in which the country uses the negotiations to achieve reforms in domestic regulations. Under such a strategy, the government uses the foreign pressure in the negotiation to overcome the political opposition of vested domestic interests to regulatory reforms favored by the government. The Japanese government frequently used this tactic in bilateral negotiations with the United States. The Chinese government used this tactic brilliantly in the negotiation of its accession to the WTO. Such a strategy was also pursued by most countries that participated in the negotiation of the Telecommunication Agreement under the GATS.

In pursuing any of these strategies, a government can adopt a very proactive stance by making far-reaching requests of other countries in pursuit of a grand bargain or a hard to get stance by making few requests and by resisting foreign demands as long as possible in order to get other countries ultimately "to pay more" for its "concessions." "A hard to get" strategy can be successful in achieving its immediate aim, i.e. in getting other countries to make more far-reaching commitments in exchange for a difficult commitment by the country involved. But in a multilateral negotiation, the country risks isolating itself and therefore hampering its ability to shape the course of the negotiations as the majority of countries hammer out the elements of an agreement. During many of the past rounds of negotiations the United States typically pursued a grand bargain strategy, while countries with defensive agricultural interests often employed a hard to get strategy.

In pursuing a grand bargain strategy, a good complementary strategy is to place considerable emphasis on coalition building among countries with similar interests. Such a strategy requires an active process of seeking out other countries and accommodating their interests in the formulation of negotiating proposals. Australia was successful in the Uruguay Round in building a coalition around the so-called Cairns Group in pursuing a far-reaching agriculture agreement. Similar coalition strategies were used in the negotiation of the GATS agreement in the Uruguay Round.

DEFENSIVE STRATEGIES

We have previously looked at outward looking negotiations aimed at solving a problem faced by exporters. We will now examine possible responses by an importing country to foreign requests for a change in its regulations. Our response to the foreign request will be influenced by the legitimacy of the request, the relative political and legal difficulty in responding to the request, and relative bargaining power. The role of a negotiating strategy in this situation is to develop the means for increasing relative bargaining power and establishing the legitimacy of maintaining protection. In the final analysis, however, we need to consider that both sides have options, and we therefore have to consider the consequences of saying no. An important concept in evaluating such requests is the concept of BATNA, the Best Alternative to an Agreement. We need to consider whether the political or economic consequence of our refusal to negotiate is worse than the economic or political difficulties created by a negotiated agreement.

The Power to Say No

Current ideas of national sovereignty give a country the right to say no to foreign requests, even when the foreign request is a request to honor commitments under trade rules. Saying no may have consequences, but as long as the country is prepared to live with those consequences, it has the right to say no. There may be a number of reasons why we may want to say no. The request may involve an action that is inconsistent with our economic philosophy. Changing the targeted regulation may not be in our economic interest or it may be too difficult to change the regulation for political, legal or even constitutional reasons. We may simply consider the request as not being legitimate.

The power to say no is even stronger in WTO multilateral trade negotiations than in bilateral negotiations. Decisions in the WTO are made on the basis of consensus. In principle, consensus means that all countries that are members of the WTO have to agree. In practice, it probably means that the vast majority of countries and all important countries have to agree. This right to say no gives individual countries considerable leverage in multilateral negotiations in the WTO. The same is true, of course, under regional and bilateral free trade agreements.

How can we minimize the consequences of saying no? The consequences of saying no will depend on the importance of the issue to the other country, the relative merits of their request and our decision to say no, and the relative bargaining power of the two sides, i.e. the relative strengths of the options available to the two sides involved in the negotiation. Just saying no is most likely to be a successful strategy when the issue is not particularly important to the other side, when we do not have important export interests in the other country, when the request of the other side is not backed by international trade rules or is not seen as legitimate by the world trading community.

Before exploring strategies we can adopt to strengthen our ability to say no while minimizing the consequences, it is useful to consider the issue of bargaining power. We are programmed to thinking that bargaining power is a function of the size of the country, but that is not necessarily true in the case of trade. What matters in trade negotiations is not the relative size of the countries but the relative size of their actual and potential trade. A large country may have little bargaining power if its imports are relatively small, while a small country may have a large amount of bargaining power if its imports are relatively large. Thus India had limited bargaining power for many years because its imports were quite small, while smaller countries like the Netherlands, Chile, Switzerland, or Hong Kong had much more bargaining power than would have been suggested by their size because they were large importers. At the same time a small country that has professionally well trained negotiators who are successful in building the legitimacy of their case may have more bargaining power than a large country that lacks negotiators with those skills.

This brings us to strategy. How can we bolster our decision to say no? One obvious answer is to find allies among opinion makers in the other country or in third countries. Finding allies in a bilateral dispute is clearly more of a challenge than in multilateral negotiations, but it can be done. For example, if we can persuade another country that it has an indirect stake in the case as a result of similar export interests, the country may be willing to submit an amicus brief in the case. Other countries may also be able to strengthen the legitimacy of our case by speaking out in our behalf at international meetings. In multilateral negotiations, building coalitions is at the core of most successful negotiations, just as it is in drafting successful legislative proposals in national legislatures. How do representatives from small and poor districts get a hearing in national legislatures?

Another strategy we can adopt to fend off foreign demands is to ask other countries for commitments we know they cannot make. We may have very little interest in getting other countries to make such commitments. The sole objective of the demand is to be able to say "if you can't do X, you can't expect me to do Y." We might call this the red-herring strategy.

Another defensive strategy is to articulate a principle that makes the foreign request illegitimate, and then to build support for that principle among other countries and among external opinion makers. We might call this the philosophical defense strategy. For a long time countries that did not want to liberalize in agriculture argued that trade rules should not affect domestic agricultural policies. Since trade measures were designed to protect these very same agriculture policies, no progress was made on agricultural trade barriers over many years.

In Annex 2 below, a case illustration is presented of the ability of countries to say no in the context of the Financial Services Understanding.

The Consequences of Saying No—Moves and Countermoves

To better understand the consequences of saying no, we need to examine the options available to a country whose request we have refused. As previously discussed, the essence of trade negotiations is the exchange of commitments that involve the mutual liberalization of barriers to trade. When we say no to a request from another country to help solve a problem faced by their exporters, they will be less inclined to help us solve a problem faced by our exporters. Two countries that trade actively with each other undoubtedly have a large number of mutual problems to address, and a country's willingness to help its trading partners is unlikely to depend on the resolution of a single issue. The net impact of saying no on any one issue therefore will depend on the relative importance of the issue and our response on all the other issues on the negotiating table. One way of minimizing the consequences of saying no on one issue is to be more helpful in solving another issue.

Another potential response of the country we have refused is to initiate dispute settlement proceedings, if they believe that the measure at stake involves a violation of a commitment we have made in a trade agreement or a trade rule. We therefore need to consider the relative strength of our and their legal position, and the consequences of losing the case. If we are confident that we can win the case, this would bolster the legitimacy of our position and make it much more difficult for the other country to press their case or to take any action against us for refusing to address the issue. On the other hand, if we are likely to lose the case, the question is whether the problems associated with resolving the problem are greater than the problems we may face if the other country is given the right to retaliate against us. Are we in a better position to address the issue domestically after we have lost the case than we are now?

The other country may decide not to wait for a dispute-settlement ruling and take some form of retaliatory measure. There are a number of ways it may be able to do so legally under the trade rules by initiating an action sanctioned by the trade rules. For example, they could initiate a safeguard action on one of our export products that have been creating difficulty for their industry, or they may decide to initiate a stricter enforcement of a sanitary measure on one of our exported agricultural products. As long as such actions are in conformity with the provisions set out in the WTO agreements, and the country has the domestic political option to act or not act, it can put pressure on us without violating any rules. Beyond such actions within the rules, the country could decide to take an illegal retaliatory measure that would put economic pressure on us while we initiate a dispute-settlement proceeding against them.

We also need to consider responses by a country that is frustrated by our ability to block consensus in the WTO on adding a particular issue to the negotiating agenda or in concluding an agreement that has been under negotiation. One of those responses is to pursue the issues involved in other international negotiating venues in which we are excluded. While we may be able to avoid being bound by any such agreement we may also lose our ability to influence the development of international norms on that issue. The bottom line is that every country has options, but each option has its own consequences.

Cooperative Defensive Strategies

A foreign request for a change in our regulations may well have economic merit, even from the point of view of domestic enterprises. There may be a number of reasons why our country's regulatory agencies may have failed to reform regulations that are outdated as a result of changes in technology, market structure or system of governance. The reason may have been regulatory inertia, or political difficulties associated in overcoming the vested interests created under the existing regulatory structure. In such cases, we can use the external impetus to pursue regulatory reforms that are in our economic interest but difficult to implement. Many countries have developed the fine art of blaming foreigners for reforms that are desirable but politically difficult. It can be a useful tactic, but it is also a double-edged sword because ultimately the legitimacy of the reform depends on public belief that it is in the country's own economic interest. China's use of the negotiations with WTO members on its accession to the WTO, for example, is a classic case of a country making the most of negotiations with foreigners to advance a domestic regulatory and economic reform agenda.

In responding to a foreign request for a regulatory change, we should ideally first ask ourselves whether changes in the targeted regulations would ultimately be in our economic interest. Maybe the specific changes suggested by the other government would not be in our best economic interest, but an alternative set of changes that would address some of their concerns could be turned into a desirable reform. If the trade negotiators on the other side are doing their job well, they will present all the arguments why the desired change would not only remove a barrier to their exports but would also improve the performance of our economy or increase the competitiveness of our own industry.

Preparing the Negotiations—Building Support

The negotiating process begins with the first exploratory discussions of the issues with stakeholders at home and abroad. While these preliminary discussions are not what we normally consider as a negotiation, for all practical purposes they are a part of the negotiating process.

This section will examine the process for building supportive coalitions and for selling negotiating proposals to negotiating partners.

Building Supportive Coalitions

Trade negotiations are a process of progressively building consensus among an expanding circle of stakeholder groups with varying degrees of interest in the outcome of the negotiation. Building coalitions among like-minded groups at home in support of particular negotiating proposals and agreements is a critical aspect of that process.

The negotiation of the services agreement in the WTO, for example, was advanced by a number of crosscutting international coalitions of stakeholders that supported the negotiation of a services agreement under the aegis of the global multilateral trading system. Business leaders, academics, and government officials from both developed and developing countries that favored an agreement met periodically to brainstorm the issues, to coordinate lobbying efforts, and to map out negotiating proposals and initiatives. It included stakeholders from such diverse countries as the United States, the European Community, UK, France, Sweden, Japan, Australia, New Zealand, Hong Kong, Singapore, Colombia, and Chile. Similarly, the working level negotiators from many of these countries constituted an informal group called the friends of services, who regularly coordinated their interventions in the meetings of the negotiating group on services.

Once potential coalition partners have been identified, then it is important to reach out to them to discuss the pending negotiations, and where possible to coordinate positions or even to draft joint negotiating proposals. A coalition partner may support efforts to prepare negotiations in some or all of the following ways:

- Help brainstorm possible solutions (options) to present in the negotiations.
- Reach out to their constituents (members) to involve them in collateral legislative, lobbying, media, or other supportive activities.
- Raise funds to finance studies, conferences, promotional materials, or press campaigns in support of the negotiations.
- Provide market information, scientific studies, and economic data in support of the negotiating objectives.

One of the most important skills a negotiator can have is the ability to build coalitions and alliances with other parties that have similar, or at least, compatible interests. This is particularly important for small developing countries with a limited amount of imports. In trade negotiations, the volume of current and potential imports gives a country negotiating power, i.e. in trade negotiations, buying power equates to negotiating power. Even large countries may have only limited amount of negotiating power if the value of their imports is relatively small. On the other hand, even a small country can exert considerable negotiating power if it is a significant importing country. What a country cannot achieve on its own through a large volume of trade, however, it may be able to achieve as part of a coalition of countries that together can exert considerable negotiating clout.

Some countries limit their coalition-building efforts to regional neighbors. This can sometimes be a mistake because neighboring countries may not have the same economic interests on a particular issue, and the negotiation of a common position may therefore unnecessarily dilute the effectiveness of negotiating proposals in advancing the country's economic interest. It may also be a mistake in spending too many resources in building coalitions with neighboring countries that lack much negotiating power. It would be much better in such situations to seek out influential countries in other parts of the world that have similar interests on a particular issue.

Coalition partners in broad domestic stakeholder coalitions can include key officials from government departments or agencies, key executives from corporations or trade associations, experts from academia or think tanks, and key legislators and their staffs. International coalition partners can include officials from other governments, executives from foreign corporations and trade associations, and foreign academic experts. The negotiation of the GATS was supported by a loose international coalition of officials, businessmen and academic experts who met periodically to map a joint strategy for advancing the negotiations, and who organized conferences and other events around the world to expand the consensus. This coalition was crucial in building up negotiating momentum and sustaining the negotiating process once the negotiations developed their own momentum. Negotiators should also identify members of the press who develop an interest in the negotiations and become educated on the issues, and can be counted on to write informative, in-depth articles on the negotiations.

Negotiators should ideally establish different coalitions for different purposes. Thus a coalition within the government at home may be critical to the development of an interagency consensus, while a coalition of like-minded countries in the WTO may be equally critical to building support among WTO negotiators. International coalition building is particularly critical to smaller countries, which can gain influence only through coalitions that include powerful countries. During the Uruguay Round, many smaller developing economies were able to exert considerable influence on the course of the agriculture negotiations through the Cairns Group of countries, named after the Australian city where they first met. The negotiation of the GATS during the Uruguay Round was significantly enhanced through the coordinated efforts of a group of small and big countries called the friends of services.

Equally important is contacting stakeholders with conflicting interests. Can they be approached and "neutralized"? E.g. Can you offer information, trade-offs, or other assurances that will minimize or eliminate their adverse influence on the negotiation process?

Negotiations need to be viewed as an interlocking chain of events that start with the formation of coalitions to explore negotiating ideas. The formation of supportive coalitions and the development of negotiating proposals should be treated as an interactive process. In order to succeed, a negotiating proposal has to receive the support of a coalition of stakeholders at home and a coalition of countries internationally that together are influential enough to prevail. Building a coalition and negotiating a common position among the members of the coalition is thus a steppingstone towards the negotiation of a successful outcome. Negotiating supportive coalitions at home is a key stepping stone to the development of the country's initial negotiating position. Negotiating supportive coalitions abroad is a key stepping stone towards the development of negotiating proposals and the negotiation of an international agreement.

Formally, the development of a negotiating position in the home country and the negotiation of an international agreement are two separate and sequential phases of the negotiation process. In reality, a successful outcome to negotiations is enhanced if international coalition building and the development of a national position take place at the same time because it will allow negotiators to factor the interests of likely international coalition partners into the development of the country's initial negotiating position, and help assure that the country's initial negotiating proposal will receive support from other countries participating in the negotiations.

Selling the Negotiating Proposals

Once negotiators have developed a negotiating proposal, they must persuade stakeholders at home and abroad on the merits of the proposal. In part this is done through meetings with stakeholders and conferences as well as the preparation of position papers, published statements, press releases and websites. Documents can be targeted either at the general public through the mass media or at targeted groups through specialized publications serving particular services industries or professions. Negotiators might also make public speeches to stakeholder groups, testify at legislative hearings and post white papers on the organization's website.

Internationally, bilateral consultations with foreign negotiators are the most common method of broadening support among negotiators. Negotiators also have the option of distributing the written text of oral interventions made at meetings of the negotiating group or the international dissemination of white papers.

Each of the various types of written and oral methods of communication have their own requirements that determine structure and format.[4] A position paper, for example, should have a brief summary that briefly covers: the what, where, when and why; a background section that outlines the issues that give rise to the proposal; a full description of the proposal; and a section that describes what will be gained as a result of the proposal. This paper can serve as a handout at meetings with stakeholders and at conferences.

Building public support for proposals contained in requests and offers under the request/offer procedure is a major challenge since the requests and offers contain long lists of proposed changes in a broad and diverse range of regulatory measures. Nevertheless it is important to find a way to characterize the nature of the requests and offers in order to build support among stakeholders. Negotiators may wish to summarize the industries targeted through the requests and offers, and what domestic and foreign exporters will be able to do once the regulatory changes are implemented. Negotiators may also wish to describe what is not contained in the requests and offers to reassure regulators and stakeholders in import-sensitive sectors.

The collective request procedure adopted at the Hong Kong Ministerial will substantially facilitate the task of building public support by focusing requests on key features that are widely supported.

How Negotiations on Trade in Services in the WTO are Organized

We discussed earlier how the negotiations on trade in services in the WTO are structured. In this section we will examine how the negotiations unfold, beginning with the initial exchanges of information between the negotiating parties and proceeding in stages to the framing of the issues and the bargaining process.

Pursuing Negotiations Through the Request/Offer Process

As indicated previously, the negotiation of specific national commitments is initiated through the tabling of requests and subsequent bilateral consultations with the countries that have received the requests. These bilateral consultations offer the country making the requests an opportunity to explain the rationale for the requests, and they offer the country receiving the

---

[4] For an extended description of the most effective structure and content of these various written documents and oral presentations, visit the website of the Institute for Trade and Commercial Diplomacy (www.commercialdiplomacy.org), and look for the instructional modules on written and oral communications.

requests an opportunity to ask follow-up questions that will help clarify the nature of the request and help fill in missing details.

The exchange of requests is followed at a subsequent stage by an exchange of offers. The initial offers should signal to negotiating partners the services and the modes of supply where the importing country believes that it may be able to liberalize restrictive provisions, and the services and modes of supply where the importing country will have great difficulty in meeting the requests, either because the domestic industry is not ready for international competition or because domestic policy reasons will make it difficult to change the targeted regulations. Similarly, the importing country may want to signal which horizontal regulations it may be willing to reform, and which are likely to be very difficult to change. A willingness to negotiate can be signaled by including some kind of offer with respect to the service and mode of supply, and the horizontal measure, even if that offer falls far short of what other countries asked for in their requests. Difficulty in meeting a request can be signaled by excluding the service, mode of supply or horizontal measure from the offer. Offers can include proposed commitments not included in the request if there is a reason to believe that the requesting country may benefit from the offer. They may have deliberately left the commitment out of the request in the belief that other countries with more leverage will be making a request in that area.

The exchange of offers is followed by another round of bilateral consultations, during which negotiators seek to clarify the nature of the various offers and the reason why the offer did not address other liberalization measures included in the first round of requests. These consultations provide the basis for the preparation of a second round of requests, which should provide the negotiators an opportunity to become more precise in their requests, and to abandon requests that are considered a low priority, or requests that are clearly not achievable. In turn, the second round of offers should provide an opportunity for the other side to respond to the updated requests.

The second round of requests and offers may be followed by further exchanges of requests, and each round of requests and offers is followed by further bilateral consultations. At some point in this process, the members of the negotiating committee will ask the WTO Secretariat to compile a consolidated list of offers, which then becomes the basis for the final round of negotiations.

The Negotiations on Rules

Multilateral negotiations of rules usually go through several phases. In the first phase, the issue identification stage, one country typically identifies an issue or problem, which it believes needs to be addressed through the formulation of a rule, or some other form of common action. In order to persuade other governments to embark on an analysis of the issue that could lead to the negotiation of a rule, proponents have to demonstrate that the identified problem or issue is more than a one time or rare event, that it is potentially a problem for every (or most) countries, that it is a serious rather than a trivial problem for member countries, that the nature of the problem and the potential remedy are fairly consistent over time and across countries, and that the problem can be solved through a negotiated rule or agreement. If the problem is rare, member countries will be reluctant to spend the time to analyze and negotiate the issue and to restrict their future freedom of action. If it is only a problem for one or some countries, but not for a majority of countries, it will be difficult to get an agreement to study the issue, much less to negotiate binding multilateral commitments. (In such a case a bilaterally negotiated commitment may prove more feasible.) If the nature of the problem and the appropriate remedy changes from event to event, opponents will argue that while there may be a problem, rule making is not the answer.

In the second phase of the process leading to negotiations, the analysis phase, the negotiators analyze the nature of the problem and the potential remedies. This phase of the negotiation is designed to create a clear understanding of the problem and how it may be addressed. In the WTO discussion of an issue at this stage of the process is often entrusted to a study group. Members will study historical occurrences of the problem, identify patterns, examine analogies to similar problems that have been addressed through negotiated agreements, and evaluate principles that could serve as the basis for rule making. If member countries are persuaded by this work that the problem is serious, consistent over time, widespread among member countries, and can be remedied through some form of agreement, then discussions will move toward the search for a negotiating framework to address the issue.

In the third phase of the process leading to negotiations, the pre-negotiation phase, member countries hammer out the terms and mandate for the negotiations. In the WTO the issue at this stage is often entrusted to a working group or a committee that has a formal standing within the organization. The work of the group is to define the problem to be addressed, identify the nature of the solution to be pursued through negotiations, the specific elements of the issue to be addressed, the components of a negotiated solution, and a timetable and venue for the negotiations.

In the fourth phase, the negotiating phase, member countries negotiate the actual language of the new trade rule. Such negotiations usually start with a consideration of negotiating proposals tabled by member countries. Where there are many such proposals, the Secretariat may be asked to compile the proposals into an integrated document, and provide members with an analysis of the various proposals. A discussion of these proposals can lead to a second tier of proposals, which incorporate comments made by members during the review of the initial proposals, or which seek to bridge the gap between competing proposals.

Negotiation of Sectoral Agreements

Sectoral agreements such as the GATS Agreement on Basic Telecommunications contain rules, the establishment of a framework for the negotiation of national commitments, and a set of national commitments that are incorporated in the country's schedule of commitments. The negotiations therefore contain features discussed above under both the section on the negotiation of rules and the section on negotiations of requests and offers.

Sectoral agreements provide a comprehensive and coherent approach to the liberalization and reform of regulations in a particular sector. Instead of approaching the negotiations on an issue by issue and a country by country basis, a sectoral negotiation makes it possible to discuss the basic objectives of regulation in the sector, and where countries can reach consensus on regulatory objectives, to provide a set of best practices for attaining those objectives and a model schedule of commitments that can serve as a template for the negotiation of individual national commitments. Negotiations along these lines therefore begin with a discussion of regulatory objectives, the impact of technological changes and market structures on the achievement of these objectives, the barriers to trade created by existing regulatory provisions and how the reform and liberalization of restrictive regulatory measures can be structured to accommodate the needs of member countries at various stages of development and at various stages of implementing reform. Agreement on a model set of rules and a model schedule of commitments then provides the basis for the negotiation of an initial set of national commitments with respect to both the rules and the reform/liberalization of regulatory barriers to trade and competition.

Opening, Managing, and Concluding Negotiations[5]

This section will explore the organization and choreography of opening, managing, and concluding a negotiation. A well-run negotiation follows a number of well established steps for choreographing the negotiating process. Some of the steps are designed to assure that the negotiating team is solidly grounded in terms of its relationship with the home constituencies. Other steps are designed to achieve an efficient organization of the negotiations and to create a positive feedback mechanism that will facilitate progress in the negotiations. Some of the steps in a well-choreographed negotiation can help minimize irritants that could distract and derail the negotiations, and create a sequence of events that will allow negotiators to make progress on an incremental basis. A well-choreographed negotiation creates positive psychological and physical feedback mechanisms that will encourage participants in the negotiations to expand their horizon and to address the issues under discussion with a great deal of creativity.

Organizing the Negotiating Team

A governmental delegation will most often consist of a "head of delegation", who serves as the lead negotiator, experts on various issues, and representatives of various departments and ministries. The head of delegation should organize the team well ahead of the start of negotiations, giving each team member a clear set of responsibilities. This will not only assure that every team member feels like a full participant who will take responsibility for the outcome, but it will also lighten the load on the lead negotiator and assure better preparation of the negotiating issues.

It is of critical importance in negotiations for a team to reflect a unified position at all times. Nothing will undermine a negotiating team's credibility more than an aura of disunity, disagreement, or other forms of dissension. If disunity or disagreement are observed, negotiators representing other countries will move to exploit those differences or will simply be confused by the team's inability to present a unified and coherent proposal or response.

---

[5] Much of the material in this and the next section is taken from a manual published by the Institute for Trade and Commercial Diplomacy on its website (www.commercialdiplomacy.org). The manual, co-authored by Monning and Feketekuty (2002), builds on ideas developed by Roger Fisher of the Harvard Negotiating Project, and disseminated through various books, including Fisher and Ury (1991), and Fisher and Ertel (1995).

Drafting the Negotiating Instructions

In pursuing discussions with domestic and foreign stakeholders, negotiators are usually acting under the general guidance that they have received from their superiors. Since no formal commitments are being made on behalf of the government involved during these discussions, they usually take place without formal negotiating instructions. Once the negotiations move from informal discussions to formal negotiations, however, negotiators become bound by negotiating instructions that usually go through a formal process of approval in the home government. Most governments have a legally established procedure for approving negotiating instructions, involving not only superiors within the Trade Ministry (or Foreign Ministry), but also senior officials in other key departments and ministries within the government, and in some cases the head of the government.

Negotiating instructions constitute both a delegation of authority to speak on behalf of the government, and a script for the negotiations that sets out the country's positions on the issues, the arguments negotiators should put forward in support of those positions, the information they should seek to obtain from negotiating partners, and what they may agree to during the negotiating sessions covered by the instructions.

The negotiating instructions should set out the country's opening position for the negotiations and spell out the flexibility that can be exercised by the negotiators. As a general rule, negotiators should be given some degree of flexibility in exploring possible negotiating outcomes, but only a limited degree of flexibility to agree on an outcome that substantially differs from the negotiating position outlined in the instructions. After all, the instructions, and the negotiating proposals on which they are based, reflect carefully crafted compromises among stakeholders at home inside and outside of the government, and these stakeholders should be given an opportunity to participate in the evolution of the country's negotiating position. Besides, it is normally advantageous to allow some time for reflection on new negotiating outcomes, because it is usually difficult, if not impossible, to think through all the ramifications and implications of new proposals. Of course, as the negotiations move to a final conclusion, the negotiators have to be given a well-defined range of outcomes that they are authorized to accept. Even then, it is common for negotiators to seek and obtain final instructions from their superiors before finally concluding an agreement.

Pre-negotiating the Negotiations

Every negotiation actually begins before the negotiators sit down at the negotiating table. Through phone calls, email messages and other communications, the negotiating parties need to discuss and decide on the following:

- Meeting logistics (when and where, who participates).
- Exchange of background information that can be reviewed before the negotiation session.
- The Agenda—a list of the topics to be covered in the negotiations, the sequence of topics and the amount of time that should be scheduled for each topic. A scheduling of different topics may allow the two parties to decide who should participate during various negotiating sessions.
- Rules of the negotiation.
- Confidentiality.

- Media contacts.
- Use of interpreters.

Negotiators can also use the pre-negotiation period to learn as much as possible about the expectations of their counterparts. By exchanging information about expectations, the participants can avoid being caught by surprise when the formal sessions are convened.

The Preliminary Steps of the Dance

Before launching into the negotiation proper—the substantive issues that have brought the parties to the table—the negotiators will want to go through a basic check list to insure a productive negotiating session.

- Introduction of team members. It is useful to build an early rapport with the negotiators on the other side even though there may be serious and contentious issues that divide the parties.
- Review of logistical arrangements, agreements on confidentiality/media issues, and the agenda.
- Review of mutual expectations regarding the objectives or desired results of the negotiating session—to exchange information, exploration of issues, identification of possible solutions, concluding a final agreement.

Opening Statements

An opening statement is an important "first intervention" in a formal negotiation, working group, or conference setting. The opening statement provides parties with an opportunity to identify key issues and interests as well as to articulate parameters for potential agreements. This is not a process where a party "reveals a bottom line," but rather an opportunity to stress the importance of the outcome to the interests of the party and to establish early in the proceeding exactly what the party making the opening statement has been directed to pursue by his/her nation or other organizational hierarchy.

After a few negotiating sessions, participants can grow weary of the repetitive enumeration of each side's views and positions on the issue. Nevertheless, a country's position, no matter how often it is repeated, remains one of the anchor points in a negotiation, and it is important to be clear about the starting point for each negotiating session. Repetition of the country's position also provides an opportunity to ask whether any aspect of the position has changed since the last session. Miscommunication and false assumptions can easily set a negotiation back, so it is important always to be very clear about the two positions that frame the negotiation. Patience is a key characteristic of a good negotiator, and a certain amount of repetition is the price you pay for being a negotiator.

Exploring the Positions and Interests of the Parties

The opening statements provide a platform for a subsequent exchange of clarifying questions on the respective positions and the underlying interests of the parties. A good way to start the process is for the head of each delegation to summarize the position of the other side and to seek confirmation that they have understood the position of the other side correctly. This provides each side the opportunity to clarify and elaborate on their initial statement of the position, and to ask clarifying questions of the other side.

As discussed earlier, negotiating positions need to be distinguished from interests. The negotiating position, which is what a negotiator is instructed to ask for at any particular phase of the negotiation, is dictated not only by the organization's interests, but by the negotiating strategies and tactics of the parties. Interests underlie positions. Interests are the commercial interests, policy objectives, bureaucratic imperatives, or legal requirements that a negotiator must satisfy in a negotiation in order to obtain the approval of the home constituencies. Interests are at the very core of what drives parties in a negotiation.

In trade negotiations, it can be safely assumed that all parties at the table seek to advance their economic interests. But there may be a multitude of other important interests that compel the parties to take the positions they do. The ranking and prioritization of interests will differ between parties. Clear recognition of the differences in priorities and interests can enable the skilled negotiator to develop creative options (solutions) for a negotiated agreement.

The interests of stakeholders are determined by the impact of the targeted policy measure on the commercial interests of competing enterprises and workers, the policy objectives served by the targeted policy measure, the broader economic impact of the measure, and institutional and bureaucratic interests. Interests are also shaped by the domestic and international legal provisions that apply to a measure under negotiation. A stakeholder's perceived interests may or may not coincide with that stakeholder's real interests, depending on the availability and accuracy of their information. A successful commercial diplomat therefore analyzes the issues not only to better understand the issues at stake, but also potentially to educate foreign negotiators on their real interests, particularly where such interests coincide.

Framing the Issues

A complete understanding of the issues and the perceived and real interests of stakeholders in all the countries participating in the negotiations forms an essential basis for framing negotiations. In the course of preparing for negotiations, a commercial diplomat may find it necessary or desirable to redefine the negotiating issue periodically as more information sheds new light on the issue. For example, as negotiators learn more about the policy issues underlying a targeted measure, they may find that their understanding of the problem was faulty and that the more accurate information calls for a different approach to the problem. Alternatively, the negotiator may conclude that the issue should be redefined to better address the needs of new potential allies or to provide a closer legal fit.

Creating Multiple Solutions to Satisfy Interests

One of the key elements to effective negotiations is the development of multiple options or solutions to satisfy the interests of the negotiating parties. The best negotiators distinguish themselves by their ability to create and generate multiple options in both the planning stage and at the negotiating table. This is the area of interest-based negotiation where a negotiator's creativity and capacity to think beyond a single solution is paramount. The shortcoming of many positional negotiators is that they become fixated on single solutions or positions that blind them to other possibilities. Such singular thinking can lead to stalemate and impasse in the negotiation process.

In Annex 3 of this Appendix, a case illustration is presented of the different positions involved in the original GATS negotiations.

Introducing a Written Text Document

The "dance" of negotiation can involve protracted dialogue and discussion that may seem unproductive as parties restate positions and appear to offer nothing to advance the process. In most productive negotiation sessions, the parties will eventually commit areas of agreement or consensus to writing. Once parties begin working on text, there is often a qualitative change in the course of the negotiations. A written text that records agreement in a particular area need not be long or address a long list of issues, and should be viewed as a building block.

A negotiator can actually expedite this productive stage of negotiations by introducing a written text document that reflects the outcome of the discussions. When such a text is presented to counterparts, it should be presented with the intent of inviting their feedback. Other negotiators may propose changes that do not alter the substance of the text but that make the document read better. These are obviously welcome changes and give your counterparts a hand in the crafting of the document. They see their words in the document and are more likely to support and sign an agreement that has their input and "fingerprint." Some proposed changes might be fundamental and go to the very substance of the negotiations. Even if the proposed change is unacceptable, it can be used as a platform for exploring other variants and options that may satisfy all parties.

It is useful to obtain signatures or initials on text documents and proposals that are agreed to confirm support. This can be done with the assurance that final agreement will depend on the satisfactory resolution of other issues not covered by the text. Besides establishing a record of what has actually been agreed, the act of signing or initialing interim agreements or building blocks helps to establish a "culture of agreement" and the feeling that progress is being made.

Drafting Durable Agreements

The following are the key elements that should be contained in an enforceable agreement.

1. Title—include suggestion of achievement in title (e.g. "Trade Agreement Between Chile and Brazil;" "Agreement on Reconciliation of Multilateral Environmental Agreements (MEAs) and Trade Agreements Between the United States and the European Union.")
2. Preamble—One or several paragraphs "media statement"—describes the achievement in layman's terms—designed to make it easy for media and public to understand significance and key elements of agreement.

3. Identification of parties.
4. Numbered paragraphs dealing with procedural and substantive agreements.
5. Implementation provisions.
6. Penalty provisions.
7. Conflict resolution provisions.
8. Signatures of the principal negotiators, date, and location.
9. Translator's declaration if a certified professional translator translated the document.

Skills to Employ at the Negotiating Table and Good Negotiating Habits

This section addresses good negotiating habits that help to facilitate good communications among the negotiators, create a positive atmosphere conducive to progress in the negotiations and facilitate the identification of win/win solutions to the negotiations.

ACTIVE LISTENING

Active listening is one of the most important skills to be developed as a negotiator. It sounds like common sense, but many negotiators do not make good listeners. Negotiators often become so convinced of the wisdom of their own arguments, and become so intent on convincing others of their particular point of view that they naturally tend to interpret what they hear through the prism of their own view of the issue, and to think others agree with them, when in reality they don't. A healthy degree of skepticism is therefore a healthy trait in a negotiator. When in doubt, ask to confirm what you thought you heard.

Another aspect of listening is to place information provided by other negotiators into the proper context. Is it information about the official position of the organization that the negotiator represents? Or, is it information about the underlying interests of the organization? Is it an argument why you or others should support the position the other negotiator is advocating? Is it a statement about the underlying beliefs of the organization your negotiating partner represents? Or perhaps is it information about the personal views of the negotiator? It obviously makes a huge difference whether a statement provides information about the organization's position, belief, or interest, and whether it is an official view or a personal view.

A few years ago the American representative to the Development Committee of UNCTAD made the statement that the United States did not believe in special and differential treatment as the right approach to economic development. Some delegates interpreted that statement as an indication that the United States would oppose S&D in the Doha Round, which was not what was said. The Ambassador did not say that it was the position of the United States to oppose the extension of S&D. A belief says something about a country's philosophical predisposition, but not what it intends to do on an issue.

How can we tell what the negotiator meant? We have to listen for the introductory comment. Does the negotiator say it is my country's "position" or does the negotiator say it my country's "belief"? Does the negotiator say that the country's objective is to expand opportunities for a particular group or avoid injury to another group, which are statements about "interests." In private conversations the negotiator may be even more direct in describing the interests they are seeking to satisfy. Does the negotiator say that others should agree with a particular proposition "because" it would accomplish a variety of wonderful objectives? The word "because" is a tip-off that what follows is a recitation of reasons why other parties should agree to the proposition being advocated. Those reasons do not say anything about the country's own objectives or practices.

The most confident negotiators use the art of active listening to enhance their understanding of their counterparts' interests. Active listening is more than just listening. Active listening includes the act of communicating to counterparts that you have heard what they said. By communicating understanding the negotiator is not accepting or acquiescing to the counterparts' proposal. By actively restating what the speaker has said, you communicate that you have indeed heard what was said.

ASKING QUESTIONS—INFORMATION IS POWER

Combined with the skill of active listening is the skill of asking. This may sound like a basic tenet of negotiations at any level, but many inexperienced negotiators use every opportunity to advance their proposals, their options, and their ultimatums at the table. By failing to use the negotiation setting as an opportunity to learn, a negotiator will remain uneducated about counterpart interests:

Asking for information or clarification conveys interest and a willingness to understand the other party's interests.

- Questions can draw information from counterparts. Information that has not been offered or volunteered by a counterpart in an opening or affirmative statement may be shared or revealed in response to a question.
- Questions and responses will contribute to building the information base for the negotiations. The broader and more complete the base of information, the better equipped a negotiator will be to fashion proposals, options, and solutions that can result in a successful outcome.

Examples of intentional "leading questions." Leading questions are those designed to get your counterpart talking/sharing information:

"How did you arrive at that position?"
"What is your proposal based upon? If we understand the basis of the proposal, we will be better equipped to share it with our superiors, home office, etc."
"What information did you rely upon to reach that conclusion? Would you share a copy with us?"
"Please explain further..."
The use of the single word "*Why*" can be a trigger to uncover underlying party interests...

Patience in the negotiating process can give a negotiator the upper hand in terms of command of information, finding out what is really important to counterparts, and determining areas where trade-offs or compromise might be appropriate.

SHARING INFORMATION

Sharing information goes against the grain in negotiations because we are taught that information is power. Yet a successful negotiation is one in which both parties are satisfied that their interests have been met and that their problems have been accommodated to the extend possible. The only way each negotiating partner can be creative in identifying negotiating outcomes that will achieve this result if both sides have a clear understanding of each other's interests and problems. This can be accomplished only through an effective exchange of information.

During the preliminary phase of building consensus on the launching of negotiations on services in the Uruguay Round, the author, who was the principal US trade official responsible for the services negotiations, had a critical conversation with a senior Indian official on India's basic concern about the launching of negotiations in services. The official pointed out that India faced a continuing large influx of workers from the countryside into the cities, and that the only sector in which enough jobs could be created was in services. Even if the liberalization of barriers to trade in services could be justified in terms of improved economic efficiency, India could not afford the social disruption this would create. The author pointed out that the United States was principally concerned about liberalizing business services, rather than the consumer services that provided the job opportunities for unskilled workers, and that India needed more efficient business services to increase its productivity in manufacturing. Moreover, India had un-employed university graduates that could find employment through the electronic export of their services should India liberalize its telecommunications regulations. An exchange of critical information thus led to a way for accommodating basic Indian as well as American interests.

USE OF SILENCE

One of the more powerful skills to be employed in the negotiation process is the tactical and timely use of *silence*. In many cultures, protracted silence creates a socially uncomfortable atmosphere. People will offer words and verbiage to fill the silence. Counterparts may offer further information, concessions, or compromises simply to fill the vacuum.

TAKING BREAKS FROM THE NEGOTIATING TABLE—"GOING TO THE BALCONY"

Getting away from the table can be one of the most important and underutilized tools to increase negotiating power. Negotiators, even when representing large organizations, often make com-mitments or concessions without having fully discussed them with teammates or superiors. "Going to the balcony" is a terminology intended to mean the physical act of leaving the negotiating area by going out on the balcony, or going to a balcony where one might still observe the proceedings but from a more distant perspective. Taking a break allows parties to achieve a number of important negotiating objectives, including:

- To review an oral or written proposal... "You have put a lot of time into developing this proposal, let us take a few minutes to review it... Or, depending on the weight and volume of what has been introduced by a counterpart, a negotiator may need a week or a month recess for economists, scientists, or other experts to review the proposal and the underlying data upon which it has been based.

- To develop or formulate a response. Thinking "on your feet" or in the heat of the moment may lead to unwise decisions and incomplete formulation of a counterproposal or response. Taking a break and leaving the room may allow a negotiator to work on the formulation of a response or counter-proposal that protects and advances the party's interests.

- To regain your composure. If a negotiator feels that the negotiation is moving too quickly or simply does not feel right about the pace of the negotiations, a break can be useful to evaluate what has transpired. A break can facilitate negotiations by allowing a counterpart to hear from teammates.

ORGANIZING BRAINSTORMING SESSIONS

An organized brainstorming session can serve a number of functions. First, it gets team members comfortable working with each other and empowers all team members to be contributors to the process.

In working with teammates or counterparts, there are some useful techniques that can be employed to elicit reactions, ideas, and counter-proposals. An error commonly made is for parties to advance a proposal as an ultimatum or as a non-negotiable, singular solution. By inviting a teammate or counterpart to evaluate a proposed option, the negotiator gives the counterpart the *power of choice*. They have the power to accept or reject the proposal. When a negotiating partner summarily rejects a proposal, ask them to offer a counterproposal, to offer a modification of the proposed option that would make it acceptable.

By employing this tactic, a negotiator can engage team members or counterparts constructively in the formulation of options for consideration, comment, and acceptance or refinement. A useful technique for eliciting a teammate's or counterpart's input is to ask: "What if we did X, or what if we agreed to do Y?" By posing the option in the form of a question, the counterpart's opinion is sought and their counterproposal or modification may lead to a viable option or proposal. Often, a minor modification that preserves the essence of your proposed option may work to gain the acceptance of a counterpart.

USE OF OBJECTIVE CRITERIA

Objective criteria represent a set of independent or external standards that are introduced to support the legitimacy or fairness of a party's proposed option or solution. Objective criteria can be viewed as factual information drawn from any number of sources. The introduction of objective criteria at the negotiating table is a form of submitting evidence in support of an argument or proposal. The goal is to persuade the other parties that a proposal is reasonable and consistent with findings of independent, neutral experts.

Objective criteria can also be understood as the introduction of fair standards. By relying on a non-party to the negotiations who in the normal course of business produces scientific or market studies, the parties can agree on the standards or norms that will serve as guideposts in the negotiation process.

A party may be skeptical that a certain proposal is fair. Objective outside criteria in support of a proposal will convey legitimacy that counterparts can use to persuade their constituencies or superiors.

Some examples of sources for objective criteria include:

● Market values.
● Prevailing wage rates.
● Industry standards and practices.
● Expert studies.
● Academic research and reports.
● Rules and regulations.
● Precedent decisions (decisions made by legal or authoritative bodies or similar types of issues or cases.

PRACTICING ROLE REVERSAL

Role reversal can be an invaluable tool in achieving a better understanding of the negotiations. Practice Role reversal. Have members of your own team play the role of counterparts. Insist that they assume the role by speaking in the first person. Ask them directly what are their concerns, goals and objectives, interests... What would work for them and why?

BUILDING NEGOTIATING MOMENTUM

In negotiations achieving agreement on some of the easier issues creates a good building block for tackling more difficult issues. Reaching agreement on anything creates a psychology of success, and as the negotiators reach agreement on more and more issues, they tend to become less hesitant to tackle the most difficult issues. By accumulating points of agreement, a good negotiator can create a negotiating momentum that pushes the negotiations forward.

LISTENING TO AND RECORDING ALL PROPOSED OPTIONS

In brainstorming sessions with teammates and with counterparts, it is important to record all proposed options. The use of charts or posted paper is an effective means as it will preserve the proposal for ongoing review and comment and create a record of the session.

Without agreeing or acquiescing to a proposed option that has been generated by a teammate or counterpart, you can gain valuable information and expose potential weaknesses by asking the contributor, "How did you arrive at that solution or proposal? What is it based upon? Is there a factual, scientific, or other objective basis for your proposed option?"

If the presenter can offer further evidence or criteria in support of their proposal (or if you can in response to a similar question, the information shared may be useful in winning support from constituents or superiors who may be skeptical. The further information or lack thereof can fortify or reduce the value of a proposed option.

CROSS-CULTURAL DYNAMICS, GENDER, AND LANGUAGE

International negotiations necessarily involve cross-cultural interactions that may affect the flow of a negotiation and the understanding of various parties to process, proposals, and agreements.

In the field of international trade law and practice, a *diplomatic culture* has developed that has served to minimize some of the barriers that cross-cultural dynamics may pose in business or other non-governmental negotiations. Diplomatic culture can be described as the universal culture of professional diplomats who often speak in a common language (English, French, Spanish) even if that language is not the diplomat's native language. Diplomats often maintain common habits associated with international diplomacy including Western dress, common educational backgrounds, and familiarity with procedures and protocols associated with international law or rule-making.

But even those who present themselves as part of this diplomatic culture may maintain strong cultural identification and habits with their native culture. Culture is manifest in many ways including orientation to time, decision-making process, formality of negotiation process, formality of decisions (oral agreement vs. written contract.), importance of age, language, preferences, and attitudes toward food, music, sports, body language, etc. A cultural issue that may affect the negotiation process is the difference in the role of men and women in various cultures. Gender dynamics may be of little importance or of profound significance depending upon the culture.

Language and the choice of language used in international negotiations is also an important variant in the potential success or failure of a negotiation process. Today, the diplomatic culture increasingly relies on English as the common language for inter-governmental negotiations. This may, of course, vary if all participants are south European, Latin American or from a Francophone country or the former Soviet Union. The important lesson to be learned with respect to language as a variant in international negotiations is that people possess varying degrees of fluency. If a person is not negotiating in their native language, the potential for misunderstanding increases.

Negotiators often are confused or misunderstand the intent of a counterpart negotiator even when negotiating in a shared common language. When negotiating with a party or parties who do not share a common language, the potential for misunderstanding increases. Even with skilled, professional interpreters, a literally accurate interpretation may not convey the intent or nuance of the speaker.

How can a negotiator be sure that his/her words are being understood as they are intended? Speaking slowly, rephrasing what the counterpart negotiator has said in the negotiator's own words, reviewing written text, and use of interpreters (oral) and translators (written) represent non-exclusive options to minimize error or misunderstanding.

DEALING WITH DIRTY TRICKS AND ULTIMATUMS

Most serious negotiators bring a level of sophistication and professionalism to the negotiating table, but there are always circumstances where a desperate or aggressive negotiator will employ dirty tricks, ultimatums, or intimidation.

The key to dealing with unprincipled negotiators is to *recognize and identify* the tactics being used. By being mindful of the types of tactics that are sometimes used, you can evaluate the impact that such tactics are having on the negotiation process and utilize one of the following techniques:

- Identify and focus on the tactic. Explain to the counterpart that you do not appreciate intimidation, abusive language, or ultimatums. You can also convey that you remain fully prepared to continue in a good faith negotiation but will not accept conduct that is disrespectful or designed to intimidate. In many instances, identification of the perceived tactic will result in a denial by the counterpart, but often you will realize a change in behavior as well. By clearly articulating what you perceive to be unacceptable behavior, this will change the atmosphere of the negotiation and registers that you will not succumb to such tactics.

- Utilize counter-tactics to counteract the behavior. In the face of an ultimatum (a "take-it-or leave-it" offer), you can request a break to review the offer. Return to the table to draw the party back into the negotiation by asking them how they arrived at that final offer. Use questions to draw the counterpart back into the game of a give and take negotiation.

- Make contact with the counterpart's superior. In the most egregious case of disrespectful, demeaning, or insulting attacks by a counterpart, indicate that you will not participate in a negotiation where such behavior is manifest. A party can refuse to continue in a negotiation where such tactics are employed and contact the offending official's superiors to request that the offending personality be replaced at the negotiating table before you will continue in the process.

- Demand respect for your team. By treating counterparts with a modicum of respect you can appropriately demand that respect be reciprocated.

Often, the tactics described above reflect the conduct of a highly emotional, defensive, and inexperienced negotiator. While such tactics may have worked in some instances, you need to make it clear that such conduct is unacceptable in the present negotiation.

BUILDING A REPUTATION

At the end of the day, a negotiator will be evaluated as fair or untrustworthy. If you gain a reputation as being unfair or unprincipled, this reputation will follow you and will be difficult to overcome. There is a difference between appearing tough but principled, and being unscrupulous and unprincipled. You build your reputation as a negotiator in large measure by your ability to follow through and implement commitments made during negotiations.

As discussed earlier, building rapport and a good working relationship with counterparts will generate long-term benefit. Remember, that you are dealing with people who have their own professional aspirations, honor, and pride. Often, the key ingredient in building a strong working relationship is to build a friendship away from the negotiating table. Sharing meals, gifts, and providing hospitality to negotiating partners who have journeyed to your city will translate into more productive work at the negotiating table. Your ability to reach out to the people at the table, regardless of the severity of conflict between principals, demonstrates a maturity and confidence that will win respect and help the parties to navigate the difficult terrain of the negotiation.

CREATING A WIN-WIN MENTALITY

Bilateral negotiations aimed at the mutual reduction of trade barriers take place in an overall win-win framework, but they inevitably involve gains for some domestic stakeholders such as exporters or domestic consumers of imported products, and losses for other stakeholders such as domestic producers of competitive products in each country. Negotiators on both sides are expected to maximize the gains and to minimize the losses for their side. While economists would argue that both sides gain, whatever the impact on winners and losers in each country, the political economic reality is that losers are often in a position to block outcomes that do not take into account their interests. While winners can always trump losers where the potential gains are large enough, it is useful in a democratic society to persuade losers that the outcome is just. This usually means accommodating them in some way, while persuading them that a successful negotiating outcome is in the interests of the country as a whole. A good negotiator is able to gain their support through a combination of offers and threats—an offer to make less of a cut in the trade barrier than might be possible if they acquiesce and a threat to ignore their interests if they choose to oppose the agreement actively.

Negotiations over the mutual reduction of trade barriers thus always involve hard bargaining, both at home and internationally. In light of the stakes for winners and losers, they inevitable take on a zero-sum mentality. Negotiators in such a situation must always remind themselves that the desired outcome is a win-win solution for both sides in the negotiations, consistent with an acceptable distribution of gains and losses among stakeholders. The role of the negotiator is to let the other side know what is required to achieve a successful outcome, both in terms of the expected gains for exporters and what would constitute unacceptable losses for import competing industries. Equipped with information about each side's needs, the two negotiators then have the task of identifying an outcome that will maximize the potential increase in trade, while meeting the domestic political requirements of each side.

The most important requirements for a successful outcome in such negotiations are a detailed analysis of the interests of stakeholders in both countries, and comprehensive consultations with affected stakeholders on desired and achievable results. Good information about stakeholder interests in the other country will strengthen a negotiator's hand in negotiations with counterparts, and provide the raw material for developing win-win solutions. Consultations with stakeholders will earn the negotiator the support of stakeholders when the negotiated agreement is tested politically at home.

Conclusion

Success in negotiations, whether on services or any other issue, depends not only on innate bargaining skills and on the power of the countries involved, but also on a detailed and comprehensive analysis of the issues, persuasive oral and written communication skills, and the ability to build alliances. These are skills that can be learned and mastered by any competent professional in the field.

Successful negotiations follow certain guidelines that create an atmosphere of trust conducive to a search for win-win solutions and an orderly sequence for addressing the full range of outstanding issues in a negotiation. When these guidelines are followed by the participants in a negotiation, they create a positive feed-back loop that adds a dynamic momentum to the negotiating process.

The challenges involved in services negotiations are great, because barriers to trade in services are enmeshed in domestic regulations. In services an orderly process for sorting out the issues is therefore especially important, because such negotiations inevitably touch on issues considered the sovereign prerogative of any national government to protect its consumers and the smooth functioning of its domestic economy.

Notwithstanding the challenges, negotiations on services have become extremely important for economic growth because the efficiency of all economic activity and the competitiveness of a country's manufacturing sector in the globalized, information-technology based economy of today depends on the efficiency of a country's services sector.

Annex 1

CASE ILLUSTRATING USE OF STRATEGY IN NEGOTIATIONS[6]

By the time the U.S. began to seriously address the issue of the OECD Study on services, the importance of launching negotiations on services had risen very considerably in U.S. priorities because a high exchange rate for the dollar had put the whole manufacturing sector in the United States on the defensive and the United States needed to use the services industries, counting for over 60 per cent of the economy, to build political support for the launching of a new round of multilateral trade negotiations in the GATT. Some elements of the strategy concerned the orientation and management of the study, and other elements concerned parallel actions outside the OECD. While the U.S. focused its efforts during the initial phase of the study on developed counties, it subsequently extended its efforts to developing countries.

Specifically, the strategy consisted of

- Using the study to identify real trade problems in services and to show that these trade problems were similar in kind to many barriers to trade in goods that had been successfully addressed in trade negotiations.

- Working with the private sector in the United States to identify services industries in other countries that had real interests in expanding trade opportunities abroad and could be persuaded to communicate those interests to their respective governments.

- Demonstrating the practicality of using traditional trade negotiating techniques and trade rules to address trade problems in services by: (a) using bilateral trade discussions to address a few obvious trade barriers in individual services and using the leverage provided by mutual problem solving negotiations in trade to negotiate trade expanding modifications of regulatory measures; and (b) adding services to the agenda of bilateral free trade area negotiations with Canada and Israel, and negotiating model provisions for trade in services in these agreement, with an eye to their possible adoption in subsequent multilateral negotiations.

- Establishing the legitimacy of negotiations on trade in services by: (a) working with economists from a representative group of countries on the applicability of traditional trade theories to trade in services and the economic benefits that could be derived; and (b) organizing weekend conferences of key opinion leaders from key countries to discuss the scope and

---

[6] The U.S. negotiating effort was led by the author. For detailed accounts of the implementation of the strategy see Aronson (1986), Drake and Nicolaïdis (1992), and Feketekuty (1988).

strategic role of services and trade in services in the new world economy driven by globalization and information technologies.

Building a global consensus on the launching of negotiation on trade in services was something beyond the normal challenges faced by trade negotiators. It called for an extra level of effort, but at the same time the number of people directly involved and the resources that were used were quite modest. While the United States had an advantage in terms of its economic weight in the global economy, many of the techniques that were used to build the global consensus can be applied by other countries to advance their interests on issues that potentially concern a wide range of countries.

Can any country develop the means for implementing a good strategy? Can a country with limited means mobilize enough resources to develop wide support outside the negotiating room for its desired negotiating outcome? Resources obviously do make a difference, and a small country will find it more difficult to mobilize support for a global undertaking, but it is not impossible. There are many examples where even one individual was able to move the world. A few talented individuals can devise and implement successful strategies for mobilizing stakeholders and countries with similar interests, if they have the requisite knowledge and skills. Most countries have charismatic, knowledgeable and energetic individuals who have the requisite skills to provide leadership on a global level. Such individuals are often found in small countries, since individuals in small countries may learn from an early age how to overcome the lack of power through the energetic application of knowledge and skill. Development of the right alliances can empower even small countries to play an important role, as was demonstrated by the Cairns Group of small and large agricultural exporting countries, who banded together during the Uruguay Round negotiations to achieve a break through on agriculture.

Annex 2

A FORMULA COMMITMENTS IN SERVICES: THE FINANCIAL SERVICES UNDERSTANDING[7]

The following case illustrates the ability of some countries to say no, while working out an accommodation that met some key requirements of another group of countries.

Borrowing from the growing practice in the GATT for reducing tariffs, the services negotiators grappled with how "formula" obligations, which would entail the same level of obligations to market access and national treatment, might be achieved in the Uruguay Round. This posed an enormous challenge, since no numerical equivalent of protection could possibly be arrived at in the context of services. In general, attaining a level of market access and national treatment that represented across-the-board liberalization was a very difficult proposition, as many countries viewed the Uruguay Round as merely the initial stage of putting together a framework of rules and disciplines, followed by subsequent rounds of negotiations that would address market access and national treatment obligations in a more serious way.

Financial services negotiators from OECD countries had a different view. They were determined to develop a formula of market access obligations that would become part of the GATS

---

[7] This case was prepared by Richard Self, who served as the U.S. negotiator of the GATS Agreement.

itself, in the form of an annex. To a certain extent, the bond among this group of negotiators was a bureaucratic one, in that it represented the particular agenda of Finance ministries who viewed trade agreements that covered financial services with skepticism. As the framework of the GATS slowly evolved, the Finance representatives inventoried those elements that represented digressions from the objective of liberal trade, from the flexibilities in the GATS for developing countries, the prudential exception available to finance regulators, and the asymmetries created by the MFN rule that would place more burdensome obligations on more liberal regimes compared to those that largely excluded foreign competition. This skepticism was shared largely by interested financial services companies in these countries, in particular the United States, who saw the MFN obligation as nothing more than a "free ride" for countries with protected markets which could exploit the more open markets through this rule.

In response to these concerns, the OECD financial services negotiators proposed an annex to the GATS that would obligate each WTO member to assume a threshold of liberalization in financial services. For instance, every country would assume the obligation to the cross-border provision of reinsurance, something that most regulators permitted at the time. Other obligations included the freedom to provide financial information and to assure national treatment in the placement of government-agency deposits in banking institutions. There is some question whether the proponents of the financial-services formula saw any chance of its adoption under the rule of consensus that prevails at the WTO. However, its rejection could have set the stage for an end to their participation in the Uruguay Round.

Indeed, the formula met predictable opposition from developing country members, who opposed such provisions as a digression from the structure established for making commitments for all services, which were to be undertaken on a request-and-offer basis, taking into account the particularities of the regulatory system of each country. Ambassador David Hawes of Australia, who at the time presided over the services negotiations, faced a dilemma. It was clear that there was no consensus for the financial-services formula proposed by most of the OECD countries. At the same time, the complete rejection of this proposal, which had generated considerable support in the powerful world of finance ministries and their constituents, threatened to end the involvement of a group of very important players in the world of trade. Hawes came up with a solution that preserved the annex of commitments through an "Understanding," which took the form of an optional approach for scheduling commitments by WTO members who chose to do so. Thus, the elements of the proposal were retained as an attachment to the GATS, but they did not constitute obligations. Rather, they were subject to negotiations among WTO members. Flexibility was allowed for the assumption of some parts of the Understanding, allowing for the exclusion of others. The Financial Services Understanding became part of the "Draft Final Act" of 1991, which constituted a proposal by the Director General of the GATT to its members for their consideration as the Uruguay Round legal text. With only a few exceptions, The Draft Final Act, with its Financial Services Understanding, became the GATS as it is known today.

The Understanding is the basis on which all OECD countries inscribed commitments in financial services. No developing country chose to make commitments under this provision, despite laborious efforts by OECD financial services negotiators to persuade them to do so. In the final analysis, the greatest significance of the Understanding is that it kept Finance Ministries of industrialized countries engaged in the Uruguay Round, albeit with different levels of enthusiasm. While it can never be established with certainty that the outright rejection of the "formula" liberalization proposal would have brought a large-scale desertion from the process by some of the critical players, Hawes' ability to preserve its elements in some form helped neutralize their position, by giving their proposal a measure of credence in the GATS.

Annex 3

NEGOTIATING THE NORTH–SOUTH DEAL IN THE GATS NEGOTIATIONS[8]

In the early stages of the Uruguay Round, there was a fundamental difference of opinion between developed and developing countries over the inclusion of investment as part of any services framework that would emerge. Developing countries, led largely by India, were concerned about the inclusion of services in the GATT because of this issue alone, fearing it would be a precursor of a larger agreement on investment in the GATT. At this pre-Internet stage of the negotiations, the ability to provide services in other countries rested largely on the ability to invest—what was later to be called a "commercial presence"—in the host country. There were both competitive and regulatory reasons for this. To give one obvious example, most financial services from abroad were (and are) prohibited unless they were provided through a branch or a subsidiary of the foreign services supplier. Clearly, any agreement that did not include investment was going to have no value at all, and yet there was considerable opposition by developing countries to the inclusion of investment as a matter of general principle.

The issue came to a head at the mid-term Ministerial in Montreal in December 1988. Prior to the Montreal meeting, services negotiators attempted to forge a common text that would reflect a consensus of views among the participants. This proved difficult, especially in light of the differences over the matter of investment in services. Indeed, despite considerable efforts leading up to the Montreal meeting, negotiators had a text that contained over 100 brackets.

Negotiators managed to bridge their differences and reach an agreed text through intensive negotiations at Montreal by addressing specific issues of interest to developing countries, again with India completely in the lead, while incorporating the investment principle. The first was to acknowledge that the temporary entry of natural persons—what was to become the fourth mode of supply—had equal footing with that of commercial presence. While the four modes of supplying services under GATS were established subsequent to the Montreal meeting, the conceptual basis for giving temporary entry and establishment equal footing in a negotiating context was agreed at Montreal.

In addition, developing countries wanted numerous provisions in the services agreement to reflect the special needs of developing countries. As their leader, Ambassador Shurang Shukla of India put it, development should "permeate" the framework. Indeed, many of the bracketed provisions in the draft text contained various references to developing countries. The United States, in particular, found these references too numerous to be acceptable. The final text that emerged from Montreal certainly contained its share of development-related provisions, which survived in GATS Articles IV and XIX. Nonetheless, the developing countries accepted a

---

[8] This case example was provided by Richard Self, who served as the U.S. Negotiator of the GATS Agreement.

reduction in the amount of provisions relating to development concerns at the Montreal gathering. In a showdown at the level of Ministers, the Indians abandoned a provision that would have duplicated the GATT's Enabling Clause for services, and this proved to be the final breakthrough that established consensus at Montreal.

Of course, the drafting of the GATS itself was still in its infancy, but the Montreal meeting was an important turning point in resolving fundamental issues of interest to both developed and developing countries. To a large extent, it represented the abandonment of services as strictly a North/South issue, as it had been for the first two years of the Uruguay Round. Thereafter, the negotiating process was less factionalized, and there was little debate over the inclusion of investment and the temporary entry of natural persons in the final agreement.

Box A.1. The Experience of Brazil in Trade in Services Negotiations

Flávio Marega[*]

Since the end of the Uruguay Round and with the creation of the World Trade Organization (WTO) in January 1995, Brazil has come a long way in trade in services negotiations. For a developing country like Brazil, the negotiation of the General Agreement on Trade in Services (GATS) was, in itself, a mixture of academic exercise and challenge of putting together new definitions, concepts, and expressions, created by the negotiators in Geneva, with regard to this "new form" of trade. Together with India, Egypt, Argentina, and some other developing countries, Brazil has played an important role in establishing the text of the GATS as it stands today, especially with regard to the concepts related to the specific concerns of developing countries such as: progressive liberalization, increasing participation of developing countries, Annex on Movement of Natural Persons, etc.

Together with the Trade-Related Aspects of Intellectual Property Rights (TRIPS), the trade in services agreement negotiated during the Uruguay Round became known as a new issue in trade. Indeed, this area was completely new for Brazil and Brazilian negotiators at the time. The GATS was truly an exercise of breaking new ground in the multilateral trading system. As a matter of fact, my generation was the first one to get to know and to become more familiar with the new concepts and expressions that today are included in the GATS, such as: modes of supply, domestic regulation, measures, schedules of specific commitments, which are much less tangible, so to say, compared to those related to trade in goods included in the General Agreement on Tariffs and Trade (GATT). As a result of that exercise of breaking new ground in the multilateral trading system, when the WTO came into force in January 1995, the work of the GATS negotiators had not ended. On the contrary, the work had only just begun, because we had to go back to our countries and start to explain to Government officials, private sector, and the academia about the content of this new agreement.

Currently, more than ten years after the creation of the WTO, the GATS has become well known in most specialized sectors in Brazil. Government officials involved with trade negotiations are quite familiar with the main features of the GATS. The private sector realizes that the existing multilateral rules are no longer restricted to trade in goods. And there are many academic studies about the GATS in Brazilian universities, especially focused on the perspective on how this "new form" of trade operates. But there are three main challenges that Brazilian services negotiators continue to face in the ongoing Doha Round negotiations: (1) regulatory sectoral regimes are still in the making; (2) the need to craft schedules of specific commitments that truly reflect the current regulatory regime in Brazil; and (3) the lack of statistics on trade in services as defined by GATS, so as to better identify "imports" and "exports" of Brazilian services.

Regulatory Sectoral Regimes in the Making

It is widely recognized that the privatization of the telecom sector in Brazil was a success story. From being a state monopoly until the early 1990s, the telecom sector in Brazil has become a vibrant and competitive private initiative, which includes the participation of many foreign services suppliers. However, there are other important sectors that are still undergoing regulatory changes (financial services, energy, postal, and sanitation services, just to give a few examples). First, this situation will require a strong and cooperative relationship between the Brazilian executive and legislative branches, in order to pass legislation in the Congress that is consistent with Brazil's multilateral commitments. Second, there must be a continuous effort by Brazilian officials to make sure that new legislation is not at odds with GATS and other international obligations on trade in services, adopted by Brazil.

Preparation of the Schedule of Specific Commitments that Truly Reflects the Current Regulatory Regime in the Country

As a consequence of regulatory sectoral regimes in the making, an ongoing challenge to Brazilian services negotiators is how to correctly craft our schedule of specific commitments, so as to reflect the current legal framework that exists in the country. With the aim of helping with this important task of preparing Brazil's schedule of specific commitments, in 2001, the Brazilian Government decided to create the Interministerial Group on Trade in Services (GICI-SV). The GICI-SV congregates all federal regulatory agencies and government bodies that regulate services, together with the National Confederation of Industries (CNI) and some State Federations of services suppliers. The GICI-SV has two main functions: (1) report on advances in negotiations (WTO, Free Trade Area of the Americas— FTAA, MERCOSUR-EU Free Trade Agreement, etc.); and (2) help with the preparation of Brazil's schedule of specific commitments.

Lack of Statistics on Trade in Services as Defined by GATS

The third challenge faced by Brazilian negotiators is related to the lack of reliable statistics on trade in services. The methodology for trade in services currently used by the Brazilian Central Bank (BACEN) is based on the Manual on Balance of Payments of the International Monetary Fund (IMF). This methodology is clearly insufficient when it comes to providing Brazilian negotiators with precise information on "imports" and "exports" of services, due to its high level of aggregate data. Therefore, the third challenge faced by Brazil and Brazilian negotiators is related to the need of organizing statistics on trade in services as defined by GATS (modes of supply and sectors/sub-sectors). In 2002, the Brazilian Government created an interministerial group (with representatives from the BACEN, the Ministry of Industry, Trade and Development, the Ministry of Foreign Relations and the Institute of Applied Economic Research—IPEA) to build a national statistics system on trade in services. Hopefully, the new methodology to be adopted by BACEN will allow Brazilian trade negotiators to have more accurate information about "imports" and "exports" of services and, therefore, help with market access negotiations in the WTO, FTAA, MERCOSUR-EU Free Trade Agreement, etc.)

In addition to the efforts to enhance statistics on trade in services (and consequently the capabilities of Brazilian negotiators), since 2002, the Ministry of Foreign Relations (responsible for trade negotiations) and the Ministry of Industry, Trade and Development have been undertaking a joint effort to identify existing market-access and national treatment restrictions/limitations in services offers submitted by the most important WTO Members in the Doha Round market-access negotiations. The goal of this joint work is to provide Brazilian negotiators with a complete overview of the restrictions to trade in services that still exist in the markets of WTO Members.

Note: * The author has been a trade in services negotiator for Brazil covering: WTO/GATS extended negotiations in telecommunications, financial, and maritime services (1995–6), MERCOSUR (1996–7), FTAA and MERCOSUR-EU Free Trade Agreement (2001–2).

References

Aronson, J. 1986. "Negotiating to Launch Negotiations: Getting Trade in Services Onto the GATT Agenda." Pew Program in Case Teaching and Writing in International Affairs, University of Pittsburgh.

Drake, W. J. and K. Nicolaidis. 1992. "Epistemic Communities and International Policy Coordination." *International Organization* 45 (Winter).

Feketekuty, G. 1988. *International Trade in Services: An Overview and Blueprint for Negotiations.* Cambridge, MA: Ballinger for The American Enterprise Institute.

Feketekuty, Geza. 2001. *A Commercial Diplomat's Brief Guide To Analyzing A Trade Policy Issue.* Arlington, VA: Institute for Trade and Commercial Diplomacy. Available at: www.commercialdiplomacy.org

Feketekuty, G. and C. Morton. 2001. *Analyzing and Managing the Politics of Trade.* Arlington, VA: Institute for Trade and Commercial Diplomacy. Available at: www.commercialdiplomacy.org

Fisher, R. and W. Ury. 1991. *Getting to Yes: Negotiating Agreement without Giving In.* London: Penguin Books.

Fisher, R. and D. Ertel. 1995. *Getting Ready to Negotiate: The Getting to Yes Workbook.* London: Penguin Books.

Monning, W. and G. Feketekuty. 2002. *International Trade Negotiations: A Training Manual.* Arlington, VA: Institute for Trade and Commercial Diplomacy. Available at www.commercialdiplomacy.org

INDEX

Abidjan 385
ABN Amro Bank 330
ABSs (asset-backed securitizations) 333
abusive language 583
academic experts 557, 568
   foreign 569
access charges 348, 349, 350
accidents 375
   work-related 522
accountability 271
accountancy sector 67, 242
   barriers 204
   nationality/residency requirements 205
   restrictiveness indexes 205
accounting requirements/rates 297, 414
Accra 425
acquisition 228, 230
adjustment costs 233, 380, 390
   aggregate, regulatory convergence 239
   distribution of 370
   effects on 16–17
   managing 383
   market access opportunities that ease 360
   need to take into account 5
   potential of 4
   sectors that help reduce 376
   undue 354
Adlung, R. 48 n., 52 n., 59 n., 61 n., 64 n., 65 n.,
   68 n., 71 n., 72 n., 76 n., 364, 372, 374,
   437 n.
administrative capacity 257, 474
administrative costs 112
ADSL (Asymmetric Digital Subscriber Line)
   systems 395, 397, 400
advisory bodies 550
AFAS (ASEAN Framework Agreement on
   Services) 245, 247
affiliates 151
   exchanges between 142
   locally established 147
   modeling of links between parents and 201–2
   ultimate beneficial owner of 150
   see also foreign affiliates
Africa:
   countries bound to introduce competition 61
   financial sectors 15, 300, 304, 308, 309
   openness to foreign entry 309
   trucking sector 368

   see also COMESA; Sub-Saharan Africa; *also under*
      various country names, e.g. Kenya; Lesotho;
      Malawi; Nigeria; Senegal; South Africa;
      Uganda; Zimbabwe
after-sales service 357
Agency for International Development (US) 552
agglomeration 94, 101
   effects of 87, 96–7
Agricultural Bank of China 332
agriculture 97, 503, 566, 587
   far-reaching agreement 564
   protectionist policies 4
   seasonal workers 513
"aid-for-trade" agenda 22, 24, 28–30
Air Asia 369
air-traffic rights 238
air transport 52–3, 112, 143, 185, 192, 237, 360, 362,
   365, 369, 374, 384
   arrangements to respond to anti-competitive
      behavior 374
   cargo 258
   complication to treatment in GATS 366
   costs of provision between countries 367
   coverage in GATS 366
   economies of scale and scope a feature of 341
   entry of low-cost carriers into markets 369
   exceptions to MFN in GATS 365
   flying operations exempted from coverage in
      GATS 362
   important exemptions that remain to be negotiated
      or reviewed in 359
   insurance 310
   international 193, 206, 212
   liberalization of 81
   preferential quotas 226
   provision to consumers of one country when they
      buy tickets in foreign country 360
   quarantine regulation of international
      trade in 366
aircraft repair and maintenance 366
airfares 213
airline markets 208
airlines:
   capacity offered from third countries 366
   costs of running 340
   exclusion of foreign carriers 366
   foreign 367, 372
   provision of services 346

airlines: (*cont.*)
   quantitative limitations on foreign ownership 255
   quotas 366
airports:
   congested, landing rights at 372
   core services 346
   incumbents dominate access to 372
Alexander, I. 17
Allianz 328
allocation of resources:
   existence or removal of barriers affect 200
   global 22 n.
   scarce 342, 372
allocative efficiency 341, 346
   "first best" pricing to ensure 348
   need for 349
allocative inefficiency 339
Amazon 88
ambulance services 447 n.
American Airlines 419
American Express 328
Americas 212, 213
   see also FTAA
Andean Community 165, 249 n., 255, 256, 269 n.
   Decisions: (439) 239 n., 254 n., 326 n.; (510) 270 n.
Anderson, J. E. 214
Ansett 208
Antigua 473, 535
anti-competitive practices 214, 352, 353, 374, 409
   competition policy deals with 462
   control of 463
   possibilities for 427
   procurement policies to address 464
   regulation designed to stop 415
anti-corruption plans 391
ANZCERTA (Australia-New Zealand Closer Economic
      Relations Trade Agreement) 21, 242, 245, 257,
      258
   Services Protocol 258 n.
APEC (Asia-Pacific Economic Cooperation) 79, 181,
      185, 187, 256, 257
   indexes compiled from 205
Apple iTunes 465
arable land 88
Araujo, M. C. 351
arbitration 265, 266, 267
architectural services 205
Argentina 590
   banks liquidated 312 n.
   port reform 368–9
   privatization of electricity distribution 17
   restrictiveness index scores 191
   significant foreign presence 294, 298
Aronson, J. 542 n.
Aronson, J. 586 n.

ASEAN (Association of Southeast Asian Nations) 21,
      24, 37, 274–8, 258
   airlines compete on routes outside own region 367
   liberalizing trade in the region 222
   see also AFAS
ASEAN/AFTA 267
Asia 421
   financial crisis (1997) 426 n., 428
   openness to foreign entry 309
   phase-in commitments to telecom liberalization 61
   restricted in banking services 204
   telecom markets with competition 17
Asia Financial Holding 328
Asia-Pacific countries 190, 212, 213
   see also APEC
Asian Development Bank 328
asset management 259, 290, 327
assets 150, 229
   bank 300
   complementary 414 n.
   disposal of 228
   financial 289
   firm-specific 94, 95–6
   higher-risk 299
   intangible 94, 95–6
   limitations on total value of 292
   little information provided on 290
   low-risk 301
   non-produced, non-financial 145
   specialized 95
   value of 57
assimilation 480, 511
asymmetric costs 99
asymmetric information 68, 104, 112, 114, 231, 491,
      492
   financial institutions characterized by 307
   regulatory requirements and licensing regimes
      respond to 226
   response to problems of 117
AT&T 414 n.
ATMs (automatic teller machines) 303, 315, 432
au pair workers 513
auctions 108, 109, 352 n., 412
   competitive 113, 117, 304
   global 228
audio capabilities 464
audio-visual activities/services 145, 238, 259
   preferential quotas 226
audit 255
Australia 50, 416, 568, 588
   airlines 208
   barriers on accountancy services 204
   foreign index score 190
   FTA between US and 238 n., 270, 319, 324, 326 n.
   impediments in financial services 204

margins 200
ownership of New Zealand banks 300
quantitative restrictions 107
see also ANZCERTA; Cairns Group; SAA
Australia-New Zealand Closer Economic Relations
    Agreement 266 n., 267
Australian Productivity Commission 178 n., 179, 205,
    206, 215 n., 352
Austria 205, 211
authentication 469
autonomy loss 294
"averaging" problems 267
aviation-related activities 258

BACEN (Brazilian Central Bank) 591
Bach, D. 465 n.
Bach, S. 475
"back office" activities 367
backbone carriers 422 n.
backsliding countries 255
Baekert, G. 295 n.
Bahamas 535
Bahrain 309
balance of payments 437
    difficulties 70, 295
    severe crisis 294
    see also BOP
Baldwin, R. E. 492
Bamako 385
bandwidth 397, 398
    large, for short distances 399
    switching capacity 392
Bangalore 419
Bangkok 303
Bangladesh 301
Bank of America 328
Bank of Communications (China) 327, 328
Bank of East Asia 329, 330
Bank of Japan 162 n.
Bank of Korea 15
Bank of Tokyo-Mitsubishi UFJ 330
Bank Supervisory Law (China) 327
Bankers' Association 551
bankruptcy 353
banks 289, 319–24
    commitments on acceptance of deposits and
        lending 309
    cost-cutting 296
    cost of recapitalization programs 299
    discretionary licensing based on economic
        needs 310
    foreign affiliates of 297
    foreign participation in 311
    inefficient or otherwise handicapped 312
    international transactions 179

Internet 469 n.
language requirement for board members 59
larger and better-known, heavy indebtedness 15
liquidated 312 n.
multilateral development 552
national private 298
preferential treatment of 252
reserve requirements 293
restrictions on 189, 190, 204, 209, 226
restructuring of 15
savings 301
shareholding 329
state-owned 15, 290–1
under-provision in rural areas 299
use of funds raised in domestic market to undertake
    external lending 299
see also central banks; foreign banks
Barbados 6, 9, 419, 535, 536
Barbuda 473, 535
bargaining power 234, 312, 565
    limited 24
    unequal 77
Barlow, J. P. 469 n.
barriers 12, 61, 96, 113–14, 177, 444, 543, 545
    agricultural 566
    analysis of 103, 105, 126
    avoiding natural monopoly elements from
        becoming 359
    best addressed through problem-solving
        negotiations 544
    capital outflow 299
    certification requirements can serve as 117
    characteristics of 178–83
    common market free of 254 n.
    common types of 104, 105
    complete absence of information about size of 511
    created by existing regulatory provisions 573
    cultural 487
    differences taken to be indicative of 197
    discriminatory 119
    dismantling of 365
    e-commerce expansion 468
    effects of 85, 195
    elimination of 4, 19, 29, 32, 97, 354
    explicit 4, 26, 32
    export 3
    external 30, 261, 264, 266, 267
    FDI 104
    foreign, information about 554
    formal 272
    frequency measures of 170
    FTA participating countries permitted to raise 263
    identifying and measuring 84
    implications of, and rationale for 80
    implicit 214

barriers (*cont.*)
  import 563
  importance of information about size of 506
  international services transactions 3, 35–6, 169–220
  "invisible" 406
  key transport sectors 81
  labor mobility 104, 487–9
  legal 487
  legislative 342
  legitimized 30
  linguistic 487
  major 104, 408
  market-access 373, 466, 527
  measurement of 183–5
  measures not ideally suited for documenting 185
  mutual liberalization of 566
  policy 3
  preferential liberalization of 229
  problem as a means to raise output 112
  producers stand to gain from 127
  production distortion induced by 106
  providers can respond by finding alternative
      modes 125
  purpose of 111
  quantitative 60, 81
  reducing the number of foreign products 123–4
  reduction of 10, 103, 542, 585
  regulatory 81, 98, 227, 342, 354, 556, 573
  removal of 9, 200, 215, 216, 217, 228, 307, 309, 341,
      378
  severe 57
  significant 372
  small firms interested in export-oriented
      growth 411
  stable, low 527
  technical 247 n.
  trade and investment 261, 262
  transparency of 305
  wide variety of 107
  see also entry barriers; NTBs
Barth, J. 344
basic telecommunications 28, 238
  financial markets generally much more competitive
      than those in 306–7
  conditions governing access to and use of 69
  extended negotiations on 56 n., 72 n.
  far-reaching liberalization in 259
  frequency measures for 204
  impact of policy reform on sectoral
      performance 201
  independent regulators for 19
  low teledensity or service rationing 16
  negotiations in 232
  networks 69
Basle accords (1988) 232–3, 329

BATNA (Best Alternative to an Agreement)
      concept 564
Bayraktar, Nihal 335 n.
BCCI (Bank of Credit and Commerce
      International) 299
BD3 (*OECD Benchmark Definition of FDI,* third
      edition) 147
Beardsley, S. 463 n.
beepers 430
Beesley, M. 350 n.
Beine, M. 509
Belgium restrictiveness 205
Belize 535
Bell South 423
benchmarks 67, 104, 105, 255, 345, 377, 415
  free trade 197
  international 409
  mobile termination fees 417
  tariff equivalent 192
  theoretical 184
  world levels 369
Benkley, Y. 460 n.
Berger, A. N. 296 n.
best practice 373
  international 255, 297, 315
Bettcher, D. 437 n.
Beviglia-Zampetti, A. 243 n., 251 n.
Bhagwati, J. N. 89, 109
Bhattasali, D. 327
bilateral agreements 31, 64, 270, 516, 543
  elaborate structure of 366
  foreign firms excluded from 514
  international air services regulated by 208
  relatively successful 79
  since BTA 409
  work programs based upon 513
bilateral air service arrangements 185
bilateral negotiations 77, 400, 529, 543, 547, 548,
      560, 586
  more formal 545
  problem-solving 545
  tactic used in 564
bilateral systems 53
bilateral trade 197 n.
  data 210
  flows 338
billing systems:
  customized 395
  less expensive approaches 398 n.
binding arbitration 265, 266, 267
BIS (Bank for International Settlements) 293
BITs (bilateral investment treaties) 247, 380
BOC (Bank of China) 328
Bogotá 375
Bohai Bank 328, 329

Bolivia 351
bonds 332–3
 selling 290
boom and recession 531
BOP (IMF Balance of Payments) statistics 6, 141,
  147 n., 162 n., 164, 508 n.
 allocation of items to modes of supply 146
 international dissemination of 159
 trade in services data availability and
  dissemination 157–9
 transactions recorded in 151 n.
 see also BPM5; EBOPS
border integrity 520
border workers 155
Borjas, G. J. 506
Bosworth, M. 192 n., 253 n.
Botswana 391
bottleneck facilities 339, 348–52
 access regime to endure access to 352
 competition upstream of 347
 flexibility to manage 341
 monopolist owns 343
bottom-up approach 54, 72, 253
Boylaud, O. 206
*BPM5 (IMF Balance of Payments Manual, 5th
  Edition)* 139, 140, 145–6, 152 n., 153, 162,
  165, 591
 EBOPS consistent with 142, 143, 144, 155
 export statistics of a number of major
  components 158
 measurement of FDI within 147
 number of countries reporting supplementary
  items 163–4
 principles and framework 157
brain drain 11, 31, 506, 525, 528
 beneficial 507
brainstorming sessions 568, 581, 582
Brazil 313, 373, 590–1
 case-by-case authorization requirement 310
 discrimination 191, 205
 exports 9
 foreign index score 190–1
 foreign ownership 300
 legislation that favors open-source solutions 464
 significant negotiating leverage 24
 tariff equivalent for business/financial services 197
 success in opening up to foreign firms 294
 trade in services negotiations 45
Breining, C. 524, 526 n.
Bressie, K. 56 n.
BRI (Bank Rakyat Indonesia) 301
Britain, *see* United Kingdom
broadband 394, 397, 408, 409
 experiments with data delivery 399
 leading edge users of 396

provision of networking for data 398
 residential networks 395, 427
 service providers 352 n.
 small businesses 395
 wireline access 427
broadcasting 122, 399
 foreign 107, 226
 regulatory system for specialized networks 397
brokerages 290
Bronckers, M. C. E. J. 60 n.
Brook Cowen, P. 345
Brown, D. 201, 202, 215, 217
BTA (Basic Telecommunications Agreement 1997) 40,
  204, 260, 389, 392–5, 398, 401–3, 415, 418, 419,
  421, 423, 425, 470, 548, 564
 ability to phase out clearly implicit in 409
 central feature of 402
 commitment on voice services 406
 demands for more market opening as part of 426
 existing market-access commitments under 421
 help to clarify the meaning of commitments 410
 hotspot for negotiations 399
 market access commitments of OECD countries
  in 423
 regulatory principles 412, 413
 significant implications for commitments 397
 world capital markets and foreign investors 413
Buenos Aires 368
build-out 412
 faster 411
 slowing 414
building regulations 67
Bulgaria 310, 313
bulletin boards 464
bundling of services 371
burden-sharing 64
Bureau of Economic Analysis (US) 162 n.
bureaucratic measures 107
Burt, T. 465 n.
Burundi 447 n.
buses 375, 378
Bush, George W. 381
business cycle 198
business models 465
business services 146, 155, 158, 197, 364
 FDI restrictions 187
 outsourcing 77
business trips 357
business visitors 153, 270, 513

cable-modem networks 397, 400
cable systems 433
Cable & Wireless 423 n.
cabotage 192, 210, 365
Cairns Group 216, 312 n., 564, 569, 587

California 29
  electricity 81, 353
  law 467
  regulatory failure 352
call centers 87, 88
"calling party pays" system 416
Cameroon 425
Canada 31, 79, 93, 447 n., 531
  childcare services 87
  domestic index score 191
  foreign index score 191
  preferential treatment of banks 252
  quantitative restrictions 107
  residents temporarily working abroad from 483
  scoring system designed to pick up most able
     migrants 489
  US resident permitted to drive in 120
  welfare effects 216, 217
  see also GAAP; NAFTA
Canada-Chile FTA 256, 257, 258
Canada-US FTA 246 n., 266 n., 534, 586
Canadian Economic Development Agency 552
Cancun Ministerial Conference (2003) 73, 74, 473
capacity:
  backbone 422
  building 376–7, 444
  more rapid expansion of 419
capacity constraint 367
capital 311
  abroad 92
  abundance of labor relative to 88
  additional, foreign banks call upon parents for 297–8
  allocation of 181, 296
  assumed to be immobile 89
  costs of 95
  countries that import 217
  countries that lose 216
  demand for 538
  depreciation of 229
  discriminatory restrictions on movement of 225
  endowments of 527, 530
  financial, access to 344
  firm-specific 229
  foreign entry allowed to access new sources of 299
  insurance industry plays significant role in
     mobilizing 301
  international 215, 298
  investing 370
  monopolistically competitive firms employ 215
  payment to, fixed 377
  provision of 141
  replaced with cheaper skilled labor 503
  restrictions on transactions 70
  see also foreign capital; returns to capital; also
     under following headings prefixed "capital"

capital account 294
  opening 293
  removal of restrictions 294
  restrictions on 294, 295 n.
capital accumulation 229
  increased incentive 217
capital adequacy requirements 293 n.
capital constraint 17, 368
capital controls 554
capital costs 357 n.
capital flows 86
  cross-border 294
  exchange and 319
  international 201, 218, 217, 294
  restricted 293, 294
  volatile 294
  see also capital inflows; capital outflows
capital inflows 16
  controlling 294
capital-intensive sectors 447
capital markets:
  direct finance institutions in 290
  encouraging institutions 301
  international, access to 298
  world, benefits of BTA for dealing with 413
capital mobility 24, 89, 247, 492 n.
  cross-border 295
  full 81
  imperfect 215
  international 202, 215, 216, 217, 295
  perfect 215, 216, 217
  spillover benefits from 11
capital outflows 295
  large 15
  reduced barriers to 299
capital stock:
  allowing all nationals to hold 530
  changes in 202
  expanded 218
  fixed 215
  increase in 217
  risk premium that will vary depending on size of 215
  world 215, 217, 218
Caprio, G. 291 n., 295 n., 307 n.
cargo 368
Caribbean 31, 79
  countries bound to introduce competition 61
  initiative to establish a single regional prudential
     regulator 354
  mobility of service providers 535–6
CARICOM (Caribbean Community and Common
    Market) 245, 247, 256, 257
  inventories of measures 270 n.
  Protocol 255, 270 n., 535
  Secretariat 270 n.

CARICOM/USAID 165
carriage of passengers 143
carrier rentals 143
cartels 214, 374
Carzaniga, A. 437 n., 487
case-by-case judgments 182
casualty rates 375
catch-up 503, 504
    productivity 538
Cattaneo, O. 484
Cawley, Richard 422 n.
CBRC (China Bank Regulation Commission) 327–8,
    330, 332
CDMA (Code Division Multiple Access) systems 400,
    418, 428
Cecchini Commission Report (1988) 296
cell phones:
    downloaded songs 396 n.
    powerful micro-processors 396
    subscribers 427
Celltel 424
cellular service providers 352 n.
Central America 254, 319
    remittances 496
    US bilateral trade agreements with 401
    see also under various country names
Central Bank of the Philippines 162 n.
central banks 162 n., 560, 591
Central and Eastern Europe 79–80, 197, 242, 308, 309
    countries acceded to EU on individual basis 234
    cultural interchange for young people from 513
    EU pre-accession agreements with 245
    need to build institutions quickly 299
    see also Bulgaria; Czech Republic; Hungary; Poland;
        Slovak Republic; Slovenia
CEPA (Closer Economic Partnership Arrangement) 329
certification requirements 28, 104, 121, 105, 117, 119,
    417–18, 469, 523
    clear and reliable 528
    full 121
    language not legally binding 242
    weaker 120
CGE (Computable General Equilibrium) model 200,
    201–2, 214–18, 494
    simple static 491
chaebols 15
Chan, C. 352
Chandra, R. 437 n.
charters 143
Chicago 422 n.
Chicago Convention 53
childcare services 87, 88
Chile 30, 375
    bargaining power 565
    bilateral trade agreements 401, 543

capital account opened 294
    decline in welfare 216
    discrimination 205
    financial crisis 294
    financial market reformed 294
    foreign banks 300
    free trade agreement with US 239, 242, 256, 257,
        259, 316, 317, 319, 324, 325
    government retained right to issue competing
        licenses 18
    household ownership of telephone 21
    index scores 190–1
    margins 200
    price impacts due to restrictions on foreign
        banks 210
    restricted markets against foreign maritime
        suppliers 205
    stakeholders from 568
    strong banking system after banking crisis (early
        1980s) 300
    subsidy auctions 412
    success in opening up to foreign firms 294
Chile-EC FTA 317
Chile-MERCOSUR FTA 238 n.
Chile-Mexico FTA 238 n., 267
China 9, 38
    airlines 208
    coastal region 357–8
    financial sector 326–35
    foreign FSPs 294–5, 297
    labor costs 495 n.
    logistics sector 369
    margins 200
    policy obligations to maintain services to isolated
        areas 378
    precommitment to expanded national
        treatment 302–3
    rebates that favor domestic products 466
    restrictiveness index 187
    schedule of reforms in transport sector 365
    significant negotiating leverage 24
    specialty occupations 484
    successful trade-policy reform 37
    supply of temporary workers 500
    tariff equivalents 197
    Wal-Mart buys in large volume from 389, 419
    welfare effects 216, 217
    WTO accession (2001) 295 n., 297, 303, 369, 381,
        406, 564, 567
    see also Agricultural Bank; Bank of
        Communications; Bank Supervisory Law;
        BOC; CBRC; China Postal Saving Bank; CIRC;
        Commercial Banks Law; CSRC; ICBC;
        Northeast Reconstruction Bank; PBoC;
        People's Bank Law

China Postal Saving Bank 332
chip transistors 459–60
choices 296
    consumer 111, 367
    GATS 439
    policy 359, 375
CIF (cost, insurance and freight) exports 357
CIRC (China Insurance Regulatory Commission) 330
Citibank 329, 330
citizenship 67, 515
    reliance on 270 n.
civil aviation 258 n.
civil servants 141
civil society activism 272
Claessens, S. 296 n., 306 n.
clarification issues 470, 472–3
Clarke, G. 300
client trust 88
Clinton administration 242 n.
closed markets 372
CMEA (Council for Mutual Economic
        Assistance) 525
coalition-building 64, 564
    strategy for 559
    supportive 567–9
coalitions 312, 557
    formation of 558, 559
Coe, D. T. 228 n.
Colecchia, A. 204
collaboration:
    inter-agency 444
    international 469
Collantes, V. A. 525 n.
collusion 188, 214, 353, 375
    risk of 369
Colombia 191, 197, 568
COMESA (Common Market for Eastern and Southern
        Africa) 21, 24
Commander S. 509, 528
commercial application 400
commercial banks 298
    foreign-equity participation in 311
Commercial Banks Law (China) 327
commercial change 259
commercial negotiation 348, 408
commercial presence (GATS mode 3) 6, 49, 50, 60, 87,
        99, 138, 147, 169, 179, 182, 217, 247, 262, 302,
        402, 492 n.
    allowed through branches 310
    banking services provided by locally established
        banks under 560
    capital outflows related to 295
    establishment of 153, 181
    establishment of 235
    foreign entry through 368

impact of trade-policy reform 370
important role played by foreign affiliates in
        providing 202
information available 160–2
information to construct frequency ratios 186
interim indicators of 147
liberalization in 497
limitations 452
limited via FDI 206
market access via 363
measures affecting 210
movement instrumental to supply through 155
not possible to determine magnitude of 164
quotas imposed on foreign suppliers 105
regulations that discriminate against FSPs 291
services exclusively delivered via 104
commercial presence commitments 364, 447
    countries unwilling to make status quo 313–14
    exchange of 382
    full 309
commercial services 134–7, 138, 146
Commission of the European Communities 243 n.
commitments 59–60, 67, 185, 189, 205, 313, 319–25,
        380, 382–6
    binding 525, 572
    bound-liberalization 269
    clarity and predictability to 315
    considerable freedom to achieve economic
        objectives 292
    credibility of 127
    dearth of 78
    exchange of 382
    GATS-specific 154
    horizontal 60, 363
    implications for national policies 292–3
    international 354, 376, 382
    legal scope of 55
    legally binding 238
    limited in scope 381
    modification or suspension of 61–3
    multilateral 261, 262, 572
    national 547, 560, 562
    need to barter sector-by-sector, country-by-
        country 77
    negotiable 48
    negotiation of 272
    new 473–4
    number in relation to maximum possible number
        of 186–7
    partial 364
    phase-in 61, 65 n., 66 n., 305, 406
    regional 259
    scheduled 54, 192, 246, 253, 255, 304, 364
    scheduling of foreign investment 402
    standstill 266

telecommunications 390, 391
three categories 548
trade-policy 346
unilateral 315
see also commercial presence commitments; market-
access commitments; national treatment
commitments; specific commitments
common property resources 375
Commonwealth Bank of Australia 328
Commonwealth countries 513
communications 144, 146, 158, 364
cables and satellites for 19
FDI restrictions 187
global, affordable 419
importance of 419
internal 395
modern data 419
restrictions on entry and foreign ownership 113
robust infrastructure 391
significant network externalities in 392
sophisticated 389
written and oral 570
see also telecommunications
comparative advantage 78, 87–8, 89, 94, 100, 344,
527, 532
benefits of specialization according to 491
denial of the role of 214
different types of services 99
efficiency gains based on 367
exploiting 521
modal 24
modes where developing countries tend to have 77
source of 95
standard approach 93
compatibility 417
compatible protocols 462
compatriot communities 483
compensation 150, 155, 261, 379, 413, 488
binding arbitration where members cannot agree on
level of 265
foreign investors 380
smaller countries excluded from negotiations 264
specific schemes 532
trade-related schemes 531
compensatory policies 529–32
competence 524
competition 23, 177, 297, 307, 377, 394–400
absence of 339
abuse of monopoly bottleneck facility to thwart 347
allowing 345
barriers to 200
basic telecommunications 426
benefits of 372, 390
BTA commitments to 412
changes in intensity of 230

to 398
countries bound to introduce 61
cross-border 382
cut-throat 114
decision to liberalize 417
delaying 463
disciplines 69
distorting of 412
domestic benefits from introducing 353
downstream 348–51
effect provided by FSPs 296
effects in local markets 378
emphasizing 17–21, 370
encouraging 329
enhanced 12, 302, 492
evolved 395
exposure first in regional market 224
fair 426, 433
FDI increases welfare by increasing 111
fragile 352
full 14, 415, 426
future 302
genuine 3
global 224, 230, 395, 426
"hit-and-run" 511
hybrid model of 375–6
immediate 312
importance of 5, 17–19
including foreign operators in 346
increased, fears about the impact of 294
international 376
introduction of 201, 375, 378, 399, 419, 427
"invisible" barriers to 406
lack of 15, 304
larger welfare gains arise from increase in 113
limited 327, 391
long-distance 425
making it work 19–21
methods of regulating not conducive to promoting 344
mobile 342, 425
more intense 367
non-discriminatory 430–1
opening up essential services to 15
opportunities and pitfalls of 419
parts of industry capable of sustaining 346
path to 390
perfect 499, 532
political disincentives for 411
potential "hit-and-run" 483
preferential liberalization may exert more durable
effects on nature of 223–4, 229
regulatory 475
reluctance to unleash 313
restrictions on 17, 113, 228, 229, 304, 395, 414
rules least burdensome for 406

competition (*cont.*)
  scope of 354, 379
  setting a binding future date for 406
  shipping 374
  significant 428
  stifling 232
  sufficient 341
  sustaining 372
  telecommunications 342, 423–5
  threat of 342
  trade negotiations, risks and benefits of 397
  transparent 433
  transport market 359
  upstream 347, 351–2
  vigorous 375, 427
  yardstick 345
  see also competition conditions; foreign
     competition; transition to competition
competition conditions 308
  effects of government policies on 198
  how existence or removal of barriers will affect 200
  modification of 59
  no less favorable 58
  privatization conducted without concern to
     creating 13
competition laws 374
competition policy 196, 374, 375
  design of institutions 376
  problem of 372
  risk well understood in 423 n.
  role of 352–3
  telecom regulation 462–4
competitive bidding 21
competitive disadvantages 300, 314
competitive law exemption 375
competitive markets 107, 339, 378, 406 n., 422, 425
  creating 395
  hard-earned lesson from 424 n.
  perfect 89
  potential 353
  realization of full benefits prevented 15
  restrictions on FDI in 110–11
competitive pressure:
  intensified 305
  lack of 18
competitive tenders:
  international 30
  reallocation of licenses as result of 374
competitiveness 174, 367, 426, 586
  depends on performance 376
  export 356
  global-quality transport services critical for 368
  international 368
  regional 224, 230
complementarities 101–3, 392, 497

computer networks 394, 395, 397
  evolved into Internet 396
computers 103, 144, 146, 151, 155, 158
  concentration of industry 96
  exports of 146
  new companies 394
  phones becoming interchangeable with 396
  processing power 397, 459–60
concentrated markets 229
concentration 96, 98
  credit 293 n.
  risk 315
concessions 24, 265, 345, 378, 390, 420, 497, 514, 563
  getting other countries to pay more 564
  reciprocal 77
  scheduled 487
confidence 290, 584
  e-commerce user 469
  investor 454
confidentiality 574
conflicts 438
congestion 359, 371, 372, 375
  controlling 399
  exaggerated 375
connectivity 399, 462
  global 414, 420
  grey market for 425
  low cost 420
  predominant form in developing countries 394
  vast increase in 400
consensus 565, 588, 590
  building 559
  country frustrated by ability to block 566
  global 587
construction services 99, 144, 155, 158, 197, 273
  employment officers' strict check-ups on sites 514
  foreign supply of workers 513
consultations 377, 379, 546
  bilateral 543, 547, 560, 570
  extensive, with industry 554
  formal 550
  problem-solving 545
  stakeholder 585
consumer applications 464
consumer protection 467, 557
consumer surplus 107, 108, 111, 114, 116, 118, 119,
    124, 125
consumption 105, 107, 119, 125, 137, 537
  increased 121
  local, spillover benefits of 122
  services provided in country of 178
  simultaneous 5
  socially efficient level of 123
  tariff-induced 106
  too low 107

consumption abroad (GATS mode 2) 6, 16, 49, 50, 87, 88, 138, 146, 169, 182, 236, 246, 247, 360, 492 n.
  capital flows related to 295
  e-commerce 472–3
  financial services 291
  full commitments to 309
  information to construct frequency ratios 186
  least restricted mode of supply 205
  liberalized 310
  most liberal of modes 364
  no conditions or limitations on 363
  quotas sometimes implemented through foreign exchange restrictions 105
  rights of commercial users to have access to local national network 403
consumption distortion 106, 111, 112, 123
containers 369
contestability 463, 475, 519, 530
contracts 156, 378
  bilateral 352
  commercial 414, 416
  enforced 127, 475
  long-term 352, 423
  students 528
Contreras, Patricio 38, 315
convention industry 389
convergence:
  around best regulatory practice 233
  divergence and 238–46
  trade- and investment-facilitating 231
  see also regulatory convergence
cooperation 64, 231, 234, 353, 376
  economic 360
  enhanced 293 n.
  global 4
  infrastructure services 4
  inter-agency 444
  international 4, 470
  regional 4
  regulatory 243 n., 244, 272, 381
  see also regulatory cooperation
cooperatives 301
coordination:
  domain names 467
  need for in networked environment 470
  quality of 462
co-production agreements 226
copyright 145, 464
Corden, Max 492–3
cores and peripheries 96, 97
corporate networks 394–400
Correa, C. 58 n.
corruption 108
  credibility of measures designed to combat 391
  low levels of 390

opportunities for 112
  pervasive in developing countries 391
Corson, W. 531
cost-benefit approach/analysis 106, 108, 111–12, 125
cost impacts 211
cost savings 21, 296, 340
cost-setting 409
cost-sharing 422
Costa, E. 460
Costa Rica 40, 324, 326, 391
  telecommunications services commitments 389, 428–35
Côte d'Ivoire 425
Council for Trade in Services (GATS) 53, 62, 69, 72, 73, 264, 265, 282, 283, 284
  Negotiating Guidelines and Procedures adopted by 70
Council of Community Statistics 164
counter-productive pricing 410
"country-of-destination" principle 467
country size 346
courier services 259
Cowhey, P. 410 n., 412, 414 n., 415
CPC (UN Central Product Classification) numbers 55–6, 143, 154, 16
"cream-skimming" 16, 411
credibility 22, 24, 127, 306, 360, 530–1
  anti-corruption plans, reinforcing 391
  market reforms 419
  policy 238, 354, 379, 380, 382
  regulation 369
credible threat 342
credit 293 n.
  access to 301, 332
  better assessment procedures 296
  centralized 299
  foreign banks and 297, 299
  non-bank 291
  private 291
  small firms obtain 300
  stability in times of crisis 294
credit cards 97, 296, 468
Credit Cooperatives 327
creditors 290, 291
  foreign 15
crisis-proneness 307
critical mass 97, 260, 503, 508, 509
cross-border trade (GATS mode 1) 5, 16, 49, 50, 59, 84, 86, 89, 91, 138, 169, 182, 242, 262, 304, 305, 367
  countries must lock in current openness of 4
  attracting foreign investors and strategic partners in 307
  basic rationales for trade policy reform to allow 302

cross-border trade (*cont.*)
  case for more ambitious approach in 77
  commitments 364
  core banking, core insurance and securities 315
  e-commerce 466, 472
  feasible 125
  financial services 291
  foreign providers of 205
  full commitments to 309
  granting market access to foreigners in 354
  growing shared interest in 24
  impact of trade-policy reform 370
  infeasibility of delivery 20
  information to construct frequency ratios 186
  interplay between investment and 246
  lack of comprehensive data on 201
  less efficient than direct provision 126
  liberalizing 77–8, 301, 310
  links between investment, movement of labor and 269
  maintaining some limitation on 297
  market-access commitment in relation to 295
  means of securing the right to 236
  national treatment unbound 363
  not feasible 124–5
  quotas common in transport sectors 105
  regulatory presumption in favor of 269
  restrictions on 247, 235, 315
  RTAs complement disciplines on 236, 246
  sales and 146
  service provided at higher cost through 124
  substitute for 87
  supervisory authorities increasing attention to 299
  switching to 125, 126
  trade pacts since BTA have expanded on 402–3
  trade policy reforms that free up 293
  unrestricted 81
cross-cultural dynamics 582–3
cross-subsidization 350, 351, 378
  implied end to 16
  unfair 425
crowding-out effects 452
cryptography 468
CSRC (China Securities Regulatory Commission) 330
Cull, R. 300
cultural identity:
  erosion of 480
  threat to 492
cultural services 145, 146, 155
culture 515, 525
  diplomatic 583
  exchanges 484
  interchange for young people 513
  international migrants face problems of 487
  permanent migrants assimilate into 511
  problems 510

  threats to 483, 492, 510
currency 142
  foreign 303
customer inertia 408
customer service 400, 419
customs:
  agents 178
  inefficient operations 369
customs duties 466, 474
  goods and services free from 473
customs unions 222, 263, 264, 265
  concerned by re-balancing 267
cybercrime 469
cyberlaws 468–9
cyberspace 465, 467, 469–70
  dissemination of content in 464
  primacy of national law vis-à-vis multilateral
    disciplines as they apply to 473
Czech Republic 300, 310, 313

Dacom 427
Dakar 385
damage rates 369
Dar-Es-Salaam 385
data 395
  entry operations 419
  packet-switched transmission 404
  processing 6, 367–8
databases:
  access 472
  protection 465, 468
DBS Group 330
Deardorff, A. V. 214
debit cards 97
debt 15, 290
deception 467
Decker, P. T. 531
Dee, P. 171 n. 185 n., 204 n., 215 n., 217 n.
defensive strategies 564–7
  cooperative 567
delivery:
  electronic 473
  fast 357 n.
  modes of, trade policy substitution between 124–6
  significant reductions in costs of 369
delivery channels 147
Dell Computer 398 n.
De Long, Brad 460 n.
demand 113, 118, 176, 177, 419
  access 351
  determinants of 210
  domestic and imported goods 499
  domestic service 124
  elasticities of 396
  excess 521, 537

information 368
matched with supply on second-by-second
    basis 351
pent-up 410
perfectly elastic 377
price sensitivity of 348, 351, 353
production 538
residual 107
unfilled 410
volatile 353
see also labor demand
demand curves 106, 107, 124
demand elasticity 203
  assumed 197
  estimated 195, 196
demand-and-supply analysis 174
demandeur countries 271, 420
demography 427
"demonstration effect" regionalism 242
dental services 447, 452
Denton, T. 467 n.
Department of Justice (US) 422 n.
depositors 290, 291
deposits 309
  foreign competitors able to set higher rates for 299
depreciation 142, 229
deregulation 353, 381, 426
  financial services 291
  significant 206
  substantial 369
derogation 261
De Rus, G. 346
Deutsche Bundesbank 162 n.
Devarajan, Shantayanan 41
developing countries 20, 28, 197, 261, 273
  administrative burdens for 256
  administrative capacity an important factor for 257
  advantages of international agreement 4
  aggregate output 501
  agricultural exports from 374
  areas of export interest to 76
  arrangements between 267
  benefit from experience of other countries 29
  bilateral relationships between industrialized
    and 210
  binding commitments to ensure temporariness of
    skilled personnel from 31
  cheap labor-intensive goods from 492
  coincidence of interest between industrial and 78
  commitments in maritime transport 364, 381
  commitments on access for international
    services 417
  communications regulators in 400
  competitive exporters of health tourism 451
  cooperating with advanced industrial countries 234
  corruption pervasive in 391
  cross-country evidence from case studies 418–19
  deals unlikely to be available to 476
  declines in welfare for a number of 216
  demand for network capacity 410
  design of arrangements for aid to 5
  difficulties in financial sector 20
  disciplines on trade and competition policy into
    RTAs with 242 n.
  economic cooperation between developed and 360
  economically advanced 73
  exchange of commitments 382
  export interests of 72
  facilitating liberalization within 80–1
  failure to rebalance retail pricing structures 351
  growth rates 6, 9
  high-end bandwidth available 397
  imports of labor-intensive goods from 481
  inland areas of 377–8
  interconnection policy 408, 409
  interests in transport services 368
  justification to act to limit power of
    incumbents 419
  labor-intensive manufacturing industries 356
  landlocked 385
  larger 24, 401
  likelihood of attracting foreign investment 390
  limited or weak regulatory capacity 348
  loss to 508
  main beneficiaries of increase in quotas 502
  maintained or increased employment 17
  major problem for 413
  margins relatively high 200
  modes where they tend to have comparative
    advantage 77
  move away from public monopolies 17
  needs of small and medium-sized service
    suppliers 72
  negotiation 26, 527–9
  non-discriminatory government procurement
    for 273
  out-of-pocket payments for health services 451
  poorer 22
  potentially mixed implications for poverty 496
  predominant form of connectivity in 394
  rates for international services 411
  regulations to prevent exploiting comparative
    advantage 521
  scope to become providers of information
    services 368
  services sectors decline 503–4
  share in gains 11
  significant increases in GDP 10
  significant stake in construction 273
  small exporters 546

developing countries (*cont.*)
  strong interest in movement of labor 270
  telecom investment in 17
  trade negotiations 21
  wage parity beneficial to 521
  welfare effects 216, 217
  wish to gain access to markets 420
  workers sometimes skeptical about benefits of
     liberalization 16–17
  see also LLDCs
DFID (UK Department for International
    Development) 493, 526
differences 95, 107
  exploiting 510
  legal systems 88
  policy 233
  regulatory systems 88, 98
  technological 88
digital literacy 462
digital signatures 469
digital subscribers 425
digitally enabled automated exchanges 460
digitized goods and services 462, 473
direct investors 147–8
dirty tricks 583–4
disaggregation 143, 144
  geographic 161
disclosure 293 n., 297
discount 212, 357
discrimination 60, 84, 119, 202, 206, 235, 266, 343
  absence of 261, 262
  arbitrary or unjustifiable 63
  de facto, potential for 476
  elimination of 261, 262, 263, 471
  explicit 261, 264
  foreign banks/firms 190, 191, 205
  implicit 476
  non-price 408
  racial 503
  reduced 373
  removing 307
  waived selectively 226
disincentives 411
displacement:
  fears of 483, 511
  measures to compensate workers 531
  unskilled workers 530
dispute resolution 408–9, 416, 470
dispute settlement 138, 439, 449–50, 545, 547, 566
  investor-state 247, 380
  state-to-state 238, 247
disrespectful conduct 584
distress 530
distribution 50, 372, 515
  accessibility, quality and cost of 356

  costs of 465
  FDI restrictions 187
distribution networks 95
  establishment of 102
  specialized 19
divergence 238–46, 269
diversification 30
diversified portfolios 298–9
divestiture 423 n.
Dobson, W. 308 n., 315 n.
doctor-deficit countries 526
doctors 524, 525, 526
  rich patients on whom to practice 527
Doha Round (2001) 66, 73, 271, 464, 473, 590, 591
  action necessary to ensure smooth and
     expeditious progress 22
  areas for improvement in 308, 313
  indication that US would oppose S&D in 578
  innumerable references to technical assistance 80
  international telecommunications/IT issues under
     consideration 389
  mobile services and interconnection principles 410
  possible impacts of 493
  priority in 28–30
  regional commitments 259
  scheduling commitments 315
Doha negotiations 4, 33, 40, 81, 543, 560, 562
  communications services 396
  current, target for 365
  mobile services 410
  suspension of 75
  telecom 38, 420
  TM, limited 514
domain names 464
  bad-faith registration of 470
  coordination and administration of 467
  dispute resolution body 470
dominant carriers 408, 416
Dominica 9, 82, 535, 536
Dominican Republic, *see* DR-CAFTA
Doove, S. 186, 193–5, 206–8, 212–13
downloads 465
downstream markets 349, 351
Drager, N. 437 n.
Drake, W. J. 542 n., 586 n.
Drucker, P. 459 n.
drugs trade 464
DR-CAFTA (US-Central America-Dominican
    Republic Free Trade Agreement 316, 319, 324,
    325, 326 n., 389
  commitments of Costa Rica on telecom
     services 428–35
  commitments of Costa Rica on telecom services in
     context of 428–35
due process 246

dummy variables 197, 203
duopoly 114, 424
    cellular services 390
durable adverse consequences 22
duties 58
    reductions of 264
    see also customs duties

earnings:
    Latino 496
    less remittances 538
    repatriated 508 n.
East Asia trade agreements 315
East Asian Insurance Congress (XVth Conference,
        Jakarta 1990) 298 n.
Eastern Europe, *see* Central and Eastern Europe
EBOPS (Extended Balance of Payments
        Services) 140, 164
    allocation of items to modes of supply 146
    components 143–5
    full implementation of 163
    main principles 142–3
    trade in services data 157–8
EC (European Community) 316, 447, 568
ECE-Eurostat Joint Meeting on Migration Statistics
        (2003) 157 n.
Echandi, Roberto 40, 391, 428–35
ECLAC (UN Economic Commission for Latin
        America and the Caribbean) 165
e-commerce 30, 259, 437, 513
    "duty-free" 81
    promoting 236, 247
    regulation 41–2, 459–79
econometric models 193, 201, 206
    partial-equilibrium 208, 210
    see also CGE
economic development:
    assistance agencies 552
    sustainable 434
economic integration 260–8 36–7, 111, 281–3
    conditions on agreements 261
    understanding 262–8
economic interest 141
economic variables 358
economies of density 371
economies of scale 68, 97, 98, 249 n., 338, 339–41,
        371, 372, 508
    capital investments in activities associated with 371–2
    costs reduced due to 95
    definition of 341
    economy-wide reduction in 217
    empirical estimation of extent of 346
    financial institutions learn to exploit 296
    interaction between transportation costs and 96
    large 392

production subject to 10
    reaping 224, 231, 491
    regulation, exploiting 32
    significant 18, 29, 228
    static and dynamic 230–1
    unit costs reduced by facilitating 296
economies of scope 338, 340, 341, 346
    advantages of incumbent may be reinforced by 371
    definition of 341
    financial institutions learn to exploit 296
    incumbent advantages reinforced by 371
    large 392
eco-tourism 87, 88
ECPR (efficient component pricing rule) 349
Ecuador 31, 79
EDI (electronic data interchange) 460
education 452, 496, 528, 532
    average levels of 511
    high-technology 419
    higher 259
    inter-generational spillovers from 490
    medical 527
educational credentials 244
educational exchanges 484
EEA (European Economic Area) 256, 257, 267
EEC (European Economic Community) 263, 517 n.
efficiency 54, 189, 291, 299, 300, 400, 411, 418, 491,
        507, 509, 586
    average 212
    comparative advantage-based gains 367
    economic 515
    effects of two different modes of supply 101
    important considerations in design of policies 378
    key components of policy cocktail required for 492
    managerial 296
    market, negative impact on 391
    network 462
    productive 18
    promoting 9–17, 302
    resource use 450
    services have a significant impact on 133
    skills that bolster 307
    suppliers encouraged to begin improving 406
    transport-system 377
    see also allocative efficiency; technical efficiency
efficient suppliers 223, 228, 229, 237, 251
    world 266, 274
EFTA (European Free Trade Association) 257, 258 n.
EFTA-Mexico FTA 247
EFTA-Singapore FTA 245–6, 247
Egypt 309, 311, 313, 590
El Salvador 311, 324, 496
electricity 29, 68, 81, 114, 191, 206–8
    inappropriate subsidization of prices 351
    industrial supply 195

electricity (*cont.*)
  measurement of regulation and impacts on
      industrial prices 214
  promoting trade in 353
  significant deregulation and structural reform 206
  switching costs 341
electricity distribution:
  privatization of 17
  retail 346
electricity generation 347
  important consideration in 346
  physical characteristics of 353
  regulatory regime to promote competition in 352
  structural separation of transmission and 351–2
  technical issues 351
  withholding capacity 353
electricity transmission 346
  costs of installing and maintaining long-distance
      lines 340
  losses 341
  structural separation of generation and 351–2
electronic banking 296, 304
electronic delivery 85–6
  see also e-commerce
electronics 397
email 97, 403
embassies 155
emerging markets:
  foreign bank participation 300
  indices of openness in financial services industries 305
  informational constraints 299
  key, industries in 305
  sharp rise in foreign bank participation 300
emigration 91, 525
  temporary 31
  wages do not rise as it occurs 504 n.
employment 149, 514–19
  costs of shifting between sectors 531
  foreign crews on ships 360
  increasing opportunities 16
  indirect effects on 451
  maintained or increased 17
  new opportunities created 370
  possible reduction in 17
  premium, displacement of local workers from 483
  pressure on 354
  rules on 363
  unskilled 510
employment law 515
encryption 469
energy services 19, 259
engineering 93, 94, 101, 395, 397
  price-cost margins 211
  restrictiveness indexes for 205
English, E. Philip 221 n.

English language 422 n.
entertainment 94, 389
entrepreneurship 508
entry:
  allowed 352
  cellular 424
  competitive 18
  costly 229
  credible (at 375
  de novo 228
  deterring 232
  difficult to constrain incumbent through
      threat of 372
  discouraging 230
  excessive 375
  exit and 92
  fixed costs of 227
  "hit-and-run" 342
  incumbent may be able to completely deter 229
  limited 114, 228
  low-cost carriers 369
  non-discriminatory limitations on 342
  openness to 309
  preferential temporary privileges 247
  preferred mode of 228
  regulation of 20
  restrictions on 16, 18, 114, 228, 298, 375
  sequential 229
  simultaneous 229
  temporary privileges 270
  temporary workers 523
  "too much" 408
  widened scope for 18
  see also entry barriers; foreign entry
entry barriers 4, 12, 19, 29, 32, 112, 113–14, 119, 408
  avoiding natural monopoly elements from
      becoming 359
  formal 272
  preferential liberalization of 229
  removed 228, 378
  significant 372
  transparency of 305
ENTs (economic needs tests) 57, 443, 452, 489, 517
  most economists would advocate abolition of 523
environmental problems 359, 375
environmental services 6, 259
  FDI restrictions 187
EPAs (Economic Partnership Agreements) 4, 21,
    22, 32
equity 19, 290, 348
  competitive auctions of 113, 304
  higher shares 313
  restricted 304
  targets for 377
  see also foreign equity

Erber, G. 475
Ertel, D. 573 n.
ESCWA (UN Economic and Social Commission for
     Western Asia) 165
Eskinazi, R. 460 n., 469 n., 470
ESM (emergency safeguard mechanism) 70, 221, 237,
     239, 306
  operational feasibility 245
Estache, A. 17, 345, 346, 349, 350, 375
estimation 209–10, 212
EU (European Union) 21, 74–5, 247, 264, 267, 365,
     463, 464, 474, 475
  acceding countries 234, 297
  candidate countries 159
  common code of practice for ENTs as suggested
     under 523
  countries in pre-accession mode 242
  database protection 465, 468
  demandeur role 420
  EBOPS classification binding for member states 164
  exports of 9
  GATS offer to talk to Doha Round 525
  GSM mandatory standard for Europe 417
  harmonizing accounting standards with 23
  migration remains low 488
  mobile termination charges 409–10
  model schedule approach endorsed by service
     industry bodies 78 n.
  national competences 524 n.
  political pressure to exclude labor mobility from
     bilateral and regional agreements 270
  pre-accession agreements 245
  privacy laws 468
  pro-competitive regulatory framework required to
     achieve integrated market for
     telecommunication services 259 n.
  realizing single market program for
     services 243 n.
  reference interconnection offer required in 408
  resistance to relaxation of European privacy
     regulation 476
  RTAs to which Members are party 239
  treatment of e-commerce as services 472
  welfare 216, 217
EU-Chile FTA 265
EU-Mexico FTA 247, 257, 258
  trade preferences under 251–2
Euro-Med 257, 258
European Commission 422 n., 524 n.
  mobile-network operators' market power 410 n.
  recurring tendency to insert disciplines on trade and
     competition policy into RTAs with developing
     countries 242 n.
European Parliament 164
Eurostat 157 n., 158 n., 159, 161

Joint Working Group on Foreign Affiliates
     Statistics 164
  New Cronos (reference database) 160, 162 n.
  Statistics in Focus series 160, 162 n.
exams 523
exchange rate 142, 293
  controls 294
exchange visitors 484
exclusivity arrangements 229
exit 92
  orderly 312
expansion 419
  e-commerce 462, 463, 466, 467, 468, 472, 474
  fiscal 426 n.
  market 95
  monetary 426 n.
  productive capacity 15
  telecommunications 354
expertise 185, 221
  banking 298
  financial 299
  foreign 296, 301
  international 354
  regulatory 354
explanatory variables 193
exports 6, 88, 89, 149, 312, 377–8
  agricultural 374, 587
  business 9
  CIF delivery 357
  computer services 146
  countries seek improved access for 76
  cross-border 6, 99
  direct 99, 101
  electronic 580
  elimination of barriers to 3
  financial services 158
  higher output drives down prices relative to
     imports 502
  increased 94
  key markets 434
  prices received for 377–8
  stimulating 93
  world 134
express delivery 259, 472
expropriation 380
external harm 118, 119
externalities 68, 117, 231, 531
  positive 96, 122–3, 223, 228
  subsidies can help to internalize 340
  see also network externalities

Fabra, n. 353
face-to-face contact 87
factor flows 48, 235
  integration agreements liberalizing 268

factor markets:
  different modes of supply have different
    effects on 16
  liberalizing 235
factor mobility 89, 128, 235, 480, 490
  temporary mobility as 493–6
factor participation 12–13
factors of production 89, 377, 500
  demand for 499, 537, 538
  reallocation of 92
  relatively abundant 270
fair trade 471
fairness 64, 581
  procedural 307
false assumptions 575
fast-food franchises 95
FATS (Foreign Affiliates Trade in Services)
    statistics 139, 146, 156, 157
  availability and dissemination of 160
  commercial presence primarily concerned
    with 146 n.
  confidentiality issues 165
  firms covered in 148
  importance of 164
  principles for recording 147–9
FATS variables 149–50, 163
  attribution (classification) of 150–2
fax services 403, 404, 414
Fay, M. 338
FCC (Federal Communications Commission) 394,
    414 n., 415
FDI (foreign direct investment) 3, 13, 33–4, 78, 86, 87,
    99, 139, 148, 157, 217, 224, 228 n., 497
  aim of attracting greater volumes of 249 n.
  allowing 101
  attracted because returns to investment artificially
    raised 304
  barriers to 104, 181, 215
  countries that provide higher levels face lower
    costs 212
  entry of foreign FSPs providing services via 291
  explained by differences between countries 95
  foreign providers of mobile services via 206
  gains from 95
  inducement to 230
  intangible firm-specific assets helpful in
    explaining 95
  international capital in the form of 215
  inward, attracting 266
  lack of comprehensive data on 201
  limited commercial presence via 206
  market-access commitments affected or nullified by
    decisions on 466
  measurement of 147
  national treatment for 313

not allowed 101
outward, capital account restrictions on 295 n.
policy encouraging 10
potential providers of cellular services via 206
restrictions on 110–11, 113–14, 187
signaling effects 269
smaller countries find it difficult to attract larger
  doses of 256
statistics 147, 160–2, 163, 164
federal political systems 245
Feketekuty, Geza 542–92
Ferrantino, M. 171 n.
fiber optics 395, 397, 404, 460
Fidler, D. P. 58 n., 437 n.
fiduciary issues 492, 523, 524
file sharing 465
filters 468
final goods and services 94
finance/financing 111
  barriers to competition in 200
  health system 451
  measurements 198–200
  subsidy 112
financial institutions 290
  CEOs of 489
  chain reaction affecting 312
  exploiting economies of scale and scope 296
  foreign 95, 297
  licensing criteria imposed on 293 n.
  re-capitalizing 17
  restructuring of state-owned banks not sufficient to
    change behavior of 15
  strengthening of 291, 303
  weak or undercapitalized 228
financial markets 294
  generally much more competitive than those in
    basic telecommunication 306–7
  international 291 n., 391
  not liberalized substantially 15
  opening at regional level 259 n.
  opening to allow cross-border trade in financial
    services 291
  strengthening of 291
financial sector:
  difficulties in 20
  first movers 230
  increased entry into 13–14
  inherently unstable 290
  international standards in 243 n.
  recapitalizing and modernizing 298
financial services 72 n., 112, 144, 146, 149, 197, 231,
    238, 364
  common occurrence to help restructuring 228
  concentration in cities 96
  delivered through electronic means 259

FDI restrictions 187
fully open 338
GATS has achieved a higher level of bound
    liberalization 259
GATS negotiations on 259 n.
impact of trade policy reform in 295–302
impediments in 204
indices of openness in 305
informational and stability problems in 82
international trade agreements and 37–8, 289–337
liberalized 13, 81
margins for 200
market access commitments in 204
new areas of 259
regulation of 469 n.
reported exports of 158
restrictions on entry and foreign ownership 113
sectoral experimentation in 245
unnecessary or needlessly burdensome requirements
    in 227
unrestricted cross-border trade in 81
Financial Services Understanding on Commitments
    (GATS) 259 n., 271, 313 n., 566, 587–9
financial speculation 400
Findlay, C. 185 n., 356 n., 365, 366, 369, 376,
    377, 380 n.
fines 514
Finger, J. M. 525 n.
Fink, Carsten 37, 201, 214, 221 n., 222, 223 n., 274–8,
    356, 265, 356 n., 374, 380 n., 383, 463 n.
Finland 20, 205
first-generation services 399
first-mover advantages 224, 229, 230, 344
fiscal deficits 15
Fisher, Roger 573 n.
fixed costs 93–4, 198, 340, 342, 349, 351
    access charge used to recover 348
    alternative methods for recovering 348
    firm-specific 95–6
    measures affecting 227–8
    plant-level 95, 96
    significant 18
flexibility 22, 267, 341, 408, 449, 516, 574, 588
    almost unlimited 53
    choice of technologies 433
    desire for 525
    policy 237, 261, 360, 383–6
    pricing plans 412 n.
    regulatory 126
    trade agreements require trade-offs involving 127
    traffic management 396 n.
FLG ((Financial Leaders Working Group) 315
flying operations 366
FOB (free on board) delivery 357
FOB/CIF value differentials 210

foregone trade 106
foreign affiliates 84, 95, 148, 150
    activities of 134 n.
    compensation of foreigners employed in 155
    establishment of 137
    important role played by 202
    located in or attracted to host countries 217
    significant increases in activity by 215 n.
    supervised on consolidated basis 297
    see also FATS
foreign banks 57, 58, 189–91, 210, 329–30
    channels by which entry influences domestic
        financial development 295
    "cherry picking" most desirable markets and
        customers 299
    limits on ATM offerings 315
    managers originating from 298
    more likely to "cut and run" during crises 299
    national treatment of 560
    ownership reduces profitability 296 n., 300
    provision of more stable source of credit 297
    restricted from participating in national ATM
        networks 303
    risk that might shift funds from one market to
        another 299
    significant entry associated with reduction of
        profitability 300
    small firms obtain credit from 300
    stabilizing impact of 300
foreign capital:
    access in times of crisis 294, 298
    caps on participation of 364
    channeling into weak or undercapitalized financial
        institutions 228
    de facto regime with respect to 311 n.
    limits on 57, 292
    restrictions on participation 60
    sudden influx of 426
foreign competition 368, 372, 521
    attractive means of protecting suppliers from 20
    case for protecting incumbent from 344
    consumers benefit from 114
    domestic service squeezed out of market by 124
    increased 118, 557
    likely to lead to decline in domestic prices 16
    potential, domestic monopolist faces 109
    protecting local providers/suppliers from 84, 105
    resistance to 64
foreign entry 294, 295, 297
    authorities persuaded to liberalize 299
    banks, trade policy reforms that permit 300
    benefits more widely distributed 374
    costs of 117, 303
    distinction between permitted equity participation
        by foreign FSPs and 302

foreign entry (*cont.*)
  market access via commercial presence limited by cap on 363
  restricted 303, 341
  threat of 344
  through commercial presence 368
foreign equity 17, 105, 298, 303, 304
  ceilings 57, 452
  limitations imposed 309, 311
  limits on shares or values of 362
foreign exchange entitlements 105
foreign factors 12–13
foreign FSPs 293, 297, 298–9, 300, 301, 303, 315
  competitive pressures from entry of 305
  discrimination against 291, 307
  distinct disadvantage in providing retail services 302
  entry providing services via FDI 291
  market access 294, 307
  permitted equity participation by 302
  restricted 294–5
foreign interests and issues 554–5
foreign investment 84, 89
  attraction of 367, 390
  commitments on rights of 402
  opening up to 454
  regulated pricing 114–17
  restrictions on 391, 426
  risk of undermining basis of transfers 378
  substantial inflows of 368
  wireline-based telephone services 426
  see also FDI
foreign investors 454
  attracting 307
  benefits of BTA for dealing with 413
  compensation to 380
  investment decisions 315
  multiple 148 n.
  post-establishment national treatment 226
  rate of return for 391
  restrictions on 426
  screening or registration process involving various degrees of burden for 182
  strategic 390
  ten-year window of opportunity for 313
foreign legal consultants 244
foreign market access:
  improved 21, 314
  increased for domestic producers 126
  potential 356
  restrictions on 100
foreign markets 108
  collusive agreements that affect 375
  comprehensive inventory of potential restrictions in 255
  firms shut out of 127

most important mode of supplying services in 249
  problems in 315
  smaller 375
foreign ownership 300
  binding levels below current levels 314
  ceiling on 427
  limitations on 226
  majority 309, 313
  one hundred per cent 298, 303
  restrictions on 113, 225
  right to 402
foreign products 122
foreign suppliers 105, 107, 119, 152, 153, 174, 545
  access to bottleneck facility on reasonable terms 347
  discriminating against 343, 547, 373
  domestic incumbent competing with 177
  effective management control 391
  health care 450
  impact on local suppliers 450
  liberalizing course of policy change 255–6
  local operations 359
  maritime 205
  market access 293, 406
  measures restricting ability to engage in cross-border trade 235
  percentage taxes on 203
  protecting the acquired rights of 270
  regulations may affect entry and operations of 178
  restrictions on 452, 547
  selective servicing by 299
foreign-worker schemes 489, 514–16, 522
  exit-enforcement 520
  no social security rights 532
  wage parity regulations 521
foreigners 156
  auctioned off rights for 108
  certification procedures 120, 121
  compensation of 155
  competing with local skilled workers 16
  cost of access to domestic markets by 103
  government wants to completely exclude 110
  granting market access to 354
  how they should be screened 119
  investment in country-specific skills 127
  local certification requirements 117
  opportunity cost of acquiring goods from 106–7
  prohibited from securities industry 303
  qualified and unqualified personnel 118
  quantitative barriers targeted only at 60
  restrictions on 107, 111
  temporary movement of personnel 124
  transfers of monopoly rents to 13
forest products 88
Foster, V. 351
France 204, 205, 568

franchises 99, 122, 144, 145, 398 n.
  fast-food 95
Francisco, J. 486–7
Francois, J. 197, 374
fraud 467, 475
free-rider problem 77, 381–2, 588
free trade 97, 103, 109, 111, 123, 124
  benchmarks of 197
  bilateral agreements 565
  consumer lobbies for 127
  government commitments to 406
  regional agreements 545, 565
  see also DR-CAFTA; EFTA; FTAs; NAFTA; South
    Asian Free Trade Area Negotiations
freedom of movement 256, 258
Freeman, R. B. 506
freight 143, 340
  air 357 n., 371
  ocean 357 n.
  quotas 226
  security requirements, international transport 368
frequency-based measurements 170, 185–91, 204–8
frictional measures 227
frontier cost method 211
fruit-pickers 153
FSA (WTO Financial Services Agreement 1997) 37,
    260, 302, 305 n., 308, 315, 316
  elucidation of rationales for commitments 306
  lessons from 310–13
  main reasons for liberalization commitments in 314
  major liberalizers of core banking and insurance
    services in 300
FSPs (financial services providers) 289, 290
  liberalizing cross-border supply of services by 301
  transport or telecommunications networks 344
  see also foreign FSPs
FTAA (Free Trade Area of the Americas) 234, 257, 543
FTAs (free trade areas) 238 n., 246 n., 247, 251–2, 256,
    257, 258
  GATT rules 222
  participating countries permitted to raise barriers
    against non-members 263
  regional/bilateral negotiations 547
Fujian 357

GAAP (Canadian General Adjustment Assistance
    Program) 531
Gabon 309
gains:
  economic, scope for 493
  efficiency 367
  liberalization 374, 504, 530
  preferential agreements 224
  productivity 369
  proportional to size of liberalization 504

real 359
  reaped through MFN liberalization 224
  specialization 87, 93, 359
  temporary movement 498
  theoretical, from larger economies of scale and
    scope 392
  welfare 113, 217, 270, 296 n., 378
gains from trade 88–90, 97–8, 116, 510
  and effects on income distribution 94–5
Gamberale, C. 343, 348, 375, 383
Gambia 81, 309, 447 n.
gambling services 55
GATS (General Agreement on Trade in Services) 4, 28,
    32–3, 34, 39, 234, 354, 360–7, 374, 542, 560
  basic structure 48–83
  binding arbitration 265, 266
  bound liberalization 238
  breadth in scope and coverage of 33
  central obligations imposed by 235
  coverage of air transport services in 366
  credibility of policy statements 379
  cross-border trade and foreign entry in financial
    services 304
  dispute-settlement process 545
  evolving law of 450
  exclusions from 52–3
  financial services liberalization and 289–95, 302
  frequency ratio for offers to liberalize trade
    in 192
  health services and 41, 437–58
  international e-commerce affected by rules
    under 472
  key provisions of 439
  knowledge and understanding of provision 377
  lack of statistics as defined by 591
  limited success in promoting regulatory
    cooperation 381
  major political threat inherent in bringing current
    schemes into 518
  managing the process from health policy
    perspective 443–4
  measures covered by 50–1
  mechanism for lending credibility to liberalization
    programs 37
  models that could inform future development of
    disciplines 257
  monitoring health implications of 444
  natural monopoly and 342–3
  non-discrimination and MFN rules 415
  pace of development of commitments 438
  partial or full commitments 204
  pre-commitment to future multilateral
    liberalization 231
  provisions contrasted with Article XXIV of
    GATT 222

GATS (*cont.*)
"public morals clause" that gives flexibility under 473
range of services covered by 85
rebalancing 263, 267
reciprocity offered by 380
relevant to natural monopoly markets 339
RTAs and 222, 236
scope of 441–2, 449
US commitments under 473
US negotiator of the Agreement 587 n.
see also commitments; Council for Trade in Services; modes of supply; *also under following headings prefixed* "GATS"
air transport 362, 366
financial services 290, 587–8
movement of natural persons 515
telecommunications 401–2
GATS Articles 548
I (trade in services) 49, 442, 514–15
II (MFN) 64, 65, 66, 71, 73, 234 n., 254, 402
III (MFN) 63, 69, 236 n., 254
IV (developing countries) 63 n., 72, 589
V (economic integration) 36–7, 65, 66, 222, 236 n., 242, 244, 245, 260–8, 271, 273, 281–3
VI (domestic regulation) 58, 63, 67, 69, 70, 234 n., 236 n., 237, 242, 293, 343
VII (recognition) 66, n., 234 n., 244, 245
VIII (provisions applying to monopolies) 63, 68–9, 342–3
IX (restrictive business practices) 63, 65
X (emergency safeguard measures) 70
XI (restrictions on capital transactions) 70, 281, 295 n.
XII (trade restriction) 62, 70, 281, 295
XIII (government procurement) 70, 71
XIV (public morals/general exceptions) 62–3, 66, 281, 292
XV (subsidies) 63, 70
XVI (market access) 54, 55, 57–8, 60, 63, 67, 71, 73, 239, 243, 291, 317, 326 n.
XVII (national treatment) 54, 55, 58–9, 60, 67, 71, 73, 243, 281, 291, 402
XVIII (additional commitments) 59–60, 63, 73, 406
XIX (negotiating guidelines) 72, 73, 75, 589
XX (schedule of commitments) 54, 60
XXI (modification of schedules) 62, 264, 265, 282, 283–4
XXIV (regional integration) 244
XXV (production, distribution, sale and delivery) 50
XXVII (measures taking virtually any form) 51
XXVIII (supply of a service) 515 n.
XXXI (modification of schedules) 236 n.
GATS institutions/miscellany:
General Council 53 n., 73

Preamble 66
Service Sectoral Classification list (W120) 77–8
UK Visa Scheme 518
Understanding on Commitments in Financial Services 259 n., 271, 313 n., 566, 587–9
Working Parties 67, 70, 222, 265, 266
GATS negotiations 21, 145
aimed at further liberalization 437
delivering openness and credibility 24–6
forum for national commitments 543
international 40, 360
list of service sectors generally used as basis for 143
North-South deal 3, 589–90
pending in number of key areas 221
rules 70–1, 444, 562–3
temporary presence of natural persons 31
GATT (General Agreement on Tariffs and Trade) 32, 33, 37, 292 n., 483, 525, 590
Article III 58
Article XX 62
Article XXIV 24, 222, 244, 261, 263, 265, 516
Article XXVIII 264
central obligations imposed by 235
concern about inclusion of services in 589
Director General 588
Harmonized System for tariff concessions 55
international e-commerce affected by rules under 472
Kennedy Round 531
multilateral trade negotiations 586
pragmatism characterized early years of 517 n.
scope in merchandise trade 50
Secretariat 49, 55
Sectoral Classification List 55
structural differences between GATS and 71
successful negotiations 103
tariff reductions under 61
Working Parties 265, 266
see also GATS; Tokyo Round; Uruguay Round
GDP (gross domestic product) 90, 197
fall in 501–2
gains of 11
importance of overseas employment to 486
real 501, 502
significant increases 10
variations in 356
general equilibrium model 498, 499, 532
see also CGE
generation 352
Geneva 72, 75, 590
International Trade Center 552, 553
geographic price averaging 411
German Employment Service 513
Germany 31, 79–80
foreign guest-workers 513–14, 516

green card for Indian IT specialists 525
  price impacts 211
  residents temporarily working abroad from 483
  subcontracting schemes 520
Ghana 40, 309, 389, 419, 423–5
Giannetti, M. 300
Glaessner, T. 306 n.
global brands 315
global markets 126, 420
  cross-border communications 411
  higher rewards for countries in 419
  important for long-term economic success 389
global supply chain 418
globalization 148 n., 543, 587
  health sector 437
  important aspects of 437
  indicators of 147, 164
  spread of 438
  workers' attitudes towards 506
GNP (gross national product) 217
  higher per capita 191
  welfare effects as percentage of 215, 216
GNS/W/120 (services sectoral classification list) 143
Goldman Sachs 328
Gomez-Lobo, A. 375
Gonenc, R. 193, 206
Gonzalez-Hermosillo, B. 259 n.
good faith negotiation 584
good governance 271
  promoting feature 256
governance-enhancing features 253 n., 255
government intervention 475
  withdrawal of 291
government services 145
GPA (WTO Government Procurement
    Agreement) 246, 272, 273
Grameen Bank 301
grandfathering 64, 313–14, 315
gravity-model estimates 185, 197, 214
Great Depression (1930s) 126
Greece 205
green cards 486, 525
greenfield investments 228
Grenada 535
Grenadines 535
Grieshaber-Otto, J. 437 n.
Group of Three 257
growth 54, 291, 296
  accelerator effects on 12–13
  export-oriented 411
  important determinant of 338
  indirect effects on 451
  induced 235
  IT as research and production driver for 426
  key components of policy cocktail required for 492

  lending stimulates 300
  marked impact on 356
  productivity 497
  reforms can promote 9–17
  services have significant impact on 133
Gruen, N. 379
GSM (Global System for Mobile
    communications) 400, 417
GTAP (Global Trade Analysis Project) model 210, 498,
    499, 532, 537, 538
Guangdong 357
Guangdong Nanhua Bank 329
Guatemala 324, 351
guest-workers 513
Gulf states 486
Guyana 81, 309, 535, 536

H visas 482, 484, 486, 523 n., 533, 534
Haggard, Stephan 426 n.
hairdressers 137
Haiti 24, 535, 536
Hamilton, C. 494
Hanaro Telecom 427
Hang Seng Bank 329, 330
Hanslow, K. 217 n.
Hardin, A. 181–2, 187–9, 201
harmonization 232
  accounting standards 23
  direct 234
  early 475
  eliminating policy differences through 233
  international 23, 224, 232, 468
  multilateral 475
  policy 239–42, 264
  promotion of 5
  pursuing at multilateral level 272
  regional 224, 232
  upward 233 n.
  see also regulatory harmonization
Hart, M. 246 n.
Harvard Negotiating Project 573 n.
Hatcher, M. 78 n.
Hawes, David 588, 589
health insurance 511
  social 522
health services/care 40–1, 437–58
  access to facilities 489
  child 337
  commercialization of 450
  electronic delivery of 259
  foreign suppliers/companies 450, 455
  receiving abroad 144
  residential 447 n.
  temporary mobility 524
Hertel, T. W. 491, 499, 532

heterogeneity across services 99
Hicksian Equivalent Variation 538 n.
Hicksian optimism 492–3
high-fashion textiles 357
high-risk groups 520
high-technology companies 26
higher education 259
highly-skilled workers 257, 482, 507, 509, 528
Hilary, J. 437 n.
historic costs 409
Hoekman, B. 3 n., 71 n., 178, 185, 186–7, 192, 198, 200, 204, 215, 223 n., 474 n.
hold-up problem 127
Holitscher, M. 467
Holmes, L. 181–2, 187–9, 201
Holz, C. 327
homogenous commodities 357 n.
Honduras 325, 496
Hong Kong 15, 159, 197, 329
   airlines 208
   bargaining power 565
   cost-price gap smallest in most sectors in 215
   eligibility for new full banking licenses 311
   margins 200
   openness 205
   restrictiveness index 189, 190
   shipping 358
   stakeholders from 568
   welfare increase 217
Hong Kong Ministerial Declaration (2005) 66, 72 n., 75–6, 562, 570
hospital services 447, 452
hotels 200
hours of work 531
household surveys 156
households 289, 296, 537
   access to rural credit 301
   benefits as users of financial services 296
   distribution of gains 173
   lower cost of capital to 307
   narrowband and broadband 397
   relatively better off and urban, decline of income falls on 497
   target for subsidies 379
HSBC (Hong Kong and Shanghai Banking Corp.) 328, 329, 330
hubs 371, 374
human capital 455, 530
Hummels, D. 527 n.
Hungary 300, 308 n., 313
   success in opening up to foreign firms 294
hybrid approach 54, 253
hyperinflation 142

IBM 398 n.
ICAIS (International Charging Arrangements for Internet Services) 416, 421–3
ICANN (Internet Corporation for Assigned Names and Numbers) 42, 459, 467, 470, 471
ICAO (International Civil Aviation Organization) 366
ICBC (Industrial and Commercial Bank of China) 328
ICC (International Chamber of Commerce) 467 n.
ICE (Costa Rican Institute of Electricity) 429, 430
ICFA (ISIC Categories for Foreign Affiliates) 151, 163
ICT (information and computer technology) 484
identity theft 469
Iida, Keyia 232 n.
illegal activities:
   e-commerce 467
   employment 514
   immigration countering 28
   migration commitments to combat 79
   music downloads 465
ILO (International Labor Organization) 517, 522
   International Labor Migration Database 157 n.
   see also ISCO-88
IMF (International Monetary Fund) 82, 159, 299–300, 311 n.
   extensive international programs 293
   memorandum items 164
   see also BOP; SIMSDI
IMF-World Bank Comprehensive Financial Sector Adjustment Programs 243 n.
imitation 221
immature financial systems 290
immigration 156, 489, 497
   Europeans' resistance to 532
   illegal 28
   medical 525
   permanent, guest-workers program 513
   restrictions 511
   rights of 258
   skilled 508
   unskilled 31
Immigration and Nationality Act (US 1990) 533
immigration officials 515, 520
impartiality 293
imperfect markets 104, 112
imports 149, 235
   air and ocean freight rates for 357 n.
   backbone 200
   capital 217
   carried by liners 214
   differences between actual and predicted 197
   duty-paid 58
   high tariff 226
   higher output drives down prices of exports relative to 502
   increased, gains from 89

intermediate products 357 n.
labor-intensive goods from developing
    countries 481
low zero-tariff 226
maritime 214
quotas filled 107
reduced 183
relatively large 565
small 565
transport charges for 374
incentives 10, 22, 88, 97, 101, 411, 537
appropriate systems 301
economic 405
long-run concerns about 507
rent collecting 304
strong, to lower prices 342
income 499
aggregate 497
demand depends on 537
factor 538
generated by e-commerce 466
growth of 359
high(er) 212, 452, 500
indirect effects on 451
low(er) 211, 212, 301, 400, 496
market access an important determinant of level
    of 358
national 89, 197 n.
per capita 197
real, large differences 487
redistribution of 92, 106
remitted 91, 497
retained by temporary workers 539
top-up 530
trading partners 197
transfers of 359
income distribution 95
effects on 101
evolution of 92
gains from trade and effects on 94–5
impacts on 92
international 91
national 92
subtle and complicated effects 101
targets for equity in 377
income support 531
income tax 466
from visitors 522 n.
incorporation 148, 273, 314
incumbency effects 229
incumbents 22
advantages reinforced by economies of scope 371
can impede access to markets 343
case for protecting 344
determining costs of 409

difficult to constrain through threat of entry 372
favoring 177, 179
foreign 81
government-owned 344
governments susceptible to pressure from 57
guaranteeing the rights of 314
inefficient 424
loss of power 396
market power of 375
market share loss 370, 378
maximizing profits by restricting output 339
relatively efficient 19
relatively inefficient 18–19
rents retained by 367
sharing network economies with new entrants 408
strong incentive to lower prices 342
suppliers may lose market share 359
technical standards 229
techniques to ensure costs kept low 345
independent regulators 424
independent service providers 154
independent variables 197
India 11, 590
boosted as global technology power 41
branches licensed and supervised in home
    countries 309
call centers 87
commitment in FSA to allow increased number of
    branches 313
concern about inclusion of services in GATT 589,
    590
deeper domestic bond market 332
discrimination against foreign banks 190
doctors to UK 524, 525, 526, 527
exports 9
foreign FSPs restricted 294–5
foreign index score 190
green card for IT specialists from 525
influx of workers from countryside into cities 580
IT workers 509
labor costs 495 n.
limited bargaining power 565
mode 4 proposal 517
negotiating leverage 24
restrictiveness 205
specialty occupations 484
suggestion for creating GATS visa 519
tariff equivalents 197
unemployed university graduates 580
indices:
investment-related 196
openness in financial services 305
restrictiveness 170, 184, 185–91, 204–8
Indonesia 301
foreign banks 190, 298

Indonesia (*cont.*)
  margins 200
  price impacts 210, 211
  restrictiveness 187, 190, 205, 210
  tariff equivalents 197
  temporary labor 487
  welfare effects 216, 217
Industrial Bank (Fujian) 328
inefficiencies 523
  allocative 339
  induced by tariffs 106
  monopoly 392
  operational 18
  pricing 413 n.
  static and dynamic 113
  technical 212, 339
  telephone system 394
inequality 92
infant-industry argument 224, 230, 312, 384, 492
infant mortality rate 338
infectious disease 437
InfoDev 459 n.
information 579
  attempt to censor 468
  better 185
  consumer 19, 20
  cost structure of firms, difficulty of obtaining 18
  global 472 n.
  help to avoid duplication of 456
  identification of 456
  imperfect 290
  large amounts of flows of 396
  market 391, 419
  necessary to inform policy 455–6
  new possibilities for dissemination of 464
  sharing 580
  information valuable 582
  see also asymmetric information; *also under
    following headings prefixed* "information"
information exchange 64
information-gathering 296, 456
information kiosks 419
information services 144, 146, 149, 155, 158,
    411, 433, 553
  developing countries' scope to become providers
    of 368
  supply of 432
information technology, *see* IT
information transfer 528
infrastructure 38–9, 338–55, 371, 464
  access to 462, 463
  communications 425
  cooperation on 4, 32
  coordination of 22
  core sectors 274

  costs of 184
  crucial 223, 229
  effects of reform 378
  essential 372, 373, 374
  fixed-network 424
  global information 472 n.
  global-network 414 n.
  investment in 383
  key services 3
  least cost 30
  liberal entry of providers 379
  major investments in 476
  network 398, 403, 410, 411, 414 n.
  private sector provision 378
  quality of 358
  rapid rollout 14
  robust communications and information
    technology 391
  separating ownership and control of 373
  sophisticated communications 389
  specialized industry 96
  telephone 395
  wired 399
innovation 92, 396 n., 397, 428
  encouraging 462
  fostering 465
  institutions that encourage and reward 88
  IPRs play critical role in 464
  key driver of 395
  rapid 397
  scheduling 313, 314
  slowing 414
  technological 304, 412, 419
inputs 212
  access to 376
  capital 350 n.
  factor 501
  imported 356
  intermediate 215, 229, 377, 499, 537
  labor 493
  purchased 377
  trade in 92–3
insider lending 14
institution building 376
institutional changes 61
institutional investors 427
insurance 111, 144, 146, 158, 180, 192, 290, 291, 324–5
  accident 512 n.
  aviation 303, 310
  compulsory 313
  direct 204
  entitlements 452
  foreign equity in 303, 311
  health 511, 522
  majority foreign ownership in 313

marine 310, 313
market opened gradually according to accession
    schedule 330
medical 512 n.
participation in opening to 309
significant role in mobilizing capital 301
transport 303, 310
uniformity in commitments 315
see also insurance companies; social insurance
insurance companies 87, 100–1, 104, 120
foreign affiliates 95
non-life 311
intangible services 137
integration 233
costs and benefits of agreements on trade in
    goods 221
deeper 5, 21, 22–3, 24, 31–2, 272, 470, 471, 473,
    474–6
intermodal, restraints on 369
international competition fostered as a result of 230
members to several agreements 262
network 98
North-South 233
policy 5, 476
problems 510
regional 230, 235, 263, 264, 267, 273–4, 267
shallow 471, 474
social 490
threats 510
see also economic integration; market integration
intellectual property, *see* IPRs; TRIPS; WIPO
Intelsat system 399
Interagency Task Force on Statistics of International
    Trade in Services 162, 166
Inter-American Dialogue (2004) 496
interconnection 19, 408–10, 417, 419
access of public to information on procedures,
    agreements or offers related to 432
across national borders 353
implementation of appropriate policies 463
international norms 470
manipulating to detriment of competitors 424–5
non-discrimination in provision of 416
regulated 432
regulations 395, 396, 398
unlicensed bands 418
interest groups 92, 303
governments may generate domestic support for
    liberalization from 312
protectionist 127
vulnerability to pressures from 312
interest rates 293
higher spreads 291
net margin 209
preferential 293

real, high 356
risk premium 217
rural borrowers may pay lower 16
spreads 210
interference 399
intermediaries 227
deposit-taking 289
intermediate goods and services 96
specialized 97
intermediate products 357 n.
intermediation services 20
internalization 524–5
international agreement 4
international assistance 22
international carriers 417
International Commercial Diplomacy Project 548 n.,
    573 n.
international competition:
financial sector 329–30
fostered as a result of integration 230
international diplomacy 583
international engagement 21–32
International Financial Institutions 333
international investors/investment 427, 497
international law 273, 422 n., 583
international markets 367
emerging 79
national markets segmented from 20
new ways to contest 462
international negotiations 81, 360, 583
appropriate approach to 76
health sector 438
role of 308–9, 353–4, 379–82
international product classification, *see* CPC; GNS;
    ISCO
international roaming 410
international standards 29, 30, 67, 147, 224, 232,
    243 n., 363
elaborate planning on 397
financial sector 243 n.
land transport well below 358
see also ISO
international switched (phone or fax) service 414
international trade agreements 433
International Trade Center (Geneva) 553
international trade negotiations 558
commitments made through 339, 354
international transport:
air 193, 206, 212
land 371
telecoms 416
international treaties 470
internationalization 206
Internet 50, 97, 247, 419, 426, 460, 555
backbone providers 423

Internet (*cont.*)
  bad-faith registration of domain names 470
  bilateral arrangements for traffic exchange 422
  content regulation 468
  dramatic growth of 459 n.
  emergence of 399
  expanded scope for activities that may infringe on
    IPRs 464
  explosion of creativity innovation associated
    with 465
  explosion of viruses 469
  fraud 467, 475
  global online population 462
  governance 466–7, 470
  high-speed wireless provision 427
  penetration and potential for e-commerce
    expansion 463
  piracy 465
  pornography 468, 475
  prices of new services over 413 n.
  rise of 394, 396–8
  security 469
  smooth operation of networks linked by protocols 467
  tax on producers who do not use as mode of
    supply 473–4
  traffic flow 421
  video-conferencing 412
  voice services 406
  web traffic between countries 421
  see also ICAIS; ICANN; ISPs; ITE; VoIP
Internet banking 469 n.
Internet cafés 425
interpreters 59, 575, 583
intimidation 583, 584
intra-corporate transferees 153, 155, 270, 273, 484,
    497, 507
  industrial countries anxious to secure assured
    mobility for 527
  pre-employment requirements apply to 519
intra-sectoral activities 291
inventories 183, 254 n., 255, 269, 270 n.
  large, costs of financing 356
investment agreements 273
investment decisions 14
investment in services 246–51
investment-restrictive measures 255
investor confidence 454
inward FATS 147, 150, 160
IOSCO (International Organization of Securities
    Commissions) 293 n.
IP-addresses:
  administration/allocation of 467
  unique, allocation of 462
I-Pods 396 n.
IPOs (Initial Public Offerings) 301, 328

IPRs (intellectual property rights) 247 n., 464–5,
    469 n., 472
ISAC (US Industry Sector Advisory Committee) 260
ISCO-88 (ILO International Standard Classification of
    Occupations) 154, 517
ISIC (International Standard Industrial
    Classification) 151, 154, 160, 163, 192
ISO (International Standardization Organization) 243
ISPs (Internet Service Providers) 395, 464
  competition in provision of networking for 398
  entrepreneurial 425
Israel 9, 586
IT (information technology) 425–6, 428, 543, 587
  globalized economy 586
  green card in Germany for Indian specialists 525
  growing convergence of telecommunications
    and 460
  importance of 419
  regulation of 426
  robust 389, 391
ITA (Information Technology Agreement) 472 n., 477
ITE (Internet traffic exchange) 416, 421
  complaints about 422
ITU (International Telecommunications
    Union) 42, 139 n., 185, 205, 206, 211,
    393 n., 459, 544, 554
  international interconnection norms agreed
    under 470
  joint supply of international phone services using
    accounting rates 414
  regulatory approaches developed under auspices
    of 453
  Telecommunications indicators 425
  World Telecommunications Standardization
    Assembly (2000) 422

Jacquet, P. 308 n.
Jamaica 535, 536
Japan 422 n., 447 n.
  airlines 208
  estimated tariff equivalent for business/financial
    services 197
  restrictiveness index 190
  shipping 358
  stakeholders from 568
  tactic used in bilateral negotiations with US 564
  unilaterally accelerated foreign-entry
    provisions 307
  welfare effects of removing barriers 216
Japan-Singapore FTA 246, 247, 257, 258
Jiangsu 357
Jinan City Commercial Bank 328
job markets 520
Johnson, M. 208
joint projects 165

joint ventures 111, 179, 303, 452
  foreign ownership 297
  measures that restrict or require specific types
    of 292
  requirements 57, 60
Joy, C. 437 n.
Juhel, Marc H. 39, 384–6
junior doctors 526 n., 528

Kalirajan, K. 204, 208–9, 215 n.
Kampala 385
Kang, J.-S. 210
Kangasniemi, M. 509, 526 n., 528
Kapstein, E. 531 n.
Karsenty, G. 488
KCC (Korea Communications Commission) 426
Kemp, S. 205
Kennedy administration 531
Kenya 301, 309, 311, 369
  fixed-line telephony penetration 425
Key, S. 291 n., 307 n., 308 n.
Kim Dae-Jung 311 n.
King, R. G. 295 n.
Kletzer, L. 529
Klimenko, M. 412
know-how 17, 296
"know your customer" rule 302
knowledge:
  industry-specific 185
  local 302
  specialized 95
  technological 88
knowledge-based services 20
knowledge flows 228
knowledge-intensive industries 231
Kono, M. 293 n., 308 n., 312 n.
Korea 40, 212, 389, 419
  bilateral free trade agreement between Chile and 543
  decline in welfare 216
  deeper domestic bond market 332
  discrimination 190
  Final Schedule of Commitments on Telecom at
    WTO 405
  financial crisis (1997) 15
  foreign index scores 190
  FSA offer 311
  market access and capital flows restricted 294
  restrictiveness 15, 187, 190, 205, 210
  severe balance of payments crisis 294
  telecommunications competition 425–8
Krajewski M. 437 n.
Krugman, P. 97
KT (Korea Telecom) 426, 427
Kufuor, John 424
Kuwait 311

La Plata 368
labor 86
  abundance of 88, 99
  foreign, restricted 303
  illegal flows 79
  marginal product of 494–6
  monopolistically competitive firms employ 215
  options available to suppliers of 359
  outflow of 501
  perfectly elastic in supply 504 n.
  perfectly mobile between sectors 505
  provision of 141
  specialized 96
  surplus 17
  value added available to 377
  world stock of 494
  see also skilled labor; unskilled labor; *also under*
    following headings prefixed "labor"
labor costs 195 n., 340
  differences across countries 88
labor demand 97, 101
  agricultural 513
  extent of change in wages will depend on 538
  temporary workers 521, 537
  unskilled 497
labor-intensive areas/activities 88, 99, 447
  imports from developing countries 481
  manufacturing industries in developing
    countries 356
  quotas 105
labor law 520
labor legislation 67
labor-market officials 515, 520
labor markets 93, 261, 503
  access to 257
  flexible 356
  integration agreements 282–3
  reasonably competitive 493
  reform of 426 n.
  relatively harsh 483, 511
  schemes used to fill gaps in 513
  single 506
labor mobility 1, 24, 79, 84, 89, 156, 215, 247
  across countries 99
  barriers to 487–9
  covered only by 257
  discriminatory restrictions on 225
  international, barriers to 104
  intra-regional, promoting 270–1
  LDCs 510–11
  links between cross-border trade, investment
    and 269
  prospects for promoting under trade
    agreements 274 n.
  related provisions in RTAs 257

labor mobility (*cont.*)
  right to 258
  spillover benefits from 11
  temporary 26–8, 104, 125, 257, 483–98
  treatment of 256–8
  see also presence of natural persons
labor productivity 15
  privatization and introduction of competition
      significantly increase 201
labor unions 483, 511, 551
Laffont, J.-J. 411 n.
land transport 237, 258, 341, 366
  access quality 369
  competition to discipline prices in broader market
      for 372
  foreign companies 370
  international air-freight supplier 371
  merger of operators 375
  preferential quotas 226
  quality of 369
  well below international standards 358
  see also road transport
language 525
  common 197 n., 583
  international migrants face problems of 487
  local, tailoring services to meet 344
  not legally binding 242
  requirement for bank board members 59
  test of 524
Lardy, N. 327
Larouche, P. 60 n.
Latin America 230
  banks 300, 308
  countries bound to introduce competition 61
  direct insurance 204
  effects of infrastructure reform 378
  liberalization 37
  mode 4 issues 44
  monopoly privileges to telecom operators 18
  openness to foreign entry 309
  remittances to poorest nations 496
  restricted entry and free equity participation 302
  restricted foreign entry but unconstrained equity
      participation 303–4
  successful trade-policy reform 37
  telecom markets with competition 17
  trade agreements 315
  urban transport and suburban rail services 385
  see also under various country names
laws:
  trade-related 58
  zoning 67
lawyers:
  allocation between home and abroad 89–91
  originally worked in home and remained at home 92

partnerships and practices between accountants
    and 205
LDCs (least developed countries) 41, 75
  flows of workers to 506–7
  integrated framework for 30
  powerful tool for boosting export performance 419
  skilled labor from 507–10
  unskilled labor from 510–11
  see also LLDCs
learning:
  cross-country 456
  dynamic 228
  social 475
learning by doing 221, 230
leased transmission circuits 394, 399, 403, 408
Leebron, David 232 n.
legal changes 61
legal procedures 232
legal services 87, 205
  nationality requirements 205
legitimacy 559, 564, 581, 586
Leroux, E. 259 n.
Lesotho 301, 309, 447 n.
  labor costs 495 n.
  remittances 497
less-skilled workers 481
  indigenous, threatened 529
  mass permanent migration of 480
  temporary movement of 257
Lessig, L. 465, 467 n.
leverage 290, 300, 571
  see also negotiating leverage
Levine, R. 295
LG Electronics 428
LG Telecom 427
liabilities 289, 290
liberalization 3, 60, 102–3, 247, 453–4, 491
  across-the-board 587
  aggressive 530
  alternative approaches to 222
  assessing the impact of 92
  autonomous 73, 255
  benefits of 5, 10, 13, 16–17, 30, 75, 81, 82
  bilateral 481
  bound 259
  broader-based, firms less likely to resist 224
  candidates for 522
  capital account 294
  capital flows 319
  choice of modality in Western Hemisphere 279–81
  commitments compared 138
  complex 104
  consequences of 35–6, 169–220
  contrasting approaches to 279
  coordinated 127

costs can potentially more than offset gains
cross-border 381
electronic commerce 474
estimating potential benefits and risks of 438
extent reached in specific sectors/markets 138
facilitating within developing countries 80–1
FDI assumed to result from 201
financial 15, 81, 289–95, 301, 305, 315
formula-based 255, 589
   from 119
full 114, 272, 309
fully effective 102
future 28, 224, 306, 310, 312
gains from 374, 504, 530
GATS can be a vehicle for 381
GATS-based, TM 518
global 10
gradual 230, 426
growing consensus on the benefits of 29
health-related services 439
help to overcome resistance to 260
immediate 28
intensity of 77
internal 261, 267, 268
investment 222, 273
labor movement 270
liberalization port services 374
likely to lead to decline in domestic prices 16
limited 505
main gains from 374
meaningful 259
measures to support industry damaged by 531
MFN 224, 230, 231, 274
modalities of 253–6
modest 306
most prominent attempt at 382
multilateral 22, 224, 230, 231, 237, 251, 258–60
mutual 566
negative list approach to 239, 253, 255
negotiated in context of WTO accession 381
non-preferential 227, 228–9
non-scheduled 56
not possible or viable 104
number of reasons to pursue via trade agreements 128
opposition to 268
partial 97, 114, 530
phase-in 245
phenomenon most likely to occur in early stages
   of 299
predicting and assessing implications of 99
procurement 272, 273
progressive 228, 439, 443, 444, 449
reciprocal 4, 5, 21, 24
regional 221, 224, 230, 231, 236–60, 268–81, 481
resistance to 238

risk that it may not yield a more stable source of
   credit 299
road transport 381
sector reform involving 463
sensitivity about timing and extent of 532
simple rules for 84
small increments 268
standstill and 267
substantial 367
sunk costs and sequence of 229–30
tariffs can simplify negotiations over 110
telecom 61, 65 n., 81, 426
transitional 245
unanticipated impacts of 305
unilateral 77, 126–8, 255, 307, 380, 455, 481
unlikely unanimity regarding merits of 92
value of spreading out 383
welfare benefits of 512
workable 353
see also commitments; liberalization effects;
   preferential liberalization
liberalization effects:
   concerns about universal service 411
   distributional 95
   economy-wide 10–11
   national health systems 450
   sectoral 9–10
   terms of trade 382
license fees 144, 145, 146, 158
   lower 229
licenses/licensing 57, 58, 66, 69, 105, 120, 225, 432, 522
   auctions of 61, 113, 228, 304
   compulsory 464
   country wishes to restrict total number of 404
   criteria imposed on financial institutions 293 n.
   discretionary 310, 313
   eligibility for 311
   fixed-wireless systems components 399
   foreign 205, 226, 345
   GATS entry 520
   import 108
   language not legally binding 242
   licenses reallocation of 374
   national regulations regarding 258
   operating, incorporation and possession 251 n.
   professions 489
   publicly available criteria for 413
   quota 109
   recognition of 237
   requirements applied to natural monopolist 343
   restrictions on 107, 179, 189, 227, 304
   specifications for 345
   spectrum allocation and 399, 418
   temporary, of engineers 244
life insurers 297, 303

Limao, N. 338, 359
limitations 292, 490
    foreign equity 309, 311
    horizontal 452
    market access 423–4
    non-discriminatory entry 342
    quantitative 255
    vertical 452
liner shipping 365
liquidity 290
listening 582
    active 578–9
Littlechild, S. 350 n.
Liu Mingkang 327–8
living standards 356, 496
    improving 338
Lo, W. C. 327
loans:
    and assistance 531
    foreign competitors able to set higher rates 299
    refusal to rollover 15
    see also NPLs
lobbies 57, 108, 127, 173
local call prices 463
locational services 19
location-specific investments 342
lock-in problem 352
logistics sector 366, 368, 369
    improvements in 378
    third-party providers 356
London 96
long-distance services:
    electricity transmission 340
    telecoms 346, 395, 398, 411, 414 n., 415, 416, 425, 427
    transport 369, 371
long-run incremental costs 408
Los Angeles 421
loss-making public enterprises 15
losses 124
    early years 379
    social 106, 125
Lovelock, P. 17
Low, P. 308 n.
low-grade service jobs 530
low-income/low-wage countries 211, 367, 493, 495
lower-skilled occupations/workers 487, 519
loyalty programs 374
Lumenga-Neso, O. 228 n.
lumpy investments 342
Luo, W. 366, 369
Luxembourg 212

McCulloch, N. 493
McDonald's 95, 398 n.

McGuire, G. 189–91, 204, 205, 210, 377
macroeconomics 531
    instability 311
    policy 292, 293
mail-order 475
mainframe computer industry 398 n.
major suppliers 408
    bankruptcy of 353
    risk of abuse of dominance by 272
Malawi 301, 369, 447 n.
Malaysia 81
    discrimination 190, 205
    environmental services 6
    foreign equity limits in insurance 311
    indigenization policy 314
    price impacts 210, 211
    restrictiveness 190, 205
malnutrition 338
management:
    improved 17
    new techniques 451
Mann, C. L. 466 n., 468, 474 n.
manufacturing industry 486, 503, 586
    displaced unskilled employees 529
    effective rates of protection for 10
    labor-intensive 356
    production 97
    trade in goods 357 n.
Marega, Flavio 45, 590–1
marginal costs 109, 114, 348
    constant 113
    optimal mark-up of price over 215
    social 123
marginal products 90, 92, 494–6, 521
    wages equal the value of 521
    workers paid the value of 493
marginal revenue curve 113
margins 198
    cost-price 215
    interest 209
    price-cost 14, 208–9, 211
    shipping 210
    wholesale trade 200
maritime services 185, 192
    auxiliary 365
    foreign suppliers 205
    impact of restrictions on 210
    international 201 n., 214
    negotiations past end of Uruguay Round suspended 365
    provision from home base in one economy to consumers in another 360
    restrictive trade policies and private anti-competitive practices 214
    unilateral policy action 374

maritime transport 237, 259, 268, 273, 553
  application of MFN principle 365
  commitments in 364, 381
  developing and transition economies'
      commitments in 364
  economies of scale and scope a feature of 341
  exemptions 359, 362
  liberalization of 81
  preferential quotas 226
mark-ups 116, 117, 215, 374, 414 n.
  reducing 296
market access 19, 54, 57, 222, 255, 268, 269, 273,
      291–2, 317, 362, 587
  additional opportunities that ease adjustment
      costs 360
  barriers to 307
  basis for checklist with regard to 58
  binding offers on 406
  broad 304
  challenge to interpreting 413–17
  choice of rules for 121
  common conditions in transport services 364
  contestability of 475
  definition in GATS 363
  developing countries' wish to gain 420
  directly inhibiting and/or nullifying 232
  e-commerce, concerns associated with 466
  enhanced for foreign insurers 296
  essentially prohibited 192
  exception in a country's schedule on 402
  existing GATS framework on 315
  foreigners 119, 294, 354
  full and unconditional 374
  future 527
  future, binding under WTO law 312
  GATS rules on 455
  granted to foreign firms 402
  granting to foreigners 354
  identifiable measure of security of 311
  impeded 239
  implications for focus on national treatment
      compared to 373
  important determinant of level of income 358
  improved 525
  increased 126
  "invisible" barriers to 406
  larger 95
  less constrained 192
  MFN basis 79
  national 548
  negotiations 548
  opportunities 380
  overlaps between national treatment and 60–1
  preferential 22
  priority over national treatment 374

  restricting 226, 294, 404–5
  restrictions 449
  significant limitations on 423–4
  sovereign regulatory conduct subjected to 272
  special 257
  standstill 430
  statistics necessary to evaluate opportunities 138
  subjecting all service sectors to disciplines 313
  unconditional 401
  via commercial presence limited by cap on foreign
      entry 363
market-access commitments 54, 192, 187, 205,
      442, 444
  affected or nullified by decisions on FDI or
      taxation 466
  avoiding non-discriminatory limitations on
      entry 342
  countries agree to undertake 253
  cross-border trade 295
  determining how to schedule 402
  distrusted 406
  exceptions in schedule of 404
  exchange of 78
  expanding 431
  financial services 204
  interaction of Reference Paper and 415
  OECD countries in BTA 423
  relatively modest levels of many 64
  resale 410
  scheduling of 398
  significant 400, 401
  strong 400
  violated 416
market-clearing price 353
market concentration 229
market dominance 229
market exclusivity 14, 463
market-expansion effects 95
market failure 272
  attributable to four kinds of problems 231
  building regulatory institutions needed to remedy 3
  countering problems that arise from 492
  domestic regulations to deal with 20
  due to natural monopolies or oligopolies 68
  one form that needs to be addressed directly by
      multilateral disciplines 343
  regulation arises essentially from 19
  responding to 84, 104
  very specific 492
market forces 96, 365, 428, 475
  competitive 391
market integration 357–8, 359
  full 224
  international 462
market-niche effect 94, 95

market opening 294, 377
  complemented by appropriate regulatory
    structures 339
  de novo 268
  demands for more 426
  foreign participation 372
  hybrid approach to 237
  implications of 80
  mutual 21
  negative-list approach to 237
  non-preferential 22
  reason to defer 22
  reciprocal 80
  seeking through trade negotiations 420
  vehicle to advance 380
  vested interests that could resist 224, 231
market power 423
  abuse of 374, 375
  capacity to exercise into complementary parts of
    network 464
  considerable 353
  created for foreign partners 414 n.
  high levels of 406
  incentive to employ, to discourage new
    entrants 408
  incumbents 375
  large firms that have 112
  main reason for differences between wages and
    long-run productivity 493 n.
  mobile wireless operators able to exercise 409
  shippers with 374
  significant 416
  supply constraints conducive to exercise of 353
  transitional measure to deal with 408
market saturation 447
market segments 96, 230, 400
  competitive 353
  economics of 391
  extra-normal profits in 16
  interconnection rules 409
  monopoly 346
  private leased circuit 394
  profitable 299
  scheduling commitments for 398
market share 315, 330, 334
  healthy 427
  incumbent suppliers may lose 359, 370
  long-distance 427
marketing:
  innovative schemes 400
  less expensive approaches to 398 n.
Marko, M. 204, 206, 212
Markusen J. R. 95, 101 n., 235 n., 497
Marrakesh Agreement (1994) 71, 233 n.
Martinez Peria, M. Soledad 300

Mattoo, A. 3 n., 59 n., 61 n., 64 n., 75 n., 204, 223 n.,
  232 n., 236 n., 291 n., 308 n., 309 n., 310 n.,
  311, 332 n., 338, 343, 348, 364, 365, 375, 379,
  380, 382, 383, 473 n., 474, 483, 492, 523, 524
maturity 584
Mauritius 9, 308 n.
MBSs (Mortgage-backed Securitizations) 333
MCI transmission capacity 423 n.
media contacts 575
medical services 100, 447, 452
medium-sized economies 509
mercantilist negotiations 21
merchandise trade 357
MERCOSUR (Mercado Común del Sur) 21, 24, 234,
  238 n., 239, 245, 247, 249 n., 256, 257, 258,
  264, 266, 267, 269 n.
  Montevideo Protocol on Trade in Services 253 n.,
    326 n.
mergers 300
  assessment of proposals 369
  horizontal 369
  proposed 422 n.
  vertical 369
mergers and acquisitions 228
  implications for competition 462
Metcalf's Law 460 n.
Methodological Soundness Questionnaire on the
  Balance of Payments (Eurostat/OECD
  2006) 164–5
Mexico 252, 316, 324, 373, 414 n., 531
  cross-border trucking between US and 382
  decline in welfare 216
  foreign ownership 300
  index scores 191
  labor costs 495 n.
  limits on foreign participation 311
  market-share caps 245 n.
  price impacts 211
  remittances 496
  restrictiveness 205
  scale of domestic banking problems 299
  settlement rates for 415
  significant foreign presence 294, 298
  US settlement costs to 416
  see also NAFTA
Mexico-EC FTA 316, 317, 319, 325
MFN (Most-Favored Nation) status 4, 21, 32, 63, 68,
  71, 77, 138, 223, 228, 229, 230, 231, 234, 235,
  237, 239, 239, 251, 254, 264, 360, 448, 516, 525,
  529, 547, 560
  asymmetries created by 588
  bargaining handicaps of 274
  country liberalizes on basis of 224
  discriminatory arrangements that contravene 366
  equity participation 311 n.

gains can be reaped through liberalization 224
limited constraint on "strategic" violations of 268
market access on basis of 79
members prevented from discriminating among
    trading partners 291
members unable to agree on application to maritime
    transport 365
monopoly providers act consistently with 342
national offers and market conduct 402
principle of 362
"raising the cost" for GATS signatories to
    violate 263
regulation designed to stop anti-competitive
    behavior in manner consistent with 415
MFN exemptions 64, 261, 262
  based on requirements set out in GATS Article
      V 261
  maintained 308 n.
  removal of 74–5, 291
  renegotiation of 72
  temporary 291
  ten-year time-frame for 65–6
  transport services 53 n., 362
Michigan Model 217 n.
micro-credit lending institutions 301
Microsoft 464
microwave-relay systems 399
Middle East 502
middle-income countries 510
middle management 507
middlemen 108
midwives 447
migrant worker programs 513–14
migration:
  development-friendly policy 31
  fear that it could unleash potentially overwhelming
      forces 515
  general legislation 258
  historical disposition towards 511
  illegal 79
  11, 31, 490, 493, 497
  labor 155
  long-term 490
  mass permanent 480
  poorest workers may gain because attracted by
      possibility of 496
  selection and screening of migrants 31
  skilled 4, 31
  statistics 156
  stepping stone to 28
  temporary 5, 156, 482–3, 499
  unskilled 31
  very small economies more likely to gain from 509
  see also permanent migration
Milgrom, P. 352

military personnel 141
Millennium Development Goals 338
minimum wage 521
Ministries:
  Finance 588–9
  Foreign 574
  Health 444
  PTT 390
  Trade 574
mirror servers 423
mirror statistics 145, 159
miscommunication 575
mistakes 119
misunderstanding 583
Mizuho Corporate Bank 330
MNCs (multinational corporations) 78, 160, 217
  assumed to produce a differentiated
      product 214
  less local training 507
  location decisions of 357 n.
  modeling of links between parents and
      affiliates 201–2
  profits at zero 215
  setting up in smaller countries 101
  vertical product chains 357 n.
mobile systems 342, 416, 417
  allowed to price higher and flexibly 400
  cellular firms 424
  phone-number portability 427
  pre-paid services 412
  rapidly expanding use 425
  termination charges 409, 410
  terrestrial and satellite-based 424
  wireless 399, 409
  see also GSM; MVNOs
Mobitel 424
mode-switching 125, 126
modems 397, 400, 417
modernization 430, 434
modes of supply 5, 16, 34, 35, 54, 67, 70, 72, 84, 89,
      139, 242, 363, 364, 560
  allocation of BOP/EBOPS items to 146
  asymmetric costs across 99
  complementary 101–3
  simplified approach to allocate services transactions
      statistics to 140
  substitute 100–1
  tax on producers who do not use Internet as 473–4
  WTO members male policy bindings in 239
  see also commercial presence; consumption abroad;
      cross-border trade; presence of natural
      persons
Mombasa 385
monetary costs 512
money supply 293

monitoring 369
  cargo 368
  movement of people 368
  suppliers 353
  tourism statistics 156
  traffic exchange 405
Monning, W. 573 n.
monopoly 14, 98, 109, 113, 247, 375, 378, 399,
    426, 435
  abuse of power 341, 347
  breaking, termination of incoming foreign
    calls 415
  considerable declines in telecom work force 17
  control over termination 414
  converting to duopoly 114
  eliminated 310
  extension of rights 69
  foreign-owned 374
  inefficiencies of 392, 394
  insurance 315
  justified 392
  law that would terminate 60
  national, reduction of importance of 5
  nationwide 427
  network-based industries prone to 272
  pro-competitive regulation to deal with 82
  regulated 84, 114
  specifically disciplines on granting or extending 442
  targets specified in license 14
  total 447
  trade-policy reform and provision of services 344–7
  see also monopoly pricing; natural monopoly; public
    monopolies
monopoly pricing 177, 341
  controlling 350 n.
  goal of restraining 350
  inefficient 394
  measures to contain 346
  problem continues to be important 342
  regulation to control 346, 354
  regulatory methods to guard against 344, 345
Montreal Ministerial Conference (1988) 589, 590
Montserrat 535
Moore's law 397, 460 n.
moral hazard 491, 492
Morocco 316, 319, 324
Mosely, P. 301
movement of people 179, 269
  customers 99
  monitoring 368
  restrictions on 189
movie stars 101
MRAs (Mutual Recognition Agreements) 120, 232,
    242, 243–5, 275, 277, 278
  pursuing at multilateral level 272

MSITS (*Manual on Statistics of International Trade in
    Services*) 138, 140, 146, 147, 148 n., 149, 150,
    151, 164, 165
  Annex 139, 143, 152, 153–4, 157 n.
  core recommendations of 145
  phased approach to implementation 162–3, 166
multilateral bargaining 260
multilateral initiatives 20
multilateral negotiations 79, 381–2, 420, 547, 586
  comprehensive 557
  more formal 545
  power to say no in 565
  process closely associated with 464
multilateral rules 20, 68, 78, 265, 459
  binding, challenges faced for implementation 470
  case for 469–70
  common 138
multimedia 400
multi-modal services 365
multinational companies, *see* MNCs
multi-sectoral negotiations 312
Mundell, R. 100
Murphy, C. 470 n.
music industry 465
mutual funds 301
mutual recognition, *see* MRAs
MVNOs (mobile virtual network operators) 410

NAFTA (North American Free Trade Agreement) 4,
    21, 31, 40, 103, 252, 236, 239, 244, 246, 247,
    254, 255, 257, 259–60, 265, 267, 317, 391, 534
  Mexico-US and liberalization of cross-border road
    transport 381–2
  ratchet clause developed in 324
  sectoral experimentation in financial services 245
  sub-national governments and lists of non-
    conforming measures 256
  trade preferences under FTA 251–2
NAFTA-TAA program (1993) 531
nannies 87, 88
national carriers 414
National Financial Work Conference 332
national health insurance schemes 156
national income 197 n.
  maximizing the value of 89
national interests 182
  assembling information on 552–4
national markets 20
national regulations 23, 224, 233, 258, 470
  inadequate, potential for 474
national security 492
national sovereignty 414 n., 470
  current ideas of 564–5
national treatment 54, 58–9, 119, 120, 239, 255, 291,
    360, 362, 364, 587

defined 292
exceptions to 516
existing GATS framework on 315
expanded, precommitment to 302–3
focus on, compared to market access 373
foreign operators 354
full 53
future, binding under WTO law 312
GATS rules on 455
governments free at any time to grant or
    withdraw 56
measures violating 262
negotiations on 548
overlaps between market access and 60–1
principles of 402
priority of market access over 374
quantitative restrictions or denials of 48
regulation designed to stop anti-competitive
    behavior in manner consistent with 415
restrictions 449
subjecting all service sectors to disciplines 313
national treatment commitments 187, 205, 253, 304,
    442, 444, 548
avoiding discrimination against foreign
    suppliers 343
member has not made 474
nationality 57, 59, 489, 539
company 273
requirements 205
natural monopoly 19, 68, 231, 232, 339–43, 372
conditions that can lead to 338
definition of 341
existence of 19–20
industry segments characterized by 228
policy problem associated with 341
proper response to 463 n.
tendency to 359
NBFIs (nonbank financial intermediaries) 289
NCA (Ghana National Communications
    Authority) 424
necessity tests 242, 523
negative list approach 239, 253, 255
negotiating leverage 53, 77, 269, 560–1
significant 24
negotiation strategy 556–9, 563–7, 586–7
Nepal 24
Netherlands 205, 565
network-based industries/services 228, 231
network costs 18
network effects 341
network externalities 229, 315, 392, 460 n.
breadth a key factor for 508
networking revolution 459 n.
networks 94, 97–8, 370
access to and use of 432

backbone 421, 422–3 nn.
communication 460, 463
global 414
incumbent 463
inefficient duplication 18
infrastructure 410
international 341, 404
national 405
open-access 460
packet-switching 460
production 357
rules-of-the-game adopted for guaranteeing smooth
    operation of 467
slowing down the growth of 475
social 488
specialized 19
supply 95
transport 340, 344, 368
unbundling 18, 423
see also computer networks; corporate networks;
    distribution networks; telecommunications
    networks
new entrants 16, 17, 18, 229, 311 n., 359
competition from 395–6, 406
complaints about access 423
easier to build own backbone wired network 395
imposing requirement on 20
incumbents share network economies with 408
inferior conditions of operation to 81
interconnection regulations to 395
more competitive, protecting suppliers from 352
pricing behavior 374
sunk costs can be used strategically by first movers to
    deter 229
transmission capacity available on cost effective
    terms 395
see also potential market entrants
new markets 370
foreign providers likely to enter 369
new technologies 344, 369, 374, 408, 451
ability to absorb 508
access to 307
impact of 398 n.
knowledge of 88
making health more amenable to trade 447
tried and tested in offshore markets 344
New York 96, 419
New Zealand 568
banks almost entirely foreign-owned 300
restrictiveness index score 190
safeguarding agreements between Australia
    and 266 n.
success in opening up to foreign firms 294
see also ANZCERTA; Australia-New Zealand
Newbery, D. 353

newly industrializing countries 197
NGOs (non-governmental organizations) 550,
    551, 555
Nguyen-Hong, D. 206, 211
Nicaragua 9, 324, 496
Nicolaidis, K. 243 n., 542 n., 586 n.
Nicoletti, G. 186, 193, 206
Nielson, Julia 232 n.
Nielson, J. 484
Nigeria 309
Noam, E. 414 n.
non-conforming measures 239, 247, 254, 269
    negative lists of 253, 256
    "revealed" 255
non-discrimination 84, 119, 138, 183, 246,
    309 n., 430–1, 432, 529
    conditions for workers 257
    interconnection provision 416
    regulatory conduct 272
non-establishment right 269
non-interference 417
non-professional essential personnel 270
non-scheduled sectors 56
Nordic countries 266 n.
norms 475
    guarantee not to violate 476
    international interconnection 470
    multilateralization of 234
North American trade agreements 315
    see also NAFTA
North Atlantic region 422
Northeast Reconstruction Bank (China) 329
NPLs (non-performing loans) 295 n., 301, 330–2, 333
NTBs (non-tariff barriers) 103, 169, 178, 267
    pervasiveness of 104
    quantity-based measurements of 183–4
    tariffs more transparent and porous than 522
nurses 447, 490, 509, 523
    overseas 523 n., 525

objective criteria 581–2
objectivity 293
obligations 239, 271
    access 50, 54–7
    assumption by source countries 79
    burdensome 588
    competition 416
    competitively neutral 434
    conditional 63, 66–9
    core 64
    far-reaching 383
    "formula" 587
    general 138, 441–2, 448, 449
    government 406
    interconnection 409

    legally binding 60
    MFN 402, 448
    national-treatment 59
    non-discriminatory 434
    phasing out 409
    policy 378
    rollout 14
    screening of service providers 271
    source-country 79
    standstill 67, 430
    transparency 69, 434
    treaty 430
    unconditional 63–6
    see also USOs
OECD (Organization for Economic Cooperation and
    Development) 42, 161, 164, 204, 236 n.,
    242, 246, 256 n., 377, 463 n., 468 n., 543,
    554, 559, 586
    all nations essentially bound to unconditional
        market access 401
    Benchmark Definition of FDI 147
    business exports 9
    decisions to enter foreign markets driven by
        reputational concerns 315
    e-commerce issues 459
    estimate of effects of restrictiveness for group of
        countries 193
    financial services 447, 587, 588
    *Handbook on Economic Globalisation
        Indicators* 147 n., 152 n.
    impact of telecommunications regulations 213
    indexes compiled from 205
    International Direct Investment Statistics 162 n.
    liberalization commitments 311
    market access commitments 423
    Measuring Globalization (2001) 160, 162 n.
    memorandum items 164
    newly open markets in international services 415
    protection skewed towards supporting unskilled
        wages and employment 510
    rationales for negotiating goals of 314
    regional agreements among countries 267
    restrictiveness index for telecommunications 206
    *Statistics on International Trade in
        Services* 159, 162 n.
    telecommunications 447
    temporary access to foreign service providers 11
    temporary migration schemes 31
    Trade Committee 542
    Workshop Report (Internet Traffic Exchange
        2001) 422 n.
    see also SIMSDI
Ofcom (UK telecoms regulator) 409, 410 n.
offshore markets 344
oil crisis (1973/4) 513

oil reserves 93
oligopoly 19, 68, 231, 232
  development of 299
  foreign 223, 228
  network-based industries prone to 272
"one way bypass" problem 415
one-year rule 141, 153
OneTouch 424
Ongena, S. 300
online betting 473
Onse Telecom 427
open markets 231
open-skies agreement 258
opening statements 575
openness 22, 54, 377
  foreign entry 309
  future 28
  indices of 305
  key infrastructure services 338
  mutual 238
operating costs 341
opportunity costs 89, 100, 106–7
optimum regulatory areas 239
ordinary least squares 211
Ouagadougou 385
output 90, 91, 111, 116, 149, 499
  aggregate 114, 493, 501
  drives down prices of exports relative to
      imports 502
  efficient 123
  expanded 95
  fall in 216
  incumbent firm will maximize profits by
      restricting 339
  large increases in 215 n.
  limitations on total quantity of 292, 362
  perfectly elastic demand for 377
  pressure on 354
  problem with trade barriers as means to raise 112
  restricting quantity or quality of 338, 341
  too little 339
  world 493, 507
outsourcing services 77, 368
  prime destination for 419
outward FATS 147, 150, 151, 160
outward looking strategies 563–4
Overseas Doctors Training Scheme (UK) 528
ownership rights 375
Oye, K. 529

packet-switching networks 460
Pakistan 81, 308 n.
Pan American Health Organization/World Health
    Organization (2002), 437 n.
Panagariya, A. 225 n.

Panda bonds 333
Panel and Appellate Body Rulings: *United States-*
    Gambling Services 56 n., 58 n., 59 n.
Papademetriou, Demetrios G. 43, 533–4
para-tariffs 511
patents 145, 465
Pauwelyn, J. 58 n.
PBoC (People's Bank of China) 327, 329
PC operating systems 464
PCS (international telephone service) 425
PECC (Pacific Economic Cooperation
    Council) 185, 186–7
peer pressure 301
peering agreements/arrangements 422 n., 423
Pena, M.-A. 253 n.
pension rights 489
People's Bank Law (China) 327
performance 133, 290, 354, 397
  adversely affected 463
  competitiveness depends on 376
  differences in ownership and legal form affect 314
  economy-wide 9, 229, 237, 251
  export 419
  financial 304
  foreign bank 300
  input controls 182
  growth 13
  market 414 n.
  port 359, 368
  range of requirements on foreign services
      providers 226
  sectoral 9, 201
  transport and distribution services 356
  wholesale market 353
perishable products 357
permanent migration 31, 91, 482–3, 490, 508
  may eventually become less threatening 511
political problems 510
perpetual infancy 22
personal services 145, 146, 155
Peru 30, 87, 98, 308 n.
  publicly funded IT projects 464
  universal-service levy 20–1
Petrazzini, B. A. 17, 379
phase-in issues 61, 65 n., 66 n., 245, 305, 406, 413
Philippines 81, 308 n., 311
  commitment in FSA to allow increased number of
      branches 313
  discrimination 190
  index scores 190
  insurance industry plays significant role in
      mobilizing capital 301
  margins 200
  nannies from 87
  nurses 509, 525

Philippines (*cont.*)
    private telecom operators 463 n.
    restrictiveness 189, 205, 210
    software development 6
    temporary labor 486, 487
Philippines Overseas Employment Administration 487
philosophical defense strategy 566
"phishing" scams 469
photocopying 464
physical capital 455
physical contact 99
PLAB (Professional and Linguistic Assessment Board)
    test 524
point-to-point operating 371
Poland 31, 300, 310, 313
policy 5, 53, 17–21, 476
    agricultural 566
    coherence 293–5
    compensatory 529–32
    integration 5
    intervention 82
    macroeconomic 292, 293
    regulatory 378–9, 469
    see also competition policy; trade policy; *also under*
        following headings prefixed "policy"
policy change 255–6
    actual future effects of 498
    binding commitment to 383
    credibility of 379
    political resistance to 547
policy reform 293, 339, 359, 360, 511
    credibility of 354
    impact of 201, 295–307, 338, 367–70
    opportunity to pursue, deepen or lock in 221–2
    political resistance to 370
    priorities for 376
    successful 343–7, 370–6
    unilateral 365
political asylum 489
political power 80
political pressure 303, 435
political will 391
Pollitt, M. G. 373
pollution 359, 375
poor people/areas 383
    access to essential services 14
    adverse effect on access to credit 301
    effects on prices of services for 15–16
    improved transport access 377–9
    protecting 19
population censuses 156
population density 346
pornography 468, 475
portfolio allocation 293 n.
ports 210, 372

access to and use of facilities 365
handling costs 359
liberalization of services 374
performance in 359
positive impact of reform in 368
reasonable and non-discriminatory terms to
    incoming ships 381
restrictions on provision of services 214
vertical mergers between shipping companies
    and 369
Portugal 212, 294
postal services 192
potential market entrants 56, 58, 69, 372, 373
poverty:
    alleviation, potential contribution of foreign FSPs to
        addressing 301
    effective reduction strategy 351
    potentially mixed implications for 496
    temporary mobility and 496–7
precedents 242
precommitment 302–3, 310, 312–13
predatory pricing 374
predictability 56, 390, 433
pre-employment requirements 519
preferences:
    consumer 357
    de facto 226
    establishment of 223
    local-content 124
    regional 224, 231, 237, 250
    scheduling 54
    service quality 369
    social 474, 475
    trade 251–2
    see also regulatory preferences
preferential liberalization 4, 21–2, 32
    economic considerations 223–35
    multilateral consistency of 266
    multilateral constraints on 260–2
    policy flexibility towards 261
premium services 412
pre-paid phone cards 400
presence of natural persons (GATS mode 4) 6, 49, 50,
    57, 60, 87, 88, 138, 139, 140, 146, 152, 165, 166,
    169, 182, 258, 303, 360, 367, 590
    case for more ambitious approach in 77
    elements related to 156
    exchange of commitments 382
    fewer commitments on 364
    financial services 291
    five categories 270
    framework for negotiating liberalizing
        commitments 78–80
    indicators for assessing/measuring 154, 155
    information to construct frequency ratios 186

labor mobility covered only by 257
length of stay related to 153
likely gains from liberalization 498
limitations 292, 452
market access to supply of construction services
    through 273
statistics on 154–7, 163
suppliers and users move necessary experts in and
    out of a country 403
temporary movement 31, 42–4, 153, 155, 480–541,
    590
press releases 552
pressure groups 434
price caps 350 n., 412 n., 415
    charges for terminating calls 427
    retail 353
price-cost margins 14, 208–9, 211
price-fixing agreements 374
price-impact measurements 192–5, 206, 208–14
price setting 408
price wedges 169, 186
prices:
    access 350
    affordable 396
    average-cost 117
    coefficients relating restrictiveness to 193
    consumer 17, 414 n.
    decline in 227
    determinants of 107, 193
    distinctive 174
    driving down 462
    effect of trade restrictions on 193
    effects on services for the poor 15–16
    escalated 411
    exorbitant 396
    export 356, 377–8, 382
    factor 16, 356
    FDI increases welfare by lowering 111
    fixed 105
    gap in 108
    help to keep down 125
    higher 106, 377–8
    import 109, 356, 382
    inflated 339, 411
    prices input 10
    freeing 291
    lower 118, 342, 374, 411, 419
    market 141, 177, 419
    observed 184
    plunged 393, 397
    predicted 195
    real 397
    regulated, foreign investment with 114–17
    relative 499, 537
    retail 349, 350, 351

takeover 229
transport 374
wholesale 353
world 105, 356, 376
primary markets 290
Primo Braga, C. A. 178, 460 n., 463 n., 464 n.,
    469 n., 470, 474 n.
principal supplying interest 264
privacy 468, 475, 476
private carrier agreements 374
private hospitals 452
privatization 17, 113, 182, 425
    complete 345
    concerns over 427
    conducted without concern to creating conditions
        of competition 13
    electricity distribution 17
    end of government support 16
    gradual 426–7
    labor productivity significantly increased by 201
    more favorable effects from introducing
        competition before 201
    overly long monopoly periods 413
    partial 390
    reduction in workforce after 17
    sector reform involving 463
    time to 206, 208
problem-solving 397
problem-solving negotiations 544
    bilateral 545
procurement 71, 247 n., 272–3, 442
    policies to address anti-competitive
        practices 464
    preferential policies 105
procurement markets 237, 246
producer surplus 107, 111, 114, 118, 119
    decline in 227
product lifetime 357
product markets 235
product mixes 369
product variety 94–5
    local, protection preserving 122–4
    optimum/optimal 122, 124
production 50, 123, 137
    allocated to various host-country locations 214
    bundling of more than one service 340
    concentrated in one place 96
    costs firms minimize 537
    decline in 500 n.
    demand for 538
    foregone 89
    instantaneous links to 419
    network economies in 341
    shut down 124
    simultaneous 5

production costs:
  firms minimize 499
  marginal 106
production distortion 112
productive capacity:
  indistinguishable 93
  over-expansion of 15
productive investments 307
productivity 97, 101, 356, 493
  boost to 16
  catch-up 503
  difference between home and host countries 537–8
  existence or removal of barriers affect 200
  gains in 10, 14
  growth in 497
  higher 116
  important determinant of growth 356
  increases in 94
  indicator of 495 n.
  marginal 521
  per worker 369
  proportionate gap between host and home
    countries 510
  social 113
  telecom 463
  temporary workers earn a wage for labor related
    to 537
  see also labor productivity
professional services 64, 112, 357
  inhibiting trade in 105
  quotas in 105
  regulation of 117–21
  unnecessary or needlessly burdensome
    requirements 227
professionals:
  granted improved access 270
  licensed 489
  middle-level, agency-provided flows of 490
profitability:
  enhancing 230
  foreign ownership reduces 296 n., 300
  international traffic 415
  relative 198
profits 353, 466
  aggregate 114
  competed away in markets now more open 378
  economic, large 414
  excess 493 n.
  extra-normal 16
  international services 415
  maximizing 89, 339, 348, 350 n.
  monopoly, loss of 349
  reluctance to eliminate 415
  taxing 304
  zero 215

proportionality 231, 272
  necessity test aimed at ensuring 242
protection(ism) 4, 122, 126–7, 182, 223, 225, 227, 233
  battle against 21
  effective rates of 10
  higher current levels 11
  how multilateral trade rules might shift legitimate
    from 20
  identifying relative levels across sectors and
    countries 214
  inextricably linked with domestic regulation 104
  infant industry 492
  instruments of 103–10
  masking 232
  not all regulations should be viewed as 183
  perpetual 22
  policies in agriculture 4
  preserving local product variety 122–4
  producer lobbies for 127
  tax a useful index of stringency of 110
proximity 5, 229
  geographic 231, 233, 237, 257
  linguistic 233
  need for 137
  physical 237, 258
prudential regulations 20, 29, 30, 69, 292, 296, 304
  adequate, liberalization not accompanied
    with 554
PTOs (public telecommunications operators) 206
PTT (Post, Telegraph and Telephone) ministries 390
public monopolies:
  cross-subsidization within 16
  move away from 17
  possible reduction in employment in 17
  reason for persistence of 15
public morals 473
public policy objectives 247
public purse 510
public-private partnerships 470
public-sector unions 435
public transport 16
Punta Del Este 542
purchasing power 496

QFII (Qualified Foreign Institutional Investors)
  scheme 330
qualifications 20, 66, 69, 225, 226, 525
  clear and reliable certification of 528
  educational 237
  foreign 67, 205, 489
  improvements in 30
  professional 237, 244, 523
  recognition of 237, 258, 513, 524
  registering 511
  technical 523

unnecessary or needlessly burdensome
requirements 227
quality 344, 375, 397
aspects of transportation 357 n.
ensuring 343
improvement in 16, 296
infrastructural 358
land transport access 369
road 369
uncertainty about 512
quality standards 50, 84, 104, 105
mandatory 233
quantitative indicators 139 n.
quantitative restrictions 48, 107, 227, 362, 466, 511
non-discriminatory 236, 239
quantity discounts 348
quantity-impact measurements 195–7
quotas 107–10, 226, 227, 499, 500, 521
airline 366
allocation of 519
auctioned 123
country-specific 366
countrywide 514
developing main beneficiaries of increase in 502
distortions caused by 112
elimination of 80
freight 226
import 107
imposed on foreign suppliers 105
industry-by-industry 514
inflows of temporary workers 537
job, exceeded 514
licensing 109
numerical 522
pervasive 105
preferential 226
relaxation of 501 n.
small relaxation in 512
temporary workers 520

Radelet, S. 356, 377
radio bands/frequencies 399, 417
radio messages services 430
rail transport 29, 81, 143, 341, 372
commitments in 364
competition in 373
economies of scale and scope a feature of 341
railway gauges/lines 232, 340
Ramsey pricing 348, 350, 351
ratchet mechanism 255, 269, 311 n., 324
rates of return 215
changes in 202
foreign investors 391
real income 97
impacts on 359

real wages 215, 493, 504
differences between sectors 505
equalization of 505
pushing down 97
reallocation of resources 368
rebalancing 263, 267, 351, 411, 412, 463
reciprocity 64, 312, 380, 497
benefits from 126
implicit 546
recognition agreements 228
Recommendations on Statistics of International
Migration, see SNA; UN
recreational services 145, 146, 155
FDI restrictions 187
other 473
red-herring strategy 565
redistribution 92, 106, 532
Reference Paper on Telecommunications (WTO) 351,
354, 372, 376, 381, 382–3, 470, 474, 548
challenge to interpreting 413–17
interconnection consensus in 408–10
major achievement 406–7
universal service as key challenge 410–13
reform(s) 401, 463
buttressing 21–32
can promote efficiency service 9–17
catalysts for 297
complementary 201
credible 81, 420
demands for 29
effects of flaws in programs 13–15
financial 15, 291, 301, 412
international negotiations help to support 379–80
labor market 426 n.
managing 14
opportunity to harness the potential of 269
plurilateral 208
promise of 29
redistributions affect prospects of 493
reinforcement of process 5
sector 63
sense of urgency in 313
sequencing of 5, 201
significant effects of 369
structural 206, 327–9
telecom, market-oriented 463
temporary 298
unfinished agenda 330–5
unilateral efforts 238
widespread, likely to benefit nearly everyone
eventually 492
work-in-progress 295
see also policy reform; regulatory reform
regional agreements 79, 270, 565
since BTA 409

Regional Internet Registries 467
regional negotiations 400, 529
regionalism 36–7, 221–86, 529
regionalization 30
regression models 203
regulation(s) 58, 84, 179, 225, 317–19, 341, 359, 433
   absence of 232, 343
   access 347, 348
   access-impeding 253
   adequate, lack of 15
   air transport 366
   arising from market failure 19
   comparable 228
   cooperation on 4, 32
   costs of 104, 409 n.
   differences across countries 98
   differing demands for 474
   direction for change in 380
   disciplines on 66–9
   discriminatory 105, 178, 202, 226, 227, 253, 291
   distinguishing legitimate from illegitimate 183
   e-commerce 41–2, 459–79
   economic case for 231
   effective 370, 374, 378, 423
   efficient 19–21, 238
   elimination of 548
   emphasizing 17–21
   entry 398 n.
   exploiting economies of scale in 32
   final price 20
   financial 15, 469 n.
   flexible 413
   foreign 190
   foreign requests for change in 564
   foreign workers 516
   geared to solving market failures 492
   good 354
   governments have flexibility to implement their
      own 119
   imperfect 119
   improved 297
   industry-specific 352
   innovative 427
   integrating trade opening with combination of
      competition and 14
   interconnection 395, 396, 398
   international 30
   Internet content 468
   lack of 372
   lifted 426
   maintaining credibility of 369
   market-oriented 406
   measurements of 214
   monopoly pricing 346
   multilateral 175, 475

   needlessly burdensome 227, 231, 232
   non-discriminatory 178, 237
   ostensibly valid purpose 185
   outdated 567
   phone networks 394
   price-cap 350 n.
   price impacts of 208, 213
   pricing 348, 349, 350
   privacy 475, 476
   pro-competitive 30, 232, 344, 348, 383, 391, 406
   professional services 117–21
   qualitative 291
   quantitative 291
   rate-of-return 350 n.
   reasons for applying to transport sector 375
   reduction of 548
   restrictiveness of 181, 184, 203, 263
   services exempt from 397
   social purpose 15–16
   sound 30
   strengthening 327
   strong 475
   technical 226
   telecom 397, 462
   trade policy and 112, 124
   trade-related 58, 104
   transition to competition 408
   transparency of 297, 315, 390
   unilateral 415
   vehicle-axle loads enforcement 369
   visa 489
   voluntary 525–6
   wage parity 521
   see also national regulations; prudential regulations
regulatory agencies 290
regulatory authorities:
   capacity to engage private sector 468
   creation of 390–1
   independence of 431
   major 417
   national, monitoring behavior of suppliers 353
regulatory convergence 224, 231, 234, 239, 244
   preferential 234
regulatory cooperation 4, 222, 224, 232, 233
   regionalism and 231
regulatory environment:
   e-commerce and 459–62, 469
   international 476
   search costs associated with learning about 475
   technical support and resources to improve 82
regulatory failure 18, 353
regulatory frameworks 431
   critical role 15
   mutually compatible 544
   pro-competitive 259 n.

soundest 233
  supporting e-commerce 469
regulatory harmonization 120, 264, 293 n.
  benefits from 224, 234
  initial selectivity in choice of partners for 245
  integration often requires certain degree of 22–3
  negotiations as vehicles for pursuing 354
  progress difficult at regional level in matters of 242
regulatory impediments:
  addressing 271–2
  nature of 223
regulatory intensity 231–3
regulatory mechanisms 313
regulatory powers:
  health-related services 449
  negotiation of multilateral disciplines on 450
regulatory preferences 226
  foreign 224, 233, 242
regulatory reform 119, 346–7, 354, 412, 553, 557
  competitive effects 378
  different experiences with 234
  direction of changes in 360
  direction that GATS may provide to 380
  international trade negotiations can facilitate 339
  model schedule for 354
  policy advice and assistance for 80
  trade liberalization not possible or viable unless
    accompanied by 104
  widespread 201, 206
regulatory regimes 554
  ambitious efforts to harmonize 474
  convergence of 224, 231
  national 470, 471
  stringent 213
regulatory weaknesses 311
reinsurance 303
  cross-border provision of 588
reliability 397, 413
  codes on 417
  guarantees 395
  uncertainty about 512
relocation expenses 531
remittances 91, 155, 451, 496, 497, 508 n., 509, 537
  factor incomes adjusted for 538
rent-seeking activities 108
  appropriation 113, 114, 304
  extraction 127, 228
  fostering 465
  incentives to collect 304
  leakage 116, 117
  offshore transfer 374
  quota 107–8, 109, 227
  retained by incumbents 367
  scarcity 521
  transfer to foreign oligopolists 223, 228

workers can share 493 n.
repatriation 31, 528
  accepting and facilitating 28
  binding commitments on screening, selection and
    facilitating 31
reporting requirements 297
reproduction costs 465
reputation 95
  building 584
  undermined 315
request-offer approach 72, 74, 560–2, 570–1, 588
  formulae vs. 76–7
resale 290, 398, 399
  full competition in 426
  market in spectrum 418
  simple, international 416
  wireless operators 410
reservation systems 340, 366, 367–8
residence 6, 143, 524
  discretion to grant, refuse and administer
    permits 258
  one-year rule for determining 141, 153
  trading partners 145
residents and non-residents 137, 139
  statistics of trade in services between 140
resistance 126
respect 584
Rest of the EU region 502
restaurants 94
  fast-food 99
  foreign franchises 122
restrictiveness/restrictions 107, 179, 180, 181, 264, 365
  common effect of 223
  discriminatory 60, 206, 254 n.
  foreign investment in telecommunications 420
  geographic 297, 303
  horizontal 487
  identified, inventories of 183
  indexes of 170, 184, 185–91, 204–8, 209–10, 211,
    212
  market access 226, 294, 404–5, 449
  measures of 203
  national-treatment 449
  non-prudential 209
  official 488
  ownership and control 182
  policy 377
  regulatory 297, 488
  see also quantitative restrictions
restructuring:
  consolidation and 327
  corporate 426 n.
  financial sector 228, 426 n.
  public sector 426 n.
  state-owned banks 15

retail trade:
  food distributors 208
  margins 200
  price caps 353
retraining 121
returns on investment 113
  artificially inflated 17
  higher 391
returns to capital 356, 500
  higher, welfare increases from 502
  real 217
  total 350 n.
  wage payments and 172–3
returns to scale:
  constant 97, 235
  increasing 87, 93–8
revenue 108, 227, 393, 414
  customs 474
  little or none to lose 223
  long-distance services to subsidize universal
    service 411 n.
  lost 226
  optimal way to raise 112
  restrictions that do not generate 107
  sales tax 474
  tariff 107, 125
  tax 106, 107
  total sales 198 n.
reverse engineering 221
"revolving door" model 490
Richards, J. E. 414 n., 415
ring tone downloads 427
Rischard, J. F. 470 n.
risk-adjusted returns 299
risk-premium elasticity 215, 216, 217
risk premiums 413
risk-taking 397
risk-reward ratio 391
risks:
  aggregation of 307
  commercial 303
  concentration of 305
  credit 299
  critical role in managing 290
  diversifying 290, 296
  downside 223, 228
  economic 298–301
  limiting 451–2
  low rating 345
  political 515
  pooling 111, 307
road transport 360, 362, 364
  commitments from developing and developed
    economies 364
  cross-border liberalization of 381

cross-border, liberalization of 381
economies of scale and scope a feature of 341
longer-distance trucking 369
MFN exemptions 362
operators from one country setting up business to
  supply services in another 360
sufficient competition from network 341
Rodrik, D. 493
role reversal 582
rollout obligations/targets 14, 463
Romer, P. 491
Rosario 368
Roy, M. 72 n.
Royal Bank of Scotland 328
royalties 117, 144, 145, 146, 158, 466
RTAs (Regional Trade Agreements) 36–7, 221–86, 381
  financial services liberalization in 315
rule design 222, 238
  greater coherence in 247 n.
rules 364
  advancing at regional level 268–81
  agreeing on architecture of 269–70
  applied in predictable manner 127
  disclosure 297
  e-commerce 475
  efforts devoted to developing 221
  employment of professional staff 363
  GATS 70–1, 443, 444, 448, 449, 455
  industry-specific 352
  interconnection 406, 409
  international 232, 308, 382–3, 549
  investment 247
  liberalization 84
  local, compliance with 294
  manipulated to protect suppliers 104
  market access 121
  MFN 415, 516
  national 413
  negotiations on 444, 559, 571–2, 574
  non-discrimination 119, 415
  privacy 476
  regional attempts at developing 221
  rights to fly 366
  sound and clear 433
  special, to certain sectors 258
  trade 428
  traffic 67
  wage parity 513
  wholesale-market design 353
  WTO 472, 512
  see also multilateral rules
rules of origin:
  absent 223, 228
  liberal 228, 249, 273, 274
  restrictive 229, 270 n., 273

sectoral, discriminatory 249 n.
  stringent ownership-related 230
rural areas:
  access to financial services 301
  borrowers may pay lower interest rates 16
  development in 358
  remittances to 496
  subsidies from urban to 411
  under-provision of retail banking 299
Russia:
  prospective WTO accession 36, 171
  tariff equivalent for business/financial services 197
Rutherford, Thomas 36

SAA (Australian Special Adjustment Assistance) 531
SAARC (South Asian Association for Regional
    Cooperation) 257
Sachs, J. 356, 377
safeguards 516, 525, 531
  see also ESM
safety codes 417
Saint Lucia 535
St Kitts and Nevis 535
St Vincent 535
sale and delivery 50
sales 198 n.
  cross-border 6
  reduced 227
sales tax 466, 474
Samsung Electronics 427
Sanchez, S. M. 300
Santiago 375
Sapir, A. 493, 532
satellite services 399, 417
Saudi Arabia 486
Sauvé, P. 223 n., 232 n., 236 n., 246 n., 251 n., 253 n.,
    259 n., 382 n.
savings 301
  access to 299
  basic services 301
  mobilized 307
  pooling 290
Scancom 425
scarcity 521
scheduling commitments:
  different market segments 398
  text for use in 315
scheduling issues 60–3
Schuele, M. 189–91, 205, 210
Schuknecht, L. 311, 473 n., 474
science and technology 513
screening 31, 119, 121
  bad 118
seafarers 48
search costs 475

seasonal workers 155, 513
Seattle Ministerial Meeting (1999) 72, 473
secondary markets 290
second-generation services 399–400, 428
sectoral modeling 201
sectoral negotiations 548, 572–3
securities services 180, 290
security 468–9
  clearance for potential entrants 520
  internal 515, 516
  threats to 520
Self, Richard 587 n., 589 n.
self-regulation 304, 468, 475
semiconductor chips 466
Senegal 309, 425
sequences 18
sequencing 5, 201, 294, 370–6
service providers:
  arrangements that discriminate against 261
  exclusive 238
  foreign 224
  key to meaningful access for many 272
  obligations to screen 271
  restricting number of 225–6, 228–9
services trade:
  basic economics of 84–129
  guide to negotiations 542–92
  measuring 133–68
  reforms appropriately sequencing 3
  reforms can promote efficiency 9–17
  regionalism in 221–86
  regulatory intensity of 231–3
SET (Secured Electronic Transactions) protocol 468
settlement:
  and clearing services 290
  international 413–17
settlement rate system 422, 426
Shanghai 357
  Pudong Development Zone 327
Shapiro, C. 414 n., 460 n.
sheltered sectors 530
Sherman, L. 401 n., 410 n.
shipping 98
  bulk 365
  coastal 365
  eliminating restrictions on 211
  foreign lines 372
  international 365
  low charges 211
  markets for 374
  restrictions affecting 365
shipping companies:
  foreign 370
  vertical mergers between ports and 369
shipping costs 356, 357 n.

shocks 92
  banking system more resilient in the face of 297
  difficult to absorb 290
  insulation against 532
  robustness of financial system to 297–8
shop opening hours 67
shortages 521
  key 454
  skilled 26, 486, 510
Shukla, Shurang 589
Sierra Leone 309, 447 n.
silence 580
Silicon Valley 96
SIMSDI (OECD/IMF Survey of Implementation of
    Methodological Standards for Direct
    Investment) 160–1, 164
Sinclair, S. 437 n.
Singapore 197, 319, 568
  bilateral trade agreements with 401
  discrimination against foreign banks 190
  foreign participation in local insurance
      companies 311
  margins 200
  openness 205
  price impacts due to restrictions on foreign
      banks 210
  unilaterally accelerated foreign-entry
      provisions 307
  see also EFTA-Singapore; Japan-Singapore; US FTAs
Singapore Issues 233 n.
Sjamsoeddın, Munir 298 n.
SK Telecom 427
skepticism 16–17, 578, 582, 588
skill-intensive sectors 447
skilled labor/workers 88, 257, 482, 497, 500, 501, 502,
    507–10
  abundance of 100
  cheaper, capital replaced with 503
  critical mass of 503
  effective supply of 537
  employment in transport operations 363
  foreigners competing with 16
  migration removes 496
  see also less-skilled workers
Slovak Republic 310, 313
Slovenia 310, 313
small developing countries:
  important consideration for 342
  international trade negotiations with 433, 434
small markets 20, 375
SMEs (small- and medium-sized enterprises) 385, 397
Smith, A. S. J. 373
Smith, R. 437 n., 446
Smith, T. 205
SNA (*System of National Accounts 1993*) 150, 153, 165

Snape, R. 253 n.
social capital 122
social costs 108, 111
  lower 112
  tariff 123, 125
social dysfunction 530
social gains 124
  unambiguous 117
social identity 492
social impacts 301–2
social insurance 92
  short-run 522
social policy 383, 516
social protection systems 532
  long-run 522
social security systems 156
  contributions 514
  entitlements to benefits 522
  preservation of 532
  repatriating payments 528
societal values 468
software 87, 89, 273, 394, 472
  application of patents to 465
  electronic transmission of 146
  global leader 419
  interoperability of 464, 465
  open-source 464
software development 6, 460
Solomon Islands 309
solvency 104, 293 n.
  outlining best practices with respect to 315
Sony 428
Sorsa, P. 310 n.
South Africa 190, 412
  foreign index scores 190
  full mode 3 commitment 309
  remittances from miners working in 497
  significant negotiating leverage 24
  tariff equivalents 197
  telecommunications 6, 14
  trucks 369
South America 254
South Asia 197
  welfare of permanent residents 500 n.
South Asian Free Trade Area Negotiations 543
South-east Asia 245
South-eastern Europe 165
South-South RTAs 224, 230
sovereignty 127
Spacefon 424
Spain 31, 79, 463 n.
spam email 469
specialists 487
  close links between investment and 257
  logistics 368

specialization:
  benefits according to comparative advantage 491
  gains from 87, 93, 359
  international 462
specialties 484, 526 n.
specific commitments 54–7, 68, 69, 262, 268, 342–3, 360, 391, 400, 442–3, 515 n.
  benefits of 309 n.
  country unsure about effects of making 446
  effect of general obligations linked to 449
  expanding 474
  GATS rules on making 449
  measures that that would nullify or impair 67
  national 547, 560, 562
  negotiation on 70, 72, 138
  products traded electronically 472
  schedule of 402–6
  target dates for initial offers of 73
  violated 264
spectrum allocation 418
  adequate, availability of 410
  licensed 399, 418
  scarce 352 n.
  unlicensed 399, 418
spillovers 11, 111, 122, 123, 490
  knowledge 96
  positive 508
Sprint 422 n.
SPS (Sanitary and Phytosanitary Standards) 243 n.
stability-efficiency trade-offs 299
staffing 398 n.
stakeholders 549–59, 567–70, 574, 576, 587
  gains and losses for 584–5
Standard Chartered Bank 328, 329, 330
standard-setting process 233, 234 n., 402, 417–18
standards 66 n.
  accounting 23
  agreed 139
  common 120
  compatibility 232
  country-specific 105
  different 120
  environmental 67
  external 581
  harmonized 23, 120, 233, 234
  improvements in 30
  independent 581
  industry-led 417
  labor 242 n., 515
  low 30
  mandatory 233, 417, 418, 428
  minimum, mutually acceptable 232
  national 224, 232, 233, 475
  operational, rigorous 315
  optimal 233

policy-related 233
  professional 32
  protocols and 467
  prudential 82
  regional 224, 232, 475
  regulatory 120, 232
  road-safety 232
  safety 105
  standards stringent 476
  statistical 147, 153
  technical 428, 448
  transparent 417
  vehicle 378
  voluntary 417
  weak 120
  see also international standards; quality standards; SPS; technical standards
state monopolies 18
  privatization of 13
state ownership 290–1
Statistics Canada 162 n.
Steiner, F. 206
Steinfatt, K. 259 n.
Stephenson, Sherry 37, 44, 222, 236 n., 253 n., 276–81, 535–6
Stern, R. M. 201, 202, 214, 215, 217
stock exchanges 291
stock markets 330, 408
Strauss, Robert 550
stylized facts 236 n., 463
sub-central governments 550
subcontracting schemes 513, 519–20, 521
submarine cable systems 433
Sub-Saharan Africa 64, 74, 412
  transport costs 81
subsidiaries 148, 427
  wholly-owned 297
subsidies 59, 124, 237, 239, 245, 340, 378
  agricultural, reduction in 454
  deemed to have injurious effects 246
  delivering efficiently 379
  funded from a broader tax base 380
  funding for universal service 397
  generic provisions on 246
  housing 530
  import-displacing 71
  inefficient 411
  often more successful than direct regulation 20
  preferences granted through 226
  production, for local programs 123
  rural or isolated areas lack resources to maintain 378
  trade-distorting 63
  trade restrictions vs. 111–12
  transparent and cost-oriented 412

subsidies (*cont.*)
  urban to rural areas 411
  see also cross-subsidization
subsistence 503
substantial sectoral coverage 261, 262, 263, 266, 267, 281
substitutes/substitution 87, 100–1, 174, 198, 235, 427
  close 89, 124, 177
  imperfect 177
  perfect 100
  trade policy 124–6
substitution effect 16
sunk costs 20, 230, 234
  absence of 342
  large 372
  location-specific 223, 229, 344
  prevalent 342
  significant 22 n.
  substantial 379
supervision:
  fragmented 15
  improved 297
  lack of 15
  mechanisms efforts to develop 313
  prudential 14, 297
  strengthening 327
supplementary indicators 139
suppliers 298
  advantage with local consumers 369
  alternative 338
  barriers to entry against 12
  competitive 347, 348, 351, 352
  constraints on establishment of 466
  core-qualification criterion 59
  dominant 232, 416
  encouraged to begin improving efficiency 406
  exclusive 68
  independent (self-employed) 153, 154
  inferior 223, 228, 229
  interacting by modern data
    communications 389, 419
  international air-freight 371
  limitations on number of 292, 362
  market share loss 359
  monopolistic 19, 68, 69, 343, 378, 406
  movement of consumers to location of 262
  national 272, 312
  new 359
  preferential treatment of 123
  privileged 81
  production subsidy discriminates in favor of 123
  protecting 20, 84, 312, 313
  proximity of 137, 229
  quota-type limits placed on number of 57
  reduction in number of 375
  rules manipulated to protect 104

scope for binding margins of preference granted
    to 272
  small- and medium-sized 72
  sole 345
  temporary movement of 262
  third-country 227, 270 n.
  vulnerability of 312
  see also efficient suppliers; foreign suppliers; major
    suppliers
supply 110, 121, 179, 367
  commercial establishment 360
  expanded 111
  foreign 176, 177
  inefficient 9–10
  labor 500, 504 n., 538
  matched with demand on second-by-second
    basis 351
  options from outside the region 378
  perfectly elastic 377
  prices adjust to ensure demand equals 499, 537
  security and quality of 353
  volatile 353
  workers restrict 493 n.
  also cross-border trade; modes of supply
supply curves 123
  aggregate 505
  foreign 111
Suriname 535, 536
surplus 17, 521
  see also consumer surplus; producer surplus
surveillance 265
Sutton, B. 414 n.
Sweden 20, 568
switching capacity 392
Switzerland 205, 565
synergies 453

TAA (US Trade Adjustment Assistance Act 1962) 531
Taiwan:
  financial markets 294
  margins 200
  welfare effects of removing barriers 216
  welfare increase 217
Tang, P. J. G. 507
tangible goods 137
tariff equivalents 169, 170, 174, 176, 177, 196, 203
  benchmark 192
  estimated 197
  judgmental values 203
  maximum 192
  reductions in 491
  very large 197
tariffs 10, 61, 81, 104, 105–7, 169, 226, 264, 272, 411,
    466, 522
  cut across-the-board 76

distortions caused by 112
goods ordered over the net subject to 474
inefficiency induced by 106
key difference between quotas and 109
preferential arrangements 224
prohibitively high 110
reduction of 80, 84, 374
revenue collected from 108
risen to cover costs of provision 378
social cost of 123, 125
zero 103, 472 n.
see also GATT
Tarr, David 36
tax avoidance 273
taxes 476
  ad valorem 176
  bilateral treaties 273
  collected, increase in 502
  consumption 112
  discriminatory 84, 104, 127, 474
  e-commerce 465–6, 475
  exemption of one mode of delivery from 124
  foreign programs 123
  import 103
  indirect 465
  percentage on foreign suppliers 203
  preferences granted through 226
  removal of 359
  social security 511, 522
  temporary movement of personnel 124, 125
  transport services 473
  useful index of stringency of protection 110
TBT (Technical Barriers to Trade) Agreements 243
TEA (US Trade Expansion Act 1962) 531
teachers 490
technical assistance 29, 30
  dedicated activities 272
  greater doses from major donors 271
technical efficiency 341, 345, 348
  ensuring 346
  free entry contributes to 375
technical standards 67, 69, 225, 229, 343
  differences across jurisdictions in 20
technological capabilities 395
technological change 18
  continuous 234
  impact of 573
  main driver of increased inequality 92
  rapid 206, 259
technological progress:
  another chapter in history of 464
  autonomous 201
  rapid 463 n.
technology 368
  advanced equipment production 428

basic, understanding 391
changing very rapidly 342
digital 465
faster upgrades 396 n.
global power 41
improved, access to 111
mandatory standard 418
operators encouraged to adopt best 21
rapidly changing 390
rural applications of 399
see also new technologies
technology transfer 13, 367
  promotion of 303
  vehicle for 17
  wireless, in low population markets 398 n.
teenagers 427
telecommunications 6, 23, 40, 59, 61, 62, 112, 185, 206, 347, 352, 372, 389–436
  barriers to competition in 200
  costs of installing and maintaining switching 339–40
  cross-border services 205
  economies of scale and scope a feature of 341
  estimate of price elasticity of demand for 196
  fixed-line operators 342
  fully open 338
  growing convergence of IT and 460
  higher prices 213
  liberalizing 13, 14, 17, 81
  long-distance 346, 395, 398, 411, 414 n., 415, 416, 425, 427
  mobile 18, 342
  overall expansion in quantity and variety of services 354
  principles established for 380
  provided by single, publicly owned monopoly 350
  quality-cost aspects of 212
  quantitative impact of barriers in 195
  regulation of policies 205
  regulatory approaches developed for 453
  restrictions on number of operators 226
  thwarting development of effective downstream competition in 351
  total costs of providing services 211
  voice 192
  world services market 393
  see also basic telecommunications; telecommunications networks
Telecommunications Act (Korea 2002) 426
telecommunications networks 69, 340, 344, 392–4, 409, 421, 424
  crossing national boundaries 402
  fixed 195, 206, 346
  interconnection 19
  international 404

telecommunications networks (*cont.*)
  mobile 410, 417
  public 432
  residential broadband 427
  wired 391, 392, 395, 399, 400, 409, 411, 412
  see also ITU; wireless systems
teledensity 201
  low 16
  sector reform tends to increase 463
TeleGeography 421 n., 422 n.
telegrams 470
telegraphs 393
Telekom Malaysia 424
telemedicine 437
telephone companies 390
  ability and incentive to cut off competition 395–6
  required to lease transmission capacity 394
telephones/telephony 18, 403
  analog services 399
  change of numbers 408
  extremely high cost of international calling 411
  fixed-line 14, 351, 425
  household ownership of 21
  international calls 402, 414, 427
  local, still require interconnection 409
  long distance 342
  mobile 195–6, 206, 342
  network engineering 397
  network technology 393
  prices of local calls 16
  waiting lists for 410
telex 393
Telkom 14
Telmex 415, 416
temporariness 79
  unskilled migration 31
temporary movement of personnel 11, 126, 155, 156
      454, 480–541
  health professionals 451
  tax on 124, 125
terms of trade 377, 419, 497
  effects of liberalization 382
  improvements in 501
territorial boundaries 141
text messaging 427
Thailand 11, 299
  commercial banks 298
  decline in welfare 216
  discrimination 190, 205
  foreign entry 302, 303
  foreign index scores 190
  margins 200
  restrictiveness 187, 205, 210
  ten-year window of opportunity for foreign
      investors 313

trade policy 37, 298
third countries 249 n.
  airline capacity offered from 366
  efficient competitors 229
  high tariff imports from 226
  insights into trade barriers found in surveys done
      by 554
  investors 249
  negotiating leverage vis-à-vis 274
  suppliers 227
  trade and investment barriers against 261, 262
third-country effects 235, 268
third-generation services 400, 428
third-party logistics providers 356
thrifts-institutions 301
Tianjin 329
Tier I carriers 421
time-series data 211
Tirole, J. 411 n.
Tokyo 395
Tokyo Round (1973–1979) 542, 549, 550
Tong, D. D. 327
top-down approach 55, 253, 254, 377
Toro, J. 353
total factor productivity 228
tourism 6, 24, 54, 94, 99, 357, 364, 389
  boosted 419
  health 451
  statistics on arrivals and departures monitored 156
TP Asuransi Bintang 298 n.
TPA (US Trade Promotion Authority) 260
Trachtman, Joel P. 232 n., 243 n.
trade agreements:
  bilateral 273
  commitment to 127
  focus on liberalizing trade 126
  important commitment advantages 127
  international, financial services and 37–8, 289–337
  multilateral 79
  North-South 3
  plurilateral 273
  preferential 225 n.
  unilateral liberalization vs. 126–8
  see also RTAs
trade associations 557, 268, 569
trade benefits 64
trade controls 475
trade-diversion effect 126
trade flows 235
  bilateral 338
  integration agreements liberalizing 268
trade negotiations:
  benefits of 390
  developing countries 21
  international 339, 354, 558

trade-offs:
  complex and intrusive 127
  cross-sectoral 308
  different approaches to 127–8
  efficiency 299
  gains from integrated markets and costs of
      transition 233
  inter-modal 26
  scale economies and competition 230
  socially optimal 233
  stability-efficiency 299
trade pacts 402–3, 408
trade policy 37, 375, 474
  cross-border trade and 293, 302
  instruments of protection 103–10
  reform in financial services 295–302, 306–7
  regulation and 112, 124
  restrictive practices 214
  "starts at home" 376
  substitution between modes of delivery 124–6
Trade Practices Act (Australia 1974) 352
trade restrictions 67, 69, 123, 255, 375
  subsidies vs. 111–12
  unilateral policy action can remove 374
trade theory 92
  basic propositions of 89
  extension of 223
  neoclassical 235
trade volumes:
  bilateral 197
  relatively high elasticities of 359
trade wars 126
trademarks 145, 464, 470
TradePort 185
traders and investors 270
trading costs 97
trading partners:
  affluent, external assistance from 22
  countries tap into regulatory expertise of 354
  distance between 197
  low degree of restrictions necessary 210–11
  major 197, 418
  market-access opportunities 380
  MFN Members prevented from discriminating
      among 291
  right to discriminate between 291 n.
  statistics 145–6
traffic volumes 358, 371
  affected adversely by macroeconomic crisis 369
  two-way flow 366
training 532
  advanced, junior doctors 526 n.
  average levels of 511
  benefits to support 531
  compulsory 531

disparities in 30
  duplicative 524
  full course requirement 512
  knowledge, experience and 111
  less local 507
  long-term 531
  medical 527
  on-the-job 523
  placements for junior doctors 528
  pre-departure 31
  strong public-sector orientation that stresses 527
  worker schemes 525
TRAINS (TRade Analysis and INformation
      System) 183
transaction costs 77, 476
  diminished 475
  transparency helps to reduce 271
transactions 291
  balanced statistical statement that summarizes 141
  capital account 294, 295
  certainty and predictability for 433
  cross-border 305, 466
  direct investment 147 n.
  directly between providers and users of funds 290
  electronic 460, 469, 472
  facilitated 290
  financial 147 n., 290
  increasing 356
  international 5, 89, 141, 178, 179, 294, 466
  international financial 554
  Internet 475
  online 460, 467, 468
  recording 141, 142
  residence of transactors 141
  residents and non-residents 140
  restrictions on 295
  service contract 155
  suggested aggregation of 145
  summarized with rest of world 139
  value of 57, 292, 362
Transatlantic aviation space 258 n.
transfer pricing 117, 142
transfers 527
  capital 530
  electronic 469 n.
  income to relatives back home 496
  migrant workers 155
  permanent 530
  skills and technologies 367
transition to competition 391, 406, 408
  global 415
transitional economies 408
  commitments in maritime transport 364
  demand for network capacity 410
translation services 59

TransMilenio Project 375
transmission capacity 395, 396, 423 n.
  leasing 394, 415
transnational corporations 437
transparency 56, 63, 67, 232, 255, 265, 291, 296, 317,
    360, 372, 418, 432, 555
  additional obligations 69
  disciplines on 238, 239
  enhancing 256
  gains in 237
  higher standards of 304
  lack of 79, 105, 467
  measures to improve 423
  need for 390
  obligations 69
  outlining best practices with respect to 315
  procedural 242
  procedures to enhance 246
  regulatory 271, 297, 307, 557
  relative 420
  tariff 109, 110
transport costs 81
  changes make significant difference to value
      added 377
  cross-border 105
  determinants of 338, 358, 359
  high 357
  interaction between scale economies and 96
  internal 357–8
  international 416, 422
  lower 357, 359
  reductions in 359
  small differences/changes in 356, 357
transportation 23, 64, 98, 146, 356–88, 503
  barriers to competition in 200
  eight modes of 143
  international 105, 231
  tariff equivalents highest for 192
  see also air transport; land transport; maritime
      transport; rail transport
Trans-Tasman Mutual Travel Arrangement 257, 258 n.
travel/travelers 143–4
  international, costs of 357
  long journeys 356–7
  substitutability of destinations 357
Trewin, R. 211
Trinidad and Tobago 535, 536
TRIPs (Trade-Related Aspects of Intellectual
    Property) 233 n., 246 n., 590
  international e-commerce affected by rules 472
trucks 105, 368, 369, 382
Tunisia 309
Turkey 190, 197, 205
turnover 149, 508
two-part pricing 348, 350, 351

UBO (ultimate beneficial owner) 150
UBS (Union Bank of Switzerland) 328
Ufficio Italiano dei Cambi 162 n.
Uganda 301
ultimatums 583–4
UN (United Nations) 153, 156
  see also CPC; ECLAC; ECWA; UNCTAD; UNSD;
      UNWTO
uncertainty 110, 298–301, 383, 512
  legal 467
UNCTAD (UN Conference on Trade and
    Development) 161, 164, 554
  data on FDI 160
  Development Committee 578
  FDI barriers identified by 181
  Foreign Direct Investment Database 162 n.
  Handbook of Statistics 139 n.
  inventories of identified trade restrictions 183
  World Investment Report 162 n.
under-consumption 107
underwriting 290
undesired messages 475
unemployment 80
  extended benefits 531
  long-lived 506
  transitional 531
  university graduates 580
unequal treatment 425
unhealthy lifestyles 437
unilateralism 77, 126–8
unincorporated enterprises 148
United Kingdom 29
  anti-competitive conduct 353, 409
  barriers on accountancy services 204
  derailed railway reforms 373
  doctors from abroad 524, 525, 526,
      527, 528
  employment with agency does not qualify as
      employment for GATS visa 519
  entrepreneurs and skilled workers with innovative
      ideas enter 513
  GATS Visa Scheme 518
  nurses from Philippines 525
  rail transport 81
  recognition of medical training given in any
      WHO-accredited institution 524
  regulatory regime to promote competition in
      electricity 352
  residents temporarily working
      abroad from 483
  stakeholders from 568
  working-holidays for young people from
      Commonwealth countries 513
  see also DFID; Overseas Doctors Training Scheme;
      White Paper

United States 66 n., 316, 365, 447, 475, 476, 542, 550, 586, 588, 589
advantage in terms of economic weight 587
air and ocean freight rates for imports 357 n.
barriers on accountancy services 204
bilateral trade agreements 401
carriers charge for international traffic to websites 421
cross-border trucking between Mexico and 382
demandeur role 420
discrimination against foreign firms 205
disposition towards migration 483
domestic index score 191
evolution of income distribution 92
explosive growth of backbone network 423 n.
exports of 9
e-commerce transactions 472
FATS statistics 164
financial sector difficulties 20
foreign index score 191
hub of global multinational business networks 414
huge demand for unskilled labor 497
H-1A visa scheme 523 n.
inflated rates for international phone services 411
Internet traffic transport 421–2
labor costs 495 n.
laws that prohibit gambling over wires across state lines 473
long-distance transmission facilities 396
low-income migrants and families 496
major trading partners 197
margins 200
maritime imports 214
market power 416, 422
Mexico and liberalization of cross-border road transport 381
MFN exemption 291 n.
model schedule approach endorsed by service industry bodies 78
opposition to S&D in Doha Round 578
patents and business processes 465
phone networks 394
political considerations 43–4
preferential treatment of banks 252
private telecom operators 463 n.
recruitment of nurses 523
regulatory and judicial disputes 408
relatively harsh labor market 483, 511
residents temporarily working abroad from 483
restrictiveness 189, 205
severe shortages of skilled labor 26
sharp decline of leadership 559
shipping 358
social security 522
stakeholders from 568
tactic used by Japan in bilateral negotiations with 564
technology meeting non-interference specifications 417
telecommunications 447
temporary movement of service providers 533–4
termination charges 409, 410 n., 415, 417
transparency 555
transport charges for imports 374
welfare effects 216, 217
see also Agency for International Development; Bureau of Economic Analysis; Department of Justice; DR-CAFTA; FCC; Immigration and Nationality Act; ISAC; NAFTA; Panel and Appellate Body Rulings; TAA; TEA; TPA; US FTAs; USTR
Universal Postal Union 139 n.
universal service 410–13
university education 93–4
UNSD (UN Statistics Division) 159, 162 n., 164
unskilled labor/workers 497, 510–11
effective supply of 537
less likely to adapt to Western culture 510
liberalization of restrictions on 502
potential benefits of mobility 503
temporary 500
UNWTO (UN World Tourism Organization) 162 n.
upstream markets 349
urban bus sector 375
Uruguay 190–1
Uruguay Round (1986–94) 40, 53, 55, 70, 71, 72, 185, 186, 254, 259, 261, 262, 266 n., 308, 389, 497, 514, 580, 587, 588, 589, 590
Australia successful in building coalition around Cairns Group 564
commitments made 203, 365, 380, 381
Final Act (1991) 264 n., 588
health ministries not actively involved in negotiations on GATS 444
important achievements of 138
most immediately palpable result of 64
Negotiating Committee on Trade in Services 542
negotiation of the GATS agreement 564, 569
telecom in 400–1
Ury, W. 573 n.
US FTAs 410 n.
Australia 238 n., 270, 319, 324, 326 n.
Canada 246 n., 266 n., 534
Chile 239, 242, 256, 257, 259, 316, 317, 319, 324, 325
Jordan 238 n., 242 n., 247, 257, 258
Singapore 239, 242, 256, 257, 259, 316, 324
USOs (universal-service obligations) 20–1, 302, 348, 349, 350, 351, 380, 383, 431, 462
have to be managed carefully 463
USTR (US Trade Representative) 260, 549

Valletti, T. 349, 350
value added 149, 343, 397, 403
    competition in 390, 398
    mobile telephony 343
    quantum decline in 509
    service exempt from restrictions and pricing 413
    special features 395
    telecommunications services markets 426
    transport costs changes make significant difference
        to 377
variable costs 223
    measures affecting 226–7
    usage charge to recover 348
Varian, H. R. 414 n., 460 n.
VAT (value-added tax) 465, 466
Venables, A. J. 95, 97, 101 n., 338, 359
Venezuela 308 n.
    discrimination against foreign firms 205
    domestic banking problems 299
    index scores 191
    tariff equivalents 197
Verikios, G. 215 n.
vertical integration 349, 368
    preferable to retain 373
vertical separation 18
vested interests 81, 224, 231
    political power of 80
    protectionist 21
    resistance by 434
videotape capabilities 464
Virgin group 369
visas:
    commitments on 257
    costs of 511
    dedicated procedures 270
    discretion to grant, refuse and administer 258
    GATS 519
    H 482, 484, 486, 523 n., 533, 534
    lack of transparency in schemes 79
    not renewable 31
    regional trade-related 270
    regulations embodied in policies 489
Vodacom 412
VoIP (Voice over the Internet) 390, 398, 413
vouchers 21

wage parity 513, 521–2
wage premia 530
wages 513–14
    changes in 504, 538
    different 493
    equalized across sectors 538
    higher 500
    increasing 16
    low(er) 88, 92, 97, 184, 356, 367

    prevailing 513, 521
    reduced 531
    skilled 502, 507
    unskilled 507, 510
    see also real wages
Wal-Mart 389, 419
Walmsley, T. L. 480 n., 483
    see also WW model
Wang, Yan 38, 335 n.
warehousing costs 369
Warren, T. 185 n., 195–6, 205, 212, 215 n., 377
waste disposal 259
water:
    distribution/treatment services 259
    reticulation systems 340
wealth generation/redistribution 467
websites 396, 416, 421, 422, 423, 416, 552, 555
    carriers charge for international traffic to 421
    foreign operators 468
    growing diversification of content 423
    hosting 419, 465–6
    legal action against 465
    major 423
    mirroring for 422 n., 423
welfare 96, 119, 121, 227, 529
    capital does not experience 492 n.
    consumer 414 n.
    decline in 216
    economic 200, 208, 218, 499, 538
    enhancing 223, 227, 228
    entry deterrence may promote 230 n.
    gains in 113, 217, 270, 296 n., 378
    global 91, 474, 491
    impact of FDI restrictions on 113–14
    implications for third parties 235
    increases from higher returns to capital 502
    larger gains 17
    maximizing 350 n.
    mode-switching contributes to decline in 126
    national 91, 113, 114
    permanent residents 502
    positive gains 296 n.
    reducing effects of liberalization 217
    social 20, 114, 127
    source of loss 217
    substantial gains 270
    trade restrictions can improve 123
    world 500
welfare effects:
    increase in world capital stock 217
    percentage of GNP 215
    removing services barriers 202
    sizable 216
    tariff for small country 105
Westel 424

Western Hemisphere 190, 197, 239, 244, 245, 246, 317
    basis in GATS most noticeable amongst 251
    choice of liberalization modality 279–81
    compliance with production of negative lists
        problematic 256
    NAFTA-type agreements 242, 316
    regional and bilateral free trade agreements 308 n.
    RTAs concluded in 255
Whalley, J. 185 n., 204 n., 494
Whichard, Obie 35
White Paper (rail sector organization, UK Dept for
        Transport 2004) 373
WHO (World Health Organization) 437
    accreditation of medical training facilities
        internationally 524
    work on GATS and policy recommendations 445–6
wholesale business 398
    food distributors 208
    markets 394, 423
    pricing pool 352
WiFi systems 399
win-win mentality 584–5
winners and losers 390, 585
    potential 498
Winters, L. A. 480 n., 483, 492, 493, 495, 505, 509,
        512 n., 514, 519, 523 n., 525, 528
    see also WW model
WIPO (World Intellectual Property Organization) 42,
        459, 470
wireless systems 411
    data communications/transfer 425, 427
    explosion in 460
    fixed 399
    interconnecting networks 409
    leadership in technology 428
    low population markets 398 n.
    mobile 404, 409
    networking 399–400, 459 n.
    terrestrial 399
Wood, A. 507
Woodruffe, J. 437 n.
Wooton, I. 374
work permits 156, 513
    workers employed without 514
working conditions 451
World Bank 225 n., 274 n., 294, 297, 301, 333, 356,
        357, 373, 497, 553, 554
    extensive international programs conducted by 293
    Financial Sector Assessment Programs 82
    World Development Indicators 139 n.
WorldCom 422 n.
worms 469
WTO (World Trade Organization) 3, 42, 143, 157 n., 221,
        233 n., 234, 242, 256, 413, 416, 437 n., 514, 543, 554
    commitment to reform in 24

country frustrated by ability to block consensus 566
creation of (1995) 590
dispute settlement mechanism 439, 449–50
domestic liberalization processes 310
e-commerce issues 459, 460, 471–3
extension of treatment to non-WTO Members 257
financial services liberalization outside 315
foreign workers registered with 516
impact on infrastructure layer of global information
        system 472 n.
indexes compiled from 205
member rights to promote and protect health 450
members' commitments 153
national treatment problems for new and
        inexperienced members 58
policy bindings 239
regulatory codes 417
request-offer approach 72, 74, 76–7, 560–2, 570–1,
        588
RTAs and 222
specification and implementation of strategy 377
spectrum licensing 418
trade deals at 390
trade-related e-commerce issues 470
    see also Doha; GATS; GATT; GPA; Hong Kong
        Ministerial Declaration; TRIPS; also under
        following headings prefixed "WTO"
WTO accession 24
    and aggregate benefits 171–2
    asymmetries inherent in non-reciprocal
        negotiations towards 381
    China (2001) 295 n., 297, 303, 369, 381, 406, 564, 567
    negotiations since end of Uruguay Round 365
    Russia, prospective 36, 171
WTO institutions/miscellany:
    Enquiry and Contact Points 63 n.
    Financial Services Agreement (1997) 259 n.
    General Council 53 n., 268
    International Trade Statistics 139 n., 162 n.
    Ministerial Decision (1998) 81, 473
    Regional Agreements 235, 268
    Scheduling Guidelines 57 n., 58
    Secretariat 74, 562, 571, 572
    Sectoral Classification 517
    Work Program on Electronic Commerce 460
    also BTA; Reference Paper on Telecomunications
WTO negotiations 44, 310, 365, 568
    capacity building especially relevant to participation
        in 376
    e-commerce 471–2
    how organized 570
    how structured 547–8
    multilateral 557, 565
    non-reciprocal 381
Wunsch-Vincent, S. 58 n.

WW (Walmsley/Winters) model 498, 499, 500 n., 502, 504, 532, 537, 538

xenophobia 483, 511

Yach, D. 437 n.
Yahoo 416, 423
Yi, S. 315

Zacher, M. 414 n.
Zambia 24, 447 n.
Zanini, Gianni 221 n.
zero-sum mentality 585
Zhang, X.-G. 215 n.
Zhu, T. 327
Ziegler, V. 463 n.
Zimbabwe 369